Purchasing Manager's
DESK BOOK
of
PURCHASING
LAW

Third Edition

SUPPLEMENTS/ANNUALS NOTICE

This Prentice Hall product is updated periodically to reflect the most important, latest changes in the field. If you have ordered this volume directly from us, you have received the latest supplement/annual, are on our subscription list, and will receive future supplements/annuals.

If you have purchased your copy from a bookstore or other source, you may obtain the latest supplement/annual on a free 30-day review basis. Please send your name, company name (if applicable), title (if applicable), address, and name of product to:

> Marketing Director, Supplements/Annuals
> Prentice Hall
> 240 Frisch Court
> Paramus, NJ 07652

In addition to your supplement/annual, you will receive future mailings alerting you to new products in your field.

Purchasing Manager's
DESK BOOK
of
PURCHASING LAW

Third Edition

DONALD B. KING
JAMES J. RITTERSKAMP, JR.

PRENTICE HALL

Library of Congress Cataloging-in-Publication Data

King, Donald Barnett.
    Purchasing manager's desk book of purchasing law. — 3rd ed. /
Donald B. King. James J. Ritterskamp, Jr.
      p.   cm.
    Includes index.
    ISBN 0-13-671462-5 (hardcover)
    1. Sales—United States.   2. Contracts—United States.
3. Purchasing agents—Legal status, laws, etc.—United States.
I. Ritterskamp, James J. II. Title.
KF915.R58´ 1997
346.7307´2—dc21   97–30492
                                                                   CIP

© 1998 by Prentice Hall, Inc.
All rights reserved. No part of this book may be reproduced, in any form or by any means, without permission in writing from the publisher.

This publication is designed to provide accurate and authoritative information in regard
to the subject matter covered. It is sold with the understanding that the publisher is not
engaged in rendering legal, accounting, or other professional service. If legal advice
or other expert assistance is required, the services of a competent professional
person should be sought.

*—From a Declaration of Principles jointly adopted by a Committee of the American Bar
Association and a Committee of Publishers and Associations.*

Printed in the United States of America

10 9 8 7 6 5 4

ISBN 0-13-671462-5

9 780136 714620   90000

ATTENTION: CORPORATIONS AND SCHOOLS
Prentice Hall books are available at quantity discounts with bulk purchase for educational,
business, or sales promotional use. For information, please write to Prentice Hall Special
Sales, 240 Frisch Court, Paramus, NJ 07652. Please supply: title of book, ISBN number,
quantity, how the book will be used, date needed.

PRENTICE HALL
Paramus, NJ 07652

On the World Wide Web at http://www.phdirect.com

Publisher's Note

The first edition of *Purchasing Manager's Desk Book of Purchasing Law* was written by James J. Ritterskamp, Jr. and published by Prentice Hall in 1987. It was supplemented each year by the author.

Unfortunately, Jim Ritterskamp became ill during the preparation of one of the supplements, and passed away in April, 1992.

Before his final illness, he designated Donald B. King his co-author. It was King who finished preparing that supplement, and who prepared the second edition, its subsequent supplements, and this third edition.

Jim Ritterskamp was a highly regarded expert in his field, and a diligent and concerned author. We miss him.

Acknowledgments

I am pleased to acknowledge the fine efforts of James J. Ritterskamp, Jr., an attorney and a purchasing manager, for his establishment of the first edition of this work. I also appreciate the support of his family, Mrs. Ritterskamp, and his sons, Douglas and James, in these continued efforts. In addition, there is the inspiration of my great uncle, Leonard L. King, who was for many years the purchasing agent for the Illinois Central Railroad and whom I had the opportunity to visit with on numerous occasions in his office and home as I grew up.

In this third edition, I also wish to acknowledge some former students and now attorneys for their contributions: Kathy Rader on Letters of Credit, Brian Sandler on International Sales, Mr. Sukang Zou on Legal-Cultural Considerations in Contracting in China, Shawn Zhao on Roles in Contracting in China, Elisa Robinson on NAFTA, and Gloria McCollum on Special Remedies. Mark McColl's past assistance was also important. My utmost thanks to my current research assistants, Mr. Lingling Zou and Mr. Thierry Guastarino, for their overall assistance throughout this book. Karen Tabak, CPA and expert witness, also contributed to specialized parts of this book.

In addition, the efforts of Mary Dougherty, Faculty Secretary, also were invaluable in producing this edition.

This book is dedicated to the memories of:

Mr. Leonard L. King,
a purchasing manager for the Illinois Central Railroad for over thirty years.
My great-uncle and a good friend of the family.

Mr. James J. Ritterskamp, Jr.,
a purchasing manager for Washington University for many years and author and
beloved by his family.

About the Authors

Donald B. King has taught Commercial Law and Comparative Law for thirty-nine years. During this time he has written or edited twelve books, and over forty articles and essays. The Commercial Transactions casebook he first coedited in 1968 is now in its fifth edition. He has coauthored books on "Sales Law" and "Negotiable Instruments and Payment Systems," and authored a book on "Secured Transactions." He also has written books on "Consumer Protection Experiments in Sweden" and "Consumer Protection in China." Professor King also was the editor of books on "Commercial and Consumer Law from an International Perspective" and "Essays on Comparative Commercial and Consumer Law." His teaching has been concentrated in the fields of commercial law, consumer law, secured transactions, products liability, and comparative law. He has taught at the University of Washington, Dickinson Law School, Wayne State University, and Saint Louis University. He also was a Visiting Professor at the University of Cincinnati, Stetson Law School, and Sichuan University in China.

He is founder and Honorary President of the International Academy of Commercial and Consumer Law, a select group of sixty international authorities. He has done comparative research and given lectures on commercial and consumer law in a number of countries throughout the world.

He received his Bachelor of Science degree in psychology from Washington State University and his Juris Doctor from Harvard Law School. Professor King has also earned a Masters from New York University and a Masters in psychiatric social work from Saint Louis University. He is a member of the Missouri, Washington State, and Supreme Court bars, is an elected member of the American Law Institute and was recently given the honor of "Life Member," an honor held by less than 600 lawyers out of 847,000 lawyers in the United States. Professor King also has been elected a President of the Central States Law School Association for 1995 , which consists of over forty law schools from thirteen states. The Saint Louis University Du Bourg Society has named him an Honorary Dean, Honorary Vice President, and Honorary Trustee.

James J. Ritterskamp, Jr. coauthored and contributed to several books on purchasing, and wrote a monthly column, "Ritterskamp Views the Law," which was carried in numerous purchasing magazines, including *Purchasing Management, Midwest Purchasing,* the *St. Louis Purchaser, Purchasing Professional,* and the *New South Purchaser.* He was best known for his legal seminars conducted for the National Association of Purchasing Management, for Regional Purchasing Management Associations, and for private organizations throughout the country.

He served as president of numerous professional associations, including the Purchasing Management Association of St. Louis, the National Association of Educational Buyers, the National Association of College Stores, and the National Association of College and University Business Officers. He taught accounting, law, purchasing, and economics at Washington University and Vassar College.

He received his Juris Doctor degree from the School for Law of Washington University in St. Louis. Before graduating, he was appointed Assistant Purchasing Agent of Stores at his alma mater. He progressed from that rank to become Vice Chancellor for Business and Secretary of the Board of Directors in 1956. In 1961 he became Vice President and Treasurer of the Illinois Institute of Technology in Chicago. Later he became Vice President for Administration at the University of Chicago. From 1966 to 1981 he served as Vice President for Administration and Treasurer of Vassar College in New York. In 1986, he came out of retirement to become President of Rocky Mountain College in Billings, Montana for one year.

Preface

The first and second editions of this landmark book on law for purchasing managers or agents were well received and succeeded in satisfying the author's goals: *The authors want this book to be a friend and a source of comfort to you as a purchasing officer when you are faced with legal involvements in your daily routine.*

Since that time, there have been a number of changes and additions to the law:

- As the new millennium approaches, both society and the law have become more complex.
- A "new business ethic" has been made enforceable by law.
- A shift in contract theory makes more contracts enforceable.
- New developments are taking place in regard to the "battle of the forms."
- Standard form contracts are more subject to attack, and courts may eventually enforce only the terms actually agreed upon.
- Buyers' remedies have become expanded and strengthened.
- Use of electronic data interchange for contracting is greater than ever.
- The purchase of computers and/or software programs has given rise to new legal problems.
- Personal liability of officers continues to be a problem.
- A new law prevails in the United States with the adoption of the convention on the International Sale of Goods.
- Environmental law regulations create new responsibilities and personal liabilities.
- New Federal legislation affects the manner in which the purchasing manager handles staff.
- Legal and cultural considerations are important if the purchasing office buys goods from abroad.

Other minor changes have also taken place.

Therefore, this *Third Edition* is necessary. It still has the goal of being "an old friend" to the purchasing manager or agent. This "old friend" should make you more comfortable with the current modern law and its trends. It also will give you the assurance that you possess a working knowledge of those portions of the law that relate to purchasing activities. Familiarity with the law will enable you to negotiate with confidence and be steadfast in insisting that contractual obligations be met by each supplier. Legal actions and courtroom battles should be avoided if each purchase is to be legally sound. In the unusual event that a lawsuit is inevitable, you and your organization, together with your legal counsel, will go into court in the best possible position to assert and defend your rights.

Several *caveats* and *explanations* from the first and second editions, still hold true:

1. The authors have been unable to find in the English language a suitable heterogeneous pronoun for use in this book. Nor does inventing one like *{s}he or he[r]* or *per [person]* seem appropriate here. Occasionally, such awkward phrases as *he or she* and *him and her* are used in recognition of the fact that the purchasing profession has well integrated the sexes. More often, however, the single pronoun *he* is used to signify both sexes. In so doing, your author pleads Section 1-102(4[b]) of the Uniform Commercial Code, which reads:

   Words of the masculine gender include the feminine and the neuter, and, when the sense so indicates, words of the neuter gender may refer to any gender. It is in this context only that the masculine pronoun is employed.

2. The expressions *your company, your organization, your business, your firm,* and *your corporation* refer to your employer. They are used interchangeably to relieve the monotony of repetition. The principles of purchasing law explained herein apply to purchasing officers in single entrepreneurships, partnerships, profit and not-for-profit corporations, and—unless otherwise indicated—in governmental agencies.

3. *Nota bene* is a Latin expression meaning "take particular notice." It is meant in this book to be a helpful hint or a suggestion. The sections headed *"Nota Bene* to the Purchasing Officer" contain practical suggestions from a former purchasing officer who applies legal learning to the purchasing profession. They are not intended to be legal advice.

4. Your author recognizes that any treatise on legal topics intended for the nonlawyer should avoid the use of legal terminology and legal theories. This text does not completely meet that criterion for the simple reason that it is intended for purchasing officers. Most purchasing officers believe in calling a spade a spade, and they want to know the complete

truth about a product and why it is useful. Therefore, the book does not go out of its way to avoid legal terms or the rationale of legal theories. The purchasing officer "wants it like it is," and that is how it is offered. Whenever a legal term is used for the first time, a reasonable nonlegalese interpretation follows.

5. Some actual reported law cases are contained herein. The facts of these cases, along with the reasoning of the court in reaching the decisions, have been abbreviated considerably. This reduces the number of pages to be printed and makes the book more cost-effective. The authors apologize to the members of the bench who may have been quoted out of context.

6. The authors admit to being human: **Errors of fact, of substance, and of law are thereby possible; therefore, responsibility for damage resulting from any such errors is disclaimed.** The reader is advised to read the content of Chapter II, "The Role of Your Legal Counsel," which states: **You should rely on any principle of law only after it has been verified by your legal counsel.**

With these provisos in mind, the authors also want to emphasize that the law is challenging and exciting. It is interesting, too, especially when it touches your daily routine. Read on and enjoy!

Donald B. King
James J. Ritterskamp, Jr.

Contents

SECTION A

INTRODUCTION

I

Complexities of Society
and Law

THE SECOND MILLENNIUM CHALLENGES

The year 2000 is not only landmark for civilization, but it should stimulate some reflection as well. Not only will there be numerous events commemorating it, but also a variety of writings. The inauguration of the second millennium should cause everyone to reflect on several levels.

In looking at the development of civilization over these many decades, one realizes the complexities of our current times. Indeed, the development of production and trade over the last century alone has been quite phenomenal. In addition, the productive capacities not only of the United States, but of nations throughout the world has created a tremendous array of goods. In this regard, the purchasing manager must be more knowledgeable than ever.

In recent decades, several other developments have taken place which make the job one of more choices-but also one that requires more knowledge, skills, and legal awareness. One of these is the more rapid evolution of the law and changing theories that may have practical results. This means that purchasing managers not only must be cognizant of some of the more traditional legal theories and rules, but also of those that are currently being established or evolving. Another major consideration is the explosion of technology, which finds manifestations in the purchasing environment and the laws relating to it. Again, the purchasing manager's knowledge must be expanded to cover these developments.

Finally, there is a tremendous expansion of international trade and of the laws governing it. The purchasing manager now has a much wider variety of markets from which.to choose, but he or she also must be aware of the laws that govern transactions in which the goods are purchased from abroad.

The reflections of the purchasing manager over the past and into the new millennium must include these ever accelerating developments. These developments, however, should not be viewed as simply isolated theories or rules, but instead in a perspective of history in which things are constantly in a state of change. With these changes come legal changes as well.

On a higher level, reflections of the millennium may also make one realize that one's role is only a small part of history. The purchasing manager's job is to do the best job possible. But like all others, once this is done, one should not allow stress or worry to enter in. It is hoped then that this book may give the purchasing manager insights into the intersection of law and various aspects of his or her work. Once aware of the legal manifestations, the purchasing manager can make better decisions. In addition, he or she can converse with the corporation's legal counsel in a much better way, where or whenever necessary.

THE ROLE OF THE PURCHASING MANAGER

Modern purchasing managers or agents have a challenging yet difficult role. They must bring to the job a variety of talents and a wealth of knowledge. Their character must be held high despite the questionable conduct of others with whom they deal.

Purchasing managers must exercise sound economical judgment and a keen sense of the more specific markets for goods. They must use strategy in their purchases and sales, yet maintain the trust and good will of all those with whom they deal over time. They must handle current relationships and long-term future ones as well. This would seem to be all that could be required from any one person.

But purchasing managers exercise even more skills. Psychology and an understanding of human nature are essential when dealing with other sellers and buyers. It also is necessary for managers to cooperate with other officers of the corporation or business. Further, they must use psychology and managerial skills in dealing with those in their own purchasing office.

In addition to all these skills, they must have some understanding of the general legal effects of their actions. Purchasing managers must move ahead with their decisions with a sense of confidence that they are operating with the support of the law. They must know that the law is backing them in negotiations and commitments. While this does not require them to be lawyers, because such may be available within the company or among outside consultants, it does require them to have a general sense of commercial law as it touches on their activities. In this regard, this book can be their source of general knowledge and sometimes specific reference.

It almost would seem to be too much to require-a breath of economic, psychological, and legal knowledge, as well as pragmatic and organizational skills and a sense of human understanding. But this is the modern role of purchasing managers. All too often, it is not recognized or fully appreciated by others that purchasing managers play such a complex role. Yet it is certainly a role that requires these many skills, and a broad base of knowledge—which includes the law.

THE COMPLEXITIES OF PURCHASING LAW

To have a good perspective of the law's continued development, a purchasing manager should keep in mind the broad changes in society that contribute to the law's development. Indeed, purchasing agents are especially aware of some of the complexities of modern-day life, business, and law. Some of these changes include the expansion of governmental activity, the growth of industry, technological advances, the development of the consumer protection movement advances in communications, and new developments in theory and jurisprudence.

Historically, there has been some concern about the complexity of the law. Indeed, in the mid-1800s, David Dudley of New York called attention to the tremendous complexity of the law and the expansiveness of the case law in that period.[1]

He would, of course, be appalled at the law today, which is in a much more expansive and complex state. Nevertheless, even then he strongly believed that the law had become unmanageable and that it ought to be simplified. Hence, he advocated codification of the law, helped establish the New York Law Revision Commission,[2] and was instrumental in the drafting of a number of model codes. Some of these were adopted within his native state, some in others, and some by other countries to replace more traditional law with emerging new legal systems.[3]

Another person who was concerned with the complexity of the law, especially in the commercial law field, was Karl Llewellyn. He noted, in testifying before the New York Law Revision Commission, that the commercial law had

---

[1]For discussion of Field's activities in codification and controversies concerning them, see Schlesinger, "The Uniform Commercial Code in Light of Comparative Law," 1 N.Y. Law Rev. Comm. Rep. U.C.C. 87-123 (1955).

[2]Ibid.

[3]Note 14 supra.

become more complex and uncertain.[4] Indeed, he pointed out that, "because of this uncertainty, lawyers from large companies could simply balk at entering into reasonable solutions or settlements with others."[5] Karl Llewellyn's purposes for the great Uniform Commercial Code were "to bring order into the complexity that existed, to bring some simplification and clarity into the law, and uniformity."[6]

In addition, we should note that the statutory law in the common law countries and civil law countries has greatly expanded in recent decades. This is discussed more in viewing the origins and modern developments of commercial law in Part I.

Another background factor that must be kept in mind is the development of the consumer protection movement. While there were only sporadic attention and a few laws at the earlier stages, it was not until the 1960s that major societal interest in consumer problems evolved in the United States. Ralph Nader and others spearheaded the interest in this area. As a result, consumer rights are more recognized than ever. To effectuate such rights, it has been necessary to add special legislation to the overall commercial law. This has meant expanding various fields of the commercial law, amending various aspects of the commercial law, and reevaluating and developing theory in regard to consumer transactions. The quest for consumer rights can be found in countries throughout the world as new consumer legislation is enacted.[7]

It also must be noted that considerable changes have taken place in legal theory or jurisprudence. This indirectly has an effect on change in or the expansion of law since it often requires a reanalysis of problems, laws, and new developments. Even within the past quarter century, these legal theory movements have included critical legal studies, the feminist theory of law, the economic analysis of law, and the revival of secular and natural law theories.[8] The influential lay and economics movement has had a tremendous impact on North American legal literature and law schools, resulting in a different legal approach than the traditional one to some major economic and social problems.

ORIGIN OF LAW IN THE UNITED STATES

The first body of law in the United States was imported. Our early settlers found themselves in need of some law. They decided to embrace the law prevailing in

---

[4]See Llewellyn, "Statement to the N.Y. Law Revision Commission," 1 N.Y. Law Rev. Comm.. Rep. U.C.C. 25-36 (1954).
[5]Ibid.
[6]U.C.S. § 1-102.
[7]E.g., King, *Essays on Comparative Commercial and Consumer Law*, pp. 245-338, Rothman Co., 1992.
[8]See Scott and King, *Sales,* pp. 1-11 to 1-15, Casenote Publishing Co., 1992.

their native lands, rather than to create new laws on an *ad hoc* basis. Those who
settled on our east coast brought from England a body of law known as the "common law"— the law that was common to England. The French and Spanish settlers of the southern and western parts of our country imported the "civil law" of
Continental Europe. The civil law, also known as the Code Napoléon, has many
features that distinguish it from the common law. Most of the variances between
the two have been reconciled in favor of the common law. However, the state of
Louisiana has maintained many of the features of the civil law in their present-
day legal structure. (See Chapter X.)

The Common Law and the Law Merchant

The common law of England was and continues to be the most predominant
influence in American law. There are many places in this text where the common
law rule is discussed, and where it is shown to be applicable today. Although the
common law began as unwritten, it has been perpetuated by recorded court decisions and by writers, the most well-known of whom is Blackstone. Acts of British
Parliament over the years added structure to this informal legal framework. The
common law brought to this country was to become the foundation of our legal
system. The various branches of our government have improved it by adding,
amending, deleting, and modernizing.

It is of particular interest to the purchasing officer that English common law
included the *Law Merchant*. You will recall from Medieval history that early trade
was governed by the traders themselves. They formed associations, or guilds, to
manage and operate their trading businesses. The guilds provided the avenues by
which traders settled their trade balances. They also established the rules and the
forum for traders to settle their disputes. Such disputes were settled according to
the *Law Merchant*. Much of early law applying to buyers and sellers is found in
the *Law Merchant*. It was made part of English common law in 1677, and came to
America with the balance of the common law.

COMMERCIAL LAW IN THE UNITED STATES

Commercial law is state-oriented. Each state jurisdiction has the authority to
develop its own body of laws to deal with commercial transactions. As long as a
law does not violate the federal and state constitutions, a state is at liberty to regulate and govern the business environment as it chooses. Needless to say, this
freedom of each state to legislate business law according to its own need leads to
many problems for those engaged in interstate commerce.

There were no problems when our country was in its infancy. Business was
done on a local basis and each business entity was small. All commerce was con-

ducted within the borders of the state where the business was located. But as the country began to grow and businesses began expanding, problems soon developed because each state had control over the legal atmosphere under which business was transacted. The problem was not the general tenor of the law as it affected business within the state, but rather with the differences in the law among the several states. A businessperson doing business in two or more states had to be aware of how each legal topic was treated within the state where the transactions took place. One could not be assured that a legal problem would be treated in the same manner in more than one state. In fact, diversity of the law among the states was more the rule than was the uniformity of the law.

STANDARDIZING STATE LAWS

The difficulties business people engaged in interstate commerce had in coping with the diversity of commercial law among the several states did not go unnoticed. The American Bar Association in the early 1890s decided to do something about the problem. The Association created a group that became known as the National Conference of Commissioners on Uniform State Laws. Commissioners from each of the states then in existence were appointed to this group. The charge given the Commissioners was to write a model law on a given commercial law topic, which would then be submitted to the legislature body of each state for adoption. The thought was that if each state legislative body adopted the same model law, diversity between state laws would be eliminated. The National Conference went to work on this immense task. Support became available from other sources, and the conference ceased to be dependent upon American Bar Association for financing.

The first model law produced by the National Conference was the Uniform Negotiable Instruments Law, which appeared in 1896. Four other model laws were produced within the next 13 years including the Uniform Sales Act and the Uniform Bills of Lading Act. These model acts were sent to every state legislature with the suggestion that they be approved by the legislature "as written" so that all states would have the identical statute on the topic as part of their law. The endeavor met with a good deal of success, although not with the speed the Commissioners had hoped for. Two of the model laws, including the Negotiable Instruments Act, were eventually made part of the law of every state.

This endeavor to make uniform the commercial law among the states worked reasonably well for a period of about 30 to 35 years. However, the preciseness of the uniformity that had been hoped for did not materialize. When the various legislatures adopted the model acts, there were always a few sections that were "tinkered with" and slightly revised to satisfy the tastes of individual legislators. As time wore on, the state courts would be required to interpret the law in cases brought before them. The court's interpretation of any particular section of the law did not always coincide with the interpretation of the same section by the court in another jurisdiction. In addition, amendments to the model laws were commonplace. By 1936 the diversity of the law, state by state, was almost as prevalent as it was when the uniform laws first appeared. Interstate commerce was again burdened with diversity of law among the several states.

GENESIS OF THE UNIFORM COMMERCIAL CODE

The fact that the volume of business transactions had tremendously increased in the three decades since the first uniform law had been written compounded the problem of the diversity of the state laws. Rapid improvements in transportation and communications accelerated the pace of business. It was evident that a whole new effort was required to modernize business law to keep pace and to provide uniformity between states. In 1942 the National Conference of Commissioners on Uniform State Laws, in conjunction with the American Law Institute, went to work on the problem once again.

There were suggestions that a federal sales act be written so that every business transaction, no matter in which state the contract was created or was to be performed, would be governed by the same set of laws. The suggestion had merit, but the idea was abandoned because of constitutional problems and a strong desire to keep business law under the jurisdiction of the several states. So the Commissioners went to work once again to prepare a model law that could be adopted by the states to bring about uniformity. They stayed with it and came forth in 1951 with the first version of what is now known as the Uniform Commercial Code. The Code as first written was adopted by the state of Pennsylvania in 1954. However, substantial revisions were made, and it was not until 1958 that the Code's present general format was established. Massachusetts was the first state to adopt the 1958 version. Since then all the states, except Louisiana, have adopted it. Arizona, Idaho, Mississippi, and South Carolina were the last to adopt it *in toto*. Their adoptions became effective in 1968. Louisiana has adopted portions of the Code, but not Article 2 (Sales), which is that part of the code most applicable to purchasing law.

It required a major effort to bring this degree of uniformity to state law. And despite the effort, the Code on the statutory books of the various states is not one hundred percent uniform. There are a few minor differences in it as adopted, but only in Article 9 are the differences substantial. The Falk Foundation gave the American Law Institute a splendid grant in 1961 to finance a permanent editorial board to review and, yes—to police—the various state codes for any amendments made or proposed to the official text. At least uniformity of the Code would be protected and an alert issued in the event any state decided to alter it. Judicial interpretation of the Code will vary; there is no way that this can be controlled. But for the present, statutory uniformity seems assured.

The Content of Uniform Commercial Code

The Uniform Commercial Code is a compendium of the statutory laws pertaining to commercial transactions. It covers many of the topics that were contained in the uniform laws referred to previously. They have been rewritten and modernized for today's business use. There are nine topical subdivisions, which are titled "Articles."

Article 1	General Provisions
Article 2	Sales
Article 2A	Leases
Article 3	Commercial Paper
Article 4	Bank Deposits and Collections
Article 4A	Electronic Transfers
Article 5	Letters of Credit
Article 6	Bulk Transfers
Article 7	Warehouse Receipts, Bills of Lading, and Other Documents of Title
Article 8	Investment Securities
Article 9	Secured Transactions, Sales of Accounts, and Chattel Paper

The writers of the Code sought to make the average business transaction, from beginning to end, regulated by a single body of law. It is apparent that these goals have been achieved. Transactions originating by a purchase, for example, are all to be regulated by the Code. This text will confine itself to a thorough analysis of Article 2, Sales, which contains the most pertinent law involved in the daily purchasing routine.

The Uniform Commercial Code replaces the older, uniform laws. The title section of the Code, which explains the scope of coverage, concludes with the statement that it is "Replacing Inconsistent Legislation." The Code suggests to the various state legislatures that when the Code is adopted a specific repealer should be included. It then gives a list of those prior laws that should be repealed, including the Uniform Negotiable Instruments Act, the Uniform Warehouse Receipts Act, the Uniform Sales Act, the Uniform Bills of Lading Act, and ten other acts which are not of great importance to the purchasing officer. Thus the Code takes over the entire jurisdiction of those areas of commercial law that were formerly covered by individual, specialized acts.

APPLICABILITY OF THE CODE

Despite the fact that one of the goals of the writers of the Code was to place all of the law regulating a business transaction in one body of the law, the Code itself is not a freestanding legal system. Its jurisdiction is confined solely to the topics covered by its text. Other general principles of law governing topics that are not covered specifically by the Code are to supplement its provisions. Section 1-103 of the Code calls attention to this fact:

> Unless displaced by the particular provisions of this Act, the principles of law and equity, including the law merchant and the law relative to capacity to contract, principal and agent, estoppel, fraud, misrepresentation, duress, coercion, mistake, bankruptcy, or other validating or invalidating cause shall supplement its provisions.

There is continued case law expansion of commercial law in terms of the sale of goods. A new article on leasing, Article 2A, has been added to the Uniform Commercial Code. A special committee studying Article 2 has proposed other amendments to the law of sales, and a special reporter has been appointed to revise that part of the Code. This is discussed in more detail in the part dealing with changes. Some believe that computer and software law should be added to the Sales Articles or even should be in its own Article (Article 2B). Some of the current legal problems arising out of computer contracts are discussed in Chapter 25. In addition, there may be an article on the sale of services at some future time. In terms of commercial paper, there are amendments to Articles 3 and 4. There is also Article 4A on the electronic transfers, and federal legislation on the electronic transfer of certain types of consumer transactions. In addition, more consumer laws have been enacted in recent times.

MODERN SOURCES OF THE LAW

The federal government and each state government contain three branches: (1) the legislative branch, (2) the judicial branch, and (3) the executive branch. Each branch contributes to the body of law by which purchasing officers must live.

1. The Legislative Branch

Those who wrote our Constitution placed the power to make law in the hands of the legislative branch of government. The Congress of the United States and the legislatures of the several states enact statutes, to which those affected must adhere. This is the true source of modern law.

2. The Judicial Branch

The federal and state court systems are charged with the duty of interpreting the law and applying it to adversary cases (lawsuits) brought before them. The judicial branch is not actually a source of the law, but, because it has the power to interpret the law, it must be reckoned with as a source. The ability to interpret a law gives the courts the opportunity to add meaning to a law. Interpretations could alter the intent, the application, and the restriction of the law. The complete impact of any law cannot be ascertained until it has been litigated in court by adversaries.

Decisions rendered by courts in lawsuits also develop into a body of law. Attorneys refer to this as *case law*. When a court decides a case, the principle of law applied in the decision becomes fixed in that jurisdiction. This is referred to as the doctrine of *stare decisis*, which interpreted loosely means, "Let the decision stand for future cases of a similar nature." Thus, the final answer, or the bottom line, of a legal problem facing the purchasing officer will probably be found in a case previously decided in court. Most courts are greatly persuaded in deciding a case by prior case law but they are not obligated to follow existing case laws, and are at liberty to reverse them. An excellent example of this freedom to reverse a previous decision is found in the case of *Brown v. Board of Education*, decided in 1956 by the Supreme Court of the United States. After the Court had for more than 63 years given credibility to the doctrine of *separate but equal* educational facilities for the races, the Court announced in the Brown case that the rationale applied in previous cases was no longer valid. Thus, it overturned existing case law and made possible the integration of educational facilities.

3. The Executive Branch

The executive branch of the government, at both federal and state levels, has the duty to administer the law. It was not contemplated that any statutes or laws would be generated in this branch of government. This principle was followed for a period of time, but at the turn of the 20th century, it was changed. At that time, the Congress of the United States began enacting complex statutes and creating commissions to administer them. The statutes involved such complicated subjects that Congress could not write into the text all the details of their application. So it delegated authority to the commissions it had created to do this job. These commissions became part of the executive branch of the government. They are now spewing out thousands of rules and regulations implementing these statutes. Typical among them are the:

1. Internal Revenue Service.

2. National Labor Relations Board.

3. Federal Trade Commission.

4. Interstate Commerce Commission.

5. Occupational Safety and Health Administration.

There are many others. Their rules and regulations have the same effect as law until overturned by a court of law. The purchasing officer therefore needs to be cognizant of these sources of the law at both the federal and state levels.

Your Legal Counsel

Any listing of the sources of the law for purchasing officers would be incomplete without mention of the legal counsel engaged by your company or organization. This important source is discussed in Chapter II.

JURISDICTION

Law in the United States is established and enforced by jurisdiction. A jurisdiction is a boundary within which a law is applicable. It could be a geographic boundary, one established by the topic of the law involved, or both.

Geographic jurisdictions include the boundaries of a municipality, a town, a county, a state, or a nation. In the United States we have fifty separate and distinct major jurisdictions formed by the state boundaries. We also have the federal jurisdiction, and jurisdictions for Puerto Rico, the other territories, and the District of Columbia.

Topical or subject matter jurisdictions are constitutionally mandated. The Constitution of the United States and its various amendments give specific authority to the federal government to legislate and control particular areas of our lives and businesses. This is the federal jurisdiction. Those powers not specifically delegated to the federal government, nor prohibited by the Constitution of the United States from state authority, are reserved for each state to control. Each state then has a jurisdiction because of a topic of the law that is applied and enforced within its geographic boundaries. This is the state jurisdiction.

The bulk of business law, which is the area that most directly concerns purchasing activities, is under state jurisdiction. There are, however, some federal and local laws that affect the purchasing officer's workplace. Contracts with and for the federal government, for example, have specific rules that must be followed. This makes such contracts subject to special rules of law within an almost special federal jurisdiction.

In addition, international law and the laws of foreign countries are becoming a factor for some purchasing officers. Since more foreign sources of supply are being developed, the law of those countries will play an increasing part in the purchasing law specialty, unless the purchasing officer is successful in having the law of his or her state made applicable to the contract.

Jurisdiction is primarily the problem of legal counsel. It determines in which court suit may be brought or defended, and which law is applicable to the situation.

COMMERCIAL DOCUMENTS

To aid in understanding the issues and application of the law, it may be well to briefly note what different documents may be involved in various commercial transactions or various parts of them as covered by the Code. Purchasing agents are familiar with the documents involved in the sales transaction per se and sometimes with some of the financing ones as well. While this may seem elementary, it is useful to note how the Code affects them.

The Sales Contract

The sales contract, covered primarily by Article 2, may consist of any number of things. It may be simply a phone or personal conversation, or it may be an exchange of telegrams or letters. In many instances it may consist of an order form followed by performance or an acknowledgment form. There is no set form required for these, although some provisions are advisable. Large companies and merchants generally have their own printed forms. In some cases these forms will conflict in part and yet there still remains the possibility of a sales contract. Other times, the sales contract will consist primarily of a printed order or agreement which the buyer signs. There are often spaces to be filled in for price, specifics on the item, and the buyer's name and address. Generally there are a number of printed clauses and conditions. In addition there are often descriptive advertisements, folders, instructions, and warranty booklets or papers. These too may become part of the overall sales contract.

Interestingly, when problems with the sales contract arise that are not covered by conversations or papers, trade usage or course of dealing or prior course performance may be brought in to solve the problem since this is part of the agreement under Section 1-201(3). In addition, the gap may be "filled in" by special provisions in Part 3 of Article 2 of the Code.

In many situations, financing of the transaction will be required. When this is so, other commercial documents may be necessary. The purchaser may wish to buy on credit from the seller, or he may seek independent financing. In either case he generally will be signing commercial paper and a security interest.

Negotiable paper—notes, drafts, checks, and other paper—has evolved in certain forms over the years. The paper need not have a particular form, but must meet certain requisites set forth in the Code. As a practical matter, the forms generally are very similar. The main purpose is to promote further financing since the paper is usually transferred or sold by the merchant to another party such as a bank or finance company. The latter may sell it to other banks or finance companies.

Forms of Negotiable Paper

Promissory Notes. A note is a written, unconditional promise to pay a sum of money either on demand or at a set time to the order of a named party or to bearer. There is some unique, but not difficult terminology, used in commercial paper. The buyer who signs the promise to pay is called the *maker* of the note — which makes sense since he "makes" the note by signing it. The party to whose order the promise to pay is made is called the *payee*. The note is sometimes referred to as *two-party paper*. The note may simply contain the promise to pay and several terms relating to payment and allowance of collection costs. It is sometimes called *a short form promissory note*. Some notes contain more terms and are called *long form promissory notes*. None of these terms may condition the promise, however, or they will make it nonnegotiable. The promissory note is often used for long-term commercial financing and shorter-term consumer loans.

The promissory notes, like other commercial paper, may be endorsed by the payee and sold to another party. The endorsement is a negotiation of the paper. If the payee simply signs on the back "Pay to the order of John Thirdparty," it is called *a special endorsement*. It may be negotiated further only by John Thirdparty. Or the endorsement by the payee could be the signing of his name with "For Deposit Only" in which case it would be a *restrictive endorsement* and must be so applied. If the note is payable to bearer, it may be negotiated by delivery alone. Once commercial paper is properly negotiated, the new holder of it may be a holder in due course if he takes in good faith, for value, and without notice of claim or defense. The endorsement carries with it certain contractual liabilities, and the negotiation and sales of the paper also carry certain warranties.

The manner of signing is also most important as indicated in Article 3. Failure to indicate the office or position may result in personal liability, even though signing under the company name.

Drafts. Another type of commercial paper used in the commercial transaction is the *draft*, which is an order directed to a party to pay. In commercial transactions, involving the shipment of goods over a distance, the draft is frequently used. The seller, or drawer, draws up the draft and sends it to the buyer's bank along with the bills of lading. These are turned over to the buyer as soon as he pays the draft if it is one requiring immediate payment. This is called a *sight draft*, because it is payable on sight.

Some drafts, however, are made payable in three days or in 30 days. These are called *three-day* and *thirty-day sight drafts*. This type serves both to give the seller his money and to give the buyer credit, which is done by the buyer's writing "accepted" across its face and signing it. The buyer signs bills of lading to him so that he gets his goods. The draft, once signed by the buyer, is negotiable paper. Therefore, the bank or other financier which becomes a holder in due course is willing to buy or discount it and pay the seller cash. It might be asked why the buyer could not simply sign a promissory note for the 30 days, since this could be sold to the bank which would become a holder in due course and would give the seller cash. This could be done, but traditionally a draft is used in this type of commercial transaction. The draft, as well as the promissory note and other commercial paper, is covered by Article 3 of the Code.

Checks and Bills of Exchange. Another type of familiar commercial paper is the check or bill of exchange. The check is signed by the buyer or drawer and is given to the seller or payee for goods. The buyer's bank on which it is drawn is called the *drawee*. The check is in effect a demand draft in which the drawee is a bank in which the buyer maintains an account. The check is covered by Article 3 of the Code, with the bank-customer relationship covered also in Article 4.

Letters of Credit

A letter of credit is another document that may be used in a commercial transaction where the parties are at a distance, and the seller is concerned about assurance of payment. Instead of relying on the credit or on payment by the buyer, he may want to have a reputable bank in effect guarantee the payment. This can be done by requiring the buyer or customer to get his bank to issue a letter of credit. Logically enough, the bank is termed the *issuer*, and the seller who benefits from it is called the *beneficiary*. The letter of credit states that the issuer will honor the drafts upon compliance with the terms of the letter, which generally call for the proper bills of lading and any other necessary shipping documents.

The application for a letter of credit by the customer is often on a preprinted form containing a number of conditions. The letter of credit itself, however, is usually much simpler and in more of a letter form. No particular form is necessary under Article 5 of the Code. In some cases the seller of the goods will want the assurance of payment from a bank in his own city or country, and it will be a *confirming bank*. The letter or confirmation also need not be used in any particular form.

Secured Transaction Documents

Security Agreement. In commercial transactions where payment is over a considerable period of time, the seller may wish to keep some interest in the goods. This is called a *security interest* and is covered by Article 9 of the Code.

The security interest is created by the debtor signing a security agreement. This is generally a printed form labeled as "Security Agreement" with a number of conditions related to care of the goods and seller's rights on any default. Although earlier forms labeled as conditional sales, or chattel mortgages, or bailment leases can still be used, they are still subject to Article 9, and it is preferable to use newer forms especially designed to incorporate advantages that may be gained under the Code.

The security agreement document is similar to a contract, but has property aspects in that some courts may require words of grant, and has some commercial paper aspects in that it may have a clause waiving defenses as to third party transferees.

The Financing Statement. In addition to the security agreement, a separate document, known as the *financing statement*, is recorded under the Article 9 notice-type filing. This is very brief and simply describes the property covered, and lists the creditor and the debtor. Generally a creditor also will mark an X in the box indicating that any possible proceeds of the property are covered, although under the Code amendments this coverage will be automatic.

While the security agreement or a copy of it can theoretically be filed as a financing statement if signed by both debtor and creditor, in most states the recording officials require that it be on their prescribed printed form. It is neither fully safe nor desirable to attempt to use the financing statement or a copy of it as the security agreement. Therefore, clearly, two separate documents are necessary: a security agreement and a financing statement. In addition, there are separate forms for continuing the security interest, amending it, and terminating it.

Bills of Lading Documents

In commercial transactions involving the shipment of goods, bills of lading are utilized. These documents control the goods and set forth the conditions of their transportation. In the *straight bill of lading,* which is nonnegotiable, the goods are consigned to a given person. The *order bill of lading* is made to the order of a person or his order and is negotiable. The standard forms have been utilized. The terms on the bill of lading are affected by Article 7 of the Code or the Federal Bill of Lading Act and the Interstate Commerce Commission. Warehouse receipts are also documents that control the goods and set forth conditions for their care. These are relatively standard, printed forms with numerous conditions for their care. The Code does not require any particular form, but sets forth certain requirements.

Combining Commercial Documents

In transactions involving the sale of goods over a distance, almost all of these separate commercial documents may be utilized in conjunction with each other. In some commercial transactions, the sales contract and security agreement may be combined. In some, the security agreement will include a promissory note separated by only a dotted line. In many commercial transactions, the draft is often sent with the bills of lading. All these documents are subject not only to the requirements of their particular article of the Code, but to the supplemental and general principles of good faith, unconscionability, and custom and trade usage as well.

Freedom of Contract

Freedom of contract is recognized in modern commercial law as serving a most valuable function. In today's world, where there has been a collapse of the Communist system, this underlying basis of contract and purchasing law should be kept in mind. It is encouraged in the Uniform Commercial Code in a number of ways. One is the tremendous emphasis placed upon trade usage and commercial practices; Section 1-205 is devoted to this subject and Section 1-201(3) defines agreement as including these matters. Another is found in the flexibility of the code in permitting new business practices to develop. Still another is the large scope of freedom under the Code to make agreements as the parties so desire.

Setting Outer Limits for Contracts. It may be said that freedom of the contract is divided into three major areas under the Code. First there is a category of the outermost limits beyond which freedom of contract cannot go. This area is the more exceptional one and serves to set outer boundaries around the large area of freedom of contract. In part, these are set by legal standards of good faith, unconscionability, reasonableness and care. In Section 1-201, the principle of freedom of contract is explicitly limited by good faith, diligence, reasonableness, and care, as prescribed by the act.

In addition to the more general limitations upon the unlimited right of agreement, the Code comment points out that freedom to contract "is subject to specific exceptions found elsewhere in the act." Although it does not set forth precisely what the specific exceptions are, the Statute of Frauds is mentioned as a primary one. It is pointed out that while the section on the Statute of Frauds does not expressly preclude oral waiver of the requirement of a writing, a "fair reading" would deny enforcement to such waiver. Other examples that are noted as being exceptions to the freedom to contract are that parties cannot make an instrument negotiable except as so provided in the article on commercial paper, and cannot change the meaning of various terms such as "holder in due course" or "bona fide purchaser" or "due negotiation" as utilized in the Code. It may be said that these are certain mandatory aspects of the Code as contrasted to permissive ones. This may, however, be a matter of labeling and the real issue may rest upon the fundamental importance and basic underlying policy of the provisions.

In addition to these very basic standards of fairness in dealing and standards of a highly important or mandatory nature from a policy viewpoint, certain provisions of the Code explicitly state that the provision "may not be varied." This category includes:

- Section 1-102(3) on general limits on power to vary.

- Section 1-105(2) on choice of law.

- Section 1-208 on the option to accelerate at will.

- Section 2-302 on unconscionable contracts or clauses.

- Section 2-718 on liquidated damages and penalties.

- Section 2-719 on variation in limitation of remedies and sales.

- Section 5-116(2) permitting the beneficiary to assign his rights to proceeds, even though the credit is nonassignable.

- Section 9-318(4) on clauses forbidding assignment of rights.

- A major portion of Part 5 of Article 9 on rights of the secured debtor after default.

It may be said that most of these provisions, which cannot be varied, are to protect a party who is in a position where he cannot effectively bargain or exercise freedom of contract. In these settings where freedom of contract has been abused, such as that relating to rights of the debtor upon default, the Code prohibits "artificial freedom of contract."

Contracts Containing the "Unless Otherwise Agreed" Clause. A second major category that the Code sets forth in relation to freedom to contract is the class of clauses often labeled as "unless otherwise agreed" clauses. This category allows for freedom of contract and allows the terms that the parties actually agree upon to prevail. It also promotes upholding contracts with missing terms by supplying terms the parties may have forgotten to mention. A number of the Code sections carry the clause "unless otherwise agreed." This clause is found in a number of situations in the sales area where a particular rule of law of the Code states the usual commercial practice. It also may be said to represent situations where the usual and normal practices would be accepted by a party as part of the agreement, or would not even be thought of as being otherwise by a party, unless it were made a matter of specific agreement or exception. It also is found in a slightly lesser degree in other articles of the Code where the expectations of the parties would generally be in accordance with the Code rule, unless there were some special notation or agreement made as to the exception. In the comments it is pointed out that one of the principal purposes of the clause "unless otherwise agreed" in a Code provision is to "avoid controversy as to whether the subject matter of a particular section does or does not fall within the exceptions to Subsection 3," which is the section relating to variation by agreement except for matters of good faith, diligence, reasonableness, and care.

Contracts Whose Provisions Can Be Varied by Agreement. A third classification in the realm of freedom to contract may be said to be those clauses where there is no explicit statement as to whether or not the section can be varied, and there is no basic underlying problem as to good faith, unconscionability, or reasonableness and care as prescribed by the Act. The large majority of Code sections would fall into this category. This large category promotes freedom of contract. The drafters wished to make it clear that freedom of contract was allowed generally. In the comments it is stated that "the general and residual rule is that the effect of all provisions of the Act may be varied by agreement."

CONTINUING COMMERCIAL LAW DEVELOPMENTS

As the Second Millennium approaches, as in all legal history, there are new developments occurring every year. In these times of complexity and accelerated change, major developments take place more often than before.

As mentioned earlier, the Uniform Commercial Code, with its drafting beginning in the 1940s, is in need of some changes. There are new businesses, as well as technological and legal developments. Even theory changes over the course of time. The Sales Article of the Uniform Commercial Code is now being revised and is further being changed to cover computer software and licensing, and some special principles are being added.

Commercial law history also has been made with the adoption of the Convention on the International Sale of Goods by this country and many others. This development is discussed in Chapter XXXII.

With the development of the North American Free Trade Association, there is now a growing body of regional country law throughout the world and despite some crisis, it will undoubtedly continue to grow. The already well-established European Community is effectuating many of its goals and expanding.

II

The Role of Your Legal Counsel

INTRODUCTION

This is the shortest chapter in the book. Its limited number of words carries an important message for purchasing officers.

Most business and not-for-profit organizations have an attorney who regularly handles the bulk of their legal matters. This individual is referred to as the organization's legal counsel. Your company's legal counsel is your primary and best source of legal advice. He or she is acquainted with the important legal details about your company, such as the charter, the legal structure, and the purposes for which it is authorized to operate. Counsel knows the laws of the state in which the company is organized and operates. This is a great advantage. No matter how generally accepted a legal principle is, nor how uniform a law is, any state jurisdiction can have a unique application or interpretation of it. Counsel will know the distinctive features that prevail in your jurisdiction.

Those of you who have undergone the rigors of a court litigated trial can attest to the fact that there is more to it than meets the eye in a lawsuit. Counsel for both parties will offer several different theories of the law to aid in the prosecution or defense of the charges. Counsel will know what facts are relevant to the trial. Facts that you might classify as having no value may be seized upon by counsel and employed to further your case. You are in good hands when your legal counsel is solving your legal problems.

Counsel is a great ally in the successful operation of a purchasing department. Get to know that individual. Have him or her get to know your operations, the forms you use, and the procedures you follow. Once this friendly relationship has been established, it becomes a simple matter to obtain competent legal advice on a troublesome situation. Little time will be required to orient counsel on how you operate. You will both be able to get to the core of the problem immediately.

Legal counsel and the purchasing officer form a magnificent team. Their cooperation secures legal advantages and protections for the organization or company involved and ensures that a minimal amount of legal difficulties arise from the purchasing operations. Your author commends you to the good offices of your legal counsel.

CORPORATE LEGAL SERVICES

A number of companies have their own legal counsel. Indeed, some of the very large companies may have over a hundred attorneys on their staff. Although this size is found more often in large companies that handle a variety of matters including patents, it is not unusual for large companies to have a fairly large legal staff. By contrast a smaller company may, especially after experiencing some litigation, decide to hire one or two attorneys. The cost of corporate legal counsel varies considerably in different parts of the country. The East Coast and West Coast salaries are generally much higher. In the Midwest, however, a company may hire a recent law school graduate for $40,000 - $50,000 a year. A lawyer with some experience may cost from $60,000- $80,000 per year, while a more experienced counsel salary may exceed $100,000. Although this may seem relatively expensive, the cost is relatively low when compared to the high hourly rates that must be paid to outside counsels as mentioned shortly.

The value of having corporate counsel is the availability and ease of consulting them. They are almost always present and have the company as their sole client. Purchasing managers should get to know corporate counsel well as they may have need to consult him or her on a fair number of occasions. The other value of corporate counsel is that copies of documents that may carry some legal implications may be sent to corporate counsel as well as to other departments of the company. Thus, if the purchasing manager would generally send an original and five copies, he or she simply needs to change the procedure to an original and six copies—one of which is to the corporate counsel.

Some companies use both inside and outside legal counsel. Inside legal counsel is most often used for evaluating long-term contracts, including those involving purchases. Inside legal counsel also handles a number of nonlitigation legal matters. On the other hand, if the company is involved in a litigation, corporate legal counsel often work with counsel hired from the outside. There are several reasons for this practice. One is that the company's interests are adequately protected by the corporate counsel being on the case. Still, corporate counsel may not have as a specialty the field of litigation; outside counsel brings this particular expertise and skill to the case. Finally, outside counsel may be more familiar with the judges in that particular area of the country and likewise may be better able to relate well to local juries. In addition, if the litigation is in another state, corporate counsel may not be a member of the bar of that state. Although special permission is sometimes possible from the court for counsel of another state to argue a case, even that sometimes requires that a local attorney also be hired for the case as well.

OUTSIDE LEGAL SERVICES

In some situations the company may not have its own counsel within the company, and an outside lawyer may be consulted. In other situations, the company's lawyer may choose to have outside lawyers represent the company, either for specialist work or for strategic litigation purposes. If it appears that the case may be tried in a distant locale, with a local jury, it may be wise to hire a lawyer from that area. Still, in other situations, the purchasing manager may have a need to consult outside counsel for his own reasons or needs. In any event, several things should be understood in regard to employing outside counsel.

One is that the law has become highly specialized. While some attorneys handle general practice (and all who have passed the bar are authorized to do so), many handle only certain types of cases. Thus, some handle only tax matters, others only corporate law, others commercial contracting, others real estate development, and so on. Even within these categories, there are more narrow specialties. If the matter requiring a lawyer is complex, it may be best to get a lawyer who specializes in that area. Indeed, in some of the more complex cases, the manpower and expertise of a particular law field may be desired. On the other hand, if it is a relatively simple or general matter, a general practitioner may be sufficient and less costly. Also, some attorneys prefer not to litigate or appeal in court, while others thrive on such work.

Another thing to bear in mind is cost. Contrary to some popular belief, there is no fixed fee schedule. Legal charges are whatever is agreed upon by the client and attorney. While one may look to some reasonable yardsticks in regard to what is a fair fee for given work or a fair hourly charge, much depends on the experience of the lawyer and the demand for his services. It also sometimes depends on mere whim! Some lawyers, with relatively little experience, simply demand a large fee!

Lawyer fees generally fall within one of several categories. One is the hourly fee, which can vary considerably from one lawyer to another. While 30 years ago an average standard fee was $35 per hour, it now is $75 to $125 per hour. Some lawyers, especially those in law firms in larger cities, may charge much more. Rates ranging from $200 to $600 an hour are not unusual in large cities. If this seems high, it should be pointed out that some lawyer fees in foreign countries are even higher!

Sometimes an attorney charging such rates is well worth it. His expertise and skills may result in better advice or a better outcome. Other times, he is no better than a more moderately priced lawyer. The amount of the legal fee will be determined by the agreement between the individual or company and the lawyer or law firm. It is important to ask about legal fees, discuss them, and agree upon them before hiring outside counsel. Where outside counsel is billing at an hourly rate, it also is not inappropriate to ask for a relative detailed accounting of that time and activity.

Another fee category is charging by the task to be done. He may indicate a certain charge to incorporate a business, to handle a contract, or to take a specific type of case to its conclusion. Again, the charges of lawyers vary considerably and are subject to whatever the parties agree upon.

Finally, some lawyers may make contingency fee arrangements. If they settle or win the case, they take a percentage of the recovery. If they lose, they get nothing and there is no charge to the client. Contingency fees are found most often in regard to personal injury cases, but can be used in business situations as well. Again, the fees (in this situation the percentages asked) vary with each lawyer. It used to be a general standard that it would be 25 percent if the case were settled or 33 percent of the amount of recovery if the case went to court and the lawyer won it. In more recent times, many lawyers ask for 33 percent of a settlement or 40 percent of recovery if it goes to court. In some cases, usually involving personal inquiry or bad faith business practices, the verdict may be in the millions. The winning lawyer on a contingent fee becomes an instant multimillionaire.

Consequently, purchasing managers should consider a variety of factors when hiring outside counsel.

ALTERNATIVE DISPUTE RESOLUTION

In the last several decades, it's become increasingly recognized that means for settling disputes other than litigation may be advantageous in many cases. The high costs and delays found in litigation thus may be avoided. Also, alternative resolution devices may keep long-term relationships going and leave both parties more satisfied and without the bitter taste of losing.

Of the various alternative dispute resolution mechanisms, two of the most common are mediation and arbitration. Parties may preagree to this by putting a clause providing for it in their contract in case of later disputes, or they may agree to it later once the dispute has arisen. The former seems more desirable, because it establishes the means before a dispute arises that so angers parties that they jump at litigation.

MEDIATION

Mediation may be defined in various ways and with various stages, but basically it means that the parties will try to reach a settlement themselves with the help of a third party, called a *mediator.* Generally the mediator meets with each party separately so as to ascertain their views of the problem, feelings, needs, and desires before bringing them together in an attempt to get them to work out a solution.

If the parties desire to use this technique, they may place a clause in their contract to the effect that, in case of disputes regarding the contract or their contracts generally, they shall first attempt to settle their differences through mediation. Various mediation services exist and can be named by the parties in this contract clause.

Mediators must have skills in fact finding, analyzing, creativeness, communication, psychology, and persuasion. The mediator (a highly skilled person) should be named before the mediation by agreement. If the mediation is part of a mediation service or association, it will normally have a fee schedule; still the total costs of mediation will be considerably less than litigation.

One of the first things a mediator does is to set the stage. The mediator should try to set a positive tone, so that the parties feel at ease and confident that there is a good chance to work things out together. Some of the hostility surrounding the dispute should be put aside. There must be an openness to resolution, realistic factors should be considered, and a cooperative search emphasized. Also, the parties should be told what the procedures of the mediation will be, how information will be gathered, the approximate schedule of sessions and breaks, the confidentiality involved, the rules of the procedures, and some of the various types of settlement that may be available.

After setting the stage, the mediator may ask both sides to explain how they see the problem. The mediator may ask questions designed for elaboration, clarification, or response to emotional contest, or for reinforcement of some matters. The questions may subtly elicit the reasons behind the conflict, as well as the values, the social or cultural differences, the biases, and the inabilities to communicate.

After this informational stage, the mediator may seek to identify the issues. This phase takes place by way of discussion, summary, and asking if any other issues appear. In identifying the issues at hand, the mediator also must seek out any hidden interests or motivations that create issues.

From an issue-identifying stage, the mediation may move to a discussion stage. Even then, the mediator often helps both sides mutually create an agenda and procedure. The discussion may take place with the two parties and mediator present, but part of it may take place with the mediator talking separately with each as well.

The search for remedies may then take place. Sometimes changes in structural roles, time patterns, or physical or environmental factors may be important. Other times, the resolution of factual matters is most important. Indeed, other experts may be called on in this regard. Other times values, emotions, stereotyping, and lack of communication are crucial factors to be looked at in shaping the remedy. Once the parties agree on a remedy, the mediator often works with them to reduce it to a writing, so as to solidify it and prevent any future misunderstanding.

ARBITRATION

In contrast to mediation, by which the parties work out their own solution, *arbitration* is often more formal and confrontational. In it, the parties submit their disputes to a neutral third party, who then decides the case. It is generally less costly than litigation, and it is not subject to court backlogs of cases that sometimes take several years.

Parties may include an arbitration clause in their original contract. This clause usually provides that, if any dispute arises under the contract, it may upon demand by either party be submitted to arbitration. Litigation of the dispute is expressly precluded by such a clause.

The clause also generally names the person or arbitration agency to be used. But even if one has not mentioned arbitration in the contract, the parties may still agree to submit the dispute to arbitration.

The fees are generally those set by agreement, and the arbitration organization may have a fee schedule. Again, the costs generally are much less than litigation. Arbitration is relatively formal. The parties, sometimes represented by their lawyers, make their presentations. It is similar to a court hearing, but with more leeway as to the evidence received.

In some arbitrations, the arbitrator may encourage the parties to compromise. In some there may be a compromise type of decision by the arbitrator. However, often the arbitrator chooses between the two positions presented by the parties. Just as in litigation, there is a winner and a loser!

REELING IN LEGAL BILLS

Legal reform has become a catchy political phrase. The Republicans included legal reform as part of their "Contract With America" and passed a version of tort reform within the first 100 days of Congress in 1995. President Clinton has expressed doubts about the legislation and has indicated he will veto the bill.

Is legal reform necessary? Maybe, but with some planning, it's possible to cut down on legal bills without the help of Congress. Purchasing managers sometimes become involved in disputes that concern the company. Some helpful hints for the company to keep legal expenses down include the following:

- *Outline what you plan to spend in the litigation.* Many law firms are much more receptive these days to alternative billing resolutions. When you make initial contact, attempt to get an outline of what the attorney plans to do, and how much the various stages of processing the suit will cost. Some firms are willing to take a flat fee for services.

- *Meet with your attorney.* Don't be afraid to ask for progress reports. Although it's true that a daily—or even weekly—assessment is unrealistic, a meeting every few months is a good way to judge where you're at and if the budget is still holding.

- *Get involved.* Some consultants believe it is often helpful in civil cases if principals meet face-to face sans lawyers. Also, attempt to find out more about the law, and its terms. You might be able to offer some insight into your attorney's strategy.

- *If you are in need of a foreign lawyer, communication is a key.* Make sure you provide your attorney with clear instructions on how to proceed, and be careful to choose an attorney that is skilled in the area in which you need assistance. Both Martindale-Hubbell and the ABA provide directories, or guides, of international firms. Still, it is most advisable to consult with others who have had occasion to utilize these firms.

USE OF A FOREIGN LAWYER

If the purchasing manager or his company needs to consult a foreign attorney, several things must be taken into account. For one thing, the fluctuation of exchange rates makes it important to specify in what currency the fee shall be paid.

In instances where the purchasing manager, some officer in his company, or the company attorney consults a foreign lawyer, it should not simply be assumed that the foreign attorney will charge a "reasonable rate" in American terms. One should always inquire as to the rate and reach an agreement as to the rate or amount to be paid. Despite what the foreign attorney says as to rate schedules governing the matter, it almost always is subject to agreement between the parties just as it is in hiring an outside attorney in the United States. No commitment or work should be given until there is such an agreement with the foreign attorney.

In a number of countries, there are fee schedules which the foreign attorney follows if there is no other specific agreement. While these are generally set by what might be fair in ordinary circumstances, there are some situations where they may work out unfairly. One example is where a foreign lawyer was contacted and asked to incorporate a subsidiary company in his home country. Although he did only a few hours work before the company informed him that they had changed their minds, he sent a huge bill based on a fee schedule which set the fees by the amount involved—in this case sixty million dollars was the amount of capital the subsidiary would have had. The fee schedule allowed that amount regardless of the few hours put in or the fact that the company later decided against it. Large contract amounts can also create large lawyer fees, regardless of the simplicity of the transaction.

Sometimes a foreign attorney may charge by the hour. While American companies may be used to American attorneys charging from one hundred to five hundred dollars an hour, some foreign attorneys charge from five hundred to a thousand dollars per hour. If one doesn't inquire first, that fee may have to be paid. While unfavorable exchange rates may make the fee higher, in many instances it is simply a matter of very high fees being charged. This is all subject to negotiation and agreement with the attorney in advance of any work.

Nota Bene **to Purchasing Officer:** Never make a commitment with a foreign lawyer for legal work or even ask him to perform any without a written agreement as to the fee. If the work is in stages or if contingencies are involved, the fee for each should be agreed upon. The currency that is to be used in setting and paying the fee also should be specified.

LIMITING OVERALL LIABILITIES

Costly lawsuits have forced companies to stretch their creativity. It appears that a new, but somewhat questionable, tactic being used by an increasing number of companies who are looking to limit their exposure to litigation is to "initiate" a class-action suit against themselves. Contacting plaintiffs' attorneys, the company encourages a class-action suit against itself and then negotiates a settlement with the attorney. This settlement, which must be approved by a court as being a fair one, covers companies against those who may get sick later, limiting future lawsuits and capping damages.

For more information on this subject, please refer to the following article: Barry Meier, "Lawsuits to End All Lawsuits, Settlements May Limit Victims' Future Right to Sue," *N.Y. TIMES,* January 16, 1996, C1. Some companies also have deliberately gone into reorganization bankruptcy to limit their liabilities through a structured plan.

SECTION B

LEGAL ASPECTS OF THE PURCHASING-EMPLOYER RELATIONSHIP

III

Creation of the Agency
Relationship with the
Employer

In the beginning.... "I need a new fur coat" announces a 17-year-old daughter to her parents one evening. A hasty family summit meeting is called, and the decision is made by her parents to proceed with the purchase of a coat. The next morning, after being counseled by her parents as to the appropriate price range, the young lady is sent off to the local emporium to make the purchase. She is told to charge the purchase to her parents' account. (Mother called the store's management to tell them her daughter had her blessing to make the purchase.) After trying on many coats, evaluating each carefully as to quality, style, and appearance, the daughter makes a selection and is asked to sign the charge slip prepared in her parents' name. The store promises to deliver the coat in a few days, after the necessary alterations have been made, and—as promised—the coat arrives at the parents' residence in good condition. At the end of the month an invoice from the store arrives in the mail showing the daughter had successfully completed her mission to the tune of $500 of fur and cloth. Resignedly, father writes a check, and the transaction is completed.

This type of family commercial transaction is not unusual and occurs repeatedly. What is significant about it is that the 17-year-old daughter accomplished her mission in a manner similar to the way a purchasing officer performs the purchasing function for a business entity. A division of the business organization expresses the need for a certain item to the purchasing department, and the purchasing officer sets about to satisfy that need. Potential suppliers are contacted; quality, price, and service are evaluated. The purchasing officer makes the decision as to where the item is to be purchased, and an order is placed. In due time the supplier makes the delivery and sends an invoice for the agreed amount. The invoice is approved, and the treasurer of the company sends a check to the supplier to pay for the purchase.

Both the 17-year-old daughter and the purchasing officer are in the enviable position of being able to buy things and have someone else pay the bill. However, the reader should note that this delightful situation existed only because the sellers of the merchandise had advance assurances that their invoices would be paid when rendered. This advance assurance to the sellers, which is so critical to the completion of the transaction, is made possible by the law and more specifically, by the "Law of Agency." The sellers knew in advance that the 17-year-old daughter and the purchasing officer were making the purchases in the name of someone else *and* that they had the authorization of that "someone else" to make their purchases. The legal validation of the transaction, because of these understandings, is found in agency law.

AGENCY DEFINED

Agency is a term used in the law to describe the relationship that is created when one person appoints another person to act on his or her behalf in transactions with third parties. The typical agency relationship involves three parties. The party who initiates the arrangement by making the appointment is known as the *principal.* The second party is the person appointed by the principal as the *agent* to represent the principal. The *third party* is the one with whom the agent conducts the business of the principal. And it is the legal relationship among these three with which the law of agency is involved.

The 17-year-old daughter in our fur coat transaction was an agent who acted for her parents. Her parents were the principal. And, of course, the third party was the local emporium that had the fur coat available for sale. The store knew the daughter was making the purchase for and in behalf of her parents, and it was willing to enter into the transaction because of this knowledge. As a matter of fact, the store sold the coat to the parents and expected them to pay for it.

THE PURCHASING AGENT

The purchasing officer, to whom this book is addressed, is also an agent. The principal employs a purchasing officer to be responsible for the organization's procurement function. There are many duties assigned to this function, but the primary duty is to make available the materials, supplies, and services that the organization requires in its operations. The purchasing officer must deal with suppliers and make contracts to purchase certain items. Such contracts are made in the name of the employer, who eventually pays the invoice for the purchase. So here again we have the typical tripartite agency relationship: (1) the employer as the principal who appoints (2) the purchasing officer as its agent to deal with (3) the third party supplier.

The title "Purchasing Agent" was long used in the business world to designate that individual selected to head the purchasing function. It was an appropriate legal title to designate the agent selected to assume the responsibility for the procurement function—the person in charge of "purchasing" for the company or institution. Many purchasing officers continue to carry this title, although the more modern titles reflect the additional management functions that are associated with procurement. Thus we have, for example, Vice-President for Materials Management, Director of Purchasing and Stores, Purchasing Manager, and Director of Procurement. Professional purchasing associations are now known as purchasing management associations; and under the auspices of the National Association of Purchasing Management, there is a professional accreditation program where one can earn the designation "C.P.M."-Certified Purchasing Manager.

The trend to give greater recognition to the manifold responsibilities associated with the procurement function is both desirable and merited. However, from a legal standpoint, the title Purchasing Agent accurately describes the individual who deals with third-party suppliers and makes legal commitments in the name of the principal. No matter what title the purchasing officer operates under, when that individual does business with suppliers for the company, those transactions are accomplished because he or she is the purchasing agent of that organization.

THE AGENT'S ROLE IN BUSINESS

Every individual of legal age and sound mind is capable of dealing with third parties in his or her own name and without agents. One may contract, buy, sell, rent, lease, obligate, barter, dispose, and propose with anyone with whom business may be done. This ability to contract for oneself is an individual right we all enjoy.

Business was conducted in a similar fashion in pioneer days. The blacksmith was a businessman selling a product and a service to one and all. When he needed some metal, nails, or a new forge, he scouted about and bought what he wanted. He did it in his name and for himself. He was a single entrepreneur. But our blacksmith found he needed assistance as his business grew and prospered. He employed others to assist him, and when these assistants began dealing with other business people outside the smithy on behalf of the blacksmith, some avenue had to be found to enable these employees to act effectively for him and in his name. Agency was the answer. It permitted the single entrepreneur to carry on his business by authorizing employees to act for him as his agent. Those employees authorized to act for him and in his name with other parties were agents.

Today's business entities take on several forms. There remain many single entrepreneurs, as our blacksmith, who assume all the risks of a business venture and who retain all the profits generated. There are partnerships, where two or more individuals join together, provide the necessary capital, and jointly share the risks and the profits. And finally, there is the corporation, where a group of individuals band together and form a distinct entity, separate and apart from themselves. The individuals provide capital for the separate entity, but it alone bears all the risk because there is a shield protecting the group of individuals from liability. The risk the individuals assume is limited solely to the amount of capital they provide the corporation. At intervals, through the declaration and payment of dividends, the profits generated by the corporation may be handed down to the individual owners according to the percentage of capital provided the corporation.

The corporate form of business organization is prevalent in both the for-profit and the not-for-profit sectors of business endeavors. The corporation is a different breed from the single entrepreneur and the partnership because it is a creation of the state government and depends upon the state government for its continued existence. The owners of single entrepreneurships and partnerships have the right to conduct a business as responsible citizens of our free society, but the corporation is dependent upon the largesse of the state for its powers and privileges.

Furthermore, the corporation, because of its unique origin as a creature of the state, faces another problem. John Marshall, Chief Justice of the Supreme Court of the United States, in the famous 1819 Dartmouth College case, described a *corporation* with these words:

> A corporation is an artificial being, invisible, intangible, and existing only in contemplation of the law.

Now if this legal entity, called the corporation, is invisible and intangible, it is obvious that it cannot perform an act for itself. How then does it do business? It must do business through agents, who are not artificial, but are both visible and tangible. It takes a natural person to perform an act for a corporation. That person performs the act in the name of the corporation as an agent for it. Confusing as it may appear at first glance, a corporation may act as an agent for a person or another corporation. But any actions a corporation may take for its principal must still be done by a natural person acting as the corporation's agent.

Thus agents, including purchasing agents, are essential to all forms of business organizations, from the blacksmith to the multinational corporation. Agents make it possible for a business to expand its activities because more than one person is able to commit the company in transactions with others. Through the prudent use of agents, business volume has reached the proportions it now enjoys.

THE APPOINTMENT OF AN AGENT

The principal-agent relationship may be brought into existence in many ways. There are no hard-and-fast rules in the law governing the appointment of an agent. A written contract, though desirable, is not essential. There are no magic words specified, such as, "I hereby make you my agent," to bring the relationship into existence. In fact, a person may be made the agent of another quite informally. For example, assume that an individual is employed by your company and assigned to the purchasing department. Duties are given to this individual. If these duties consist of filing requisitions and copies of purchase orders, typing letters, and sharpening pencils, the individual retains an amateur status as an employee. But when told by the manager to go to the office supply house to purchase a comfortable seat cushion for his or her chair, the individual steps over the line marked "employees only" and enters the agency arena. If the seat cushion is to be a personal purchase for the manager, the individual is acting as an agent for the manager. However, the individual will be an agent for the company if the instructions are to charge the purchase to the company. Verbal instructions can bring into existence the principal-agent relationship. No formal ceremonies need occur to make someone an agent of another. It can come about almost by accident rather than design.

There are advantages to having the appointment of an agent reduced to writing. Agency is more than a simple employment whereby one hires out to work for another. The transfer of some of the powers the principal possesses to another person is not to be taken lightly nor done in a carefree manner. Thought should be given to just what powers—as well as the range and limits involved— are being handed over to the agent. The delegation of power should be specific so that both parties realize and understand what is expected of each other. The principal-agent relationship is personal and based upon trust. Therefore the creation of the agency merits a written agreement to enable both the principal and the agent to comprehend fully what is intended. The written agreement will serve well as a guide to each party for their future conduct.

THE APPOINTMENT OF A PURCHASING OFFICER

The appointment of the chief purchasing officer is customarily heralded as the employment of a senior administrative official for the hierarchy of the company or organization. The individual selected may come from outside the organization or be promoted or transferred from within. Regardless of the process, it is generally regarded as an employment, and most of the details of the selection are devoted to the employment contract. Scant attention is paid to the fact that a principal-agent relationship is created at the same time. Part of the explanation for this lack of attention to the agency is due to the fact that the employment is for the full-time services of the individual. Part of the responsibilities of the position include administrative duties, supervision of other employees and of internal operating procedures. Only a portion of the services rendered will be devoted to agency involvements. Basically, the officer is first a full-time employee of the employer. And because of this fact, the agency relationship goes unnoticed or is thought of only as an offshoot of the employment.

The job description will spell out the duties and the responsibilities of the job. It is usually here that the agency relationship is first noted. If the duties include the negotiation and execution of contracts with third-party suppliers for the purchase of goods and services, there is at the very least a presumption that an agency relationship is also created. Agency is the only avenue by which the purchasing officer may accomplish the duties of purchasing goods from third party suppliers and make the various arrangements incidental to the sale. It is in this almost incidental manner that the creation of the principal-agent relationship between the employer and the purchasing officer occurs.

One might hope that the purchasing officer will be given a more direct and specific appointment as an agent vested with the authority to contract for the employer. However, the important factors in the appointment of a purchasing agent from the legal viewpoint are (1) that the employing company or organization has the intention of granting the purchasing officer the authority to make purchase contracts, (2) that the purchasing officer accepts this contracting authority and utilizes it with third-party suppliers, and (3) that the employer recognizes and accepts the commitments made by the purchasing officer. If these factors are present, the employee-purchasing officer is also an agent of the employer. The lack of a written agency contract does not prevent the principal-agent relationship from coming into existence.

THE APPOINTMENT OF BUYERS
AND OTHER ASSISTANTS

Buyers and assistant purchasing agents are generally considered to be sub-agents of the employer-principal Their appointment occurs in the same manner as the chief purchasing officer. They are hired first as an employee, and their duties are assigned either verbally or in a written job description. Again, if their duties include negotiating with third-party suppliers, they fall into the agent category too. Because their conduct is subject to the direction of the chief purchasing officer—an agent—such subordinate individuals are referred to as subagents. Note that technically they are subagents of the principal employer, and not subagents of the chief purchasing officer.

THE TERMINATION OF THE AGENCY RELATIONSHIP

The chief purchasing officer, assistants, and buyers are at once employees and agents of the employer. As employees, they are subject to the customary rules and procedures in hiring and firing. As employees, they may gain or earn some manner of job security. Or they could be employed for a term of years under a contract that would guarantee continuity of employment for the contract period. The employer seeking to dismiss the employee is governed by the rules of the company and the laws of the state, or by the terms of the employment contract.

The agency relationship, however, has no protection from any tenure considerations that might be available to employees. An agent may be dismissed at the will of the principal. This is because the principal-agent relationship is a personal one. The principal places in the hands of the agent powers to act for him and in his name. Complete confidence and trust in the agent are "musts." It follows then, that if the principal loses confidence in the agent, he must have the ability to withdraw any delegated powers immediately, notwithstanding any employee tenure or contract considerations. An employee-agent may cease to be an agent long before the employee relationship is terminated, or the term of the employment contract expires.

IV

Authority of the Purchasing Officer

One of the important subjects in the Law of Agency is the authority that is vested in the agent by the principal. "Authority," in agency law, is the license given by the principal to the agent to act for the principal. It denotes the privilege, the power, and the right to perform an act or acts. The law imposes no restrictions on the authority a principal may grant to an agent. It may be very broad and general, or it might range down the scale to a single act. If the authority is continuing, a time limit for its expiration may be set, or it may be open-ended. The amount of authority granted depends entirely on the wishes of the principal, for it is the principal's own authority to act that is being delegated to the agent. Thus the principal has complete control over the scope of authority the agent possesses.

Every purchasing officer, as an agent, should be aware of the authority granted by the principal (the employer). This authority states what may be done in the name of the employer. It tells, in positive terms, what portion of the employer's own authority has been delegated to be performed. This delegation of authority is similar to the delegation of authority (and responsibility) that is discussed in management circles, but it is also something more. It is the delegation of legal authority to *commit* the principal in transactions with third-party suppliers. It gives one the power to obligate the principal in contracts. It is the authority required to be able to perform that portion of the procurement function that requires the agent to contract for and obtain the requirements of the company or organization. And this is what purchasing is all about.

TYPES OF AUTHORITY IN AGENCY LAW

Agency law recognizes that several types of authority may exist or arise in an agency relationship. Four of these types are of particular significance to the purchasing officer:

1. Express (actual) authority

2. Implied authority

3. Emergency authority

4. Apparent (ostensible) authority

The first three are the types of authority that the purchasing officer possesses. The fourth, as we shall see, may exist in individuals not working in the purchasing department.

1. Express Authority

Express, or *actual authority* is the authority that is given specifically to the purchasing officer. This authority is bestowed when "the boss," as a representative of the principal-employer, tells the purchasing officer what he or she is to do for the company. This is done when the purchasing officer is appointed to that position. As stated previously, this may be accomplished either informally or in writing.

It should be noted that the requirement of express authority of any agent applies equally to "the boss" mentioned above. The so-called boss must have the authority to grant express authority to the purchasing officer. It should be noted further that there may be documents or guidelines that limit or control the authority granted. These extraneous documents could include corporate bylaws, board of directors' guidelines, or directions from the president of the company (see "Apparent Authority" on page 48).

Here is an example of a statement of express authority that might be given to the top procurement officer of a corporation or organization:

> The vice-president for materials management is responsible for the procurement of the raw materials, supplies, component parts, equipment, and outside services required by the company (school, hospital, or governmental unit), and for the allied transactions involved therein.

This statement may be nothing more than a job description. However, in the eyes of the law, it is the grant of express authority to the purchasing officer to purchase the requirements of the company he or she is serving. It is specific enough to tell everyone that there is vested in the procurement officer the authority to purchase raw materials, supplies, equipment, and outside services for the principal.

The statement tells the purchasing officer, in positive terms, what he or she may do. There are no "thou shalt nots" contained in this statement, nor are negatives customarily stated in any grant of authority. You, as the purchasing officer (the agent) are told in specific terms what you may purchase for your company. Note, for instance, that the above statement is silent on the purchase of real estate. This omission is construed to mean that this procurement officer is not authorized to purchase real estate. An additional delegation of express authority to purchase real estate would have to come from the principal if a building were to be purchased for the organization by the vice-president for materials management. One cannot interpret the omission to indicate that real estate was probably overlooked in the statement but is covered by the fact that the vice-president for materials management is authorized to purchase everything else for the company. Not so, because, in legal terms, the authority of an agent is said to be "strictly construed" and limited to that which is expressly stated.

The Advantages of Written Authority. The purchasing officer—as any agent—should be thoroughly cognizant of the specific authority granted him or her. For this reason, it is preferable that the specific grant of authority be expressed in writing. There can be no misunderstanding of what the agent's express authority is if it is in writing. The time could come when either the agent or the principal, or both, might wish to be able to produce the exact wording of the authority that was vested. Not only would the writing be able to settle disagreements between principal and agent, but it might also be helpful as a defense against third parties making unreasonable claims against the principal.

A state law may suggest another reason for the purchasing officer's authority to be reduced to writing. California, for example, has a law that reads as follows:

> An oral authorization is sufficient for any purpose, except that an authority to enter into a contract required by law to be in writing can only be given by an instrument in writing. (California Civil Code Section 2309.)

One surmises that this statute was legislated with real estate transactions in mind, since most states require all real estate transactions to be in writing. But the California statute does not specify real estate, nor does it exempt other types of transactions that the law requires to be in writing. There is, for example, in the Uniform Commercial Code, a section known as the "Statute of Frauds," which requires that every contract for the purchase and sale of *goods* having a value of $500 or more be in writing to be enforceable in a court of law. If we couple the legal requirement of a written contract under the Statute of Frauds with the California Section 2309 requiring a written instrument for the authorization of an agent to sign such a contract, we then strike deep into the territory of the purchasing officer.

This is because "goods," as used in the above section of the Uniform Commercial Code, includes every tangible item other than real estate. Goods then includes raw materials of all types, equipment, component parts, supplies, and everything else on the purchasing officer's shopping list, except contracted services. It would follow then that every contract for goods a purchasing officer signs costing $500 or more is unenforceable in a court of law unless the purchasing officer's authority to sign it has been previously established by a written instrument.

At the present time it appears that California is the only state having such a law. Other states with similar "equal dignity" laws, as they are termed, specify that their law is applicable only to real estate transactions. North Dakota's law is worded identically with California's, except that it specifically exempts the Statute of Frauds section of the Uniform Commercial Code.

One might conclude that only California purchasing officers have the legal requirement to have their authority to purchase reduced to writing. However, circumstances might develop where someone doing business with a California supplier might be called upon to produce a similar written instrument of authority. In any event, a written expression of the scope of the purchasing officer's authority is good insurance for both the principal and the agent to have.

2. Implied Authority

This is the second type of authority you possess as a purchasing officer. *Implied authority* is implied by the law at the time the principal grants your express authority. It is designed to give you the legal rights and power to carry out the purposes for which you were appointed as an agent for the principal. Implied authority supplements and adds to your express authority. It makes it possible for you to perform your job as a purchasing officer.

Several examples will be of aid in understanding the reason for implied authority. Referring back to the sample statement of express authority, it is stated that the vice-president for materials management "is responsible for the procurement of raw materials. . ." There is involved in the procurement of raw materials, or any other commodity for that matter, the need to negotiate and execute a contract for the purchase. The statement of express authority is silent on the negotiation and execution of contracts, and this is where the law steps in. It gives the agent that essential authority. The law will say that if the express authority authorizes the agent to purchase a commodity, there is implied the authority to negotiate the terms and details of that purchase. This will include (1) the quantity to be purchased, (2) the quality and other specifics, (3) the place and time of delivery, (4) the price to be paid, and (5) the payment due date. All these items are negotiated under the implied authority the law gives to the agent. Furthermore, there is the implied authority to sign the purchase contract in the name of the principal.

Thus, from the express authority of "procurement of raw materials," comes a list of implied authorizations to effectuate the purchase.

One might continue a list of examples of implied authority by pointing out that if the purchase is F.O.B. (free on board) the seller's place of business, transportation contracts may be completed by the purchasing officer. If the goods need to be insured, an insurance contract must be arranged. A warehousing contract may be necessary as well, if the purchased commodities must be stored. All of this may be done by the purchasing officer under the implied authority given by the law.

It can be seen, then, that the law gives the purchasing officer whatever authority is reasonably required to accomplish the mission specified in the statement of express authority. This carte-blanche grant of implied authority is always subject to restriction by the principal. The principal (the purchasing officer's boss) could state: "The president must sign all contracts for the company," and out of the window would go the purchasing officer's implied authority to sign purchase contracts. Or the company might have a rule that all insurance must be negotiated and placed by the treasurer. This would curtail the purchasing agent's ability to insure goods purchased. The company might have a traffic department charged with arranging the transportation of all incoming and outgoing material and equipment. This would limit the authority of the purchasing officer with respect to negotiating transportation contracts. (Extraneous documents or rules limiting the agent's authority are discussed in the previous section on "Express Authority.")

The purchasing officer should be reminded that the law specifies that an agent does not have implied authority to sign promissory notes. If our vice-president for materials management above would be asked to sign the principal's name to a promissory note to cover the cost of a purchase made, it could not be done without the principal's giving express authority to sign it. This is predicated upon the fact that a note is a negotiable instrument. As such, it could fall into the hands of an innocent holder in due course through endorsement. Such a holder of a note must be assured that the maker of the note is the one primarily bound to pay the face amount of the note. Had an agent signed the note under an implied grant of authority, a cloud of questionable validity would be cast over the note. Other than this specific exception of promissory notes, and the specific limitations the principal may impose, there are no obstacles in the path of the purchasing officer's having all the reasonable and proper types of implied authority needed to accomplish the express authority assigned.

3. Emergency Authority

Emergency authority is the authority to take an action for which the agent does not have the express or implied authority to perform for the principal. This action may even have been specifically prohibited by the principal. It is with fear and trepidation that we include this type of authority as one the purchasing officer possesses. Our reluctance stems from the fact that it is not granted by the principal, and because the situation under which it is available for use is most difficult to define or establish. Its exercise must be very limited. As the name implies, it is an authorization to act in only unusual and unique situations. The justification for its exercise must be to protect the principal's property or rights at a time when a consultation with the principal is not possible. "On-the-spot situations where, but for immediate action, all would be lost" best describes its applicability.

4. Apparent Authority

Any listing of the types of authority found in the Law of Agency is not complete without the inclusion of *apparent* (perhaps a more descriptive word is "ostensible") authority. Apparent authority, when found to exist, is not deliberately granted to the agent. It is created unintentionally by the principal through actions or conduct toward the third party.

     Apparent authority is the subject of frequent lawsuits, and many times these lawsuits involve the purchasing function. Because its existence may lead to unfortunate results, special attention is given to the creation, control, and avoidance of this type of authority in a succeeding section.

SUMMARY OF THE PURCHASING OFFICER'S AUTHORITY

The express authority granted by the principal and the implied authority given by the law to carry out the express authority are the two types of authority the purchasing officer possesses. These are the tools by which the commitment powers of the employer-principal are transferred to the purchasing officer. When these powers are properly applied to purchase orders and contracts by the purchasing officer, they have the same effect of creating binding obligations as if the principal had signed personally. This is what the Law of Agency makes possible.

    Nota Bene **to Purchasing Officer.** It is desirable to have the authority given to you reduced to writing so that both you and your employer know exactly what power has been transferred to you. This writing need not be a formal document, but it should be as precise as possible. However it is accomplished, the written statement will prove to be of value to you and your employer. You will know precisely what you may do in the employer's name, and the employer will know the limits of the authority that has been delegated to you. It will also be of aid in settling third-party supplier disputes over the nature and extent of the scope of your authority.

Do not be alarmed if your authorization is not initially in writing, or if the scope thereof is vague. Many purchasing officers are in a similar situation. Neither their appointments as agents nor the scope of their authority are mentioned or are only vaguely alluded to when they are employed and given the purchasing officer's responsibilities. It is only when a legal argument develops with the principal or with the third-party supplier that attention is paid to these formalities. The author urges you to talk with your superior officer and convince him or her that a written appointment and a specific grant of authority will serve both of you well.

Should you have a voice in the preparation of this statement of authority, it is suggested that it be written in as broad terms as possible. Avoid restrictive phrases that might lead to disagreement in interpretation. "Purchase all of the company's requirements for goods and services" is to be preferred to "Purchase the supplies and equipment required by the company," since the latter may or may not be construed to include raw materials, component parts, services, and so forth.

AUTHORITY OF ASSISTANT PURCHASING OFFICERS AND BUYERS

Assistant purchasing officers, buyers, and others in the purchasing department who have responsibilities dealing with suppliers are involved in the same considerations of authority as is the chief purchasing officer. The same authority may be given them, although in their case, it is customary to limit the express authority granted beyond the limits placed on the chief purchasing officer. These limitations may be made in any manner and to varying degrees. Some buyers may be limited in their authority by giving them authorization to purchase only specific types of commodities, such as office supplies, maintenance products, one or more raw materials, computer software, and so forth. The detailed subdivision of commodities has no limit and may be customized for each type of business or organization.

Dollar limits of authorization to sign a purchase order may also be established. A contract exceeding the established dollar limit will then have to be signed by a superior officer. Another alternative is to give the buyer no authority to commit the company, but only to negotiate the purchase, with the final authorization reserved to a contracting officer. There is no limit to the variations of limited express authority that may be placed in effect.

It is suggested that this more limited delegation of authority given to subordinates be reduced to writing. The more strings that are attached to a limited authorization, the more important it is for there to be a clear-cut understanding of what may and what may not be done. A written statement of these details needs no clarification. The buyer, the chief purchasing officer, and the principal will benefit from this practice.

Nota Bene **to Chief Purchasing Officer.** It is suggested that you and your superior officer have a very clear agreement as to your liability for the action of your subordinate assistants and buyers. You need not be reminded that the authority to commit the company carries with it the potential for affecting the bottom line of the income statement. Commitments also have a major effect on the balance sheet. You, as the chief purchasing officer, can never avoid the management responsibility for the work of your department as it reflects in these two financial statements. It is you who assigns the duties and supervises the work of the personnel in the department. Their actions in committing the company reflect on your performance as their supervisor.

However, you should be given the protection of avoiding the legal responsibilities connected with commitments to suppliers made by assistants and buyers. The authority that is vested in them, however limited it may be, should be authority granted by the principal employer and not by an unauthorized subdelegation of your own authority.

To accomplish this, you need the express authority of your superior officer to subdelegate authority to the buyer and vest that buyer with corporate powers. The buyer must be a subagent of the principal-employer and must not be your own personal agent. There is an important difference here: It is *your* express authority to subdelegate to buyers. Then the legal responsibility for the buyers' actions remains with the corporation, while you as the supervisor retain the management responsibilities.

APPARENT AUTHORITY IN AGENCY LAW

In a previous section it was noted that any listing of the types of authority in Agency Law would be incomplete without the mention of *apparent* authority. Apparent authority is authority that is not intended to be created, but is thrust upon the principal by the law. It is the result of a conclusion reached by the law because of the actions and conduct of the principal. The principal is caught in the unhappy situation of denying the creation of the authority, while at the same time the law states that such authority was apparently created. In a courtroom battle, a decision that apparent authority existed is a decision against the principal, and it is one in favor of the third party who dealt with the alleged agent.

Indulge in the following fantasy for a few minutes to understand how apparent authority may lead to problems for the principal.

The president of a corporation tells his favorite secretary to go to a local office equipment house and buy a nice new desk, a plush comfortable chair, and an electric typewriter in a color pleasing to the eyes. The secretary dutifully accepts the mandate and presents the president with the invoice for the items. The invoice is sent to the company's treasurer for payment. Two weeks later the secretary is sent back to the office equipment house to buy the president a desk and a chair to match hers. She is also told to have a desk, chair, and typewriter sent to her apartment so that she might work at home occasionally in the evening or on weekends. The invoice for all these items is paid by the company treasurer

All is well for a period of time, but then a disagreement develops, and the secretary is dismissed. Three days after her dismissal an invoice arrives at the company's office from the office equipment house. The invoice is for two armchairs and a three-piece sectional lounge which were ordered by the ex-secretary and delivered to her apartment.

The president tells the purchasing officer of the company to return the invoice to the office equipment house and remind them that he, the purchasing officer, is the only one in the company authorized to make such purchases. The owner of the office equipment house responds that he had some idea this might be the case, but that he became confused when the secretary appeared not once but three times to purchase equipment for the company. He pointed out that the first two invoices were paid promptly, and that now he could not understand why there might be a problem with the third purchase. He admitted that on the first visit the status of the secretary as an authorized representative of the company was somewhat in doubt in his mind. However, they had been unsuccessful in selling equipment to the purchasing officer, so they decided to take a chance and deliver the first order. The quick payment of the invoice for the first order removed any doubts in his mind about the authority of the secretary. The two succeeding purchases merely followed the pattern of the first one and reconfirmed his belief that the secretary had authority to do this buying.

The law as applied by the court in such a case would probably sustain the position of the owner of the office equipment house, although there is no doubt the purchasing officer had the express and exclusive authority to make purchases for the company. It had become apparent to the office supply house that the secretary was vested with some similar type of authority. The fact that twice the purchases had been made by her, and that the invoices were promptly paid by the corporation gave credibility to that belief. The court would deny the claim of the corporation that it had not vested authority in the secretary. It would state that the corporation is estopped (that is, prevented) from denying the existence of such authority. This is because it had ratified and acknowledged the fact that some authority had been vested in the secretary by paying the first two invoices. The court would conclude with the observation that "because of the actions of the corporation, the office equipment house was entitled to believe the secretary apparently had the authority to make purchases and obligate the company."

Note that the court is the one that determines that apparent authority existed. The corporation is denying that fact, but to no avail. Their actions established in the secretary the apparent authority to commit them to contracts of purchase with the office supply house. Remember, though, that this apparent authority of the secretary existed only with the office equipment house. The authority does not extend beyond the third-party supplier to whom the corporation had paid the first two bills. The secretary does not have carte blanche to use her apparent authority to make purchases at a jewelry store, for example. The apparent authority is created only with the third party who had had some dealings with the alleged agent. (Note that in the above fantasy the corporation does have the legal right to file suit against the secretary to recover the value of the unauthorized purchases.)

APPARENT AUTHORITY AND PURCHASING

Personnel in the average purchasing department of any company or organization witness many instances where apparent authority is created. This phenomenon is referred to in purchasing circles as *unauthorized procurement*. Despite the best of intentions, many well-managed (in other respects) corporations fall prey to the bad habit of permitting personnel outside the purchasing department to make purchases. Each time this occurs, the company employee who makes an unauthorized purchase has had created in him or her apparent authority to commit the company with that particular supplier. As a result, the company will find that it has many agents outside the purchasing department who possess the authority to commit it in purchase contracts with various suppliers—and this despite the fact that the corporation procedures manual states quite clearly that "all purchase commitments will be made by the Director of Procurement."

Purchasing would be the first to admit that there are occasions when it appears prudent to have someone outside the purchasing department deal with a supplier. Items that have reason to be selected personally by the user are typical examples. The surgeon on the hospital staff could make an excellent argument to having the right to personally select the surgical knife used in brain surgery. The new corporate treasurer could claim the right to personally select the color and design of the drapes that will adorn her office. The welder could make a valid claim to the right to personally select the safety goggles needed in his work so that they will fit properly, be comfortable, and be able to be seen through. And then there are the many emergency repair situations where a very specific type of valve or fitting needs to be selected by the maintenance person and brought back to the plant immediately. These are just a few examples of circumstances where it is judicious to have a nonpurchasing department employee get involved with a supplier.

However, the nonpurchasing department employee getting involved with the supplier is not the problem. The need for personal selection of items will always be with us, and purchasing is prepared to accommodate that need. What happens after the selection is made by the employee *is* the problem. Often, after the selection has been made, the employee will place an order for the item and arrange to have the supplier deliver it. Or if the item is not too heavy or bulky, it can be handed to the employee and he can tote it back to the office personally. In both instances the supplier will be told to "send the invoice to the company."

This creates a problem because an unauthorized purchase has been made. If the invoice is paid by the company without comment, an agent of the company with apparent authority to obligate it has been unintentionally appointed. That is not a desirable conclusion for the legal welfare of the company or for the organization that creates this agency.

PROBLEMS CREATED BY UNAUTHORIZED PROCUREMENT

Both the purchasing officer and his or her company suffer when unauthorized procurement occurs. It is a costly procedure and should not be allowed to exist. Here is a list of some of the problems created when unauthorized purchasing does occur:

1. Official corporate procedures are violated because the commitment was not made by an authorized purchasing officer. Successful avoidance of one regulation tends to create the feeling that others can be avoided too.

2. It gives impetus to the desire of some to diffuse centralized procurement. Vendors are opportunists, and, if it becomes apparent that one need not go through the purchasing department to do business with the company, others will attempt to do the same.

3. An unauthorized purchase is made outside the established purchasing routine. Steps must be taken to get that purchase into the routine when it is discovered. This involves recording the purchase, charging the department, and paying the invoice. This consumes additional time for the purchasing department, the accounting department, and the treasurer's office.

4. More money may have been paid for the item because the purchasing department did not have the opportunity to negotiate the purchase.

5. More money may have been paid for the item because the purchasing department might have been able to select alternate suppliers who sell to the company at a lower price.

6. Cash discounts may be lost because the invoice will arrive without much identification. It may take several days beyond the discount period to discover who made the purchase, and who is to be charged for it. Another possibility is that the invoice may be handed to the employee when the purchase is made, and that person may mislay it or throw it away.

7. Delivery of the item to central receiving causes problems because no one there is aware of the purchase. Identifying the purchaser consumes extra time of the receiving department personnel.

8. The accountant and the treasurer will have no control of the total commitments outstanding against the company. Since there is no record made of an unauthorized purchase, the company has no idea what its liabilities are to outside vendors.

9. It creates in the employee who made the purchase apparent authority to further commit the company with that supplier. If this employee possesses a trace of larceny in his makeup, the cost of this unauthorized purchase could increase exponentially.

Listing these costly problems of unauthorized procurement is a waste of valuable space in a text addressed to purchasing officers. Personnel in any purchasing department are well aware of the added work involved when notice of an unauthorized purchase is received. (This notice could be a month or more after the purchase was made, which makes it all the more difficult to identify.) It is surprising, however, that senior management does not join with the purchasing officer more readily, and take the necessary steps to correct the problem. In the above list, there are many opportunities to reduce operating costs if the practice is eliminated. Cost effective rewards are present for those who dare to say—"only purchasing has the authority to commit the organization for a purchase."

ELIMINATING UNAUTHORIZED PROCUREMENT

A program to eliminate unauthorized procurement from your workplace should begin with the full support of senior management. Removing the freedom of employees of other divisions of the organization to purchase items will not be a popular move, and the groundwork should be prepared at the top. The purchasing officer's case with senior management is best made by presenting a detailed report of the cost savings that will result if the practice is discontinued. Some suggestions for this cost-savings report can be obtained from the list of problems in the previous section. This cost-effectiveness presentation may be enhanced by demonstrating some of the potential problems that could arise from the creation of the apparent authority to commit the company that is placed in so many non-purchasing department employees when unauthorized procurement runs rampant. You may have already encountered some of these problems in your company. Real, live examples of the dangers of apparent authority are the best convincers. Put all these points together, plus a reaffirmation of good management practice, and you should be able to get senior management on your side.

Let us assume the decision has been made to proceed with the program. You may or may not wish to have some statement come from top management to the various departments in the company, stating that the centralization of all procurement of the company in the purchasing department will be strictly enforced henceforth. Such a published statement will reinforce your own program, but it has the disadvantage of acting as an irritant to some people who resent being told what they may not do. This is especially true in not-for-profit institutions where freedom of action is a jealously guarded right. The climate in your organization must be your guide in deciding whether a "broadside" from the top is desirable.

It is you, the purchasing officer, who must take the lead in the elimination program and do most of the work. If unauthorized procurement has been with you for some time, it will not disappear after one broadside from top management. Months of patient and repetitive reminders will be required. The employees and departments who are the persistent offenders may need to be reeducated on the purchasing procedures of the organization. Suppliers, too, will require reeducation vis-a-vis the role of the purchasing department in doing business with your company. There are countless purchasing officers who will tell you it is a never-ending battle.

Your first priority is to make certain that the established purchasing procedures are proper, and that provision has been made to meet all the needs of your company. One of the justifications ("alibis") offered by department heads for making unauthorized purchases is that the established purchasing routine is a bottleneck when some item is needed in a hurry. This is a reminder to the purchasing officer to make certain that requisitions are handled expeditiously in the department so that this allegation may be denied. A capable purchasing officer recognizes that there are valid reasons for emergency purchases to be made. Provision for their accommodation is essential. We know, too, that there will always be some requirements that fall into the "personal selection" classification. Provisions for these types of purchases must also be available. Remember that when these out-of-the-ordinary types of purchases occur, the essential factor is that authorized purchasing personnel make the commitment to the supplier, or that the employee dealing with the supplier convey purchasing's authorization. This avoids creating a veil of apparent authority to commit in the nonpurchasing department employee. A second advantage of having the purchasing officer make the actual commitment to the supplier is that a record of the purchase is made at the time the commitment is made. This record serves as a reminder to purchasing to get that commitment into the regular purchasing routine.

One of the more successful methods of controlling the emergency purchase is to utilize a special emergency order form designed to record and identify such transactions from the beginning. This form should be in sets, serially prenumbered with a prefix such as "EO" to distinguish it from the regular purchase order. The department in need of making an emergency purchase must communicate with the purchasing department *before* the purchase is made. Purchasing assigns an emergency purchase number to the transaction and records on it the following information:

1. Supplier

2. Date

3. Items required

4. Account to be charged

5. Departmental requisition number that will be used to confirm the emergency purchase

If the employee making the purchase is located near the purchasing department, the original of the emergency order form can be picked up and given to the supplier when the purchase is made. If the order is to be telephoned, the serial number will serve as the authorization to the supplier. In the latter event, the original of the emergency order may be mailed to the supplier or discarded. This procedure keeps the supplier on notice that it is the purchasing department that is authorizing the purchase. There is no danger that "apparent" authority will be created in the employee of the using department.

The using department should be required to send a confirming requisition to the purchasing department with a copy of the emergency order attached. The requisition is then processed in the customary manner, and the purchase order sent to the supplier. The purchase order must note in an obvious manner that it is confirming the emergency order, and that the supplier should not duplicate it. If the using department does not promptly send the confirming requisition to purchasing, a stern reminder should be forthcoming. Purchasing's copy of the emergency order in an "unconfirmed" file will jog the memory.

Emergency orders can be used for personal selection purchases if the purchase must be made immediately or on the spot. In our previous examples, the surgeon, the treasurer, and the welder might make their visits to the suppliers' places of business, make their selections, and then return to their respective offices and have a requisition prepared to make their purchase. In this manner, there would be no violation of purchasing procedures and no creation of apparent authority. However, if these same individuals believe their purchase must be made when they make their visit to the supplier, and if purchasing concurs in that belief, an emergency order could be prepared for any one of them to take with them.

There is another type of purchase that can be accommodated by the emergency order. This is the so-called rush order that appears when the using department fails to properly anticipate its needs. The emergency order routine is an ideal method to circumvent the normal purchasing routine, if circumvention is inevitable. It keeps the control of the purchase in the hands of the purchasing department and provides a record that ensures that an orderly confirmation will follow. The purchasing officer is advised not to use this rush order procedure any more than is absolutely essential. The using departments could become chronic violators in anticipating their needs if a simple method is available to rescue them.

The advantages of the use of an emergency order system are obvious.

1. Purchasing has the opportunity to review the vendor selected and the item to be purchased before assigning the emergency order.

2. The supplier is put on notice that purchasing is the one committing the company for the purchase.

3. A record of the purchase is made before the commitment is made.

4. Purchasing may readily identify an invoice if it has the emergency order number displayed.

5. Purchasing may follow up on wayward departments that do not promptly send a confirming requisition.

6. Purchasing, by the number of emergency orders issued to particular departments, may readily identify those departments that do not anticipate their needs and resort to the emergency order routine repeatedly.

With this procedure, purchasing is able to accommodate most of the needs of the company. At the same time, it is able to protect against the use of apparent authority by nonpurchasing department employees. This will give the principal-employer the full protection of the law against unauthorized acts and unauthorized agents.

You, the purchasing officer, will be busy keeping the various departments in line. However, the more successful your program of prompt accommodation of genuine emergency needs, personal selection purchases, and rush orders is, the more quickly unauthorized procurement will disappear from your company or organization.

CORRECTING PAST EVILS

Nonpurchasing department employees who successfully made unauthorized purchases in the past will continue to be clothed with apparent authority to commit your organization. However, suppliers will get the message that purchasing department authorization is required as your program proceeds to eliminate unauthorized procurement. The result will be that most suppliers will not make unauthorized sales without first making the offending employee obtain purchasing department approval. If the suppliers will do this for you, they will automatically defrock those employees of their apparent authority by their refusal to sell.

Communication with the suppliers will be required if you desire to "wipe the slate clean" of apparent authority. A simple letter to each supplier, where apparent authority was created, will suffice. The letter need state that only invoices showing a purchase order number will be approved for payment. Therefore, the supplier is advised to make certain that the purchase authorization is in hand before accepting an order. This will place the supplier on notice. One such letter will take away any semblance of authority to commit the company from all those employees who successfully made unauthorized purchases from that supplier.

THE OCCASIONAL CURRENT OFFENSE

No doubt there will continue to be a few occasions where unauthorized purchases are made, and your company will want you to confirm them. This is an almost inevitable fact of purchasing life. Proceed with the confirmation, but send a note to the supplier with the purchase order or the payment. The note might state:

> We are accepting responsibility for this purchase even though it was made without purchasing department approval. We ask for your cooperation in the future by contacting the undersigned for authorization if you intend to request payment from our company. Only the purchasing department is authorized to obligate this organization.

Such a note will snuff out any vestige of apparent authority that the supplier might claim to arise from the payment of the invoice for the unauthorized purchase.

Nota Bene **to the Purchasing Officer.** Justice is not served if the onus of an unauthorized purchase is placed solely on the shoulders of the supplier. It is true that it takes a willing supplier to make possible an unauthorized purchase that violates your purchasing procedures. But the real culprits are your coemployees who commit the offense and your company that makes it possible for the offense to be committed. Punitive actions should be taken at the source, and that means it is an in-house problem. If top management is sincere in their support of your program, they should take appropriate action against the persistent offending employee and his or her department head. It is not the supplier's responsibility to enforce your corporate procedures.

There are some—primarily government agencies—who have a unique method of making the recalcitrant employee cease and desist from making unauthorized purchases. The employee is required to pay the invoice for the purchase personally! No opportunity is afforded for a confirming requisition to come from the department. Another institution, we are told, requires the offending employee to have the president cosign a confirming requisition for an unauthorized purchase or pay it personally. Although this may be an excellent opportunity to get to know the president better, it could be done under more pleasant circumstances. This procedure, while it has great promise of being effective, can hardly be categorized as professional management practice.

Suppliers who persist in selling to unauthorized employees, rapidly lose favor with the purchasing officer. Such suppliers risk future, legitimate business by their actions. They also risk not being able to obtain payment of their invoice for an unauthorized purchase. The next section illustrates the legal effect on a supplier who fails to make certain that he or she is dealing with an authorized agent of the company to be invoiced.

DEALING WITH AN AGENT

It is a well-established rule of law that a person dealing with an agent has the responsibility of ascertaining the scope of authority that agent possesses. At first blush, this may appear to be a harsh rule that imposes an undue burden on the individual dealing with an agent. However, the rule is essential if one considers the potential harm that might develop were the rule not so stated.

Assume you walk into a meat market that you have never been in before and tell the butcher, "I would like to purchase six prime beef rib roasts, about 10 pounds each, for the XYZ Corporation. We are having a large dinner party tomorrow night for some out-of-town customers. You can send the bill for the roasts to our treasurer at 123 Main Street." (We also assume you do not work for the XYZ Corporation and that you are desirous of getting some good beef at a very low cost to yourself.) Now, no matter how pleasant a personality you might have, that butcher is not going to allow you to walk out of his shop with 60 pounds of prime beef under your arm without making certain he will be paid for it! To allow you to get away with such an act would be sheer folly on his part. He might want to do business with you in the worst way and could insist that you show him your money to pay for the roasts. If you persist in having the bill sent to the corporation, the butcher should then call someone at the XYZ Corporation to make certain you are for real. He must determine whether or not you have the authority to commit the corporation for such a purchase. If he obtains a negative answer, he knows you are trying to bilk him out of 60 pounds of good beef. But the obligation to ascertain the scope of your authority remains with him, no matter how much he wants to sell his beef. This is the law.

When two individuals engage in a business transaction, there is the presumption that they are dealing with each other at arm's length. If one person is the seller, that individual will want to be certain about the buyer's financial stability if credit is to be extended. Due inquiries will be made at credit rating bureaus, the bank where the buyer has an account, and perhaps with the certified public accountants who certify the buyer's financial statement. A seller is not at all shy about making such inquiries.

But suppose the buyer announces to the seller that the purchase is not being made for personal use but instead for another person—the buyer's principal—whom the buyer represents as an agent. No doubt the seller will want to make the same credit inquiries into the principal's financial stability; but first, the seller should make inquiries into the agent's authority to commit the principal to the contract. There is no point in checking on the principal's financial integrity if the principal will not be bound to the contract. The seller is placed on special alert when the buyer announces the sale is being made to someone not at the negotiating table. This alert, the law believes, is sufficient warning to the seller to take the necessary steps to ascertain the actual authority the agent has to obligate the named principal. Should the agent not announce the fact that he represents someone else, the seller is entitled to the assumption that the agent himself is the other party to the contract and should govern himself accordingly.

It is obvious that this legal battle—that the person who deals with an agent has the responsibility of ascertaining the agent's authority—is great protection to the principal. It protects everyone who has not appointed an agent. This is very basic. The law, in the previous example, will protect the XYZ Corporation from having you successfully declare yourself as their agent. And so does the law protect every other company or organization against having unauthorized—and often, unknown—agents commit them to contracts. The only manner in which the law may offer this protection is to make it incumbent upon the person dealing with the alleged agent to be able to prove that there was reason to believe the agent had authority to commit the principal.

We should take an additional step forward and note that the law even protects principals who have appointed agents against unwarranted extensions of the authority created in them. A principal may appoint an agent with limited authority to represent the principal in some transactions. An example of the protection offered can be found in our previous hypothetical situation involving you and the butcher in the meat market. Assume the XYZ Corporation had employed you, to prepare and serve the dinner for the out-of-town customers. It was suggested to you that prime rib might be an appropriate entree for the meal, but that first you should ascertain the cost, and then a decision would be made. You are authorized to make inquiries about prime rib costs and report back to the company. Armed with these credentials, you walk into the same meat market. This time you walk in as an agent for the XYZ Corporation, but with limited authority—authority to investigate and report back.

Let us assume that you again order the six roasts notwithstanding the instructions given you. Let us justify your actions because our butcher friend gave you a very low price per pound. You make the purchase and walk out of the store with the six roasts. Our butcher friend in the meat market took your instructions to send the bill to the XYZ Corporation without checking on your authority. When you talk with the individual at the XYZ Corporation in charge of the dinner, you are told they have decided to serve fresh mountain trout. You report that you have already purchased the prime roasts because of the very low price offered. The response is, "Return the roasts. We are serving fish at the dinner." The butcher refuses to accept a return of the six roasts. The XYZ Corporation refuses to pay the butcher's invoice. What happens?

The answer to this question is that you will be eating prime ribs of beef for some period of time. You were an agent for the XYZ Corporation—that much is true—but you did not have the authority to make the purchase. The XYZ Corporation can return the invoice to the meat market unpaid, because they did not give you authority to purchase the meat. The butcher cannot collect from XYZ because he failed to ascertain whether or not you had the necessary authority. But that does not stop the butcher from collecting the sum due from you personally. You bought the meat from the butcher, and since you cannot get the XYZ Corporation to pay for it, you are responsible. The legal rule continues to protect the principal even though it had appointed you an agent, but with limited authority, remember. The law will hold the corporation responsible only for the authority granted to you. The law also protects XYZ Corporation against the meat market because our butcher friend failed to ascertain the scope of authority you had been given by XYZ. The butcher may only look to you for payment.

This legal rule makes possible the widespread use of agents in business. It protects the principal against unauthorized and unknown agents. It protects the principal against agents with limited authority who dare to exceed that authority. The law protects the agent who acts within the scope of authority by making each authorized act the action of the principal. It absolves the agent of all liability for action taken within the scope of authority granted, provided the principal is disclosed. And finally, the third party knows that if the agent has the authority to commit the principal, there is created a firm and valid contract with the principal. These are the assurances that this legal rule gives each of the three parties to a transaction negotiated by an agent.

Let us note, too, that the results are unfortunate if any one of the three parties fails in its obligation under this rule. If the third party fails to ascertain the agent's scope of authority, there will be no enforceable contract with the principal. The third party will be able to hold only the unauthorized agent to the contract. If the agent signs a contract in the name of the principal without having the proper authority, the agent is personally liable to the third party. And then we come to the principal who reaps the greatest benefit from this rule of law, but who also stands to lose the most if he fails in his obligation. The principal is securely protected against the unauthorized acts of his agent and against third parties who do not bother to ascertain the scope of authority claimed by an alleged agent. The principal rests in the enviable position of being assured that he will be responsible only for the actions of a specific agent authorized to perform specific acts for him. But, if the principal becomes careless by acknowledging responsibility for unauthorized acts or for the actions of unauthorized agents, the roof will cave in on him. The principal must remain steadfast in acknowledging the authorized acts of his authorized agents and in disavowing unauthorized acts of unauthorized agents. The failure to promptly disavow all unauthorized acts and agents could give the principal king-sized problems. Any ratification of these unauthorized actions, without proper renunciation of the implied consequences, opens the door to future claims of apparent authority. (See the previous sections on apparent authority.)

DEALING WITH A SUPPLIER

One of the practical applications of the principles of authority in agency law occurs each time you make a purchase. A representative of the supplier with whom you are doing business will conduct the negotiations with you. And that representative—the salesperson who calls on you and handles your company's account—is an agent of that supplier. The only instance in which that representative will not be an agent is when that supplier's business is organized as a single proprietorship enterprise, and the owner of the business is the individual who calls on you and handles your account. Then you will be dealing directly with the supplier. But if the owner of the single proprietorship entity employs sales personnel to represent the business, and if one of these representatives handles your account, you will be involved with an agent. Thus the odds are high that you will be doing business with an agent when you make a purchase.

Keep in mind that when you transact business with an agent the scope of authority that agent possesses is of importance to you. Remember, too, that it is the rule of law that "he who deals with an agent has the responsibility of ascertaining the scope of authority that agent possesses." It follows, then, that if you are to rely on representations or assurances that the supplier's agent makes, you must be certain that agent has the authority to commit the principal—the supplier—to these assurances.

It is not always an easy chore to ascertain the scope of authority a sales agent possesses. Of course, you could ask the salesperson what authority has been given by the principal-supplier, but his answer will prove nothing in the eyes of the law. The law has taken the position that the average salesperson, or "drummer," as many courts term a salesperson, has very limited authority. The law books are replete with legal instances where a drummer has been defined as an agent with limited authority. The courts go on to state that this limited authority consists of the authority to solicit invitations to do business with his principal (the supplier), and carry these invitations back to the home office where they might either be accepted or rejected. In short, the average salesperson does not have the authority to enter into a contract with you. As we shall see shortly an exception to this generalization might occur if the principal created apparent authority in the salesperson. Although you have the authority to commit your company, the sales representative cannot commit the supplier. When you say to the sales representative, "We will buy a dozen of your product," that person will say to you, "Great! Now I will go back to my office and find out whether we want to sell you a dozen of our product." This is not a good way to do business. There must be a better way, and there *is* a better way.

Note that in the above reference to the law's view of drummers, the home office of the supplier is the key. And that key at the home office can open two doors for you. One door offers the possibility that you might be able to obtain a letter from the home office of the supplier stating that the sales representative calling on you has the authority to commit the supplier to a contract and to negotiate all angles of the sale. If you can obtain such a letter, you will be entitled to rely on this statement. It comes from the home office and is signed by someone who has the authority to do so. That is where the authority is lodged.

The other door the home office key can open for you is to make the home office come to you. Make them submit written proposals to you to do business with them. These proposals then fall into your hands as offers to do business and are not mere invitations. Then you have the option to accept or reject them. The use of this door makes the salesperson not much more than a messenger. But many suppliers prefer to do business in this manner. They prefer to have someone in the home office call the shots. Then the sales representative is no more than an intermediary and has no authority to commit the supplier.

There are other clues that may be of help in ascertaining the scope of authority a sales representative possesses. When you receive a quotation you requested from that supplier, note who signed it. If your sales representative's signature is on the form, and if it is obvious the form was mailed from the home office, this is a good indication that the salesperson has authority to contract with you. Such a quotation is an offer to sell to you, and an offer is one-half of a contract. That proves that the sales representative has authority to contract, and that is all you need to know. However, if the quotation from the supplier is signed by someone else—beware! You are on notice that someone in the home office is prepared and authorized to contract with you. This is not conclusive proof that the salesperson does not have authority, but you should be on the alert because of the other signature.

In the absence of written proof of authority, what else is available? The calling card of the salesperson might show a title, such as sales manager, vice-president for sales, or even president. Such imposing titles might—but not always—carry with them authority to obligate the supplier. It is difficult to be a vice-president for sales and not have the authority to commit the company in a sales contract.

It is equally difficult to be a sales manager without having the same, authority to commit. But then again—just to caution you—if that sales manager reports to the vice-president for sales and the vice-president retains all authority to make commitments to customers, you have a sales manager with limited authority handling your account. (See previous discussion of express authority. It is applicable to sales agents too).

It is also possible to conduct a test on the actual authority your salesperson possesses. The test could be conducted in an innocent manner without your friend being aware of it. For example, assume that you wish to purchase a package of 12 of an item, and the salesperson states that the catalog price of a standard pack of 12 is $600. Ask the salesperson, "If I only need 10, would you break a standard package and sell me 10 for $500?" If the response is, "Well, I would have to check with the boss before I answer that question," you have your answer on that sales representative's authority: It is limited.

On the other side of the coin, if the response is, "Sure, we'll be glad to sell you 10 for $500," that implies some semblance of authority. If you place the order for 10, and they are delivered, you have some indicia that the sales representative does possess authority. Note that there is also an interesting byproduct in this situation. You were the third party in the principal-agent relationship at the supplier's company. The principal (the supplier, not the sales representative), by delivering 10 at the standard package price, has ratified the agent's actions even though the salesperson may not have had the authority. Let this happen several times, and you as the third party could build a strong case that the salesperson had *apparent* authority to obligate the principal. Apparent authority may work as a useful tool for you as well as one that can be used against you and your company. Repeated instances of a salesperson's making commitments to you that are ratified by the home office can only help establish the fact that you are entitled to believe the salesperson has the apparent authority to commit his principal.

But why resort to such legalisms and extracurricular methods of ascertaining the scope of the authority of the salespeople that call on you? There is a procedure you have available to you that is close to being foolproof. Let us first examine the following hypothetical case and then discover how to protect your company and yourself.

> Loose, a purchasing officer, requests quotations on 600,000 half nuts. Eager, a salesman for the Nutt Company who handles Loose's account, calls on him shortly after Loose has received all his quotations. Loose tells Eager, "Your company's quotation is the lowest I received, but there is one question. My storeroom people tell me they will go nuts with all of those half-nuts around. Could you space deliveries?" Eager takes the quotation and writes on it, "in three deliveries of 200,000 each." Loose sends the Nutt Company the purchase order, which reads, "600,000 half-nuts per your quotation." The next day, 600,000 half-nuts arrive at Loose's storeroom.
>
> Loose calls Eager at the Nutt Company to protest, but he is not available, so Loose talks to P. Nutt, the president of the Nutt Company. (Nutt had signed the original quotation.) Nutt tells Loose that if he wants the 600,000 half-nuts in three deliveries, the price will have to be increased by 10 percent. Loose points out that Eager had promised him three deliveries at no additional cost and had amended the quotation to include that fact. Nutt responds, "Eager had no authority to amend my original quotation. I prepared that quotation for you. Eager had nothing to do with its preparation and he cannot change it in any manner without my concurrence."
>
> The court would decide in favor of P. Nutt if this hypothetical case reached the proportions of a lawsuit. Loose would be the loser because he had failed to ascertain the scope of authority Mr. Eager possessed. He was on notice that Eager was an agent of the Nutt Company. He was relying on Eager's written amendment of the quotation and should have been certain of Eager's authority to do it. The law places this obligation on Mr. Loose.

Every alert purchasing officer will see in the above case how Mr. Loose erred and got himself into a bit of trouble. Mr. Loose's purchase order should have read (the added words are italicized): "600,000 half-nuts per your quotation, *in three deliveries of 200,000 each, as promised by Mr. Eager*."

Those additional words typed on the purchase order place the proverbial monkey squarely on Mr. Nutt's back. He cannot deliver all 600,000 half-nuts at one time, and thus irritate Mr. Loose's storeroom people. He must either accept Mr. Eager's commitment to make three deliveries or risk cancellation of the order. It is true that he has no obligation to make the three deliveries at no increase of cost. He might call Mr. Loose after receiving the purchase order and point out that Eager did not have the authority to alter the quotation. Mr. Loose's response could be, "You had better take Mr. Eager out to the woodshed and discipline him. Your agent made a commitment to me, and I expect you to honor that promise." If Mr. Nutt continues to protest, Mr. Loose has the option to turn to the supplier who made the second lowest quotation.

Mr. Loose kept all his options open by including Mr. Eager's promise of three deliveries on his purchase order. This is the method to ascertain an agent's authority which was referred to above. The principal loses the right to plead "lack of authority" if he wants the order. He is unable to make the sale and make his point for additional payment, too.

***Nota Bene* to Purchasing Officer.** Your legal counsel will be pleased with you if you follow this practice with every important verbal commitment made to you by a supplier's representative. The above hypothetical case, as amended by the additional words on the purchase order, illustrates how your written documentation may defend you against the lack of authority vested in an agent. But the same approach is good business practice in every purchase you make, no matter whether the salesperson has authority or not.

Practically all, if not all, your purchases are made by use of a purchase order. The purchase order is a written document and becomes part of the final contract with your supplier. Make certain all the terms of the purchase are contained in that writing. Do not allow verbal representations made by the supplier's representative to go unrecorded, especially if you plan to rely on such representations. Your legal counsel will tell you that verbal representations that amend or add to a written contract are difficult to prove in a court of law. The court regards the written contract as the best evidence available to establish what you and your supplier agreed upon when you made the purchase. It is difficult to persuade a court to believe that there is more to the contract than what is on paper, especially if the "more" are oral representations made by the supplier's representative.

You have a good system going for you when you place on your purchase order all the representations made to you during the negotiations. The supplier cannot ignore these written promises. He may protest what you have written on the purchase order, but then you will have the opportunity to make your own election of whether to proceed with the purchase on his terms. Without the written protection, your election may be reduced to proceeding on his terms whether you like it or not. Protect your company and yourself by taking the time to get what the salesman or saleswoman said on the purchase order. Then you couldn't care less whether or not the salesperson had authority.

DEALING WITH A PURCHASING OFFICER

The sales representative of a supplier faces similar problems in determining authority when doing business with a customer through a member of the purchasing staff. Not all buyers and purchasing officers are vested with complete authority to contract for their company. It is not uncommon to find that members of a purchasing staff will have varying degrees of authority. And, of course, the same legal duty is on the shoulders of the sales representative to ascertain the scope of authority possessed by the one with whom he or she is transacting business.

Generally, sales personnel have one advantage over purchasing people when it comes to determining the authority of the person on the other side of the desk. Purchasing personnel work in their home office, and the salesperson is the one who visits that office. Therefore, the opportunity of checking out authority is a simple procedure. It involves only one conversation with the chief purchasing officer while on the site. Communication is not dependent upon the mail.

Most purchasing offices have available for suppliers printed brochures that explain how to do business with the organization. Included in such helpful printed pieces will be some mention of which buyer is responsible for purchasing the type of item handled by the supplier, that buyer's name, and where he or she is located. Most brochures are quite specific in telling the supplier that an official purchase order will be issued over the signature of the authorized purchasing officer when a purchase is made. Such assurances are adequate to alert the salesperson that an official commitment of the organization has been made. The salesperson is advised not to attempt to jump the gun by acting as if a sale has been made before the official purchase order is made available. In fact, a salesperson almost never has to be concerned about the purchasing officer's authority when a purchase order, duly executed, is in hand.

V

Duties of an Agent

The law places many duties on an agent, the number and scope of which far exceed those that are placed upon an ordinary employee. The reason for this added burden lies in the fact that the principal-agent relationship is founded on the trust that is placed in the agent. The principal hands over to the agent the power to commit him in contract. The transfer of such power by the principal to another person is a significant action and it obviously requires a good amount of faith on his part. It is not done without considerable thought. Great care must be exercised in the selection of an agent. Once the agent is appointed, the principal must depend upon that person to act properly at all times. The principal hopes that the agent will never betray this trust or abuse the authority granted. The principal is unable to look over the agent's shoulder and monitor each individual act, because the agent acts independently. All the principal can do is to trust that the selection process was a successful endeavor and hope for the best.

You now know that agency is a creation of the law. It is the law that makes possible the transfer of the principal's authority to the agent. The law makes the actions of the agent those of the principal, just as if the principal had done them personally. At the same time, the law recognizes that the principal has had to place a high degree of trust in the agent, and that the principal is at the complete mercy of the agent that this trust will be honored. To give the principal some assurance that it will not be abused, the law places on the agent certain duties that are designed to keep the agent in line. These duties are unwritten; they are not spelled out in the agent's contract even if the agent has a written contract, but they are part of the contract nonetheless. They are implied by the law and impressed upon the agent when he or she accepts the appointment. One must accept the legal duties of the job when one accepts the appointment. It is as simple as that. Any violation of these duties that causes injury to the principal gives the principal a cause of action against the agent for damages. Such violations are regarded as a breach of the agency contract.

The duties that have been established by the law over the years include the following:

1. Duty of loyalty to the principal

2. Duty of obedience to the instructions of the principal

3. Duty to perform with reasonable care

4. Duty to account to the principal

5. Duty to inform the principal

6. Duty of confidence

7. Duty to bring the necessary skills and training to the agency

The succeeding sections will discuss these duties primarily as they apply to purchasing personnel.

DUTY OF LOYALTY

At first blush, one might assume we are taking off on a patriotic expedition when we discuss the duty of loyalty. That is not a totally inaccurate analogy. The duty of loyalty requires the agent to set aside all other conflicting interests when acting for the principal. Unswerving loyalty is demanded and expected. The agent must not only act *for* the principal but act *as* the principal would act at all times.

This places a strong responsibility on the purchasing officer to make certain there are no personal interests involved when a purchase is being negotiated. One of the foremost considerations is never to have a personal financial interest—"a piece of the action," if you will—in a supplier's organization. One should not purchase from a supplier if a proprietary interest is held personally or by a member of the family. One hundred percent of your efforts and interests must be used for your principal's interests, and that is impossible if you stand to gain personally from a purchase made from a particular supplier. You need to be free to push for any advantage you can get for your principal. This freedom of action is not present if you or your family might suffer pecuniary damage should you push too hard. The old saying, "You cannot carry water on both shoulders" is most apropos here. You must go into a negotiation for a purchase with only your company's interests at stake.

Doing business for your principal with your own company—or with a relative—is known as a *conflict of interest*. We hear much about conflict-of-interest situations in government circles and we know that such activities are looked upon with scorn by the public. They are equally frowned upon when they arise in private business circles. When it becomes known that a purchasing officer is doing business with a company in which he has a financial interest, the reputation of the purchasing officer suffers. If an award is made to that supplier, the competitors will do a considerable amount of talking with members of the industry. That talk will not be complimentary to the purchasing officer. Even if the supplier in which the purchasing officer owns an interest is the low bidder, the competitors who lost the order will never believe that they themselves made a higher quotation. Only the "conflict of interest" will be mentioned as the reason why they did not get the award. It is a no-win situation for the purchasing officer.

Several years ago *The Wall Street Journal*[1] carried a lengthy article concerning the purchasing officer of a well-known manufacturer of chips and other popular snacks. It appears that this company required large quantities of corn that had to possess special characteristics. The purchasing officer found an area where this type of corn could be grown. Soon he had the farmers in this locality grow corn to meet the company's specifications. The farmers, in turn, sold their corn through an agent which was a corporation in which the purchasing officer owned a majority of the capital stock. The purchasing officer bought the corn required by his company from this corporation. There was no accusation that he paid more for the corn that he would have paid to competitors of the corporation in which he was a major stockholder. Nonetheless his company filed suit against him charging that he "placed himself in a position of conflict of interest, breached his duty of loyalty and/or his fiduciary duty to his employer."

Interviews by *The Wall Street Journal* representatives brought out the negative effect the purchasing officer's actions had on competitors of his personal corporation. One competitor stated: "It got to the point we didn't make offers anymore because you just knew you wouldn't get (the company's) business." This, of itself, might tend to negate the claim that he paid no more for the corn than would have been paid to competitors. If competitors quit making offers to sell, competition had to be decreased. However, the *Journal* concluded with the observation:

> The irony of the case may be that the company, by upsetting an arrangement that was effective, regardless of its ethical considerations, may be at least temporarily raising its cost of doing business. It also cost the company its ace commodities buyer because this purchasing officer was dismissed.

Situations of this type do not come to light very often. This one does serve

---

[1] *The Wall Street Journal*, November 14, 1978.

as an excellent example of how employers take seriously the duty of loyalty of their purchasing staff. Employers are convinced that no matter how honest a purchasing officer might be, doing business with a self-owned supplier is not conducive to good business practice. If the purchasing agent gets a bad name for doing business with a supplier in which he has a financial interest, his company knows that it too will be criticized. The public will charge management with negligence in allowing the situation to persist. Condoning the purchasing officer's actions brings even more criticism than having it exist without the knowledge of management.

Many companies now require their purchasing staff to sign an annual "Conflict-of Interest" statement. The statement is an affirmation to the employer-principal that the purchasing officer received no benefits from suppliers with whom the company did business, nor did the purchasing officer have any conflicting financial interests in their suppliers. There is also a place on the form to allow the purchasing officer to state any "Exceptions" that might have occurred. A purchasing officer should not be insulted by being asked to sign such a statement. Ethical practices of the purchasing profession dictate that conflict of interest situations are to be avoided, and, if they are inevitable or arise quite by accident, a full disclosure to the principal-employer should be made immediately. This will maintain the purchasing officer's good name and the employer's confidence in him or her.

Once the conflict of interest statement is signed, it is kept on file by management. If some charge of conflict of interest in a previous transaction is made against the purchasing officer, management will investigate. If the allegation is proven to be true, the company has every reason to summarily dismiss the purchasing officer. Not only was the duty of loyalty violated, but the agent also completed a false statement to the employer. Nothing will destroy the employer-principal's trust in an agent so completely and quickly.

Needless to say, commissions to a buyer, kick-backs, and other types of fraudulent—and yes, criminal—actions are also covered by the duty of loyalty. These types of violations of this duty will be covered in detail in Chapter VII.

***Nota Bene* to Purchasing Officer.** There are occasions where an apparent instance of conflict of interest will arise. The moment the fact is brought to your attention, make a full disclosure of all the facts to your superior officer. Do not wait until the annual conflict of interest form is presented to you. Do it immediately! If your management tells you to proceed with the supplier despite the apparent conflict, have someone in your department handle the negotiations or at least have another staff member sit in with you and the supplier. Have that person also review all the documents of the transaction and get a concurrence on your decision. Having the second party may also serve as a witness for your good actions. If you are a one-person department, use your superior officer as the review person.

One other suggestion is apropos here. No matter how trivial an apparent conflict of interest situation might appear to you, it may assume great significance in the eye of another person. Therefore, full disclosure to your superior officer is the best direction no matter how minor it might be. Even a *slight* conflict is nevertheless a conflict. Divulge it before others have the opportunity to enlarge its scope into proportions beyond reality.

DUTY OF OBEDIENCE TO INSTRUCTIONS

It is a time-honored tradition of the law that every principal has the right to give instructions to an agent on how the agency is to be performed. In fact, one of the most quoted lines of demarcation between the agent and the independent contractor is the degree of control the principal has over the manner in which the work is done. If the principal engages someone to do some work and that person's performance is not subject to the control of the principal, that person is an independent contractor. The distinction between an agent and an independent contractor is of no great moment to this book on purchasing, but it is of importance to those in the personnel and payroll departments. Their interest in differentiating between the two may assist in understanding the distinction. An agent is an employee, and the compensation earned by the agent is subject to withholding taxes and social security taxes. Payments made to an independent contractor are not subject to these withholdings.

The duty of obedience to instructions on how the agency is to be performed is well understood by purchasing officers. Your tenure in your position is at stake! You do your work as directed by the boss. The alternative is to work elsewhere. But in a serious vein, it is the principal's privilege and right to give the instructions as to how the agency is to be accomplished. The law associates this right with the right to appoint an agent. The principal has the *right* to appoint an agent, but does not have the *duty* to do so. If the appointment is a right, then the principal also has the right to instruct the agent as to how the work of the agency will be done. These instructions will include what is to be done, what is not to be done, and the method and means by which it will be accomplished. Ignoring or violating these instructions is a breach of the agency contract.

DUTY TO EXERCISE REASONABLE CARE

An employee is expected to perform his or her assigned work tasks properly. Careless or slovenly performance is not tolerated in the work place. If an employee persists in doing the work carelessly, the employer has every right to dismiss that individual.

An agent has a similar duty to avoid negligent action in performing the duties of the agency. The duties of an agent customarily demand a higher degree of skill and judgment than that expected of the average employee. Then too, an agent's action can have far-reaching consequences both on the resources of the principal and of the third parties with whom the principal transacts business. Consequently the law places the duty of reasonable care on the agent at a level consistent with the skill and judgment demanded for the performance of those duties.

The guideline for this duty is found in the *prudent person rule*. Simply stated, this rule says that a person is expected to act as a reasonable prudent person might act in a similar situation or under similar circumstances. This tells you, the purchasing officer, that you are expected to act with care when negotiating for your organization and to spend the company's funds wisely by obtaining the maximum value in each purchase. You will contract with care and exercise due diligence in protecting your company's resources. You should not act carelessly and expose the company to unnecessary hazards. It is your duty as an agent to act with the same skill as if you were transacting business with your own funds and resources.

Many purchasing officers are not aware of the vital impact a purchase may have upon an organization. One of the unusual and unfortunate examples of the effect a purchase might have on people occurred some years ago at a Midwestern university.

> The university had abandoned football during World War II. The field and the wooden bleachers were not maintained, and serious decay had occurred. At the conclusion of the war it was decided to reactivate the sport. In the spring of the year, the plant engineer was instructed to get the field and the spectator bleachers in shape for the opening game of the season the last week in September.

The purchasing officer of the university received a requisition from the plant department for 1000 pcs. 2 x 10-12 Northern Pine S4S. The boards were to be used to replace the planks of the bleachers on which the spectators sat. These bleachers, on the north side of the field, were 30 rows high and accommodated some 4000 spectators. They had been built 25 years previously, and the original planks were badly decayed and splintered.

Much to the consternation of the purchasing officer, available lumber of the quality and quantity that was requisitioned was not immediately available from the usual sources of supply. He was told that there would be a waiting period of at least six to nine months before his needs could be met. The purchasing officer then resorted to long distance telephone calls and met with much the same story.

One lumber yard offered to sell some 3 x 12-12 white oak planks that were in stock. When all other inquiries brought negative results, the purchasing officer ordered the white oak at a premium price. Delivery was made, and despite two weeks of continuous drenching rains, the plant department finished the replacement of the seats two days before the opening game.

The day of the first game of the season was beautiful, and by 1:00 p.m. 4100 spectators were in the bleachers using the new seats. After a scoreless first half, early in the third quarter the university's star halfback took a hand-off from his quarterback at his own 10-yard line and ran for a touchdown. As the halfback broke loose, the 4100 spectators rose to their feet en masse. The sudden shift of their weight caused the bleachers to collapse sideways, gently and slowly, but completely. Several hundred loyal alumni suffered injuries. Fortunately, no one was killed.

Subsequent investigation showed that the long period of rain had loosened the ground surrounding the supports of the bleachers. This, coupled with the added weight of the 3 x 12 white oak planks caused the supports to give way when the spectators shifted their weight in unison.

The fact that the added weight of the 3 x 12 oak planks contributed to the accident illustrates how simple it can be for a purchasing officer to be the proximate cause of a calamity. This particular purchasing officer did everything in his power to fill the requisition from the plant department, which had asked for the almost impossible. Those of you who remember the months following World War II will recall that purchasing any acceptable lumber was a unique accomplishment. Most available lumber had not been seasoned—it was possible to have lumber delivered with some of the branches and leaves still growing from it. And yet this university purchasing agent came up with beautiful seasoned 3 x 12 pieces of white oak, only to discover that the purchase had led to a severe accident.

This purchasing officer, however, took his duty to exercise reasonable care and avoid negligent action seriously. He made every effort to protect his principal and himself against such an occurrence. Before the substitution was made, he consulted the plant engineer and insisted that an engineering study be made to determine if the bleacher structure could handle the added weight.

The study was made and the results were affirmative. Unfortunately, the study was made during a dry period in early summer, and the quicksand type of soil surrounding the supports of the bleachers was not apparent to the engineers. Nonetheless, the purchasing officer exercised "that degree of care a reasonably prudent person would use in a similar situation," and thereby protected himself against a charge of negligence. He had the foresight to anticipate a potential problem that might arise from a purchase.

It must be emphasized here that we are discussing the duty of an agent to avoid negligent action in the day-to-day purchasing routine. The purchasing officer, as an agent, is not an insurer of work. The officer may make errors of judgment and that can be expected of any prudent person. But gross negligence—an indifference to consequences—is covered by this duty. The purchasing officer may be found guilty if it is violated. This negligence and the usual tort type of negligence will be discussed in detail in Chapter VII dealing with the liabilities of a purchasing officer.

DUTY OF ACCOUNTABILITY

Some agents have the authority to make collections for their principal. Any monies collected by the agent must promptly be accounted for. This means that the agent must acknowledge the collections made and hand them over to the principal, as required.

The duty to account to the principal may also be applied to a purchasing officer. Many buyers have had advertisements come to them in the mail that offer a gift of some type if a quantity of the advertiser's product is purchased: "A beautiful clock radio or a Thanksgiving turkey if you order a 54-gallon drum of our product" are examples of such handbills that come in the mail. Should the purchasing officer place an order for the barrel of "whatever," whose radio or turkey comes with the item? The intent of the advertiser is that the agent placing the order will want the gift for personal use badly enough to place an order for the product. But the duty to account to the principal makes the radio or the turkey the property of the principal. This places the purchasing officer in the untenable position of keeping the gift and violating the agency contract.

Needless to say, all such gifts, commissions, rebates, and fees received from suppliers are the property of the employer. The duty to account imposes this on an agent. One of the most illustrative examples of this occurred some years ago in a Midwestern county that included a very large metropolitan area. The county clerk had the responsibility of purchasing the voting machines used in elections. Two of the manufacturers of voting machines either rebated a part of the purchase price or else paid a commission to the county clerk for the sales made. The county sued the clerk to recover these sums paid and won its case in court. The court stated in its opinion:[2]

> Since a fiduciary [an agent] is bound to act solely for the benefit of his principal, equity will intervene to prevent him from accruing any advantage—however innocently—from transactions conducted in

---

[2]*County of Cook v. Barrett,* 344 N.E. 2d (ILL. 1976).

behalf of the principal. So, when a fiduciary, who has acted for his principal, receives a gift, or bonus or commission from a party with whom he transacted business, that benefit may be recovered from him by the beneficiary [the principal] of the fiduciary relationship. [Bracketed words are the author's.]

The report of the case does not indicate the reasons why the money went to the clerk, but it does clearly state the duty of an agent to account to the principal.

***Nota Bene* to the Purchasing Officer** . The purchasing officer would be wise to avoid doing business with a supplier that insists on giving personal gifts or rebates for the purchase of his product. The offer and acceptance of such gifts could be interpreted as commercial bribery—giving of a bribe by the supplier and acceptance of a bribe by a purchasing officer. It is unfortunate that some suppliers believe that this is the manner by which the sale of their product may be assured. One is tempted to ask if their product is of such poor quality or so highly priced that it cannot be sold on its own merit.

If by chance it is important for you to do business with this type of supplier, try to negotiate a lower price for the product without the personal gift or rebate. The price should be lowered at least by the value of the gift. If the supplier insists that the sale can only be made at the listed price, and that a separate rebate check has to be sent, insist that the check be made payable to your company or organization. Should there be continued resistance to this suggestion, try to find an alternate supplier at all cost. If that gift or check comes to you personally, you may be in for trouble. The check could come back to haunt you as a bribe you accepted.

DUTY TO KEEP THE EMPLOYER INFORMED

Every agent has the duty to inform his or her principal of all information of importance that comes to the agent in the course of business dealings. The law also specifies that if the agent is informed, it may be assumed that the principal has been informed. Thus, if the agent receives information that the principal should be told, the law makes the agent receiving the notice responsible for getting that information to the principal. The person who had the original duty to inform the principal is relieved of that liability when it is given to the agent.

A purchasing officer is seldom confronted with situations involving the duty to inform. But let us resort to a hypothetical situation to understand the application of this duty.

Let us assume that you are being sent to Oklahoma to investigate several tracts of land being considered by your company as potential sites for a large warehouse. Furthermore, let us assume that while walking over one of the sites, the divining rod you are carrying tells you there

is an unusually large quantity of oil underground. Can you report back
to the company officers that this site is unsuitable for the warehouse
and then purchase the plot of ground for your own personal oil well?

The legal answer to the question posed is no. You were acting as an agent for
your company when you obtained this information about the oil cache. Your duty
to inform your principal obligates you to pass along all information that came
into your possession during the period of time you were pursuing your company's business. Should you elect not to mention your discovery and then purchase the land for yourself, and your company later discovers the true facts, you
will be obligated to sell the land to the company for what you paid for it. You violated your duty to inform your principal of all the pertinent facts you discovered
when investigating that site.

DUTY OF CONFIDENTIALITY

We know that the principal-agent relationship is based upon trust—a trust that
the principal places in the agent to act properly for him at all times. The duty of
confidence that the law places on the agent is one corollary of this element of
trust. The principal, because this duty is placed upon the agent's shoulders, is
given some assurance that the more sensitive information of his business affairs
will not become public knowledge because of the agent's access to it. The agent
has the general duty to keep such matters confidential. It is believed that the communication between principal and agent will be more open if this confidence is
maintained.

The duty of confidence assumes a position of greater importance when the
trade secrets of the principal are given to the agent. A "trade secret" in the law is
a unique process or formula that a person develops to manufacture a product or
deliver a service. It is a trade secret because presumably no one else in the industry knows how to produce the product in that particular manner. Generally—but
not always—a trade secret is not subject to patent or copyright protection. The
only restriction on its use by others is that they do not know what constitutes the
secret. When a trade secret is made known to an agent, the agent's duty of confidence assumes greater proportions. The information given the agent becomes
very similar to a *privileged communication,* as does information a patient reveals
to a doctor and a client to a lawyer. Neither a doctor nor a lawyer may reveal such
information to others who might seek it. The law protects such confidential data
as a privileged communication in the belief that a doctor will be better able to
treat a patient if all the facts of the illness are made known. It is presumed that the
patient will talk more freely knowing that the doctor has a legal obligation to
maintain the confidence.

Trade secrets given an agent are accorded much the same status. The principal will reveal the trade secret to the agent to enable the agent to more completely perform the duties of the agency. The principal feels secure in telling or showing the agent the secret because the law imposes the duty of confidence on the agent.

But trouble can develop if the principal and the agent part company and go their separate ways. The agent is in possession of the trade secret. Should the agent be engaged by a competitor of the first principal, the trade secret is in danger. Or, if the ex-agent forms a new company to engage in a competing business, may the trade secret be utilized? Obviously, the temptation to use it is great, and so are the legal restrictions imposed upon its use. A New York court enunciated the duty of confidence quite clearly in a 1940 case:[3]

> The essential point to be borne in mind is that the duty of the agent not to use confidential knowledge acquired in his employment in competition with his principal is implicit in the (principal-agent) relation. It exists as well after the employment is terminated as during its continuance. It is an absolute duty and not a relative duty.

There has been and is considerable litigation over the duty of confidence. It poses a difficult question for the court. On the agent's behalf, the court is aware that the agent must be free to work and to work for whomever he chooses. To keep the agent bound to the original principal forever because of his knowledge of the trade secret is tantamount to legalizing slavery once again. And yet the principal has every legal right to have his trade secret protected against disclosure and use by the agent and his competitors. Most of the reported cases of such litigation insist that the principal's trade secret be a genuinely unique process, and that reasonable limitations be placed on the agent insofar as engaging in competition is concerned. A genuine trade secret will be protected by the court for a reasonable period of time, but not forever.

Nota Bene **to the Purchasing Office.** A purchasing officer could well be an agent invested with trade secrets developed in his company, and would be under similar obligations stemming from the duty of confidence if these secrets were revealed to him. Many principals will take an additional step to protect themselves. Rather than depend upon the agent's implied duty of confidence, they will have the agent sign an agreement to the same effect. Then the duty is contained in a written contract that spells out precisely what limitations are placed on the agent if he or she leaves the employ of the principal. If you are asked to sign such a statement, it is suggested that you consider at least these two points:

> 1. Have the trade secret clearly expressed and its parameters bound as tightly and closely as possible. Vagueness in its description could lead

---

[3]*Rubner v. Gursky,* 21 N.Y.S. 2d 558 (1940).

to an attempt to widen its coverage and cause you greater problems in
your attempts to go to work for a competitor.

2. Keep the effective time of the restriction not to compete to a minimum. Try to make it applicable only for a year at the most; a shorter
span is to be preferred. Do not allow it to run for years on end.

DUTY TO POSSESS THE NECESSARY SKILLS AND TRAINING

Implied in every agency contract is the condition that the agent possess the essential skills and training to perform the required duties. It is an obvious requirement for any employee to have the skills to perform the job for which he or she is
employed. It is even more mandatory that an agent have such skills, because the
power and authority that the principal grants must be exercised properly. Thus
the law makes it a condition that a person accepting an appointment as an agent
assure the principal that he or she possesses the necessary qualifications to be
such an agent.

Purchasing officers are fortunate to have available the Certified Purchasing
Manager's program of the National Association of Purchasing Management. The
"C.P.M." designation, awarded by peer experts in the purchasing field, gives the
purchasing officer that credence necessary to meet the challenge of this duty. For
those who do not yet possess this certification, the professional development
courses offered by the regional associations of the Purchasing Management
Association give each purchasing officer the opportunity to develop the skills
essential to become certified. Many colleges and universities offer courses in purchasing management and purchasing techniques. There is ample opportunity for
every member of a purchasing staff to obtain the needed training to satisfy this
duty.

***Nota Bene* to the Purchasing Officer.** The above listed duties of an agent
form an imposing array. Your obligations to your employer-principal place upon
you the need to exercise the highest degree of care when performing the duties of
your job. You must exercise your judgment countless times a day, and there is no
quantitative measure that can be applied to determine whether you pass or fail as
a purchasing officer. The duties of an agent should remind you that your first
duty is to your employer-principal. Your employer's trust has been placed in you,
and you must act to merit that confidence. Your conduct must be above reproach.
Give no one the opportunity to claim that you are not acting in your principal's
best interest. Be positive and aboveboard in all your actions. A wholesome attitude will dispel allegations that you are acting in your own self-interest.

Above all, remember that you are not an insurer to your principal that all your decisions will be 100 percent correct. You cannot guarantee to your principal that you will not make errors in your work. Remember that those who criticize your decisions have the benefit of hindsight observation. Your duty as an agent is to act as a reasonably prudent person would act under similar circumstances. Your employer can expect no more of you.

VI

Duties and Liabilities of
the Principal

DUTIES OF THE PRINCIPAL

The previous chapter seemingly established a "bill of rights" for the principal, with the enumeration of the duties imposed upon the agent. The law has not forgotten the agent, however, and has placed certain duties on the principal to give the agent some protection too. These duties include:

1. The duty to possess the authority delegated to the agent

2. The duty to compensate the agent

3. The duty to reimburse the agent

4. The duty to indemnify the agent

5. The duty not to unreasonably interfere with the agent's work

The Duty to Possess the Authority Delegated to the Agent

It is an obvious fact that the principal may not delegate to an agent the authority to do an act which it has no authority to perform for itself. But if the principal does happen to get an agent involved in such an episode, the agent must be protected by the principal. The agent is entitled to assume that the principal has the right to do what the agent is appointed to do for him. Should it later be proven that the principal did not have such authority, the agent may still claim his or her rightful compensation for doing the work. Lack of authority on the part of the principal does not render the agent's contract null and void.

Situations involving this duty do not arise very often. Those situations that do present themselves usually involve the question as to whether a corporation has performed an *ultra vires* act—an act which the charter of the corporation does not permit. For example, assume a newspaper corporation receives a charter from the state to publish a newspaper. To increase the circulation of that newspaper, the company runs a series of contests giving large monetary prizes to the winners. Further, assume a claim is made that the contest is more than a mere game of skill—that it is a game of chance and constitutes a type of lottery. If the state in which this newspaper is incorporated has not legalized gambling and games of chance, the attorney general could take action against the newspaper and those managing the contest. That legal action could be a criminal charge and also a civil charge that the corporation is performing an *ultra vires* act. If gambling is legalized in the state, only the civil charge of an *ultra vires* act could be brought. The penalty for the corporation in that event could be as severe as the loss of the corporation charter.

Those agents (the officers of the corporation) who conducted the contest are protected to some extent by the duty imposed upon their principal—the corporation. Any monetary fines assessed against the officers can be recovered from the principal. The principal gave them the assurance that when they were appointed agents, the principal had the authority to conduct such a contest. When it developed that the corporation did not have such authority, it amounted to a breach of contract of the corporation's duty to the agent and a breach of the agency contract. The agents were entitled to rely on presence of this authority, so if they were damaged by its absence, they were entitled to be reimbursed for any damages they may have suffered. If their actions of conducting the contest were also found to be in violation of the criminal laws of the state, they could not expect the corporation to go to jail for them. The person who commits the crime must suffer the consequences.

The Duty to Compensate the Agent

Unless it is made abundantly clear to the agent that the work is to be done on a gratuitous basis, the principal must compensate the agent for services rendered. Purchasing officers have their salaries established in the same manner as other employees of the company or organization.

The Duty to Reimburse the Agent

The law also imposes on the principal the obligation to reimburse the agent for all reasonable expenditures made while furthering the principal's business. The reimbursed expenses must be reasonable and necessary. It is desirable for the agent to have the expenditures authorized in advance by the principal, but it is not essential. The expenses that are reimbursable are those that are reasonable, necessary, and related to the mission of the agency. Of course, the duty of reimbursement could be limited by agreement between the principal and the agent.

The Duty to Indemnify the Agent

The duty of the principal to indemnify the agent applies to those situations where the agent is unexpectedly held personally liable for an authorized act. It is the general rule of law that the act of an agent becomes the act of the principal when the act was authorized by the principal. Most often, then, the agent is not involved in any settlement between the principal and the third party with whom the agent contracted. The duty to indemnify rarely arises, and then, only when the agent through some strange circumstance is unexpectedly held as the person making the contract. In such instances, the principal may be called upon by the agent for indemnification.

The Duty Not to Unreasonably Interfere with the Agent's Work

An agent customarily is given a considerable amount of discretion in performing the duties of the agency. Most agencies are created as a continuing relationship for the performance of a particular function in a company. In most instances, no one can predict every problem that might arise, and that the agent might be called upon to satisfy. Consequently, the agent will be required to exercise his or her own personal judgment to solve the problems as they arise. Part of the trust or confidence the principal places in the agent is the authorization to use his or her own best judgment when it comes to situations that don't have specific handling instructions. Couched somewhere between the agent's duty to obey instructions and the principal's duty not to unreasonably interfere with the agent's work lies a broad discretionary area. Purchasing officers are well aware of the amount of discretion they have when making a purchase. Seeking sources of supply, selecting a suitable quality of the product for the intended use, negotiating terms of delivery, payment, and guarantees, and buying economical quantities all fall into the area of discretionary decision making. Purchasing is a profession that calls for the exercise of a high degree of judgmental determinations. The principal, therefore, must recognize the duty not to unreasonably interfere with the agent's performance, as long as the agent keeps within the principal's instructions as to how the agency is to be performed.

LIABILITIES OF THE PRINCIPAL

The above listed duties of the principal may become liabilities if they are not observed. The principal also voluntarily assumes other responsibilities and potential liabilities when a purchasing agent is employed. Each act the agent performs for the principal that is within the scope of authority granted becomes a responsibility of the principal. The commitments that a purchasing officer makes to suppliers become the commitments of the principal. The law forces the principal to honor the contracts that have been made in his name by the agent

The principal also may become unexpectedly bound to a contract that has been made by an unauthorized agent. (This was discussed in Chapter IV, where the topic of apparent authority illustrated the potential liability of the principal in such instances.) A principal must be continuously alert to the possible consequences of allowing someone without authority to continue to deal with third-party suppliers in his name. Contractual liabilities can result.

Vicarious Liabilities

There are liabilities a principal incurs through no fault of his own, other than having engaged an agent to represent him and that agent acts negligently while performing the duties of the agency. A *vicarious* liability is one imposed upon a person by the law because of another person's actions. The liability is placed upon the mantle of the innocent party because of his relationship to the person who committed the offense. This principle is applied in the principal-agent relationship. The negligence of the agent can be imputed to the principal under certain conditions.

Common law termed this imputation of the agent's liability to the principal the doctrine of *respondeat superior* ("let the master respond"). This Latin phrase is more loosely translated today as "let the master respond, too, by payment of damages to the injured party for injuries caused by the negligent action of his agents and employees." This common law doctrine is firmly entrenched in American law. It is applied continually, and there is evidence that its applicability is expanding. However, the principle does not generally apply to independent contractors in most states.

The doctrine of *respondeat superior* goes into operation when an agent commits a tort and thereby incurs a liability to an injured party. (See "Exposure to Tort Liabilities," Chapter VII for an explanation of tort liability.) The agent is responsible to the injured party for the damages suffered *and*, under the *respondeat superior* doctrine, the principal also becomes liable for the same damages. The agent has the liability because he caused the injury. The principal has the same liability because he has a vicarious liability for the acts of his agent. The principal's liability is not based upon his fault or wrongdoing. He is simply the victim of a legal principle that imposes *liability without fault*.

Liability without fault is unusual punishment and contrary to most legal principles. The law justifies this principle in several ways: First, it says that the principal selected the agent and did so voluntarily. That he happened to select an agent who committed a negligent act and injured someone suggests that the principal was not careful in the selection process. This is tenuous reasoning, because we all know that accidents happen while exercising the greatest amount of care. They are inevitable. The second line of reasoning has to do with the control exercised over the agent. We saw earlier that a principal controls the work of the agent. The agent is told what the duties of the agency are, and how those duties are to be performed. The law, then, observes that if the agent committed a negligent act, the principal did not exercise the proper controls over his actions and should be responsible for the unfortunate results. Again, the logic in this assumption is weak.

The third approach to vicarious liability is more meritorious. The law observes that the principal receives the benefits of the work of the agent. Therefore, the conclusion to this observation is that he who receives the benefits of the labors should also assume responsibility for any mistakes the agent makes while pursuing the interests of the principal. This approach is based on much sounder reasoning.

Finally, the law reasons that in most instances the principal is in a better financial position to assume the costs an injured party suffers when an agent commits a negligent act. At least it is believed (and probably correctly so) that the principal has sufficient financial substance to be able to purchase the necessary insurance to provide restitution for the damages suffered by the injured party. Both of these financial-ability rationales have some merit. At least, they are honest expressions of what goes through the thinking processes of the juries and the courts. (See also the discussion of the "deep-pocket" theory in "Exposure of Tort Liabilities," Chapter VII.)

Like it or not, the principle of vicarious liability is with us and is firmly implanted in our law. There are two conditions that must be met in any negligence situation for the principal to be subject to vicarious liability because of the agent's actions. The first is that the agent must have been acting within the scope of authority granted at the time the negligence occurred. The second condition is that the agent was furthering the principal's business interests when the faulty action took place. It is not enough for the offender to be the principal's agent, nor is it generally adequate for the agent to be using equipment or premises of the principal when the accident occurred. There must be direct evidence showing that the agent was furthering the business of the principal at the time the incident occurred to assign vicarious liability.

When vicarious liability is imposed on the principal, the agent is not relieved of responsibility for the negligent act. It does mean that *both* the principal *and* the agent may be held responsible. The injured party may file suit against either the principal or the agent, or against both of them. However, the injured party is not entitled to double the amount of the damages. If both parties are joined in the lawsuit, the court will hold both parties jointly and severally liable for the damages awarded the injured party.

Liability for Criminal Acts of the Agent

The common law was firm in its conviction that a principal was not liable for the criminal acts of his agent unless the principal had directed the agent to commit the criminal acts. But our laws reflect the public concerns about our environment and about the social responsibilities of business, and they now provide that certain acts will result in criminal penalties for both the agent who perpetrates the crime and the company by whom the agent is employed. Typical examples are found in laws relating to pollution, treatment of hazardous waste, pure foods and drugs, unfair labor practices, antitrust prohibitions, and a host of other forbidden activities.

The text is not devoted to the manifold legal involvements of business, but the above list of liabilities of principal-employer should emphasize to the purchasing officer that being the "boss" is not all wine and roses. Your principal assumes many responsibilities for your behavior and conduct, and it behooves you to act in a manner that reduces these risks. You are under a *personal* obligation to act as a reasonably prudent person at all times to avoid any personal liabilities. There is also the obligation to your principal-employer, because the exposure he faces from your actions are equal to or greater than your own.

VII

Personal Liabilities
of the Agent

The title of this chapter is foreboding: It implies that the agent assumes certain liabilities. It also indicates that these are *personal* liabilities, which means that the agent's personal fortune is placed "on the line" as the duties of the day are performed. These frightening conclusions are not intentional. The chapter is designed to call the agent's attention to areas where there might be exposure to liability, how such liability might arise, and how it may be successfully avoided.

BREACH OF THE AGENCY CONTRACT

The duties of the agent as set forth in Chapter V served to alert the purchasing officer to the consequences of noncompliance. These duties are implied by the law and become part and parcel of your agency contract with your employer. Failure to comply with them is a breach of contract, and subjects you to liability for the consequences. Compliance is an obligation you assume when you agree to become an agent for your company or organization. Your employer-principal is entitled to rely on your adherence to these assignments, because they are part of every agent's contract. When you ignore a duty, you incur a liability. The extent of that liability depends upon the extent to which the damages that your employer-principal suffers are directly attributable to your neglect.

EXECUTION OF CONTRACTS AND PURCHASE ORDERS

Each time you sign a purchase order or execute a contract to purchase or a lease, your personal signature is used to signify the act of commitment of the company. Does the use of your very own "John Henry" involve you in the contract personally? The answer to this question is an emphatic no, providing all four of the following prerequisites are met:

1. The name of your principal is shown on the document.

2. The fact that you are signing as an agent for your principal is clearly indicated.

3. Your agency relationship is shown.

and last but not the least,

4. You are acting within the scope of your authority when the document is signed and the commitment is made.

When all of the above conditions are met, you have little to fear because your own personal and private signature appears on the document.

The first three items above indicate that there is a proper format for signing a contract or a purchase order, as illustrated below.

WIND CORPORATION

Joseph Blow

Director of Purchasing

"Wind Corporation" identifies the principal—the company that is being committed to the contract. The word "by" to the left of the signature demonstrates that "Joseph Blow" is signing the contract for the Wind Corporation and is not personally committing himself. It shows that he is signing the document as an agent. "Director of Purchasing" describes the agency relationship Joseph Blow has to Wind Corporation.

Many companies print their name and address at the top of the purchase order and do not repeat it above the director of purchasing's signature in the lower right-hand corner. This is also regarded as meeting the first condition—identifying the principal. The law wants the identity of the principal disclosed in clear, unmistakable terms to enable the other party to the contract to know with whom they are contracting. A purchase order with "Wind Corporation" centered and in clear legible type at the top of the form meets that criterion.

Omission of the word *by* in the signature block of the purchase order is another common variance. This is not a grievous omission because, with the principal clearly identified, it is obvious that Joseph Blow is signing for the Wind Corporation. The use of the word *by*, however, leaves no doubt in the reader's mind that Joseph Blow is signing on behalf of Wind Corporation. This is the traditional manner a signature block is prepared, but there is no violation of duty or misidentification if the word *by* is omitted.

A Legal Signature

The law is very permissive as to what constitutes the legal signature of an individual. A fair statement would be that the law recognizes any type of signature as long as the person making it *intended* it to be his or her signature. There is nothing in the law that requires the use of full names in a signature. Initials can substitute for one or both given names. Even an initial is an adequate substitute for the surname. The law is so loose in this respect that a signature does not have to be legible to be adequate. All that is required is that the signature or mark be intended as the person's legal signature and that it was meant to be affixed to the document.

This also answers the question as to whether a signature need be made in pen and ink. Obviously, a pen-and-ink signature is more permanent and perhaps more legible than one made with a pencil or crayola. But it does not follow that a pencil signature is not a valid signature. A typewritten signature is also acceptable (but difficult to prove in a courtroom), as is a mark or cross made by a person unable to write. Another person may even sign for an individual as long as it is done in the person's presence and at his or her direction.

You will note that no mention has been made of having one's signature on a rubber stamp. This is not because it is illegal to use one. Signatures made by a rubber stamp are valid as long as they are stamped by the person or in the person's presence. But a rubber stamp signature is a very poor gadget for a purchasing officer to have in the office. The opportunities for perfect forgeries are limitless. A rubber stamp is therefore not a wise investment for a purchasing officer. It is much better for someone else in the purchasing organization to be authorized to sign purchase orders, if the chief purchasing officer is so busy that the purchase of a rubber stamp is contemplated.

***Nota Bene* to the Purchasing Officer.** It should be noted that many checks these days have facsimile signatures. Modern office equipment has developed to the point where a facsimile signature of a treasurer or a cashier can be prepared and reproduced millions of times by mechanical processes. Such signatures are legal and proper, as stated above. The reproduction of such a signature is done under very controlled circumstances with more than one person observing the signing, and a careful note is made of the check numbers and amounts for which a facsimile signature is used. The plate containing the signature is locked in a safe or vault when not in use.

The sheer magnitude of the numbers of checks to be signed makes this practice popular today. There are obvious risks, but the weight of the number of checks that would have to be signed manually makes the risk taking seem prudent. Many firms limit the use of facsimile signatures to payroll checks. Payroll checks may have to be prepared weekly or bimonthly, and this makes the task of signing them assume massive proportions. Since payroll checks are drawn against a special payroll account that contains only a limited amount of money, it makes the practice of mechanically signing the checks less risky. However, most banks still require a special resolution of the board of directors of the company using this check-signing practice to authorize its use.

A purchasing officer might ask the question, "If facsimile signatures are acceptable for checks, why should they not be used for purchase orders, too?" The author can suggest at least three reasons why a manual signature is preferred for purchase orders:

1. A purchase order is one-half of a contract. The intent to be bound in a contract is better expressed by affixing one's signature to the document personally. It has been—and still is—the traditional method of expressing agreement to the written word.

2. A purchase order should be proofread by an experienced purchasing officer before it is mailed to the supplier. The time when the signature is affixed provides an excellent opportunity to reread the purchase order to make certain there are no important errors. If the purchasing officer who negotiated the purchase signs the order, he has one last opportunity to review the transaction. If someone else signs, it affords an excellent opportunity for independent review of the transaction.

3. There is immediate and positive criminal liability for the person who forges a *check*. This is a strong deterrent to such action. There is no immediate criminal liability attached to the forgery of a *purchase order*. A more extensive and rigorous prosecution is necessary to convict the forger of a purchase order.

Delegating Order-Signing Responsibility

The application of a signature to a purchase order is the final act required to commit a company or an organization to a contract. The actual commitment occurs when the order is signed and released. The person signing must be someone who has been granted the specific authority to commit the company. The chief purchasing officer usually has this authority. It is either granted by an express action of the principal, or it is implied by the law as part of the power essential to perform the duties of the agency. Such authority is absolute and not subject to question.

Assistant purchasing officers and branch office purchasing agents may also have the authority to sign purchase orders. Other personnel in the purchasing department may be given similar power. It is not unusual to have buyers sign the purchase orders for the transactions they have negotiated. The larger the purchasing organization, the more individuals there are who possess contracting ability. Delegation of this authority by the principal is proper and essential.

The chief purchasing officer is reminded that the delegation of authority to commit the principal-employer by signing purchase orders is a significant action. He or she should not unilaterally decide who in the department should have such authority and then grant it. It is preferable for the principal to delegate this authority directly to the individuals, with the understanding that those receiving it continue to report to the chief purchasing officer. The organizational chart of the purchasing department might indicate to which subordinate staff level the authority to commit is delegated. Those in that select area will have their appointment letter specify this authority to commit. They then have direct authority from the employer-principal, but they continue to be subagents because they are under the supervision of the principal's agent—the chief purchasing officer.

An alternative to this procedure is for the chief purchasing officer to be given the *express authority* by the principal to subdelegate commitment authority to eligible subordinate purchasing officers. Those persons designated by the chief purchasing officer under this authorization will remain subagents of the employer. Their actions thus are actions done in the name of the principal and with his blessing.

It is recommended that this delegation of authority among the purchasing staff to sign purchase orders be limited to one of the above two methods. Both direct authorization by the principal and direct authorization to the chief purchasing officer to subdelegate signing authority make the subordinate officer a subagent of the company or organization. This is the desirable result. It avoids the questions: "Whose agent are you?" and "For whom are you signing this purchase order?"

Problems could arise if someone in the purchasing department signs a purchase order without having this direct and positive authorization. Assume for a moment that an assistant purchasing officer has authorization to sign orders. About the time the orders requiring signatures are placed on this officer's desk late one afternoon, the telephone rings, and the officer is asked to come down to the receiving department to inspect a delivery. The orders must be mailed before the day closes. Not wishing to keep the staff overtime, the officer tells a clerk to sign the orders in his name and get them in the mail. One order the clerk signs has a mistake in the quantity ordered of an unusual chemical. The order reads "500 g," and it should read "500 mg." The order is mailed with the mistake unnoticed.

The assistant purchasing officer was not authorized to delegate this commitment authority to the clerk. Nonetheless the clerk was an agent—but an agent of the assistant purchasing officer! The clerk was authorized to sign the purchase orders by the assistant purchasing officer, and that was, in law, the creation of an agency relationship. Thus it was the assistant purchasing officer's agent who signed the faulty order. The company is bound to the commitment. The clerk, signing as an agent of an authorized officer, affixed the legal signature of that officer. The company could not plead lack of authority because this assistant purchasing officer did have the authority to commit the company.

The company's only recourse is against its assistant purchasing officer. This officer exceeded his scope of authority by appointing a personal agent to do his work. The officer is responsible for the consequences of his unauthorized act. What are the consequences? This might be difficult to determine. The answer would depend on whether or not the error would have been discovered if the authorized person had signed the purchase order himself One imagines that the officer, under pressure to get to the receiving department, gave the quantity specified "500 g" scant attention and signed the order without correcting the mistake. Nonetheless, his unauthorized act exposed him to censure, and perhaps more.

***Nota Bene* to Purchasing Officer**. Everyone gets under pressure at times, and the signing of purchase orders could become an unwanted chore. It is so easy to turn to a clerk or your secretary and direct them to sign the orders. But when you do this without the authorization of your superior officer, you expose yourself to some personal liabilities if things go wrong. The above situation is a good example of the risks the purchasing agent takes in assigning a major responsibility to an unauthorized person. Had the assistant signed the purchase order personally without noting the error, it would have been "just one of those things" that occur in a day's work. At most, he would have been subject to a reprimand. But when the task to sign is given to a clerk, the officer can be charged with violating his agency contract and thereby expose himself to personal liability.

It is suggested that, if there is an occasional need to have some unauthorized person sign purchase orders, you get blanket approval in advance. Let your superior officer know that the pressures of your job require you to do this occasionally. If there is objection to the suggestion, then ask your superior officer if he or she will sign the orders for you on such occasions.

It is also suggested that, if you are the chief purchasing officer and have subordinates authorized to sign, you issue strict instructions of the procedures to be followed in the event one of them is unavailable to do the routine signing. Instruct them to hand over the task to another authorized person in the department. And if there is no other authorized person available, then the orders are to come to you for signature. You might find this an onerous task to perform, but it is a delightful opportunity to review your subordinate's work at his or her request! You cannot be accused of spying on your staff's work if they ask you to assist them in this manner.

Exceeding the Scope of Authority

The fourth condition an agent must satisfy to avoid personal liability is that the contract must be within the scope of authority the agent possesses. There is no personal responsibility if the contract covers an area over which the agent has the authority to act, *and* if the other three conditions have been met—(1) disclosure of the principal, (2) notice that the signing is by an agent, and (3) identification of the agency relationship. If an agent exceeds the authority granted, there is then personal liability; but that liability is contingent upon the response of the principal to the unauthorized act.

The principal has two options available if an agent signs a contract for the principal without the authority to do so. The first option is to ratify the agent's actions. Ratification of the agent's unauthorized action does not require the principal to do anything. The contract was executed in the principal's name by the agent. It is a contract for the principal, and, if the principal is willing to perform his part of the bargain, no problem will arise. It produces the same result as any other contract the agent might negotiate for the principal that is within the scope of authority.

The second option available to the principal is to disavow the unauthorized act. This leaves the agent as a party to the contract. The principal will point out to the third party that the agent did not have the authority to commit him (the principal) to the obligations of the contract. The third party may accept or reject the principal's assertion of lack of authority. If the third party accepts the principal's statement, the principal's name will be eliminated from the contract. This leaves only two names—the third party's and the agent's. It becomes the agent's personal contract, and the agent must assume the obligations of the principal. A personal liability of the agent has been created because of the unauthorized act. If the agent disputes the principal's contention of lack of authority, the only recourse available is the courtroom.

If the third party elects not to believe the principal's contention of lack of authority, it is the third party's responsibility to bring action in court to force the principal to perform his obligations under the contract. Should the principal hold fast to this defense, it will be up to the court to make the decision. The third party will plead "apparent authority" in the agent. If the court accepts the principal's defense, the principal will be released from all responsibility under the contract. This places all the responsibility on the agent.

The court could come down with a decision against the principal. In such an instance, the court would find that the principal's actions toward the third party led the third party to believe the agent did have the authority to obligate the principal. (See the section in Chapter IV, "Apparent Authority in Agency Law.") Such a decision will result in the principal being held to the contract that was signed by the agent.

But this verdict does not release the agent of personal liability for the unauthorized act. The court's decision will have rested upon the principal's actions toward the third party. This has nothing to do with the relationship between the principal and the agent. The court will have found that in the eyes of the third party the agent had the apparent authority to act for the principal. But the court will not say to the agent that he had such authority. At this point the principal has a legal cause of action against the agent to recoup the losses suffered in the losing court battle with the third party. Now the principal must prove to the court's satisfaction that the actual authority to commit was not granted to the agent. If the principal prevails, the agent will be forced to repay the losses the principal suffered.

These possibilities may be better understood by the following hypothetical case:

> The Backeast Corporation is considering building a warehouse in one of the western states. The president of the corporation has had some correspondence with a real estate dealer in Wyoming concerning possible sites. Finally, the president sends his purchasing officer, Gay N. Eager, to Wyoming to meet with the real estate agent. Eager is instructed by the president to carefully inspect and evaluate all three sites and report back to the board of directors.
>
> Eager is not at all impressed with the first two sites, but the third one impresses him very much. The real estate agent says to Mr. Eager, "You really have a great eye for selecting a site for your company's warehouse. This is by far the best value of the three sites, but I am afraid that unless you act this afternoon, it will be gone. I am showing this site to another buyer tomorrow morning."
>
> Eager tries to call the president back home at the office, but because of the time differential, he found that the president had left the office for the day. He was convinced the company should have this site, so he signed the contract to purchase it: "Backeast Corporation, by Gay N. Eager, Purchasing Agent." He gave the real estate agent his personal check for $10,000 which was 10 percent of the purchase price.
>
> When Eager returned to his office two days later he was ushered into the board room and made his report to the directors. After considerable discussion, the board voted not to purchase the site, and Eager was told to cancel his contract.
>
> Eager called the Wyoming real estate agent and informed him of the decision. The real estate agent would not listen to a cancellation of the contract. He said that the other prospective buyer had visited the site the next morning and had offered him $135,000 cash for it. When the real estate agent refused to renege on his contract with Eager, the

potential buyer had bought another site owned by another person who was represented by a different real estate agent.

The owner of the site of Eager's desire and the real estate agent filed suit against the Backeast Corporation and Gay N. Eager to enforce the contract.

The Backeast Corporation has two options. First, the board of directors could ratify Eager's action and go through with the purchase. This election would free Eager of any personal responsibility. Backeast's second option is to defend the lawsuit in Wyoming. The corporation could plead the defense that Eager had no authority to commit them to the contract. The president would point out that Eager was given specific instructions to investigate and report back to the board of directors. His action of signing a purchase contract was beyond his authority. If the court believes the president's account of the situation, the charge against the Backeast Corporation will be dismissed. This will leave Eager as the only defendant. If the court then decides to enforce specific performance of the contract, Eager will be the proud, but unwilling, owner of some land in Wyoming. This is one possible outcome of the lawsuit.

The other possible verdict would be against the Backeast Corporation. The real estate agent might be able to prove to the court that he was led to believe that Eager had the authority to commit Backeast. The correspondence the real estate agent had with the president of Backeast would be introduced as evidence. From this correspondence the court might deduce that the real estate agent had been led down the primrose path by the president of Backeast by being led to believe that Eager had the authority to commit the company. If this line of reasoning was accepted, the Backeast Corporation would become the owner of the Wyoming land.

But the Board of Directors had already decided they did not want the land. After being forced to purchase it by the court, the corporation has the option of looking to Mr. Eager to relieve them of the property. The corporation was forced to purchase the land because Mr. Eager had exceeded his authority as Backeast's agent. This is sufficient reason to make Eager take over their interests in Wyoming. If necessary, a court order could be obtained to make Eager reimburse the Backeast Corporation for their expenditures. Of course, the Backeast Corporation would have to give Mr. Eager a clear title to the land to allow him to become a Wyoming taxpayer.

***Nota Bene* to the Purchasing Officer.** It is doubtful that any agent would deliberately exceed the authority granted by the principal. The legal consequences resulting from such action are too foreboding to imagine any person in his or her right mind committing such an act deliberately. If the act is not deliberate, why does it occur? There are two possible reasons: (1) The agent is unaware that what he is doing exceeds his authority, or (2) the agent knows he is exceeding his authority but performs the act because he honestly believes he is acting in the best interests of his principal.

In Chapter IV emphasis was placed on the point that you should have your own express authority specifically delineated. The major reason for this is to enable you to understand clearly the limits of the authority you possess. You are then less prone to commit an act that exceeds these limits. The agent caught exceeding his authority has usually not had the advantage of a written definition of this authority. The authority given verbally affords the agent the opportunity to say that he thought he heard someone say he could do what had been done. It is much better to know the scope of your authority than to attempt to interpret someone else's words.

Now, if the reason the agent deliberately exceeds the authority is to protect the principal's best interests in an urgent situation, remember that there is *emergency* authority, too. Should your principal attempt to hold you personally liable for a deliberate violation of your agency contract, your defense could be that you exercised your power of emergency authority. If you are able to establish that, but for your unauthorized act, your employer-principal would have incurred serious damage, you have an excellent defense. In fact, the more plausible your explanation, the more possible it is that your principal will reward you for the act rather than attempting to find you liable.

EXPOSURE TO TORT LIABILITIES

Definition of a Tort

Every individual citizen—doctor, lawyer, merchant, or purchasing chief—has a legal duty to act in a careful manner in whatever he or she does to avoid injury to others. When someone acts in a negligent manner, and that negligence results in injury to another person or another person's property, a personal responsibility for the consequences arises. This personal responsibility is there whether the negligent act occurs during or after working hours, and whether it occurs on or off the employer's premises. No matter where or when, the person who violates the duty of due care is responsible for the consequences of this negligence.

The law refers to a wrongful act that injures another person or another person's property as a *tort. The Random House Dictionary of the English Language*[1] defines a tort as "a wrongful act, not including a breach of contract or trust, which results in injury to another's person, property, reputation or the like, and for which the injured party is entitled to compensation." A tort is a private wrong for

[1]*The Random House Dictionary of the English Language*, p. 1496, Random House, 1967.

which the injured party may seek redress by collection of monetary damages.

A tort is not a criminal act. A criminal act is one that is committed against society. It violates a public law. The legal action against a criminal wrongdoer is brought into the court by a prosecuting attorney in the name of "The People of the State" or "The People of the Commonwealth." It is the federal, state, county, or city government that files and prosecutes the case. Conviction for committing a crime results in punishment by a fine to be paid to the governmental unit, or it results in imprisonment for a period of time. The punishment could result in both a fine and a prison term for the same offense.

A tort, on the other hand, is a wrongful act committed against an individual. Legal action against the *tort-feasor* (the individual committing the negligent or tortious act) is a private lawsuit brought by the injured party. Payment of monetary damages to the injured party is the penalty if a tort-feasor is found guilty

Two Prevalent Misconceptions of Tort Liability

The basis of a successful lawsuit for damages in tort is that the defendant committed a wrongful act. This must be proven in court by the plaintiff by a preponderance of the evidence. There are two types of wrongful acts—*misfeasanc*e and *nonfeasance* are the legal terms applied. "Feasance" according to *The Random House Dictionary*[2] means, "The doing or performing of an act." *Mi*sfeasance means the act was done improperly. *Non*feasance means the act was not done at all. A tort action may be successfully maintained if either misfeasance or nonfeasance by the defendant is proven.

One popular misconception of tort liability is heard when someone recounts an incident where he or she slipped and fell on the floor in a public place—say, a large department store. It is not unusual for the listener to observe "My, that ought to be worth thousands of dollars." To use a Latin phrase, that observation is a *non sequitur*—it simply *does not follow* that this would be the outcome. Thousands of dollars of damages do not automatically flow to the person who fell. First of all, the fall must have resulted in injury or damage. Dust on the seat of the trousers is not damage. A torn trouser is damage, as is a broken arm an injury. But more important is the answer to the question, "Why did you fall?" It is essential for the injured party to prove that the fall was occasioned by the negligence of the department store. This negligence could be either misfeasance or nonfeasance. Putting a high-finish wax on a tile floor, which results in the floor becoming very slippery to walk on is misfeasance. The floor was maintained improperly. Nonfeasance could be the failure to repair a wide crack in the floor, which caused the person to twist an ankle, which in turn caused the fall. The department store had a duty to keep its floor in good condition because it invites

---

[2]*Ibid..*

people to walk on it, but it did not carry out this duty. That is nonfeasance and could result in liability. To recover damages for an injury, one must prove the defendant committed an act of negligence. There must be more than a fall on the floor to hold the department store responsible.

The other popular misconception of the responsibility for tort liability prevails among some employees and agents. It is the misbelief that only their employer or principal is responsible for the injuries they cause by their negligent acts while at work. This misconception comes from the fact that the law makes an employer *also responsible* for the torts committed by his employees while furthering his business interests. There is a joint responsibility for such negligence, and neither the employee nor the agent is released from liability in such situations. The plaintiff (the injured party) is free to file suit against either the employer or the agent, or both may be joined as codefendants. If the plaintiff prevails in a suit where both are named as defendants, the court will direct that the employer and the agent are jointly and severally liable.

The "Deep-Pocket" Principle: One reason for this misconception is the so-called deep-pocket principle. This is not a legal principle but an action based upon common sense. Legal counsel for the plaintiff, in a tort action, has the obligation to obtain the greatest amount of damages for the client. Most tort actions are tried before a jury. If the agent is sued as an individual, a feeling of compassion could develop among the members of the jury for the agent, who is the defendant. An underpaid purchasing officer with a large family to support could bring out the best in the jurors. They might say to themselves, "There but for the grace of God go I" as they look at the poor hapless defendant. If the jury finds such a defendant guilty, and they are considering the amount of damages to award the plaintiff, they will say, "Let's not hit him too hard because he can ill-afford it." However, if legal counsel has selected the employer-principal as the defendant, a different feeling may prevail among the jurors. They will see nothing but an artificial, invisible, and intangible corporation as the defendant. Corporations are known to have many assets and much liability insurance. The person the jurors will therefore focus their attention on will be the individual plaintiff who was so cruelly injured by the careless defendant. They will want to be certain that the injured party is given fair treatment and is fully recompensed for the injuries and the suffering incurred at the hands of the defendant. Thus, the deep-pocket principle dictates that the defendant whose pocket contains the most money and who is the least subject to sympathetic consideration will be named in the lawsuit. Most often this is the principal-employer and not the agent. This gives the false impression that only the principal is responsible for the agent's negligence that occurs on the job. We know that this is not true.

The *deep-pocket* approach and the rule of *joint and several liability* where there is more than one defendant have created much criticism of our entire tort

and several liability" means that either defendant may be called
ne hundred percent of the damages awarded a plaintiff. When a cor-
a responsible governmental agency) is named as a codefendant
he negligence of their purchasing officer, for example, the corpora-
/ winds up paying the entire damages. There is little chance that the
defendant (the purchasing officer in our example) will have adequate
...bility insurance to meet such huge damage awards. Therefore, payment of the damages falls on the corporation. Corporate liability insurance premiums are inordinately high for this reason.

Some states have substituted, or are considering substituting, the *comparative liability* principle for joint and several. This would require the jury and the court to assign a percentage of liability to the corporation and the balance to the individual, according to their comparative contribution to the tort. It is hoped this might cut down the eventual size of any jury verdict for damages, since the corporation would be required to pay only a portion of the total award, thus reducing the corporation's liability insurance costs. It could add, however, to the cost of the individual's (the purchasing officer in our example) insurance.

THE PURCHASING OFFICER'S RESPONSIBILITY FOR TORTS

There are many types of torts, including torts against the person and against property, the torts of fraud, slander and libel, and business torts. A purchasing officer, as an individual in our society, has the same personal exposure to liability for torts committed as does every other human being. It is not the purpose of this text to delve into these manifold areas of liability, so we will confine our discussion to those types of torts that relate most closely to the purchasing profession. This will limit our discussion to two general areas of liability— those torts that may arise in the daily routine of purchasing goods and services, and those that may arise from the operation of an automobile.

Torts That May Arise in Purchasing

The purchasing officer of the Midwestern university who purchased the heavy planks for the stadium bleachers, which we recounted in Chapter V, came very close to committing a tort. The purchase of the heavier seating planks contributed to an accident that caused injuries to many people. A jury could have found that purchasing officer guilty of a wrongful act in making the purchase because the added weight contributed to the collapse of the bleachers. What saved the purchasing officer from that charge was the fact that he exercised that degree of care expected of a person in a similar situation. He had an engineering study made of the strength of the bleacher supports. The fact that the engineering study proved to be incorrect was unfortunate, but it did save the purchasing officer from the charge that he committed a negligent act. (As an aside and to give the reader an example of how the duty of care never "quits" in your work as a purchasing officer, we point out that the same duty of care was on this purchasing officer when the engineering firm was selected to make the study. If it had been discovered that the engineer was not qualified to make an intelligent study of the stress on the supports of the bleachers, the purchasing officer could have been charged with negligence in the selection process.) The collapsible bleacher incident is a good warning to all purchasing officers to be alert when making a purchase. *Alert* in this instance means to use foresight and anticipate potential consequences before they occur. *Anticipate the consequences* means to not send "Hot-Rod Harry" in a beach buggy to pick up a highly explosive liquid in a glass bottle from a supplier located three miles off the main highway on a bumpy unpaved road. The duty of reasonable care is always with the purchasing officer.

There is another area of tort liability that the average purchasing officer may be exposed to in some degree—libel or slander. *Libel* is the written defamatory word, and *slander* is the spoken defamatory word. A purchasing officer is frequently called upon to express an opinion about a supplier's product or an opinion about the supplier. The person usually asking the question is another purchasing officer, which aggravates the situation.

The purchasing officer whose opinion is sought is usually quite willing to give a candid and honest response to the inquiry. But care must be taken in that response so that the supplier cannot claim he has been damaged by lies said about his product or about himself

Libel, to a supplier, is the written word that disparages his product or his reputation without legal justification, and which results in damage to his business. Slander is the spoken word that does the same thing. Damage, to a supplier, is the loss of a sale and the loss of the resulting profit. A purchasing officer who gives a negative evaluation of a supplier's product in a manner that cannot be proven opens himself to the charge of making a libelous or slanderous statement. The immediate damage of such a statement is obvious if it is made to another purchasing officer. There is a strong likelihood of a lost sale for that supplier.

Our purpose is not to discourage you from responding to inquiries about a supplier or his product. That is against the self-imposed professional obligation to counsel with your peers. But we are suggesting you recognize the potential risk if you answer such inquiries improperly. Truth is one of the successful defenses to a charge of libel or slander. Respond only with the facts about a supplier's product that you or your company have established. Say only what you are able to prove. Choose your words carefully. Be precise and accurate. Do not extend facts beyond their worth or allow your words to do it in an innocent manner. To say, for example, that "the paint dries slowly and remains tacky" could imply that the paint remained tacky for six months after being applied. It would be more honest and direct to say, "The paint took two days to dry and remained tacky during that period of time." Do not say, "Supplier A is going bankrupt. I hear he takes 90 days and more to pay his bills." Say instead, "Supplier A takes 90 days to pay his bills to our company." Do not repeat what others may have told you in conversation as fact. Stick to the facts that *you* know. Remember, the person to whom you are making the statement may be related to supplier A or is one of his close friends!

You have heard the comment, "Never put it in writing" when you are making a negative recommendation about a person or a product. There is a good deal of merit in that advice, but it is not protection against liability. A defamatory expression that is untrue and causes damages creates equal liability whether it is written or spoken. However, an oral statement is more difficult to prove in a court of law than is a written statement. Keeping it verbal does have some legal advantage.

A major problem that arises from a written statement is its possible subsequent use. The person to whom the recommendation is sent may show it to the person about whom it is written. Showing a negative recommendation of his product to the sales person is a quick and decisive way to terminate the interview and get that person out of the office! But it also creates untold problems for the writer, because there is no way to deny what is written. Although not everyone will show a letter of recommendation, it does remain a possibility that can be avoided if the spoken word only is used.

But there is one advantage to putting the recommendation in writing. Your words can never be misquoted by adding to, subtracting from, or amending. If you have a provable argument and get it on paper, you need have no fear of being found guilty of libel. The written word is the best evidence that is available to you to prove exactly what you said. But when you put it in writing you need to be able to depend upon the person receiving the information to keep it confidential.

BUSINESS USE OF AN AUTOMOBILE

Traffic accidents are commonplace today. Most of us have been or will be involved in a fender-bender or worse during our life span. Purchasing officers have no exemption from this hazard. In fact, they have more than the normal exposure to this risk because of the frequent travel they must do to accomplish their work. Visiting suppliers' showrooms and manufacturing plants to inspect products, attending meetings, going to branches, and picking up emergency replacements are some of the reasons they are called upon to travel, much of which is done in an automobile. The automobile used may be their own personal car, a company-owned car, or a rental car. No matter whose car is used, potential liabilities arise to both the purchasing officer and the principal-employer should an unfortunate accident occur. A tort liability is assigned to the driver of the auto whose negligence caused the accident. If that driver was engaged in a business pursuit, his principal is also involved because the law places vicarious liability on the principal.

There is liability insurance protection available to both parties—the principal and the purchasing officer. The insurance is designed to assume the monetary damages arising from the negligence. It is important that you understand the risks you are exposed to should an accident occur, the available insurance protection, and the exceptions to coverage that may exist.

Driving Your Own Automobile

We will first assume that you are driving your own car on a business errand and have an accident that is attributable to your failure to exercise due care under the circumstances. This makes you responsible for the damages caused the injured party. These damages could include bodily injury, loss of earning power if the injured party was incapacitated, and property damage. You will look first to your personal auto liability insurance to pay for these damages and, of course, hope that there is adequate insurance to cover everything. Its adequacy will depend on the policy limits that are expressed therein. There are two limits expressed: one for bodily injury and the other for property damage. The bodily injury limit will be expressed as an amount per person and an amount per occurrence or per accident. The per-accident limit covers the event that more than one person in the auto you damaged was injured. It is customarily double the amount of the per-person limit. The property damage limit covers the cost of repairing the car you hit and any other property that may have been damaged by the accident. Courts are prone to award large damage settlements for injuries because hospital and physician services are so very expensive these days. Furthermore, if the injured party is a wage earner and is unable to work because of permanent injuries, the damages awarded will be sufficient to replace that earning power for the balance of that person's life span. This is not an attempt to paint a gloomy picture for you in the event you are in an accident, but to warn you in advance that you will have more worry-free miles of driving if you are certain the limits in your insurance policy are set high enough. Your insurance agent can advise you as to what is an appropriate limit of coverage. Be certain that your insurance agent knows you use your automobile for business purposes. (See discussion of business use insurance rider in next section.)

Strange accidents do occur, and even more strange consequences may follow. We heard the tale some years ago of a driver who suddenly swerved his car to avoid hitting an animal in the downtown area of a large metropolis. His car hit a fireplug and sheared it off its mounting. A strong stream of water began flowing. The terrain was such that the water backed up against the ground floor display window of a department store. The weight of the water broke the window. Before the water could be turned off, the basement and the ground floor of the department store were flooded. The basement was used as a storage area for their merchandise. Thousands of dollars of damages resulted, and the property damage liability coverage of the auto insurance was woefully inadequate to meet the damages. Granted, this was an unusual situation, but when such a situation occurs, the necessary insurance coverage may not be there.

Insurance known as *excess personal liability* is available for a small additional premium over the regular auto liability premium. It is written in amounts of $1 million or more, and acts as an umbrella over the basic liability coverages. It contains a few additional coverages not found in the basic policy. This is a coverage that is recommended for purchasing officers. It would have been very helpful to the driver who hit the fireplug. Because such catastrophic occurrences are infrequent, the premium cost is low. Excess personal liability insurance is a good bargain.

We must not forget the vicarious liability your principal-employer assumed when you "hired on" as a purchasing officer. Your principal, for all practical purposes, was in your car with you when you had your unfortunate accident. Someone will inevitably and quickly determine that you were on a business errand when it happened. The injured party or parties may look to your employer for recovery of the damages. Your principal's liability insurance usually has coverage for this potential liability under the caption "nonowned automobiles." This coverage will defend and protect your employer against the claims of the injured party. It does not protect you or your insurance company. It covers only your employer. Should you both be joined in a lawsuit for damages, it is your insurance company who will defend you, and your employer's insurance company will defend the employer. If damages are apportioned between you, each insurance company will pay the directed portion of the award. Keep in mind that your employer will be involved only if you were on a business errand at the time of the accident. If your employer is successful in convincing the court that you were not engaged in a business expedition when the accident occurred, you will then stand in court alone as the only defendant.

Driving a Company-Owned Automobile

Now let us assume you were driving a car owned by your employer when an unfortunate accident occurred as a result of your negligence. Despite the fact that you were driving a company car when the accident occurred, in the eyes of the law you continue to be personally responsible for the damages the injured party suffered. It was your negligence that caused the accident; you were the tort-feasor (the person committing the tort), and the law will hold you responsible for the damages you caused.

This time, however, you will not got to court alone. Your company will become the principal defendant in this lawsuit because it owned the car involved in the accident. Since you, the driver, are an agent of the company, it is clear that there is company liability. Of course, the injured party has the option of filing the lawsuit against you, against your company, or against you both.

There is every reason to believe that your company or organization will have insurance covering any liability that arises from the operation of its automobiles. (In fact, it is appropriate for you, as a responsible agent of your company, to make certain that such insurance coverage is in existence at all times.) This insurance protection is designed primarily to protect the company against claims made *against it* that evolve from the operation of the automobile by its officers, agents, and employees. The insurance will cover any direct liability the company may have, such as the failure to have the auto in safe operating condition, plus liabilities that may be imputed to it because the auto was operated by its agent at the time of the accident. (See the section in Chapter VII titled "Vicarious Liabilities of the Principal.")

Assuming that your principal is adequately protected by insurance, the next question that you will want an answer to is, "Does the employer's liability insurance protect me, the agent, too?" The definition of *insureds* in the employer's insurance contract will give you this answer. It is customary to find that the insureds listed in the contract include the directors, officers, agents, and employees of the employer. If this is the case, you have the assurance that your company's liability insurance protection is riding with you when you are at the wheel of a company car. The company's insurer will defend you and pay any damages assessed, if you are involved in an accident that was caused by your negligence.

Most states now have compulsory auto liability insurance laws. These laws require an owner of an automobile to have liability insurance on the car and the driver at all times. An uninsured car cannot legally be on the public streets where this law is in effect. This has removed many of the problems formerly associated with the use of a company car by an agent. There were instances where an employee could get involved in a situation that exposed him to personal liability when driving a company car. The following account of a purchasing officer's expedition will illustrate one of the problems raised.

> Mr. Buyer took the company station wagon to examine a new piece of equipment in a supplier's showroom. After concluding his visit, Mr. Buyer decided to drive two miles beyond the supplier's showroom to a shoe store that was having a sale on his favorite brand of shoes. En route from the supplier's showroom to the shoe store, Mr. Buyer had an accident that was occasioned by his negligence. The injured party

sued Mr. Buyer and his company for the damages incurred because of
Mr. Buyer's negligence.

Here our friend Mr. Buyer got involved in an accident while driving a company-owned car on a personal shopping trip. He was not on company business at
the time of the accident. One theory attaching vicarious liability to the employer
for the negligent acts of an employee is that the employee was "furthering the
employer's business interests" when the negligent act took place. The facts here
indicate that this was not the case. Notwithstanding the absence of this prerequisite, the courts today will assess the damages against Mr. Buyer's employer and
the employer's insurance company. The court will justify this result by pointing
out that the employer's insurance attaches to the car, and even though Mr. Buyer
was not on a business errand, he had the *assumed permission* of the employer to
make the personal trip. At the least, the employer had the opportunity to prevent
Mr. Buyer from using the car for personal purposes, but failed to do so. The rationale is not too clear, but it is in line with the modern approach to assess the owner
of the car for any damages caused by an employee while driving the car because
it was made available for the employee's use.

You as a purchasing officer should be alert to the policy your company or
organization has concerning the personal use of company-owned autos. Most
governmental agencies and many not-for-profit organizations forbid employees
to use agency cars for personal purposes. And many corporations in the private
sector find that their insurance costs decrease when the same prohibitions are
applied. Violation of such company policies might result in the dismissal or reprimand of the employee. It could also conceivably lead to a claim for damages
against the offending employee if an accident occurred while on a personal
errand in violation of company policy. The measure of damages would be the
damages paid by the company insurance carrier to the injured employee. Such a
legal recourse is highly unlikely. Dismissal of the employee would be the logical
conclusion from such an incident.

It is hoped that the splendid protection the employer's insurance coverage
gives to the purchasing officer and other staff members will encourage the purchasing officer to make certain that the company insurance is always kept in
force. If the company-owned auto is not insured, the company and the
employee's own insurance are the only protections against personal injury liability claims. Furthermore, it is to the interest of all parties, including the company,
to make certain that there are adequate policy limits of coverage. The awards
made by courts today in personal injury claims can be astronomical. An insurance carrier is responsible only for the damages awarded up to the policy limits.
Any additional damages awarded must come from the employer or from the
employee.

It is not necessary for the employee to have a nonownership clause in his personal insurance contract, because he is covered by his insurance when driving anyone's car. But it is a good idea for those who drive their own car on business errands to notify their insurance carrier *that they use their personal cars* on occasion for business purposes. This business use insurance rider may increase the premium costs slightly in some states, but it is a worthwhile protection to have.

The reader should also understand that the nonownership clause in your employer's insurance contract does not cover any damage to your personal car when it is used for business purposes. Your own collision insurance (if you have such coverage in your personal insurance) must pay for such losses. However, the property damage coverage in your personal insurance contract will pay for any damage to a company-owned automobile if you happen to be held responsible for it.

Renting an Automobile

A purchasing officer may be required to rent an automobile, when traveling out of town on business—or, for that matter, on a pleasure trip. The car rental agency will give you the opportunity to accept, at an added premium, or reject the optional insurance coverages. One of these optional coverages is personal accident insurance that will cover injury to you and to any passenger in your car. You are the best judge of whether you have sufficient personal health and accident insurance to pay the cost of any injuries you might suffer. Your chance of injury is no greater whether you are driving your own car or a rented car. Ordinarily, a person renting a car will reject this particular optional coverage.

It is suggested, however, that you give careful consideration to the second option of additional insurance offered you by the rental car agency. This is known as *collision damage waiver* insurance. Its purpose becomes clear when you read the fine print on the reverse side of the rental agreement. There you will note that public liability insurance is included in your rental price. Most rental agencies will also tell you that they carry insurance on their own vehicles, which will protect you if damaged while you are in possession of one of their vehicles. However, this insurance on the rental agency's car is subject to a deductible. This means that you, the renter, will pay the first—say $500—damages to the rented car. Sometimes the deductible is much higher—say, $3000. If more damage is caused than the deductible amount, the rental agency pays the difference. The collision damage waiver with an additional per diem premium is offered to you to eliminate your responsibility for the deductible amount of damage to the rented car. The amount of the deductible varies. The recent trend in the auto rental business is to eliminate the deductible and require the renter to assume responsibility for the full value of the rented car if the collision damage waiver insurance is not accepted. Electing the waiver and paying the additional premium results in the rental agency's assuming 100 percent of the damages to their car, unless the agency can prove you deliberately damaged it.

Accepting the waiver and paying the additional premium saves you some worry. You rent a car in the evening and drive away in it without checking the condition of the fenders and other parts of the car. The next morning you notice the right front fender is damaged. Did it happen while the car was in your possession, or did a previous renter cause the fender-bender? With the collision damage waiver accepted, you couldn't care less. The problem with this is that the additional premium charged for such protection is fairly substantial.

There are now two other options available to most people who rent cars. The first option is one's own car liability insurance. Many automobile insurance companies now extend the liability protection in your policy to so-called *contractual liability* for the responsibility their insureds assume when renting an auto. The term *contractual liability* is applied because the person renting the car contracts with the rental company to assume any collision damage to the car. It is suggested the reader contact his or her private insurance carrier to determine whether this coverage is provided in your policy. It is also suggested you determine whether there is any deductible attached if this feature is included.

The other option available for covering this hazard is found in some types of credit cards. Those credit cards that extend this coverage require that you pay your rental bill with that credit card and then the coverage by the credit card company is automatic. However most of these cards providing this coverage will state that they will cover only what your regular auto liability insurance does not cover.

Your employer's nonownership clause will protect it against public liability claims that arise while you are using a rental car for business purposes. This will include damage to the rented car. If the rental car is used for personal purposes, your own liability insurance covers you while driving. Your property damage insurance will cover the damage to the rented automobile if you are the cause of the damage, that is, if you drove the rental car in a negligent manner and caused the accident. If the damage is caused by another person, that person must pay for the damage to the rented car. If the damage was caused by persons unknown, your responsibility for the damage becomes a contractual liability. You assumed complete responsibility for the rented car when you signed the rental contract. Some personal insurance carriers set a limit on their responsibility for the contractual damage you assume in such circumstances. Therefore, if you do not intend to accept the collision-damage waiver offered by the rental agency because it is almost duplicate insurance, check with your personal insurance agent to make certain that you are fully covered for any type of damage to the rented car—at least, that you are insured to cover your responsibilities in the rental contract.

Your employer may have an operational policy that tells you not to accept the collision damage waiver insurance if you are charging the rental to the company. If you are told to reject the waiver, your employer is either self-insuring the risk or has nonownership insurance coverages that will assume the deductible amount of collision damage to the rented car.

***Nota Bene* to the Purchasing Officer.** You should know the answers to the following about the liability insurance your employer carries:

1. Are you a named insured?

2. What are the policy limits of coverage for liability?

3. Does the policy contain nonownership provisions?

4. Are you covered by the insurance whenever you are driving the car, or are there restrictions on this coverage?

5. How, where, and what do you report if an accident occurs while the car is in your possession?

In addition to this information about your employer's insurance, you should also be told about your employer's policy on personal use of a company auto. Most often, occasional or incidental personal use will be permitted, but you should know this for a fact. If the employer's policy is to ban completely personal use of a company auto, it is suggested that you adhere to such a restriction.

With this information, your own personal auto liability insurance should be planned to protect any deficiencies in the company's insurance, and to protect you fully when driving for business purposes. It is not prudent to drive any automobile without being fully protected, whether driving for personal use or on company business.

If you are the chief purchasing officer, every member of your staff should be given the above information. They should also be counseled on how to write their own personal auto insurance, if they have occasion to use an auto for business purposes. And perhaps most important, they should be given written instructions on the company policies on personal use of company-owned cars.

Government Procurement Officers

There is a quirk in our laws pertaining to tort liability. A maxim in the old English common law was, "The King can do no wrong," which was interpreted to mean the King—the government itself—and some government officials were not subject to the usual tort liabilities that the ordinary citizen encountered. This legal concept was brought to the United States with the common law, and, although we are a democracy with no king, the federal and state governments enjoy this tort immunity.

This immunity applies to the federal government, the state government, and municipal corporations in their exercise of governmental functions. Elected officials are covered under the same immunity when performing strictly governmental functions. The federal government and some state governments have voluntarily waived their rights to this immunity. Special courts and special procedures are provided for injured parties to seek reimbursement for their damages.

Most agents and employees of governmental agencies (except federal employees) do not enjoy this immunity. Some governmental agencies are authorized to purchase auto liability insurance for their fleet of cars. It is suggested that if you are a state or municipal purchasing agent you check with your agency to determine if this coverage is available to you when driving an agency car for business purposes. It is also important to know if there is any coverage when you drive your personal car for government business purposes. If your agency has no insurance coverage and relies on its governmental immunity as the protection against liability claims, then your personal insurance is the only protection you have. Your insurance agent should be apprised of this fact when your liability insurance is written.

EXPOSURE TO CRIMINAL LIABILITIES

A crime is considered to be an act against society because society suffers when a crime is committed. Criminal laws are designed to deter criminal activity by exacting punishment for those who violate such laws. Punishment may be a fine payable to the governmental unit, imprisonment, or both.

Any person who commits a crime is subject to the penalties meted out by the courts. No one is exempt from these penalties, except minors who are given special treatment because of their age. Corporations cannot be imprisoned for committing a crime, but they can be fined. In extreme cases they may also have their charter revoked and are then forbidden to do business. When a corporation is involved in criminal activity, it is the officers or the agents of the corporation who committed the crime for which the corporation is liable, and therefore they may be held personally responsible for the corporate crime and be punished by imprisonment and/or a fine, even though the activity occurred while furthering the business of the company. Nor is the officer or the agent absolved of responsibility if the crime is committed on behest of a superior officer. Although an agent could claim it is his duty to follow the instructions of the principal, the court would respond that the agent is relieved of the duty to follow instructions when told to perpetrate a crime. The continued employment of the agent if the principal's instructions are disobeyed is now protected in most states by statutes referred to as *protecting whistle blowers*. Therefore, the court would not regard the threat of losing one's job as an adequate defense. Furthermore, if the agent did commit a crime at the behest of the principal, not only would the agent be subject to punishment, but the principal too would suffer the same penalty as "an accessory before the fact."

Purchasing officers have several occupational exposures to criminal liability including exposure to antitrust liability, which is discussed in the succeeding chapter. Miscellaneous occupational exposures follow later in the chapter in summary form. Self-inflicted criminal liabilities are considered in Chapter IX.

Purchasing a Licensed Product

Some products require special licenses to purchase and to store. Radioactive chemicals, for example, require a license. Tax-free alcohol is under the strict surveillance of the Alcohol Tax Unit of the Internal Revenue Service. Narcotics and other addictive drugs are under similar controls. These and other controlled products must be purchased in accordance with the regulations of the governmental agency having jurisdiction over them. They must be stored under proper conditions that protect the environment, safeguarded against theft, and strictly accounted for. It is not unusual for the purchasing department to be the repository of these responsibilities. The chief purchasing officer is advised to see that the regulations for their procurement are carefully followed, and that the rules for protection of the items are not violated. Care must be exercised in accounting for their use. These accounting records should be retained in a secure vault or safe. Violation of any of the rules usually calls for criminal punishment. Do not take these governmental regulations lightly; the government finds the products to be of such a sensitive nature that their distribution is regulated.

ENVIRONMENTAL HAZARDS LIABILITY

Some purchasing officers face the prospect of purchasing products which when used may create problems that conflict with the protection of our environment. Products which generate PCBs (poly chlorinated biphenyl) and dioxin are typical examples of products that create environmental hazards. Disposal of any wastes generated by the manufacturing process that contain these chemicals must be accomplished with great care and in strict accordance with state and federal regulations. There are regulations that pertain to the packaging and transportation of these items as well as their ultimate disposition.

The purchasing officer is advised to secure copies of the appropriate regulations regarding such products and to follow such rules assiduously. Consult the regional offices of the agency or agencies having jurisdiction over the items and enlist their support in your problem. No longer is it prudent to take a chance and dump at night. Such actions are now regarded as evidence of lack of social responsibility on the part of your company and are to be avoided. It is also regarded as injurious to the health of the nation and subjects your entire organization to liability. It is illegal and subjects the company, its *officers*, and *agents* to criminal prosecution.

It should be noted, too, that one never loses "title" to or ownership of hazardous waste. Even though all of the rules for packaging and storage were followed in its disposal, should some problem with it develop in the future, it is your company's responsibility to correct that problem. Hazardous waste sticks to the owner like fly paper. It could come back to haunt you. Make certain all regulations are followed carefully.

The Occupational Safety and Health Administration (OSHA) is a federal agency charged with the duty of protecting the health of employees against occupational hazards. It imposes many regulations both on the health conditions in the workplace as well as on the safety of the equipment and materials used in the industrial scene. The purchasing officer is advised to become thoroughly familiar with its rules and regulations. There are civil and criminal penalties that can be assessed against an employer and its agents for violations. The purchasing officer's ability to purchase the proper equipment that conforms to OSHA's standards will reduce the principal's exposure to liability. By doing so, the purchasing officer will also reduce his or her personal exposure to the same penalties.

Recent trends in court cases that involve violation of one or more of the plethora of environmental laws surrounding us show that the courts are becoming more willing to attach liability for violations on the shoulders of individual officers and directors of offending corporations. Part of this trend is occasioned by increased public awareness of the need for ecological control and protection of our planet. Part of the trend is also due to increased enforcement efforts by the various agencies involved, particularly against corporate offenders, and those who are responsible for the actions of such corporations.

For example, a radio news report carried a story that four individuals were due to be sentenced today following their original conviction four years ago for operating an improperly ventilated factory. Thermometers were manufactured in this factory. Mercury is one of the ingredients of a thermometer and the handling of it requires proper ventilation. Without giving all of the minute details, it seems the factory had been warned several times by OSHA (the Occupational Safety and Health Administration) through their inspectors that it was operating under unsafe conditions. Fines had been levied against and paid by the company, but no improvements in ventilation had occurred, probably because of the heavy cost involved. In a subsequent inspection, the inspectors issued summonses to four of the operating officers of the company, including the plant superintendent, for the improper ventilation. One supposes the government agency grew tired of having the bad conditions persist after the fines had been paid and decided to "get the attention of" the operating officers by personally serving them with summonses. The threat of incarceration and/or heavy personal fines against the operators of the corporation is one approach to having a bad situation corrected.

Federal Environmental Laws

There are many Federal environmental laws on our books. Here is a partial list:

1. Comprehensive Environmental Response, Compensation and Liability Act of 1980. This act is often referred to by its acronym of CERCLA. The reader has probably heard references of "Superfund" which is the appropriation bill to fund CERCLA.

2. Resource Conservation and Recovery Act of 1982 which has a section termed "Imminent Hazard" that can be used to punish violators of our environment.

3. The Clean Water Act

4. The Refuse Act

5. The Safe Drinking Water Act

6. The 1980 Clear Air Act

7. The Toxic Substance Control Act

8. The Hazardous Materials Transportation Act

This is not a complete list. It does not include so-called "safety" acts such as the Federal Food, Drug and Cosmetics Act, the Occupational Safety and Health Administration Act, and the act that created the Environmental Protection Agency. It also does not include the various environmental control acts passed by the state legislatures. Many of the state acts are more strict than their counterpart Federal acts.

Who Is Liable and Responsible?

It has been fairly simple to make corporate America accountable under these various pieces of legislation. There are those who say it has been almost too simple because some corporations will pay their fine and proceed with "business as usual." Because our law has consistently held the corporate "entity" as being separate and distinct from the shareholders, directors, officers and employees, responsibility and liability for violations has been assessed against the corporation itself. And yet, many years ago, Chief Justice John Marshall of the Supreme Court of the United States told us a corporation is an artificial being, invisible, intangible, and existing only in contemplation of the law.

Those not well versed in corporate law will ask, "How can a corporation be found guilty of a violation of the law if it is invisible and intangible?" The question is answered with the statement that the corporate "entity" is construed as the violator of the law by the law. But it is equally clear that the corporation must have "actors" or "agents" who actually commit these violations. And it is these individuals, these actors for the corporation, whom the government agencies and the courts are beginning to "ferret out" and hold liable for the acts they perform in the name of the corporation.

Recent Pertinent Litigation

Two cases in the Federal courts have extended such liability to these corporate actors.[34] In the Shore case an officer was held guilty of violating the law and in Northeastern Pharmaceutical, individual officers who had arranged for an illegal dumping and burial of hazardous waste were found guilty. These are the only two cases that went so far as to convict officers of a criminal act, but there are other instances where owners have been individually found guilty. Newspaper accounts continually refer to such actions.

Nota Bene to the Purchasing Officer. The word to the purchasing officer who must arrange for disposal of hazardous waste for his or her organization is simple—follow the law. There are no known shortcuts to immunity. You must follow the law and act within its parameters. If you do not know what the law is, call one of the agencies and get a full explanation. Involve your legal counsel. The two of you should be able to plan a compliance program that will keep you and your corporation free from legal liability.

An additional note of caution. The courts are attaching liability for environmental violations to executives of corporations who had no knowledge that their corporation was violating the law. Such executives are being convicted of a criminal action because "they had it within the power of their corporate office to prevent subordinates from violating the law." The lesson to a purchasing officer is clear—make certain your subordinates are living within the law. It is your legal duty to give them proper supervision so that such violations will not occur.

Finally, be a "buddy" of your corporate entity. If you know of, or observe, other divisions of the company violating the environmental laws, do what you can to correct the situation. Of course, be certain you are interpreting the law and the corporate procedures properly before you move. If you are convinced violations are occurring, "speak out and point out." Hopefully you will receive nothing but

[3]*New York v. Shore Realty*, 759 F.2d 1032.
[4]*United States v. Northeastern Pharmaceutical*, 810 F.2d 726.

cooperation and gratitude. Should you run into backlash because of your inter-
vention, you are working for the wrong type of corporation. Our people in this
country and our government are "proenvironment" today. We must all get on this
bandwagon.

SIGNING CHECKS AND NOTES

An officer of the company, including a purchasing manager or agent, may
become personally liable by signing a check or promissory note in a certain way.
This is true even though he is authorized by the company to sign and is signing
for a proper purpose.

   For example, in one case, an officer of a company signed a promissory note
for the company. The company's name was on one line, and on the next line was
the individual officer's name. The court held that the officer was personally liable
to the purchaser of the note when the company was unable to pay it. The court
noted that the officer should have signed his title or office as well. It noted that his
intention to sign only for the company was undisclosed, hence he was personally
liable. While it may seem clear to a lay person that he is signing for a company,
the law holds him personally liable.

   The same type of issue has arisen when the corporate officer signs a check
for the company, but does not indicate his title or office. Sometimes the officer is
saved from personal liability by the court looking to overall circumstances and
finding an inference to rebut this personal liability. In one case, the corporate
name, address, and logo were in the upper left-hand corner, together with prior
invoices that were used. The court found the officer not personally liable. Still it
would have been better to prevent this type of lawsuit from ever arising in the first
place.

   Under the traditional Code, these charges of personal liability still arise as
to promissory notes or checks signed in this fashion. Under the revised Article 3,
the problem is resolved when the check identifies the company. However, this
does not apply for other commercial paper such as promissory notes.

   What is the best way for a purchasing manager or other company officer to
sign? The Code comments suggest that the company name, followed by the word
by and the officer's name and office or title. For example:

   Standard Machines, Inc. by Paul Manners, Purchasing Agent

would be the best way to sign.

   The harshness of the Code in terms of the personal liability of an officer is
illustrated by three comment examples. In each the intention of the original parties was that the company be liable but not the officer who signed, but in each the
holder in due course is asserting that the officer is personally liable:

Case 1. Doe signs "John Doe" without indicating in the note that Doe is signing as agent. The note does not identify Richard Roe as the represented person.

Case 2. Doe signs "John Doe, Agent" but the note does not identify Richard Roe as the represented person.

Case 3. The name "Richard Roe" is written on the note, and immediately below that name Doe signs "John Doe" without indicating that Doe signed as agent.

The comments point out that in each case Doe is liable on the instrument to a holder in due course. In none of the cases does Doe's signature unambiguously show that Doe was signing as agent for an identified principal. The reason given is that a holder in due course should be able to resolve any ambiguity by proving that the original parties did not intend him to be liable on the note. But he must prove it! Why bother to have such troublesome issues as to personal liability even raised, when a proper signing can avoid it.

VIII

Liabilities of a Purchasing Manager Regarding the Staff

GUIDANCE FROM PERSONNEL AND LAW DEPARTMENTS

The many rules ranging from discrimination to medical leave that affect the employees of the purchasing manager's department are extremely complex. Although the purchasing manager can understand general parameters of these matters, it is the personnel and legal departments of the company that should have greater expertise as part of their function. The purchasing manager should not hesitate to ask for general guidance from each of these departments in regard to all of these various matters mentioned in this chapter. With these guidelines, he can have a better understanding of some of the problems that might arise. Also, he should seek their confirmation and advice in regard to such matters if they are ever raised by any of his employees. If it is necessary to dismiss an employee he should also consult with these departments to be sure that no violations occur.

In addition, these departments may be able to give him some good advice to avoid problems arising from sex or age discrimination. He should also remain alert as to any problems that he sees or any complaints from any of the employees. In regard to sex discrimination, even general environmental factors which may not seem important or may seem trivial, are sometimes taken into account and can result in a finding of such discrimination.

DISCRIMINATION GENERALLY

Think of the word "discrimination," and the image that is likely to come to mind for many Americans is a picture of the great civil rights movements of the 1960s and the struggle of African Americans to gain equality in a society that viewed the world through tinted glasses. The great focus of that time was on racial discrimination, but the legislation spawned by the work of Dr. Martin Luther King and others is broad based. Federal law protects not only race, color, and national origin from employment discrimination, but also religion and "sex," or gender.

Under Title VII of the 1964 Civil Rights Act, it is illegal for employers to discriminate based on race, color, religion, sex, or national origin. Title VII—which covers private employers, local and state governments, and educational institutions with 15 or more employees—makes it illegal to discriminate in the hiring and firing of employees, and in other terms and conditions of employment (e.g., employment compensation, job assignment and the use of company facilities).

For example, as noted above, it is illegal to discriminate against an employee based on his or her religion. An employer is therefore prohibited from such activities as refusing to allow the observance of a Sabbath or religious holiday, or scheduling an examination that conflicts with an employee's religion, *unless* the employer can prove that abiding by the employee's wishes would cause an undue hardship. An employer is allowed to claim that it is an undue hardship if the accommodation of an employee's religious needs requires costs that exceed the ordinary administrative expenses.

The 1964 Act is probably the most well known, but there have been several other Federal acts passed since that time that all deal with various forms of discrimination. The Age Discrimination in Employment Act, Title I of the Americans with Disabilities Act, and the Civil Rights Act of 1991 have all been passed since Lyndon Johnson signed off on the original Civil Rights Act. The following paragraphs offer a brief look at some of the legislation governing this area.

The Age Discrimination in Employment Act (ADEA)

Under this 1967 law, persons 40 years or older are protected from discrimination in hiring, termination, compensation, and promotions because of their age. The Older Workers Benefit Protection Act (OWBPA), which became effective in 1991, emphasizes that employee benefits and plans are subject to the ADEA. The ADEA applies to private employers with 20 or more employees.

The Equal Pay Act (EPA)

This legislation was actually passed before the Civil Rights Act of 1964. Enacted in 1963, the EPA, as amended, prohibits an employer from discriminating in compensation between men and women who perform essentially the same job. In addition, an employer may not lower the salary of either sex to come in compliance with this law. Violations in this area may also be violations of Title VII.

The Americans with Disabilities Act (ADA)

Title I of the ADA prohibits private employers with 15 or more employees from discriminating against qualified individuals that have a mental or physical impairment. An individual is qualified if they have the skill and knowledge to perform the job with or without reasonable accommodations. An employer is required to make a reasonable accommodation, which can include such things as making existing facilities accessible to employees with disabilities or restructuring and modifying jobs, if it is not going to pose an undue hardship. An undue hardship would mean that accommodation is significantly difficult and expensive in light of a business' size and financial wherewithal. An employer does not have to make an accommodation if it means lower quality or production standards.

The Civil Rights Act of 1991

In the wake of some controversial decisions by the Supreme Court, Congress passed additional legislation to protect against unlawful employment discrimination. This amendment to the Civil Rights Act of 1964 is aimed at intentional discrimination and disparate impact actions.

All of these acts are enforced by the United States Equal Employment Opportunity Commission (EEOC). The EEOC investigates complaints of employment discrimination against private employers. It is the EEOC's mission to seek full relief for every victim of discrimination. Remedies against an employer that has been found to have discriminated against an employee may include compensatory damages, back pay, and the payment of attorney's fees; placement in the position the victim would rightfully have occupied were it not for the discrimination; and preventive actions to ensure that this doesn't happen again. It is illegal to retaliate against a person who files a discrimination charge or participates in an investigation.

For further information on these Federal laws, purchasing managers may contact the EEOC at the following address: U.S. Equal Employment Opportunity Commission, 1801 L Street N., Washington, D.C. 20507; or call 1-800-669-4000.

AGE DISCRIMINATION AND THE
PURCHASING MANAGER*

Age Discrimination and the Law

Legal issues involving discrimination related to race, sex, age or disability as well as sexual harassment are complex. Many questions have yet to be clarified as the laws evolve. The question of age discrimination in particular is governed by a number of statutes. Title VII of the Civil Rights Act of 1964 and the Age Discrimination in Employment Act of 1967 (ADEA) makes it unlawful for an employer to refuse to hire an individual or to discharge an individual or to discriminate in any manner based upon age, with several exceptions. Additionally, the law prohibits the retaliatory discharge of individuals who testify on behalf of those alleging discrimination or harassment. The ADEA was amended by the Older Workers Benefit Protection Act enacted in 1990 (OWBPA) which involves benefit costs. Furthermore, workplace issues may be covered by the Employee Retirement Income Security Act (ERISA) relating to pension plans as well as the Americans with Disabilities Act (ADA). This latter law addresses issues that may be particularly important to older workers who become ill or disabled. The ADA requires that employers allow workers to return to work after an injury once they are able to perform substantially all of their duties, although they may not have completely recovered. In the many thousands of cases resolved by the courts over the past two-and-one-half decades, the burden of proof has shifted back and forth between the employee and the employer in proving or disproving age discrimination. Age discrimination may be found by the courts if it can be shown that:

    a) the employee was age forty or over,

    b) the employee was performing his or her duties,

    c) the employee was fired, demoted, reduced in salary, or otherwise negatively treated,

    d) younger employees (those younger than age 40) were treated more positively.

In proving such allegations, statistics may be utilized to support claims that a significantly greater number of older employees were fired, transferred, or demoted than younger employees. However, the courts have yet to provide clear and concise guidelines for managers and supervisors in terms of statistical analysis and in terms of evidence.

---

*By Karen Grossman Tabak, CPA and consultant.

What Can Managers Do?

While there is no way to guarantee a successful defense against charges of age discrimination, there are steps purchasing managers can take to limit the extent of potential liability to the organization from accusations of discriminations.

1) Ensure that your firm has a clear, written policy defining and prohibiting both discrimination and sexual harassment.

2) In conjunction with the human resources department, familiarize yourself and your subordinates with the policies. This should be an ongoing process.

3) Clarify the internal procedures to be taken when employees believe they or their colleagues are the subject of discrimination. Consider posting complaint procedures.

4) Inform the human resources department or top management when complaints of discrimination arise.

5) Document performance-related problems and maintain accurate records! Often supervisors are reluctant to include negative comments in employee evaluations. Thus, when termination occurs with an older employee due to poor performance, there is little evidence to support the company's position of poor performance.

6) Avoid age-bias in training programs. Be sure that employees of all ages are selected to attend training programs.

7) Create an environment that discourages discrimination. Avoid stereotyping older employees and reinforce the commitment to a discrimination-free workplace.

Cost of Age Discrimination Law Suits

Age discrimination cases are costly. There will be legal fees in defending the company as well as the cost of experts. Should a company be found guilty of age discrimination, they may be liable for actual, compensatory, and liquidated damages. An often overlooked cost is the time required of company personnel in preparing the defense and gathering documents, as well as testifying in court. While some of these costs may be covered by the company's insurance policy, the distractions of employees and the emotional toll may cost the employer more than the damages awarded by the court.

Computation of Damages

When damages are awarded by the court, they fall into several types.

a) *Actual damages* or economic damages may include compensation lost to the trial date, interest on these funds and the present value of lost compensation in the future.

b) Damages may also be awarded to the plaintiff for emotional distress. These are called *compensatory damages*.

c) *Liquidated damages* will be awarded if the jury determines that the discrimination was willful. To obtain the liquidated damages, the actual or economic damages are doubled.

The computation of the actual damages in age discrimination cases is usually handled by an economist. Economists are trained in the analysis of wage increases and interest rates. Accordingly, they are able to determine an appropriate settlement that leaves the plaintiff in the same situation as if he or she had not been discharged or demoted.

Lost Income to Trial Date

The first computation the economist makes is the determination of lost income from the date of discharge/demotion to the trial date. To make this calculation, the economist determines:

the period of time from the date of discharge to the trial date;

the annual compensation received by the employee prior to discharge including fringe benefits such as medical insurance, life insurance, pension benefits, and other retirement programs;

and any compensation received by the plaintiff including fringe benefits from replacement employment.

The economist then makes an assumption as to the growth of wages had the plaintiff remained in the original position. If the economist assumes the wages would have grown during the period, the calculation of the lost income to the trial date is then the computation of the future value of an annuity using the formula:

$\Sigma(pmt(1+r) + pmt(1+r)^2 \ldots + pmt(1+r)^n]$ − compensation from replacement employment

where pmt = the annual compensation received from employment before discharge r|= the annual growth rate in wages

n = the period of time from discharge to the trial date

If the economist determines the compensation would not have grown during this period or chooses to take a more conservative approach, the calculation is simply to multiply the annual compensation the employee would have received had the action not taken place by the period of time from the date of discharge to the trial date and then deduct any compensations received from replacement employment. Additionally, there may be interest computed on this money as the plaintiff has theoretically been denied the benefit of this money.

Present Value of Future Income Lost

To determine the value of the compensation lost into the future, additional assumptions must be made. First, there must be an assumption about the ability of the plaintiff to find employment with a new employer (or to remain employed at a lower-paying position within the company) and the level of compensation the plaintiff will receive. Furthermore, there must be a determination as to the salary and benefits the employee would be receiving had he or she not been discharged or demoted. The difference between these two amounts—the compensation from the new position minus the compensation from the old position—will be the annual rate of loss. Next, the economist will make an assumption as to the number of years the employee would have remained in the work force. This determination can be made by asking the plaintiff his or her estimated retirement date, or by assuming that the plaintiff would have retired upon becoming eligible for full social security benefits based upon year of birth and the social security laws. The retirement age is 65 for those born in 1937 and before; however, for those born after 1937, the age at which one qualifies for full social security benefits (called full retirement age) rises gradually from age 65 to age 67. Individuals born in 1960 will not qualify for full social security benefits until age 67. As an alternative assumption, the economist may assume the plaintiff would have delayed retirement and taken advantage of increased social security benefits by working to age 70 or beyond. Perhaps the most difficult decision is that of the appropriate discount rate. Remember that in a settlement, the plaintiff will receive the money at the settlement date and then be able to invest this money. The settlement must be large enough to hypothetically set up an account that will allow the plaintiff to annually withdraw an amount equal to the difference between their salary, based upon not being terminated, and their new compensation. We assume they continue to withdraw an amount that grows as their salary would have grown and by the time they reach the assumed retirement age, the balance of this hypothetical account will be zero. We know that this account will earn interest, and we also know that wages will grow over time. Accordingly, we must determine the difference between the rate of interest the plaintiff will earn on the money in a secure investment and the rate of future wage increases. The difference will become the net real discount rate. To maintain consistency in taxability of both the settlement and the earned income, we use an investment vehicle that is also taxable such as United States Government bonds. Hence, the discount rate will be the difference between the interest rate on United States government bonds and the growth rate in wages. Historically, this is below 2.5%. However, the Internal Revenue Service is currently reconsidering the taxability of such settlements and the related interest. Should the IRS determine that these amounts are not taxable, then consistent treatment requires that we reduce the annuity payment amount to take into account the effects of taxes. Additionally, we use an investment vehicle that is not taxable, such as municipal bonds. This will lower the net real discount rate. To compute the amount of money needed to compensate the plaintiff, we use the formula for computing the present value of an annuity:

$$\sum[pmt/(1+r)+pmt/(1+r)^2 \ldots + pmt/(1+r)^n]$$

where pmt = the difference between the compensation the plaintiff would be earning had he or she not been discharged and the compensation the plaintiff is assumed to be earning

n = the number of years to retirement

r = the discount rate, in the case, the difference between United States government bonds and the growth rate in wages or 2.5%

The combination of the loss to the trial date and the present value of future lost income will be the amount of the actual damages.

Clearly, age discrimination can be costly. Careful attention to managing employees and the demographics of the workforce is now an important requirement of all supervisory personnel.

THE FAMILY AND MEDICAL LEAVE ACT

In 1993, Congress passed the Family and Medical Leave Act (FMLA). This law requires companies with 50 or more employees to provide up to 12 weeks of unpaid leave for a "serious health condition" of an employee or a member of his or her immediate family. Likewise, an employee who celebrates the birth or adoption of a child is eligible for leave under this law (29 U.S.C. 2601-2654).

The FMLA applies to all public employers, as well as private employers with more than 50 workers on the payroll during each of the 20 or more work weeks in the current or the preceding calendar year. Employees must work at sites with more than 50 employees, or companies with 50 or more employees within 75 miles of this site, and have at least 12 months experience, and at least 1,250 hours at their jobs in the past 12 months preceding commencement of their leave to be covered by the FMLA (29 U.S.C. 2611 (2), (4)).

A "serious health condition" is an "illness, injury, impairment, or physical or mental condition that involves inpatient care in a hospital, hospice, or residential medical care facility; or continuing treatment by a health care provider." (29 U.S.C.2611 (11)).

It should be noted that the employee only needs to give his or her employer verbal notice that the employee needs leave, and the employer must let the employee know that the leave counts against his or her FMLA entitlement. When the leave is finished, the employee must be returned to his or her old position or a similar one with the same pay and conditions. Employers are in violation of the law if they do not allow leave, or try to discourage it, or if they discipline an employee who takes leave.

This law is likely unfamiliar territory for most firms, and many problems can be avoided if both sides cooperate. Employees should let their employers know that they need leave as soon as they can. It also behooves them to find out exactly what their benefits are before an emergency takes place, so they'll know exactly where they stand.

Caveat Bene: When employees don't ask enough questions, misunderstandings later occur. The purchasing manager should, in consultation with the company attorney, provide employees with information concerning this Act and these benefits.

PUNITIVE DAMAGES FOR DISCRIMINATION

The purchasing manager should realize that not only may there be high compensatory damages covering salary over several years, but also there may be punitive damages as well in these discrimination cases. Indeed the amount of punitive damages is generally left to the jury and is therefore highly uncertain. In many instances, they may even result in hundreds of thousands or even millions of dollars of damages.

Several reasons may be a basis for a finding of punitive damages in these cases involving personnel. If there is a deliberate or willful violation of the federal act itself, this is generally considered to be enough to give rise to such damages. Even if there is no ill-will or malice, the deliberateness in committing a violation of the act may give rise to such damages.

Punitive damages may also arise if there is an intent to discriminate or to act wrongfully. Although the matter of intent is sometimes more difficult to prove, circumstantial evidence may indicate that it is present. Also the jury will assess the credibility of the witnesses on the stand as to whether there was such an intent. This makes it especially important not to allow any circumstances to arise that could be thought to show such an intention even though none really existed.

The requirement of intentionalness is also sometimes found to be satisfied by court where the action has been "wanton and reckless." This means that if one is very careless in proceeding in these regards, the necessary element for punitive damages may be present.

The matter of punitive damages is a matter for legal expertise. But the purchasing manager's reasonableness, carefulness in the proceedings, and avoidance of any arbitrary action is crucial. In this regard the purchasing manager should bear in mind that while he or she may consider the actions to be appropriate, to outsiders it may seem to be wrongful and outrageous. It is the jury that makes the decision as to the outrageousness of the action. While sometimes it is possible for the appellate court to reverse the jury, generally the courts give the juries a wide range of discretion in fixing the amount of punitive damages.

IX

Antitrust Liabilities of Purchasing Officers

The general field of antitrust is a vast area of the law, replete with intricate and detailed concepts and principles. Volumes could be written on the subject, most of which would add little to the purchasing officer's ability to conduct the day-to-day operations of a purchasing department. Consequently, this chapter will be abbreviated to include only a discussion of the highlights of antitrust legislation and the obvious areas where purchasing personnel might run afoul of this branch of the law. Some practical advice will be offered as to how to avoid getting your company or organization into some of the legal entanglements that lurk in the law through your purchasing operations. It is suggested that those purchasing officers who believe their company may be exposed to antitrust liability seek the advice of their company's legal counsel. The liability exposure is much too complicated to attempt to avoid it by your own individual efforts. It requires the advice and counsel of specialists in the subject.

MAJOR ANTITRUST LEGISLATION

It is remarkable that despite the wide area of potential involvement in antitrust problems there are only four basic pieces of federal legislation on the subject. The four are:

1. The Sherman Antitrust Act (1890)

2. The Federal Trade Commission Act (1914)

3. The Clayton Antitrust Act (1914)

4. The Robinson-Patman Act (1936)

Most states have similar types of legislation that are patterned after their federal counterparts.

The Sherman Antitrust Act

The Sherman Act is the first piece of antitrust legislation. Passed by Congress on July 2, 1890, it was named after its author John Sherman, the brother of General William T. Sherman of Civil War prominence. The Sherman Act is noted for its brevity. This has led to the criticism that it contains broad phrases designed to give a "shotgun" effect to anything that might impinge upon our free enterprise system and lessen competition. Its two major provisions are:

> Section 1. Every contract, combination in the form of trust or other-wise or conspiracy in restraint of trade commerce among the several states or with foreign nations, is hereby declared to be illegal.
>
> Section 2. Every person who shall monopolize or attempt to monop-olize, or combine or conspire with any other person or persons, to monopolize any part of the trade or commerce among the several states or with foreign nations, shall be deemed guilty of a misde-meanor.

Section 1 is aimed at restraint of trade in any form, while section 2 goes after the end result of restraint of trade, which is monopoly. Section 1 forbids joint activity, while section 2 forbids both individual and joint activity. The law was patterned after the common law doctrine on restraint of trade and sought to con-demn only those restraints which seriously interfered with competition and free enterprise. The Act provides penalties for those who are guilty of violating it. These penalties include both fines and imprisonment. A corporation can be found guilty of a violation and forced to pay monetary damages. As we shall see shortly, the Robinson-Patman Act also provides for monetary damages for viola-tions but it does not include imprisonment as a penalty. Consequently, where there is an apparent gross violation of an antitrust law an effort will be made to secure a Sherman Act conviction because of the sterner penalty available.

The Federal Trade Commission Act

In 1914, the Federal Trade Commission Act created the Federal Trade Commission and gave it the power to determine the precise meaning of *restraint of trade*. The act seeks out unfair methods of competition as well as unfair or deceptive acts in commerce.

The Clayton Act

The Clayton Act declares price discrimination to be unlawful. Its price discrimination provisions were later amended by the Robinson-Patman Act. The act also forbids the leasing or selling of a product on the condition the buyer not deal with a competitor of the seller or the lessor. It outlaws exclusive-dealing types of restrictions on sales. There is another section in the Act that governs corporate acquisitions that might lead to a monopoly.

The Robinson-Patman Act

Chain stores—retail outlets of consumer products located in various areas that were owned by a single corporation—gained prominence during the 1930s. The corporation that owned the chain stores centralized the purchase of various resale items. Large-volume purchasing gave them the advantage of obtaining their needs at lower unit costs than if they bought for only one store. These lower acquisition costs permitted their retail prices to be lowered to attract customers. This type of activity made the small corner neighborhood store, owned and operated by a single entrepreneur, an unprofitable venture. Scores of such small stores had to close their doors because of chain store competition during the early years of the Depression.

The Robinson-Patman Act, passed in 1936, was called an antichain-store law. It was designed to give the small corner grocery store an equal competitive advantage to the chain-store operation. Those who supported the passage of the act had no good will toward the chain stores. The act is more a trade-regulation law than a trust-busting statute. It is dull, difficult to read, more difficult to understand, and often impossible to apply. We will only synopsize the one section of the act that applies to purchasing officers—Section 2, which amended the Clayton Act.

Section 2 has the following six divisions, designated by letters:

> *Subsection (a)* outlaws direct and indirect discrimination in price by a seller. Mere differences in price are not unlawful, but only where those price differences substantially lessen competition. Price "differentials which make only due allowances for differentials in the cost of manufacture, sale, or delivery resulting from the differing methods or quantities in which . . . goods are sold or delivered" are not prohibited.

> *Subsection (b)* provides that a seller may escape the penalties of subsection (a) if he can prove "that his lower price or the furnishing of services or facilities to any purchaser . . . was made in good faith to meet an equally low price of a competitor . . ."

Subsection (c) flatly prohibits the paying of "a commission, brokerage, or other compensation or any allowance or discount in lieu thereof" to the buyer. The section makes it unlawful for the seller to pay the commission *and the buyer* to receive it. (This section is being interpreted more strictly by the courts and not all fees and commissions may be illegal.)

Subsection (d) prohibits payments by a seller to a buyer for any facilities or services furnished by him unless such payments are equally available to all other customers.

Subsection (e) makes the furnishing of any facilities or services to a buyer by the seller illegal unless such facilities or services are made available to all of the seller's customers.

Subsection (f) is aimed directly at a buyer:

"It shall be unlawful for any person in commerce, in the course of such commerce, knowingly to induce or receive a discrimination in price which is prohibited by this Section."

This is quite specific that the buyer must not accept a *prohibited* discrimination in price, nor may he *knowingly* induce such a discrimination. This subsection and subsection (c) are the only places in the Robinson-Patman Act where the buyer is specifically charged with the duty not to perform an act because it is deemed illegal to do so. The buyer is liable only for knowingly inducing or receiving a price discrimination which is condemned by subsection (a), and for receiving with or without knowledge a commission or an allowance prohibited under subsection (c).

This is the general outline of the antitrust legislation that is on the law books at the present time. You are reminded that much of the law on the subject is found in the reported cases involving antitrust litigation. The federal courts and the Federal Trade Commission have added considerable volumes to the present laws through their interpretation and application of the above legislation. This so-called "case law" expands the general statements of the law contained in the four acts of Congress mentioned above.

It should be noted that a charge of violation of the Sherman Antitrust Act is a criminal charge brought into court with the "United States of America" as the plaintiff. Charges under the Robinson-Patman Act may be brought in the name of the United States of America by the Federal Trade Commission or by private parties who claim to be damaged. In the latter case, payment of treble damages to the injured parties is provided if the accused is found guilty. If the Federal Trade Commission brings the suit and wins, a cease and desist order will be issued against the offender. A cease and desist order makes it illegal for the company to continue its discriminatory activity. The order also carries with it a $5000 fine plus a possible $5000 fine per day for each day the company continues to violate the cease and desist order.

THE PURCHASING OFFICER AND THE SHERMAN ACT

Purchasing officers have a genuine interest in advancing the purposes of the Sherman Act. The title of the Act reads "An act to protect trade and commerce against unlawful restraints and monopolies." Affirmatively stated, the law is directed at preserving the free enterprise system and encouraging competition in American business. Monopolies eliminate competition, and restraints on trade tend to restrict the effects of competition. We know that competition is the lifeblood of effective procurement, and purchasing must see to it that it is preserved as a way of life in business. Every purchasing officer has a heavy stake in the Sherman Act's goal of protecting the competitive nature of our business climate. The Sherman Act is basically purchasing's friend and not its foe.

Yet purchasing itself must be cautious not to abuse its "friend" by engaging in practices that are contrary to its principles. The purchasing officer with powerful buying power must use that power properly and not engage in activities that might tend to limit the ability of suppliers to compete for his or her business. It is true that a purchasing officer's exposure to possible liability under the Sherman Act is somewhat limited, but it is nonetheless real. Most of the publicity given to Sherman Act violations has involved the sales function where suppliers combine to control the price of their product. There are, however, specific purchasing situations that, if coupled with the essential ingredients of a Sherman Act involvement, could lead to liability under the act. We will list a few of these scenarios, that illustrate some of the potential liabilities of the purchasing function and the purchasing staff. No claim is made that the list is complete.

Reciprocity

Reciprocity as a buying motive is given credence in some purchasing circles and yet it is a purchasing policy that has run afoul of the Sherman Act because it tends to stifle competition. Here is a hypothetical case illustrating how this scene could be set:

> Company A produces a product known as "Bark." Three other companies—Green, White, and Pink—make a similar product. Sales of Bark are almost equal to the combined sales of its three competitors. The largest bulk of all sales the industry makes are made to chemical companies throughout the country.

One of the essential ingredients of Bark and its three competitors is a chemical known as "Zee." The purchasing officer of Company A decides to purchase Zee only from chemical companies that buy their Bark. This fact is made known to the sales representatives of the chemical companies who see to it that their purchasing officers purchase Bark. Naturally this affects the sales of Green, White, and Pink. The three competitors of Company A complain and launch a legal attack against Company A.

A case similar to the hypothetical case above actually occurred. Company A in our hypothetical case had suit brought against it by the United States of America for violation of sections 1 and 2 of the Sherman Act. Before the case went to trial, Company A agreed to what is known as a *consent judgment*. A consent judgment is one that the defendant agrees to have imposed upon him by the court without the merits of the case being litigated. Consent judgments are usually agreed to when the defendant sees the handwriting on the wall, which says that it will probably lose the case if the full facts against it are aired; or that the defendant believes it is more prudent to accept the consent judgment rather than to spend the time and money necessary to fight the charge in court.

This consent judgment against Company A placed a number of restrictions on the company and its personnel, too numerous to quote verbatim. Here are a few of the restrictions, stripped of legal verbosity:

1. Company A is enjoined and restrained from purchasing products from any supplier on the condition that such purchases will be based upon Company A's sales to such supplier.

2. Company A is enjoined and restrained from selling products to any customer with the understanding Company A's purchase of products from such customer will be based upon Company A's sales to such customer.

3. Company A is enjoined and restrained from communicating to its customers that in purchasing products preference will be given to any supplier based upon Company A's sales to such supplier.

4. Company A is enjoined and restrained from communicating to its customers that in compiling bidders lists preference will be given to any supplier based upon Company A's sales to such suppliers.

There were many more "thou shalt nots," all to the effect that in no way will the company engage in the practice of using reciprocity as a buying motive. The restraints in the judgment were to be effective for a period of ten years, and Company A is required to submit yearly reports to the court indicating its compliance with the judgment.

Each member of Company A's purchasing staff received a copy of this consent decree. The letter of transmittal from the chief executive officer of Company

A concluded with this warning:

> Managers of groups, divisions and departments must make it clear to their employees, particularly to those having sales or purchasing responsibilities, that this compliance program has the full, complete, active and continuous support of corporate management. As indicated, this decree is binding not only upon Company A, its officers and management, but upon every employee, and violation of the decree by any employee renders him subject to the penalties applicable in cases of criminal contempt; i.e., such fines or imprisonment as the court, in its discretion, may deem appropriate. Thus, there is a real and immediate risk of prison sentence for any employee who willfully violates this decree. The decree means what it says, and the company will not tolerate violations. The decree is a fact which every employee having sales or purchasing responsibilities, or in communication with suppliers or customers, must recognize. Employees must also understand that management expects them to comply with the letter of this decree. Violations of company policy and of the law generally come to light in one way or another and will not be condoned by the company, whether or not they result in criminal prosecutions by the government.

> It is the duty of management at all levels to communicate these views to all concerned in a way which will leave no doubt that both the letter and the spirit of the company's commercial relations policy and of the consent decree are to be observed completely and without exception. [Signed by the chief executive officer]

These concluding remarks from the chief executive officer of Company A are not idle threats. Any purchasing officer of Company A who violates this federal court Consent Decree could be found guilty of criminal contempt. These purchasing officers have a "heavy-heavy" hanging over their heads each morning when they report for work. One may assume reciprocity is no longer a buying motive at Company A.

Reciprocity can be a problem for the large company. It becomes a problem that attracts legal action when it is actively pursued by either the purchasing or the sales division. *Active pursuit* implies outright solicitation of potential customers from whom purchases have been made. Active pursuit also implies that the purchasing department maintains lists of the dollar volume of sales made to customers with the list used as the basis of awarding purchase contracts. And active pursuit may also be accomplished by sales representatives who tell their potential customers that they can be of assistance in getting business from the purchasing department if the customer will reciprocate. Much of this type of activity goes on under the banner of "trade relations," which was at one time very popular among the larger corporations. But affirmative action to secure reciprocal trade relations with other large corporations disaffects the smaller companies who are competitors and leads to complaints to those in government who are the trust busters. When a purchasing officer with a strong buying power attempts to help the sales department by agreeing to purchase only from their customers, there is an "attempt to monopolize . . . part of the trade or commerce . . . " If that attempt has a reasonable chance of success, there is an apparent violation of the Sherman Act. This is why an outspoken affirmative action program of reciprocity is to be avoided if at all possible.

***Nota Bene* to the Purchasing Officer.** Doing business with one of your company's customers is not illegal in itself. Furthermore, deliberately making an award to a customer is justifiable, for example, in the case of tie bids, with one bidder a customer and the other a noncustomer. Making the award to the customer because he is a customer is entirely appropriate. Certainly you as a purchasing officer cannot avoid and ignore a prospective supplier simply because he is a customer of your company. That customer may be the single source of the product you are buying, or the customer's product may be far superior in the field. Remember that purchasing is part of the management team whose duty it is to look after the welfare of the entire organization. This includes the sales of the company product, as well as satisfying the legitimate needs of the company with the best product available on the market. Your author heard the chief counsel of the largest corporation in a particular industry classification tell his assembled purchasing staff if at all possible find alternate suppliers who were not customers to avoid doing business with their customers. Our opinion is that this may be an overly cautious approach, although we would be the last to criticize the advice given by the chief counsel of any company. *Your* legal counsel knows the legal climate in which *your* company operates and is in the position to recommend your best course of action.

The purchasing officer of a small- or medium-sized company has little to worry about legal entanglements if reciprocity is used as a buying motive. You have limited influence in the marketplace, and your chances of creating a monopoly are minimal. Your author does not like to see reciprocity used as a buying motive by professional purchasing officers, but your company's need for business may make its application necessary. Maintain a low profile in its use, and the consequences will be minimal or nonexistent.

The purchasing officer of the large corporation faces a different outlook on the use of reciprocity. We do know that an active program of reciprocity that was practiced by several large companies resulted in successful prosecution of Sherman Act violations. Now the facts and circumstances surrounding those companies may be different than those of your company, but you may never know whether the facts in your case are sufficiently different to enable you to avoid conviction until you are brought to trial. But why take the risk? The law does not deny you the right to purchase from your customers if you are acting in good faith to meet the legitimate needs of your company. But it does prohibit you from deliberately conspiring with your sales department to use the company's buying power to produce additional sales to customers who might not have considered buying your company's product under ordinary circumstances. It is suggested that you consult your legal counsel before embarking upon an affirmative action program of reciprocity.

Boycott

The Sherman Act is aimed specifically at conspiracies or concerted actions that result in a restraint of trade of one type or another. A group boycott is a typical example of concerted action. Should a group of purchasing officers agree that they will not purchase from a particular supplier and then carry out that agreement, there has been a violation of the Sherman Act. If any individual purchasing officer of that group decides not to buy from that supplier, that is a legal act. The free enterprise system gives the buyer the right to choose with whom he will do business. No supplier can claim foul play when a purchasing officer elects not to do business with him. It is only when that purchasing officer talks with other purchasing officers and persuades them to join him in not doing business with that supplier that the Sherman Act goes into operation. Then there is a conspiracy that interferes with free enterprise. This type of concerted action injures that individual supplier, and it makes no difference how salutary the purpose of their boycott is. The boycott may have a great humanitarian purpose, but that is not germane. These purchasing officers would be found guilty of depriving the supplier of the right to sell his product in a free and open market. That violation of the Sherman Act would override their good intent in developing the boycott.

Collusion

A group boycott is one form of collusive action that is frowned upon by the Sherman Act. Any type of concerted action that interferes with a person's right to enjoy a free and competitive market is suspect. One can imagine many types of actions a group of purchasing officers might take to bring a particular supplier to his knees. One example would be to agree to return purchases from the targeted supplier and file false claims for damage or for nonconformance of the goods delivered. This would increase that supplier's cost of doing business. Another type of collusive action would be to agree not to pay for purchases made for 90 or 120 days to create a cash flow problem for the supplier. While these examples differ in their nature, they all have one common fault—concerted action that damages the ability of the supplier to enjoy a free and competitive market. Such conspiracies are illegal.

Group Buying

Business and service organizations in the same fields of endeavor have common purchasing requirements. Retail drug stores, department stores, farmers growing corn or wheat, hospitals, and colleges and universities are typical examples of this fact. Such common requirements may be the basis for the formation of a formal or informal group-buying unit. These various groups—groups of competitors, if you will—could pool their purchases of a common item or items and make one large purchase to cover all their needs. A single purchase could be made in a quantity far larger than a purchase for one member, which would qualify for a quantity discount from which all members could benefit.

The Sherman Act does not make group buying illegal per se. Group purchases can be made in a manner that will promote, rather than suppress, competition among suppliers. And the Sherman Act is in favor of competition. Following are some suggested policies a group of buying activity should consider to avoid any charge of restricting competition:

1. Eligibility for membership in the group should be uniform and reasonable. If membership in the group is available to the entire industry it will preclude any charge of being a tool to gain an unfair advantage on competitors.

2. Selection of suppliers for the group purchases must be as fully competitive as possible. All the suppliers interested in bidding on the group's purchases should be permitted to do so, providing the buying specifications are met.

3. A very limited range of products, or only one product, should be in a single contract. The wider the range of products included in a contract, the fewer the number of suppliers that will be found able to quote on the entire list. This limits competition.

4. A contract award to a supplier should be for a limited period of time—probably no more than one year. At the expiration of that period of time, the contract should be rebid.

5. A contract should cover a limited geographic area. A national contract excludes many regional suppliers, which limits competition. It is an unreasonable restraint of trade on the regional supplier to be forced to "go national" or forgo bidding on the group contract.

6. Participation by members in the group-buying contracts should be optional; there should be no coercion placed on members who want to award a particular contract independently.

7. All negotiations and purchases must comply with the requirements of section 2 of the Robinson-Patman Act. (These requirements are discussed in the succeeding section.)

The experienced purchasing officer will note that several items on this list are not conducive to getting the lowest possible price from the suppliers bidding on the contract. A very limited range of products, a contract for a limited period of time, a contract for a limited geographic area, and voluntary participation by members all tend to make the contract less attractive to a supplier. But these conditions are essential to avoid charges of restraint of trade or of restricting competition. It is when attempts are made to circumvent these essentials by clever devices or by clever wording that the long arm of the Sherman Act begins to reach out. Outright adherence to the criteria is recommended for group-purchasing arrangements.

The type of group-buying unit that is formed to handle purchases has little legal consequence. The group may be unincorporated and operate as a limited partnership; it may be incorporated as a separate entity, or it may be a true cooperative organized under the cooperative laws of the state. Savings generated by the group-buying activity can be recognized by each individual member by simply paying less for the item. Or the cooperative unit may assemble the savings and hand back to its members a "patronage dividend" for the earnings remaining after expenses of operating the cooperative are paid.

It should be noted that section 2(c) of the Robinson-Patman Act prohibits the payment of "a commission, brokerage, or other compensation or allowances in lieu thereof" to the buyer. A patronage dividend payment to members of a cooperative group-buying unit does not violate this section of the law because the act has a specific exemption for patronage dividends. As pointed out previously, the Robinson-Patman Act was known as the antichain-store law. Independently owned stores organized cooperative buying groups during the Depression years of the 1930s to combat the chain stores' buying power. These cooperatives distributed their earnings in the form of patronage dividends. The framers of the Robinson-Patman Act made certain that this was an acceptable practice for small stores by including the following section in the Act:

> *Section 4. Cooperative Associations:* Nothing in this act shall prevent a cooperative association from returning to its members, producers or consumers the whole, or any part of, the net earnings or surplus resulting from its trading operations, in proportion to their purchases or sales from, to, or through the association.

This exemption for cooperative associations is applicable only to the payment of patronage dividends. Cooperative associations must adhere strictly to all other sections of the Robinson-Patman Act.

There are in existence today many hospital and educational cooperative buying groups. At least one such group has been challenged in court, accused of violating the Sherman Act, the Clayton Act and the Robinson-Patman Act. The charges were brought against the supplier who received the major contract from the group-purchasing association. This supplier was the largest supplier in the field, with national distribution facilities. The plaintiffs, who brought the suit, were four much smaller regional competitors of the defendant. They claimed, with sufficient persuasiveness to convince a lower federal court, that the contract tended to create a monopoly and constituted an unlawful restraint of trade. (The case was later reversed by the Federal Court of Appeals.) The details of the contract are most unique but too voluminous to repeat here. Suffice it to say that the contract with the supplier ignored many of the seven essentials for a palatable cooperative buying arrangement mentioned earlier. The contract also added a few additional twists that caused the court much concern, including an ingenious method of encouraging members to patronize the cooperative. Yes, cooperative associations must abide by the provisions of the Sherman Act, even if they are for the benefit of not-for-profit institutions.

THE PURCHASING OFFICER AND THE ROBINSON-PATMAN ACT

Lowell Mason, a former commissioner of the Federal Trade Commission, once stated to a group of purchasing officers that the Robinson-Patman Act "dares a purchasing officer to do his job properly." Commissioner Mason was referring to section 2(f) of the act which states:

> It shall be unlawful for any person engaged in commerce . . . knowingly to induce or receive a discrimination in price which is prohibited by this Section.

Any person refers to a purchasing officer, *a discrimination in price which is prohibited by this section* refers to section 2(a) of the Act where it is declared unlawful for a seller to discriminate in the pricing of his product between different purchasers. Putting subsections (a) and (f) together and paraphrasing them, the Act says: "A purchasing officer should not try to talk a supplier into a lower price for his product than that paid for the same product by the purchasing officer of a competitor."

This almost tells you, as a purchasing officer negotiating with a supplier, that when you get that supplier down to the price your competitor paid, you had better "shut up shop and go home." The Robinson-Patman Act is there staring at you and daring you to try to get another penny off the supplier's price. If you succeed in that endeavor, you may have violated the Act, and your company will then be in for big trouble if its competitors complain to the Federal Trade Commission. Good purchasing officers find this to be repugnant. Part of your job is to make purchases for your company at the lowest possible cost. You are unwilling to accept what your competitor paid as the best price for your own company. Yet the Robinson-Patman Act seems to dictate this conclusion.

We need to take a practical look at the Robinson-Patman Act to understand more fully what its purpose is and how to rationalize its provisions in light of the purchasing officer's role in business to bargain for the best possible price. We stated previously that it was an antichain-store law when it was put on the books in 1936. Section 2 was not new law because it amended and broadened a similar provision in the Clayton Act which was passed in 1914. Thus, price discrimination had been declared unlawful 22 years before the Robinson-Patman Act was born. The Act is aimed at the powerful purchasing power of the chain store. The chain could offer a seller a very large order for its product and it could dangle this bait before the seller's eyes for a price concession. Business was in the midst of a depression during the middle 1930s, and a seller was always interested in adding to its sales volume. The chain store's offer to buy the large quantity was very attractive, and, more often than not, the seller accepted the offer by making a price concession to get the sale.

On the other side of the street was the individually owned corner grocery. If it wanted to offer the same product to its customers, it had to negotiate with the same seller but with a much smaller quantity to purchase. It was buying for only one store. As a result it had to pay more for the same item. This enabled the chain store to resell the product to its customers at a lower price than that of the corner grocery.

This differential in acquisition cost is what the Robinson-Patman Act sought to eliminate. The Act, in plain language, seeks to strip the chain store of its powerful purchasing power and bring it down to the same bargaining position as the corner grocery. Quantity purchasing power, without any cost justification on the part of the seller, is an evil in the eyes of the Robinson-Patman Act. It destroys the ability of the corner grocery to compete with the chain successfully, and eventually puts the small store out of business. That was what the Act wanted to prevent. So today, we have this law on the books as a guarantee there will be competition between sellers at all levels of retail trade. But it is also a law and a fact of life that the modern purchasing officer must learn to live with. Some of us must go into negotiations with our supplier friends with "one arm tied behind our back" to avoid using the full strength of the purchasing power our companies possess to get a better price.

We in purchasing must keep in mind that the law is aimed primarily at the seller of the goods. The goal is to prevent the seller from offering the same goods to competing buyers at different prices. Only sections 2(c) and 2(f) apply to the purchasing officer, and the restrictions contained in these two sections are not as broad as the restrictions placed on the seller in the balance of the Act. This is small consolation, but it is of some advantage.

Section 2(c) and the Purchasing Officer

Section 2(c) makes it unlawful for the buyer to receive "a commission, brokerage, or any allowance or discount in lieu thereof" from the seller. We have seen in Chapter VIII on the personal liabilities of the purchasing officer that it is illegal to receive any commissions on the purchase of goods from the seller. Therefore, the provision in this act merely codifies in another form the prohibition against commercial bribery. It also gives *your* competitors the right to police your action in acceptance of such commissions. It places liability on your employer-principal if the payments are made directly to your company. This is one of the reasons why we recommend that the entire transaction of a purchase be confined to one piece of paper, and that the purchase involve only the receipt of the goods and the payment to the supplier. Side deals and "kickers" in a transaction should be avoided.

Section 2(f) and the Purchasing Officer

This is the other section in the Robinson-Patman Act that is aimed directly at the purchasing officer. "It shall be unlawful for any person . . . knowingly to induce or receive a discrimination in price which is prohibited by this Act." This is a clear statement of responsibility that you, the purchasing officer, cannot avoid. It calls for a careful analysis of its provisions so that you may readily recognize (1) discrimination in price, (2) discrimination in price that is prohibited by the Act, (3) discrimination in price that is not prohibited by the Act, and (4) "knowingly inducing or receiving" a price discrimination prohibited by the Act.

1. A Discrimination in Price. A discrimination in price occurs when a seller charges different prices for his product to two different purchasers who are competitors. One purchaser is discriminated against and the other receives the benefit of the discrimination. The same product must be offered to both purchasers to constitute price discrimination, e.g., the product offered to both must be of like quality and of the same grade. Selling a lesser quality at a lower price is not discrimination. The differences in quality must be real, however, and must be in the physical components. It cannot consist solely of artistic taste. Two identical automobiles with identical accessories cannot be sold at different prices because one is painted a beautiful beige and the other a hideous purple, without it being considered discriminatory pricing. A 1965 case decided that different labels on cans of the same product did not constitute a difference in quality sufficient to warrant a difference in price. There must be genuine reasons for differing prices for a product, otherwise the price differentials discriminate in favor of one buyer and against the other.

A purchasing officer knows that there are many other ways in which a price differential may be effected. A 2 percent discount for payment in 10 days could be a discriminatory price if that same discount is not offered equally to other buyers unless based strictly on the credit involved. Likewise, if the seller's credit terms are: "10th net proximo," and you ask for "25th net proximo" because your company pays all its bills on the 26th day of the month, the seller would discriminate against his other customers if he granted your request.

More expensive or extensive packaging for one customer would be discriminatory. Differing F.O.B. terms, partial deliveries, or warehousing a part of an order by the seller, would fall into the same category. Anything in a purchase that is of value to the buyer and adds costs to the seller constitutes a discrimination in price, if the goods are identical.

An interesting question of discriminatory pricing is raised when a seller gives a buyer advance notice of the impending price rise of his product. We all know that a supplier will make the decision to raise the price of his product, but it may be several weeks or a month before the new price lists can be printed and distributed. During that interim, the sales representative handling your account hears a rumor from the home office that his price change is about to happen. To curry your favor, or because you are a good customer, or because the sales representative may need an order quickly to meet a quota, the word is passed on to you. You believe the report and place an order in time to "get in under the wire" to avoid the price increase. If the sales representative was telling the truth and the price does rise as predicted, you have been given a discriminatory price by the supplier unless all of the supplier's customers were given similar advance warnings.

2. A Discrimination in Price Prohibited by This Section. Thus far we have been looking at some examples of what might constitute the "discrimination in price" that is mentioned in section 2(f) of the Robinson-Patman Act. These examples assume that one purchasing officer has been given the favor of a lower price than that given to other customers of the supplier. There has been no distinction made as to whether the "other customers of the supplier" are competitors of the favored purchasing officer. We have merely illustrated by example discrimination in price by a seller among the seller's several customers.

Not all discriminations in price made by one seller are illegal. These discriminations may be unfair to the other buyers and may be the result of superior purchasing ability by the favored buyer, but they are not all illegal. Only those price discriminations that are prohibited by Section 2 of the Robinson-Patman Act are illegal. Subsection 2(a) states clearly that an unlawful price discrimination is one "where the effect of such discrimination may be to substantially lessen competition." Thus, if a discriminatory price does not affect competition, it is a legal price discrimination. The act does not concern itself with all price discriminations—only with those that "may . . . substantially lessen competition."

There are three words in this quote from the act on which we should focus our attention. The verb *may* tells us that the effect on competition need not be an accomplished fact before the price discrimination becomes illegal. The possibility of the lessening of competition is sufficient to bring about the differential within the Act. Speculative results open up avenues of argumentation and keep us from getting a firm grip on the problem. This is one of the reasons why the Robinson-Patman Act has given concern to everyone. Here the use of *may* means that it need not be proven that the price differential actually lessened competition, but only that it *might* do so.

Competition here refers to the competitors of either buyer or the seller. It is not essential that the affected competition be both the buyer's and the seller's. Only one group of competitors need be involved to bring about the charge.

The one good word used is *substantially.* This narrows the extensions of the Act considerably. In a competitive marketplace, every act anyone performs probably affects competition. If you, the buyer, have competitors and you make an economical purchase, you have given your company an advantage over its competitors. And if you are able to obtain competitive bids on a purchase, your suppliers have competition too. The low bidder gets a jump on his competitors. Therefore every purchase you make has some effect on competition. But the price differential you secure from the supplier may cause as little effect on competition as a ripple created by a grain of sand being thrown into Lake Michigan. That is far from having a substantial effect on the water. The fact that there must be a *substantial* effect on competition eliminates a large percentage of your purchases from being involved with a prohibited price differential under the Act.

3. Price Discrimination Specifically Permitted by the Act. There are several allowable price discriminations provided for in the Act, even though they might substantially lessen competition. The first is contained in subsection 2(a) and it reads:

> Nothing herein contained shall prevent differentials which make only due allowance for differences in the cost of manufacture, sale or delivery resulting from the differing methods or quantities in which such commodities are to such purchasers sold or delivered . . .

The language in this subsection is typical of the entire Act. This is what prompted a previous statement by your author that the Act is "difficult to read, more difficult to interpret, and often impossible to apply." The hasty reader will come away from the reading of this section believing that quantity price differentials are allowable. Quantity price differentials are allowable by the above-quoted section only to the extent that there are *provable differences in cost* to the seller because of the larger quantity involved in the order. The Federal Trade Commission and the federal courts are very emphatic that there must be a provable cost justification for any allowable price differentials to exist. Provable cost justification could mean that there should be a statement to that effect by certified public accountants.

Moreover, because a quantity price differential favors the larger purchaser over the smaller, it affects the ability of the smaller buyer to compete in the marketplace if the price differential is given. This quickly affects the competition that the large buyer faces—it lessens such competition. And remember that the lack of ability of the small buyer to compete with the large buyer is one of the most motivating reasons the Robinson-Patman Act was enacted. Consequently, the courts have been very stern in insisting that any differential claimed to be allowable be thoroughly and completely justified by provable cost savings when the seller attempts to justify a lower price under this subsection.

The same section 2(a) has another bit of prose that tells of a second type of allowable price differentials.

> Nothing contained herein shall prevent price changes from time to time wherein response to changing conditions affecting the market for or the marketability of the goods concerned, such as but not limited to actual or imminent deterioration of perishable goods, obsolescence of seasonal goods . . .

This does not offer a seller much comfort because it refers to price *changes* rather than price *differentials*. Any such changes for the reasons specified must be offered to all buyers, which merely brings them under the general rules of the Act. The first buyer to accept such a price change would have only a temporary advantage over his competitor in such circumstances.

The last provision for allowable price differentials is found in section 2(b):

> Nothing shall prevent a seller . . . showing that his lower price or the furnishing of services or facilities to any purchaser or purchasers was made in good faith to meet an equally low price of a competitor, or the services or facilities furnished by a competitor.

This gives the supplier the opportunity to meet a competitor's price. The law limits that opportunity only to meeting the lower price—that is, by not going below it in order to become the low bidder. You will note that the lower price must be made in good faith. This places the burden on the seller to prove that his competitor actually made a lower price quotation to you, the buyer. This can be proven by the seller if you are willing to give him a copy of his competitor's price quotation, or if the seller discusses the price with his competitor. The latter alternative is a dangerous one for the seller, because it opens him to a charge of collusion, which is banned by the Sherman Act. The careful supplier may insist that you reveal his competitor's quotation, but that remains at the buyer's discretion.

4. Knowingly to Induce or Receive a Discrimination in Price. The final prerequisite in the law that is necessary to find a purchasing officer guilty of a violation is that the discriminatory price was *knowingly induced or received.* Unfortunately the law itself does not define the word *knowingly.* It sets up no standard of *knowledge,* and one must therefore make assumptions about what was intended.

It is obvious, though, that there are two facts about a price that a buyer must know before he or she can be accused of violating this section of the law. First, the buyer must know that the price he is receiving is discriminatory, and, second, he must know that it is one that is prohibited by section 2(a). Since we have already seen that a mere price differential is not illegal in itself, it is then necessary to show additionally that the purchasing officer knew that the price received was prohibited by the Act. This knowledge is a question of fact, and fortunately for the buyer, proving this is difficult in the usual purchasing processes.

Of course, if a purchasing officer is buying a large quantity of goods and he induces the supplier to quote him a special price without regard to the supplier's price list, there is a strong presumption that the purchasing officer is acting at his peril. The buyer could be charged with negligent disregard of the principles of the act, which requires that there must be a justification of a supplier's special price. The large quantity to be purchased does not in itself satisfy the need for justification of the special price. There must be a *cost justification.* The purchasing officer could be held accountable for not making an inquiry of the supplier for this information.

A purchasing officer is a professional at the bargaining table. The law recognizes this and will place on the purchasing officer a duty to use his professional abilities to the fullest. This suggests that in cases where the buyer's knowledge of the transaction is at stake, the law will make a presumption of the extent of knowledge that the reasonably prudent buyer should possess:

> The buyer is presumed to know that which any buyer of his experience and training would know if he made the reasonable inquiries in good faith that any professional buyer would make under similar circumstances.

This standard of performance may lack specificity but it expresses, in general terms, what every professional buyer is expected to know. Some of the obligations that may be read into this standard are as follows:

1. The buyer cannot remain passive in the negotiations. He must make all inquiries the reasonably prudent buyer would make under the same circumstances.

2. The buyer should not deliberately avoid asking for the facts if he is afraid he will get the wrong answers. If he is afraid to make the inquiry, the odds are that the question is indeed a pertinent one.

3. The buyer should not be content to resort to mere routine to satisfy himself that the seller is complying with the law. Using a rubber stamp with the words "The seller assures the buyer that the price quoted is in compliance with the Robinson-Patman Act" stamped on every purchase order is *not* acting in good faith.

4. If the supplier quotes a price that the buyer *knows* is below the list price, the buyer should make reasonable inquiries to ascertain the basis for it. If the answer is cost savings, the buyer should ask for a letter to that effect from the supplier. (There is one word of caution the author offers here to the purchasing officer. Do not press the supplier for all the facts involved in the alleged cost savings. If you are given all of the facts, you may be held accountable for the correct interpretation of them. This is not your responsibility, nor can it be presumed to be within the scope of your professional knowledge. Leave the accounting interpretations for the accountants to handle.)

5. If the buyer has serious doubts about the validity of a "cost savings" justification, he could ask for a C.P.A.'s (Certified Public Accountant's) certificate to that effect. This is drastic action, which should be reserved only for large purchases where a penalty for treble damages would be costly.

6. Beware of a response from a supplier that says, "You are getting a special inside price." When there is no cost-savings justification, and you are getting a discriminatory price, remember the words of the act: It is unlawful . . . to receive a discrimination in price which is prohibited by this Section." Your supplier places a noose around your neck with such a sales argument.

7. Whenever you are aware that you are being offered a discriminatory price, your author suggests that a reasonably prudent professional purchasing officer would seek the advice of legal counsel before placing the order.

Of course, actively pursuing a prohibited discriminatory price places the purchasing officer in jeopardy because he is knowingly inducing the lower price. A federal court found one purchasing officer guilty of doing this in a case decided in 1971.[1] The purchasing officer was negotiating for a large quantity purchase and had invited four suppliers to quote him. One bidder had already responded with an 11 percent discount off list price when a fifth potential supplier visited the purchasing officer seeking to participate in bidding for the business. After discussing the prospective deal, the fifth supplier observed, "We are thinking in terms of a 15 percent discount." The purchasing officer responded, "Well, forget it. I have already got one at 20 percent off the existing list price." At a later discussion, the fifth bidder was told, "You are not in the ball park. You might as well go back home if that is all you have to offer." During all these conversations, the best offer the purchasing officer received was the 11 percent quotation. Eventually, number five submitted a 28 percent discount, which was accepted. Before long, the fifth supplier and the purchasing officer and his company were in court.

The court absolved the supplier of any wrong doing. The court believed the supplier had acted in good faith in meeting his competitor's price. The court said that even though the supplier was not guilty of offering a prohibited price, the purchasing officer and his company were guilty of *inducing* a prohibited price. The buyer claimed the court was placing him "at his peril whenever he engaged in price bargaining." The court responded that the hard bargaining of the buyer did not control the decision, but rather that it was his misrepresentation of the other bids.

Hard bargaining then is permissible according to this court, but just how hard it may be is the logical question that follows. Most purchasing officers at one time or another have used the ploy to a supplier, "I have a better quotation than the one you just gave me." You use that approach when you have the feeling that you and your company are being taken advantage of by the supplier. And yet, when you use it in a transaction that may run afoul of the Robinson-Patman Act, it is then knowingly inducing a prohibited price and not mere hard bargaining.

There are other techniques used by purchasing officers that probably border on the illegal too. For example, suppose a purchasing officer threatens to import a product if a supplier does not reduce his price for the same product. No one would deny a buyer the right to buy in a foreign market. That is legal. But using threat against the supplier as a means of inducing the supplier to give a price not offered to the supplier's other customers does seem to run afoul of the act. And by the same rationale, a threat to have the buyer's company manufacture the product would seem to be a prohibited inducement as well. But if a buyer has the option to "make or buy" it is perfectly legal to elect the make option. It is only when the threat to make is used in the hard bargaining with the supplier that the law becomes a hazard. It is apparent that the purchasing officer is well advised to

---

[1]*Kroger Co. v. F.T.C.*, 438 F.2d 1372 (1971).

keep such options within the family and not use them in bargaining with the supplier. Remember too that the supplier is probably fearful of reducing his price because of the Robinson-Patman controls on him. If you threaten him, and he does not get the award, you become a target for a treble damages suit.

ATTENDING ASSOCIATION MEETINGS

Concern has been expressed that attendance at a meeting of a professional purchasing association constitutes a violation of antitrust laws. There are corporations that have gone so far as to prohibit their purchasing personnel from being members of such professional groups to avoid these charges. It is your author's opinion that such fears are without substance if the association involved is organized and operates as a professional organization.

It is true that a meeting of area purchasing personnel could provide a forum for the organization of a collusive action against a supplier or a group of suppliers. It would be a natural place to plan a boycott of a supplier. It is true, too, that a meeting of purchasing officers of, for example, insurance companies or paper manufacturers would bring together industry purchasing officers who purchase the same commodities from many of the same suppliers. This would be an ideal forum to plan illegal activities. But the same charge could be leveled against a meeting of the Chamber of Commerce of a given locality if a number of purchasing officers—or sales personnel—regularly attended such meetings.

The important point to remember is that it is not illegal per se for a number of purchasing officers to gather together to break bread or to have liquid refreshment. Nor is it illegal per se for several purchasing officers to meet at a picnic area in a park each day and then jog together. Simply because one is a purchasing officer one does not lose the civil rights that every other individual enjoys. This is not one of the occupational hazards of being a purchasing officer. What is important is that every purchasing officer who assembles—no matter where —with professional peers, remember that there are certain professional matters that should not be discussed openly with each other. These taboos could include, but not be limited to, the prices paid for a commodity, the performances of a particular supplier, the special services received from a supplier, and any negative experiences with a supplier that might call for retaliatory action. The more specific the topic of the conversation is, the closer one comes to the possibility of concerted action of the group. And this is where the group might lead itself into troubled waters.

Professional associations are designed for the professional development of their members. The programs they offer, therefore, must be directed either to that purpose or for the entertainment and relaxation of those attending. Topics and programs that do not fall into these categories should be avoided. Even the members sitting at a round table that seats eight or ten while attending a meeting should avoid table conversations that violate these professional conduct rules. Each attendee must keep in mind that as a professional purchasing officer there are topics to be avoided or conversations that have legal connotations. These have no place at a professional meeting.

Your author firmly believes in the values received from the professional development of the various purchasing associations. These include local, regional, and national Purchasing Management Association meetings, regional and national meetings of the National Association of Educational Buyers, and various regional and national meetings of various hospital associations for their purchasing personnel. These programs are all aimed at improving the professional skills of the purchasing officer. Plant visits, entertainment, and sightseeing tours may also be included in the programs. All these activities are legal and should be encouraged and supported. The sharing of knowledge, experience, and training helps make purchasing a pure profession. The purchasing officer who participates increases his or her value to the employer. All employers should recognize this fact and encourage their purchasing personnel to join such associations and participate in the activities thereof.

In the same breath, your author also reminds each member of a professional purchasing association of his or her obligation to be supportive of the legal objectives of the group. Each person is also reminded to be very cautious not to degrade the good name of his or her association by indulging in illegal activities at the meetings. Each member should be a watchdog and be prepared to blow the whistle on any member who dares to use the group for self-serving illegal purposes. The daily work of a purchasing officer involves encroachments into sensitive areas, and great care must be taken to avoid charges of unfairness and lack of good faith. The purchasing officer must apply this same strict approach to association activities.

Exemption from Antitrust Liabilities

There are no exemptions from liability contained in the Sherman Act, the Clayton Act, and the Federal Trade Commission Act. Charities, not-for-profit institutions, including educational and hospital organizations, and any other type of organization that customarily receives tax exemptions are all covered. Purchasing officers of these groups must adhere to these laws as does every purchasing officer of a for-profit organization.

There is an exemption from liability in the Robinson-Patman Act. It was passed in 1938 as an amendment to the 1936 act. The amendment reads:

An act to Amend Public Law 692: That nothing in the Act approved June 19, 1936, known as the Robinson-Patman Antidiscrimination Act, shall apply to purchases of their supplies for their own use by schools, colleges, universities, public libraries, churches, hospitals and charitable institutions not operated for profit.

X

Purchasing Ethics
and the Law

A question could be raised about the inclusion of a chapter on ethics in a text addressing itself to the legal aspects of purchasing. Ethics, per se, is not a legal code, nor is it a compendium of laws relating to a particular occupation. But it is closely akin to the law because in many areas where ethics end, the law begins. In short, when one goes beyond ethical practice there may be a law that forbids such activity.

ETHICS DEFINED

Any definition of *ethics* will include: "A body of moral principles or values that relate to an occupation." Ethics could also be defined as: "The rules and standards for right conduct and good practice that are found to be generally acceptable to a particular profession." A code of ethics could be established voluntarily by a group of practicing professionals, it could be imposed upon the professional group by the law, or it could be established by a combination of both sources. The medical and the legal professions both have standards of ethical practice that have been set for them by peer groups and supplemented and enforced by legal principles. Since both professions require state licensing to practice, adherence to their ethical codes is mandatory for their continuing ability to pursue their profession. An infraction of ethical standards of practice might result in censure, temporary suspension of their license, or revocation of their license.

PURCHASING CODE OF ETHICS

Groups of purchasing personnel have established codes of ethics for the general guidance of their members. Adherence to such ethical codes is not mandatory, as it is for the legal and medical professions, but it is highly desirable. Since no state licensing is involved, anyone may become a purchasing officer by the simple act of employment in an organization. Furthermore, adherence to any standards of ethical practice is not required for continuing employment. An employer may dismiss a purchasing officer for a gross violation of an ethical standard, but such dismissal is not mandatory. It is left to the discretion of the employer.

CERTIFIED PURCHASING MANAGERS

Purchasing officers have long sought to make their occupation a profession. In literature and among themselves they refer to their vocation as the purchasing profession. To their credit, strong efforts are being made to establish professional credibility. The largest association of purchasing officers—the National Association of Purchasing Management—has established what is known as the Certified Purchasing Manager program. This program gives a person who is capable of passing an examination on basic purchasing principles and techniques prepared by a group of practicing purchasing officers the title "Certified Purchasing Manager." Those who receive such an award are entitled to affix the initials "C.P.M." to their name, not unlike the degree designation M.D. affixed to a physician's name and the professional courtesy designation Esq. affixed to an attorney's name. There are also requirements for recertification after a number of years have passed since the original C.P.M. designation was granted.

The C.P.M. program is gaining recognition in the business world as an assurance that the one possessing it meets the minimum prescribed educational standards of the position. This recognition will increase over the years, but only for its present limited purposes.

Unfortunately there is no mandatory state licensing of those employed as purchasing officials, and at present (to your author's knowledge), there is no policing of C.P.M.s. For example, a person may not lose the C.P.M. designation if convicted of a commercial bribery charge. It is to be hoped that at some future date there will be even more recognition of the designation as business leaders learn more about its meaning and as the various associations improve its quality values. However, there is a strong need for an effective monitoring program that will restrict or revoke the designation for those who fail to merit it. This would be a splendid supplement to the program.

Several national purchasing associations have adopted and published codes of ethics, which their members subscribe to and attempt to practice in their daily business routine. These codes have been prepared by practicing purchasing officers and have been kept current by occasional revisions that are dictated by changing business climates. These ethics codes are written for several purposes:

1. To promote efficiency in the purchasing function.

2. To create a business atmosphere where honesty and integrity prevail.

3. To portray a wholesome approach to conducting business transactions and to attempt to dispel the prevailing view that a negativistic attitude surrounds the purchasing function.

4. To discourage attempts of offers of bribes from suppliers by making it most apparent that none will be accepted or tolerated.

5. To provide a guide for good business conduct for the purchasing officer.

It could be said that a purchasing code of ethics is the business expression of the golden rule.

The National Association of Educational Buyers

The Code of Ethics of the National Association of Educational Buyers (N.A.E.B.), an organization composed of college and university purchasing officers, sets forth ethics dealing with company goals, dealings with others, and general association and societal standards. The first two centering on company objectives state:

1. Give first consideration to the objectives and policies of my institution.

2. Strive to obtain the maximum value for each dollar of expenditure.

The third through ninth concern dealing with others:

3. Decline personal gifts or gratuities.

4. Grant all competitive suppliers equal consideration insofar as state or federal statute and institutional policy permit.

5. Conduct business with potential and current suppliers in an atmosphere of good faith, devoid of intentional misrepresentation.

6. Demand honesty in sales representation whether offered through the medium of a verbal or written statement, an advertisement, or a sample of the product. .

7. Receive consent of originator of proprietary ideas and designs before using them for competitive purchasing purposes.

8. Make every reasonable effort to negotiate an equitable and mutually agreeable settlement of any controversy with a supplier; and/or be willing to submit any major controversies to arbitration or other third party review, insofar as the established policies of my institution permit.

9. Accord a prompt and courteous reception insofar as conditions permit to all who call on legitimate business missions.

The last three standards relate to broader matters:

10. Cooperate with trade, industrial and professional associations, and with governmental and private agencies for the purposes of promoting and developing sound business methods.

11. Foster fair, ethical and legal trade practices.

12. Counsel and cooperate with NAEB members and promote a spirit of unity and a keen interest in professional growth among them.[1]

This code was written specifically for purchasing personnel of educational institutions, but the principles enunciated therein are equally applicable to purchasing officers of for-profit organizations. Each ethic contributes to a standard of good conduct that helps provide an ethical business atmosphere. None can be said to prescribe legal duties, and yet in all but Ethic (9) there are legal principles either supporting the ethic or are standing by in the wings as legal deterrents to those who dare to go beyond the proscribed limits.

Ethics (1) and (2) are restatements of an agent's legal duties to the principal. Suppliers' gifts and gratuities mentioned in (3) is a topic important enough to be discussed separately in the two concluding sections of this chapter. However, we do not need to be reminded here how excesses in this type of activity may lead to the criminal penalties associated with commercial bribery and income tax evasion. Granting all competitive suppliers equal consideration as suggested by Ethic (4) reminds us of the Sherman Antitrust Act.

Ethic (5) and (6) warn both the buyer and the seller that deliberate misrepresentation is not tolerated by the law. Suppliers are recognized as having the propensity to "puff their wares" but those who go beyond allowable limits in their sales presentations find the law of warranties and tort law dealing with fraudulent misrepresentation awaiting them. Ethic (7) jogs the buyer's memory that there may be patent or copyright laws protecting the supplier's original design.

Ethic (8) " . . . be willing to submit to arbitration any major controversies" presents a legal controversy in itself. Opinions among the purchasing profession differ widely on this ethic, as salutatory as it may appear at first blush. Those who

---

[1]Reprinted with the permission of the National Association of Educational Buyers, Woodbury, New York.

oppose arbitration point out that if a purchasing officer has gained specific legal rights for the company in the contract negotiations, these rights should be secure. Why should any one right be surrendered if a controversy develops in the purchase and if arbitration is invoked? It has been said often that no one wins in arbitration. The arbitration of a dispute often results in a settlement that represents a compromise of the positions of each party. Any compromise involves the giving up of contract rights by each party, and that results in no one party coming out as winner. Some purchasing officers do not subscribe to this agreement to submit any major controversy to arbitration. State government purchasing officers and their legal counsel particularly object to any agreement to arbitrate controversies. Arbitration cases are not tried in a court of law and the usual legal rules of evidence are not followed closely. Furthermore, certain rights that the state government possesses are not recognized in the informal arbitration processes. Legal counsel for state institutions do not like to see their purchasing officers always agree to arbitration because of this fact.

Those purchasing officers in favor of arbitration point out the time delays and the expense involved in court litigation. They recognize that arbitration is an excellent alternative to litigation. Arbitration is also more in agreement with those purchasing officers who emphasize the importance of good supplier relationships. Rather than take a supplier to a court of law to settle any differences, these buyers prefer to sit down and work it out in an informal type of arbitration.

Cooperation with trade, industrial and professional associations, as suggested by Ethic (10), is proper but too much cooperation again may run afoul of the Sherman Antitrust Act. Ethic (11), "Foster fair, ethical and legal trade practices" is one of the goals of this text on Purchasing Law.

Ethic (12) also has a laudable purpose, but once again the purchasing officer is advised that there are certain legal topics that may be discussed with purchasing peers, and then there are other topics that cannot be tolerated. Ethic (12)—like the other ethics discussed above—may have either a rainbow at the end of the trail or a lawsuit if there are excesses in its usage.

It is hoped that the reader will understand from this brief summary that ethics are not laws in themselves, but that there is a law that is applicable if conformance to the ethical standards is not maintained.

The National Association of Purchasing Management

The code of ethics promulgated by the National Association of Purchasing Management sets forth the following ethical standards. The first four relate primarily to company objectives and require the purchasing manager:

1. To consider, first, the interest of his company in all transactions and to carry out and believe in its established policies.

2. To be receptive to competent counsel from his colleagues and to be guided by such counsel without impairing the dignity and responsibility of his office.

3. To buy without prejudice, seeking to obtain the maximum ultimate value for each dollar of expenditure.

4. To strive consistently for knowledge of the materials and processes of manufacture, and to establish practical methods for the conduct of his office.

Five through eight require him:

5. To subscribe to and work for honesty and truth in buying and selling, and to denounce all forms and manifestations of commercial bribery.

6. To accord a prompt and courteous reception, so far as conditions will permit, to all who call on a legitimate business mission.

7. To respect his obligations and to require that obligations to him and his company be respected, consistent with good business ethics.

8. To avoid sharp practice.

The last two relate to broader responsibilities. He is:

9. To counsel and assist fellow purchasing agents in the performance of their duties, whenever occasion permits.

10. To cooperate with all organizations and individuals engaged in activities designed to enhance the development and standing of purchasing.[2]

It is interesting to note that this list, which was prepared by purchasing experts primarily in the commercial field, is similar to the N.A.E.B. list, which was prepared by purchasing personnel in the not-for-profit educational field. One must conclude that the authors of both codes regarded these factors as those having the greatest importance in the ethical practice of purchasing.

GIFTS FROM SUPPLIERS

The purchasing profession has had a cloud over its head for a long period of time. This cloud is made up of gifts, favors, and gratuities that come from suppliers and are accepted by purchasing personnel. Despite the fact that there are serious questions about the propriety of the acceptance of these gifts, the cloud has per-

---

[2]Reprinted with the permission of the National Association of Purchasing Management, Tempe, Arizona.

sisted. At one time in the history of the purchasing profession, such gifts were looked upon as one of purchasing's perquisites. Acceptances of such "perks" was not considered a violation of any duty of the purchasing officer, heard bandied about as to what constituted the acceptable maximum value of a gift from a supplier. Such phrases as these were used in purchasing circles: "Accept only if it is a reward for past favors," "Accept it in the spirit of the season," "Accept it if it is not intended to influence your future buying habits," "A bottle, not a case," and "If you cannot eat it or drink it within 48 hours, return it." Most suppliers fell into line with the practice, and it became a custom. Gifts became "perks" to be expected, especially during the Christmas season. Specialty companies were organized to select and sell appropriate gifts as presents for suppliers to buy at wholesale prices. One purchasing trade publication ran a survey on the types of gifts being given to buyers. The results of the survey were published so that one and all could see what was the "in" gift for the purchasing officer during the current year. Some suppliers would call the purchasing officers of their best customers to ask what gift they wanted from Santa Claus. This avoided giving a gift that was not needed or that was "something I have always wanted—but not very much." Gift giving and gift receiving became a firmly established custom in most circles.

There were a few companies who told their buyers not to accept gifts from suppliers, and to send out letters a month before Christmas advising suppliers that accepting gifts from suppliers was forbidden by management. This enforced abstinence management policy was not received gracefully by one chief purchasing officer because, at the same time purchasing had to write these no-gift letters to suppliers, his entire purchasing department was busy filling requisitions from their sales department for gifts to be given to the company's customers.

There were also some individual purchasing officers who did not like the idea of accepting gifts from suppliers. They were embarrassed about receiving such presents because of their business relationship. But most of them nevertheless accepted the gifts for fear of insulting the donor if they rejected the favor. It takes a strong will to tell another person that the gift he or she has selected with great care is not acceptable to the donee. Since most of their peers were accepting gifts without question, it might appear prudish to reject it.

Occasional questions about the propriety of a gift were raised if the gift came from a prospective supplier who had not done any business with the purchasing officer. This made it rather obvious that the intent of the gift was to buy some business, and there was concern that the gift might be regarded as a bribe. Questions were also raised by some purchasing officers if the value of a gift seemed excessive. A gift considered to be *too expensive* might be an indication that the buyer had not done the proper amount of work at the bargaining table and was paying too much for the supplier's product. The expensive gift could be a payoff for a lucrative piece of business. This gave the purchasing officer some concern because it could be regarded as a bribe to induce the continuation of the "honeymoon contract." A too-expensive gift that would be considered a bribe was never clearly defined. The loose talk about "a bottle but not a case" came close to being the guideline, but no one would ever say whether the line should be drawn at 2 or 11 bottles—or at any other quantity.

In legal terms, the amount or value passing from the supplier to the buyer, practically, does not distinguish between a gift and a bribe. The common law regard bribery as the giving or receiving of anything of value with the intent to influence the performance of an official act or duty by a government officer. It was the intent of the gift, and not the value, that marked the difference. A payment to a traffic policeman to induce him not to issue a traffic summons for doing 65 miles per hour in a 40-mile zone is a bribe. The policeman's duty is to give you a citation for violating the law, and your offer of a payment is intended to deter that officer from doing his job. But suppose this same traffic officer returned the wallet that you left in his car when you got out your driver's license while he was writing your ticket. You are grateful for the return of your wallet because it had some valuable papers in it, and you offer him a reward. Although the policeman would not accept the reward, you were not guilty of offering him a bribe because the intent of your payment was to say "thanks" for a kind favor and not to deter him from doing his job.

Intent then distinguished a gift from a bribe. When your supplier offers you a gift, is it a reward for past favors performed, or is it intended to help him get the next order from you? If it is the latter, it is a bribe, because bribery laws have been extended to include the acts of both public agency and private corporate officials. (No longer is a bribe reserved exclusively for government officials.) If it is a reward for past favors, it is a true gift, unless the gift is made under an agreement with the supplier that it would be forthcoming if the supplier received a specified contract, or some similar arrangement. The line of demarcation between a gift and a bribe is very fine in some situations.

It is apparent that the manner in which the acceptance of a gift from a supplier to a purchasing officer can be interpreted has a wide range of possibilities. It could be regarded as

1. an accepted commercial custom,

2. a practice subject to one's own moral values,

3. a questionable ethical practice,

4. a violation of professional standards,

5. a breach of the agency contract,

6. a misdemeanor, or

7. a felony.

Where any particular gift might fall on this scale of 1 to 7 depends upon many factors, including the intent of the supplier giving the gift and the understanding (or intent) of the purchasing officer who accepts it. *Intent* is a very intangible commodity, difficult to interpret precisely, and much more difficult to understand. Part of its vagueness can be attributed to the different groups of people that might apply it. The supplier giving the gift and the purchasing officer accepting it may place the action at 1 or 2 on the scale. The supplier's competitors will surely rate it 6 or 7. Public reaction would probably be higher than lower on the scale.

There was an apparent reluctance on the part of the purchasing profession to establish a firm ethical standard regarding suppliers' gifts. This can be partially explained by the fact that it was a fairly well-established commercial custom. There may also have been some feeling too of "let us not kill the goose that laid the golden egg." In any event, in 1959 the National Association of Purchasing Management (it was then known as the National Association of Purchasing Agents) adopted and promulgated the code of ethics that was previously reported in this chapter. The fifth ethic on their list concludes with the following phrase: " . . . and to denounce all forms and manifestations of commercial bribery." This could be more positively phrased for those who seek to eliminate the supplier gift problem completely.

The N.A.E.B. published its code of ethics shortly thereafter. This group addressed the gift problem more directly, but fell short of eliminating the custom in its original statement: "To decline personal gifts and gratuities which might in any way influence the purchase of materials." This expression states clearly that a purchasing officer may retain a gift from a supplier if it does not influence the purchase of materials. Both this code and that of the National Association of Purchasing Management reflect the prevailing view of purchasing personnel at the time they were published.

Bribery and the Law

The State of New York, meanwhile, put some rather clear legal definitions of commercial bribery in its laws. Section 439 of the 1959 Penal Laws read in part as follows:

> An agent, who being authorized to procure materials, supplies, or other merchandise either by purchase or contract for his principal, receives directly, or indirectly, for himself or for another, a commission, discount, gift, gratuity or bonus from the person who makes such sale or contract, is guilty of a misdemeanor.

Section 439 was a tough law. Any "gift," by whatever name one chose to call it, passing from a supplier to a purchasing agent was outlawed. The intent of the gift was not germane. The agent receiving a gift from a supplier was guilty of a misdemeanor. There was no ambiguity about the meaning of this law. Even the allowance of a personal discount on the purchase of the supplier's product fell into its purview. And it made no difference if the discount was given to the spouse or the mother-in-law of the purchasing officer. It covered all angles of any favor. Section 439 is symptomatic of what can be done if the public decides that the receiving of gifts—and the giving of them—is a commercial custom that must be eliminated. The law was subsequently amended and is reported, as amended, later in this chapter.

The N.A.E.B. took a giant step forward in 1979 when it amended the ethic to read: "Decline personal gifts and gratuities." There is no ambiguity in this wording. A professional purchasing officer of a member institution is expected to decline any gift offered by a supplier, regardless of the reason, purpose, or intent of the gift. The association is to be commended for this bold step forward to professionalism.

Some commercial organizations have also taken firm steps to eliminate the practice completely. Here is a quote from a publication for the employees of one of America's largest corporations on the subject of ethical responsibilities:

> Neither you, nor any member of your family, may solicit or accept from a supplier money or a gift that may reasonably be construed as having any connection with our company's business relationship. Gifts include not just material goods but services and discounts on personal purchases of goods and services. If you are offered money or a gift, or if one arrives at your home or office, tell your manager right away. Appropriate arrangements will be made to return or dispose of what has been received, and the supplier will be reminded of our company's gift policy.[3]

The same company sends the following letter to each new supplier:

> We welcome you as a supplier.
>
> As a new supplier you should be aware of a principle we think has been helpful to all concerned. No employee or member of his or her family may accept a gift or a gratuity from a supplier or prospective supplier. This supports our objective that our employees be unbiased in their business relationships with our suppliers and avoid even an appearance of partiality.
>
> I will appreciate your telling appropriate people in your organization our position regarding gifts and gratuities to preclude the possibility of any offers. We consider total compliance with this request an

---

[3]Reprinted with the permission of the International Business Machines Corporation from *Business Conduct Guidelines.*

essential element of our business relationship.

Thank you for your interest in our company. We look forward to a mutually advantageous business relationship.

These are straightforward approaches that clear the air on the topic. It allows no room for interpretation on how to get around the policy. It even provides the procedure to follow if some errant supplier attempts to circumvent the company policy. As more and more organizations join in this approach, and, as the major professional associations take a firm stand, the cloud that has long hovered over purchasing's head will be dispelled. "No suppliers' gifts accepted here" is the proper ethical standard for purchasing officers. When this becomes a uniform policy, purchasing will have made another step toward professionalism. And it will be a major step.

If the purchasing profession does not voluntarily do this, we will see more laws being passed, such as the Bank Bribery Amendment to the Program Fraud and Bribery Section, Chapter 31 of Title 18 of the United States Code. This amendment was passed by the United States Congress late in 1984. Stripping the amendment of much of its detail, it loosely reads:

> Whoever being an officer, director, employee, or agent of any financial institution directly or indirectly asks, demands, seeks, accepts, receives, or agrees to receive anything of value for himself or any other person from any person for or in connection with any business of such financial institution
> or
> Whoever directly or indirectly gives, offers, or promises anything of value to any officer, director, employee or agent of any financial institution for or in connection with any business of such financial institution . . . shall be fined not more than $5000 or three times the value of anything offered, asked, given, received or agreed to be given or received, whichever is the greater or imprisoned not more than 5 years, or both . . .
> . . . but if the value of anything offered, asked, given, received or agreed to be given or received does not exceed $100, shall be fined not more than $1000 or imprisoned not more than 1 year, or both.

One gets the impression from this law that Congress wants to stop every type of gift giving and receiving between suppliers and bank purchasing officers. The law implies that if a supplier takes a bank purchasing officer to lunch, both he and the purchasing officer are risking a $1000 fine and a year in jail. Such penalties make the lunch expensive!

***Nota Bene* to the Purchasing Officer.** There may be those who continue to believe there is nothing wrong in accepting gifts and gratuities from suppliers. They are probably correct in the assumption that there is nothing *legally* wrong in accepting modest handouts. Also, some distinction may be made between gifts and items of advertising of modest value (e.g., calendars). In fact the present Internal Revenue Code gives some degree of credence to any personal gift to a customer of $25 or less by allowing the supplier to deduct up to that sum as an expense of doing business. But the damage purchasing personnel do to their professional status by accepting these gratuities is irreparable. Purchasing officers need to take an affirmative stand on eliminating this nonprofessional practice. We should recognize that a *gratuity* is another word for a tip. Tips are for waiters, waitresses, taxicab drivers and coatroom attendants. Tips have no place in the purchasing profession. Once and for all time the words should be explicit, succinct, loud and clear—*no gifts accepted here!*

DELIBERATE VIOLATIONS OF THE LAW

A text addressed to professional purchasing personnel should not be burdened with a discussion of the illegal activities of a few of its members. This section is tucked in at the end of this chapter on ethics to give the reader the assurance that law enforcement agencies are doing their part to weed out nonprofessionals from our ranks. Most states now have commercial bribery statutes that make it a misdemeanor or a felony to give or receive a bribe. An edited version of New York State's section 180.05 in the Penal Laws entitled "Commercial Bribe Receiving" is:

> An agent . . . is guilty of commercial bribe receiving when without the consent of the . . . principal, he solicits, accepts or agrees to accept any benefit from another person upon an agreement or understanding that such benefit will influence his conduct in relation to his principal's affairs.

You will note that there must be *intent* to influence conduct to constitute a bribe. The crime is considered a Class B misdemeanor, which means that a conviction could lead to a sentence of imprisonment of from three months to one year. (Any crime that carries a penalty of imprisonment for more than one year is a felony.)

There is a similar statute for commercial bribing in section 180.00 for those who dare to corrupt a purchasing officer:

> A person is guilty of commercial bribing when he confers, or offers or agrees to confer, any benefit upon any . . . agent ... without the consent . . . principal, with intent to influence his conduct in relation to his . . . principal's affairs.

Some comments have been made that these commercial bribery statutes are not enforced to any great extent, and also that they have been proven to be rather ineffective in curbing abuses. However, there are other avenues open to law enforcement officers to bring penalties upon the heads of those who dare to go to excesses in this type of activity. The law enforcers are not dependent solely on commercial bribery statutes. A former purchasing agent of a large manufacturing company received a jail term of 177 days and a $5000 fine, according to *The Wall Street Journal*[4] for taking kickbacks from suppliers. The conviction was based upon 39 counts of using the mails to defraud. *The New York Times*[5] reported that a former meat purchasing agent of a supermarket chain was found guilty of income tax evasion for failing to report cash kickbacks as income on his federal income tax return. These cases illustrate that there are other laws that may step in to assist in prosecuting those who violate their duty of loyalty as an agent.

It is a sad commentary on the purchasing profession that there are those who invite criminal liabilities by their deliberate, illegal activities. Each member of the profession must take an active and positive position against such self-inflicted criminal liabilities, which cast a bad name on purchasing.

NEW BUSINESS ETHICS

Although ethics and law are sometimes thought to be separate, commercial law incorporates some business ethics and makes them enforceable. For the purchasing agent who is faced with unethical action by the other party to the contract, he or she may want to utilize the law in this regard.

There is a new "business ethic" which is made a part of the Uniform Commercial Code by virtue of several major principles:

1. The ban against unconscionable clauses and conduct

2. The requirement of good faith

3. Use of custom and trade usage of decent dealers

These ethics placed in the Code are enforceable. Indeed, there have been a number of case decisions written on them. In some cases, as mentioned shortly, they have not only provided for alteration or voiding of an unfair contract provision, but for very substantial compensatory and punitive damages as well.

PROHIBITING UNCONSCIONABLE CONTRACTS AND CLAUSES

The principle prohibiting unconscionable contracts and clauses is another extremely important one that runs throughout purchasing and commercial law.

---

[4]*The Wall Street Journal*, February 27, 1975. Reprinted by permission of *The Wall Street Journal*, and Dow Jones & Company, Inc., 1975. All rights reserved.
[5]*The New York Times*, January 10, 1975.

Unprecedented in terms of statutory law, the Uniform Commercial Code contains a specific section, Section 2-302, dealing with unconscionability, which has a general application. To properly understand this section its modern origins should be briefly noted. It was a response to one-sided, harsh types of contracts, whether between businesspeople or between a business and a consumer.

At the turn of the twentieth century, legal commentators began to note that many contracts were in fact very one-sided and that the terms were not yet negotiated by both parties. The phrase "contract of adhesion" means simply that one party does not, in reality, have a chance to bargain on the various terms but must simply adhere to the contract furnished to him by the other party. These phenomena became acknowledged in academic circles but did not receive significant recognition in the courts.

In the meantime, on a more general basis, some courts attempted to alleviate situations in which strict enforcement of a contract would have a harsh and unconscionable effect. In many instances, this could be accomplished by finding that a particular term of the contract did not mean what it literally seemed to mean.

It is in this overall setting that the Code provision was drafted. Section 2-302 of the Uniform Commercial Code provides that a court may refuse to enforce an unconscionable aspect of an original agreement The court may achieve this result in one of several ways:

1. It may refuse to enforce the entire agreement if this seems necessary or desirable.

2. Or it may simply enforce the contractual arrangement without the unconscionable aspect.

3. In still other cases, a court may simply limit the application of the clause or agreement that it feels is covered by this provision in any manner so as to avoid an unconscionable result.

This new approach is illustrated by the text in Section 2-302 dealing with the proof of unconscionability. A court is required to hear evidence as to the "commercial setting, purposes and effects" of the contract in making its determination. In this manner, a court may consider the overall setting, the expectations of the parties found in the purpose of the agreement, and the effect that enforcement would have. It seems clear that a number of factors will be brought into evidence whenever the point of unconscionability is raised.

The concept of unconscionability rests primarily upon a test of one-sidedness in the sense both of oppression and unfair surprise. These criteria of one-sidedness or unconscionability, even though admittedly difficult to define, place emphasis upon the overall setting and on the particular relationship of the parties.

The element of oppression takes into account the overall setting in a number of ways. Oppression may be found in factors such as one party's control of bargaining power. It may relate to the extent to which a party has control of the particular contract terms by the use of standardized contracts. Such contracts used throughout a particular industry may be oppressive and limit the other party's freedom of contract. For example, monopolistic use of disclaimers by the auto industry is evidence of oppressiveness that is against public policy and unconscionable. While it is clear that one-sided clauses in standardized contracts used in a number of types of sales may restrict any real freedom of contracting and are unconscionable, attorneys have not yet utilized the concept of unconscionability in as many types of contractual relationships as they might.

It may be found that one party has control over the particular bargaining situation and includes one-sided terms with harsh results even though it is not an "industry-wide" clause. Should a party be held to this type of clause? While it is true that he might be able to find a seller who would not demand such a clause, should he be forced to search out such a seller or be held to the one-sided term? As a realistic matter, he often cannot do this and his freedom of contract is severely limited. In many situations of this type there may be unconscionability because of oppression. In such situations, of course, there is often also unfair surprise and unconscionability may be found on either basis alone.

Unfair Surprise

The other primary criterion for determining unconscionability is "unfair surprise." This also rests upon a consideration of the overall setting and the relationship of the parties. Where one of the parties is unfairly surprised in some aspect of the contractual relationship, then that part of the contractual relationship may be considered unconscionable. In looking to this criterion, many elements of the setting must be taken into account. One of these, of course, is the manifestation of the agreement and the form in which it is embodied. Where there is a writing, which is often the case, the question whether it is a form contract or one filled out stage by stage by the parties themselves may make a difference. The "understandability" of the language is also important. Is the language comprehended by the individual in the relationship, or is the contract so phrased that it is obscure or unclear? The degree to which vital terms are apparent may also make a difference. Are they hidden or are they placed in such a position in the overall form of printed or typed sentences so as to be easily missed?

A serious question was asked by Karl Llewellyn, whether "unconscionability" was too vague and how it would be defined by courts. It is not defined in the Code. The Chief Reporter and draftsman of the Code gave an interesting answer:

Business lawyers tend to draft to the edge of the possible. Any engi-

neer makes his construction with a wide margin of safety, so that he
knows for sure that he is getting what he is gunning for. The practice
of business lawyers has been, however—it has grown to be so in the
course of time—to draft, as I said before, to the edge of the
possible . . .

Let me rapidly state that I do not find that this is desired by the
business lawyers' clients. In all the time that I have been working on
this Code, and before, one of the more striking phenomena has been
to me that the lawyers insist on having all kinds of things that their
clients don't want at all

Continuing in the New York Law Revision Commission Hearings:

Llewellyn did state that he felt the definition of unconscionability
would come to be established through case law precedent. If the court
finds the contract or any clause of the contract to be unconscionable,
it may refuse to enforce the contract as if the stricken clauses had
never existed. That is Court action, and it is reversible . . . and it
makes precedents and guides, he said.

Since that time there have been a number of court decisions on "precedent."
On one hand, the definition of unconscionability is still not as clear as one might
like for the purpose of certainty. In some similar situations, involving similar contract clauses and settings, courts have come out with conflicting results. On the
other hand, the courts have come up with a common theme—there are two types
of unconscionability: one is substantive and the other is procedural.

Procedural "surprise" involves the extent to which the supposedly agreed-
upon terms of the bargain are hidden in a printed form drafted by the party seeking to enforce the disputed terms. Characteristically, the form contract is drafted
by the party with the superior bargaining position.

Substantive unconscionability is generally found in "overly harsh" or "one-
sided" results. Often there is not only a one-sided result, but also an absence of
reasonable justification for it.

Case Examples of Unconscionability

In a famous case, *A & M Produce Co. v. FMC Corporation,*[6] a produce company
purchased machinery which turned out to be very inadequate. The contract contained a disclaimer of warranty clause in bold print and a disclaimer of consequential damages in small print.

After discussion of the unconscionability doctrine, the court applied it to
the facts. Procedural unconscionability was found in the long preprinted form
with no suggestion to read the back. Oppressiveness was found in the "not bar-

---

[6]*A & M Produce Co. v. FMC Corporation,* 186 Cal. Rpts 114, 135 Cal. Agy 3d 473 (1982).

gained for" terms which took away any real remedy. The court upheld the lower court determination of unconscionability.

Both buyer and seller were businesses; they were in a different category as to size. Application of unconscionability to contracts between businesses is less frequent, but still quite proper. Of course, where they are of similar size, there is sometimes more of a chance to "bargain" on the various terms, which may then reflect on allocation of risks the parties desire. But other times there may be both procedural and substantive unconscionability even between businesses in settings where there is "unfair surprise" or no bargaining takes place. The court looks to reasonableness in judging terms. A business using forms ought to be sure its customers understand the terms using fair and reasonable terms; the business will avoid unfair surprise.

An atmosphere of haste and pressure in contracting between businesses can bring procedural unconscionability into play. In another case, *Industralease Automated & Scientific Equipt. Corp. v R.M.E. Enterprises, Inc.,*[7] the court considered the issue of whether disclaimers of express or implied warranties are unconscionable under circumstances where the equipment fails to operate. The buyer, a picnic grove owner-operator, entered into a lease for the use of rubbish incinerators. Seller subsequently informed defendant that the initial lease was "no good" and asked that he sign "new papers." The new lease contained an unqualified disclaimer of express and implied warranties. The incinerators were delivered and installed properly but did not work. Buyer demanded removal of the incinerators from his property, but the seller refused to accede and insisted upon timely receipt of the monthly payments. The trial court held that the disclaimer was not unconscionable as a matter of law. On appeal, the court found that the new contract which eliminated the warranties was entered into under an "atmosphere of haste and pressure" which was "clearly pervasive." The court also found that since the summer season for defendant's operations had already begun, defendant was clearly disadvantaged at this point in the bargaining. The court held that the disclaimer of warranties was unconscionable under the circumstances and that the express warranties to the defendant concerning the incinerators had been breached.

Construction Associates, Inc. v. Fargo Water Equipment Co.[8] demonstrates both procedural and substantive unconscionability. J-M Pipe had sold pipe to Fargo Water Equipment under a contract limiting the remedies available upon breach of its warranty and excluding liability for consequential damages. Fargo in turn sold the pipe to Construction Associates who was unaware of this dis-

---

[7] *Industralease Automated & Scientific Equipt. Corp. v. R.M.E. Enterprises, Inc.,* 396 N.Y.S 2d 427 (1977).
[8] *Construction Associates, Inc. v.. Fargo Water Equipment Co.,* 446 No.W.2d 237.

claimer. The pipe eventually developed several leaks and a trial court awarded Construction Associates expenses for repair.

When J-M Pipe appealed, the court held that the clause limiting remedies was procedurally unconscionable because J-M Pipe, a large, international conglomerate, had taken advantage of its superior bargaining power over Construction Associates, a small, local company. Additionally, the clause was substantively unconscionable because it left the nonbreaching party with no effective remedy.

In many cases, the two criteria of oppression and unfair surprise are both present and intertwined. Due to the general problem of insufficient time and other factors, an individual may not have the opportunity to read fully a printed contract of sale. However, even if he were to read it, he may not be able to understand it or to comprehend fully its legal effects. Because the contractual limitations or disclaimers represent an undesirable or disagreeable aspect of the relationship from a public relations viewpoint, they are not fully explained or made fully comprehensible; hence they are not used in the advertising or sales promotions. Even if the buyer were to read and understand these terms, since they may be of a standardized nature for the particular product or type of product involved, there is no real freedom to negotiate terms or to appreciate fully their meaning. In setting forth these criteria, the Code is laying down general tenets that must be viewed in light of the overall setting and the particular relationship of the parties involved.

Imposing a New Business Ethic

It may be said that the law requires the parties to act with a certain minimal ethical conduct and responsibility. This "new business ethic," which is imposed and which is given emphasis through the unconscionability section, means in some cases that an entire industry, from manufacturers to dealers, must see that a reasonable and fair bargain exists and that no unconscionability is present. It may also mean that a manufacturer must see that those who represent the firm act within this new positive ethic. In terms of the relationship of the parties, positive ethical responsibilities are also quite apparent. There is an ethical duty upon those who draft contracts to make them clearly understandable and to make important aspects conspicuous. Nevertheless, this is not in itself sufficient to satisfy the ethical duty, but it represents only one portion of "fair dealing." It is incumbent upon those selling a product to be sure that the individual knows these limitations and appreciates them. Again the ethical duty of fair dealing and the ethical duty of nonoppression are intertwined, and absolute limitations may be prohibited in light of the overall setting.

Section 2-302 is phrased in terms of unconscionability at the time of the making of a contract. A question may then be presented whether a court should enforce a contract even though the enforcement would be unconscionable in light of subsequent factors. To a certain extent, this is not as serious a problem as it might initially seem to be. For one thing, some of the sections or principles relating to excuse of performance may be applicable. A court may also find, without too much difficulty in some cases, that a contract was unconscionable at its making from its operation in particular circumstances. Further, the concept of good faith may be used in that an unconscionable enforcement might be deemed to be an enforcement that is not in good faith. Although this requirement of unconscionability at the time of the making of a contract raises serious issues, in many cases an unconscionable contract, when enforced, will contain at least some element of unconscionability in its making. Further, the question of unconscionability in the making must be viewed in terms of what may happen with the ultimate enforcement. The emphasis on the formation stage is directed primarily toward nonintervention in such matters as changing economic factors, which may be part of the legitimate business risk of supply and demand knowingly undertaken by the parties.

REQUIRING GOOD FAITH IN ALL TRANSACTIONS

Another basic principle running throughout the Code is the requirement of good faith in all transactions. The Uniform Commercial Code gives special emphasis to the concept of good faith by providing both expressly and impliedly for it throughout the entire code. Section 1-203, Obligation of Good Faith, states:

> Every contract or duty within this act imposes an obligation of good
> faith in its performance or enforcement.

It is part of the new business ethic that permeates all commercial areas covered by the Code. In sales and contract areas, however, it assumes major significance.

While good faith may be found in certain aspects of the law, such as those relating to good faith purchasers and holders in due course, it has not served as a generally recognized legal requirement in the contract setting. It may be found to exist, however, in an indirect manner under various theories in some special situations. For example, where good faith has been so lacking in an intentional and positive misrepresentation as to the essential aspect of an agreement, then it may be said that the fraud involved makes the contract voidable. Or if good faith is lacking in the sense that misrepresentation occurs, the theory of misrepresentation may be applicable.

Some contract doctrines also have brought about similar results. In some situations, where there is a lack of good faith on the part of one of the parties, the doctrine of duress or the doctrine of mistake may alleviate the situation. Nevertheless, these theories have been applied in relatively extreme situations, not in the ordinary setting. Good faith in the performance of obligations also has been implied by a small number of courts to satisfy the requirement of consideration. Good faith performance also has been injected into the contract relationship as an implied promise. The use of moral obligation as an element of consideration has existed in only a few extreme cases, and even if viewed as containing an element of good faith, such obligation is not as comprehensive as the good faith that is to permeate a transaction under the Code.

While it is true that some disguised traces of the good faith concept have existed in contract and commercial law settings, as well as in special status situations such as good faith purchases, its introduction into the statutory law by the Code represents a significant change. Since the direct assertion of good faith as a requirement is basically new, it represents a major change within the new conceptual framework for both contract and commercial law.

Section 1-203, governing all other sections of the code, expressly adopts the obligation of good faith: "Every contract or duty within this Act imposes an obligation of good faith in its performance or enforcement." It was the intention of the drafters that this provision be construed broadly. After listing certain situations in which good faith was especially applicable, the drafters pointed out that "the concept . . . is broader than any of these illustrations and applies generally . . . *to the performance or enforcement of every contract or duty within this Act.*"

In showing the presence or absence of good faith, the comment states that the section is to be implemented by Section 1-205 dealing with usage of trade and course of dealing. This latter section places emphasis upon factors found in the overall setting. A usage of trade may be found in any practice or method of dealing that is regularly observed in a particular place or trade so as to give rise to an expectation that it will be observed in individual transactions. The course of dealing looks to the relationship of the parties and to any sequence of previous conduct between them that may be regarded as part of the basis for their understanding.

Distinction Between Merchants and Nonmerchants

The viewing of good faith in terms of the relationship of the parties may be further seen by the distinction between merchants and nonmerchants. This is mentioned in the comments of the general section relating to the obligation of good faith and is made more explicit by reference to the definitional section. For the nonmerchant, the standard in Section 1-201(19) is primarily one of "honesty in fact." For the merchant, however, not only is "honesty in fact" required, but also an "observance of reasonable commercial standards of fair dealing in the trade." In making this distinction, the Code is placing emphasis upon the abilities of the parties and the ethical responsibilities that each may be expected to undertake.

While this general obligation of good faith is placed into the law and is part of every setting and relationship, it is emphasized especially in certain situations. For example, it is expressly mentioned in relation to the modifications of contracts, primarily because it is recognized that these types of settings are such that one party may be tempted to operate in an unethical way without good faith. Likewise, where good faith is especially important due to the power of one party over the other, as it is in a long-term contract specifying the price, the requirement of good faith is specifically mentioned in Section 2-305. Other than the good faith requirements for bona fide purchasers, buyers in the ordinary course of business, in Section 1-201 or holder in due course, in Section 3-302 specific reference made either in the text or in the comments involves facets of performance or enforcement. Good faith must be exercised in accelerating payment, in Section 1-208 in performing requirements contracts in Section 2-306. Again it should be noted that these situations are viewed in terms of the particular setting and the relationship of the parties.

Honesty in Fact

Certain problems of a definitional nature, however, may ensue from the good faith requirement. The basic test of good faith, "honesty in fact" set forth in Section 1-201(19), presents a number of problems. To a large extent, it is subjective in nature. Nevertheless, viewing it in this manner does not clearly define its nature. Is the test that the individual does not feel a sense of dishonesty or guilt? Or is it that he uses certain methods with the knowledge that they do not meet societal norms? In addition, it would seem that evaluation of whether the standard is met may be the result of certain objective factors. For one thing, lack of "honesty in fact" must be determined objectively by the fact-finder in each case. This means, in effect, that the fact-finder will be looking to what he, if a judge, or they, if a jury, think the individual's state of mind is at any given point in the transaction. Also, when the fact-finder uses his judgment to determine as to whether a party's state of mind is one that constitutes "honesty in fact," he may define honesty in accordance with his own ethical standards. In this latter way, another thread of objectiveness is woven into what is primarily termed a subjective standard. In weaving this thread, the fact-finder may also be influenced by varying community standards of what does or does not constitute "dishonesty." Nevertheless, a subjective type of "honesty in fact" is a viable standard despite the issues that may be raised concerning it. Although the determination of good faith in the conduct of a sales contract is not an area in which much experience has been amassed, it does not present insoluble problems.

Reasonable Commercial Standards

The standard of good faith in Section 2-103(1)(b) required of one who is defined by the Code as a merchant in Section 2-104 may also create certain practical problems. Several questions immediately arise. By what criteria are "reasonable commercial standards" to be ascertained? For in some instances, what seems reasonable to one individual in a commercial setting may seem unreasonable to another. To one small group of businesspeople, a particular practice might seem to be reasonable; to others in the community, it might not. In addition, there is a question concerning the degree or scope that should be permitted to business judgment in determining what is a reasonable method. In addition to the problems of individual differences, if the guidelines of a group concerning the scope of permissible conduct are local and differ from those having a more national foundation, by which is the standard to be measured? There may be questions concerning what persons or groups in a particular community are to be considered in setting the standard.

Even though numerous problems arise from the use of the term "reasonable commercial standards," the application of such standards maybe feasible. Evidence of commercial standards and business practices may be obtained through the testimony of those engaged in a particular business. Thus, if a practice is widely accepted, a failure to follow it may indicate a failure to meet "reasonable business standards." This may be especially true in a business setting where each party seeks to maximize its own advantages within reasonable limits of conduct. Still, the question of reasonableness will depend upon testimony concerning what is practical in situations such as those found in the particular case before the fact-finder. In any event, it should be emphasized that it will be important for the practitioner to place emphasis upon factors relating to the overall setting and the particular relationship of the parties.

Fair Dealing

Another aspect of the good faith standard that is imposed upon those falling within the broad classification of merchants is that of "fair dealing." This aspect of the good faith standard may also cause certain problems of a definitional nature, especially in a business setting where a certain "give and take" is often considered permissible. Since a certain amount of "praising" or "overselling" of a product or opinions relating to its desirability may be expected and since a certain amount of inspection and caution on the part of the buyer may be standard in some settings, the problem of "fair dealing" is further complicated. Nevertheless, it is increasingly recognized that the old doctrine of caveat emptor should not predominate in a society where there is an inadequacy of skill, knowledge, and time to inspect the ever-growing number of complex products. Then, too, it is recognized in some situations that the exaggeration or the misrepresentation of a product, even in the form of an opinion, may be deceptive.

Despite the many issues that arise from a determination of "fair dealing" and its many intricacies, it can be made a viable concept. In applying it, one must recognize that it is part of the ethical standard found in the new conceptualism of commercial law. Emphasis, therefore, must be placed upon a number of pertinent factors in the overall setting, including not only general practices, but also the particular market conditions and the opportunities for fair conduct. Similarly, the relationship of the parties, including any inequality in knowledge or skill, should be considered in determining whether there has been fair dealing.

Making the Contract

It should be noted that the general principle of good faith, set forth in Section 1-203 of the Code, is in terms of the performance or enforcement of the contract. This may raise certain questions as to matters related to good faith in the making of the contract. It may appear on the surface that good faith in the making of the contract is not necessary, since only the good faith in performance and enforcement of the contract obligation is mentioned. Indeed, this argument may be made by some when it is asserted that there was a lack of good faith in the making of the contract. It would, however, be strange if the drafters should exempt the entire making of the contract from any requirements of a business ethic or good faith.

It should also be noted that the concept prohibiting unconscionable contracts and clauses is applied to the making stage of the contractual relationship. This means that in many instances where a lack of good faith is evinced by a failure to point out fine print clauses or the use of oppressive clauses in the making of the contract, the principle of unconscionability may serve somewhat the same role that the principle of good faith serves. In essence, the contract lacking good faith in the making may well be unenforceable because there has been unconscionability in the making of it.

It also may be argued that the contract where there is a failure of good faith in the making is not enforceable, since this would be a failure of good faith in the enforcement. While it may be asserted that, had the drafters so intended, they would have included the term "making" in the good faith provision, a serious question is raised by this point. If there has been actual bad faith in the making of a contract with the intent to later enforce it if necessary, has there been a failure of good faith in the performance of the contract and its later enforcement? Is it feasible to separate the transaction into various stages when bad faith has permeated it? It would seem quite possible to argue that in cases of bad faith in the making of the contract, when enforcement of those rights is anticipated, that there is actually a type of bad faith running throughout it that carries through in the enforcement of the contract itself. Also the requirement of "fair dealing" just discussed may bring good faith into the making of the contract stage. It seems unfortunate that some of these problems are not dealt with in a more direct and effective manner in the Uniform Commercial Code.

EMPHASIZING DECENCY IN TRADE TRANSACTIONS

The legally enforceable "new business ethic" of the Uniform Commercial Code is implemented further by the emphasis on custom and trade usages which are automatically made a part of every agreement under Sections 1-201(3) and 1-205. The drafters have emphasized that only ethical trade usages are applicable. It is noted in Comment 5 to Section 1-205:

> Under the requirement of subsection (2) full recognition is thus available for new usages and for usages currently observed by the great majority of decent dealers, even though dissidents ready to cut corners do not agree.

Thus the element of decency and fairness again becomes relevant.

CODE OF ETHICS FOR DOING BUSINESS ABROAD

Those who plan to conduct business in a foreign country may in the near future be asked to adhere to a corporate code.

President Clinton's administration has been in contact with businesses and Congress about putting in place a voluntary code of conduct that would be used to guide the efforts of American companies doing business outside the borders. A sample draft code asks companies, among other things, to avoid using child labor and to have respect for collective bargaining.

Clinton broached the idea of drafting a code for doing business overseas in May 1994 when he decided to renew most-favored-nation trading status for China. The five basic principles that were included in a draft code called for:

1. having a safe workplace;

2. practicing fair employment procedures (including not having children as part of the labor force);

3. protecting the environment;

4. encouraging freedom of expression;

5. complying with U.S. laws in the prohibition of illicit payments.

It should be noted that the document as it stands would not be mandatory, but is intended to be voluntary.

In addition to the broad principles mentioned, and specific prohibitions of the Federal Corrupt Practices Act discussed shortly, general ethical considerations as to the giving and receiving of gifts are also applicable. Although the matter of gifts has been discussed, generally, the problem is compounded when one is doing business with persons abroad because of several factors.

Sometimes persons abroad expect some gift as a part of their overall cultural and traditional backgrounds. Indeed, in some cultures some gifts are expected in the development of friendship or business relationships. In such a setting the failure to give a gift may be viewed as conveying the opposite attitude. It could even be considered as a matter of rudeness or disrespect as well as possibly ignorance.

Another problem is that the competing companies from other countries may be giving gifts and receiving them as well. In such a context one is at a competitive disadvantage in doing business. Of course, one should not engage in bribery or any violation of the Federal Corrupt Practices Act. But outside this limitation some giving and receiving of very modest and inexpensive souvenirs may be almost a necessity.

To some extent this problem may be avoided by careful planning in advance. The giving and receiving of small souvenirs in the beginning of the business relationship may be quite appropriate. These need not be very large to satisfy this requirement and should be in the nature of small souvenirs. Another possibility of further establishing a good business relationship may be to sponsor in whole or in part a trip by the person with whom one is doing business. This trip may be for the purpose of working out and establishing a further basis for business relationships and terms. It may also be for giving the other party a greater familiarity with the particular needs of the purchasing manager and his company and of the products which it makes or deals with. Trips with legitimate purposes may engender far more respect and gratefulness than gifts would ever do.

FOREIGN CORRUPT PRACTICES ACT

The Foreign Corrupt Practices Act was passed in 1977 to prohibit certain payments to foreign officials, made directly or through third parties, which are more commonly referred to as bribes or corrupt payments. During the Watergate investigations of payments to U.S. political candidates, it was discovered that numerous corporate political slush funds to foreign officials evaded normal accounting controls. Congress responded quickly by passing the Act. The U.S. is the only nation in the world that prohibits its domestic corporations from bribing another country's public servants.

The original 1977 Act included only three substantive sections. One established accounting standards which would disclose foreign payments. The other two governed payments to foreign officials and to "other" persons, who "knew or had reason to know" the payments would be passed on to a foreign official. The law contained no definitions and only a brief exclusion for payments that were "ministerial" in nature. The so-called "grease" payments often needed to pass goods through customs were allowed. The law was ambiguous, and U.S. business requested that guidelines be issued. None were forthcoming.

Continued pressure from U.S. business finally brought about the 1988 trade law which substitutes the "reason to know" language for a requirement that any payment to a third person be made "knowing that" it would be passed on to a foreign official. But new definition provisions" state that "knowing" may well include reason to know. Having "a firm belief" or being "aware" is sufficient to constitute "knowing."

Another important addition is the further clarification of permissible "grease" payments. Payments are allowed for a "routine government action," which includes obtaining permits to do business, processing papers, providing certain routine services such as police protection or telephone or power, and "actions of a similar nature." But it does not include any decision by a foreign official regarding new business or retaining old business, decisions which are more than merely routine government actions.

The law further includes an affirmative defense for several payments not prohibited. They include payments permissible under the written laws of the other nation, and reasonable and bona fide expenditures such as travel and lodging if related to the promotion or performance of the contract. The FCPA in 1988 also included some clarification of the accounting provisions.

In addition, what was known as the Eckhardt provision was removed in 1988, which prohibited bringing a suit directly against an employee without first having received a judgment finding the employer in violation of the Act.[9] Corporate officers may now find themselves scapegoats, and required to defend charges while the company remains free of any litigation.

There have been attempts to govern payments to foreign officials on the

---

[9]*See United States v. McLean*, 738 F.2d 655 (5th Cir. 1984).

international level, particularly by the Organization for Economic Cooperation and Development and the United Nations. The OECD established guidelines but the U.N. has done nothing. A few individual nations attempt to prohibit payments by their entities, but some nations encourage such payments by allowing them to constitute deductions against taxes as ordinary business expenses.

SECTION C

NEGOTIATING WITH
A SUPPLIER

XI

The Legal Arena for the Purchasing Routine: The Uniform Commercial Code

A purchase made by a purchasing officer from a supplier is a commercial transaction that involves several facets of the law. It begins with an agreement between the purchasing officer and the sales representative. Both parties are acting for and in behalf of their respective companies as agents. Their ability to act for their companies is determined by the Law of Agency. The agreement they reach is a contract. This is governed by the Law of Contracts. The subject matter of the contract most often will be "goods." (Goods are tangible items excluding land and real estate. Real estate is the term applied to buildings permanently affixed to land.) The Law of Sales governs the purchase and sale of goods. The shipment of the goods will involve the Law of Common Carriers. The Law of Warehouse Receipts will be involved if the goods must be stored. If the goods are insured, the Law of Insurance will control. Completion of the purchase requires payment by check or draft, and the collection of the proceeds by the supplier. These processes are controlled by the Law of Negotiable Instruments. A chain of commercially related transactions is initiated every time a purchase is made. Each phase of the transaction is regulated by a specific topic of the law. The legal topics involved in such a transaction are referred to collectively as *commercial law.*

As discussed in Chapter I, commercial law in the United States is found primarily in the state enactments of the Uniform Commercial Code. While mentioned earlier, the major matters covered by the Code are found in eleven major chapters or Articles:

Article 1.   General Provisions

Article 2.   Sales

Article 2A. Leases

Article 3.   Commercial Paper

Article 4.   Bank Deposits and Collections

Article 4A. Electronic transfer

Article 5.   Letters of Credit

Article 6.   Bulk Transfers

Article 7.   Warehouse Receipts, Bills of Lading, and Other Documents of Title

Article 8.   Investment Securities

Article 9.   Secured Transactions, Sales of Accounts, and Chattel Paper

Also as pointed out in Chapter I, other general principles of law governing topics that are not covered specifically by the Code are to supplement its provisions.

THE EXPRESS LEGISLATED PURPOSES AND POLICIES OF THE CODE

We have seen that the writers of the Code had two goals—(1) to establish uniformity among the laws of the states and (2) to make a commercial transaction the topic of a single body of the law. The text of the Code begins with an expansion of these purposes. Section 1-102(2) reads as follows:

> (2) [the] underlying purposes and policies of this Act are (a) to simplify, clarify, and modernize the law governing commercial transactions; (b) to permit the continued expansion of commercial practices through custom, usage and agreement of the parties; (c) to make uniform the law among the various jurisdictions.

Subsections (a) and (b) above are purposes and (c) is a *policy*. The Code has modernized the law in some areas as we shall determine shortly. Some old and venerable rules of law have been wiped from the scene. Other rules have been amended to make them more easily applied to the modern business transaction.

Subsection (b) deserves special mention. The writers, in the "Official Comment," state:[1]

> This Act is drawn to provide flexibility so that, since it is intended to be a semi-permanent piece of legislation, it will provide its own machinery for expansion of commercial practice. It is intended to make it possible for the law embodied in the Act to be developed by the courts in the light of unforeseen and new circumstances and practices.

The phrase "to permit the continued expansion of commercial practices" is intended to assure that the Code will remain flexible enough to accommodate any changing conditions of the future. It is hoped that it will keep the code from becoming outdated, as did the various uniform acts it replaced.

Subsection (b) also mentions "custom, usage and agreement of the parties." One of the recurring phrases in the Code is "unless otherwise agreed." Great emphasis is placed on the ability—yes, it is encouragement—of the parties to a transaction to reach an agreement on how the transaction is to be conducted, notwithstanding any general rules of law that might be written in the Code. There is an invitation in the Code to the parties to tailor-make their agreement as they would like it to be. As a matter of fact, subsection (3) of Section 1-102 begins this way:

> The effect of provisions of this Act may be varied by agreement, except as otherwise provided in this Act . . .

There are a few sections in the Code where the parties are obligated to follow the legal principle stated therein. In all other sections, the parties are free to agree that the stated effect of the law will be changed to suit their desires, subject to this constraint in subsection (3):

> . . . the obligations of good faith, diligence, reasonableness, and care prescribed by this Act may not be disclaimed by agreement.

It is obvious that everyone in a legitimate business transaction will subscribe to this condition.

***Nota Bene* to the Purchasing Officer.** Keep in mind the Code's words: "agreement of the parties" when negotiating with suppliers. The Code gives you *carte blanche* to strike any arrangement that your supplier will agree to, as long as you do not violate the obligation of good faith or standards of reasonableness or care required under the Code. In most instances you are free to bargain for any

---

[1]Copyright 1972 by the American Law Institute and the National Conference of Commissioners on Uniform State Laws. Reprinted with the permission of the Permanent Editorial Board for the Uniform Commercial Code.
Subsequent quotes from the Official Comments are reprinted too with the permission of the Permanent Editorial Board for the Uniform Commercial Code.

special term or condition in a purchase. You are not limited by the Code in such an endeavor. The only limitation you may encounter is that you must negotiate the term affirmatively, because the Code may be written in the negative.

LEARNING THE CODE

Purchasing officers will be living with the Code for a long time. This suggests that a thorough understanding of its provisions and how these provisions are applied to everyday purchasing routine is essential. There follows here a few general observations and several basic concepts that run throughout the Code. It is hoped that this will be of value when we get into the depths of Article 2 on Sales.

About Definitions

It is customary to begin the discussion of an important piece of legislation by giving a long list of definitions of the terms and phrases used therein. Your author finds that this practice serves no useful purpose since such a list often goes unread. The reader is interested in the definition of a term only when it is employed in the section of the law being studied. This book will follow the practice of giving a definition at the appropriate time. Those of you who wish to have their definitions served up front are reminded that Section 1-201 of the Code contains 46 definitions of terms, and sections 2-103, -104, and -105 add to this imposing number.

Code References

Writing the previous section reminded your author that it would be helpful if the reader knew how the referencing to Code sections is accomplished. A list of the nine topical subdivisions (articles) in the code was given previously in this chapter. These topical subdivisions are numbered 1 through 9. When quoting the Code, the first number refers to the Article. This is followed by a dash, followed by three numbers, which refer to the specific section of the article cited. Thus, "Section 1-201" refers to Article 1 (General Provisions), Section 201. "Section 2-103" refers to Article 2 (Sales), Section 103, and so on.

The Official Text of the Code includes "Official Comment" after each section. These Comments were prepared by the Commissioners on Uniform State Laws and The American Law Institute. They explain the purpose and the intent of the section. Your author has included some of the more pertinent Comments in succeeding chapters of this book that are of interest to the purchasing officer. These Comments are copyrighted (1972) by The American Law Institute and the National Conference of Commissioners on Uniform State Laws. They are reprinted with the permission of the Permanent Editorial Board for the Uniform Commercial Code.

For those purchasing officers interested in the full text of these Official Comments, they are included in the *Uniform Commercial Code Official Text— 1993* published by The American Law Institute, 4025 Chestnut Street, Philadelphia, Pennsylvania 19104.

GOODS

Article 2—Sales is the Article in the Code that is most intimately involved with purchasing routine. Section 2-102 of the Article begins with this statement:

> Unless the context otherwise requires, this Article applies to transactions in goods . . .

The term *goods* is defined in Section 2-105(1):

> (1) "Goods" means all things (including specially manufactured goods) which are moveable at the time of identification to the contract for sale other than the money in which the price is to be paid . . .

The purchasing officer will note that the Code states that Article 2 covers "transactions" in "goods." It also states that "goods" are "things." Keep this in mind when applying the Code to your purchases. Some of them may be for services, such as maintenance contracts. "Services" are not "things," and presumably the Code is not applicable when purchasing services. Similarly, rentals and leases are not sales "transactions," and it is doubtful if they would be covered. The law that was prevailing for service and rental contracts at the time the Code was adopted continues to be applicable.

We must watch the trend in court decisions concerning these interpretations of the Code. Some courts are beginning to apply portions of Article 2 to service contracts, at least by analogy. Others are seeking ways to convert a nonsale, such as a lease, to be a transaction within the Code. Thus there appears to be a strong desire to make more and more contracts subject to the applicability of Code provisions. How far this trend will extend is unknown. The purchasing officer is advised to look closely at the Code when having trouble with such a contract. There may be a more friendly Code section applicable to the problem. If so, the attempt to use the Code might fall on friendly and sympathetic ears. It might even be persuasive to the troublesome supplier. There have been many—and there will continue to be more—cases litigated that seek to extend the reaches of the Code, particularly in the area of warranties.

Note also that goods must be moveable at the time of the sale. This excludes land and real estate. Contracts for the purchase and sale of real property (land

and buildings) are governed by the general rules of contract law and the specialized laws governing transactions in real estate.

However, purchases of minerals, including oil and gas, or a building or the building's materials that are to be removed from land, are considered goods if they are to be severed by the seller. Growing crops and timber, though attached to the land, are considered goods because they are capable of being severed from the land without doing material harm to it. It makes no difference in the case of "crops" and "timber" whether the buyer or the seller is to remove them. They continue to be considered as goods and under the scope of Article 2 of the Code.

The reader may question why "minerals" or a "building to be severed from the land" are considered goods only if they are to be severed by the seller. The writers of the Code believed that if these items were to be removed by the buyer, the contract would be one affecting land. If so, the contract is governed by the laws affecting real estate and cannot be brought under the umbrella of Article 2.

MERCHANTS

The Code introduces to modern law a new concept of professional buyers and sellers. Throughout the Code you will find references to "merchant." *Merchant* does not refer to the usual retailer or storekeeper that we associate with the term. The name goes back to the days of the "Law Merchant," which was mentioned in Chapter I as part of the common law of England. In the *Law Merchant*, a merchant had a professional status, and his business practices were measured on a professional basis.

The Code revived this concept of professionals in business and termed them *merchants.* The official definition of a merchant is found in Section 2-104(1). There are three separate parts to the definition that your author has identified by [a], [b], and [c]:

> [a] Merchant means a person who deals in goods of the kind, [b] or otherwise by his occupation, holds himself out as having knowledge or skill peculiar to the practices or goods involved in the transaction, [c] or to whom such knowledge or skill may be attributed by his employment of an agent . . . who by his occupation holds himself out as having such knowledge or skill.

Part [a] obviously refers to a supplier who regularly sells a given product or a group of products, [b] could be a broker, and [c] must be your company or organization with you as the purchasing officer. Although we associate a merchant with one who engages in commerce for profit, the term in the Code includes not-for-profit institutions that employ purchasing personnel or other business people.

Thus any organization is a merchant if it has someone to conduct their purchasing operations.

You operate as a merchant—a professional buyer—when you are transacting business. But you have not lost your amateur standing completely. When you purchase paper napkins for your company you are buying them as a merchant. If you stop at the supermarket on the way home from work and buy some paper napkins for use at home, you are buying them as a nonmerchant and a consumer. The Code applies to all buyers and sellers, including consumers. It distinguishes merchants only for the application of special rules in certain sections. It is also of interest to note that the Code does not interfere with special consumer laws. Section 2-103 states in part " . . . nor does this Article impair or repeal any statute regulating sales to consumers . . . "

The Code definition of a merchant utilizes two tests to determine who a merchant is. The first test is familiarity with the goods involved in the transaction. Reference is made to "deals in goods of the kind" and "having knowledge or skill peculiar to . . . the goods involved in the transaction." The second test is familiarity with business practices—"having knowledge or skill peculiar to the practices . . . involved in the transaction." You will find references made to merchants because of their experience with the "goods"; other references will be made to those who have skill in the "practices" involved in the transaction; and finally there will be references to merchants who qualify as such under both the "goods" and the "practices" tests.

Purchasing officers will be glad to know that the price of being considered a merchant is not excessive. It is true that the Code does impose a higher standard of good faith on merchants in their dealings with others. But you and your supplier are both merchants, so you will both be playing the same game. The Code established special rules for merchants. These rules are not harsh. They are written under the assumption that merchants possess the necessary knowledge about the goods and the business practices found in the transaction to react properly, and that they have the essential skills to follow the rules established. This means that the contract will be completed properly, with each party contributing to, and receiving from it, their just rights. The special rules for merchants will be called to your attention as the appropriate Code sections are discussed.

COURSE OF DEALING

Another concept given express recognition is the "prior course of dealings" between the parties to the transaction. The practices the parties followed in their previous dealings with each other form an understanding that the same procedures will be followed in a current transaction.

The Code explanation is found in Section 1-205(1):

> A course of dealing is a sequence of previous conduct between the parties to a particular transaction which is fairly to be regarded as establishing a common basis of understanding for interpreting their expressions and other conduct.

This section is applicable to those situations where you, the purchasing officer, and a supplier have done business with each other prior to the current transaction. Terms and procedures written in the current contract with that supplier, which might need interpretation, may be explained by how the contract was handled previously. The "course of dealing" principle may enter a contract either by specifically including it in the contract or by tacit recognition of its existence. More often it is the latter case.

USAGE OF TRADE

Somewhat similar to "course of dealing" is the "Usage of Trade" principle. It is a slightly expanded version of what we in purchasing refer to as a "custom of the industry." Section 1-205(2) gives us this definition:

> A usage of trade is any practice or method of dealing having such regularity of observance in a place, vocation, or trade as to justify an expectation that it will be observed with respect to the transaction in question.

Note that the usage of trade principle applies to a *place* as well as to a specific *vocation* or *trade*.

The Official Comment section of the Code (hereinafter referred to as "Official Comment") indicates it is intended that this concept be used "as a factor in reaching the commercial meaning of the agreement which the parties have made." A usage of trade is to be used to explain the language of an agreement— what the parties in a particular industry intended it to mean. For example, if one reads the definition of a "ream" in a dictionary, it is explained as a "count of 480." Yet those in the printing and the fine paper industry expect 500 sheets in a ream of paper. The difference in count is a long established *custom of the trade* among these businesspeople.

Usage of trade also encompasses standards of an industry and the trade customs practiced therein. These standards can be specifically spelled out in the agreement of the parties and referred to in a specific section, or they can be applied without reference. If you are purchasing an item that is covered by specific trade practices, it is prudent to become familiar with them. The old adage, "When in Rome, do as the Romans do" is applicable here. Unless you specifically negate the application of an industry practice, it will be applied to your purchase whether you intend it to be included or not.

The words *regularity of observance* are used in the definition of "usage of trade." They are included as part of the effort of the writers of the Code to enable it to stay up-to-date and modern. One associates a custom of the industry with something having a long and venerable history and being in existence from time immemorial. But the new definition of usage of trade requires only that it be regularly observed. A new usage or custom might be developed at any time, and as long as it is regularly observed, it will fall into the category of a usage of trade as defined in Section 1-205(2).

We noted in a previous section that the Code encouraged the parties to an agreement to negotiate fully and with the freedom to reach a contract as they wanted it to be. Many of the rules in the Code, for example, begin with the words "unless otherwise agreed." A "course of dealing" or a "usage of trade" are typical examples of what the buyer and the seller may substitute for other general rules of the law stated in the Code. It is a part of the flexibility of contracting the Code wanted to ensure. But this flexibility does not extend to some absolute rules, such as the necessity of having a writing to enforce a contract for the sale of goods in a court of law. (See Chapter XVI.) For example, it would be of no avail for a party to plead in court that the course of trade in the industry was to do business by word of mouth. There may be a custom to honor one's word and never reduce an agreement to writing. This defense for not producing a writing would fall on deaf ears in a court of law.

THE IMPORTANCE OF GOOD FAITH

The final Code concept to be mentioned is one that every purchasing professional subscribes to in a code of ethics, and it is one which is practiced at all times. It is *good faith* in dealing with the supplier. The Uniform Commercial Code makes this ethic the law in Section 1-203:

> Every contract or duty within this Act imposes an obligation of good faith in its performance or enforcement.

This principle is applied throughout the Code.

Merchants have this principle especially impressed upon them. Section 2-103(b) reads:

> "Good faith" in the case of a merchant means honesty in fact and the observance of reasonable commercial standards of fair dealing in the trade.

A purchasing officer need not be reminded of the obligation to exercise good faith when negotiating with suppliers. Most suppliers, too, are sincere in their actions and reciprocate with the reasonable standards of fair dealing in their trade. But should either the buyer or the seller attempt to ignore this precept, this Code section will bring them into line quickly.

XII

Essentials of a
Purchase Contract

"PURCHASE" DEFINED

Purchasing officers have had to read the law in reverse since the beginning of time. The legal aspects of transactions in goods has always been referred to in legal circles as the "Law of Sales." Even Article 2 of the Uniform Commercial Code, which has such a great impact on purchasing personnel, is captioned "Sales." Nowhere in the law is there any reference to purchases, and yet everyone knows that there can be no sale unless there is a purchase too. Purchasing is ignored in the law while "Sales" is given all the recognition.

When we in purchasing search for the legal definition of a purchase we are forced to apply the law in reverse. Section 2-106(1) of the Code states:

> A "sale" consists in the passing of title from the seller to the buyer for a price.

Applying the reverse twist to this we can come up with:

> A "purchase" consists in the passing of title to the buyer from the seller for a price.

Title is the ownership rights in an item. An ownership right is the right to use an item in any legal manner, including reselling it. One may have title to an automobile or title to a piece of real estate. Therefore, a purchase is the acquisi-

193

tion of the ownership rights of a given commodity by the buyer from the seller for a price. In the Code a buyer is defined as "a person who buys or contracts to buy goods," and a seller as "a person who sells or contracts to sell goods." To those familiar with pre-Code law, the "passing of title" from the seller to the buyer had great legal import. The Code itself, however, disassociates the passing of title to the settlement of most legal issues.

Two parties must agree to the transaction to have a purchase and a sale. This agreement is a contract. Each time you make a purchase you enter into a contract with your supplier. The title to the item cannot pass to you and your company until there is an agreement—a contract—with the seller. Contracts are governed by the Law of Contracts and by the Uniform Commercial Code.

ESSENTIALS OF A LEGAL CONTRACT

The law of contracts specifies that there are four essentials to a valid contract:

1. Capable parties

2. Valid (legal) subject matter

3. Mutual consideration

4. Agreement of the parties, which consists of an offer by one of the parties and acceptance of that offer by the other party

Capable Parties

The first essential of a legally enforceable contract requires that both parties meet all the normal standards associated with the concept of "knowing what you are doing and possessing the competence to do it." This standard immediately eliminates an insane person, an infant, a confirmed drunkard, and a corporation.

An insane person is ruled out from becoming a capable party to a contract because the law regards that individual as being unable to give assent intelligently to an agreement with another party.

An infant is protected by the law against responsibility for the consequences of a contract entered into during his or her minority. The common law defines *minority* as a male or female under the age of 21. Many state statutes changed this to 18 after 18-year-olds were given the right to vote. Contracts with infants may not occur in the average purchasing officer's daily routine. Be cautious should you be required to deal with an infant. An infant has the ability to hold an adult or a corporation to a contract. But the adult and the corporation do not have the reciprocal privilege.

An infant has the right during his or her minority to disaffirm any contract entered into, or to disaffirm within a reasonable time after reaching majority. This is a general rule of law with the only exception pertaining to *life's necessaries*. Life's necessaries are limited to food, shelter, clothing, medical attention, and common schooling. When an infant enters into a contract for necessaries, the party providing such items might have difficulty recovering the contract price. It is customary for a court to ask that the infant pay only the reasonable value of the necessaries furnished. The law protects an infant against his or her improvidence during minority if a larger payment than the reasonable price was agreed to in the contract.

When an individual has been adjudicated a confirmed drunkard by having a guardian appointed, that person no longer has the capacity to contract. However, too many luncheon martinis do not a drunkard make. An individual who does do this on occasion has no legal excuse to be relieved of a poor agreement with a supplier because the contract was signed while in a temporary state of inebriation.

The capacity of corporations to enter into contracts needs special explanation. A corporation may be—and often is—a party to a contract, but being invisible and intangible, it cannot contract for itself. It must act through agents such as you. Once an agent with the proper authority has entered into a contract on behalf of the corporation, the corporation is bound to that contract as a party to it.

You are reminded here of the discussion in Chapter IV concerning the authority of purchasing officers and sales representatives to contract for their companies. *Capable parties* is defined as "capable parties with the necessary authority to commit their principals in the contract." When you, the purchasing officer, sign a contract for your organization, you know that you have the authority to commit the company to perform its part of the bargain. Your supplier is the other party to the contract. It is equally essential for the supplier to be committed to the other side of the bargain by a capable party. This party may be the sales person handling your account or someone in the home office. Make certain that the person is clothed with the proper authority to enter into a firm and binding contract. (See the discussion of the authority of sales personnel in Chapter IV.)

Valid Subject Matter

A contract that contains all the legal essentials is enforceable in a court of law. Should a supplier renege on a contract, you have recourse against him by filing suit for damages or for specific performance under certain circumstances. It is obvious that the subject matter of the contract must be honorable and legal if the court is to assist you. A court cannot and will not enforce a contract that is illegal per se, that involves an illegal product, or is against public policy.

A court recently tried a lawsuit that involved a contract for the sale of an Indian dance shield with genuine eagle feathers and other ornate trimmings. The court refused to order that the contract be performed by the seller, and it also refused to award damages to the buyer for the failure of the seller to honor the contract. It refused to take action because the dance shield contained genuine eagle feathers. Possession of genuine eagle feathers is forbidden by the Federal Migratory Wild Bird and Bald Eagle Protection Act. This law made the subject matter of the contract illegal, and the entire contract was therefore unenforceable.

Most purchasing officers have little problem with legal and valid subject matter in their purchases. Almost all purchase contracts cover items and commodities that have no legal restrictions on their sale. A hospital or pharmaceutical purchasing officer might be required to purchase drugs and other narcotics that cannot be sold freely on the open market. In such instances, a permit or license must be first obtained. With that in hand the purchase becomes one with a legal subject matter. The purchase of radioactive materials also requires appropriate licenses to make the contract contain a legal subject matter. Other products that have similar controlled distribution may require permits to purchase them.

In Chapter IX we discussed antitrust legislation. Occasionally a purchasing officer may find a court of law unwilling to enforce one of his favorable contracts because. its enforcement would be a violation of antitrust laws. Assume that a purchasing officer negotiated the purchase of a supplier's product at a price less than the supplier charged the purchasing officer's competitors. After getting the entire purchase tied up in a neat contract, the supplier decides to renege on the sale. The supplier announced that he was fearful the sale would be a violation of the Robinson-Patman Act. If this was a true statement of fact, the purchasing officer would have a difficult time convincing a court that damages should be awarded him because of the supplier's breach of contract. The court would determine that enforcement of it would be against public policy.

Mutual Consideration

Consideration is understood by everyone until an attempt is made to define its legal effect in the formation of a contract. Then its meaning becomes somewhat obscure, and the waters get murky as we become involved in promises and things of value. The Uniform Commercial Code, despite presenting a multitudinous variety of definitions, chose not to include "consideration" on its list, which leaves us to our own devices to gain an understanding of this essential aspect of a contract.

Consideration, in the legal sense, is something of value passing from one party to a second party in exchange for a promise of the second party. The value given must be associated with the second party's promise in order for it to meet

the legal definition of consideration. Giving someone $500 is not considera-
tion—only a gift. But giving that person $500 in return for a promise to paint
your house is consideration.

The promise of the second party is the return consideration coming to the
first party. The promise could be the giving of something of value to the first
party, or it could be a detriment to the second party. The painting of the house in
the example above is something of value passing from the second party. This is
consideration. However, if the proposal to the second party was, "I will give you
$500 if you do not smoke or drink for six months," and he abstains during that
period of time, his abstinence would be consideration. Although nothing of value
passed to you, the second party's consideration was a detriment to him. This consideration may be something of value or a detriment. However, the detriment
cannot be an act forbidden by the law. "I will give you $500 if you do not pollute
my favorite fishing stream with your company's toxic wastes" is a proposal to the
second party. He may spend thousands of dollars treating the waste to avoid pol-
luting your stream, but he cannot claim the $500 from you for doing it. It was a
costly detriment to him, but because he is under legal obligation not to pollute, it
cannot be considered as legal consideration for your $500. Anything a person is
legally obligated to do, or legally prohibited from doing, is not consideration.

Mutual consideration is the value given by each party to the other in return
for their promises to each other. Thus, in a purchase contract, you promise to pay
a sum of money to the supplier in return for the supplier's promise to deliver a
quantity of his product to you. Each of you is promising to give something of
value to the other in return for the other's promise. You have formed a contract
based upon your mutual promises. Each promise involves consideration to the
other party. The mutual promises to each other meet the requirement of mutual
consideration necessary in a valid and enforceable contract.

Mutual consideration makes a contract legally binding on both parties.
Courts of law will not enforce the other party's promise to you unless it is shown
that there is consideration coming from you to support that promise. The
promise, to be enforceable, must be supported by consideration. A court turns a
deaf ear to a request to enforce a promise unless there is consideration for it. Bare
promises, without consideration, generally are not worth the paper on which they
are written when attempting to use them in court. In a few instances, promissory
estoppel may be used to enforce a contract without consideration. But there must
be a promise, justifiable reliance, and detriment if it is not enforced.

The Uniform Commercial Code has made one change to the general rule
requiring consideration for a contract to be enforceable. That change has to do
with the modification of an existing contract for the sale of goods. Section 2-209
of the Code states that such a contract may be modified without the exchange of
consideration. Only the agreement of both parties is required to make the modi-

fication enforceable. Of course, if the modified contract covers the sale of goods having a value of $500 or more, the modification must be in writing. This change in the law does not apply to service contracts. Mutual consideration must be present to successfully modify a service contract.

Despite the fact that the law is so insistent that consideration be present to enforce another's promise, it has little concern for the adequacy of that consideration as compared with the value of what is promised. Agreed-to consideration is all the law looks at and demands. The law cares not whether one party gets a bad or a good bargain for the consideration given. Parties may negotiate freely for the promises of each other. What may be a good bargain in the eyes of one party may be someone else's idea of little or nothing. It is only when the values of the consideration become so disparate as to be unconscionable that the law will step in. Otherwise the law is satisfied with the conventional recital of "for $1 in hand paid and other good and valuable consideration" as meeting its stern requirement of consideration to support a promise.

Purchasing officers pay more attention to the adequacy of the consideration received from suppliers than do many parties to contracts. The professional buyer seeks the best value for his or her company. The components of quality and service that make up the value in a product are part and parcel of the consideration received from the supplier. This value is weighed against the sum of dollars in return when deciding whether to make the purchase. It is the purchasing officer's responsibility to make certain that there is an adequate *quid pro quo* for each dollar of the principal's resources. There is no need for the courts to decide this question, and they usually do not get into it.

Every purchase commitment is made because of the return consideration that is to come from the supplier. And, by the same token, every sale of a product is made because of the consideration that is to come from the buyer. Both buyer and supplier depend upon first, the other's promise to give consideration, and then, second, on the receipt of the actual thing of value for which they bargained. Mutual promises bring the contract of purchase and sale into existence. They create what is known as a *bilateral contract* because mutual promises have been exchanged.

Agreement of the Parties

The fourth essential of a legally enforceable contract is that there must be agreement of the parties. A legal dictionary will define agreement as "mutual assent of the parties to a contract." Mutual assent is achieved by two legal acts—an offer and an acceptance. One of the two parties will seize the initiative in the negotiations and make an offer to the other party. If the second party is in agreement with the offer that has been made, he will respond with an acceptance of that offer. The two parties are then in contract. Offer plus acceptance is the agreement of the parties and results in a contract. At this point each party knows his or her obligations undertaken in the contract and is prepared to perform these obligations. Offers are discussed in detail in Chapters XII and XIII, and acceptances are presented in Chapters XIV and XV.

These four essentials—capable parties, legal subject matter, mutual consideration, and agreement of the parties—must be present in every contract of purchase. The absence of any one of these ingredients makes the contract unenforceable in a court of law. Of course, if a contract written without one of these essentials is performed without the objection of either party, there is no problem unless the contract covered an illegal subject matter. Then the appropriate law enforcement agency will take the necessary steps to apply sanctions against the parties involved.

AGREEMENT GENERALLY

What is often not realized is that a very general agreement on something, without a written document or even extensive discussions, may be upheld by the courts. This is in part because the law favors the upholding of agreements generally. It also recognizes that some persons may attempt to renege on agreements when market forces change even though this violates their promise.

Under current law, however, as found in the Uniform Commercial Code, a couple of matters should be noted. First, there is much less emphasis placed upon a meeting of the offer and acceptance. Secondly, there is not a need for a meeting of the minds or a meeting of the offer and acceptance on a number of points. In regard to a meeting of the offer and acceptance, it should be noted that under the Code the moment of the making of the contracts is no longer essential. It becomes less relevant and the conduct or other facets of the setting may indicate that a contract does exist even though the particular moment of its creation is indefinite. Instead, there is a finding that the parties are in a relationship in which there has been a general agreement as to a transaction but not necessarily an agreement on a number of terms in that transaction. In a sense that there must be some generalized agreement, the element of mutual assent is preserved and remains part of the law. But it is only mutual assent to a relationship or assent in very general terms to a contractual relationship that is required.

Once there has been this very general agreement under the Code, there is a contract despite the fact that a great deal of indefiniteness remains. It is unnecessary for the parties to have agreed upon a number of terms such as price, performance, time of delivery, place of delivery, warranty, remedy, or other such terms which were formerly believed to be necessary. In other words, there need not have been mutual assent on many of these points, but rather entering into a contractual relationship in more generalized terms is all that is required. Indeed, there may even be an agreement to agree on such things as price. Whereas courts formerly would strike down contracts on grounds of indefiniteness even though the parties had indicated a general agreement and expectation that the agreement would be carried out, under the new contract law of the Code this is no longer does. The matters formerly covered by these terms of definiteness may now be filled in by the courts.

XIII

Offers in Procurement

The fourth requisite of a legal contract—the agreement of the parties—generally consists of two separate acts—(1) an offer made by one of the parties and (2) the acceptance of that offer by the other party. The offer comes first in the contract formation process.

"OFFER" DEFINED

An offer is a proposal made to someone to enter into a contract. It is an invitation to "come do business with me on these terms." It is a promise made to the other party that if the terms proposed are satisfactory there will be a contract. Thus, an offer is more than a mere proposal or an invitation. It is a legal commitment to the other party to form a contract if that person agrees.

SOURCES OF OFFERS

In the daily purchasing routine, offers may be originated by you or by your supplier. If you originate an offer, it will be an *offer to buy;* it will be addressed to a supplier. You will be the offeror, and the supplier will be the offeree. But the supplier might also be the source of an offer that would be addressed to you. Then the offer would be an *offer to sell.* Your supplier would now be the offeror and you the offeree. Obviously, during an extended period of negotiation with a supplier, there is the possibility that you both may make several offers. It is also possible that negotiations proceed for a considerable period of time before either of you makes an offer. And, of course, an offer could be made without there have been any prior negotiation or previous communication. A person may elect to make an offer at any time.

THE LEGAL IMPLICATIONS OF AN OFFER

An offer is a legal act. It is the first of two steps that could lead to the formation of a contract. The law is prepared to enforce the obligations one assumes in a contract. The obligations the offeror is expected to assume in a contract are promised to the offeree when the offer is made. A person making an offer must be prepared to comply with the terms of the offer if it is accepted by the offeree. The penalty for noncompliance can be one of the various types of damages a court assesses for breaching (breaking or avoiding) the terms of a contract.

Not every offer results in legal consequences. Only those offers accepted by the offeree carry legal obligations. An offer is a conditional promise to enter into a contract. It is conditional because it carries legal obligations only if the offeree agrees to the terms of the offer. The offeree's act of acceptance of an offer imposes legal obligations on him too. If the offeree does not elect to accept these obligations, the offeror has no commitments either.

Note that the contingency as to whether the offeror has legal obligations arising from making of an offer is decided by the offeree. The offeror makes the proposal in a form to give the offeree a power to turn the offer into a contract. The offeror assures the offeree that he is ready, willing, and eager to get into a contract. This is the purpose of making the offer, but it remains for the offeree to decide whether there will be a contract. It is as though the offeror has extended a hand to the offeree and says, "This is what I propose. If you agree, shake my hand and we have a contract." During the time the offeree is considering the offer, the offeror's hand continues to be extended waiting for a handclasp. The offeror could become weary from holding out the hand for a long period of time and could possibly retract it. But as long as that arm is extended there is the possibility that it could be grabbed by the offeree, and a contract be brought into existence. The law refers to the offer as an *open offer* as long as the hand is extended. This means that the offeror continues to be conditionally obligated to enter into a contract; he is bound by the promise to enter into a contract while there is an open offer. There is no opportunity to back out or amend the proposal should the offeree accept it.

ESSENTIALS OF A VALID OFFER

It is not always readily apparent that an enforceable offer has been made. A purchasing officer is exposed daily to actual offers and incomplete apparent offers.

Separating the wheat from the chaff—the real offers from the "close-to" offers—is sometimes difficult to do. "Almost offers" must be distinguished from genuine offers so that one may know when a contract can be created by an acceptance. As a guide to this decision, here are the three essentials that must be present in every genuine offer:

1. There must be an intent on the part of the offeror to make a valid and binding offer.

2. This intended offer must be communicated to the offeree.

3. The offer must be specific and definite insofar as the subject matter is concerned.

1. The Intent to Make an Offer

There must be a clear and undeniable intent to make the offer. The offeror makes a legal commitment when making an offer. There is no room in a precise legal commitment for caveats or other devices to "leave a way to get out of it." An offeror is "on the line for a contract" with an open offer. The specific intent to be in that position must be expressed. Certainly the offer cannot be made in jest.

The best method for an offeror-buyer to express the necessary intent to make an offer is to use the words, "We offer to buy . . . " If the offeror is a supplier the proper words are, "We offer to sell you . . . " These words leave no doubt that the intent to make an offer is there. The usual purchase order—especially the one beginning with, "Please enter our order for the following . . . "—is also acceptable.

A quotation form is the prevailing medium a supplier uses to extend an offer to sell. Forms that are worded properly will begin with, "We offer to sell you the following . . . " But there are other quotation forms that are not worded as explicitly. The mere heading "Quotation" at the top of a blank form leaves much to be desired. A price quotation, strictly interpreted, is nothing more than what it says it is—the communication of the prevailing price of the item listed. The intent to offer to sell the item is missing. No doubt the supplier intends to sell, but that fact would be so much more in evidence if the magic words "we offer to sell" were used.

You, the purchasing officer, can do wonders with such reluctant suppliers who seem fearful of making a firm offer to sell. Word your quotation request in a manner that forces them to "stand up and be counted" as making an offer to sell. Consider the following three circumstances:

1. You send a letter to a company asking, "Do you make a Chinese typewriter?" The company tersely responds with a catalog page illustrating a

Chinese typewriter, showing a price of $1400. Has an offer to sell been made? No.

2. You send a letter to a company asking, "What is the current price of your Chinese typewriter?" The company again responds with the catalog page. Has an offer to sell been made? No.

3. You send a letter to a company that reads, "At what price will you sell us a Chinese typewriter?" The company again responds with the catalog page showing a price of $1400. Has an offer to sell been made? Yes.

The answers "No" to the question, "Has an offer to sell been made?" is given in case nos. 1 and 2 because the typewriter company merely answered your questions with the catalog page. In the first instance they responded, "We do make a Chinese typewriter. Here is a picture of it." In the second case their answer was, "The current price of our Chinese typewriter is $1400." In neither instance did they state, "We will sell you a Chinese typewriter for $1400." While some courts might find an implied intent, many would say that the expressed intent to make an offer to sell is lacking. Should you send them a purchase order for $1400 under either of these two circumstances, they are at liberty to respond, "Our prices went up yesterday. We now will sell you our Chinese typewriter for $1700." The supplier can properly claim they did not intend the catalog page to be an offer to sell.

Now look at case no. 3. The catalog page arrives showing "$1400" in response to your query, " At what price will you sell us your Chinese type- writer?" Now their answer to your question is, "We will sell you our Chinese typewriter for $1400." Should an argument over price develop with the type- writer company, your proof of the $1400 offer to sell will come by integrating your letter of inquiry to them with their catalog page. Your letter of inquiry and their catalog page, together, make an offer to sell at $1400.

Despite the supplier's apparent reluctance to make a clear statement of an offer to sell in all three circumstances, your letter in case no. 3 forced the com- pany to make an offer. To be fair, we must agree that the supplier probably was saying in all three situations that they would sell the typewriter for $1400 but their response in answer nos. 1 and 2 lacked clear expression of this intent. This left open a loophole for them should they wish to increase their price because of changing market conditions. Their hand was not extended for you to grasp.

***Nota Bene* to the Purchasing Officer.** Encourage suppliers to word their price quotation forms so that the magic words, "We offer to sell you" or "We will sell you" appear on the form. Make certain, too, that your purchase order shows the same intent. The words, "Please enter our order" are better suited for your purchase order since you may use those words to make an offer to buy as well as to accept a supplier's offer to sell.

If you use preprinted quotation request forms, begin the body of the form with "Please quote the best price you offer to sell us the following items." This will give you the opportunity to integrate the form with a supplier's price quotation and make it an offer to sell. Should you require your suppliers to submit their quotations on a carbon copy of your quotation request, have the statement "We offer to sell the above to you at the prices indicated" appear above the place where the supplier signs the form. This removes all doubt about the intent of the supplier to make an offer to sell.

2. Communication of the Offer

An offer must be communicated to the offeree before it can become a legal commitment. The intent to make an offer is finalized by the delivery of it to the offeree. Until that is accomplished the offer remains nothing more than a figment of the offeror's mind. Even though the offer is in written form it has no legal effect until it is intentionally communicated to the offeree. For example, imagine that you have had a purchase order prepared that is an offer to buy a quantity of a particular supplier's product. Further, assume that you have just completed signing the purchase orders for the day, and the above mentioned order winds up on top of the pile. You place the stack of orders on the edge of your desk so that they may be picked up to be mailed. Before the order clerk picks up the pile, the sales representative of that supplier comes to visit you. While sitting on the other side of your desk, his roving eye reads the order to his company. You make no comment. Impatiently he asks, "Want me to take that purchase order with me to save some postage?" You respond, "No, leave it there. I believe I will give that order to your competitor who doesn't read everything lying on my desk." Although the sales representative has seen that offer to buy, it was not communicated to him or to his company by you. He of the "roving eye" stumbled upon it, and that does not qualify as necessary intent of communication. You have no legal obligations to the supplier, and the supplier has no legal right against you after that episode in your office.

Reward offers to the general public are the one major exception to the rule that an offer must be communicated directly to the offeree by the offeror. An advertisement in a newspaper or a notice posted on a wall reading, "A reward of $1000 is offered to any person who gives the necessary information leading to the arrest of the two robbers who held up the National State Bank on Thursday December 12" is recognized as a valid offer by most courts. Despite the lack of direct communication of the offer to the offeree, the courts have enforced such reward offers to assist in the maintenance of law and order in our society. The courts have also rationalized this by pointing out that a person making a reward offer cannot communicate the reward offer to a specific person because determining who that specific person is, is the very intent of making the offer!

Offers may be communicated verbally or in writing. In the daily purchasing routine both methods are employed. Many offers are extended verbally over the telephone, as well as in face-to-face negotiations with suppliers. Both the purchasing officer and the sales representative may make one or several offers during a negotiating session. If an agreement with the supplier is reached verbally, certain formalities are necessary to make the contract enforceable. These formalities, such as delivery and acceptance of the goods or a written confirmation of the agreement, are discussed in Chapter XVI, "Oral Contracts."

Written offers are equally commonplace. The purchase order is the customary communication tool used by purchasing officers to extend offers to buy to suppliers. A supplier uses a form labeled "Proposal" or "Quotation." An ordinary letterhead or a blank piece of paper may be used. Telegrams and other modern forms of communication, such as a computer, can also be used to extend an offer. The words that are written make an offer, not the piece of paper on which they may be written. The intent to make and be bound by the offer is essential.

3. Identification of the Subject Matter

The topic of the offer—what is proposed to be bought or sold—must be accurately described. A definite and precise description is required. Vagueness and ambiguity will cause an offer to fail the legal test of a valid offer.

Purchasing officers are familiar with the preparation of specifications for an item to be purchased. Specifications are designed to tell the supplier exactly what the purchasing officer wishes to buy. This is the degree of specificity required when an offer is made either by a purchasing officer or a supplier. The various options one has in preparing specifications are available. Brand names, catalog numbers, as well as detailed performance, quality, and output specifications may be used. The target is to readily identify the subject matter of the offer. Offers from suppliers should conform to this requirement of specific identity, too.

It is very important that the quantity of the item be expressed. An offer generally will fail by being indefinite if the quantity is omitted. The quantity test is expressed as being *definite* or *determinable.* An offer that reads, "All of our requirements for no. 4 fuel oil at our Main Street factory from July 1 to June 30" will not fail for lack of mention of a specific quantity. The quantity involved in such an offer is capable of being determined during the stated 12-month period. That satisfies the need for a definite expression of quantity.

Price is always important to the purchasing officer, but the law does not regard it as critical to a valid offer. If a price is mentioned in an offer, it should be specific. Thus $1 standing alone means nothing. Something more should be stated, such as "for the lot," "each," "per dozen," "per pound," or for whatever unit of measure the commodity is traded in the industry. A future price may be pegged to some commodity market or exchange on a particular day. This is adequate. A variable price pegged to established grades used in the industry is equally satisfactory.

It should be noted that the absence of a price in an offer will not cause the offer to fail. The law will substitute the "prevailing market price at the time of delivery" if the parties to an offer fail to agree upon a price.

There are some suppliers who insist that the price be the one prevailing at the time of delivery. A purchasing officer will see more of this approach during inflationary cycles and during seller's markets. It is not a desirable method of doing business insofar as the buyer is concerned because the final cost of the purchase is not known until the product is delivered. Furthermore, if a period of time elapses between the placement of the order and the delivery, the risk of any upward market price movement is placed on the buyer. Suppliers like it of course, because once the sale is made the profit margin is assured. Nonetheless, a supplier's offer that includes the phrase "price prevailing at the time of delivery" is a legal offer. It will not fail for lack of a stated price. The price is determinable when the goods are delivered.

In summary, an offer should consist of:

1. the intent to make an offer by the offeror,

2. the communication of that offer to the offeree, and

3. the essential details of the offer expressed unequivocally, including

    a. a precise description of the subject matter,

    b. a precise or determinable quantity expressed,

    c. a precise or determinable price, if price is mentioned in the offer. Absence of any statement of price will not cause the offer to fail.

While sometimes custom and usage or missing terms provisions of the Code can be used to supply details, it is always best to state these in the offer itself.

INVITATIONS TO DO BUSINESS

Now that we have determined the requisites of a valid offer, the next problem is to determine what classification to give all of those "would-be," "almost," or "sounds like" offers that pass before us.

These attempts to do business that fall short of being bona fide offers are known in the law as "invitations to treat"—the more modern term is "invitations to do business."

A purchasing officer initiates many invitations to do business in the form of a request for a quotation (RFQ). An RFQ has no legal significance whatsoever. A purchasing officer may send out as many requests as the budget for postage will permit without ever making a commitment to purchase the item. A request for quotation fails as an offer because it lacks the essential ingredient of *intent.* The purchasing officer has no intent to make a commitment to buy the item shown on the RFQ at the time the request is sent to one or more suppliers. Lacking this intent, the form is classified as an *invitation to do business.* This is an appropriate term for the RFQ because its purpose is to invite the suppliers to submit offers to "do business with me."

Suppliers, too, make great use of the process of extending invitations to do business with purchasing officers. The catalog is a typical example of an invitation to do business. It describes, lists, and often pictorializes the products the supplier offers for sale. Current prices may also be included. The purpose of a catalog is to keep the products of the supplier before the purchasing officer. It is a promotional piece of material designed to *solicit* offers to buy. It comes very close to being an offer to sell, but the courts have consistently held that a catalog is nothing more than an invitation to do business. It lacks the intent on the part of the supplier to be continually "on the line" for offering to sell every product contained in the catalog. A catalog might lie on the shelf of a purchasing office for years. The products described could be changed in description, not offered for sale any more, or no longer manufactured. Because of these factors the courts have protected suppliers by classifying catalogs as invitations to do business. Notwithstanding this protection of the law, many suppliers protect themselves from having the catalog become an offer to sell by placing a caveat in one of the front pages. One caveat often seen is "Prices shown herein are the current list prices. They are subject to change without notice. Ask your sales representative for the current prevailing price and availability."

Pamphlets, brochures, and other advertising materials are similarly classified as invitations to do business. They are not intended to be offers to sell but are designed to arouse the interest of the business community in the product advertised. One may be certain that an advertiser would not object to receiving orders as a result of promotional material, but this does not make the brochure an offer to sell. More specific language is required to convert it into an offer.

Modern reproduction methods and word processors bring sales and promotional letters closer to constituting valid offers to sell. A typewritten letter, personally addressed to a purchasing officer and signed by a facsimile signature, may be prepared on a quantity basis. Should the body of the letter convey the thought of an offer to sell, it could be regarded as a bona fide offer. The item is described in sufficient detail. The mailing of the letter demonstrates the intent to make the offer to sell, and its receipt by the purchasing officer to whom it is personally addressed constitutes proper communication. Thus all of the essentials are present and the supplier could find himself in a contract with a buyer who accepts such an offer.

Why would a supplier want to renege on delivery of the product he spent money on to advertise? Most reputable suppliers are delighted to make the sale and fill the order. There are, however, some more aggressive—and perhaps less reliable—suppliers who use promotional pieces for ulterior motives. One typical ploy is to list a price for the item that is lower than the prevailing market price. This catches the attention of the alert purchasing officer who may send the supplier an order for the item. This is exactly what the aggressive supplier wanted to determine—where the potential buyers for his or her product are.

The purchase order answered that question for the supplier. A sales representative will be sent to the purchasing officer with some poor excuse, such as "the price was misquoted" or "production costs have risen. As a result, the price has gone up 25 percent." But now, at the least, the supplier knows where a potential customer is located. That was the purpose of the advertising piece.

Most such suppliers will "get away" with using such devices because purchasing officers will usually discover that the letter did not meet all of the standards of a valid offer to sell. Such letters are cleverly prepared to avoid the breach of contract lawsuit. Consider this following letter addressed to Mr. Bull, a purchasing officer:

> Dear Mr. Bull: For a 30-day period we are offering our top-quality corn for $3.25 per bushel. *Signed*: Corn Company.

A buyer might read this letter and find that $3.25 is a bargain because top-quality corn is currently selling on the open market slightly above $4 per bushel. Suppose Mr. Bull sends the Corn Company an order for 20,000 bushels. Bull will probably receive a response acknowledging receipt of his order, but telling him that the *current* price is now $4 per bushel. Corn Company will add, "We are prepared to make immediate delivery at this price."

The Corn Company has no legal obligation to sell 20,000 bushels of corn to Bull at $3.25 per bushel. Their original letter was not a valid offer to sell because it did not meet the test of being definite. There was no mention of the quantity of corn they offered at $3.25 per bushel. One might perhaps gather that they are offering to sell one bushel at that price, but no more. Nowhere in the letter is the quantity of 20,000 bushels mentioned. That quantity appears only on Mr. Bull's purchase order, which as a matter of law is an offer to buy. It did not create a contract.

Quantity is so very important because a court may only award damages for breach of contract if the item is not unique. To measure damages the court would ask Mr. Bull to spell out his damages. Mr. Bull would point out that the Company offered to sell at $3.25 per bushel, but is now asking $4.00 per bushel. "That is

$.75 more per bushel." The court would then ask, "And how many bushels did the offer state would be sold at that price?" There is no mention of quantity contained in the letter, so the damages would be 75 cents times zero, or zero. The court would be forced to tell Mr. Bull, "Sorry, but we can do no more for you."

***Nota Bene* to the Purchasing Officer.** Experience has demonstrated to purchasing officers that most advertising pieces are designed to attract attention. Ads are written by professionals skilled in that art. Most use the skill legitimately to push the sales of their client's product. But there are also those who may use that skill in a less professional manner. The number of states that now have *consumer laws* to protect the consumer against false advertising is testimony to the need for some control over the excesses a few professionals resort to in servicing their clients. Unfortunately, consumer laws do not protect professional buyers. We must resort to good, sound purchasing judgment to protect our organizations against this type of activity of the few nonprofessionals. Careful supplier selection is our answer. This will give you and your organization the protection you need.

COUNTEROFFERS

The negotiation process between the buyer and the seller to reach an agreement for a contract may be short and simple, or it may be prolonged. The pattern by which this agreement is reached will vary. We know that the first legal step is for one of the parties to make a valid offer. The offeror may be the buyer or the seller. The offeror who makes the first offer is the one who takes the initiative by being willing to make a legal commitment to the other party. But this original offer may not be the offer that is finally accepted and becomes part of the contract agreed upon. During negotiations many offers may be made by one or both parties.

Negotiation implies bargaining and trading positions. It is accomplished by the process of making offers, one to the other. As an example, assume that a buyer is interested in purchasing 100 pairs of a type of safety goggles. The conversation might go this way:

Supplier: I will sell you 100 pairs for $30 per pair.

Buyer: I will not pay more than $29 per pair.

Supplier: Because of the large quantity involved, I will reduce my price to $29.75.

Buyer: Your glasses are better than average quality. I will pay $29.25 per pair.

Supplier: I am anxious for your employees to begin using my glasses, so I will sell them to you for $29.50 per pair.

Buyer: I will buy your glasses at that price.

In this example, the supplier made three offers and the buyer made two. The supplier made the initial offer, which was an offer to sell at $30.00. The buyer countered with an offer to buy for $29.00, which was countered by the supplier's $29.75 offer to sell, and so it continued. After the supplier's first offer at $30.00, each of the succeeding offers are referred to as *counteroffers*. A counteroffer is an offer made by an offeree to alter or change an open offer directed to him or her. The offeree becomes the offeror of the counteroffer. This makes the original offeror an offeree. A counteroffer has the same legal effect as an offer if it contains the essentials of an offer. It, too, is a legal commitment made to the other party. At the same time the counteroffer becomes an offer, it also rejects the original offer.

DURATION OF AN OFFER

The life span of an offer (or a counteroffer) is limited. It may (1) lapse, (2) be rejected, (3) be revoked, or (4) be accepted and ripen into a contract. Its eventual fate is determined by either the offeror or the offeree, depending upon the circumstances.

1. The Offer Lapses

Lapse in this context means the offer dies a natural death without action by either party. Assume that you as a purchasing officer receive an offer to sell from a supplier. On the face of the quotation form is the statement "This offer is good for 10 days." After 10 days have elapsed that particular offer no longer exists. You have 10 days to decide whether to accept it. If you take no action during this 10-day period, you will find that on the eleventh day that offer has disappeared. It lapsed automatically at the end of the 10 days.

When does the 10-day period to run in such an offer begin—from the date the offer was prepared by the supplier, or from the date it is received? The time period on a *dated* offer begins to run on the date shown on the face of it. The time on an *undated* offer will begin to run the date it is received by the offeree. The law prefers greater specificity—"This offer expires on June 30" makes the question, "When does this offer expire?" totally unnecessary.

Occasionally an offer from a supplier will state: "This offer is subject to immediate acceptance." Obviously this calls for a prompt reaction on your part. The supplier making the offer has some reason to limit the life span of that offer. It might be that he is attempting to pressure you into a quick purchase before his competitors have an opportunity to persuade you to buy their product instead of his. Or it could be for a more valid reason, such as an impending price rise of the raw materials the supplier needs to manufacture his product. The supplier needs a quick answer from you so that he may cover his purchase of the raw materials. Whatever the reason for the suggestion of an immediate response, the supplier has applied pressure on you for a response.

How much time do you have to accept an offer that calls for "immediate acceptance?" The words seem unambiguous, and yet in the normal course of business dealings they become vague. Very few purchasing officers are willing to respond to such an offer the moment they set eyes upon it. Yet that is what the term calls for—"immediate action." However, the law recognizes that acceptance of an offer is a legal act, which requires considered judgment, and it will expect that action be taken within a reasonable time after the offer has been received. Thus the precise time such an offer lapses is in doubt.

It is obvious that the supplier should have been more precise in the wording of this time limit. Yet the ambiguity of the term may be exactly what the supplier intended. If he is "looking over his shoulder" at the market price trends of his raw materials, he may want the freedom to be able to say "too late," if you do not respond immediately. However, if he is interested in getting your order, he wants the ability to accept it even if it comes two, three, or five days later, provided his profit margin is still the same because the raw material prices remained firm. The vagueness in the expression of the time limit gives the supplier the best of both worlds—he can accept your order when it arrives if it is to his advantage, or he can reject it if he finds it prudent to do so.

One may question whether the supplier has made a valid offer when he includes a time limit that is couched in somewhat vague terms. Will the offer fail because it is not definite? Your author is of the opinion that the offer is sustainable because the words "immediate acceptance" have a definite meaning in the English language. We are also mindful of the long-standing adage in the law that "the offeror is master of the offer." The offeror has the right "to call the shots" for limiting the time for acceptance. One cannot be critical of a businessperson who protects his legitimate business interests by phrasing his offer in a manner that is most favorable to his position.

This is a fact the purchasing officer must keep in mind at all times. The supplier is in business for the express purpose of making a profit. Protection of profit position by exercising the full rights of an offeror is something that the buyer-offeree must be prepared to face. If the offer to sell is so advantageous, quick action is the price the buyer must be prepared to pay. But the purchasing officer must also keep in mind that there is no law requiring acceptance of an offer where the supplier is the *master.* The option of rejecting and making a counteroffer is always available.

It is suggested that if the purchasing officer is faced with an attractive offer to sell subject to immediate acceptance, the supplier should be questioned about the meaning of the time limit. If the offer is hand delivered by an authorized sales representative, the sales person should be asked point-blank, "What constitutes *immediate acceptance*?" If the offer comes by mail, a telephone inquiry should be made to ask the same question. It is much more prudent to make a direct inquiry than it is to attempt to solve the question by general rules of law or by a legal opinion. Purchasing officers are accustomed to asking the direct question at any time and should make no apology for asking it.

Many offers to sell contain no time limit. In such instances the law states that the offer will lapse after a reasonable period of time has expired. This statement leads us to the question "What is a reasonable period of time that we can depend upon for an offer to be held open?" Unfortunately the law does not give us as precise an answer to this question as we in purchasing would like to find. Subsection (2) of Section 1-204 of the Uniform Commercial Code defines *reasonable time* with these words:

> (2) What is a reasonable time for taking any action depends on the nature, purpose and circumstances of such action.

Thus a reasonable time is a variable in the law, and not a precise number of days that might be applied to every situation and to every offer. The time span may vary, and will depend upon many factors, including the following:

1. The nature of the product involved

2. The possible volatility of the market in which the product or its raw materials are traded

3. The prior course of dealings between the parties (see Chapter X).

4. The usage of the trade and customs of the industry in which the seller and the buyer work.

5. Any other unusual factors that might exist or could arise concerning the product or business conditions

The need for the law to keep an implied time limit on the life of an offer variable can be understood by a few examples. Should I say to you, "I will sell you this double-dipped ice cream cone for $1," you must give me a rather prompt response to my offer. The offer could lapse within 5 minutes, on a warm summer day. Or, if I should say to you, "I have 100-dozen freshly laid eggs that I will sell for $1 per dozen," you again have a rather limited response time, but not quite as urgent as in the case of the ice cream cone. On the other hand, if I am selling paper products or steel, my offers will not carry with them the same degree of urgency since the product is not affected by the pressures of spoilage. Thus, because of the variable characteristics of the item involved in the offer, it is apparent that what is a reasonable time for one offer to lapse will be different than the time limit in another. Because of these and other factors, the courts are given wide latitude in determining when an unlimited offer lapses.

But the courts will protect an offeror against an offeree who takes too long to respond to the offer. Here is a chronological account of the correspondence between two parties, which was brought before a federal court:[1]

> *July 20, 1971*. An attorney for an estate wrote to the Internal Revenue Service, "I am authorized to offer to settle all federal tax obligations allegedly owed for a total amount of $13,000. I would appreciate hearing from you at your earliest convenience as to the disposition of the Department of Justice concerning this offer."
>
> *August 9, 1971*. The Internal Revenue Service responded, "We acknowledge receipt of your offer dated July 20, 1971. Your offer will be processed in accordance with our procedures. Every effort will be made to advise you promptly of the action on your proposal."
>
> *December 20, 1971*. The attorney wrote, "To date no determination on the offer has been received. I would appreciate very much your looking into the matter to see if such determination might be forthcoming."
>
> *October 4, 1972*. The Internal Revenue Service wrote, "This is to advise you that the offer has been accepted on behalf of the Attorney General."

Sometime before the October 4 letter arrived, the attorney decided that the offer to settle was unnecessary. When the acceptance letter arrived, the Internal Revenue Service was advised that the estate would not pay the $13,000. This prompted the Internal Revenue Service to bring suit against the estate for the agreed sum, claiming that a valid contract had been formed with the acceptance of the offer on October 4. The estate claimed that there could be no contract because the offer had expired before October 4. Therefore, there was no open offer for the October 4 letter to accept on that date.

The federal court agreed with the estate and ruled against the Internal Revenue Service. The court repeated the general rule of law that "an offer lapses after the expiration of a reasonable amount of time." It observed that the offer had first been made on July 20, 1971, and was then renewed by the December 20, 1971 attorney's letter. Thus the purported Internal Revenue Service acceptance of the offer came 14 and one-half months after the first offer was made and 9 and one-half months after it was repeated. The court said simply, "This is beyond a reasonable time."

The Court never defines the "reasonable time limit" that this offer "went beyond." All we get from the case is that under this set of circumstances, the nine and one-half months were more than its life span. Somewhere between Decem-

---

[1]*United States v. Roberts*, 436 F. Supp. 533 (1977).

ber 20, 1971 and October 4, 1972 that offer lapsed. We never will know the date of its death. Purchasing officers must live with this uncertainty when any sales offer is received that does not contain a time limit. There is no general rule of law that applies to all offers. The only known statutory time limit of an offer is stated in Section 2-205 of the Code, which applies only to *firm offers.* It states that if no time is stated, the offer remains open "for a reasonable time . . . but in no event may such period exceed three months." This tells us the maximum period of time that a firm offer remains open, but it says nothing about offers other than firm offers. (Firm offers are discussed in Chapter XIII.) However, it does give us a "clue" as to how the Code defines a reasonable time for an offer to remain open—three months. But even this three-month period can be shortened by a court by the circumstances surrounding the offer, the customs of the industry, and the course of prior dealings. The purchasing officer is advised not to depend on a three-month period of life for an unlimited offer to sell lying on the desk. It may die right before his eyes!

The purchasing officer is reminded that not only do suppliers make offers, but buyers do as well. A purchase order may be used to convey an offer to buy to a supplier and the same possibilities of remaining open for an indefinite period or lapsing apply. Purchase orders have been known to be sent to suppliers as offers to buy and nothing more has been heard of them. You "shot an arrow in the air, it landed on earth, you know not where" is possible. This might happen occasionally during seller's markets and short supply. While that order is outstanding without a time limit, you have an open commitment to enter into a contract. The arm of your company is extended awaiting a grasp from the supplier. How long a period of time this commitment continues to exist is subject to the same rules as an offer to sell. It remains open until a reasonable time has elapsed. If it is a priced order, the supplier might hold it until the current market price drops, and then fill it at a greater-than-normal profit. It is also possible that your company's need for the item ordered no longer exists at the time it is delivered. It is dangerous to allow such an order to remain open for too long a period of time, subject only to the whims of the supplier or the possibility it may lapse. An unaccepted purchase-order offer to buy should be followed up and some positive action taken to limit its legal existence. This can be done by placing on the order the statement, "This order is subject to acceptance within 10 days from the above date." When that time has passed by, you will be at liberty to place the offer with another supplier, if there is no acceptance. The offer on your purchase order has lapsed.

Nota Bene **to the Purchasing Officer.** This is also a topic of interest to your sales department. Quotations issued to customers without time limits could expose your company to some problems. Sixty days after a quotation has been delivered could find the price quoted to be a bargain. Some alert purchasing officer in your customer's office might decide to take advantage of it because it is now a good price.

2. The Offer Is Rejected

Rejection of an offer is the act of the offeree. Continuing our analogy of the offeror extending the hand, the offeree merely pushes away the outstretched hand and says, "Take it away! I do not want any part of your proposal." This is rejection. It might be accompanied by a direct statement such as, "I reject your offer," "Your price is too high," or something similar. Even though a statement of objection is addressed to only one provision in an offer, it nevertheless rejects the entire offer. Thus, a rejection of F.O.B. terms, packaging, cash discount terms, quantity, delivery date, color assortment, or any other part of the offer is effectively a rejection of the entire offer, even though the balance of the terms are acceptable. The offeree must accept the complete package as proposed by the offeror to constitute an acceptance.

Rejection of an offer kills it. The offer ceases to exist and is forever gone. Once rejected, the offer cannot be revived except if the offeror repeats the offer. It is futile for the offeree, once he has rejected the offer, to attempt to revive it. Any action the offeree might take will only be treated as a counteroffer to the previous one. As an example, assume that you have invited bids for 5000 electrical connectors from three suppliers. The last time you purchased these connectors you paid $8.40 each. The first supplier invited to bid comes to your office and hands you his quotation. You read it while he is still in the office. The price quoted is $10.50. You are astounded at the 25 percent increase and say, "This is highway robbery! I have never paid $10.00 for this connector and do not intend to do so now. You have wasted both your time and mine by bringing such an outrageous quotation to me." After the supplier beats a hasty retreat from your office, you look at the morning mail. The two other bids are there and both are for $10.75! You call one of the suppliers who quoted the $10.75 price and ask, "Why this sudden increase in price?" The answer is that the copper market has had three increases in price since you made your last purchase. You verify this and resignedly send a purchase order to the first supplier who quoted $10.50. A week later a letter from that supplier arrives stating, "We acknowledge receipt of your purchase order. Our selling price is now $11.10 each. Please advise if we should ship at this price."

You have no available legal recourse to force this supplier to deliver at the $10.50 price. Your verbal comments made at the time the offer to sell was delivered to your office acted as a rejection of the offer. Your purchase order could not pump life into that rejected offer to sell. It died when you uttered your harsh words about it. Your purchase order went out as an offer to buy and the supplier is now rejecting it.

We have used the pronoun "you" in this example for convenience. But you, as a trained purchasing officer, would not have been that outspoken with supplier number one. You would know that negotiation is something like a game to be played, and you would elicit all the information you could about a valid offer while reserving your decision until all of the facts were in. Furthermore, the decision-making process would be done in the privacy of your office and not with a supplier in the audience. You would play your cards in proper order—never out of turn, so as to be caught "talking when you should be listening." This is what happened in our hypothetical case.

Let us continue with this hypothetical situation for a moment to learn how an open offer "can come back to haunt you." We will continue using *you* as our main character. Suddenly you become vindictive. You never respond to supplier one's letter, but order the connectors from supplier two for $10.75. Within seven weeks after receiving supplier one's letter, your company receives an order from a customer that requires you to purchase another 5000 connectors. You telephone supplier two and learn that copper has continued to "shoot upward." This supplier advises you that the current price of the connectors is now $11.50 each. You get supplier one's letter out of the file and smugly prepare a courteous response. It states: "My apologies for not responding at an earlier date to your letter advising me that the price of the 5000 connectors is $11.10 each. The press of other business has occupied my time. Please consider this letter your authorization to ship at once the 5000 connectors at $11.10 each. Use my purchase order number in your hands as a reference on your invoice." You say to yourself, "Now I have minded my manners by answering his letter."

Supplier one may not be all that happy that he has finally heard from you. He finds that his counteroffer of $11.10 each has been wrapped into a contract by your letter. He failed to tend to his business. He allowed that $11.10 offer to remain open. The final sentence in his letter to you should have read: "Please advise us within 5 days if we should ship at this price." Then your letter would not have so successfully created a binding contract.

It is a general rule of the law that the rejection of an offer must be communicated to the offeree before it becomes effective. Rejection need not be made in the same form as the offer. A verbal rejection kills a written offer. But no matter how it is made, the rejection does not achieve its purpose until it is communicated to the original offeror. For example, when you send a courtesy note to an unsuccessful bidder thanking him for the courtesy of giving you a quotation, your note or postcard acts as a rejection of that offer. But the rejection is not effective until that supplier receives it in the mail. Should you wish to change your decision by making the award to that supplier shortly after the note of rejection was mailed, you could call him and accept his offer verbally. If your telephone call reaches him before your written note of rejection arrives in his mail, you have effectively accepted his offer and created a contract.

We have stated previously that an outright rejection of an offer kills it. But a rejection with a suggestion for an amendment, although it rejects the original offer, serves the second purpose of making a counteroffer. It is a rejection and a new offer combined. We shall pursue this interesting piece of legal action further in Chapter XIII.

3. The Offer Is Revoked

The third possibility in the eventful life of an offer is that it may be revoked. Revocation is act of the offeror. The hand that the offeror extended when making the offer, is drawn back. It is no longer there for the offeree to grasp. For the revocation to be successful, the hand must be drawn back before the offeree has grasped it.

The law permits an offer to be revoked at any time before acceptance because of the lack of consideration passing to the offeror at the time the offer is made.

The offeror, at the time the offer is made, makes a legal commitment to the offeree. He extends his arm voluntarily to express his willingness to enter into a contract on the terms proposed. If the offeror decides at any time that there is no reason to proceed with his proposal, he is at liberty to withdraw his hand and revoke the offer. Nothing has occurred legally to make him keep that arm extended. Nothing has been paid to him to help support that hand while it is extended. The offer was made freely and there is no legal reason to prevent it from being withdrawn with equal freedom. The law gives the offeror this choice because no consideration was given to induce him to continue making the offer available for acceptance. The offeror is under no obligation to hold it open.

The ability to withdraw an offer at will has led to some unfortunate results in business transactions. Consider this hypothetical situation:

> The sales department of the Hijinks Company receives a request for quotation from a customer for 200 units of one of its products. Their product requires a component part that has always been supplied by the Valve Company. Jinx, the purchasing officer of Hijinks, gets a $300 per unit quotation on this part from the Valve Company. This $300 cost is added to Hijinks manufacturing costs of $700, for a total cost of $1000, including overhead. A 50 percent markup is added to the $1000, and their customer is quoted $1500 per unit.
>
> Ten days after their customer was quoted, Jinx receives a telephone call from the Valve Company telling him that they are revoking their $300 quotation. He is told that they have just received a large order from another company that will occupy their full production capabilities for the next three months. They apologize for being unable to

supply Jinx with the requested component part during that time. Jinx no sooner hangs up the telephone from his call, than his sales manager comes striding into his office. The sales manager happily conveys the good news to Jinx that he has just gotten the order from their customer for the 200 units. The sales manager continues, "Our customer must have delivery within two months. Our plant superintendent tells me he can meet that deadline easily if you can get the Valve Company to deliver the component part within 45 days. How about that?"

Jinx is speechless—and helpless.

This is an instance where the ability to revoke at will causes real hardship. Jinx is faced with the difficult task of finding an alternate supplier to make their component part, or attempt to get the Valve Company to run a separate night shift to produce it. The $300 acquisition cost under either alternative appears to be out of the question. The profit from the sale has eroded.

You will note that nothing illegal occurred. All three parties acted in good faith and within their legal rights. The Hijinks Company made a valid offer to sell their product, and their customer accepted that offer in a proper manner. The Valve Company made a valid offer to sell their part, but then legally revoked the offer before it was accepted. Despite the good faith of each party, Jinx is caught in a vise. His company has a legal commitment to their customer, yet there is no ready source of supply for the needed component part. The timing of the offers— the acceptance and the revocation—worked against the Hijinks Company, Note that if the order from their customer had arrived one day earlier, Jinx could have mailed a purchase order to the Valve Company the same day. This would have accepted their $300 offer to sell, and Valve and Hijinks would have been in a legal and binding contract. (An acceptance becomes effective the moment it is mailed, providing it conforms in all respects to the offer. See Chapter XIV.) Also note that if the Valve Company had called Jinx before Hijinks customer had mailed their purchase order, the sales manager could have revoked the offer to sell to the customer and submitted a revised proposal. As long as the revocation from the sales manager reached the customer before their order was mailed, the revocation would be effective. Despite all these possibilities, the transaction was a disaster because Valve Company's offer could be revoked, since it had not been accepted by Jinx.

Nota Bene **to the Purchasing Officer.** The possibility is always present that an ordinary offer on your desk may be revoked. You must be alert to this fact. When there is possible exposure to loss if an offer is revoked, it is your duty to protect your company. You will find this protection by making an arrangement with the supplier that precludes revocation of the offer. You have several avenues to do this: (1) securing a firm offer, (2) writing an option contract, (3) securing a bid bond from the supplier, or (4) bringing your supplier into negotiations with your customer through the doctrine of promissory estoppel. These choices are explained in the next chapter. Do not allow what happened to Jinx to occur in your organization.

4. The Offer Is Accepted

The fourth and last possibility on the list of things that might happen to an offer is that it may be accepted and ripen into a contract. A contract is what the offeror hoped for when the offer was made. Acceptance occurs when the offeree grasps the offeror's extended hand and says, "You have yourself a deal!" (Acceptance of offers is discussed in Chapter XIV.)

FIRM OFFERS

Although an offer may generally be withdrawn anytime before its acceptance, the Uniform Commercial Code has made an exception under certain conditions. If the offer is an ordinary one which does not comply with the firm offer requirements of the Uniform Commercial Code, then there is not a firm offer. One must simply rely upon any case law exceptions such as estoppel. The Uniform Commercial Code provisions for firm offers and the requirements for them are covered in the next chapter.

AGREEMENT WITHOUT IDENTIFYING OFFER

Just as the Uniform Commercial Code does not require that one identify the precise acceptance, it also does not require identification of the precise point of offer. It recognizes that in business conversations and negotiations it may be difficult to precisely identify these factors and the precise point of the making of the contract. For this reason, the drafters of the Uniform Commercial Code have pointed out that one need not show this exact point, but rather simply show that an agreement exists. Of course, in many situations, one will be able to identify the particular statement or writing that constitutes the offer. Still it is important to realize that such identification may not be necessary where the overall context indicates agreement.

XIV

Firm Offers, Bid Bonds, and Options

We saw in the previous chapter an example of the devastating effect revocation of an offer can have on a business transaction. The ability the offeror has to revoke an offer at any time before its acceptance has long plagued the purchasing officer. You take time to prepare proper specifications for your requirements and then you seek quotations from suppliers based upon these specs. One by one the quotations arrive. You evaluate them prior to making an award. While these quotations lie on your desk, they are only offers to sell. During the evaluation process you run the risk of having one or more of them whisked from under your eyes. A supplier may decide to revoke his offer. It could be for any reason or for no reason. A replacement quotation may be submitted. If a substitute offer is submitted, the evaluation process begins again. In short, the ability to revoke an offer at will creates an uncertainty in the purchasing operation. And this uncertainty has been around since the beginning of modern business practice because the common law refused to make an offer *firm* even for a limited period of time. The lack of consideration passing to the offeror caused the common law to give the offeror the right to revoke at any time before acceptance.

Although buyers can and do make offers as well as suppliers, the common law rule harmed buyers more than suppliers. Buyers concentrate on filling a need when they issue an offer to buy. The intent is to fill that need at the lowest possible cost. The urgency of filling that need is paramount in the buyer's mind, and there is less chance the offer to buy will be revoked once it is issued. So the ability to revoke freely is more harmful to buyers than to suppliers.

Some cooperating suppliers, who recognized the problems created by this

rule of law, would place a statement on their offers that reads, "This offer is firm
for 10 days." But even such assurance did not overcome the lack of consideration.
Courts regularly ruled that these offers, too, were revocable at will. Revocation
was still possible during the stated firm period. Thus the statement only added to
the problem, because most buyers were lulled into the belief that the supplier's
word was good and it would control. The majority of the suppliers did abide by
their promise because they were professional businesspersons acting in good
faith. They wanted their word to be accepted at face value. But there were also
others who had less character. They might get caught with an open firm offer that
was not to their advantage and would want to rid themselves of a bad deal.
Despite the "guaranteed firm" clause on their offer they would exercise their
option to revoke. The courts proved to be powerless to hold them to the written
promise.

Some states passed legislation to correct this evil. New York, for example,
has this statute (Section 5-1109 of the General Obligations Law):

> When hereafter an offer to enter into a contract is made in writing,
> signed by the offeror, or his agent, which states that the offer is irrev-
> ocable during a period set forth or until a time fixed, the offer shall
> not be revocable during such period or until such time because of the
> absence of consideration for the assurance of irrevocability.

This legislation eliminated the need for consideration passing to the offeror
and was what the courts needed to hold a supplier to his word. But not all states
had such legislation, and buyers continued to be caught short on occasions.

SECTION 2-205–PURCHASING'S BUDDY

Purchasing officers, therefore, welcomed the Uniform Commercial Code and its
now popular Section 2-205. This section once and for all time sets forth clearly
the status of firm offers made without consideration. It reads:

> An offer by a merchant to buy or sell goods in a signed writing which
> by its terms gives assurance it will be held open is not revocable, for
> lack of consideration, during the time stated or if no time is stated for
> a reasonable time, but in no event may such period of irrevocability
> exceed three months; but any such assurance on a form supplied by
> the offeree must be separately signed by the offeror.

Section 2-205 provided a marked change in the prevailing law when the
Uniform Commercial Code was adopted. It brought a uniform and standard
approach to the process of obtaining quotations which are irrevocable for a
stated period of time. No longer may a supplier make an apparent firm offer and
then revoke it before the purchasing officer has had time to decide whether to

accept it. Gone, too, is the need to find some "considera-
tion" passing to an offeror before it becomes a firm offer. This section of the code
is purchasing's friend and is designed to assist in the performance of your job.
Look at the following hypothetical case to see how valuable it can be.

> Jane, the director of procurement of Tube Inc. invites bids for three
> carloads of pulpboard which is the raw material for the company's
> product. She sends detailed specifications to four suppliers, each of
> whom responds to the invitation. All bids are dated July 15, are writ-
> ten on the company's letterhead, and begin with the statement: "In
> response to your invitation to quote, we are pleased to make the fol-
> lowing offer to you:" These are the bids:
>
> Bee Co.—3 carloads pulpboard $.32 per pound delivered. This price
> guaranteed firm for 60 days.
>
> Sea Co.—Pulpboard per your specifications, $.30 per pound deliv-
> ered. Offer must be accepted within 10 days to receive this price.
>
> Jay Co.—3 carloads pulpboard, $.33 per pound delivered. Will sell
> you carload lots at this price for the next three months.
>
> Kay Co.—3 carloads pulpboard, per your specifications, 31 cents per
> pound.

Before Jane could place an order, each of the prospective suppliers sent her
the following announcement: "The price of pulpboard will be 45 cents per
pound delivered, on and after July 22. All previous quotations are hereby cancelled."

These notices were received by Jane the morning of July 22, and each was
signed by the sales manager of the company who had signed the original quotation.

> Rube, the president of Tube Inc., called Jane to his office that morning.
> During the conversation Jane told Rube of the sudden increase in the
> price of pulpboard. Rube told Jane to order 15 carloads immediately to
> cover their needs for the next six months.
>   On July 23rd Jane sent purchase orders to Bee Co. and Sea Co.,
> each for 3 carloads, noting on the order, "per your offer dated July 15."
> She sent an order to the Jay Co. for 9 carloads with the same note on
> the order.

Prior to Section 2-205 Jane would have been forced to pay 45 cents per
pound for the pulpboard. But now the Section saves the day for her. Bee, Sea, and
Jay gave her firm quotations for 3 carloads each, which were nonrevocable under
Section 2-205. None of the three could legally revoke their offers by their letters
that announced, "All previous quotations are hereby cancelled." Bee's offer was

firm until September 14. Sea could not revoke its offer until July 26, and Jay's offer was good until October 15. Only Kay Co. successfully revoked its July 15 offer with the letter. That revocation became effective the morning of July 22 when Jane received it. Kay's offer contained no assurance that it would be held firm, and was therefore subject to immediate revocation.

Special mention should be made of the nine-carload order Jane sent to the Jay Co. Jane was taking advantage of Jay's statement, "Will sell carload lots at this price for the next three months." Whether a court of law would say that Jay's offer included nine carloads of the pulpboard at the firm price is questionable. There is a definite firm offer for three carloads at the 33-cent price. The assurance that this is a firm offer can be found in the statement quoted previously. But it is feared the statement "Will sell carload lots at this price" is not an offer to sell an additional six car loads. It lacks the degree of definiteness required in an offer. Perhaps a court might say at a minimum that it is an offer for one additional carload. In any event Jane is to be applauded for making the attempt to get an additional six car-loads from Jay under the proposal. "Nothing ventured, nothing gained." Besides, Jay may be anxious to sell an oversupply of pulpboard that he has on hand.

The main point of this hypothetical case is to illustrate how well Section 2-205 serves the purposes of the buyer. Jane was able to provide the raw material for her company's product for several months at a price 30 percent below the current market because these quotations were held firm. The three suppliers could not revoke their offers to enable them to take advantage of a sudden market upswing.

Since Section 2-205 is such a friend of purchasing, we must become familiar with its provisions. It devotes most of its words to specifying what a firm offer is, and these are the details we must master. It appears that the following eight essentials are required to make Section 2-205 operative:

1. It must be a bona fide, valid offer.

2. It must be made by a merchant.

3. It must be an offer to buy or sell goods.

4. It must be in writing.

5. It must be signed.

6. It must express the assurance it will be held open.

7. It must have a reasonable time limitation.

8. The assurance must be separately signed if made on the offeree's form (for example, on a duplicate copy of a request for quotation form).

Any offer that does not meet all of these requirements is not a firm offer and can be revoked at any time by the offeror. A discussion of each of these essentials follows.

1. It Must Be an Offer

All the essentials of an offer discussed in the previous chapter must be present. Section 2-205 does not apply to invitations to do business or to any other type of incomplete offer. The intent to make an offer, a definite subject matter, and communication to the offeree are the essential elements of an offer that is covered by this section.

2. The Offer Must Be Made by a Merchant

Only those offers made by a merchant are covered by this section. We determined in Chapter X that a person who regularly deals (buys or sells) in the goods involved in an offer is a merchant. So, too, are their authorized agents. Purchasing officers and authorized sales personnel are merchants when acting for their principals. The distinction between the treatment of an offer by a merchant and a nonmerchant can be observed in these two situations, which are similar:

> *Situation 1.* On December 10 Jerk visits a local jeweler by the name of Sparkle. Jerk has a valuable diamond ring he wishes to convert into cash and asks Sparkle if he will purchase the ring from him for $10,000. Sparkle recognizes it as a valuable ring and believes it can be resold for a handsome profit. He tells Jerk, "Let me have the ring for a few days to have it appraised. Meanwhile give me some statement that you are willing to sell it for $10,000, so that I will not waste time and money in having it examined." Jerk prepares the following note: "I will sell you my diamond ring for $10,000 any time before December 20. Signed (Jerk)." The note was dated December 10.
>
> By December 15 Jerk has changed his mind. He visits Sparkle and says he has decided not to sell the ring and demands it back. Sparkle is furious because he has just about completed arrangements to sell the ring to a third party for $15,000. He offers Jerk $10,000 cash. Jerk refuses to accept the cash and files suit to recover his ring.
>
> *Situation 2.* On December 10 Jerk notices a beautiful diamond ring in Sparkle's store. It has a price tag of $12,000. Jerk expresses an interest in purchasing the ring as a Christmas present. Sparkle, anxious to make the sale, says, "You may have the ring for $10,000." Jerk hesitates and says, "I want to think it over. Give me a few days and I will be back. Will you still sell me the ring for $10,000 if I do decide to buy it?" Sparkle writes out the following note and hands it to Jerk: "I will sell you diamond ring No. 32a for $10,000 any time before December 20. Signed (Sparkle)." The note was dated December 10.
>
> By December 15 Jerk decides to purchase the ring. He visits

Sparkle at the jewelry store. Before Jerk can utter a word, Sparkle says to him, "I am glad you came in today. Another customer wanted to buy the ring you liked so much and offered to pay me my $12,000 asking price. I held him off saying that I was duty-bound to offer it to you first for $12,000. Do you wish it at that price?" Jerk was furious and showed Sparkle his note offering to sell it for $10,000. Sparkle is adamant and says, "You pay me $12,000 or I will sell it to my other customer." Jerk responded by filing suit to force Sparkle to sell him the ring for $10,000.

Valid offers to sell were made in both Situations 1 and 2. These are written offers, duly signed and communicated. The rings involved are sufficiently described. In both situations the offerors changed their minds and decided not to sell. The offerors communicated their revocations before the offerees had the opportunity to accept. The facts are almost identical, except that offeror Jerk is a nonmerchant, while offeror Sparkle is a merchant. It is this difference that will cause the courts involved to come up with diametrically opposite decisions.

Section 2-205 is not applicable to the offer made in Situation 1 because Jerk is a nonmerchant. The rule in Section 2-205 making offers firm does not apply to an offer made by a nonmerchant. The court instead of applying Section 2-205 would resort to the common law and general contract law. This permits an offer to be revoked at any time before acceptance. Section 2-205 amended this prevailing law only in those cases where the offeror is a merchant. Sparkle would be forced to return the ring.

Section 2-205 is applicable to the offer made in Situation 2. The offeror here was Sparkle, a merchant who regularly deals in rings and other jewelry. Jerk could have waited until December 19 to buy the ring for $10,000 because Section 2-205 makes it a firm offer through that date. Sparkle could not legally sell the ring to anyone else before December 20. The court's decision in Situation 2 will again be in Jerk's favor. Sparkle must sell him the ring for $10,000 if Jerk wishes to purchase it.

3. It Must Be an Offer to Buy or Sell Goods

Look first at the following hypothetical case:

Lynn Seed is the purchasing officer of the Paint & Varnish Company. She invites bids from four painting contractors to paint the interior and exterior of Paint & Varnish Company's office building, manufacturing plant, and warehouse. Her specifications include this provision: "All necessary paint and thinner will be supplied to the contractor free of charge by our company. We will provide our first-line products."

Peel Painting Company is the low bidder with a price of $49,000. Across their quotation in capital letters is this statement: "THIS

PRICE IS GUARANTEED FIRM FOR 30 DAYS." The bid is dated June 10 and is signed by the president of Peel Painting Company. The others bids are $55,000, $56,000 and $57,000.

On June 15 Lynn discusses the quotations with the president and the sales manager. Peel Painting is not a good customer of Paint & Varnish Company, while the other three bidders are large users of their products. It is decided to award the order to Peel Painting to save the $6,000. It is also hoped that the award will make Peel Painting a better customer of theirs.

When Lynn returns to her desk she reads the morning mail. In it is a letter from Peel Painting Company advising that they are forced to change their bid to $54,000.

The question raised here is whether Peel Painting Company can be required to do the job for $49,000.

A court of law would say that the $49,000 offer made by Peel Painting Company on June 10 was effectively revoked before it was accepted by Paint & Varnish Company. The quotation was a bona fide offer to sell that met all the provisions of Section 2-205, except one. The one exception is that the offer was not to buy or sell *goods*. The offer was to apply paint to the walls and ceilings. That is a sale of a *service* and not a sale of *goods*. The offer does not qualify under Section 2-205.

You will recall that in Chapter X we found that Section 2-102 of the code stated " . . . this Article applies to transactions in goods . . . " We also learned that the code defined goods as "things." Thus Section 2-205 is following that direction when it confines firm offers to buy or to sell goods. In the case above, the application of paint cannot measure up to the code's definition of goods or "things." Without the benefit of Section 2-205, the common law rule will apply. That means that the $49,000 of Peel Painting Company was properly revoked. Peel Painting was free to make another offer if Lynn was willing to consider it. But they cannot be made to do the job for $49,000 under Section 2-205 of the Code. However, if Paint & Varnish Company was located in New York or in a state that had a statute similar to the New York statute mentioned at the beginning of this chapter, the result could be reversed. You will note that the New York statute did not mention "goods" but only "a contract." Therefore Peel Painting's offer to do the work for $49,000 might be enforceable under such a statute. But it is clear that it could not be enforced under Section 2-205.

There is a gray area that exists as to whether a contract is considered *goods* or *services* and whether the goods or services come under Article 2 of the Code. When a contract calls for both goods and services, the applicability of the Code is questionable. Suppose Peel Painting had to furnish the paint for the above job. Does that make the transaction one for *goods* and thereby be covered by Section 2-205? Courts have considered such hybrid situations, and the result has been one that depends upon the specific circumstances of each case. If the preponderance of costs in the contract is for goods, the Code is ruled applicable. If the labor portion is greater, the Code is not applied. In all probability, the Peel Painting offer would continue to be for *services* under this interpretation because labor costs would exceed the cost of the paint.

4. The Offer Must Be In Writing

Earlier it was stated that an offer may be communicated either verbally or in writing. That statement remains unchallenged, but it must now be amended. An offer, to qualify as a firm offer, must be in writing. Oral offers, though valid, cannot become firm offers. The writers of the code were of the opinion that the extreme change in the law that is contained in Section 2-205 is justified only if there is a writing to establish precisely what was offered. Exact wording of a verbal offer is difficult to prove.

5. The Offer Must Be Signed

The writers of the Code provided another protection for offerors in Section 2-205. They wanted to be certain that the offeror had made a conscious decision to make an offer and to make that offer a firm offer. One method to assure this was to insist that the offer be signed. We are aware that in the pressures of modern-day business, people often sign papers without knowing the contents, or they have someone else sign for them. This could happen when the offer was signed, but at least the person signing it had the opportunity to review what was contained on the paper.

In Chapter VII a legal signature was defined. The Code adopts the same criteria for a valid signature—it must be intended to be the legal signature of the maker. Thus, any signature that meets this test is adequate to meet the Section 2-205 requirement.

The Official Comment of the commissioners who wrote the Code states that the signature required might be on a separate piece of paper. This is possible if the separate piece of paper clearly relates the signature to the piece of paper on which the offer was submitted. Thus a detailed offer to sell could come to your office unsigned. If the person submitting the offer was some distance from your office, compliance with the requirement to be signed could be made by a signed note from the offeror. The note might read: "The offer dated October 13 covering structural steel that I submitted to your office in three pages, but unsigned is a firm offer for 30 days. (Signed) The Offeror." The signature on the note authenticates the offer if the description of the offer is sufficient for a court to integrate it with the offer. The same type of note can be used to convert a signed ordinary offer to a firm offer.

6. It Must Contain an Assurance That It Will Be Held Open

An assurance that it will be held open is the magic that separates a firm offer from an ordinary offer. There must be words in the signed written offer that indicate that a firm offer is intended to be made by the offeror. Section 2-205 does not specify what words are necessary to make an offer firm. It only requires that the offer "gives *assurance* it will be held open." *Assurance* is a promise or a guaranty. "Held open" in this context means that the offeror agrees not to withdraw or revoke the offer. Therefore the Code seeks to have the offer contain a promise or a guaranty that it will not be revoked. There are many phrases used commercially to denote this concept that serve this purpose. Here are a few examples that could be used:

1. This is a firm offer.

2. Offer will be held open.

3. Open offer.

4. Firm offer.

5. Offer and price guaranteed firm.

6. Offer not subject to revocation.

7. Open for acceptance within 30 days.

8. Will remain open for 10 days.

9. Open for 30 days.

10. Offer not subject to revocation for 30 days.

11. Available for 10 days only.

12. This offer will remain firm for 10 days.

There are many other possibilities than the above. Care should be taken to make certain that the words used express the fact that the offeror is relinquishing his power of revocation of the offer. Any phrase that gives the offeree this assurance will suffice. Remember that it is the offer—the supplier's willingness to sell the product—that is made firm by Section 2-205. In a strict legal sense the statement, "This price is guaranteed firm for 10 days" does not embrace the complete offer and could be construed not to give assurance that the offer itself will be held open for 10 days. However, most courts would say that commercial custom dictates that such a statement includes the offer as well as the price. A supplier who does not intend to hold open the complete offer would have to amend his assurance to read, "The price, but not the offer to sell, is guaranteed for 10 days," or "Availability of the product is not guaranteed."

7. The Offer Must Contain a Reasonable Time Limitation

Section 2-205 contains relatively few words for such an important piece of legislation. More than one-half of the words employed in the section are devoted to the time constraints applied to firm offers. The Code states, " . . . during the time stated or for a reasonable time, but in no event may such period of irrevocability exceed three months . . . "

" . . . during the time stated . . . " gives us little problem. "This offer firm for 30 days" means exactly what it says. On the thirty-first day, the offer is no longer firm. But when does the countdown begin? On the date of the offer or on the date the offer is received by you? The elapsed time between the mailing of an offer and its receipt by the offeree could be several days. Purchasing officers are advised to accept the date shown on the face of the offer as the date the time period begins to expire or run. The offeror is master of the offer. The courts will accept the offeror's intent as controlling; the offeror's intent is shown by the date printed on the offer—as the date the offeror intended for the time period to begin.

Suppose an unreasonable period of time elapses before the offer is received. Insofar as the offeror is concerned, the time limit established on the offer has been running. If the offeree finds the shortened length of time remaining for consideration of the offer a hardship, it is the offeree's duty to call this fact to the attention of the offeror. A request for an extension of time should be made. If the offeror grants the extension, it must be placed in writing and signed for it to be effective under Section 2-205. A verbal extension does not serve the requirements of 2-205.

How does one count the number of days that have elapsed when a time limit is involved? Commercial custom tells us to exclude the first day and include the last day. Thus, an offer written on June 10 that is guaranteed firm for 10 days, will be firm *through* June 20. It is no longer a firm offer on June 21. Although June 10 to June 20 involves 11 days, we have only 11 chargeable days to the firm offer, by excluding the first day (June 10) and including the last day (June 20).

Purchasing officers are advised not to play the numbers game on dates down to the last minute, unless it is absolutely essential. Remember that your offeror has taken a business risk when a firm offer is extended to you. His costs can escalate while his offer lies on your desk. A firm offer is really an insurance policy for the buyer. If you are contracting for a raw material need for the next six months, your company will have a fixed raw materials cost for nine months, based upon a lead time of three months for delivery. Asking a supplier to quote you a 30 days firm offer adds another month of insurance, at the supplier's expense. Good faith on your part dictates that you take no more time than essential to make the award. The supplier is entitled to a fair deal too. A fair deal includes the prompt decisions—and notification—of who the successful bidder is and who the unsuccessful bidders are. The unsuccessful bidders will be able to allocate the risk they have been taking on your quotation to other potential customers, if given prompt notification of the loss of your award.

Should you foresee a need for additional time before making an award, and the time limitation for the firm offer is about to expire, you may ask the supplier for an extension. It is suggested that you ask for the extension before the present time limit expires! The supplier must agree to such an extension. Should the supplier not agree, you will then have a few remaining days to act on the original offer. Any extension of time must be given in writing and signed to make it effective under Section 2-205.

The second caveat on time limitation in Section 2-205 states that in the event that no time limit is set in the firm offer, the offer is firm "for a reasonable time." This is the same "reasonable time" we encountered in the previous chapter when discussing the lapse of an offer. Again, the same considerations of the circumstances of the offer, previous dealings, and usage in the trade apply.

Section 2-205 does, however, establish the maximum time in which an undated firm offer may run before it lapses " . . . but in no event may such period of irrevocability exceed three months . . . " This also establishes the maximum period of time a dated firm offer may be considered firm. Thus, "this offer is firm for four months" cannot be considered firm after the first three months of its life have elapsed. This is the maximum time Section 2-205 permits.

This raises an interesting question, though, of what will happen to a 4 months firm offer after three months have elapsed. If the offer is not accepted during the first three months of its life, is it capable of being accepted during the fourth month? Consider the import of the answer to this situation:

> On April 10 The Pie Company invited bids for 150 bushels of top quality peaches. Fruit Growers Company responded on April 12, "We offer to sell you 150 bushels of our top quality peaches for $30 per bushel. This offer, as well as our peaches, is guaranteed firm for four months."
>
> On July 31 The Pie Company sends Fruit Growers Company a purchase order for the peaches showing the quoted price of $30 per bushel. Fruit Growers responds, "Our current price of peaches is now $40 per bushel."
>
> Can The Pie Company get the peaches at $30 per bushel?

The answer to this hypothetical situation is yes: The Pie Company can get its peaches for $30. On July 10 the firm offer expired by action of Section 2-205, but the full life of the offer was four months. The Pie Company accepted the offer while it was still alive and is therefore entitled to the peaches at $30 per bushel. Note that from July 10 to August 10 Fruit Growers could have revoked its outstanding offer. The freeze placed on revocation by 2-205 expired on July 10, but that did not cause the entire offer to lapse.

8. *If Made on the Offeree's Form, the Assurance Must Be Separately Signed*

The authors of the Uniform Commercial Code placed a protective clause in Section 2-205 for the benefit of those who do not take the time to read the boilerplate on a printed form. This clause is placed there specifically for our supplier friends who do not take the trouble to read all the terms and conditions we take the trouble to print on our request for quotation forms. This protective clause reads, "but any such assurance on a form supplied by the offeree must be separately signed by the offeror." The offeree's form referred to is a quotation request form or a bid document that you, the purchasing officer, prepare for the bidder to complete and return. Your supplier is the offeror because he is submitting an offer to sell to your company in response to your invitation to submit a quotation. The quotation is on your form so it is a "form supplied by the offeree." The following hypothetical case illustrates the situation:

> Rose, the purchasing officer of Toy Automobile Company sends out quotation requests for 1000 automobile radios for installation in the toy automobile they make for children. One of Toy Automobile's customers is interested in buying 1000 of their product, but insists that they must be equipped with genuine auto radios.
>
> The quotation request is sent to each prospective supplier in duplicate, with instructions to submit their quotation on the duplicate copy and return. At the bottom of the form to be returned by the supplier is this statement: "We offer to sell Toy Automobile Company the above items at the price stated, in accordance with the terms and conditions on the reverse side of this form." *Signed* _____
>
> The reverse side of the quotation request form listed 10 terms and conditions. Number 3 reads, "The bidder guarantees to hold firm the price quoted for 30 days."
>
> Dial Radio Company is the low bidder with a unit price of $75. Their bid was dated April 15 and was signed by Watt Dial, the president. Based upon this quotation Toy Automobile Company quoted their customer the usual wholesale price of their toy auto, plus $75 for the cost of the radio.
>
> On May 5 two important pieces of mail arrived at Toy Auto Company. One was from the customer ordering the 1000 autos with the radios installed. The second was a letter from Dial Radio Company which read:
>
> > We are sorry to have to advise you that production costs at our plant have increased. We must withdraw our April 15 quotation to you. Our new price is $90 each. We hope you will favor us with your order.
>
> Rose immediately called Watt Dial to state that Toy Automobile had relied on the $75 price quoted. That cost was built into their costs, which determined their selling price. The proposed price change would cost Toy Automobile $15,000 and would erode their profit on

the sale. Rose continued, "Your quotation was a firm quotation. You signed the quotation form which included the term on the back of it assuring us that your price was guaranteed firm for 30 days."

Dial responded, "We never read all the terms and conditions printed on our customer's forms. There is so much trivia on these forms that we would have little time to run our business if we read all of it. I am very sorry, but I must insist on $90 per radio."

The question raised here is whether Dial Radio's quotation was a firm offer. There is no doubt that their quotation was a valid offer to sell their radio at $75 each. At any time prior to May 5, Rose could have sent them a purchase order, and they would have been in a binding contract. But on May 5, Dial Radio effectively revoked the $75 offer to sell and submitted a new offer at $90 each.

Section 2-205 was not Rose's buddy in this situation. It could not make a firm offer from the quotation Dial Radio submitted. The assurance needed to make it a firm offer was printed on Rose's form. Rose was the offeree. Section 2-205 requires that " . . . assurance on a form supplied by the offeree must be separately signed by the offeror." In this case there was no separate signature applied to condition no. 3 on Rose's request for quotation form. Watt Dial did not turn over the form to sign the clause. In fact, it is doubtful that he read any part of the reserve side of the form. His failure to do this allowed his offer to remain an ordinary offer, subject to revocation. It could not graduate to the firm-offer class without the separate signing.

At first blush, it seems harsh justice that Dial's failure to sign the term could work to his advantage. But the truth of the matter is that Rose had the power to keep this from happening. The fault lies at her doorstep. When a purchasing officer has this firm offer provision in the request for quotation form, the suppliers must be made to separately sign it. A quotation that arrives without that signature must be ruled an incomplete bid. The bid should be returned to the supplier for completion. The failure to sign it should cause that bid to be removed from further consideration. Thus Rose was at fault due to her failure to reject Dial Radio's quotation because it was incomplete.

This unusual requirement (of a second signature when the assurance of a firm offer is printed on a request for quotation form) is in the law for several reasons. The authors of the Uniform Commercial Code made a major change in prevailing law by allowing a firm offer to be created without consideration passing to the offeror. They wanted to be certain that each offeror who gave a firm offer did so with full knowledge that it was being made. The offeror who applied the statement of assurance on his own form could be presumed beyond a reasonable doubt to have intended to make that commitment. But when the statement of assurance is prepared by someone else and printed on a form that the offeror is to sign, the question, "Did he know it was there?" will immediately arise. If he signs the form without reading the assurance statement, it cannot be said that the offeror intended to make the commitment. The Code writers believed that the only method to prove that the offeror had read the assurance statement and intended to make a firm offer is to have that term signed right where it is was printed on the offeree's form. Hence the requirement that it be "separately signed." This means that the supplier must sign the request for quotation form twice—once for the offer itself, and another time for the assurance that a firm offer is being made.

The above eight requirements are essential for an offer to be firm under Section 2-205. An offer that is valid in other respects, but does not possess these essentials is an ordinary offer and revocable at will.

***Nota Bene* to the Purchasing Officer.** Section 2-205 is a law that favors purchasing. It shifts the burden of the risk of price increases to the supplier for a limited period of time. It also gives purchasing some time to evaluate quotations and reach decisions. The pressure is absent during the period the offer is kept open by the law. The other proven methods used to lock in an offering price for a period of time are writing an option contract or forcing the supplier to furnish a bid bond. An option contract is a potential cost to the buyer in the event the option is not exercised because the earnest money is forfeited. A bid bond is paid for by the supplier, but the price quoted is usually higher because the cost of the bond is wrapped into the quote. But there should be no added cost for a firm offer under Section 2-205. There is no reason for the supplier to include an add on to the firm offer if he is confident of a stable market. Furthermore, the supplier has the opportunity to protect himself against a price increase in his raw materials by securing a similar firm offer to sell from his suppliers. It appears Section 2-205 has made the need for options and bid bonds minimal because the same results may be obtained by the intelligent use of firm offers.

There are—and will continue to be—some suppliers who hesitate to give a firm offer. Such suppliers are wary of being tied into a fixed position for a period of time. There is little a purchasing officer can do to change the posture of such suppliers, except to seek alternate suppliers who will give this assurance. Sheer pressure from competitors is the one effective force that might move a stubborn supplier. If his competitors will offer this protection, the reluctant supplier may see the handwriting on the wall and capitulate.

Some suppliers complain that Section 2-205 is a one-sided law because it favors the buyer. There is some merit to this viewpoint, because the buyer has two alternative procedures available while he hold s a firm offer. If prices escalate, the quoted price on the firm offer protects the buyer. If prices decline, the buyer may decide to ignore the offer and seek new quotations that will reflect the lower market prices. Thus, the buyer has the best of both worlds when holding a firm offer. Yes, Section 2-205 is purchasing's buddy.

SECURING FIRM OFFERS

Securing a firm price quotation that will be held firm for a period of time is not always possible. Some suppliers, eager to do business with you, may voluntarily quote you on a firm basis. But such voluntary action rarely occurs in other than a highly competitive market. Usually purchasing must work for a firm quotation, if it is required.

The proper time to ask for a firm offer is when you are obtaining quotations from suppliers. This is preferred to waiting until all quotations are in and then confronting the bidders without advance warning. It is not fair to a supplier to force him to make a snap decision on a firm quotation while sitting at your desk. The quotation submitted is the *considered* judgment of all the factors and risks that might affect the supplier's performance if given the contract. If a firm quotation is to be part of his submission to you, he should have the same opportunity to review the factors involved in making it. The ethical practice of purchasing dictates that the request for a firm offer be made at the same time a price quotation is sought.

To incorporate a firm price provision in your request for quotation, a statement similar to the following should be included in your conditions:

> Prices quoted in your offer must be guaranteed firm for 30 days. This assurance must be included in the quotation you submit. Quotations received without such assurance will be returned for correction or disregarded when the award is made. Should you be unwilling to make a firm offer for 30 days, state the minimum time you will guarantee your offer and your price.

The last sentence in the above statement can be eliminated if you do not like the suggestion that something shorter than 30 days might be acceptable to you. You have every right to ask for a 30-day assurance—or even 60- or 90-days assurance. But you might be aware of the fact that the market for the product for which you are seeking quotations is unstable. If so, the last sentence might evoke a fewer number of days, but, it could get a firm offer that you might not be able to obtain if it were not included. The last sentence invites the supplier to state on his quotation, "This offer is firm for five days only" or "This offer is subject to immediate acceptance." Every supplier's offer must be firm at the time it is submitted. No supplier would dare hand you a quotation and then immediately revoke it.

A different tactic must be used if you utilize preprinted request for quotation forms and insist that the supplier quote on the carbon copy of that form. If your terms and conditions are printed on the back of the form, this condition should be included: "Prices quoted must be guaranteed firm. Quotations received without the assurance statement on the front page separately signed will be regarded as incomplete and returned for correction." Then on the front of the form state the following: "This offer to sell is guaranteed firm for 30 days." *(Signed)*. It is suggested that this clause be inserted on your form immediately above the blank provided for the supplier's signature to the complete quotation. This will lessen the likelihood of the supplier's coming up with the alibi, "I did not see it."

A 30-day time limit was used in both these examples. There is nothing magic about that number: 10, 15, 20, or 60 may be used. You must be the judge of the time you require to make a decision on the award. You might also consider this option: "Please complete the following assurance. This offer to sell is guaranteed firm for_____days." *(Signed)* This gives a supplier the opportunity to insert his own version of a reasonable time. When the supplier fills in the number of days, you can be certain the assurance is intended. But it does not satisfy the need for the separate signature. You are advised to insist on that signature, too.

A purchasing officer following either of these methods of securing firm offers must be prepared to enforce this bid condition. A supplier who does not give the requested assurance must be made to understand that his quotation will not be considered until the assurance is given. It is not fair to the other competing suppliers, who have given the firm assurance, to be forced to compete with one who has not met all the conditions. The purchasing officer who does not enforce this requirement for every supplier soon loses credibility. Other suppliers will find out that the assurance is not necessary to do business and will abandon their practice of making offers firm.

OPTION CONTRACTS

Purchasing officers are occasionally faced with the necessity of obtaining a firm offer, but are unable to find a supplier willing to make one under Section 2-205. In this event, it is suggested that an attempt be made to execute an *option contract* with the supplier. An option contract will make an offer to sell firm for the length of the option. Under an option contract consideration passes from the offeree to the offeror in return for a firm commitment. A typical option contract might read:

> For and in consideration of $500, receipt of which is hereby acknowledged, we will sell you for the next 60 days our top quality corn for $4 per bushel delivered, in units of 10,000 bushels, up to a total of 150,000 bushels.

This contract makes the offer firm for 60 days. But it is made firm by the option contract and not by Section 2-205. The option contract is enforceable because of the payment of the $500 consideration. This $500 is the cost the buyer must pay to have the assurance of the firm offer. Usually—but not always—the $500 will be applied as partial payment for the purchase. But this is not an assured event, because the application of the $500 to the purchase price is done only if the option contract provides for it. In the event the buyer does not make any purchases during the 60-day period, the $500 is retained by the offeror.

The option contract is a separate and distinct contract between the buyer and the seller. It is not a contract of sale. If the buyer elects to exercise the option by purchasing 20,000 bushels of corn, this will require another contract between the buyer and the seller. The option contract only makes a firm offer to sell possible because the seller (the offeror) is legally bound under it to enter into the sales contract.

Option contracts may be executed for any period of time. It is not covered by the three months limitation stated in Section 2-205. That section is applicable to offers that have no consideration passing to the offeror. An option contract does have the required consideration and thus it may be made for any period of time. This is one of the reasons why they are used.

BID BONDS

Another method that may be employed to make an offer firm is to have the offeror execute a bid bond. A bid bond brings a third party into the transaction. The offeror (the supplier) secures a guarantor (the bonding company) to guarantee that the offeror will enter into a contract of sale with the offeree if given the award. Should a supplier be awarded the contract and then refuse to enter into a contract of sale, the bid bond will be declared forfeited to the benefit of the offeree. The bonding company will pay to the buyer the damages the buyer incurred, up to the limit of the bond.

Bid bonds are used quite often by governmental agencies. Since a government agency must accept any supplier that wants to do business with the government, the use of the bid bond serves an additional purpose. A bonding company will not write a bond on just any person or any company. It must be assured that it has a reasonable chance of recovering any sums it might be called upon to pay to the buyer. Therefore, before a bond is written, the supplier must be able to prove to the bonding company that it has the financial resources to reimburse the bonding company. Thus, a government procurement officer who asks for a bid bond has some reasonable assurance of the financial stability of every supplier that submits a quotation.

Bid bonds are also used extensively in construction bidding. The general contractor's bids are required to be supported by either a bid bond or a cashier's check equal to a percentage of their total bid. The bid bond or the cashier's check are considered to be assurance to the owner that there will be a contract with the successful bidder when given the award. It is customary to include provision in the bidding documents to make the award to the successful bidder within a specified period of time. This period of time—between the bid opening and the time the award must be made—is provided to allow the owner and the architect to evaluate subcontractors, substitutes or alternates, and other details of the bidding documents. The bid bond is a guarantee that (1) the bid will be held firm for the specified number of days, and (2) that the bidder will enter into a contract if awarded the contract.

The guarantee that the successful bidder will enter into a contract or forfeit the bond is not absolute. There is a category of cases that deals with situations in which the low bidder has made an honest mistake in the bid submitted. Here is a hypothetical case that illustrates the problem:

> Joe College, Business Officer of the Weeflunkem University, publicly opens sealed bids for the construction of a new Chemistry Building. The four bids range as follows:

Alpha Construction Co.	$10,000,000
Beta Construction Co.	11,500,000
Gamma Construction Co.	11,600,000
Delta Construction Co.	13,500,000

> Each contractor submitted a bid bond or a cashier's check amounting to 10 percent of their total bid. Joe announced to the assembled bidders that the University and the architect would review the bids and make the award within the 30-day time period in the bid documents.

> Two days later Phi, the President of the Alpha Company, met with Joe College in his office. Phi said his company had made a mistake in their bid. He showed Joe a piece of paper that contained a list of his subcontractors' bids and his own general work:

Electrical	$1,200,000
Mechanical	2,500,000
Heating, ventilating, and air conditioning	3,300,000
General	2,500,000
Subtotal	$8,500,000
10% Overhead	850,000
	$9,350,000
10% Profit	935,000
Total	$10,285,000

Phi said that he entered the $10,000,000 bid because his firm needed a large project to keep their work force together during the next 12 months. Obviously his bid was off by more than $1,000,000 because of an obvious error in addition in reaching the subtotal. The total cost should have been $11,495,000, which is $9,500,000 plus $950,000 plus $1,045,000. He said that he would be willing to take the contract for $11,210,000. "This price is my cost and profit, less the $285,000 by which I agreed to reduce my bid when I believed the total cost plus add-ons would be $10,285,000. This is a fair figure for the University."

Joe College responded that he would not sign a contract with Alpha at any other price than $10,000,000. "If you are not prepared to sign at $10,000,000, I will declare your bid bond forfeited," he said.

Phi was astonished. He said, "You would penalize my firm $1 million because we made a simple arithmetic error in addition? Why, that is unconscionable. I will fight that all the way to the Supreme Court."

Phi correctly interpreted the attitude of the courts of law in this situation. The court would state that the $1 million forfeiture was unconscionable and would refuse to declare the bond forfeited. It would point out that the University had not changed its position because of Phi's error. There remained the three other bids that the University could accept and have their Chemistry Building built. They were not "out of pocket" for any amount if the $10 million bid was allowed to be withdrawn. It was true that the University would pay more than $10,000,000 for the construction of the building, but that would have been the result if Alpha had not made an error. The prevailing opinion in the courts would allow Alpha to withdraw the bid without penalty.

Experienced purchasing officers will raise an eyebrow about Alpha's action. Everyone recognizes that honest errors may be made. In the construction business, it is not uncommon for the general contractor to receive the subcontractor's bids an hour before the deadline for bid submission. In the haste to complete the bid and hand-deliver it before the deadline for opening, Alpha could have made an honest but unfortunate error. Phi has to be believed. But it is also interesting to note that after all bids have been opened, each contractor knows the price the competitors have quoted.- If Joe College rebids the job, the reliable contractors' bids will not change materially. But a highly competitive and aggressive contractor wanting the job has the opportunity to change his price and still be the low bidder. In other words, the honest mistake by Alpha may have been deliberate. Whether it was or not, it is incumbent upon the purchasing officer to make certain that the other three bidders are given equal consideration. This might result in not permitting Alpha to participate in a rebid.

Despite the possibility of the above arising, bid bonds have generally proven to be an excellent but costly method of securing firm bids.

THE DOCTRINE OF PROMISSORY ESTOPPEL

There are some jurisdictions that apply the doctrine of promissory estoppel to make an otherwise revocable offer become a firm offer. Those jurisdictions recognizing the principle are using it particularly in the construction industry and apply it to subcontractor bids to the general contractor. Subcontractor bids are offers to sell to the general contractor. But most courts will classify their bids as offers to sell services and not goods. Therefore Section 2-205 is not applicable. Occasionally the bids will be made orally, which runs afoul of Section 2-201 too. Some courts have worked diligently to make such bids firm. They have seized on the doctrine of promissory estoppel to achieve that goal.

Promissory estoppel, in plain language, means "You cannot do that because I acted on a promise of yours." The "you" is the offeror and the "I" is the offeree in this definition. You made an offer to me to do some work as part of a project I am proposing to do for a client. You know that I cannot accept your offer now because I must await an answer from my customer before I will need your services. But I am depending on your promise to do the work at the quoted price if I get the job. Application of the doctrine of promissory estoppel will make that promise a firm offer and it will prevent you from revoking your offer.

Let us place this in perspective by use of another hypothetical situation:

> General Contractors are bidding on the construction of an office building. Three plumbing contractors give General Contractors their proposals to do the plumbing for the proposed building. All three know that the owner of this proposed building has 30 days to make the award after the bids are opened. The Faucet Company is the low bidder. Thirty days hence General Contractors is given the contract to build the building and General gives the plumbing subcontract to Faucet by accepting his offer made more than 30 days previously.

This is all well and good, but we must look at a "what if"—what if Faucet reneges on his offer and revokes his bid? This would leave General Contractors without a plumbing subcontractor. They would have two options: (1) to attempt to force Faucet to do the work at the price quoted, or (2) to use the second lowest bid if it is still available and file suit for damages against Faucet. The damages would be the difference between Faucet's price and the price quoted by the second lowest bidder.

Some courts would grant General Contractors such damages. The decision would be based on the application of the doctrine of promissory estoppel. Such courts would say that Faucet was estopped (prevented) from revoking his bid because General Contractors relied on it to their detriment. Their detriment is twofold: (1) paying more to the second lowest bidder, and (2) giving up the right to "dicker" with the other two plumbing subcontractors. ("Dickering" is practiced by some general contractors after they receive an award from the owner. They use the lowest subcontractor's bid as the basis from which to negotiate with the other subcontractors in an effort to get a lower price for the work. It is more effective to negotiate with a subcontractor by dangling the owner's contract before him. "If you want this job, you must now deal with me because we, and only we, will determine who does the plumbing.") Giving up this privilege is a detriment to the general contractor.

One of the leading cases on the doctrine of promissory estoppel was decided in California in 1958.[1] It involved a paving contractor who made a telephone bid to the general contractor and then refused to perform when given the award. The court held that the bid was a firm offer under the doctrine of promissory estoppel and awarded damages to the general contractor. The court explained the principle of promissory estoppel with these words:

> The vital principle of estoppel is that he who by his language or conduct leads another to do what he would not otherwise have done, shall not subject such person to loss or injury by destroying the expectations on which he acted.

A federal court more explicitly stated the rule that prevails in Texas when applied to the construction industry.[2]

> In Texas, a subcontractor who submits a bid offer to a general contractor, knowing that the general contractor is going to rely on its bid, is bound unless it is clearly shown that the subcontractor's bid offer was not final.

This is clear and succinct. (Please note that this is not the federal rule but the rule that the federal court found to exist in Texas. When a federal court has jurisdiction because of diversity of domicile of the two parties or for any other reason, the federal court will apply the law of the state where the transaction took place. The contract in this case was a Texas contract, so the federal court applied Texas law.)

We observed at the beginning of this section that the doctrine of promissory estoppel has gained some acceptance in the construction industry in some jurisdictions. The result makes a revocable offer firm without resorting to any Code section. The purchasing officers for general contractors in jurisdictions that follow the principle should note that there are two requisites for application of the principle:

1. The subcontractor making the bid has reason to foresee the detrimental reliance the general contractor places on the bid.

---

[1] *Drennan v. Star Paving Co. Calif.,* 333 P.2d 757 (1958).
[2] *Montgomery Indus. Etc. v. Thomas Const. Co., Inc.,* 620 F.2d 91.

2. And the general contractor will sustain a substantial loss by such reliance on the subcontractor's bid if the bid is not performed.

Your author recommends that the general contractor tell the low bidder that his bid is being used in the general's proposal prior to submission of the total bid to the client. This precludes the general contractor from dickering after he receives the award. To do anything else would be a violation of his duty of good faith.

Be certain too that your legal counsel affirms the fact that your jurisdiction and the jurisdiction of the subcontract (if a different jurisdiction) embrace the principle of promissory estoppel. Many states, including New York for one, do not recognize it.

***Nota Bene* to Purchasing Officer.** This concludes the discussion of firm offers. In this chapter the following methods to secure a firm offer from a supplier have been offered:

1. A Section 2-205 offer

2. An option contract

3. A bid bond

4. Application of the doctrine of promissory estoppel

A firm offer that complies with the requisites of Section 2-205 is the most desirable approach to follow. It is available without out-of-pocket cost to you and to your supplier. It relies on Section 2-205 for its legitimacy, and there is no legal interpretation necessary to support it. If the offer meets all the criteria spelled out, you can be assured you have a firm offer. At the same time, you are free to negotiate with other suppliers for a more favorable bargain.

An option contract is the answer if your supplier insists on consideration from you as the asking price for a firm offer. An option contract is also the course to follow if 2-205 is not applicable, as for example, in the situation where the contract is one for services and not for goods. Most often the earnest money (or down payment) given the supplier as consideration may be negotiated to be applicable to the purchase price if you make the award to that supplier. Your risk in an option contract is that you will not exercise the option and lose the earnest money. Bid bonds are expensive, too.

The promissory estoppel approach is the inexpensive manner to firm up the offer if you are not buying goods. Most legal jurisdictions honor such arrangements if the consideration is spelled out. It is suggested such arrangements be reduced to writing so that there is no opportunity for the supplier to avoid the consequences by pleading that it was an oral contract. But keep in mind here that you are not at liberty to negotiate for a more favorable purchase from another supplier.

XV

Acceptance of an Offer

Both parties involved in the negotiation for a purchase and sale must be in agreement before there can be a legally enforceable contract. Agreement plus (1) capable parties, plus (2) a legal subject matter, and plus (3) mutual consideration are the essential ingredients for a valid contract. Agreement generally is a two-step process consisting of an offer and an acceptance of that offer. The contract is born when acceptance occurs. However, there still may be a contract even though the exact point of its formation is indefinite, as Code Section 2-204 indicates.

There is no turning back once the contract comes into being. Both the buyer and the seller obtain rights and assume duties under a contract. The failure of one party to perform his or her contract duties impinges on the contract rights of the other party. Contract rights are enforceable in courts of law. Whenever one party fails to live up to the obligations of a contract, the injured party may walk into a courtroom to seek the assistance of the law in obtaining the rights created by the contract.

DEFINITION OF ACCEPTANCE

Acceptance is the communicated assent of the offeree to the terms of an offer proposed by the offeror. The offeree grasps the extended hand of the offeror and says, "I accept the responsibilities and duties you propose in your offer. You have a deal." Acceptance is a deliberate and intended act. The offeree is agreeing to accept obligations that are legally enforceable by the other party. Acceptance of legal duties is not something that one does accidentally or in a jesting manner. It must be accomplished with the serious and positive intent to obligate and commit oneself to the terms of the offer. Consider the following situation:

> You send a purchase order to the Mail Order Catalog Company on June 10. The order reads, "100 Whatnots as shown on page 16 of your catalog, price $20 each." Five days later you receive a post card dated June 12 that reads, "This will acknowledge receipt of your purchase order no. 123 dated June 10. It will receive our prompt and careful attention. Thank you (Signed) Mail Order Catalog Company."
>
> On August 1 you send a follow-up to your purchase order. The following response is received, "We can ship 100 Whatnots immediately. The price is $32 each."

The interpretation of the June 12 post card determines whether you get $20 or $32 Whatnots. Did the Mail Order Company accept your June 10 offer to buy with this communication? If they did, you are entitled to $20 Whatnots. If the post card is not an acceptance, then the Whatnots will cost $32 each, if you want them.

A court of law will tell you that the post card is not an acceptance of your offer to buy. The most one can get out of that post card is that the United States mail service did its job of carrying your purchase order to Mail Order Company. The Mail Order Company also indicated that they were going to consider whether they would honor your offer by accepting it. Nowhere on the card did they say, "We will accept our duties that you propose in your purchase order." A New York judge some years ago was faced with a similar situation in a case that was being heard. The purchaser of some trucks received a letter from the distributor in response to his purchase order. The letter used the exact phraseology, "We acknowledge receipt of your order" for the would-be acceptance. The judge ruled the letter was not an acceptance.[1] He stated:

> I am of the opinion the mere acknowledgment of the receipt of an order is not a promise to fill it. The words "we acknowledge receipt of your order . . . " are simple English words which do not say, either expressly or impliedly, "We will fill your order;" and the orderer who receives such words has no right to assume they constitute a promise to fill his order.

It is obvious the courts want more specific words of acceptance to make Mail Order's post card an acceptance. There must be some clearly expressed intent that the company has accepted their duty to send you 100 Whatnots. For example, had the post card concluded with the statement, "We will ship on or about June 30," the court would be more willing to declare it an acceptance of your offer.

The card, as written, has no legal significance. You continued to have an

---

[1]*S.A. Ghuneim & Co. v. Southwestern Shipping Corp.*, 124 N.Y.S. 2d.303 (1953).

offer to buy outstanding. (Their post card did not reject your offer to buy.) As time moves on, the offer is in danger of lapsing. But your August 1 follow-up gave the offer renewed vigor until it was rejected by their $32 counteroffer in August.

***Nota Bene* to the Purchasing Officer.** No doubt your mail contains many similar weasel-worded communications. However, some of these post cards may be legitimate. If you mail a purchase order that is used to accept a supplier's offer to sell, and receive an acknowledgment post card, fine. Your purchase order completed the contract. The post card acknowledging receipt of it is not necessary. The supplier who mailed it was making a gratuitous gesture. But it is a different game when your order is used as an offer to buy. *Then* you do require legal action from the supplier. *Then* you want an acceptance and not an acknowledgment. You then need a communication that has substance—a commitment to enter into a contract with you.

One becomes suspicious of suppliers who use the acknowledgment route in lieu of a bona fide acceptance. Is the supplier hedging on your purchase order by only acknowledging its receipt, or is he simply guilty of using poor English to express his intent? In a volatile market, or where there is a lengthy lead time, the supplier by simply acknowledging the receipt of your order keeps his options open. If the market price of the item increases, he has the option of telling you he will deliver Whatnots at $32. If the market price decreases to $14, he has your open offer to buy at $20, which he can accept by delivery. This is the best of both worlds for the supplier.

Purchasing officers are advised to get tough with those suppliers who send this type of acknowledgment. Contact these individuals and make them give you a positive response of acceptance. If they refuse, send them a revocation of your order. Since they have not accepted your offer to buy, you are at liberty to revoke at will. A few lost orders will make this type of supplier attend to the proper use of the English language and give you an acceptance when it is required to form a contract.

Unfortunately, the word *acknowledgment* has had dual meanings in some purchasing circles. We have long used it as being synonymous with acceptance. For example, some purchasing officers send two copies of their purchase order to the supplier. The first copy is marked "Original" and the second copy is captioned "Acknowledgment Copy." The intent is to have the supplier sign the second copy to indicate that he is accepting the order, and then to return it to the buyer. In such instances, the use of the word *Acknowledgment* is improper. The copy should be termed "Acceptance Copy" because that is what you want from the supplier—an acceptance.

If you are using your purchase order to accept a supplier's offer to sell, the use of two copies of the purchase order throws confusion on the transaction. Your purchase order, accepting the supplier's offer to sell, creates a contract when mailed. You need no action from the supplier. The contract is firm and settled. There is no need for the second copy to go to the supplier unless you are curious as to whether it arrives safely. Furthermore, if you ask for an acknowledgment from the supplier you may be submitting the purchase order as a counteroffer. A court could say that your purchase order was not an acceptance, and that you were awaiting a response from the supplier before the contract would come into existence. It is suggested that you read the next chapter on the "Battle of the Forms" before deciding on the usefulness of the acknowledgment copy. In any event, purchasing officers should train themselves to think of *acceptance* when there is an offer to wrap into a contract rather than *acknowledgment.*

THE SOURCE OF AN ACCEPTANCE

Either the buyer or the seller may accept an offer. Suppliers accept offers to buy, and buyers accept offers to sell. In a prolonged period of negotiations several or many offers may be made before there is an acceptance. During the negotiation period the positions of offeror and offeree are rapidly reversed between the buyer and the seller. We saw in Chapter XII that an amendment to an offer made by the offeree acts as a rejection of the original offer and at the same time becomes a counteroffer. A counteroffer is an offer that may be accepted, too. When an acceptance is made, the last counteroffer would be the only open offer available for acceptance. Either party could be the one accepting. It makes no difference who was the original offeror.

You will see shortly that the distinction made as to which is the accepting party is of importance because both the buyer and the supplier have available alternate methods of acceptance. Either party may use one of these methods at any time to accept an open offer or a counteroffer, and catch the other party off guard. This freedom of movement requires us to be on the alert to whose offer is on the table.

Section 2-204(1) of the Code spells out a very broad guideline for creating contracts through an acceptance:

> (1) A contract for sale of goods may be made in any manner sufficient to show agreement, including conduct by both parties which recognizes the existence of such a contract.

One may deduce from this that there are no proscribed rules for an offeree to follow in making an acceptance. "Any manner" gives the offeree carte blanche to follow any method to bring an offer to the status of a contract. The offeree may accept the offer by a writing. The offeree may accept verbally. The offeree may also accept the offer by an act. All three methods are available. There are other requirements stated in the Code in the event the acceptance is made verbally. See

Chapter XVI on Oral Contracts. (There is one limitation to the general rule that an offer may be accepted in "any manner." The offeror, as master of the offer, has the privilege of specifying how acceptance is to be made.)

There are four conventional methods of acceptance which have been available to the buyer since the common law was recognized. The supplier also has four options to accept an offer to buy. Two of the suppliers' options are the same as two of the buyers'. The differing methods involve conduct of the acceptor, which of necessity would be different if the party was a buyer or a seller. The Uniform Commercial Code has also made it possible for a contract to be completed by either or both parties under special rules that differ from the application of the rules of the common law. These will be discussed after we have reviewed the conventional modes of acceptance.

BUYER'S CONVENTIONAL METHODS OF ACCEPTANCE

1. In Blank

The first method available to a purchasing officer who accepts an offer to sell is to say or write, "I accept your offer." Nothing more or less need be expressed. An *acceptance in blank* is when the offeree accepts the complete offer of the supplier as stated. It is simple and direct. There is no quibbling over words, phrases, or clauses. The supplier stated the complete proposal for the contract, and the purchasing officer bought it.

The result of an acceptance in blank is to make the offer of the supplier the complete contract. Whatever the supplier said or wrote, including all ancillary terms and conditions, is part and parcel of the completed contract. As the offeror, the supplier is not only the master of the offer, but he is also the "master of the contract." There can be no doubt as to the terms and conditions that govern the contract.

How does a purchasing officer accept an offer to sell in blank? The first method is when the supplier's representative has a handy order form in his briefcase. The proposal is placed on this form, the salesperson signs it and hands it to the purchasing officer, pointing a finger to the line underneath the word "Accepted" and says, "Sign it here." When signed, the contract comes into existence if the salesperson has the authority to obligate his or her principal. All the terms and conditions preprinted on both the front and back of the order become part of the contract. If the salesperson does not have the authority to obligate the principal, the purchasing officer has signed an offer to buy. The form may have printed on it, "This order is subject to the approval of the home office," or "This is not a valid order until countersigned by the vice-president for sales." Without that second signature on the form, it is not an offer to sell. It is only an invitation to do business from the supplier, and it becomes an offer to buy when signed by the purchasing officer.

This is not a desirable way to do business. Most purchasing officers will not go along with such pressure tactics of salespeople. The formality of a purchase order is preferred. The purchasing officer can send an order that shows on its face, "Whatnots per your quotation dated June 1, copy attached." A letter or a telegram will serve the same purpose. Another acceptance in blank is verbally to tell the supplier, "I accept your proposal dated June 1," and then to send a confirming purchase order. No matter how it is accomplished, acceptance in blank makes the supplier's terms and conditions part of the contract.

2. Repeat the Terms of the Offer

The purchasing officer may elect to accept the supplier's offer to sell by repeating the terms of the offer on the purchase order. The same result might be obtained by using a company letterhead. Use of a letterhead creates less legal problems, as we shall see in the next chapter, but use of the purchase order is the preferred form. Good purchasing practice dictates that we use it. The boilerplate printed on our purchase order form may get us involved in legal problems when we attempt to accept an offer to sell by repeating the terms of the offer. Unless we make it a point to omit all preprinted terms and conditions on the order, confusion does result.

It is unfortunate but understandable how our purchase orders become cluttered with boilerplate. We suspect that the first purchase order printed was a very simple form. Its original design contained a caption, a space for the date, and a serial number. In addition, the supplier's name and address were shown, as well as the items ordered and their prices. There was also a line for the purchasing officer's signature. These few entries left much unused space on the form, so some purchasing officers got the idea to use that vacant space to print some of the idiosyncrasies of their company. "Show this purchase order number on your invoice", "Send invoices in triplicate", and "Deliver all material to 111 Dock Street" are typical pieces of information that apply to all purchases. This type of information creates no legal problems because it has no legal significance. It represents the type of information every supplier needs to know.

But then one day the treasurer said, "The 2 percent cash discount you get on some purchases adds up to a tidy sum during a year. Why don't you get those terms on every purchase?" So the statement "Terms 2 percent 10 days, net 30" was added to the form. Then one of the buyers asked, "Why don't we make every supplier pay the cost of delivering the goods to us?" So the statement on terms "F.O.B. our receiving dock" was added. There were other good suggestions from legal counsel, and these were added. Before long, all the vacant space on the front of the form was filled. Not to be thwarted by the lack of space, the form was turned over and some of these goodies began appearing on the reverse side. It did not take too much time before we developed a fine and complete set of boiler-plate.

Please do not misunderstand. There are positive advantages to having these terms and conditions printed on the purchase order. Preprinted terms save the time involved in having them affixed specially when they are applicable. And when we use the purchase order as an offer to buy, these terms and conditions become part of the offer. This is desirable because they are all written in our favor. We want these terms and conditions working for us in a contract. When the supplier accepts our offer in blank, we have these terms included. We get a 2 percent discount if we pay the invoice in 10 days, and the supplier must pay the cost of delivering the goods to us. We are delighted with these results.

But problems arise when we use that same purchase order as an acceptance of a supplier's offer to sell. These preprinted terms become part of our acceptance. That is no problem if the supplier's terms are the same as ours. But suppose the supplier's offer to sell stated, "Terms net 10 days," and we use our preprinted order to accept that offer. We are then not accepting the supplier's offer, but we are making a counteroffer, as we determined in the section on Counteroffers in Chapter XII. Contract law has been quite insistent that an acceptance be identical to the offer, if it is to be effective in creating a contract. This principle has been known as the *mirror image* rule and it applies to substantive matters, such as price or less substantive matters, such as delivery dates, cancellation and rescheduling charges, disclaimers, and a host of other items that do not pertain to every purchase. The mirror image rule was explicitly defined in 1951 by a Minnesota judge:

> An acceptance, to be valid and to give rise to a binding contract, must be made in unequivocal and positive terms which comply exactly with the requirements of the offer. If the acceptance seeks to vary, add to, or qualify the terms of the offer, it is not positive or unequivocal and constitutes a rejection of the offer and a counteroffer. A valid acceptance must not only embrace the terms of the offer with exactitude, but it must be unequivocally expressive of an intent to create thereby, without more, a contract.[2]

Thus, if the acceptance is not a mirror image of the offer, it does not create a contract. This rule of law has long given attorneys and judges severe problems.

The Uniform Commercial Code has taken strong steps to ameliorate the impact of the mirror image rule where the contract involves the sale of goods. We will discuss this in Chapter XV. But the mirror image rule often continues in full

---

[2]*Minar v. Skoog,* 50 N.W. 2d 300, Minn. (1951).

force, untempered, in other types of contracts. What is important to note here is that the use of a preprinted purchase order creates legal problems if it is used to accept an offer to sell. There is no problem when the order is used as an offer to buy. Of course, there is the possible problem that would arise if the supplier does not accept such an offer in blank, but instead, uses a preprinted form for his acceptance. The same problems will arise. Because these problems arise through the use of the printed forms of the buyer and the seller, the problem has become known as "The Battle of the Forms."

3. The Buyer Receives and Accepts the Goods

Receipt and acceptance of the goods is considered by the law to be the buyer's acceptance of an offer to sell. It is the method of acceptance that most purchasing officers are not likely to select deliberately. Rather, it is thrust upon them by the law because a series of events has led to that conclusion. Consider these consecutive occurrences:

> Step 1. A purchasing officer sends a purchase order as an offer to buy. Payment terms printed on the order are, "Terms 2 percent 10 days, net 30 days."

> Step 2. The supplier sends back an acknowledgment of its receipt. In the same communication the supplier states, "Please note that our terms are net 10 days." (This is not an acceptance of the purchase order, but a rejection of it and a counteroffer to sell.)

> Step 3. The supplier does not wait for a response to his communication to the buyer. He proceeds to deliver the goods ordered the next day.

You will note that there is no contract in existence when this supplier makes the delivery. Only his counteroffer to sell on a no-discount basis is open.

At this point in the transaction the purchasing officer has two options. The first option is to reject the goods. There is no contract in existence, and he is at liberty to refuse the shipment without penalty. The supplier acted at his peril when the goods were delivered, because the purchasing officer had not responded to the counteroffer to sell at no discount. The supplier did not ship under contract. He could only hope the purchasing officer would voluntarily, or involuntarily, accept them.

The second option open to the purchasing officer is to accept the goods after they have been received. Please note that "receipt" of goods is to be distinguished from "acceptance" of goods. Receipt and acceptance are two distinct acts. When the supplier's truck arrives at the receiving dock of the buyer, the goods are handed over to the receiving clerk, who gives the driver a receipt for them. This is the action of receiving the goods. But they are not yet accepted by the buyer. "Acceptance" in this context means that the buyer indicated that the goods delivered are satisfactory to him, and that he regards them as his own property. This acceptance is evidenced when the buyer inspects the goods and files no protest with the supplier, or more simply, when he proceeds to utilize the goods. The act of acceptance also has a legal implication when goods are shipped without a contract. Here there is only a counteroffer to sell on the table when the supplier delivers the goods. The buyer, by accepting the goods delivered, is also said to have accepted the counteroffer to sell. The acceptance of goods in this case creates the contract, and the terms are those of the supplier—no discount.

The purchasing officer could also find that the counteroffer to sell was accepted by his company involuntarily. If the goods are received and put to use, there has been an acceptance of the supplier's counteroffer. The purchasing officer may not have intended this to happen, but since the receiving clerk knew nothing about Step 2 above, the clerk proceeded to put the goods out for use. Since it is customary for copies of a purchase order to be sent to the receiving department, a copy could have gone to receiving when Step 1 occurred. If the purchasing officer failed to place a hold on the order when Step 2 occurred, it is possible that the receiving department received and accepted the goods from the supplier in supreme innocence. Thus the purchasing officer would find the company tied into the contract with the supplier involuntarily.

This rule of law whereby the acceptance of goods is also the acceptance of an open offer may appear harsh, at times. The acceptance here was hardly an intentional act of the purchasing officer. But the law insists that it was a voluntary act on the part of the company, which acted through its receiving clerk. The company still had the choice to accept or reject the goods, but such a choice is meaningful only if the purchasing and receiving departments are working together. It is incumbent upon the company officials to make certain that the necessary coordination exists between the two departments. Here the purchasing officer should have alerted the receiving department not to accept the goods from the supplier when the counteroffer was received. But because receiving knew nothing about the problem, the goods began to be used and the law grinds out an acceptance of the counteroffer. This must be avoided.

One can almost hear the purchasing officer protesting that the goods were received before the mail delivered the supplier's counteroffer. What happens then? Well, this is a favorable event and not a dilemma. The rejection of the purchase order by the supplier is not effective until it is received by the purchasing officer. Here the goods arrived by truck before the mail brought the rejection. Therefore, the supplier is construed to have accepted the purchase order by delivering the goods. We shall see in a succeeding section that delivery is one method available to an offeree-seller of accepting an offer to buy. A delay in the mails would work to the advantage of the buyer.

Nota Bene **to the Purchasing Officer.** The purchasing officer should seek to learn the reason why a supplier delivers immediately upon receipt of the purchase order even though the purchasing officer disagrees with its terms. If the supplier sends a counteroffer, as in Step 2 above, a reasonable period of time should be allowed to pass to give the purchasing officer an opportunity to respond. But firing off a counteroffer and immediately delivering the goods without waiting for a response should raise some eyebrows. Was the supplier motivated by a sincere desire to offer the purchasing officer super-service, or was there an ulterior motive involved? This sort of "bang-bang" action is a smooth way of forcing supplier's terms upon the buyer—if the buyer falls into the trap. To send a counteroffer, deliver the goods, and hope the receiving personnel will accept and put out the goods for use without comment is a crafty series of maneuvers. This allows the supplier to get in the "last short" at the purchasing officer. But it should also be the last purchase order sent to that supplier. You should also note that no damage will come from the supplier's actions if purchasing and receiving are coordinating their actions. Receiving will not accept the goods that were fired as the last shot, and that foils this eager supplier.

4. Payment

Payment in advance of the invoice price for the goods is considered an acceptance of a supplier's offer to sell. A sale results when the payment is made, and the terms of the sale are those spelled out in the supplier's offer. A down payment will also be considered an acceptance if it is demanded by the supplier in his offer. Thus, the condition: "This offer may be accepted only by a payment of 20 percent of the invoice price" leaves no choice to the buyer. The supplier is master of this offer, and if the buyer urgently needs the goods, the required earnest money must be forthcoming. (See Chapter XVI if the offer is oral rather than written.)

A purchasing officer seldom uses payment alone as a method of acceptance, unless forced to do so. A purchase order is customarily issued to accept the supplier's offer, and a check accompanies it in the mail. The purchase order is then the acceptance, and the check is applied as part or full payment. Those who use a system of cash payments for small purchases follow the same procedure. Usually some type of written memorandum is handed the supplier along with the check.

SUPPLIER'S CONVENTIONAL METHODS OF ACCEPTANCE

Suppliers have several courses of action open to accept offers to buy.

1. In Blank

A supplier who receives a purchase order that is an offer to buy may accept *in blank* by responding with a letter or a post card. The communication might state, "We acknowledge receipt of and accept your purchase order No. 123 dated June 10." Any such expression will serve to tell the purchasing officer that the offer contained on the purchase order has been accepted.

Another in-blank method of supplier acceptance occurs when the purchasing officer sends two copies of the purchase order to the supplier, as suggested previously. The intent is to have the supplier sign the second copy as an acceptance of the offer and return it. The supplier's signature on the acceptance copy is an acceptance in blank. This is equivalent to the method followed when the purchasing officer signs the handy order form carried by the sales representative.

A supplier's acceptance in blank is the most desirable type of acceptance for the purchasing officer to receive. It incorporates only the purchasing officer's terms and conditions in the contract. There is no need to read line after line of boilerplate thrust upon you by a supplier's form. The entire contract is exactly as the purchasing officer proposed. The battle of the forms is avoided because only one form is utilized—the purchase order. The transaction is accomplished quickly and with a minimum of confusion. Would that all purchases were made and completed in this simple fashion!

One might ask why more purchases are not accomplished in this simple manner. One of the reasons is that the purchase order may contain too many terms and conditions written in favor of the buyer. A supplier receiving such a form will often ask himself, "Do I really want this order bad enough to agree to put up with all of these nitty-gritty minutia that will probably never enter into this transaction? And if they do, you can bet they will work to the buyer's advantage and not mine." A supplier who takes this attitude will respond with his own form, which has his own favorite terms and conditions. The acceptance copy of the purchase order is filed in the cylindrical file on the floor.

Another major reason why this simpler type of transaction does not occur more often is that it does not follow the pattern a purchasing officer uses in the daily procurement routine. The efficient purchasing officer will seek competitive bids from several suppliers before placing an order. These proposals are offers in themselves. They are offers to sell that require *acceptance* by the buyer—and not an *offer* by the buyer—which is what occurs when two copies of the purchase order are used. Of course, the purchasing officer has the option of rejecting the supplier's offer to sell what is contained in the proposal. A purchase order could pick up the quantity, specifications, and price shown on the supplier's quotation. The purchase order then goes to the supplier as a rejection of his price quotation and as an immediate counteroffer to purchase the same items at the same price. But the difference now is that the purchase order contains the *buyer's* terms and not the *supplier's*. Some suppliers will object to this practice, but some will accede. Those suppliers who give in to the purchasing officer will return the signed copy of the order as an acceptance in blank. Others will not return the copy, but deliver the goods. Then we have a battle of the forms. Still others will ignore the purchase order and refuse to deliver until their terms are accepted. All in all, this is not a preferred method of doing business. A better alternative is offered in Chapter XV.

2. The Supplier Repeats the Terms of the Offer

A supplier may accept an offer to buy by repeating the terms of the offer. Instead of saying or writing, "I accept your offer," the supplier will say, "I accept your offer to buy 100 gross of our no. 3 pens at $144 per gross, F.O.B. our plant, terms 2 percent 10 days net 30 days, as proposed on your purchase order No. 123." There is total acceptance of the buyer's offer, including the terms and conditions spelled out, if this acceptance is written on a post card or a letterhead.

There is a strong possibility the supplier will not use a letterhead to make this type of acceptance, but instead will take advantage of modern printing processes and have his own form available to use in such circumstances. The form will have the caption "Acceptance," "Order Acknowledgment," or something similar. It will have a complete set of terms and conditions that the supplier finds most beneficial to himself Therefore, the odds are slim that the boilerplate on the acceptance form will match the boilerplate on the purchase order. One is written "prosupplier" and the other "probuyer." And yet, if the supplier intends to accept the buyer's offer with this form, under traditional contract law the acceptance should match the offer as a mirror image. Any failure to do so makes it technically a counteroffer. But here again we have the Battle of the Forms and the Uniform Commercial Code makes some changes and permits some variations. Because this is more complex and a subject in its own right, it is suggested that we await Chapter XV for further discussion of this problem.

3. The Supplier Delivers the Goods

The supplier has the option of immediately delivering the goods after the receipt of a purchase order that is an offer to buy. Such delivery in response to the offer is an acceptance of that offer. It is a quick and reliable method of acceptance. The terms and conditions printed on the purchase order are accepted, too. The supplier accomplishes two legal acts by delivery: (1) He accepts the offer to buy and (2) He completes his obligation under the contract.

Section 2-206(1)(b) of the Code gives specific recognition to this method of acceptance by the supplier:

> (1) Unless otherwise unambiguously indicated by the language or circumstances
>
> (b) an order or other offer to buy goods for prompt or current shipment shall be construed as inviting acceptance either by a prompt promise to ship or by the prompt or current shipment of conforming . . . or nonconforming goods.

A supplier who follows this process of delivery of goods ordered without writing or saying anything is performing an act of acceptance. This section of the Code recognizes and gives statutory sanction to delivery as an act of acceptance.

You will also note that this section gives statutory sanction to acceptances in blank or when the terms of the offer are repeated on the acceptance. Acceptances by a "promise to ship" need not be in writing. The oral acceptance is also permitted.

The section's use of the terms "conforming" and "nonconforming" goods merits a digressory explanation. *Conforming goods* as defined in Section 2-106(2) are those goods that " . . . are in accordance with the obligations under the contract." *Nonconforming goods* are goods that do not meet the contract specifications. Thus, if the purchase order called for yellow apples, a delivery of yellow apples would be conforming goods. If red apples were delivered they would be nonconforming goods. A supplier may deliver nonconforming goods with the thought that perhaps the buyer will be good enough to accept a substitute, or that he may not notice the substitution. In any event, this Code section makes delivery of nonconforming goods an acceptance of an offer.

But the Code then proceeds to protect the buyer if nonconforming goods are delivered. Section 2-206(2) continues:

> . . . but such a shipment of nonconforming goods does not constitute an acceptance if the seller seasonably notifies the buyer that the shipment is offered only as an accommodation to the buyer.

This places a strong obligation on the seller to notify the buyer that nonconforming goods have been delivered. Failure to notify exacts a penalty on the supplier. If nonconforming goods are delivered without notice to the buyer, the supplier is deemed to have accepted the offer and a contract is formed. Immediately after the contract is formed, the delivery of the nonconforming goods without notice is considered a breach of that contract. This gives the buyer a cause of action (the right to bring a suit in a court of law) for damages. That is the last thing the supplier would want to have happen. Thus the section makes an honest person out of the supplier who delivers nonconforming goods. The buyer must be promptly notified. (Additional discussion of the supplier's acceptance by delivery is in Chapter XV.)

4. The Supplier Begins to Manufacture

A supplier who must first manufacture the goods ordered in an offer to buy has the option of accepting that offer by beginning the manufacturing process. This is an effective manner of acceptance, provided the supplier complies with the Code's requirements. Section 2-206(2) states:

> Where the beginning of a requested performance is a reasonable mode of acceptance, an offeror who is not notified of acceptance within a reasonable time may treat the offer as having lapsed before acceptance.

Such protection to the buyer was not available under the common law. Formerly the commencement of manufacture was an act of acceptance in itself. The buyer did not have to be notified that production had begun. Subsection (2) continues that point of law by giving code recognition to the commencement of manufacture as an act of acceptance of an offer to buy. But it places upon the supplier manufacturer the obligation to notify the buyer that manufacture will proceed within a reasonable time. If no notice is forthcoming, the buyer may treat the offer as having lapsed. This makes the supplier stand up and be counted as having accepted the offer by proper notice to the buyer within a reasonable time.

"Notice" is defined by the Code in Section 1-201(26) as "taking such steps as may be reasonably required to inform the other in ordinary course whether or not such other actually comes to know of it." The section then proceeds to stipulate how a person is deemed to have received notice:

> A person receives a notice when:
> (a) it comes to his attention or
> (b) it is duly delivered at the place of business through which the contract was made or at any other place held out by him as the place for receipt of such communications.

Thus a purchasing officer is deemed to be notified that the supplier has begun the manufacture when a notice arrives at the purchasing officer's normal place of business. It is not required that the purchasing officer actually see and hold the notice in hand.

FORMATION OF A CONTRACT BY
CONDUCT OF BOTH PARTIES

The above methods of acceptance by both buyer and seller are the conventional modes that have been recognized since the common law was brought to this country. Offer and acceptance are the "bare bones" of a contract and they continue to be the essential tools with which purchasing officer and supplier work to carry on their business transactions.

Section 2-204(1) adds a new method, or perhaps a variation of a previously accepted method, to this list. The section states that a contract may be made in any manner "including conduct by both parties which recognizes the existence of such a contract." It ignores the need to determine who is the offeror and who is the offeree. The time the contract comes into existence is immaterial. All that is required is that there be conduct by both parties indicating that they believe there is a contract in existence. The section gives the court the right to declare that there was a contract. Following are the abbreviated facts of a case heard before a federal court involving Section 2-204(1):[3]

> Perlmuter, a Cleveland printer, was called to the office of Strome, Inc. in New Jersey. Perlmuter had previously mailed to them a cost estimate of $6.80 per thousand to print 17 million flyers that were to be used in a direct mail campaign to sell costume jewelry. He met with George Strome, the president, on April 1. Perlmuter was given the copy for the flyer and color film to be reproduced. He was told to proceed with the printing. He asked for a purchase order but was told by the chief counsel of Strome, Inc. that because other matters of urgency required his immediate attention, the purchase order would have to be mailed later. Before Perlmuter flew home to Cleveland that day he called his paper supplier and ordered 100,000 pounds of paper for the flyers.

After Perlmuter left Strome, Inc., the officers prepared a certificate of incorporation to form "Strome Marketing, Inc.," which was to handle the costume jewelry venture. Then on April 10, Perlmuter received a purchase order for the 17 million flyers from Strome Marketing, Inc. He attached no significance to the word "Marketing" added to the name at the top of the purchase order. One-half of the flyers had been printed when the purchase order arrived. The flyers were delivered on time, and an invoice of $124,000 was sent. The invoice included some additional work.

> Payment was not forthcoming. In October Perlmuter found out Strome Marketing, Inc. was a "bootstrap" organization formed only to handle the jewelry venture. The venture proved to be unsuccessful, and there were no funds available to pay Perlmuter's invoice. Strome, Inc. itself continued to be financially viable. Perlmuter filed suit against them to collect the money due him. The Strome, Inc. officers said the firm was not responsible for the debts of Strome Marketing, Inc. They pointed out to Perlmuter that his contract was formed when he received the purchase order from Strome Marketing, Inc., and that he must look there for payment.

[3]*Perlmuter Printing Co. v. Strome, Inc.,* 436 F. Supp. 409 (1976).

The federal court was unimpressed with the purchase order that had come from the newly formed corporation. The court said the contract was made April 1 and cited Section 2-204. It pointed out that the section made it possible to have a contract formed by the conduct of both parties. George Strome gave Perlmuter the copy for the flyers and told him to proceed with the printing on April 1. That was conduct on his part to create a contract. Perlmuter ordered the 100,000 pounds of paper the same day. That was conduct on his part that a contract came into existence on April 1. The court then reasoned that the contract came into existence on April 1, and since there was not a Strome Marketing, Inc. corporation in existence on that day, the contract had to be made with Strome, Inc. The court awarded the verdict to Perlmuter.

In this case, it is difficult to pinpoint the exact time or the specific act that created the contract. But Section 2-204(2) says that the time the contract is made is immaterial:

> (2) An agreement sufficient to constitute a contract for sale may be found even though the moment of its making is undetermined.

It is quite clear that the framers of the Code were more concerned that the buyer and the seller complete the transaction than they were about their meeting some of the minor technicalities in the law of contracts. We will see more of Section 2-204 in the succeeding chapter, where it comes predominantly into play in the Battle of the Forms.

THE TIME AN ACCEPTANCE BECOMES EFFECTIVE

Despite the statement in Section 2-204(2) that the time of the formation of a contract created by conduct of the parties is not essential, there are instances where the time of making the contract may be important to one or both of the parties. The vast majority of contracts are made through the conventional offer and acceptance method. It behooves us then to set clear once and for all time, *when* offers and acceptances become effective. It is also important to know when a rejection and a revocation become operative.

It was stated previously in Chapter XII that one of the conditions of a valid offer is that it must be communicated to the offeree. An oral offer must be stated in the presence of the offeree. A written offer may be communicated by handing it to the party to whom it is addressed, or it can be mailed. If it is mailed, it becomes a valid offer only when the offeree receives it. Dropping it into the mailbox is not sufficient; the postal authorities must deliver that offer to the person to whom it is addressed for it to become effective.

Rejection of an offer follows the same general rules. Rejection is effective if the offeror is told personally by the offeree that the offer is unsatisfactory. An oral rejection is effective even if the offer is in writing. If the rejection is reduced to a writing and mailed, the offeror must receive it before there is a rejection. It is axiomatic that an offer cannot be rejected once it has been accepted. Such a procedure would be most unusual because both the rejection and the acceptance are acts of the offeree. Once an acceptance has been made, the offeree is locked into a contract with the offeror. Therefore for a rejection to be effective, it would have to have the power to break a contract. It has no such power.

Revocations, too, must be received to be effective. The offeror making the revocation must see that it is communicated to the offeree. If the revocation is mailed, the mail must be delivered and received by the offeree. Until a revocation is received, the offeree always has the power to accept and make a contract. Thus, offers, rejections, and revocations must be received by the proper party before they are effective.

Now we come to acceptances, and the rules vary somewhat. First, though, we must affirm that an acceptance must be received to be able to convert an offer into a contract. But "receipt" here may mean either *actual receipt* or *constructive receipt.* An oral acceptance must be told directly to the offeror and received in that manner. But a written acceptance is effective *when mailed*, in most instances. There is no need for the offeror to receive the acceptance to make the contract. The contract comes into existence upon mailing. The mailed acceptance is regarded as having been constructively received by the offeror at the time of mailing. The following events in a disagreement that was tried before the Supreme Court of New Hampshire in 1978 illustrate this principle of law:[4]

> *March 30.* The Adjutant General's Office received an application from Cushing for use of the Portsmouth Armory to hold a dance on April 29. The dance was to be sponsored by the Portsmouth Clamshell Alliance, described in the report of this case as an antinuclear protest group.
>
> *March 31.* The Adjutant General's Office mailed a signed contract offer agreeing to rent the armory.
>
> *April 3.* Cushing received the contract and signed it.
>
> *April 4.* Cushing received a telephone call from the Adjutant General advising him that the Governor had ordered withdrawal of the rental offer. Therefore the offer was being withdrawn (revoked). Cushing responded that he had already signed and mailed the contract.
>
> *April 5.* A written confirmation of the revocation was mailed to Cushing by the Adjutant General.
>
> *April 6.* The Adjutant General's Office received the signed contract mailed by Cushing. It was dated April 3 but postmarked April 5.

---

[4]*Cushing v. Thompson,* New Hampshire, 386 A. 2d.805 (1978).

The Supreme Court of New Hampshire directed that the Clamshell Alliance be permitted to hold the dance at the armory on April 29. The Court quoted from a 1904 case:[5]

> To establish a contract of this character . . . there must be . . . an offer and an acceptance thereof in accordance with its terms. . . . When the parties to such a contract are at a distance from one another and the offer is sent by mail . . . the reply accepting the offer may be sent through the same medium, and the contract will be complete when the acceptance is mailed . . . properly addressed to the party making the offer and beyond the acceptor's control.

The Court continued:

> Withdrawal of the offer is ineffectual once the offer has been accepted by posting in the mail.

The offer became effective on April 3 when it was received by Cushing. Cushing signed and mailed it the same day. The revocation of the offer was communicated verbally on April 4 and the written confirmation was received by Cushing on April 6. April 4 is the date the revocation would have been effective, but it came over the telephone too late. The acceptance became effective on April 3, when it was mailed. The contract came into existence on April 3.

The question was raised in court whether the acceptance was mailed on April 3 or on April 5 when it was postmarked. The court found April 3 to be the effective date because Cushing filed a sworn affidavit that he had signed the contract on April 3. He further testified that he had placed it in the "outbox" the same day he signed it. There was further evidence that it was customary office practice for outgoing letters to be picked up from the outbox daily and placed in the U.S. mail. (See the section following regarding proof of mailing.) Thus the legal act of acceptance was completed when the contract was placed in the U.S. mail, and that is presumed to have been the same day it was placed in the outbox.

The rule that an acceptance becomes effective once it is mailed dates back to the common law and to a case decided in the English courts in 1818 *(Adams v. Lindsell)*. The rule has often been criticized because it gives a time advantage to the offeree. Assume that an offeror decides on a specific date to revoke his offer. The next day, the offeree decides to accept the same offer. Both mail their papers and deposit them in the mail. The offeree's acceptance becomes effective immediately even though it was mailed the day after the revocation was mailed. Some courts believe this to be an injustice wreaked upon the offeror. Many legal authorities have offered rationale for the rule. One of the traditional arguments in favor of the rule has been that once the acceptance is placed in the mail, it is placed out of the control of the offeree. This was true for a long period of time, but

---

[5]*Busher v. New York Life Ins. Co.*, New Hampshire, 58 A. 41 (1904).

in 1913 the U.S. postal authorities amended this rule, which prohibited retrieval by the mailer. Now, under proper circumstances, the sender may recall a mailed letter, so this reasoning is no longer apropos.

The most compelling argument for making an acceptance effective when it is mailed is the need to find some precise period of time at which a contract is formed. The rule establishes a line of demarcation—the mailing of the acceptance. Once that line is crossed a contract is in existence. (A thorough analysis of the writings of legal authorities on this rule is contained in 155 So.2d 889 written by the District Court of Appeals of Florida in 1963.)

The rule that an acceptance is effective at the time of mailing is not a unanimous rule in the United States. California has had a specific statute on the books for some time that reads, "A contract in writing takes effect upon its delivery to the party in whose favor it is made." (Deering's *California Civil Practice Code,* 1984 edition.) The cases cited under this statute all apply to lease contracts and transfers of real estate, but there is no such limitation expressed in the statute. This is one of the many areas you should consult with your legal counsel to determine the rule prevailing in your jurisdiction.

CONTROL OF THE MANNER OF ACCEPTANCE

In common law an offeror was regarded as the *master of the offer.* Included in the rights of a master was the right to specify the manner by which the offeror wanted the offer accepted. The same privilege applies today. It has not been eliminated by the Uniform Commercial Code. In fact, the preamble clause of Section 2-206 begins with, "Unless otherwise unambiguously indicated by the language or circumstances." This is an open invitation to every offeror, whether a buyer or a supplier, to dictate the manner in which his or her offer is to be accepted.

Should the offeror elect not to specify the manner of acceptance, then subsection (1)(a) becomes applicable:

> (a) an offer to make a contract shall be construed as inviting acceptance in any manner and by any medium reasonable in the circumstances;

Please note that subsection (a) applies only if the offeror has not exercised his privilege to suggest the manner the offer is to be accepted. Subsection (a) has also eliminated some presumptions of how acceptances were to be made that prevailed prior to the Code. Then the law recognized the "deposited acceptance" rule which followed these special rules:

> (1) If the offer was telegraphed, the acceptance must be telegraphed back to the offeror if the offeree wanted the acceptance to be effective

immediately. If the offeree mailed the acceptance, the acceptance would not be effective until the offeror received it.

(2) If the offer was mailed, an acceptance mailed in return would become effective the moment it was mailed. If telegraph was used to return the acceptance, then the offeror would have to receive the telegram before the acceptance was effective.

These may appear to be minor technicalities, but there were many occasions where these rules affected the outcome of a lawsuit. Section 2-206(1) rids the law of these technicalities. A mailed response to a telegraphic offer becomes effective the moment it is mailed, unless the offeror specified acceptance by return telegram.

Nota Bene **to the Purchasing Officer.** The purchasing officer's job has been simplified by the Code when the purchase order has been used as an offer to buy. A supplier who sits on a purchase order without taking any action will have Sections 2-206(1)(b) and 2-206(2) prodding him. Section 2-206(1)(b) requires the supplier to ship promptly or send a prompt promise to ship. Section 2-206(2) requires the supplier who must manufacture the goods to send a notice of acceptance of the offer within a reasonable time or run the risk of having the purchasing officer treat the offer to buy as having lapsed. These two sections operate to the benefit of the buyer.

There is one problem that remains for the purchasing officer who depends upon these two sections to move the suppliers. There is no precise definition of the phrases "prompt promise," "prompt or current shipment," and "notified of acceptance within a reasonable time." What is a *prompt promise* and a *reasonable time* continues to be in doubt. The purchasing officer's only accurate solution to these vague phrases is to take advantage of the preamble, "Unless otherwise unambiguously indicated." When your purchase order is used as an offer to buy, you are the master of the offer. The Code with this preamble invites you to define these terms with preciseness. You have the privilege of showing on your purchase order terms such as these:

1. This offer must be accepted in writing or the goods delivered within 15 days of the above date.

Or

2. This offer must be accepted in writing or the goods delivered on or before May 15.

This type of clause makes the supplier get back to you promptly. Section 2-206 dares you to be specific as to how and when you want your offer accepted. Accept that challenge!

The preamble of 2-206 also gives you the right to send two copies of your purchase order to the supplier and ask that one copy be returned as the acceptance copy. When you request that the supplier sign and return the acceptance copy you are dictating the method of acceptance you wish to be followed. This is "unambiguously indicated" by the wording you place on the acceptance copy. We shall see in the next chapter in the discussion of the battle of the forms that the use of the "acceptance copy" procedure is the proper of the forms, and that the use of "acceptance copy" procedure is the proper manner to avoid the battle of the forms. Avoiding the battle of the forms is much preferred to winning it. If you do not engage in the battle, you do not have the chance to lose it.

There may be some who will charge you with being too aggressive and autocratic when your purchasing procedure follows these rules, which are made possible by Section 2-206. A charge could be made that these procedures will impair good relations with your vendors. The answer to such a charge is that if good vendor relations depend upon allowing the vendor to select the time and method an acceptance will be made, then good vendor relations contribute little to an effective procurement program.

PROOF OF MAILING AN ACCEPTANCE

This section is a postscript. There are occasions when a purchasing officer is called upon to establish the date a purchase order, a contract, or a notice was mailed to a supplier. It is not a simple task to prove this in court. The sheer volume of mail that is dispatched from a purchasing office makes it difficult to recall just when any individual piece of correspondence was sent. And yet the answer could be important in deciding whether a purchase order was mailed within the time limit allowed for it to act as an effective acceptance.

It is a simple matter to establish this fact if you are aware of its importance at the time of mailing. You would make certain the envelope was properly addressed and that the proper amount of postage was affixed. You would make certain that your return address was shown on the envelope. Then you would hand it over to another person in the office to mail it for you, call that person's attention to all the details of the proper address and postage, and then direct that it be dropped in a U.S. mailbox. The person mailing it for you should note the location of the mailbox and the time the next regular pickup is scheduled. These details should be noted on your calendar and on the calendar of the person mailing it. These recordings, along with your assistant's testimony corroborating your own assertion of mailing, are strong evidence to a court that the order was mailed on a particular date. Such proof is so convincing that it makes it difficult for the opposing party in court to rebut (disprove) the fact of mailing.

This, however, does not prove that the addressee received the purchase order. But most courts will accept as evidence that the addressee received it if such proof of mailing is established. Wigmore, the traditional authority on evidence states, in his *Pocket Code of the Rules of Evidence*[6]: "Whenever a human act or the manner of doing . . . an act is material to be proved, the person's habit, or the custom of a class of persons . . . is relevant, providing it involves a fair regularity or frequency of conduct as to the act in question." Wigmore then cites as an example the custom of the government post office department as evidence that a letter properly addressed, prepared and deposited was delivered to the addressed. There are many cases on record that support this point of view. Sometimes the court will ask for testimony to the effect that the mailed envelope was not returned to the sender. This is the basis for the previously mentioned suggestion that a properly addressed envelope should have the sender's return address on the face of it.

The use of registered mail, together with a request of return receipt, is proof that the envelope was both mailed and received. This is the most foolproof method of establishing the date and receipt of a mailing. It is recommended for all legal documents and as a means to establish proof of service. There are two disadvantages to registered mail. The first is the added cost. Registering requires one fee, and the return receipt request adds another fee. The second objection is that registration requires a trip to a U.S. post office. The cost of the time for registering, plus the added fees, makes the registration an expensive procedure. Certified mail may be utilized. It is less expensive and accomplishes the same purpose.

But for the purchasing officer, the greatest problem is establishing in advance that a particular purchase order will require this special attention. So often, the one purchase order that requires this special attention will not be identified at the time of mailing. That particular order goes out with the balance of the orders prepared that day without recognition. Some time later, the need for proof develops. And proving its mailing six, nine? or twelve months later becomes impossible.

This possible crisis can best be met with advance planning on the part of the purchasing officer. A mail routine must be established—a routine that is followed day in and day out with no variation. If the mail is to be placed in an outgoing box, every member of the department should use that box. The procedure for handling all mail must be the same. Your daily routine will include preparing purchase orders by some mechanical process and then placing them on someone's desk for signature. Then what happens? Who places them in the envelopes? (Window envelopes have an added advantage that the addressee's identification and address are retained on the carbon copy of the purchase order.) Who stamps the envelopes? When are they placed in the "outgoing" box? Who picks up the

---

[6]John Henry Wigmore, *Pocket Code of the Rules of Evidence,* Little, Brown & Co., 1910.

mail from the outgoing box? At what time are they picked up? Where are they taken? When do they finally get into a U.S. mailbox? What is the scheduled pick-up time from that box? These are all questions you might be called upon to answer in a courtroom trial. The more rigid your schedule, the more solid bank of evidence you can lay at the court's doorstep.

Establishing, and following, this routine regularly does not in itself prove that purchase order No. 12345 was mailed on July 10, the date shown on the carbon copy of the purchase order. But if order No. 12345 was one of 75 orders prepared and mailed that day, the chances are excellent that it got into the U.S. postal service's good hands via the usual routine. As Wigmore states, "This is circumstantially evidential that this particular letter was so mailed." It is not proof positive of the fact, but the chances are good that this is how and when it was mailed.

The evidence of following a rigid routine for outgoing mail transfers the obligation of disproving it to the opposition in court. The longer the routine has been followed, and the more rigidly and unswervingly it has been adhered to, the more difficult it is to dispute. Every purchasing office should have such a routine. If you do not have it now, it is never too late to begin. Organize your staff to follow an established routine.

A final observation: The supplier, in all probability, will have a similar mail routine to prove that his mail was sent to you. How might you refute his proof of delivery? You are first reminded that the cancellation date shown on the envelope is of little probative value. Today's post office does not cancel all letters. (How often have you received a letter that contains an uncancelled stamp?) Furthermore, much of the business mail today is run through a postage meter machine. The machine printout includes the date the postage was affixed. This date is set by the operator of the machine and can be controlled. Therefore any date stamped by the meter is open to dispute because it is not stamped at an independent post office.

Your only protection is to have all incoming mail regularly stamped by a stamping machine with the date and the time of day it is received. This is also only evidentiary, because you and your staff have control over the stamping machine. There is also the possibility that mail may be received by your department and remain unopened for a period of time. Once more, a strong and stable routine for reading your mail will assist your legal counsel in establishing the date an important document was received.

AGREEMENT WITHOUT IDENTIFYING ACCEPTANCE

Just as the Uniform Commercial Code does not require that one identify the precise offer, it also does not require identification of the precise point of acceptance.

It recognizes that in the business conversations and negotiations it may be difficult to precisely identify these factors and the precise point of making up a contract. For this reason, the drafters have pointed out that one need not show this, but rather simply show that an agreement exists. Of course in many situations one will be able to identify the particular statement or documents constituting the offer and likewise the acceptance. Still it is important to realize that such identification may not be necessary where an overall context indicates agreement.

XVI

The Battle of the Forms: Orders and Acknowledgments

Several references have been made in previous chapters to the Battle of the Forms. This refers to a problem that arises when the buyer and the seller use their own printed forms to create a contract to buy and sell goods. The conflicts that exist between the printed terms on one party's form with the terms printed on the other party's form give rise to the descriptive title, "The Battle of the Forms." The authors of the Uniform Commercial Code were aware of this problem, and Section 2-207 was written with the express purpose of solving it. The solution is complicated. Much of the complexity can be attributed to the fact that when Section 2-207 was written, some major changes were made in traditional contract law principles. These changes are applicable only to contracts involving the purchase and sale of goods, because Article 2 of the Code covers only "transactions in goods." Contracts involving services, leases, and real property are unaffected. Traditional contract law remains applicable for those types of contracts. The reasons for changes in the law for transactions in goods are better understood when we first recognize the legal difficulties that arose under traditional contract law when a purchasing officer and a supplier used their own individual forms. The solutions offered by Section 2-207 then appear more reasonable.

TRADITIONAL CONTRACT LAW

One of the essentials of a valid contract is agreement of the parties. This is achieved when one party makes an offer to buy or sell, and the other party makes a matching acceptance of that offer. Traditional contract law requires that this matching acceptance be a mirror image of the offer. (See "Repeat the Terms of the Offer" in Chapter XIV for an excellent judicial definition of the mirror-image rule.) The requirement of mirror-image acceptance is never a problem when the two parties prepare a formal contract. The terms and conditions of the purchase and sale are put down on one piece of paper with such phrases as "Party of the first part," and "Therefore be it resolved." Then both parties affix their signatures at the end of the document, and each party walks away with a copy of it. The same terms and conditions have been agreed to by both parties. The offer and acceptance are identical because they are on the same sheet of paper.

Nor does any problem arise when only one of the parties uses a printed form. The single form will be used as an offer—either an offer to buy or an offer to sell. The other party accepts the offer by performance, or by signing the offer form. For example, a purchasing officer makes an offer to buy by issuing a purchase order to a supplier. The supplier, in turn, delivers the goods. Delivery of the goods by the supplier is an acceptance of the offer to buy as spelled out on the purchase order. This includes all terms and conditions printed on it. There is no Battle of the Forms because only one form is used. A similar clean transaction results when a supplier hands the purchasing officer an order form all filled in. The purchasing officer signs the order form: This is an acceptance of the supplier's offer to sell and includes all terms printed on the sales order. This form controls the contract between the two parties. Again, there is no conflict, because only one form is used.

But a conflict will develop if both parties use their own printed forms to make the contract. The offer is made on one of the forms and the acceptance is on the other form. The terms and conditions printed on the offer form are part of the proposed contract. These printed terms must be mirror-imaged by the acceptance form to create a contract under traditional contract law. This is when the conflict between the forms becomes apparent.

The terms and conditions printed on the offeree's form that is used for the acceptance are also part of the acceptance. The likelihood of the offeree's form being a mirror-image of the offer in every detail is remote. The "big three" items on the acceptance—the quantity, the description of the goods, and the price—will probably agree with those shown on the offer form. But there the mirror-image of the offer will end. The terms and conditions printed on the buyer's form will be drawn in his favor. No doubt the terms printed on the supplier's form will be slanted in his direction. Conflicts between two such forms are inevitable. In most instances the hope that the acceptance will mirror the offer is wishful thinking.

After these forms have been exchanged by the buyer and the seller, traditional contract law says that there is no contract because the mirror-image rule has not been satisfied. The purported acceptance is regarded as (1) a rejection of the offer and (2) a counteroffer. Traditional contract law expects the buyer and the seller at this point to return to the negotiating table and hammer out their differences.

Most modern buyers and sellers long ago gave up on this ideal solution. There are not enough hours in the day to read the boilerplate printed on all the forms that come across the desk. When an acceptance arrives in the mail, the big-three terms are checked and verified. But that is about all that is read. The form is placed in the file with full assurance that a contract has been created and that another business transaction has been completed. The supplier will deliver the goods, and the buyer will receive and accept them. In due time the supplier will be paid. The transaction is completed without the two parties having formed a valid contract! The buyer and the seller are satisfied. They couldn't care less that the mirror-image rule was violated.

But let something go wrong with the transaction! It is then that the two parties rush to their files to retrieve the papers for a careful reading. This will be the first time these two parties discover that there was no contract created by the exchange of their forms. They completed the transaction and both performed their obligations, but what are the applicable terms of that deal? Particularly, what are the terms that cover the topic around which the dispute is centered? The parties are fortunate if the dispute involves a subject that was stated in the same manner in both forms. These agreed-to terms will prevail. But a battle will erupt if this is not the case. If the subject was treated differently in the two forms, the question logically arises—whose form will prevail? This is the Battle of the Forms.

APPLYING TRADITIONAL CONTRACT LAW TO A BATTLE OF THE FORMS

In such a Battle of the Forms, traditional contract law applied the mirror-image rule even when the goods has been delivered and accepted. The first party to send a form is considered to be the offeror. The second party is the offeree. The second party's form, presumably sent as an acceptance, does not create a contract. The variant term in the form causes it to reject the offer because it is not a mirror image. This rejection also makes the purported acceptance a counteroffer under the mirror-image. This counteroffer is the only offer that is open for acceptance when the goods are delivered. Then traditional contract law dictates that the counteroffer is accepted by the conduct of the other party. If it is a counteroffer to buy, then it is deemed to be accepted by the supplier by delivery of the goods. If it is a counteroffer to sell, the buyer's receipt and acceptance of the goods constitute his acceptance. When traditional contract law is applied, it is the counteroffer that contains the terms that will be applied to settle the dispute. The counteroffer is always the last form sent in the exchange. The party who sends the first form is always the loser.

Let us look at a simple hypothetical situation to fully understand this result.

> A buyer regularly uses a purchase order that contains this printed term among several: "Buyer reserves the right to inspect, test, and accept the goods ordered herein anytime within 60 days after delivery." This buyer negotiates a purchase with a supplier who uses a sales acknowledgment form. Among the numerous terms on the supplier's form is the one: "Any claim arising from this sale must be filed by the buyer with the supplier within 10 days after delivery."
>
> After some period of negotiation the buyer and the supplier reach a tentative agreement for the purchase and sale of the supplier's product. Both parties send their forms to each other. The big three—quantity, description, and price—are identical. The balance of their terms and conditions do not vary substantially except for the time limit for filing claims. The goods are delivered and paid for by the buyer.
>
> Thirty days after delivery, the buyer encounters some problems with the goods. He notifies the supplier that the goods are defective and demands that they be picked up and his money refunded. The supplier responds, "You are too late. You had a time limit of 10 days to file any claim. See my sales acknowledgment form." The buyer responds, "I had 60 days to inspect and test your product. See my purchase order."
>
> The question then is: Does the limit of 10 days for filing claims apply or is 60 days appropriate?

Traditional contract law could come up with the answer "10 days" or "60 days" to that question. Its decision would be based upon the answer to one more question: Who fired the first shot in the Battle of the Forms? Whoever sent his form first loses the battle! Here is the logic of how the law would arrive at this conclusion:

Situation I. The buyer sends the purchase order first.

Step A. The purchase order becomes an offer to buy with a 60-day claim period included.

Step B. The supplier's sales acknowledgment form with the 10-day claim period is then forwarded to the buyer. It fails as an acceptance because of the mirror-image rule. Therefore it is:

(1) A rejection of the offer to buy, and

(2) A counteroffer to sell, with a 10-day claim period.

Step C. The supplier delivers the goods. This act in itself has no legal significance. The buyer has not yet accepted the counteroffer to sell and is free to reject the goods.

Step D. The buyer accepts the goods and perhaps pays for them. This is "conduct" on the part of the buyer, which is considered by traditional contract law to be an acceptance of the counteroffer to sell. This counteroffer contains the 10-day period for claims.

Here, then, the buyer was the first to send his form and he loses the battle.

Situation II. The supplier sends the sales form first.

Step A. The sales form becomes an offer to sell, with a 10-day claim period.

Step B. The purchase order with the 60-day claim period is then sent to the supplier, presumably to accept the sales offer. It fails as an acceptance because it "flunks" the mirror-image rule. Therefore it is:

(1) A rejection of the offer to sell, and

(2) A counteroffer to buy, with a 60-day claim period.

Step C. The supplier delivers the goods. This is the legal act of acceptance of the buyer's counteroffer to buy. This counteroffer has the 60-day period for filing of claims.

Here the seller was the first to send his form and he loses the battle. The previous two examples illustrate the approach traditional contract law follows when there is a Battle of the Forms that is followed by conduct of one of the two parties. You will note that in each example the original offeror loses the battle. The offeree by sending a nonconforming acceptance effectively takes over command of the transaction. Scant heed is paid here to the common law maxim: The offeror is master of the offer. The decision reached by this process depends solely on who fired the last shot. He who waits until the other party's form arrives before dispatching his own paper wins the decision. Justice is not served when such a tenuous and fortuitous circumstance dictates the verdict.

The reader should observe the opportunity a supplier has to manipulate a transaction under traditional contract law. If a purchase order is received, the unscrupulous supplier can send off a nonconforming sales acknowledgment. At this point there is no contract. If the market price of the product increases while the supplier is holding the purchase order, he can refuse to deliver unless the buyer agrees to an upward adjustment of the price. If the market price declines, the supplier can deliver and realize an extra profit by the delay. But this latter circumstance is an opportunity for the alert buyer to give the supplier a taste of his own medicine. The buyer can refuse to accept the delivery unless the supplier agrees to reduce the price.

There are many other examples that could be given to illustrate the fact that the application of the mirror-image rule in a business world filled with preprinted forms produced unsatisfactory results. The uncertainty created by the rule kept purchasing officers (and suppliers too) from being certain that a contract had been created through the exchange of their purchase orders and sales documents. And when a contract was created, there was always doubt as to the terms of that contract. Most often the confusion resulted from relatively insignificant terms and conditions printed on these forms. It seemed, therefore, that the law was making decisions on highly technical and minute details. Such laws have no place in the business world, and business has no tolerance for it. There must be a better way—law should support and further business activity, not impede it.

THE UNIFORM COMMERCIAL CODE AND TRADITIONAL CONTRACT LAW

The second section of the Uniform Commercial Code (Section 1-102(a)) states that one of the purposes of the Code is "to simplify, clarify and modernize the law governing commercial transactions." With this in mind, the authors of the Code took note of the problems facing purchasing officers and suppliers when traditional contract law was applied in the Battle of the Forms. They decided that a major effort was required to clear this battlefield and bring peace to the participants. The peace maker offered was Section 2-207.

It was obvious to the Code authors that the peacemaker would require major surgery on some traditional contract-law principles. This did not deter them. We have seen examples previously of their willingness to change, alter, and amend traditional principles. Section 2205 on firm offers (see Chapter XIII) and Sections 2-204 and 2-206 on acceptance (see Chapter XIV) are examples of how the Code has reworked traditional principles to make the law more suitable for modern business. In 2-207 the mirror-image rule was pushed aside for the benefit of purchasing officers who print terms on the purchase orders and for suppliers who print terms on the sales proposals and acceptances. The writers of the Code also removed the availability of the last-shot principle for those offerees who send a deviant acceptance to their offerors. In this one section two major traditional contract law principles were eliminated for transactions involving the purchase and sale of goods that are made on the parties' printed forms. Substitute procedures are spelled out in the section.

INTRODUCTION TO SECTION 2-207

An introduction to this section of the Code must begin on a negative note. The reader is warned that parts of it may be hard to understand and sometimes difficult to apply. The section has not received universal acclaim. Many legal experts believe that it should be materially revised. Here are a few of the objections heard about the section:

1. It is lengthy.

2. It does great violence to traditional contract law principles.

3. It covers three distinct factual situations.

4. It contains four escape hatches or safety valves.

5. It mentions two problems, but provides a clear solution for only one.

6. It is not precise in its application.

7. One does not get a firm and positive answer from its words.

Yes, the section does draw criticism.

Notwithstanding, 2-207 is the law in 49 of our 50 states. Since it was written primarily for purchasing officers and sales personnel, we must get on with an analysis and comprehension of its provisions. We must keep in mind that the section is intended as an answer to the problems created by the Battle of the Forms. Therefore, it is applicable only when these facts are present:

1. Both buyer and seller have completed the basic negotiations for the purchase and sale of goods.

2. One party sends a printed form to the other as an offer. This form may be either an offer to buy or an offer to sell.

3. The other party responds with a writing that is intended to be an acceptance of the offer. The form agrees with most of the major items shown on the offer, such as quantity and description of the goods to be bought. However it fails to pass the mirror-image test because of one or more discrepancies among the less important printed terms and conditions.

This is the scenario under which 2-207 operates.

The provisions of 2-207 allow it to go into action either before the goods are delivered or after the supplier has delivered the goods and the buyer has accepted them. Here is the general thrust of what the section does in the scenario stated above.

Prior to delivery of the goods. It makes the second form sent operate as an acceptance even though it states terms additional to or different from those stated in the offer. If 2-207 can find enough evidence in the second form that it was intended as an acceptance of the offer, it says, "so be it." A contract is in existence. The terms of the contract, with minor exceptions, are those contained in the offer. The offeror is once more the master of the offer.

Subsequent to delivery of the goods. It says, "If the goods are delivered and accepted by the buyer, there is a contract," period. Even though the writings that were exchanged cannot be found to be a contract prior to delivery as above, delivery and acceptance of the goods do make the contract. The reader will recall that in Chapter XIV we saw that Section 2-204(1) made *conduct* of the parties (delivery and acceptance of the goods) sufficient to create a contract. Section 2-207 does the same thing—with one difference: Since the writings of the parties differ, 2-207 reconstructs their words to make a contract out of the confusion. The final contract, says 2-207 "will consist of those terms on which the two parties agree plus any term needed from other sections of the Code to settle the dispute."

The above gives the reader a general idea of what 2-207 tries hard to do. Hopefully, you will find its words more understandable if you keep in mind what it is trying to accomplish. Note that this generalization omits the safety valves, the escape hatches, and the caveats that are replete in the section.

THE TEXT OF SECTION 2-207

You are now prepared to meet Section 2-207 head-on. Here is the complete text:
Additional Terms in Acceptance or Confirmation.

> (1) A definite and seasonable expression of acceptance or a written confirmation which is sent within a reasonable time operates as an acceptance even though it states terms additional to or different from those offered or agreed upon, unless acceptance is expressly made conditional on assent to the additional or different terms.
>
> (2) The additional terms are to be construed as proposals for addition to the contract. Between merchants such terms become part of the contract unless:
>
>> (a) the offer expressly limits acceptance to the terms of the offer;
>>
>> (b) they materially alter it; or
>>
>> (c) notification of objection to them has already been given or is given within a reasonable time after notice of them is received.
>
> (3) Conduct by both parties which recognizes the existence of a contract is sufficient to establish a contract for sale although the writings of the parties do not otherwise establish a contract. In such case the terms of the particular contract consist of those terms on which the writings of the parties agree, together with any supplementary terms incorporated under any other provisions of this Act.

Now you have the official text of this somewhat confusing section of the Code.

Before we proceed with a detailed analysis of the above, note that subsection (1) and subsection (2)(b) pertain to the period that we termed "Prior to the Delivery of the Goods." Subsection (3) pertains to the time span we labelled, "Subsequent to Delivery of the Goods."

And now let us proceed to pick apart Section 2-207.

The Title

The title refers only to "additional" terms in the acceptance, yet in the body of the section *different* terms are discussed as well. Both additional and different terms in an acceptance violate the mirror-image rule. Since the section is devoted to eliminating this rule in transactions involved in the Battle of the Forms, both variants are considered and disposed of herein. In a similar vein, even though the title mentions only acceptances, offers are also included, either directly or by implication, because there must be an offer before there is something for an acceptance to accept.

Subsection (1)

Point A: "A Definite and Seasonable Expression of Acceptance."

These initial words tell us immediately that there are two writings involved in the situation to which the section is applied. An acceptance must have an offer to accept, so we assume the first writing has been an offer. This could be either an offer to buy or an offer to sell.

An offer to buy would be on a purchase order. The supplier's acceptance would be on his form titled, "Sales Acknowledgment," or something similar. To meet the test of being a "definite . . . expression of acceptance . . . ," the form ideally would begin with, "We acknowledge and accept your order." That tells the reader what the form is intended to accomplish. Not all sales acceptances from suppliers have this wording. Would that they did! The form needs more details than this sentence, however, to measure up to the *definite* standard set by 2-207. It should also show the quantity and the item or description of what was ordered. (Or, these essential details may be incorporated by specific reference to the purchase order—with phrases such as "Parts as specified on your purchase order no. #123 dated January 10.") Many suppliers will show the price, too, but that is not essential to meet the definite standard. Other details, such as the buyer's name and address, and place and time of delivery can be included. The balance of the supplier's form will probably contain preprinted terms and conditions which do not contribute to definiteness. It is the quantity and description of the goods, plus the title of the form and its expressed intention, that make it a definite expression of acceptance. The printed terms and conditions are the items that create the Battle of the Forms and make 2-207 necessary.

If the acceptance is for an offer to sell, it is the purchase order form that must be definite. Again, quantity and description of the goods are essential. The purchasing officer prefers to show the price. The title "Purchase Order" does show some indication of the intent of the form, but a statement in addition, such as "Please enter our order for . . . " is desirable. The purchase order could incorporate the supplier's proposal, "Parts as specified on your sales proposal no. 456 dated January 10" as a substitute for the quality and the description.

Note that this acceptance must be a *seasonable* expression. Section 1-204 of the Code states that "an action is taken seasonably when it is taken at or within the time agreed or if no time is agreed at or within a reasonable time." Since the time limits of an acceptance are governed by the offer, we may say that a seasonable acceptance is one that is communicated before the offer has lapsed. (See "Lapse of an Offer" in Chapter XII.)

Point B: " . . . operates as an Acceptance even though it states terms additional to or different from those offered"

These are the magic words in the section that tell us that the mirror-image rule will not be applied here. Traditional contract law principles receive a severe jolt with this statement. Today, a contract is formed by a variant acceptance, provided the acceptance is definite; and in commercial understanding, it indicates that a deal has been made.

This portion of 2-207 is of vital interest to purchasing officers and sales personnel. Its words tell you that a purchase order issued in response to a sales proposal will create a contract despite varying printed terms in the two forms. Conversely, a sales acknowledgment sent as an acceptance of a purchase order offer to buy will create a contract, too, despite variant terms. These conclusions give the parties some degree of certainty that a contract has been formed.

Some of the lesser terms of that contract, however, may come as a surprise to one or both parties.

What are the terms that will be applicable to such a contract created under subsection (1)? The answer is that they will be the terms of the original offer plus any additional terms proposed by the offeree that will be allowed to get into the contract under subsection (2)(b), which is explained below. Section 2-207 endorses the common law maxim that the offeror is the master of the offer. Whoever is the offeror—the buyer or the seller—will find that his terms prevail.

***Nota Bene* to the Purchasing Officer.** Since this book discusses the law of purchasing it is incumbent upon the author to point out to purchasing officers that the previous two points should raise an alert to you. Quite often you will invite suppliers to submit quotations. Most of these quotes come to you as offers to sell. Your award to the low bidder is communicated by your purchase order. Your purchase order then, is the acceptance of the supplier's offer to sell. Under subsection (1) of 2-207 the terms of that purchase will be those of the supplier, and your purchase will be governed by the terms printed on the supplier's quotation. More on this later.

Point C: " . . . unless acceptance is expressly made conditional on assent to the additional or different terms."

We will label this phrase, "Escape Hatch No. 1" in the section. It is an escape hatch available to the offeree. Here the section gives the offeree an opportunity prevent the creation of the contract on the offeror's terms when his acceptance form is sent. For example, if the purchasing officer is accepting a sales proposal, there can be placed on the purchase order a statement similar to this: "Your sales proposal is accepted by this purchase order only if you agree to all of the additional or different terms that are stated herein." A statement of this type on the purchase order makes it a conditional acceptance of the sales proposal. It will not create a contract until the supplier indicates that he accepts the additional and different terms. The use of the conditional acceptance defeats the purpose of 2-207 of some extent. The exchanged forms do not make a contract because the acceptance is conditional. It puts us back almost to square one when the Battle of the Forms prevailed. But it is effective in preventing the supplier's terms from becoming the terms of the contract. The supplier may use a similar statement on a sales acknowledgment form if he is accepting your purchase order offer to buy.

You are reminded that when a conditional acceptance is sent to the supplier, the supplier is free to back away from the deal. The sales proposal has not been converted to a contract by your purchase order and the operation of subsection (1) of 2-207. The conditional acceptance clause prevents this from happening. The use of the conditional acceptance clause should be carefully considered if the sales proposal is an advantageous one that you are unwilling to "let go."

The purchasing officer is also reminded that if the conditional acceptance clause is used, and the supplier does not respond, but then proceeds to deliver the goods, and you accept them, the delivery will not be regarded as an acceptance of your terms. You might think the conditional acceptance will be thought of as a counteroffer. If this were so, the delivery by the supplier would be an acceptance of that counteroffer and make a contract. This does not follow. If it did we would be back into traditional contract law days and not the modern world of Section 2-207. Delivery by the supplier should throw the transaction into the lap of subsection (3), which is explained below. The word "should" is used in the previous sentence because this is not an absolute conclusion since there were a few early cases decided under Section 2-207 that led to a contrary result. But the statement and conclusion do represent the current trend in case law. Purchasing officers are advised not to depend upon the conditional acceptance clause as a routine matter. It is only workable if you are prepared to enforce it each time it is utilized.

Enforcing it means not to accept any deliveries from the supplier to whom you have sent the conditional form until that supplier gives you written assurance your terms will prevail.

Point D: " . . . or a written confirmation which is sent within a reasonable time."

This phrase goes back to the beginning of the text of subsection (1). It establishes a different scenario for 2-207. A "written confirmation" presupposes that an oral contract has been reached by the parties, and then one or both send a confirmation of their verbal agreement. The inclusion of a confirmation in subsection (1) confuses some legal experts because most of the section applies to deviant writings. A confirmation implies a contract has already been made and is in existence. Therefore it is redundant to include it in this subsection. We assume it is here in the event of conflicting terms in the confirmations. Then the same rules of construction of the contract will apply as spelled out in subsections (2) and (3) following.

Subsection (2)

"The additional terms are to be construed as proposals for addition to the contract. Between merchants such terms become part of the contract unless . . . " Subsection (2) only deals with additional terms contained in the acceptance form. They are "additional" because they were not mentioned in the offer. Evidently the offeror believed that the topics were not important enough to be included in the offer, or else they were forgotten. In any event, the offeree attached enough significance to the additional term to include it on the acceptance form. Subsection (2) makes this additional term in the offeree's form a proposal for addition to the contract reached in subsection (1). It goes one step beyond this for merchant parties by making the additional term a part of the contract unless it is caught up in one of the various escape hatches detailed in parts (a), (b), or (c) which are covered below.

The reader is asked to note that subsection (2) covers only additional terms. "Different" terms are not considered here, although they were mentioned in subsection (1). We will have more to say about "different" terms when we come to subsection (3).

Subsection (2)(a)

"The offer expressly limits acceptance to the terms of the offer . . . " This is "Escape Hatch 2" in Section 2-207. It is available for use by the offeror. The offeror exercises this escape hatch at the time of making the offer. If the supplier is making the offer, for example, the sales proposal might include this statement:

"Your acceptance of this proposal must include all, and must be limited to, the terms and conditions set forth herein."

There is no new law created by this statement. The offeror has always had the right to demand how and when the offeree is to accept the offer if the offeree wants a contract. "The offeror is master of the offer" has been sustained by years of tradition. The Code continues this right of the offeror to control how an offer may be accepted in Section 2-206 (1). The suggested statement on the sales proposal gives the offeree, who is a buyer in this example, only one choice—take it or leave it. If the offeree takes it, the supplier's terms and conditions come right with the goods. But the offeree-buyer also has a right to seek an alternative supplier who is not so demanding. This may cost the supplier a customer. But he has, however, effectively kept the buyer from getting some of the additional terms that are on the purchase order into the contract.

Note that this example uses the supplier as the offeror and the one taking advantage of Escape Hatch No. 2. The purchasing officer, if the offeror, would have the same opportunity to use the escape hatch, but no example will be given here. The author believes a purchasing officer can protect against additional or different terms in a much more effective manner.

Continuing the discussion of the supplier using Escape Hatch No. 2, what will happen if the purchasing officer ignores the statement on the sales proposal and fires off a purchase order that agrees with all the major provisions of the sales proposal, but contains additional or different terms? Will the purchase order create a contract under subsection (1) or will the purchase order be considered to be a counteroffer to buy? The answer is difficult to find among the muddy waters of 2-207. Apparently a court of law might decide the question either way under the section. Its answer will be dependent upon all the facts surrounding the transaction. Your author inclines to the belief that a contract would be created under a strict reading of subsection (1) and the additional terms proposed in the purchase order would not become part of the contract because of subsection (2)(a). But a court has latitude in answering the question posed, and might decide that no contract was created because the purchase order was a counteroffer.

The situation can get more complex. What if the supplier after receiving the purchase order delivers the goods, and the buyer accepts them? Whose terms will prevail? Now there are three possible answers to this question:

1. The supplier's terms prevail because a contract was formed under subsection (1) and the buyer's additional terms were eliminated under subsection (2)(a).

2. The buyer's terms prevail because the purchase order was a counteroffer to buy. A contract was formed when the supplier delivered the goods and thereby accepted the counteroffer. This is the approach that traditional

common law contract principles would follow.

3. A combination of the supplier's terms and the buyer's terms plus fill-ins from the Code will be applied. This can occur if the court finds no contract was created by subsection (1) and also chooses not to follow the common law. This means the court will find that the contract came into existence under the conduct provisions of subsection (3), which are explained below. Then the terms of the final contract will be those on which the writings of the parties agree plus any supplemental terms from the Code that are necessary to settle a dispute between the parties.

The author believes answer "1" or "3" would be the decision reached. If there is definite proof the parties' forms matched sufficiently to meet the intent of subsection (1), a contract is formed and the supplier's terms prevail. If not, the court must go to "3" if the purposes of 2-207 are to be achieved. It is not possible to be certain which approach would be used by the court in any given set of facts. It is suggested that both purchasing and sales personnel avoid this method of conditioning an offer because of the muddy waters in 2-207 at this point. Similar and more certain protection can be obtained by use of subsection (2)(c).

Subsection (2)(b)

"They materially alter it; or . . . " Additional terms in an acceptance cannot become part of the final contract if they are of such substance as to materially alter the contract. This is not an optional escape hatch available to the parties. It is an absolute mandate provided in the law. However, before the offeror may depend on the law's protection in this manner, we need to know what material terms are. Unfortunately, the law gives us no positive definition.

The Official Comments of the Commissioners who wrote the Code give us some clues about materiality. They state: "Examples of typical clauses which would normally 'materially alter' the contract and so result in surprise or hardship if incorporated without express awareness by the other party are: a clause negating . . . standard warranties; a clause requiring 90 or 100 percent deliveries in a case such as a contract by a cannery; a clause reserving to the seller the power to cancel upon the buyer's failure to meet any invoice when due; a clause requiring that complaints be made in a time materially shorter than customary or reasonable."

Some of the examples given of clauses not believed to be material are: "a clause fixing a reasonable time for complaints within customary limits; a clause providing for interest on overdue invoices; a clause limiting the right of rejection for defects which fall within the customary trade tolerances for acceptance." The reader is reminded that what is and what is not material is a judgmental decision of the court. What is material may vary between jurisdictions, and it could even vary within a jurisdiction depending upon the facts in different cases. Our courts are unwilling to give guidelines on how we might decide an issue of materiality, but here are some tests that might apply in the determination of the. question:

1. Does the new (additional) term result in surprise for the other party?

2. Does the additional term create a hardship for the other party?

3. What is the dollar effect of the new term?

4. What was the significance of the new term under pre-Code law?

5. Was the additional term included in prior dealings between the two parties?

6. Is the additional term commonly used in the industry?

7. Is it one additional term or a multitude? (Forty proposed additional terms were declared material in one case.)

No matter what the tests might establish as material terms, one can be assured that if one party brings a lawsuit attempting to prove materiality of a term, it must be important and material to that party. This fact in itself might have some influence on the court's decision.

Subsection (2)(c)

"Notification of objection to them has already been given or is given within a reasonable time after notice of them is received." Here are Escape Hatches Nos. 3 and 4. Again, they are available to the offeror. Escape Hatch No. 3 may be used either prior to making the offer or at the time the offer is being made. Escape Hatch No. 4 is for use within a reasonable time after the offer has been made.

Subsection (2)(c) provides the best method for the offeror to keep additional terms from creeping into the final contract. Of the two escape hatches in this subsection, No. 3 is preferred. It can be activated in each offer with the use of a statement such as this on a purchase order: "By accepting this purchase order in writing or by delivering the material involved, you accept all the terms and conditions set forth herein. Formal objection is hereby made to any additional or different terms you might propose in your acceptance."

Such a statement on a purchase order precludes the supplier from slipping in additional terms with an acceptance of your offer to buy. You are not dependent on a decision of the court as to whether an additional term is material. This statement of objection challenges both material and nonmaterial terms. With the statement on the purchase order, a supplier's sales acknowledgment form that confirms the major details will make a contract under subsection (1) that will be based upon your terms and conditions. Subsection (2)(c) and the statement eliminate the additional terms on the supplier's form. The different terms on the supplier's form will not enter into the picture if a contract has been formed under subsection (1). Different terms are considered only when the exchanged writings do not make a subsection (1) contract, but the goods are delivered and accepted. Then a contract is formed under subsection (3), and different terms will have an effect on the final contract.

Escape Hatch No. 4 is useful only when there is no statement of objection on the purchase order itself. Escape Hatch No. 4 then gives the opportunity to object to an additional term after the acceptance has been received from the supplier. Use of the statement on each purchase order is preferred to using Escape Hatch No. 4.

***Nota Bene* to the Purchasing Officer.** The routine use of the suggested statement is the most effective manner to keep the supplier's additional terms out of the contract. However, its use does have a limitation. The statement can be used only when your purchase order is an offer to buy. Should you wish to accept a supplier's offer to sell that is contained in a sales quotation, the statement is ineffective. Your purchase order will be acceptance of the supplier's offer. It is possible to reject the supplier's offer to sell and send the purchase order as an offer to buy, ordering the identical material that was on the quotation. You would need to add a prefatory sentence to the statement such as, "Notwithstanding any prior negotiations, this is an offer to buy the material listed above." Follow this sentence with the covering statement suggested earlier. Now you have rejected the supplier's offer to sell and instituted your own offer to buy. You also eliminate any possible misinterpretation that your purchase order is an acceptance. But do keep in mind that you may be losing an advantageous offer. The supplier is now free to walk away from your purchase order. You have rejected his original offer to sell.

You are also put on alert that despite the statement on the purchase order the supplier may respond with a conditional acceptance. This is explained in Point C under subsection (1). No contract is formed if this occurs. Subsection (1) specifically recognizes a conditional acceptance as not being a definite and seasonable expression of acceptance. At this point in the transaction neither you nor the supplier have an enforceable contract. The supplier does not have to deliver the goods. If delivery is made, you do not have to accept it.

You must be careful about your next step if the goods are delivered. If you accept them, subsection (3) will become operative. That section, as you will see, creates a contract because both you and the supplier acted as if you were involved in a contract. The terms of the contract will include supplemental terms from other Code sections. When this happens, you as a buyer may lose important provisions of your purchase order, such as credit terms. There is no automatic protection that can be offered to prevent this from happening. All that can be suggested is that you read your supplier's acceptance form carefully and negoti-ate the differences. More about this later.

Subsection (3)

Point A: "Conduct by both parties which recognizes the existence of a contract is sufficient to establish a contract for sale although the writings of the parties do not otherwise establish a contract."

This is the second place in Section 2-207 that will create a contract for the two parties. Subsection (1) creates a contract from the writings of the parties. Subsec-tion (3) creates a contract from the conduct of the parties. The required conduct is that the seller must deliver the goods, and the buyer must receive and accept them. This is the same provision that we discussed in subsection (1) of Section 2-204. The difference between the 2-204 provision and the 2-207 provision is that 2-207 goes on to put together the terms of the contract under rules presented in Point B that follows. Section 2-204(1) does not offer to piece out a contract.

One must take care to note that the contract created under 2-207(1) consists of the terms of the offer plus any nonmaterial terms the offeree may have included under the provisions of subsection (2)(b). The terms of a 2-207(3) con-tract are pieced together under certain rules, as stated below. The major differ-ence between the contracts created in these two subsections is that a subsection (1) contract may be enforced in a court of law without delivery having been made by the supplier. Both the buyer and the supplier are free to file suit for damages or for specific performance once the contract is made. The parties' writings create the contract. A subsection (3) contract does not come into existence until after the goods have been delivered. It is not possible to sue for specific performance under a subsection (3) contract.

Point B: "In such case the terms of the particular contract consist of those terms on which the writings of the parties agree, together with any supplementary terms incorporated under any other provisions of this Act."

This says that the buyer's purchase order and the sales acknowledgment from the supplier will be laid side by side. Those terms and conditions in both writings that agree will be lifted and become part of the final contract. There will be added from the acceptance (this could be either party's form) those additional terms that come from subsection (2)(b). If the offeror has properly objected to such additional terms, none will be considered for placement in the final con-tract. Next, the different terms in the two forms will be crossed out. If one of the topics of the "different" terms that is crossed out is important to deciding the argument between the buyer and the seller, then the Code provision dealing with that topic will be substituted. If the substituted section of the Code is written in favor of the buyer, the buyer gains the advantage. Likewise, a supplier will gain the point if the substituted section is written "prosupplier." Some Code sections are written in favor of the supplier and some are written in favor of the buyer. Here are some specific examples of how the final outcome will be determined if the terms in the two forms disagree:

1. *Buyer's form:* "deliver to our receiving dock."
   Supplier's form: "F.O.B. seller."
   Code: Section 2-308 states, "Unless otherwise agreed, the place for delivery of the goods is the seller's place of business."

   Result: Seller will get his terms because 2-308 is substituted.

2. *Buyer's form:* "terms net 30 days."
   Supplier's form: "payable on delivery."
   Code: Section 2-310 states, "Unless otherwise agreed payment is due at the time and place at which the buyer is to receive the goods."
   Result: Supplier gets his terms because 2-310 is substituted.

3. *Buyer's form:* "Goods must be merchantable."
   Supplier's form: "Goods sold on an 'as is', 'where is' basis."
   Code: Section 2-314 states, "Unless excluded or modified, a warranty that the goods shall be merchantable is implied in a contract for their sale."
   Result: Buyer gets his implied warranty because 2-314 is substituted.

4. *Buyer's form:* "Damages for breach of warranty of merchantability shall include incidental and consequential damages incurred."
   Supplier's form: "Damages for any claimed breach of warranty shall be limited to the replacement of the defective goods."
   Code: Section 2-714 states, "In a proper case any incidental and consequential damages under the next section may also be recovered."
   Result: Buyer can recover provable incidental and consequential damages because 2-714 is substituted.

5. Here is an example that is particularly injurious to the buyer.
   Buyer's form: "Table tops shall be alcohol and acid resistant."
   Supplier's form: "There are no warranties made, including the warranty of merchantability."
   Code: Section 2-314 states "Unless excluded or modified, a warranty that the goods shall be merchantable is implied in a contract for their resale."
   Result: The buyer will lose the express warranty that the table tops shall be alcohol and acid resistant. The buyer will get the implied warranty of merchantability. That forces the table tops to be "fit for the ordinary purposes for which such goods are used." It is doubtful that "acid resistant"

would be included under the "ordinary purposes" implied warranty. Thus the buyer will lose the express warranty.

These are some examples of the supplementary terms from the Code that may be used to plug the holes left when different terms on a topic are eliminated from both parties' forms.

It is possible that the topic eliminated by different terms is not covered by a Code provision. For example, assume a New York buyer's form has the term, "All disputes arising under this contract shall be decided under the laws of the State of New York." A California supplier's form states, "All disputes arising under this contract shall be settled by arbitration under the rules promulgated by the American Arbitration Association." These "different" terms will be stricken from both parties' forms when subsection (3) is applied. However, there is no Code provision dealing with arbitration. Therefore the supplier will not get arbitration. All disputes under this contract will have to be settled in the appropriate court of law.

It is obvious from these examples that a contract put together by subsection (3) may not contain the terms one of the parties sought. In the Battle of the Forms, there are always winners and losers. This is a calculated risk one takes when a printed form is used by both parties and there is not time available to read the response on the other party's form.

Subsection (3) eliminates the "last shot" principle that has haunted us from the days of the common law. No longer will the terms of the contract be those on the offeree's form. The final terms and conditions will be pieced together by this subsection.

SUMMARY OF SECTION 2-207

The above detailed analysis of this controversial Code section shows that there are some unanswered questions remaining in dealing with the Battle of the Forms. The uncertainties that arose when traditional contract law principles were applied in the battle have been eliminated. But they have been replaced by two basic areas of uncertainty in the application of Section 2-207. The first is whether the exchange of forms by the buyer and seller creates a subsection (1) contract. The parties can never be certain the court will find the offeree's acceptance form to be a "definite and seasonable expression of acceptance." Assuming all of the basics are in agreement in the two forms, the court's decision will rest upon how substantive the differences that remain will be. The more material the differences are, the less likely a subsection (1) contract will be ordered. Differences of minor terms will not affect the decision. If the contract is not declared formed under subsection (1), then a subsection (3) contract will be put together if both parties perform their obligations. There can be a wide variance between the terms of a subsection (1) and a subsection (3) contract. Until the decision is reached, the final terms of the contract will be "up in the air."

The second uncertainty occurs when the offeree sends a conditional acceptance as provided by Escape Hatch No. 1 in subsection (1), and the goods are then delivered without the differences being reconciled. A conditional acceptance does prevent a subsection (1) contract from being created. That much is certain. But the question then arises, "Will the court apply the rules spelled out in subsection (3) to create the contract, or will it treat the conditional acceptance as a counteroffer?" Your author believes that Section 2-207 was designed to eliminate the second conclusion, which is really the application of the last-shot principle. It is also clear that the trend of current decisions is toward a subsection (3) contract. But in either event, the offeror risks losing important terms when a conditional acceptance is received. It behooves the offeror to "blow the whistle" when a conditional acceptance arrives and take time to negotiate with the offeree. This is good advice no matter whether the offeror is the buyer or the supplier.

***Nota Bene* to the Purchasing Officer.** You should understand the alternatives you have available when you are using your purchase order and your supplier is using his form—and—Section 2-207 is hanging over your heads. There are five options you have at your command as the purchasing officer in such situations:

1. Do nothing about the supplier's form except to make certain that the major terms are in agreement with your purchase order. Quantity, description of the goods, price, and delivery date should be verified. If a warranty is important to you, check that too. Then file both forms, let the delivery come and be accepted under your customary receiving procedures. There is every reason to believe that 99 percent of all of your purchases will be completed satisfactorily. You have saved a large block of your time and the time of your staff.

2. Read every bit of boilerplate on the supplier's form, match it with your own, and note the discrepancies. Negotiate these differences with the supplier until both you and the supplier are in agreement. You will not win all of your points against some suppliers, but you will never be surprised at the outcome of a purchase. However, there is the possibility that there are not enough hours in the day to follow this procedure.

3. Print on your purchase order the statement that takes advantage of Escape Hatch No. 3, and make your purchase order an offer to buy in every transaction. The complete statement should read something similar to the following:

    Notwithstanding any prior negotiations, this is an offer to buy the material listed above. By accepting this purchase order in writing or by delivering the materials ordered, you accept all the terms and conditions set forth herein. Formal objection is hereby made to any additional or different terms you might propose in your acceptance.

This statement will keep out the supplier's nonmaterial terms printed on this acceptance form. However, you must continue to guard against conditional acceptances coming from the supplier.

4. Send two copies of your purchase order to the supplier. The second copy is an acceptance copy for the supplier to sign and return to you. Your purchase order should contain a statement similar to this:

   Notwithstanding any prior negotiations, this purchase order is an offer to buy the above items, and includes the terms and conditions printed hereon and on the reverse side. It must be accepted by you. Sign and return the attached acceptance copy to signify your acceptance of our offer.

   Above the signature block on the acceptance copy, there should be this statement: "We accept this purchase order including the terms and conditions printed hereon and on the reverse side." *(Signed)*

   This provides a workable and effective system. It does require policing by your office. You will find that many suppliers will ignore your acceptance copy and send their own form. Since you have used your purchase order as an offer to buy, the supplier's acceptance form then becomes a conditional acceptance, with all the problems associated therewith. And if the material is in stock, delivery may occur before the differences are reconciled. Then the possibility of a subsection (3) contract is upon you. Coordination with the receiving department is most essential. No goods should be accepted by them until you have received the signed copy of the purchase order from the supplier.

5. A more foolproof system utilizes your "Request for Quotation" form. Print on it all the terms and conditions that appear on your purchase order. Insist that all suppliers submit their proposals on your form. The supplier should sign the form under this statement: "We hereby offer to sell you the above material at the prices shown and under the terms and conditions printed hereon and on the reverse side." *(Signed)*

Now you will have an offer to sell in hand based upon your terms and conditions. Send your purchase order to the successful bidder as an acceptance of his offer to sell. When you mail the purchase order, a contract is formed. The offer and the acceptance are identical in all respects. There are no additional or different terms. Section 2-207 will not get involved in such a transaction. Your only concern is that the supplier does not attempt to alter your printed terms when sending the quotation. That would have to be remedied at the time the quotation is being considered. And that is the proper time to "negotiate out" all deviant terms and conditions. This method is to be preferred to the four alternatives listed above.

Should you initiate a purchase with your purchase order as an offer to buy, a different procedure is suggested: Send two identical copies of your purchase order to the supplier. Make the second copy the acceptance copy. Ask the supplier to sign and return it. Have this statement above the signature: "We accept this offer to buy, and all the terms and conditions stated hereon."

Overriding Agreements. There are many suppliers with whom a purchasing officer will deal repeatedly. One suggestion for the purchase contract with such a supplier would be to prepare a master contract that would be applicable to every purchase. Include in this contract all of the terms and conditions that you and the supplier agree upon. The two of you negotiate one standard set of conditions. Make these conditions apply to every purchase and include it by reference only. This will save the time spent in negotiating terms and conditions for every purchase. Such an overriding agreement is particularly useful when purchasing via computer or other modern devices that involve direct placement of an order from the buyer to the supplier.

Another Legal Approach

Possibly in the relatively near future, the law will be more realistic and make enforceable only the terms that are actually agreed on as part of the contract created by the Battle of the Forms. The aim would be to find the contract in the terms actually agreed upon by the parties. The "boilerplate" language and fine print would not be a part of the contract. If, under these circumstances, any other terms are needed, they could be taken from trade usage, course of dealing, course of performance, or the standard Code gap-filling provisions.

This "reality" approach may become a part of the law in the near future.[1] Indeed, even now conflicting terms in the "Battle of the Forms" may cancel each other out when the drafter of both have objected in advance to the others.[2]

In the Executive Summary of the Study Group work (discussed more in Chapter XXX), a reality theory, in regard to Section 2-207 on the Battle of the Forms as a whole, is viewed favorably. It notes that "not all of the Committee

---

[1]See King, "Standard Form Contracts: A New Perspective," *Commercial Law Annual 137* (Callaghan 1991); King, "A New Perspective on Standard Form Contracts: A Subject Revisited," 2 *Commercial Law Annual 87* (Callaghan 1993).
[2]U.C.C. 2-207 Comment 6.

Forms as a whole, is viewed favorably. It notes that "not all of the Committee agree with the earlier mentioned proposal because it is too elaborate and complex." Most "favor what might be called a 'lean mean revision' . . . " The reality theory makes the contracts resulting from the standard form order and acknowledgments "lean and mean." The leanness is in enforcing the agreed-upon terms only. The meanness is to do away with the beloved legal fictions of the past and recognize the reality that the standard form boilerplate is not part of the contract.

XVII

Oral Contracts

The topic of oral contracts is given special consideration in this book because our laws contain unusual provisions concerning their enforceability. We know that oral contracts are commonplace, and that most everyone indulges in them. We place an order verbally in a retail store, and the sales person on the other side of the counter hands the goods to us. A contract of purchase and sale has been negotiated, entered into, and performed. No writing was necessary. We order verbally what we want at a restaurant, and the person serving us accepts our order—a contract is formed. We use our home telephone to order all types of products and services. A tremendous volume of business is transacted by the spoken word. In the professional work of the purchasing officer, the telephone is used to place urgent orders with suppliers and to conclude contract negotiations. Most oral contracts are performed and completed without incident. "All's well" when a verbal contract becomes a *fait accompli.* The law does not police, control, or interfere with such contracts.

But let something go wrong with an oral contract: Suppose your supplier refuses to perform his obligations under the oral contract; suppose you find it necessary to seek the assistance of a court of law to make that supplier do what he promised. It is at such a time that you discover the legal obstacles to settling your differences in a courtroom. The law had remained passive when all of your previous verbal contracts were made and performed; it was not the least bit interested in them. But suddenly, when you seek the law's assistance in enforcing or protecting your rights in an oral contract, you find it to be unconcerned and cool. The law will not consider your complaints if they arise from the purchase or sale of goods having a value of $500 or more because such a verbal contract is not enforceable in a court.

ORIGIN OF THE LAW ON ORAL CONTRACTS

The current legal principle that an oral contract for the purchase and sale of goods in excess of a stated value is unenforceable has been with us for a long period of time. Early common law in England prohibited a defendant, among others, from testifying in court on his or her behalf This gave the plaintiff an unfair advantage, because the defendant was unable to present the other side of the story in the effort to refute the plaintiff's version of the contract. The injustice of this situation was apparent, and in the 1670s the British Parliament passed a law to correct the problem. The law they passed is known as the "Statute of Frauds." It covers many topics; what interests us here is its requirement that certain types of contracts be in writing to be enforceable in a court of law. Included in the list of contracts that were required to be in writing were: (1) real estate contracts, (2) contracts that required more than one year to perform, and (3) contracts involving the purchase and sale of personal property (goods). Note that contracts for services to be performed within one year did not have to be in writing to be enforceable.

THE STATUTE OF FRAUDS

We saw in Chapter I that the common law of England was brought to America and it was accompanied by the Statute of Frauds. Most states embraced the terms of this statute. However, the amounts specified in the sale of goods to "trigger" the requirement that such contracts be in writing varied. Reams of paper have been written defending or attacking the Statute of Frauds. There are those who support the law because they believe it avoids fraud toward the other party to a contract. The opponents of the law point out correctly that the original need for the law does not exist in the United States since defendants are permitted to testify in court on their own behalf and therefore do not need this protection. Those in favor of the requirement of a written contract subscribe strongly to the principle: "Put it in writing," because it is an excellent business discipline. Most purchasing officers follow the practice of reducing to written form purchases and commitments made with suppliers. This is done not only to conform to internal office procedures, but also to record the assurances suppliers have made, such as warranties, price, delivery dates, and guaranteed performance of the products purchased. Putting down on paper the details of a verbal contract is good purchasing practice, and the Statute of Frauds encourages it.

The Commissioners who wrote the Uniform Commercial Code believed in the principles of the Statute of Frauds. They included it in the final version of the Code with only a few variations from the common law. These Code provisions are contained in Section 2-201. Thus 49 of the 50 states in our country embrace the principle that a written contract for the sale of goods is essential if it is to be enforced in a court of law. Only the State of Louisiana continues to follow the civil law in this respect, which does not require a written contract for the sale of goods. The reader may find it interesting to note that the Statute of Frauds was repealed by the British Parliament in 1954. The statute no longer exists in the country from which the United States obtained its concept. It is also noteworthy that the repeal of the statute in England occurred in the same year that the first version of the Uniform Commercial Code, including Section 2-201, was adopted in the state of Pennsylvania.

SECTION 2-201

Section 2-201 contains three subsections: Subsection (1) contains the general rule that an oral contract for the sale of goods for the price of $500 or more is not enforceable in a court of law unless there is some writing indicating that a contract was made between the two parties.

The writing must be signed by the party who would be the defendant if the contract was to be the basis of a lawsuit. Subsection (2) makes one writing do double duty where both parties to the contract are merchants. It allows the writing signed and sent by one party to be effective against the recipient under certain circumstances. This is an innovation that was not included in the original Statute of Frauds. Subsection (3) gives three substitutes for the required writing: (a) Goods to be specially manufactured for the buyer where manufacture has commenced; (b) The party against whom enforcement is sought admits in court that a contract had been made; and (c) The payment is made by the buyer, or delivery is made by the supplier. Substitute (b) is an addition to the original statute, and substitute (c) is an amended version of it.

Application of Section 2-201: Subsection (1)

A hypothetical situation will assist in illustrating the application of the legal principle involved:

> The purchasing officer of Paperless Company telephones Advantage Company and inquires, "What is the current price of your no. 747 valves?" The reply is, "$550 each in lots of 12." The purchasing officer says "Fine. Send me 24 at that price." Advantage replies, "Thanks. We will deliver them tomorrow."
>
> Two weeks later the purchasing officer from Paperless calls Advantage and asks, "What happened to those 24 no. 747 valves you promised to deliver 2 weeks ago for $550 each?" Advantage responds,

"We have no record of you placing an order. Besides, the price of our no. 747 valves increased to $750 each last week."

Paperless believes it is entitled to purchase the valves at $550 each and it files suit against Advantage to force delivery at that price or collect damages. Advantage pleads Section 2-201 as a defense. (Pleading Section 2-201 means that Advantage is asking the court to dismiss the suit because Paperless is suing on an oral contract.)

The court will rule in favor of Advantage, citing as its authority subsection (1) of Section 2-201, which reads:

> Except as otherwise provided in this section a contract for the sale of goods for the price of $500 or more is not enforceable by way of action or defense unless there is some writing sufficient to indicate that a contract for sale has been made between the parties and signed by the party against whom enforcement is sought or by his authorized agent or broker. A writing is not insufficient because it omits or incorrectly states a term agreed upon but the contract is not enforceable under this paragraph beyond the quantity of goods shown in such writing.

The court will therefore not allow Paperless to introduce oral testimony in its attempt to prove the telephone conversation with Advantage. The lawsuit is summarily dismissed because there is no writing signed by Advantage to meet the requirements of subsection (1) of 2-201.

Let us suppose that after Advantage took the original telephone call it sent a note to the Paperless purchasing officer that read: "This is to confirm our telephone conversation today wherein we quoted you $550 each for our no. 747 valves in dozen lots." Would this writing alter the court's decision? The answer is no, because the writing is only a confirmation of the price quoted. For a writing to take an oral contract out of the reaches of Section 2-201 it must:

1. Indicate that a contract for sale has been made;

2. Be signed by the party against whom enforcement is sought; and

3. It must show the quantity of goods involved in the contract.

The writing from Advantage did not meet requirements (1) and (3) above.

It is interesting to note that the last sentence in subsection (1) pinpoints *quantity* as the only contract term that must be contained in the writing necessary to take an oral contract out of the clutches of 2-201. Price, delivery, payment, quality of the goods, and warranties may be stated incorrectly or omitted entirely in an effective writing. The Official Comment of the Commissioners on this subsection states:

> All that is required is that the writing afford a basis for believing that the offered oral evidence rests on a real transaction. It may be written

> in lead pencil on a scratch pad. It need not indicate which party
> is the buyer and which the seller. The only term which must appear is
> the quantity term which need not be accurately stated but recovery is
> limited to the amount stated.

Thus, all that is required in our hypothetical situation to take the contract out of Section 2-201 is a signed writing by Advantage showing that a contract was reached for the sale of 24 no. 747 valves.

Unfortunately, Advantage sent no writing—so Paperless lost its day in court. But the purchasing officer could have protected himself against this unfortunate result by taking advantage of the rules that are established in subsection (2) which follows.

Application of Section 2-201: Subsection (2)

Subsection (2) provides a method to satisfy the Code's requirement of a writing to enforce an oral contract, when only one of the parties prepares and mails a written memorandum of the agreement. Such a possibility was not available in the original Statute of Frauds nor in any previous statutory law. It is strictly a Code innovation. Keep in mind that subsection (1) provides that a writing signed by the party "against whom enforcement is sought" satisfies the Code. But suppose we have the situation where the party who sent that writing is the one that is seeking to enforce the contract? Under prior law, his writing could not be used to hold the other party who did not sign and send it. Now subsection (2) takes care of this dilemma when both parties are merchants:

> Between merchants if within a reasonable time a writing in confir-
> mation of the contract and sufficient against the sender is received and
> the party receiving it has reason to know its contents, it satisfies the
> requirement of subsection (1) against such party unless written notice
> of objection to its contents is given within 10 days after it is received.

This subsection makes the writing by one merchant-party of the oral contract sufficient against the other merchant-party, if not objected to within 10 days after its receipt.

The full impact of subsection (2) will be better understood if we go back to the situation involving Paperless and Advantage. Let us assume that after the purchasing officer of Paperless concludes the telephone conversation he sends them a confirming order that reads: "24 no. 747 valves @ $550 each. Confirming our verbal contract reached today."

This shifts the burden to Advantage. Advantage has 10 days after receiving this confirming order to object to it in writing if it does not meet its approval. If Advantage does not object, the confirming order will be deemed adequate to satisfy Section 2-201 even though Advantage did not sign it. Paperless will be permitted to bring a suit for damages if Advantage persists in demanding $750 for each valve. The confirming order does not guarantee that Paperless will win its case in a court battle, for it must still prove that the contract was created. What the confirming order does do is to strip Advantage of the right to plead Section 2-201 as a defense. Now Paperless has an oral contract that may be "enforceable by way of action" in a court of law.

Subsection (2) demands that the confirming order, or any other type of writing dispatched, satisfy five requirements. The three requirements of a subsection (1) writing must be met plus two additional matters imposed by subsection (2). Here is the complete list:

1. The writing must indicate that a contract for sale has been made between the parties.

2. The writing must be signed by the party preparing it.

3. The writing must specify the quantity of goods involved in the contract.

4. The writing must be prepared by a merchant and sent to a merchant.

5. The writing must be sent within a reasonable time after the verbal contract was made.

Requirements (1), (2), and (3) above are the three mandates of subsection (1). Subsection (2) is applicable only when two merchants are parties to the oral contract, which makes requirement (4) necessary. The last requirement (5) needs further explanation.

In Chapter XII we learned that "reasonable time" is a variable in the law. The Code states: "What is a reasonable time for taking any action depends on the nature, purpose and circumstances of such action." Common sense suggests that if one is to achieve the purpose of recording an oral contract, a reasonable time for action will immediately follow the event. Unwritten details may quickly slip the mind. It is good advice for the purchasing officer to mail the confirming order of the verbal contract the same day or following day. Not only is it good advice to record the agreement in writing before the details become hazy in your and the supplier's mind, but it is also wise to have a written record to eliminate one legal defense if the parties go to court. Since the law states that the writing must be sent within a *reasonable* time, the party receiving the writing has the right to claim that it was not sent promptly. Issuir.g the writing the same day the contract was made removes the possibility of such an argument.

The purchasing officer must also remember that there is more than a 10-day period of waiting once the confirmatory writing is mailed. Ten days must pass after the writing has been received by the supplier. One should allow several days for the supplier to receive the confirming order and then another 10 to pass, as prescribed by the Code. Should the supplier decide on the tenth day to write an objection, another several days could pass before the purchasing officer received that objection. Thus 16 to 18 days must pass before the purchasing officer can be certain there will be no objection. Postponing the mailing of the confirming order only extends this period of waiting that many more days after the oral contract was made. In addition, postponement may give the other party the opportunity to claim it was not sent within a reasonable time.

Subsection (2) is unique: It is an addition to the centuries-old Statute of Frauds. There was no such provision in the original statute. The law in Subsection (2) is good law, and it is a step forward in the development of modern business practice. It is the purchasing officer who most often will memorialize an oral order after the conversation by issuing a confirming order. Under subsection (1), which is the approach taken in the original statute, this confirming order could be used by the supplier against the buyer in a lawsuit. This will deny the buyer the defense of an oral contract. But the same confirming order would not be available to the buyer in an action against the supplier, because the supplier had not signed it. Thus the buyer who diligently sent confirming orders could be penalized by the old law. Subsection (2) corrects this inequity. It makes the buyer's confirming order equally effective by denying the supplier the defense of an oral contract if no objection is sent within 10 days after receipt of the confirming order.

Subsection (2) upsets a longstanding, generally accepted, legal principle. We have been accustomed to the rule: "Silence has no legal significance unless previously agreed to." This rule prevents one from forcing another person to make a legal commitment under the threat of remaining silent. For example, a supplier may write: "Unless we hear from you within five days, we will assume you have accepted our proposal." This supplier cannot make your silence a legal acceptance if you fail to respond within the five-day period. The only manner your silence can be construed as a legal act is if you previously told the supplier: "You submit your proposal in writing, and if you do not hear from me within five days, you can assume I have accepted it." Then your silence could have legal implications because you consented to it. But the supplier cannot unilaterally impose this condition upon you.

Subsection (2) sends this rule on silence to the graveyard in the limited application of confirming memoranda. Unless the merchant-recipient of the written confirmation gives written notice of objection to its contents within ten days, his silence is construed as losing the defense of pleading an oral contract. Thus, the subsection takes away from the recipient an important legal right because he has remained silent.

The "Notice of Objection" Provided in Subsection (2).

Purchasing officers will use Subsection (2) to make certain an oral contract is secure and enforceable. But the occasion may arise when the purchasing officer wants to avoid being tied into an unfavorable or an unwanted oral contract. This is when the defensive provision in subsection (2) should be utilized. The concluding words of the subsection read " . . . unless written notice of objection to its contents is given within 10 days after it is received." *Its contents* refers to the written confirmation of the bargain sent by the other party. This is the Code's invitation to the recipient of the writing to deny that an oral contract was created during the conversation with the sender.

This notice of objection must be in writing. A verbal statement of objection is useless. The notice must be sent by mail or telegram within 10 days after the confirmation is received. The wording of the objection should be terse and to the point. It is possible to say too much and thereby admit that some contract was made during the conversation. We read previously that a valid confirmation (1) must show that a contract was reached, and (2) must indicate the quantity of the item to be purchased and sold. Any notice of objection should be directed to item (1). All that need be or should be written is: "No contract was reached in our conversation." Anything more could lead to other conclusions. For example: "We object to your sales confirmation notice sent following our conversation. You agreed to pay the cost of delivery to our receiving dock," will lose the defense of Section 2-201. Such an objection admits that a contract was reached during the conversation. This is sufficient to take it out of the reaches of 2-201. The written confirmation will prevail even though the recipient disagrees with the stated delivery term. Subsection (1) states: "A writing is not insufficient because it omits or incorrectly states a term agreed upon . . . " The sender of the confirmation in this instance will be allowed by a court to offer testimony proving the contract, and this could mean that the buyer loses the delivery-point argument. If conflicting testimony is offered by the buyer and the seller on delivery point, the court will follow the rules of subsection (3) of Section 2-207, and follow the Code provisions on delivery. Section 2-308 provides that the normal terms are F.O.B. the seller's place of business, unless otherwise agreed to by the parties.

In our example, it would have been prudent for the buyer receiving the sales confirmation to have responded with the terse note: "We reached no contract in our conversation." That would send both parties back to the negotiating table to iron out their differences. This is where the delivery terms should have been decided in the first place, rather than having a court of law apply the standard Code provision.

The implications from silence in subsection (2) also suggest the importance of reading and responding to the mail each day. A less than reputable supplier might follow up an unsuccessful telephone solicitation with a fake sales confirmation in an attempt to force the buyer into a contract. The prompt written response: "We reached no contract in our telephone conversation" preserves the right of the buyer to defend the claim of a sale by pleading Section 2-201. The buyer is also advised to notify the receiving department of this attempt to force a sale. Any goods received from that aggressive supplier should not be accepted by the receiving department.

Application of Section 2-201: Subsection (3)

Subsection (3) suggests three additional circumstances under which a verbal contract may be taken from the reaches of the unenforceability provision of subsection (1).

Item (a) of Subsection (3) gives a supplier-manufacturer the opportunity to do this without a writing if the goods are specially designed for the buyer. If the manufacturer proceeds with the production of the special order, or if orders are placed for its components, the oral contract is enforceable under (3)(a). But this provision applies only to the instance where the goods ordered are specially designed for the buyer. This provision will not apply if the product being manufactured is an item the supplier regularly stocks and sells to other customers. This subsection will have little practical value for professional purchasing officers and their suppliers. It is inconceivable that a purchasing officer place a verbal order with a manufacturer to make his product to the buyer's special design without giving that manufacturer detailed specifications and drawings. It is equally difficult to imagine a manufacturer taking off on the manufacture of his product to the buyer's special design without having a written agreement with that buyer. This is particularly true if that special product cannot be sold to other customers of the manufacturer.

Item (b) of Subsection (3) has limited application too. It provides that an oral contract is enforceable in court "if the party against whom enforcement is sought admits in his pleading, testimony or otherwise in court that a contract for sale was made." This provision is included primarily as a technical legal barrier to a party pleading in the alternative—that is, pleading that a contract was made, but the Statute of Frauds prevents its enforcement.

Item (c) of Subsection (3) has more practical application for buyers and sellers. It provides that an oral contract is enforceable "with respect to goods for which payment has been made and accepted or which have been received and accepted." Note that two actions are required in both payment and delivery to make this rule applicable. In the case of payment, it must be shown that not only did the buyer make payment, but also the seller must have accepted that payment. In the case of delivery of the goods, not only must the goods be delivered, but also there must be a showing that the buyer accepted the goods delivered.

The enforceability of an oral contract under Subsection (3)(c) is limited to those goods actually paid for or for those goods actually delivered and accepted.

The full quantity included in the oral contract is not proven by partial payment or partial delivery. Thus, if the oral contract called for 24 machines at $5000 each, a $10,000 "down payment" by the buyer at the time the contract was reached, will take out of the reach of Section 2-201 only two of the 24 machines. The remaining 22 will continue to require some other method of proof that they were contracted for. Such a contract is said to be "divisible" and can be divided into individual units for application of Subsection (3)(c). It is possible for the buyer to protect his or her company by writing on the check "This is a $10,000 down payment on our oral contract for 24 machines at $5000 each." The supplier will not be permitted to plead Section 2-201 as a defense if he accepts the check without making any objection within ten days. Subsection (2) and not Subsection (3)(c) will close the door on the supplier's defense.

It is, at times, difficult to determine whether a contract is divisible. A 1983 Oregon case offers a rationale applied by some courts.[1] The plaintiff, Martin Electric Company, sold seven used transformers to the defendant Mesaba Service and Supply Company. Included were five 1000-kilovolt, one 1500-kilovolt, and one 7500-kilovolt transformers. They were sold for a fixed price on an "as is, where is" basis, with the buyer being required to move them from the premises. Mesaba picked up the 7500-kilovolt transformer but refused to pick up the other six because they contained polychlorinated biphenyl oil (P.C.B.). The Oregon court decided the case in favor of the Martin Company because the contract was not divisible and severable. The sale was a package sale of seven units and there could be no allocation of price among each unit. Thus, because Mesaba picked up the one transformer, this part performance made the oral contract enforceable for all seven transformers.

The question can also arise and has arisen where only one item is included in an oral contract' and the buyer makes a partial payment. Strict construction of subsection (3)(c) might dictate that there is no enforceable contract because the down payment was not adequate to cover the purchase price of the one unit. But a California case in 1971 decided otherwise.[2]

> Lockwood, the plaintiff, sued Smigel for damages for breach of an oral contract. Smigel owned a 1967 Rolls Royce and verbally agreed to sell it to Lockwood for $11,400. Lockwood gave Smigel $100 as part payment, with the balance to be paid on the delivery of the car. Smigel did not deliver the car to Lockwood but sold it to someone else. Lockwood sued for damages. The question raised in this case was whether the $100 down payment on an $11,400 automobile took the case out of the reaches of Section 2-201 through subsection (3)(c). The California court said it did, although it admitted the wording in (3)(c)

---

[1]*Mesaba Service & Supply v. Martin,* 676 P.2d 930. Oregon (1983).
[2]*Lockwood v. Smigel,* 96 Cal. Rptr. 289 (1971).

was ambiguous. The court, in its decision, said:

> When there is a part payment instead of a memorandum, this fact evidences the existence of a contract and identifies the party to be charged—i.e., the seller who received the money. Where the buyer is claiming to have purchased no more than one unit, there can be no dispute over quantity.

Thereupon, the California court awarded damages to Lockwood for breach of oral contract. This could be the trend that will be followed in future decisions.

Summary of Section 2-201

Capsulizing the provisions of 2-201, we come up with the following:

1. An oral contract cannot be enforced in a court of law unless:

   a. There is a signed written confirmation of the contract sent by one party to the other stating: i. that a contract was reached orally, and ii. the quantity of goods that were ordered; or

   b. The supplier-manufacturer has begun manufacture of specially ordered goods.

2. Partial enforcement of an oral contract is permitted to the extent to which

   a. Payment has been made or accepted, or

   b. The quantity of goods has been delivered and accepted.

3. An objection to a written confirmation must be made within ten days after its receipt.

   ***Nota Bene* to the Purchasing Officer.** The rules of Section 2-201 which require a writing to enforce an oral contract apply only to contracts involving the purchase and sale of goods with a price of $500 or more. If the price of the goods is less than $500, no written confirmation is required. It is also true that an oral contract for services is enforceable in court without a writing if the services can be performed within one year from the date of the contract. The amount of the contract for services is immaterial. Only the *length of time the service is to be performed* dictates whether or not a writing is required for the contract to be enforceable.

   Some state jurisdictions also permit this Statute of Frauds section in the Code to be avoided under the doctrine of promissory estoppel. (See Chapter XII for an explanation of promissory estoppel.) It is suggested that the purchasing officer consult with legal counsel to ascertain whether his or her jurisdiction follows this rule.

PRACTICAL EFFECTS

Many persons feel that the Statute of Fraud results in more fraud than it prevents. Indeed, it does allow parties to get out of contracts which they had made. In a sense it is a type of technicality which allows parties in some instances to get out of contracts even though there may be witnesses to the making of the oral contract. Not only are there some cases where the Statute of Frauds permits a party to break a contract, but there may be many more instances which are never reported as well.

In some situations, as has been discussed already, there are exceptions to the Statute of Frauds. Indeed, some persons would say that the exception often "swallows the rule." Since there are a number of exceptions already, it would seem advantageous to abolish the rule rather than leaving it applicable to these exceptions and inapplicable to other situations.

NEW PROPOSALS

As has been mentioned previously, Article 2 on Sales of the Uniform Commercial Code is in the process of revision. The reporter, Professor Richard Speidel, has advocated that the Statute of Frauds be abolished. In his draft of the revised Article 2, he simply leaves out the section found in the traditional code. It is his opinion that the statute no longer serves a useful purpose and that it creates injustices at times.

The proposal for the elimination of the Statute of Frauds is a good one. Indeed, there are a number of arguments which favor its abolition.

INTERNATIONAL TRADE AND ORAL CONTRACTS

In international trade, many of the contracts are in writing. However, the question still arises as to whether oral contracts can be made which are enforceable. In this regard, it should be noted that the Convention on the International Sale of Goods does not require contracts to be in writing. This Convention applies to contracts between United States businessmen and businessmen in a large number of other countries that have ratified this treaty. As a treaty, it is automatically the law of the United States and every state. This means that in a large number of contracts where purchases are made from persons outside the United States, such contracts are enforceable even though they are not in writing. The Statute of Frauds of the traditional Uniform Commercial Code is inconsistent with this law. This means that the businessman is subject to two different laws in regard to world contracts, depending on whether the other party is within or outside the United States.

In the new "International Restatement of Contracts Law" there are also no requirements for a contract to be in writing. Thus, oral contracts are enforceable under these general principles of International Transactions. Again, the Statute of Frauds in the traditional Uniform Commercial Code is inconsistent with this law as well.

It should be noted that there are very few countries such as China which do require that a contract be in writing. This has been permitted as an exception to the General Principles of the Convention for International Sale of Goods. In addition, it should be noted that a number of businessmen do ultimately reduce their oral contracts into written form in international transactions. This tends to prevent any later misunderstanding that may arise between the parties. Further discussion may be found in Chapter XXXI.

SECTION D

TERMS OF THE CONTRACT

XVIII

Quantity

Quantity is an important term in the law of purchasing, as well as in the purchasing function itself. In law, the need for a specific expression of the quantity begins with the offer. An offer to buy or an offer to sell must be definite to constitute a valid offer. An offer that does not mention the quantity, or mentions it only in vague terms, generally is not considered to be definite (see Chapter XII, "Identification of the Subject Matter in an Offer"). In a few cases, circumstances giving rise to an implication or trade usage or past practices could indicate quantity in regard to contract formation. We noted in the previous chapter that a written confirmation of an oral contract is not sufficient to overcome Section 2-201 if it fails to mention a specific quantity. Finally a contract that does not specify a fixed or determinable quantity is unenforceable in a court of law because there is no precise subject matter in such a contract. One may readily understand the difficulty a court of law would have in awarding damages to a buyer for breach of a contract that did not specify the quantity. A fixed or determinable quantity must be expressed in a contract for the sale of goods.

There will be occasions when the purchasing officer must make a purchase while having no way of determining the actual quantity of the item that will eventually be required. The law does permit quantities to be estimated in a contract provided the same contract provides the method by which the final quantity is to be determined. Such a contract is known as a *requirements contract*. This is discussed in a succeeding section of this chapter.

EXPRESSING THE QUANTITY TERM

A purchasing officer has no problem stating the quantity of an item wanted on the purchase order when the total need is known. The required number is all that must be stated. If the number applies to a unit of measure, such as a dozen, a bushel, or a ton, the unit of measure must be clearly specified. When there is more than one possible meaning to a unit of measure, the one intended should be clearly identified. For example, one orders a ton. Is it a *short ton* (2000 pounds) or a *long ton* (2240 pounds)? No room should be allowed for the supplier to make a free interpretation of the quantity intended to be purchased.

Customs of the Industry

Some industries have established customs for expressing quantity that allow for variations. One such industry is the printing industry where it has long been established that an over- or underrun of 10 percent is an acceptable variation from the quantity ordered by the buyer. Pricing of the over- or underrun is based upon the unit price contained in the contract. Thus, if 10,000 letterheads are contracted for at a price of $300, and 10,600 letterheads are delivered, the printer will invoice the customer for $318. If 9600 letterheads are delivered, the invoice is $288. There are similar customs in other industries that allow for quantity variations, such as canneries and foundries.

The reasons vary as to why such industry customs became established. Availability, uniformity, consistency of the raw material, and spoilage during the manufacturing process are some of the more common reasons given. In the printing industry, for example, one does not simply press a button to start production. Setting margins and registering colors require trial sheets until the desired position of the printed image is established. This might waste a number of sheets of paper. Since the paper comes from the printer's supplier in standard packages, such spoilage reduces the final quantity of the finished product, thereby creating an underrun. Some printers will over order the amount of paper to allow for some spoilage. If the spoilage is minimal, more of the finished product might be available for delivery to the customer; hence, an overrun. Customs of the industry are recognized by the Code in Section 1-205(2), under the title "Usage of Trade."

The purchasing officer who does not wish to accept a variation in quantity should specify on the purchase order that "no over- or underruns are accepted." However, if the purchase order is being used as an acceptance of the supplier's offer to sell, a term in that offer to sell could be included stating: "The customs of the industry are incorporated in this proposal." This could lead to the supplier's possibly getting the industry custom into the contract under application of Section 2-207. (See Chapter XV.) The preferred course of action in such an instance is for the purchasing officer to negotiate with the supplier to get that provision removed from the contract.

REQUIREMENTS CONTRACTS

There will be occasions when a purchasing officer is faced with the problem of arranging for the purchase of an item with the following characteristics:

1. It is a repetitive need: The item is used by the organization daily or at frequent intervals.

2. The total usage of the item over a period of time may be, and usually is, variable.

3. On-site storage of large quantities of the item is difficult, expensive, or impracticable.

4. Continuity of supply of the item must be assured for a reasonable period of time.

5. The usage and cost of the item is substantial enough to make volume purchases cost-effective.

A few examples of items with these characteristics might be: newsprint for a daily newspaper, paper for a weekly magazine, X-ray film for a radiology unit in a health facility, milk and ice cream for the company cafeteria, gasoline for a fleet of delivery trucks, or fuel oil for a heating plant.

The purchasing officer will find that a *requirements*-type contract is admirably suited to such situations. This type of contract provides the opportunity to negotiate for the purchase of a large volume of an item. The quantity covered by the contract may vary within reasonable limits, provided the buyer is committed to the purchase of all the organization's need of the item from the same supplier. A long-term contract assures continuity of supply, and frequent deliveries can be arranged with the supplier. Thus, a properly drawn requirements contract satisfies the law despite the indefinite quantity term, and it gives the buyer the advantages of a volume-purchase contract.

Requirements contracts were recognized by the law prior to the adoption of the Uniform Commercial Code. But their enforcement has always given the law problems. One reason for this is of course the variability of the *quantity* term. Another pervading enforcement problem is that when wide price swings occur during the life of the contract, it becomes favorable to one of the parties and harsh for the other party. This makes it difficult for a court to order enforcement, because an unconscionable burden falls upon one of the parties. Nonetheless enforcement can be ordered, provided two tests are clearly met: (1) Can the quantity involved be determined at any point in time, including determination on a hindsight basis, and (2) is there an equal mutuality of obligation to perform on the part of both the buyer and the supplier?

The law recognizes that the precise quantity involved in a purchase and sale under a requirements contract cannot be stated at the time the contract is written. But it does insist that there be a definite statement, or a formula indicating how the quantity will be determined during the period covered by the contract. For example, the quantity involved in a heating oil requirements contract cannot be known the summer before the heating season begins. Quantities of oil used during past heating seasons give some guide to what might be required during the forthcoming season. However weather varies, and with it the consumption of oil. But at the end of the heating season, both buyer and supplier will know how many gallons of oil had to be poured into the oil tank to keep the buyer warm. The quantity required under such a contract is determinable by the time the contract expires. This satisfies the law's need for a definite quantity term to be expressed in a contract.

There must also be a rigid obligation on the part of the buyer to purchase all his needs from the supplier. This obligation must be matched by a similar commitment by the supplier to sell the buyer such requirements during the life of the contract. The above heating-oil contract is a good example of required mutuality to perform. The buyer must be required to purchase all the oil required for the heating plant from the supplier. This means that the buyer gives up the right to take advantage of more favorable "spot" oil prices that may be offered during the season by other suppliers. Giving up this right is to his detriment, and the law considers this to be consideration for the enforceability of the requirements contract. The supplier must have similar obligation. That obligation is to supply all the buyer's requirements during the period. Here the supplier gives up the right to allocate his available supply of oil to customers who might pay more for it than he is receiving under the requirements contract. It is to his detriment that he must sell his supply under the terms of the contract. This is his consideration to make the contract binding and enforceable.

Some requirements contracts are written stating minimum and maximum quantities. These are included to make the contract more appealing to both parties. Thus, in the heating oil example, the buyer could agree to make purchases from the supplier of no less than a specified minimum number of gallons, regardless of the winter weather. This is a contract "sweetener" for the supplier. He knows he has made a sale of a specified gallonage no matter how low the price of oil goes or how mild the weather is. As a contra inducement for the buyer, there will be a clause in the contract that the supplier agrees to sell "up to" a specified number of gallons. (This quantity is well above the minimum established.) This gives the buyer the assurance that no matter how high the price of oil goes he is assured that he will be permitted to purchase the maximum quantity at the contract price. The range between the minimum and maximum is the allowable range for the requirements of the heating season, notwithstanding price variations or available supply. The purchasing officer is reminded that the inclusion of minimum and maximum quantities is not required to make a requirements contract enforceable in a court of law. The allowable variations of the quantity to be bought and sold are only intended to make the contract more appealing to one or both parties.

The Uniform Commercial Code: Section 2-306(1)

Section 2-306(1) of the Code and the Official Comments of the Commissioners, continue the general approval of pre-Code law to requirements contracts. Subsection (1), which imposes the obligation of good faith on the parties and sets a standard for allowable variations, reads as follows:

> (1)A term which measures the quantify by the output of the seller or the requirements of the buyer means such actual output or requirements as may occur in good faith, except that no quantity unreasonably disproportionate to any stated estimate or in the absence of a stated estimate to any normal or otherwise comparable prior output or requirements may be tendered or demanded. This section establishes a few ground rules for determination of allowable variations in quantity in requirements contracts. It does implicitly recognize such contracts by reference; but we must remember that requirements contracts were considered enforceable in pre-Code law. Therefore their established validity is unchanged by the Code because it states in Section 1-103: "Unless displaced by the particular provisions of this Act, the principles of law and equity . . . shall supplement its provisions."

Furthermore, the Commissioners in their Official Comment give their blessing to requirements contracts by affirmatively stating that they meet the tests of both definiteness and mutuality, which are the areas most often challenged by general contract law. They state the following:

> Under this Article, a contract for output or requirements is not too indefinite since it is held to mean the actual good faith output or requirements of the particular party. Nor does such a contract lack mutuality of obligation since, under this section, the party who will determine quantity is required to operate his plant or conduct his business in good faith and according to commercial standards of fair dealing in the trade so that his output or requirements will approximate a reasonably foreseeable figure.

Note that good faith on the part of both parties emphasized in Section 2-

306(1) and in the Official Comment of that section. It is a prevailing principle under the Code (see the discussion of good faith in Chapter X). Here, it is demanded as the price for the enforceability of a requirements contract.

Drafting a Requirements Contract

The purchasing officer must exercise care in negotiating for and drafting a requirements contract. The needs of the company must be properly met, and in a manner that conforms to the law governing requirements contracts and meets the rigid test of good faith to the supplier. A list of nine drafting suggestions that will be of assistance in this procedure follows.

1. Estimating the Quantity. The first decision to be made is with regard to the probable quantity of the item to be purchased during the period of the contract. The stated quantity must be a part of the request for quotation to enable the suppliers to submit competitive quotations. It is obvious that the quantity must be an estimate; otherwise there would be no need to engage in a requirements contract. But that estimate should be as close to the actual quantity involved as the purchasing officer may reasonably foresee. It is advantageous to the buyer to make the estimate as large as possible, but the temptation of "puff the need" must be resisted. Facts known must be considered. Probably the most establishable fact is the prior usage of the product, if any. Past records of ranges and the reasons for the variances are helpful. Next, the projection of usage during the period the contract is to run must be made. Is there an unusually heavy backlog of orders that will increase the need? Are there plans to expand marketing areas of the product? Is the business forecast for your product and for your customers favorable or unfavorable? These and any other factors known to the buyer at the time must be considered before reaching a final decision regarding the quantity to be included. The purchasing officer is advised to prepare an informal memorandum listing the factors used in determining the final estimate. Such a memorandum will serve as evidence of the reasonableness of the estimate should there be a need to prove this at some future date.

2. Maximum and Minimum Quantities. Quantity boundaries were discussed previously. Their inclusion is not required for a requirements contract to be valid, but it may be found necessary to use them to attract the suppliers from whom you wish to obtain proposals. If the quantity is to be included in the contract, it is to the buyer's advantage to set the minimum as low as possible, temporized only by the fact that it must be large enough to offer a substantial sales volume to the supplier. The maximum quantity should be set high enough to give the buyer the greatest possible leeway in utilizing the contract.

The buyer is advised to keep in mind that stating a minimum quantity in a requirements contract could well be equivalent to an absolute purchase. On occasion, that will work to the advantage of the buyer; on other occasions, the supplier will benefit. In 1976 a federal court held that a statement of minimum quantity in a requirements contract constituted an absolute purchase, even though the requirements contract itself was declared to be unenforceable.[1] The facts of the case are complicated and very detailed. Here is an abbreviated version:

> A Colorado utility entered into a requirements contract with a coal mine to supply coal for their generators. The minimum quantity in the contract obligated the utility to purchase 85 percent of the total consumption of coal that its two 350,000-kW generators would require, allowing for the fact that the generators would not always operate at full potential, and that there would be downtime. The maximum quantity of coal the mine was required to supply was 100 percent of the consumption if the generators operated at full load continuously with no allowance made for either unit to be out of service. At the time the contract was signed, the utility had already decided to increase the size of the generators by about 20 percent, but they did not tell the coal mine this fact. Evidently the utility believed there was enough leeway in the maximum quantity allowance to cover their needs for the added capacity.
>
> About five months after the contract was in existence, the Arab oil embargo occurred, and coal prices skyrocketed. The supplier—the coal mine—was caught in an unfavorable contract. They discovered the utility had increased the size of the generators and filed suit to cancel the contract, claiming the utility had violated its provisions.

The federal court agreed with the coal mine and declared the utility had breached the requirements contract by not informing the coal supplier that the capacity of the plant had been increased. But the court then said that although there was no longer a requirements contract in existence, the minimum purchase provision was separable from the maximum-quantity provision. The court ruled that the utility had an obligation to purchase 85 percent of the coal that would be consumed under normal conditions by the two 350,000-kW generators. This was an absolute purchase, and it stood alone. Therefore, the court required the coal mine to deliver that amount of coal at the contract price

Although the court's decision gave the buyer a partial victory, it emphasizes the commitment a buyer makes when agreeing to a minimum quantity in a requirements contract.

3. How the Requirements Will Be Determined. The contract should express clearly and in positive terms how the quantity of requirements of the product will be determined during the period of the contract. It is the purchasing officer's duty to express this, since it is his or her company's requirements that are being purchased. For example, "All the no. 2 heating oil required by our Main Street plant from September 1 to June 30" is a precise description of the quantity and product covered by the contract. It leaves no doubt as to the source of the

---

[1] *Utah Intern, Inc. v. Colorado-Lite Elec. Assn., Inc.* 425 F. Supp. 1093 (1976).

need and how the quantity will be measured, although at the time the contract was written that quantity was unknown. The quantity covered by the contract is determinable at the end of the specified period of 10 months.

4. Mutuality of Obligation. The requirements contract must be written in a manner that makes it mandatory for the buyer to buy and the supplier to sell the quantity required. These obligations must be mutual. Here is a case that was tried in the federal court that underscores the need for mutuality of obligation:[2]

> Propane Industries sent the General Motors unit in Kansas City the following proposal on March 9, 1973:
>
>> We will supply to your factory (propane gas) during the 1973-74 winter standby season . . . as follows: Price $.17 gallon, guaranteed firm, F.O.B. your plant location.
>
> On March 21, 1973, the purchasing officer of General Motors issued the following purchase order to Propane Industries:
>
>> To cover a possible requirement of 500,000 gallons to be used as standby fuel . . . delivery within 24 hours of release on an "as required" basis.
>
> On July 30, 1973, Propane Industries wrote:
>
> Due to serious shortages of all fuels . . . we are unable to fulfill our contract with you as outlined in your purchase order.
>
> General Motors responded on August 23, 1973:
>
>> Since this contract was executed in good faith, we expect you to fulfill its obligation.
>
> In October General Motors got approval under the Energy Policy Allocation Program to obtain 75,000 gallons of gas, and Propane Industries delivered it. They sent an invoice at $.4048 per gallon. General Motors paid at the contract rate of $.17 per gallon and Propane Industries filed suit to collect the additional sum invoiced.

The federal court awarded Propane Industries the additional $.2348 per gallon. In its decision, the court first emphasized the necessity of having binding mutual obligations of the buyer and the seller in a requirements contract. It then pointed out that the purchase order did not contain an express promise of General Motors to purchase exclusively from Propane Industries. It concluded with a statement that the words "possible requirement" were ambiguous and did not commit General Motors to make any purchase.

5. Length of Period Covered by the Contract. A requirements contract should not be written for an unlimited period of time. There must be an established date specifying when the contract will expire. A contract does not meet the

---

[2]*Propane Indus. Inc. v. General Motors Corp.,* 429 F. Supp. 214 (1977).

criterion of being "definite" if the termination date is left open-ended.

A tightly drawn requirements contract should cover a period of no longer than 12 to 15 months. (A *tightly drawn* requirements contract is meant to include only those contracts that contain no escalation clause, no reopening provisions or any other types of safety valves for both parties.) Too many contingencies might occur as time progresses which might well create a hardship on the buyer or the seller. Prices might drop sharply, and the buyer would then be caught in a cost squeeze that would place him at a competitive disadvantage in the marketplace. If prices rose considerably, the supplier could be in the same position. Or if the available supply of the product covered by the contract diminished, problems for both the supplier and the buyer would arise.

Short-term requirements contracts (no longer than 12 to 15 months) will probably be enforced no matter what market changes occur. But the longer-term contracts without escalation clauses are more difficult to sustain after the lapse of a reasonable length of time. An unconscionable result might occur when enforced against the disadvantaged party. When a longer-term contract is desired to protect and assure continuity of supply, price-adjustment provisions will eliminate this charge.

6. Price-Adjustment Clauses. The buyer or the supplier in a requirements contract may insist on the inclusion of a price-adjustment clause. More often it is the supplier who will insist on such protection. Too many times in the past suppliers have seen prices rise suddenly and sharply. When this happens, their only response is to raise the price they charge their customers for their product. If they are tied into a firm-requirements contract, this option is not open to them. Consequently, when the purchasing officer suggests that they enter into a requirements contract, the supplier may refuse to do so. If the purchasing officer persists, the supplier is apt to quote a high price that has a margin of safety built in as insurance. When this happens, the purchasing officer may not get the best price available.

One solution to such a quandary is to provide for price-adjustment clauses in the contract. Provision could be made for a price adjustment every two to three months and establish a basis by which the supplier can prove he has undergone an increase of cost for his product. Or perhaps a published market price list is available to which the contract price may be pegged. If not, then look for a published list price of an industry leader. The price in the requirements contract could be expressed as a specific discount from the pegged list. Should the list price increase, the buyer will pay more for the product, but he will continue to enjoy the same percentage of discount from list. The contract will maintain that discount.

The purchasing officer is advised to remind the supplier that price adjustments are a two-way street. Should the supplier insist on a price escalation clause, the buyer should insist that a similar downward adjustment be made available if prices decline. The buyer is entitled to the same safety precautions as the supplier. (See "Price Escalation Clauses" in Chapter XIX.)

7. Market Expansion Clauses. The purchasing officer may wish to provide for the purchase of additional quantities of an item covered by a requirements contract because of a contemplated expansion of his company's market. One simple method to accommodate this is to raise the maximum allowable quantity to be purchased, if the contract has such limits. If there is doubt about the expansion becoming a reality, the estimate of quantity to be purchased should not be increased. This would give the supplier an opportunity to cry "foul." But there is nothing wrong about convincing the supplier to raise the maximum limit.

If there is a possibility of an increase in quantity to be purchased, one can consider seeking a lower price for any additional contingent purchases. A contract is perfectly proper if it sets one price for the first 5 tons purchased, and a lower price for each additional ton over 5 that might be bought.

Whatever method the purchasing officer employs to provide for a possible market expansion, good faith requires that the supplier be informed of the fact. However, do not allow yourself to be caught in the position of not being able to purchase up to your promised quantity. Inform the supplier and place in the contract the "If" part of your anticipated volume. The supplier will have then no grounds for complaint if the contingency does not materialize. The supplier gambled with you and lost.

8. Assignability. The possibility is ever present that a buyer or a supplier might transfer to another his or her duties of performance under a contract for the purchase and sale of goods. Rights that have accrued under a contract may be similarly transferred. ("Rights" include the right of the supplier to receive payment and the right of the buyer to collect damages if the contract is breached by the supplier.) The law refers to this transferability as the "assignment of duties and rights." Assignment is available to both the supplier and the buyer.

Assignment of performance in the ordinary contract for the purchase and sale of goods does not occur frequently. The supplier will attempt to deliver promptly, and the buyer will pay the invoice when due. The performance of each party's duty is completed in a relatively short span of time. Performance in a requirements contract, however, will continue over a longer period, which increases the possibility of assignment. The purchasing officer, for example, could be faced with a situation in a requirements contract when the supplier decides to cease manufacture of the product and assigns the contract to another company. The new supplier was probably one of the original supplier's competitors. It is also possible that the new supplier is one the purchasing officer rejected when entering into the contract. In any event, the assignment forces the purchasing officer to deal with a different company than the one originally contracted with and may force his acceptance of a product made by a different manufacturer.

The Uniform Commercial Code recognizes assignment as a contracting fact of life and gives it its blessing. The pertinent provisions are found in Section 2-210 which is titled "Delegation of Performance; Assignment of Rights." Subsection (1) reads:

> A party may perform his duty through a delegate unless otherwise agreed or unless the other party has a substantial interest in having his original promissor perform or control the acts required by the contract. No delegation of performance relieves the party delegating of any duty to perform or any liability for breach.

Subsection (1) makes four pronouncements concerning assignment:

1. Assignment is legal and can be done.

2. The parties to the contract may agree to outlaw assignment.

3. Assignment cannot occur if the would-be assignor has a personal duty to perform under the contract.

4. Assignment does not relieve the assignor of any responsibility of the original obligations undertaken when he signed the contract.

The purchasing officer should take careful note of the Code's inclusion of the repeated suggestion, "unless otherwise agreed." Negotiate the possibility of assignment out of the contract if you do not want it to occur.

Subsection (3) of Section 2-210 restricts the right to outlaw assignment of the rights of the party. An agreed-to prohibition of assignment applies only to the delegation of the duties of performance—the obligation of the supplier to deliver and the obligation of the buyer to receive, accept, and pay for the goods.

Subsection (4) places an obligation on the assignee (the one who is delegated as the substitute) to perform the duties accepted from the assignor. It gives a right to the person making the assignment *and* to the other party to the contract to enforce the original contract against the party who accepted the assignment. Subsection (5) of Section 2-609 reads:

> The other party may treat any assignment which delegates performance as creating reasonable grounds for insecurity and may without prejudice to his rights against the assignor demand assurances from the assignee.

This entitles the other party to the contract to make a written demand on the assignee to give adequate assurance of due performance as provided in Section 2-609. (Section 2-609 is discussed in Chapter XXI.) Failure of the assignee to give what the other party considers to be "adequate assurance of performance" within 30 days entitles the other party to repudiate the contract.

Nota Bene **to the Purchasing Officer.** The purchasing officer has the option of insisting on a "no-assignment" clause in a contract before signing it. The alternative is to ignore the matter of assignment completely. Section 2-210 gives real protection to "the other party." If you are the other party and your supplier assigns his performance to another supplier, here is the protection you get:

1. The original supplier remains responsible to you for performance on the contract, and is liable to you in the event of a breach (Subsection 1).

2. The delegated or substitute supplier has a similar obligation to you to perform in accordance with the contract (Subsection 4).

3. You have the right to demand Section 2-609 assurances of adequacy of performance when an assignment has been made. If you believe the assurances received are unsatisfactory under reasonable commercial standards, you have the right to repudiate the remainder of the contract.

One way to look at an assignment by the supplier is that the buyer, after the assignment occurs, has two companies that guarantee performance and are liable for possible breach of contract. Both the original supplier and the substitute have the obligation to you, whereas prior to the assignment you could only look to the supplier who signed the contract.

The disadvantage to the buyer of assignment is the possibility of getting another manufacturer's product. If you selected the original supplier because of the quality of his product you might be disappointed with the substitute product. On the other hand, if the original supplier assigned the contract because of ceasing production, there is little you can do but find an alternate supplier.

Your author suggests that you keep all doors open for options. A clause in the requirements contract—and perhaps in all contracts— similar to the following might be apropos:

> Neither party to this contract may assign their duties of performance under it without the express written consent of the other party.

Then, if any assignment is made, and you are willing to give approval to it, conclude your written approval with this sentence:

> This approval is granted with the full understanding that all the rights given a nonconsenting "other party" under the Uniform Commercial Code: Section 2-210 are reserved and available to the undersigned.

Then you and your company will have the best of both worlds.

9. A Variety of Products. The previous eight considerations when drafting a requirements contract presume that there is only one product involved in the contract. There is no legal objection to including more than one product in the contract as long as they are related products. Thus, a contract could call for no. 2 and no. 4 fuel oil, diesel oil, and perhaps even gasoline for the company's fleet of cars and trucks. The same care for quantity range and determination of the total need must be exercised for each product. A mistake made for one product might jeopardize the entire contract. It is prudent to keep the range of products in a single contract at a minimum. Separate contracts for the other products purchased from the same supplier could be written using the identical format. Furthermore, you will find that the administration of individual product contracts is simpler.

The purchasing officer will find that the above suggestions contained in these nine considerations for planning a purchase through a requirements contract will provide the necessary guidelines for writing an enforceable contract with variable quantities involved.

One-Time Requirements Contracts

The customary requirements contract is written to cover an extended period of time and it usually involves repeated purchases of the product. But repeated purchases for a single project may also be arranged in the format of a requirements contract. A recent case in federal court sustained such a contract.[3] A subcontractor was bidding on a project for the government. The subcontractor was to supply crushed limestone with certain characteristics to a specified depth over an area of 176,000 square feet. The government bid document stated it would pay for "the actual number of square feet of crushed stone measured in place and accepted." The bid document gave a government estimate of the amount of stone required but cautioned the bidders that it was an estimate only. The successful bidder supplied all the stone required for the job, but it amounted to considerably less than the estimate. The court ruled this to be a requirements contract calling for all the stone required, and it was not a contract for the stone mentioned in the estimate. As long as the estimate was made in good faith and was properly designated as such, the supplier had no claim for damages because less than the estimated quantity was purchased. However, some courts will allow the supplier a price higher than the contract unit price for the goods actually delivered, if the quantity is disproportionately less.

INSTALLMENT CONTRACTS

Contracts calling for fixed quantities of a product to be delivered at several specified dates in the future are known as *installment contracts*. They differ from requirements contracts because the quantities in the contract are firm. No room is allowed for variation in the quantity to be supplied and accepted.

The precise quantity in a contract may work to the detriment of the pur-

---

[3]*R. A. Weaver and Associates, Inc. v. Asphalt Const., Inc.*, 587 F.2d 1315 (1978).

chasing officer if the needs of the organization decline during the period covered. A lower contract price may offset this disadvantage because the supplier makes an absolute sale of the quantity covered by the contract. If prices quoted are identical in both the installment contract and the requirements contract, the latter is to be preferred by the buyer because of the greater flexibility afforded in quantities to be purchased.

BLANKET ORDERS

Blanket orders are sometimes confused with requirements contracts. They are quite often issued on purchase order forms. A typical blanket order might read, "Milk and cream delivered to our cafeteria, as required, not to exceed $25,000 during the period of June 1 to December 1." Such a purchase order is no more than a billing authorization for releases (deliveries) given the vendor. It is not an order for $25,000 of milk and cream.

Prior to the issuance of this blanket purchase order, a requirements contract may have been negotiated. As a consequence, the blanket order for releases was issued. There is nothing of legal significance contained in the purchase order since the requirements contract is the basic document.

PRICING ARRANGEMENTS

Purchasing officers often negotiate pricing arrangements with suppliers. For example, a purchasing officer may be faced with the need to purchase small quantities of maintenance tools—nuts, bolts, and what have you. A local hardware store will be contacted, and because of the potential volume of such small purchases, it will offer discounts off the regular retail prices on such items. The arrangement may be formalized to the point where a written document is prepared offering such discounts for a fixed period of time. No matter how formal the written document is, it does not become a valid contract unless a fixed or determinable quantity is mentioned in the arrangement along with a firm commitment to purchase that quantity. If the quantity term or the commitment to buy and to sell all hardware items required are missing, the document is no more than a pricing arrangement. Both parties are free to walk away from that document at any time. (See also Chapter XXI "Failure of Presupposed Conditions.")

XIX

Quality and Warranties

The *quality* of any product is determined by many factors. These factors might include the size, the color, the composition, the performance, the thickness, the durability, or a combination of any or all of these elements. In fact, one definition states that quality is the sum total of those properties that contribute to the usability of an item. Quality is a variable and has a wide range. The quality of any one product comes in a spectrum ranging from the best to the poorest. The buying decision on quality is not always based on the product with the *best* quality; often it is based on the product having the most suitable quality for the intended purpose.

The purchasing officer devotes considerable attention to determining the proper quality for the intended purpose. The quality decision may be made unilaterally by the purchasing officer or it may be based on the consensus of the using department and the quality control department. No matter who has the final word, it is the purchasing officer's responsibility to get the chosen factors of quality into the final contract with the supplier.

The quality factors decided upon may be placed into the contract in a variety of approaches: They may be stated on the purchase order. They may be incorporated on the purchase order by reference to a set of blueprints or specifications. They may be incorporated by reference to a supplier's catalog. They could come from the supplier on a sales proposal or by independent statement of facts made by the supplier. One final source is that quality assurances may come from the law, particularly from the Uniform Commercial Code.

WARRANTIES

In the law, the quality of a product in a contract for the sale of goods is covered primarily by the *law of warranties*. This topic, as it relates to the quality of goods, is covered in Sections 2-313 through 2-318 of the Uniform Commercial Code. Any breach of a quality specification is considered a breach of warranty. A breach of warranty may also be a breach of contract. A breach of contract is a broader term that also includes a breach of price, of quantity, or of delivery terms in a contract.

The *Random House Dictionary* states that a warranty is "an engagement, express or implied, in assurance of some particular in connection with a contract." It is a guarantee that one or more of the specifics of a contract will be as stated. The usual warranty in a contract for the sale of goods comes from the supplier to the buyer, and most—but not all—warranties apply to the *quality* characteristics of the product involved. Other warranties might include such items as title to the goods and freedom from liens and infringement claims.

Seller's warranties are a direct outgrowth of the gradual abandonment of the common law doctrine of *caveat emptor* ("Let the buyer beware.") Long ago the buyer purchased the pig in the poke, and if "the pig" died two days later from a longstanding illness, it was too bad for the buyer. The doctrine found little favor, and the law gradually changed over the years until at present the buyer is assured of many quality factors in the product purchased.

Our discussion in this chapter follows the sequence in which warranties are presented in the Code. This discussion includes the following topics:

1. The warranty of title

2. The warranty against infringement

3. Express warranties

4. The implied warranty of merchantability

5. The implied warranty of fitness for a particular purpose

6. The exclusion or modification of warranties

Warranty of Title

The first warranty offered by the Code does not pertain to the quality of the goods purchased, but to the quality of the ownership rights transferred by the seller to the buyer. Section 2-312(1) provides the following warranty for the buyer unless, as we shall shortly see, there is a specific exemption made by the supplier:

> (1) Subject to subsection (2) there is in a contract for sale a warranty by the seller that

(a) the title conveyed shall be goods and its transfer rightful; and

(b) the goods shall be delivered free from any security interest or other lien or encumbrance of which the buyer at the time of contracting has no knowledge.

Title is the term the law applies to the concept of ownership of goods. Title to real estate is evidenced by a *deed* for the property. Title to an automobile is evidenced by a certificate of title issued by the vehicle registration department of the state. But when it comes to a bar of soap or a chair the purchasing officer uses, title becomes less tangible and visible. Usually the only evidence available to establish title to the bar of soap is the supplier's invoice establishing the fact that it was bought. Nonetheless, the law says that we obtained title when the supplier sold it to us. But did the supplier have title to it when it was sold? If the supplier manufactured that bar of soap along with hundreds of other bars of soap, how may he establish his title that he transferred to us? The answer is that Section 2-312(1) of the Code requires that the supplier warrant to the purchaser that he does have title, and that the fictional transfer of title to the buyer is proper.

The section also requires the supplier to warrant that there is no outstanding lien or encumbrance against the goods sold. Thus, if there was a sheriff's lien, or a chattel mortgage on the goods when sold, the supplier is required to clear such an encumbrance for the buyer.

Subsection (2) of 2-312 provides the only grounds for exception to the supplier's absolute duty to give a warranty of title.

(2) a warranty under subsection (1) will be excluded or modified only by specific language or by circumstances which give the buyer reason to know that the person selling does not claim title in himself or that he is purporting to sell only such right or title as he or a third person may have.

"Specific language" is the only avenue open to the supplier to disclaim the warranty of title. General disclaimers that appear on suppliers' forms, such as "There are no warranties, express or implied, given in connection with this sale," will not touch the warranty of title. It survives such a disclaimer. The language used by the supplier must be to the point to be successful, as for example: "This automobile is sold subject to a $750 chattel mortgage."

The Official Comment points out that the latter part of this section is intended where a sale is made by a sheriff, an executor, or a foreclosing lien or; that the buyer is put on notice that the seller is selling only a limited right to the goods. He is not expected personally to warrant a free and clear title.

Warranty Against Infringement

Merchant sellers have an additional duty imposed upon them by subsection (3) of 2-312:

Unless otherwise agreed, a seller who is a merchant regularly deal-

> ing in goods of the kind warrants that the goods shall be delivered
> free of the rightful claim of any third person by way of infringement
> or the like . . .

Note that this mandatory warranty against infringement is imposed only on sellers who are *merchants*.

Patent infringement suits seldom arise out of a purchase made, but when they do occur subsection (3) can be of real assistance to the purchasing officer. One may think that the supplier-manufacturer who imitates a patented product is the only party responsible for damages to the patent holder. But patent law dictates that the person who uses the imitated product is also liable for damages. Therefore, a buyer who purchases the imitation will go to court as codefendant with the imitator.

As an example, consider the hospital purchasing officer who buys an innovative bed lamp from supplier A. Sometime prior to the purchase, supplier Z had patented a similar bed lamp. He files suit for damages. Supplier Z may name both supplier A and the hospital as defendants in his lawsuit. If Z wins the case, supplier A and the hospital are liable to Z for the amount of damages awarded. If supplier A proves to be financially unsound and perhaps bankrupt, the hospital will probably be required to pay the full award to supplier Z. (See the next section.)

Subsection (3) of 2-312 will be very helpful to the hospital purchasing officer in such a situation, provided the supplier is financially sound. This Code section, under the warranty against infringement, makes supplier A responsible for any damages the hospital might have assessed against it by the court. It also will make a supplier responsible for all costs in defending the infringement suit. The infringement is regarded as a breach of warranty by the supplier and as such the supplier is held accountable for all damages sustained by the hospital as a result of the breach.

In order to sustain the seller's liability for the infringement, there are certain procedures prescribed by Section 2-607 that the buyer must follow. Subsection (3)(b) states:

> (b) . . . if the claim is one for infringement or the like (subsection (3)
> of Section 2-312) and the buyer is sued as a result of such a breach he
> must so notify the seller within a reasonable time after he receives
> notice of the litigation or be barred from any remedy over for liabili-
> ty established by the litigation.

This is the first requirement imposed upon the buyer: Prompt notification of the litigation must be made. The Official Comments to the section states that the notification need only be to inform the seller that the transaction is claimed to involve a breach. It might also include an invitation to the supplier to come in and defend the lawsuit.

However, subsection (5)(b) poses another obligation on the buyer:

> (b) . . . if the claim is one for infringement or the like (subsection (3) of Section 2-312) the original seller may demand in writing that his buyer turn over to him control of the litigation including settlement or else be barred from any remedy over and if he also agrees to bear all expense and to satisfy any adverse judgment, then unless the buyer after seasonable receipt of the demand does turn over control the buyer is so barred.

The reason for this rule, which requires the buyer to turn over the defense of the litigation, is obvious. The seller's actions have been challenged by the infringement suit, and it is logical that the seller have the opportunity to defend his actions. The seller has great knowledge of the product and he can present a better defense. Subsection (5)(b) gives the seller this opportunity. If the buyer refuses this written request, the Code removes the seller's obligation to indemnify the buyer for any adverse judgment.

Nota Bene to the Purchasing Officer. The determination as to whether to turn over control of the litigation to your supplier is a decision your legal counsel should make. However, counsel's response to a great extent might depend on how well you have done your purchasing job. Section 2-312 does not relieve your company of any of the liability you might have to the patent holder. What it does do is require your supplier to indemnify your company for any damages that might be assessed by the court for the infringement. The one thing Section 2-312 cannot do for you is guarantee the solvency of the supplier from whom you purchased the product. This is where the professional purchasing officer is reassured, because, before placing the order, he has made certain that the supplier is one with whom he can do business and that he is financially sound. The purchasing officer may rest comfortably in a patent suit if he has assured himself of this fact.

Buyer's Warranty to the Supplier Against Infringement. It may seem out of place in a discussion of supplier warranties of quality to mention warranties that the *buyer gives to the supplier*. But it is fitting here to make every purchasing officer aware of the last phrase of subsection (3) of Section 2-312. We quoted above the first part of this subsection, and now here is the last part:

> But a buyer who furnishes specifications to the seller must hold the seller harmless against any such claim [of infringement] which arises out of compliance with the specifications. (The words in brackets are the author's.)

Subsection (3) protects the supplier from being led down the primrose path of patent infringement by a purchasing officer who specifies a patented product. The supplier who is given the specification can claim indemnity against such a buyer if his following the specification leads to a patent infringement suit. The same rules of Section 2-607(3) and (5) quoted above regarding notification and right to defend an infringement suit apply here in reverse. The seller must notify the buyer of the infringement litigation and must allow the buyer the privilege of defending the suit. The buyer must agree to pay all litigation costs and settle any adverse judgment that might be ordered by the court.

The likelihood of such a situation arising might seem slight, but suppliers can be found who are willing to duplicate a patented product to get an order. This may be particularly true of some foreign suppliers who might be beyond the reach of a United States court: In addition to being able to keep their assets free from attachment by U.S. law, they have the protection of Section 2-312. When the buyer asks them to duplicate a patented product, they have everything to gain and little to lose. Patent infringement problems in such circumstances are left on the doorstep of their U.S. customer whose purchasing officer told them: "Make me 1000 of these units." This is indeed the time when the old adage, "Let the buyer beware" comes into full bloom. The last phrase in Section 2-312(3) is there to haunt the buyer.

Express Warranties

A proven method of assuring that quality standards of a product are maintained is to include the essential characteristics directly in the contract. For most purchases the contract consists of the purchase order and the supplier's document. The latter document may be a proposal to sell or an acceptance of the purchase order. Some transactions will have the purchase order as the only document. This occurs when the order is issued as an offer to buy and the supplier accepts it by delivering the goods. In any event, the contract is the proper location for expressing the quality terms of the product. This procedure makes the quality terms an integral part of the contract. They become conditions for the satisfactory performance by the supplier. Any variation from these terms in the delivered goods renders the goods nonconforming. Any variation to the terms of the contract entitles the buyer to reject the goods under Section 2-601, which is discussed in Chapter XXII.

A quality term stated in the contract is an express warranty. It is referred to as a *seller's warranty* because it has to do with the quality of the goods. Responsibility for the quality of the subject of a contract for the sale of goods lies with the seller. However, a warranty of quality may be first proposed by the buyer. If this challenge is accepted by the supplier, it becomes the seller's express warranty.

This gives the buyer the opportunity to affirmatively control the quality of the goods being purchased. Specification of the desired quality may be made in the solicitation for quotations, as well as in the purchase order. Any quality assurances given by the supplier during the negotiations can be placed on the purchase order as well. The purchase order may, and should, contain all the essential attributes of quality. There is then no need to rely on other written documents or verbal commitments of the supplier. Should a legal battle over a quality term arise, your legal counsel will appreciate the fact that the terms are clearly expressed on the purchase order. This saves countless hours of intricate legal maneuvers on the parol evidence rule; whether the warranty was made before, during or after the contract was formed, and whether the warranty was part of the basis of the bargain.

Sources and Types of Express Warranties. The Uniform Commercial Code suggests several methods to create an express warranty. These are contained in Section 2-313(1). It should be noted that while these types are referred to as "seller's warranties," only those contained in subsection (1) must originate with the seller. Even these could originate from the seller's responses to questions of the buyer. Those suggested in subsections (b) and (c) may originate from either the buyer or the seller. If they originate from the buyer, the seller must accept them before they can be considered express warranties. Section 2-313(1) states:

> (1) Express warranties by the seller are created as follows:
>
> (a) Any affirmation of fact or promise made by the seller to the buyer which relates to the goods and becomes part of the basis of the bargain creates an express warranty that the goods shall conform to the affirmation or promise.
>
> (b) Any description of the goods which is made part of the basis of the bargain creates an express warranty that the goods shall conform to the description.
>
> (c) Any sample or model which is made part of the basis of the bargain creates an express warranty that the whole of the goods shall conform to the sample or model.

The common thread that runs through (a), (b), and (c) above is that the warranty must be made "part of the basis of the bargain." This underscores the advantage of including the quality factors on the purchase order. There can be no doubt, then, that the warranty is part of the basis of the bargain. Even *affirmations* or *promises* by the seller can be placed on the purchase order. Such a practice removes any doubt as to whether the buyer relied on the warranty.

Affirmation of Fact or Promise. Probably the most difficult area of interpretation facing a buyer is when he or she has to discern when the supplier is stating a fact about his product and when he is bragging about it. This distinction is important because the last phrase in subsection 2-313(2) negates a warranty when the supplier is engaged in "puffery":

> But an affirmation merely of the value of the goods or a statement purporting to be merely the seller's opinion or commendation of the goods does not create a warranty.

The Code thereby protects the supplier against his own improvidence when he is too ebullient about the quality of the product he is selling. This forces the buyer to distinguish *fact* (thereby an express warranty) from *opinion* (totally useless).

There is no definition or rule of law to guide us in separating fact from opinion. The purchasing officer must develop the ability to sort the chaff from the wheat. A cold, hard analysis of the statements made is the only answer. Obviously the statement: "This is the sweetest grape grown" is opinion, while the statement, "This is a seedless grape" is fact. But there are many possible combinations in between that are not so easily distinguishable.

A federal court was called upon to determine whether a series of statements made by a supplier regarding copying machines qualified as statements of facts and thus as express warranties.[1] The simplified facts of this case involved the purchase of 128 copying machines. The purchaser placed these machines in various customers' locations on a rental basis. Many of the machines required an unusually large number of service calls. Some broke down completely. Several caused fires. After 18 months of this frustration, the purchaser "quit" on the machines and filed a suit claiming breach of warranty. Some of the statements of the supplier which the buyer claimed were express warranties follow. The court's response to each statement is also given.

1. "The machines were of high quality." The court said this was not an express warranty because it was a statement of the seller's opinion.

2. "From experience and testing the frequency of repairs would be low." The court again held that this was an expression of general commendation of the machines and not an express warranty.

3. "Replacement parts are readily available." (This was one of the buyer's aggravations because it took 6 to 10 weeks to obtain some parts.) The court once more ruled that this was not an express warranty. The court admitted that it was a statement of fact, but that it did not relate to the copying machines sold to the buyer. It related to parts that could be installed in the machines sold. (Note that subsection (1)(a) contains the proviso "which relates to the goods sold.")

4. "Experience shows through a reasonable projection that the purchase would return substantial profits." This was no express warranty since profits are not included in a sale of copying machines.

5. "The machines were safe and would not cause fires." The court ruled this to be an express warranty.

6. "Service calls would be required only after every 7000 to 9000 were

---

[1] *Royal Business Machines v. Lorraine Corp.*, 633 F.2d 34 (1980).

run."—An express warranty, even though it applied to the future operation of the machines.

7. "The machines have been extensively tested and are ready to be marketed."—An express warranty as to the testing.

8. "The cost of maintenance and the cost of supplies was low and would remain low." Here the court ruled the statement concerning maintenance to be a statement of fact and an express warranty even though it applied to future performance. The statement concerning the supplies related to the future and did not pertain to the goods involved in the sale. This was something over which the supplier had no control. It was not an express warranty.

Nota Bene **to the Purchasing Officer.** The above court decisions make it obvious that you must have a discerning eye when reading the supplier's assertions about his product. It is suggested that you develop the legal art of cross-examination, if you have not already done so. When you come across a supplier's statement that is not affirmatively stated in a clear-cut manner, ask an appropriate question that makes the supplier "fish or cut bait." Do not allow the supplier to get away with half-truths or statements that may contain a "germ of truth." Make the supplier come forth with an answer that gives an express warranty, or else make him admit that he was simply bragging about the product.

Description of the Goods as an Express Warranty. As we stated previously, describing the goods and the quality desired is an excellent method of obtaining and securing express warranties. Subsection (1)(b) of 2-313 is quite explicit when it states: "Any description of the goods which is made part of the basis of the bargain is an express warranty that the goods shall conform to the description." One could not hope for nor seek a more positive statement. *Any* description of the goods that is recited will be an express warranty and becomes a contract condition that goes to the essence of the contract. The one and only qualifying requirement is that the description must be made part of the basis of the bargain. This qualification is met when the description is included in the basic contract. Since the customary purchase is the purchase order, the purchasing officer should have little difficulty in making certain that the express warranty is included in the bargain.

A purchasing officer reading Section 2-313 carefully may be inclined to challenge the conclusion just stated at the end of the last paragraph. This is because Section 2-313(1) begins with the words: "Express warranties by the seller," then how can the purchasing officer control an express warranty in the contract? The answer to this question is that the purchasing officer has two avenues available to him to control the express warranties in the purchase contract, but before explaining them it is prudent to make an admission. The admission is that, yes, only the seller can make a warranty concerning the quality of goods sold. He is the only party who has control over the quality of the product, so quite naturally he is the person who must make the warranty about them. But that does not mean that the buyer must accept whatever quality the supplier deigns to offer. The buyer has definite rights too, including the right to specify the desired quality factors in the product being purchased. It is at this point that the buyer has the two opportunities to control the quality factor.

First, the purchasing officer may specify the desired quality factors in the request for a quotation. Then a conforming proposal from the supplier that repeats the specific quality elements or simply states: "As per your specifications" makes these factors part of the offer to sell. When the purchase order is issued to accept the supplier's offer, all the desired quality factors become part of the final contract as express warranties. Thus, the purchasing officer suggests the express warranties and the supplier follows them. The supplier's warranties become part of the basis of the bargain.

The second avenue of quality control in a contract occurs when the purchasing officer issues a purchase order that constitutes an offer to buy. The supplier may accept this offer by delivering the goods or accepting the offer. Whatever descriptions of the goods are contained in the purchase order become part of the contract. The purchasing officer knows the available options to give an accurate description of the goods and to get the quality factors incorporated into a contract as suggested above. Size, color, shape, thickness, chemical composition, and finish can be described to become part of the seller's warranty. Performance may be specified. Durability and useful life are definable as well. Blueprints can be employed. A complete set of formal specifications is another detailed descriptive source. All of these become express warranties when accepted by the supplier and tied into the final contract.

This discussion of the opportunities the purchasing officer has to get express warranties included in a contract does not imply that the seller himself does not or cannot make warranties about his product. He may and usually does make many statements that are descriptions of the quality of the product, either in literature, in conversations with the purchasing officer, or in offers to sell. The purchasing officer should encourage such activity on the part of the supplier. The more he talks, the more the purchasing officer learns about the product and discovers those special quality factors that sell the product. But, any statements of fact on which the purchasing officer relies should be written into the final contract. There can then be no doubt as to the extent of the express warranty and to its being part of the basis of the bargain.

A Sample or a Model as an Express Warranty. Subsection (1)(c) of 2-313 contemplates the supplier who offers a sample of the product selected at random from his inventory as a true representative example of each unit to be delivered.

The code section makes the sample an express warranty that each item in the total delivery will be of identical quality. If the supplier offers a model of the product, the entire order must conform to it. Any variation from the sample or the model is a breach of the express warranty. It is suggested that the purchasing officer retain the sample or model offered by the supplier. This will make it possible to have the basis of the express warranty on hand to compare it with the delivered goods for conformity.

The purchasing officer might also propose an express warranty to the supplier by offering a sample or a model to be duplicated. This is a method of describing the product to be delivered by the supplier.

Choice of Words Used in an Express Warranty. There are no magic words to be used when making an express warranty. The first part of subsection (2) of 2-313 tells us:

> (2) It is not necessary to the creation of an express warranty that the seller use formal words such as "warrant" or "guarantee" or that he have a specific intention to make a warranty.

The affirmation of fact about the product or its description establishes an express warranty. The same affirmation or description expresses the intent of the supplier to make the warranty. The supplier cannot make the statement: "These are seedless grapes," and then later claim he did not intend to warrant the grapes as being seedless. Once the fact about the product is expressed in a sale it becomes a warranty per se.

Advantage of an Express Warranty. Most express warranties in purchasing activities are written. This gives certainty regarding the nature and extent of the warranty. The ability to compare the product delivered with the precise words of the warranty has distinct advantages in court trial procedures.

Perhaps the outstanding advantage of an express warranty is that once made it is difficult for the supplier to lose the responsibility for making it come true. Even such general disclaimers in a supplier's sales document as: "There are no warranties, express or implied, given in connection with this sale" may not prevail against an express warranty. Code Section 2-316(1) reads:

> (1) Words or conduct relevant to the creation of an express warranty and words or conduct tending to negate or limit warranty shall be construed wherever reasonable as consistent with each other; but subject to the provisions of this Article on parol or extrinsic evidence (Section 2-202) negation or limitation is inoperative to the extent such construction is unreasonable.

Thus the express warranty, "These grapes are seedless" would prevail against the general disclaimer stated above. This is a distinct advantage in these modern days of business when suppliers are inclined to disclaim all warranties and limit any possible remedies a buyer might have against them. The supplier's pride in his product has given way to the threat of damages arising from a breach of a warranty or a lawsuit for product liability.

Other Sources. Since express warranties are affirmations of fact, they also may be found in other places or media. The magazine, catalog, newspaper, radio, or television advertisement of a product may constitute an express warranty. The statements of the sales representatives likewise may have this effect, though sellers often attempt to preclude this in the written contract.

Nota Bene **to the Purchasing Officer.** Your author has extolled the advantages of using your own description and specifications in stating the desired quality of the product you are purchasing. This has been done with the full realization that a purchasing professional would not write detailed specifications for a product about which he or she was not fully informed. This "nota bene" is written as a word of caution and to suggest one disadvantage of using descriptions to create warranties. Shortly we shall discuss the implied warranty of fitness for the intended purpose. A supplier is not held to this implied warranty if the buyer provides detailed specifications. If the supplier must manufacture the product to meet the buyer's specifications, the buyer is not depending upon the supplier to provide a product suitable for a purpose! The buyer assumes full responsibility for the performance of the product that is manufactured to meet the buyer's specifications. Detailed specifications might also make a performance specification useless. If a purchasing officer tells the supplier how to construct a motor, he has no one to blame but himself if the motor fails to meet the test of 10,000 r.p.m.

The Uniform Commercial Code provides two *implied* warranties in addition to the express warranties described above. An *implied warranty* is a warranty placed upon every seller of goods by the Code. It is not necessary for an implied warranty to be specifically mentioned in the contract for it to be effective. It comes with every purchase of goods made from a merchant-seller, unless the seller has taken the precaution of disclaiming it.

The Implied Warranty of Merchantability

The first implied warranty found in Section 2-314(1) states:

> (1) Unless excluded or modified (Section 2-316), a warranty that the goods shall be merchantable is implied in a contract for their sale if the seller is a merchant with respect to goods of that kind. Under this section the serving for value of food or drink to be consumed either on the premises or elsewhere is a sale.

The only requirement to make this warranty applicable is that the supplier be a merchant who regularly deals in the goods that are the subject of the sale contract. Thus a supplier who regularly sells office furniture would not be a merchant for the purposes of this section when selling a repossessed truck.

The Official Comment to the section also points out that a contract for the sale of second-hand goods would not carry the full implied warranty of merchantability. The seller's obligation when selling second-hand goods is limited to meeting the contract description of the goods. Of course, this description would then be an express warranty as would be a guarantee of the seller that the goods will carry the same warranty as if they were new. A statement by an automobile dealer who gives a new car guarantee with the sale of a slightly used car makes the guarantee an express warranty. It would not be subject to a disclaimer.

One of the advantages of this implied warranty to the buyer is that it runs with every purchase unless disclaimed. This means that it is written in favor of the buyer. Should a situation arise when Section 2-207(3) of the Code is to be applied, the buyer will emerge victorious. Assume the buyer has a term in the purchase order that provides for implied warranties, and the supplier has a general disclaimer. Under 2-207(3) both terms would be stricken from the writings of the two parties and the Code term substituted. This places the implied warranty right back into the contract. This result suggests that the purchasing officer would be prudent to place a continuing clause providing for implied warranties in every purchase order issued. This will counteract the effect of a supplier's general disclaimer and still allow the implied warranty by operation of Section 2-207(3).

***Nota Bene* to the Purchasing Officer.** A friendly reminder that the provision for express warranties in the Code is not written in your favor, as is this implied warranty. Should you place an express warranty on your purchase order and the supplier's document contains words that substantially contradict these words, both will be stricken from the writings under Section 2-207(3). This will cause the buyer to lose the express warranty because there is no section in the Code that implies an express warranty. It pays to read the supplier's acceptance form to make certain that there is no conflict with any express warranty that you might have included in your purchase order. You should be particularly observant to catch a supplier's direct statement of contradiction to the quality term stated on your purchase order. For example, if you state: "These motors are guaranteed to be waterproof," and the supplier's document reads: "The motors sold herein are not guaranteed to perform under other than normal circumstances," these conflicting terms would be stricken by 2-207(3). Had the supplier's document said only: "There are no express or implied warranties given," Section 2-316(1)— mentioned in the previous section of this text—would probably save the express warranty.

The Code Definition of Merchantable. Section 2-314(2) provides statutory guidance as to what is considered merchantable:

> (2) Goods to be merchantable must be at least such as
>
> (a) pass without objection in the trade under the contract description; and

(b) in the case of fungible goods, are of fair average quality within the description; and

(c) are fit for the ordinary purposes for which such goods are used; and

(d) run, within the variations permitted by the agreement, of even kind, quality and quantity within each unit among all units involved; and

(e) are adequately contained, packaged, and labeled as the agreement may require; and

(f) conform to the promises or affirmation of fact made on the container or label, if any.

The Official Comment points out that the words at the beginning of the subsection "must be at least such as" leave the door open for other unstated factors that might affect the merchantability of the goods. This might be usage of trade or prior dealings, or even be from a prior court decision.

The Official Comment reminds the reader that subsections (a) and (b) are to be read together. They refer to the standards used in the seller's line of business. "Fair average" is a term customarily employed for agricultural bulk products. Subsection (c) provides a standard of quality that may be employed in a vast number of situations. The failure of a product in normal usage gives rise to a breach of warranty claim almost automatically. This subsection by the *implied* warranty has saved many buyers who failed to get an express warranty in the contract. This subsection supplements the implied warranty of fitness for a particular purpose, which will be discussed in a succeeding section.

A case involving subsection (c) illustrates its applicability. Here are the simplified facts:[2]

> The purchasing officer of Chris-Craft Industries approached a supplier to develop a different type of gasoline tank to be used in a new boat model his company was developing. The supplier suggested a slush compound tank with a painted exterior. Chris-Craft has been using hot-dipped tanks. They found the supplier's suggestion to be an attractive alternate. An order was placed. The purchase order specified that the tanks had to be approved by the Boating Industries Association (B.I.A.), an organization that establishes acceptable performance standards of components used in the industry.
>
> The tanks were delivered. They were approved by B.I.A. Chris-Craft, after thoroughly testing the tanks for pressure, accepted them and began installing them in their new boats. Within 1 month the tanks began to corrode and within 6 months, some of them began to leak. Neither Chris-Craft nor the B.I.A., had made corrosion tests.

---

[2]*Taylor and Gaskin v. Chris-Craft Industries,* 732 F.2d 1273 (1984).

> B.I.A. withdrew its approval of the tanks. Chris-Craft had to conduct
> an extensive and expensive recall program to replace the tanks with
> the older type.
>   The supplier sued Chris-Craft for the price of the tanks. Chris-
> Craft responded with a counterclaim for their costs of the recall pro-
> gram and other related costs. The damages they asked for were sub-
> stantially above the cost of the tanks.

The appellate court found for Chris-Craft. It pointed out that the tanks were
not merchantable because they were not fit for the ordinary purpose for which
such tanks were used. The court also found the tanks to be a breach of the
implied warranty for the particular purpose. Here Chris-Craft was able to prove a
breach of both warranties, but even if they had failed to prove the particular purpose breach, they were able to come in under the more general warranty of merchantability. The advantage of subsection (c) is that the buyer has two
opportunities to prove the breach.

Subsection (d) should remind the buyer that there may exist customs of a
particular trade that can alter the usual allowable variations of quality in a lot. It
also reaches those cases where the contract provides for a plus or minus tolerance. Subsection (e) applies when the nature of the goods requires special types
of containers or packaging.

Subsection (f) reminds every purchasing officer that when a label or a container has affirmations of fact or promises about the product that these too are
warranties. They may add to other warranties in the agreement.

Section 2-314(3) provides other implied warranties from usage of the trade.

> (3) Unless excluded or modified (Section 2-316) other implied war-
> ranties may arise from course of dealing or usage of trade.

The Official Comment gives as an example of this: "The obligation of the
seller to provide pedigree papers to evidence conformity of the animal to the contract in the case of a pedigreed dog or bull."

The Implied Warranty of Fitness for a Particular Purpose

This is the second implied warranty in the code mentioned above. Its application
is much more restricted than the *implied warranty of merchantability*. Specific
circumstances must be present for it to be operative. Section 2-315 reads:

> Where the seller at the time of contracting has reason to know any
> particular purpose for which the goods are required and that the buyer
> is relying on the seller's skill or judgment to select or furnish suitable
> goods, there is unless excluded or modified under the next section an
> implied warranty that the goods shall be fit for such purpose.

This section applies when the buyer has a special purpose for the goods in distinction to an *ordinary* purpose, as covered by Section 2-314(2)(c).

The language in this section indicates that these two requirements must be present for the warranty to arise: (1) The seller must have knowledge of how the goods will be used, and (2) The buyer must rely on the seller to select suitable goods for the purpose. The Official Comment offers several temporizing thoughts concerning these two requirements. One is that the seller need not have actual knowledge of the purpose if "the seller has reason to realize the purpose intended or that the reliance exists." On the other side of the contract, it is not an essential that the buyer say to the supplier, "I am depending on your judgment in selecting the product." However, the Official Comment is stern on the fact that the buyer must be actually relying on the seller's judgment to select the product.

There are other matters of importance in the Official Comment relating to this implied warranty.

1. The buyer's use of technical specifications makes the implied warranty inapplicable. Of course technical specifications are express warranties, but the buyer is not relying on the seller's skill in the selection of the product to be used by use of these specifications.

2. The buyer's use of a brand name is strong evidence that no implied warranty of fitness arises. This is not an absolute assumption and may be refuted by proof of special circumstances.

3. Normally, this implied warranty will arise only when the seller is a merchant. You will note the Code section does not make this a requirement, and it is omitted intentionally to allow the buyer the opportunity to show unusual circumstances to prove a nonmerchant made such a warranty.

4. The warranty specifies a "particular purpose," which differentiates it from an "ordinary purpose" in a merchantable warranty. The Official Comment gives an excellent example of this difference. Shoes are ordinarily used for walking on the ground. If the seller knows the particular purpose is for use in mountain climbing, this implied warranty would apply.

5. There is nothing to prevent a contract from containing both a warranty of merchantability and one of fitness for a particular purpose.

***Nota Bene* to the Purchasing Officer.** The purchasing officer is advised to "lay all of the cards on the table" for the supplier to see if he is depending on the implied warranty of fitness to arise. This is particularly true of the use he intends to make of the product and his reliance on the supplier's selection of the product to be used. The more the purchasing officer gives advice or suggestions to the supplier, the less dependence there is on the supplier's judgment. There are two safety clauses that may be shown on your purchase order. One such safety clause might read, "End use: Arctic Pipeline." The other might state, "We order the following items based upon your representative's suggestion:" These are far from being conclusive in a court of law, but the two statements certainly indicate intention to create an implied warranty of fitness for the intended purpose.

This warranty is implied by the Code and is there whenever the circumstances exist as mentioned above. It is written in favor of the buyer. It will come back into the contract under application of Section 2-207(3). (See Chapter XV.)

Exclusion of Warranties

The common law rule of *caveat emptor* has been effectively eliminated by the Code sections that provide for express and implied warranties and for the warranty of title. The Code has performed an excellent service for purchasing officers by doing this. Sections 2-312 through 2-315 provide ample opportunity for the buyer to secure the necessary protection when making a purchase. But, just as the Code has given purchasing officers the comforting protection of these warranties, it has also provided the supplier with directions as to how to take some of them away in the next section. Section 2-316(2) tells the supplier how to disclaim the implied warranties:

> (2) subject to subsection (3), to exclude or modify the implied warranty of merchantability of any part of it the language must mention merchantability and in the case of a writing, must be conspicuous. Language to exclude all implied warranties of fitness is sufficient if it states, for example that "There are no warranties which extend beyond the description on the face hereof."

This Code section not only allows the supplier to take away the implied warranties, but it also tells him how to do it! We have almost returned to caveat emptor if the supplier takes advantage of this invitation.

The Official Comment defends this action by pointing out that the provisions of Section 2-316(2) require the supplier to state the disclaimer clearly. This protects the purchasing officer against unexpected and unbargained for surprises.

The Official Comment also points out that subsection (1) of 2-316 provides another protection to the purchasing officer. Subsection (1) makes a supplier's general disclaimer of all warranties ineffective against an express warranty. (Section 2-316(1) is stated and discussed in a previous section of this chapter "Advantage of an Express Warranty.") Subsection (2), while giving the supplier the opportunity to disclaim implied warranties, places the duty to do so in a conspicuous manner so that the purchasing officer will not be surprised by the lack of an implied warranty. If the supplier does not follow this method of disclaimer, the purchasing officer may claim "surprise" and then enforce the warranty. To repeat, subsections (1) and (2) give the purchasing officer the following protections:

1. A stated express warranty can only be disclaimed by specific language directed against it. A general disclaimer by the supplier will be regarded as inconsistent with the express warranty.

2. The supplier must use conspicuous language to disclaim implied warranties, and in addition in the case of the implied warranty of merchantability must use the word "merchantable" in the disclaimer.

***Nota Bene* to the Purchasing Officer.** The protections against surprise provided for you by Section 2-316(1) and (2) will only be effective if you read your supplier's proposals and acceptances, particularly where the quality aspects of the goods are discussed. Failure to do so may place you in the position of operating in a *caveat emptor* atmosphere without the protection afforded by suppliers' warranties. One would assume that a supplier would have enough pride in his product to be willing to tell the world "I guarantee my product to one and all." This is no longer true. The high cost of product liability insurance and the potential exposure to large liability claims arising from a breach of warranty make a supplier submerge the pride he has in his product in favor of the more basic rule of self-preservation. The Chris-Craft case reported previously is an example of where a breach of the implied warranties cost the supplier many times the value of the product sold. One does not remain in business very long if called upon to pay out large sums of money to settle damage claims. No longer does the supplier say, "That is what I have insurance for." Insurance is difficult to obtain, and what is available is expensive and written for lower limits than formerly.

All of this makes the supplier's approach difficult in negotiations with the purchasing officer. His goal will be to sell his product while either eliminating or severely limiting any possible liability that might arise out of the sale. You, the purchasing officer, will be sitting across the table with the responsibility of protecting the finances of your employer. Your goal is to prevent the supplier from transferring liabilities arising out of the use of his product to your company. You must get into the contract proper and unlimited warranties pertaining to the quality of the product. Your goal and the supplier's goal in this respect are diametrically opposite. You must utilize your negotiating skills to the fullest extent.

Thus far we have reviewed two of the methods suggested in Section 2-316(2) by which a supplier may disclaim the implied warranties. We will next cover subsection (3), which gives three more possible sources for a disclaimer. The last section in this chapter calls your attention to another stout sword the supplier has to use against you—the limitation of damages. The supplier may decide to give you the warranties you seek, but then effectively limit their value to you by restricting your remedy for a breach. You may be forced to negotiate against both a disclaimer and a limitation of remedy. This all indicates how important it is for you to read the provisions of the supplier's documents.

The Term "As Is" as a Warranty Disclaimer. The first three subsections of Section 2-3l6(3) offer three more possible sources of implied warranty disclaimers. Subsection (a) specifies that the language used by the supplier, such as "with all faults" or "as is" effectively excludes all implied warranties of quality unless the circumstances indicate otherwise. The buyer is put on notice by such expressions and cannot claim to be surprised. The language of the supplier has the effect of placing the entire risk of the quality of the goods on the buyer. The buyer should make certain why there are expressed limitations(s) by asking the simple question, "What are the defects in the goods that cause you to offer to sell them 'as is?' "

Inspection of the Goods as a Disclaimer. Subsection (b) of 2-3l6(3) offers the following limitation on implied warranties:

> (b) When the buyer before entering into the contract has examined the goods or the sample or the model as fully as he desired, or has refused to examine the goods there is no implied warranty with regard to defects which an examination ought in the circumstances to have revealed to him.

Hidden defects would continue to be covered by an appropriate implied warranty unless otherwise disclaimed. Also note that both this limitation on implied warranties and the one above in subsection (a) are ineffective against an express warranty.

Exclusion by Course of Dealing. Subsection (c) of 2-3l6(3) provides that:

> (c) an implied warranty can also be excluded or modified by course of dealing or course of performance or usage of trade.

Once more the Code assumes that the buyer will have sufficient experience in the methods of doing business in a particular industry so that there will be no surprise in not having an implied warranty because of the industry's customs.

Nota Bene **to the Purchasing Officer.** The above three exclusions of implied warranties provided in subsection (3) of the Code may be overcome by express warranties. You will know what quality aspects of the product must be present to make it a worthwhile purchase. You should also know what dangerous conditions might impair the usefulness of the product. Be prepared to ask direct questions of the supplier concerning these factors. If the supplier responds with anything but direct affirmative answers you will know that you are assuming all of the risk concerning quality. If you *do get* positive answers to your questions, you have express warranties that will prevail against these exclusions. Be certain to record these answers on your purchase order.

A word of caution: Remember that the supplier's representative to whom you pose these questions must be vested with the authority to make the affirmative answers enforceable express warranties.

Limitation of Remedies. There is one more subsection to 2-316. Subsection (4) is rather infamous to purchasing officers because it gives the supplier the opportunity to restrict the importance and value of any warranty given. It reads:

> (4) Remedies for breach of warranty can be limited in accordance with the provisions of this Article on liquidation or limitation of damages and on contractual modification of remedy (Sections 2-718 and 2-719).

Thus a purchasing officer may fight hard to get a warranty from a supplier only to find its value curtailed under this subsection. (Sections 2-718 and 2-719 are discussed in detail in Chapter XXII on Remedies and Limitations.) The purchasing officer must keep this subsection in mind when negotiating with the supplier. Not only must the warranty be negotiated, but any limitations of the effectiveness of the warranty must also be avoided.

STRICT LIABILITY IN TORT FOR DEFECTIVE PRODUCTS

Breach of warranty remains in the mid-nineteen nineties as the main remedy for the purchasing manager who finds the goods purchased to be defective. But there also is strict liability in tort if the defect in the goods causes property damage or personal injury. It also covers property damage to the goods themselves if it is the result of a violent occurrence, rather than slow deterioration. While this seems like a strange distinction courts generally have drawn it. They find such damage to the goods to be covered by strict liability in tort because the damage is caused by the unreasonable dangerousness of the defect, whereas they find gradual deterioration caused by the defect to be more the subject of warranty law.

In terms of economic loss brought about by the defectiveness of the goods, such as lost profits, the issue may be whether strict liability in tort or warranty law is applicable. The general trend seems to be to hold that warranty, which allows disclaimers of liability by contract, is the applicable law. Strict liability, as mentioned shortly, does not allow for such contractual disclaimers.

Strict liability for products is best exemplified by the Restatement of Tort Section 402A:

"SPECIAL LIABILITY OF SELLER OF PRODUCT FOR PHYSICAL HARM TO USER OR CONSUMER

(1) One who sells any product in a defective condition unreasonably dangerous to the user or consumer or to his property is subject to liability for physical harm thereby caused to the ultimate user or consumer, or to his property if

(a) the seller is engaged in the business of selling such a product, and

(b) it is expected to and does reach the user or consumer without substantial change in the condition in which it is sold.

(2) The rule stated in Subsection (1) applies although

(a) the seller has exercised all possible care in the preparation and sale of his product, and

(b) the user or consumer has not bought the product from or entered into any contractual relation with the seller."

There are several "caveats" which cover special situations where the American Law Institute takes no position as to the applicability of §402A; these remain a matter of case law:

"The Institute expresses no opinion as to whether the rules stated in this Section may not apply

(1) to harm to persons other than users or consumers;

(2) to the seller of a product expected to be processed or otherwise substantially changed before it reaches the user or consumer, or

(3) to the seller or a component part of a product to be assembled."

In part, it is a development of warranty law, with the elimination of privity, and to a slight extent takes on characteristics formerly found in warranty law. Nevertheless, it is based primarily on a separate theory in tort and is explicitly separated from warranty liability. Since the Restatement section represents one of the most important modern formulations of strict liability, it is important to look at its underlying bases.

One basis given as underlying Section 402A, is that the seller "by marketing his product for use in consumption, has undertaken and assumed a special responsibility toward any member of the consuming public who may be injured by it." This portion of the statement of the underlying theory seems to reflect the undertaking by the seller of the business enterprise or risk-involved activity. It is merely the marketing of the product which will later be used and consumed, which is the undertaking itself and carries with it a certain responsibility.

A second basis for the Restatement strict liability for products is that "the public has the right to expect and does expect, in the case of products which it needs and for which it is forced to rely upon the seller, that reputable sellers will stand behind their goods." This theory places greater emphasis upon the general expectancy of the public that products on the market will be ones which are sound or which the seller will stand behind or be liable for damage caused by their defects. While there is some emphasis upon the factor that the products are needed by the public and that the public is forced to rely upon the seller for the product, there are, however, no limitations specially found as to products which are considered necessities of life or any particular reliance upon the seller.

A third reason given as underlying Section 402A is that "public policy demands the burden of accidental injuries caused by products and intended for consumption be placed upon those who market them, can be treated as a cost to production against which liability insurance can be obtained." While there may be several reasons in this more general statement, the brunt of the statement is directed toward making the loss a part of the cost of production. In doing so, it is pointed out that liability insurance protection can be undertaken or losses be treated as a cost of production.

Another basis for Section 402A, is that the "consumer of such products is entitled to the maximum of protection at the hands of someone, and the proper persons to afford it are those who market the product." This particular policy lays heavy emphasis upon the need for protection in a modern society permeated by the use of goods and the great possibility of accidents occurring.

The drafters of Section 402A are clear that it is a strict liability in tort. They do not set forth precisely, however, what must be its basis. They have said that "on whatever theory" there are the justifications for strict liability just discussed. It is clear that the drafters intend not to choose any particular basis so much as to enunciate the fact that strict liability does exist on any of the theories mentioned.

Currently there is a new proposed §402A on Strict Liability for Defective Products. This draft is the product of extensive work over a number of years by the Reporter and consultants. It is important because if redefines defect into certain main categories and will undoubtedly serve as the basis of the law for years to come.

RESTATEMENT PROPOSAL: REVISION OF §402A STRICT LIABILITY

As mentioned earlier, if goods purchased are defective, there is a basis for recovery of damages on three possible major bases: negligence, warranty, and strict liability. §402A of the Restatement of Torts 2d in the formulation of strict liability of the manufacturer and seller is often followed by the courts. This allows the purchaser to recover if the product is defective in quality, design, packaging, labeling, or carrying any needed warnings. It is likely that the courts will continue to follow this formulation until a new one has been considered and passed by the American Law Institute (ALI).

The new formulation of §402A was debated on the floor of ALI and is scheduled for further discussion. For the purchasing manager, it is valuable to have an understanding of this new development. Some of the goods or products purchased by his or her company may be defective and damage may be caused to the goods themselves, or to other goods, or to persons. The first section of the Proposed §402A is similar to the former §402A set forth on page 13 of the 1995 supplement. It states:

§1 Commercial Seller's Liability for Harm Caused by Defective Products:

(a) One engaged in the business of selling products who sells a defective product is subject to liability for harm to persons or property caused by the product defect.

(b) A product is defective, if, at the time of sale, it contains a manufacturing defect, is defective in design, or is defective because of inadequate instructions or warnings.

However, several differences are readily apparent. For one, the liability is limited to commercial sellers. Although most of the sellers to purchasing agents will be commercial ones, there may be a few instances where the seller is an individual not engaged in commercial sales. If the latter is so, the new §402A appears inapplicable. The drafters also indicate that an "occasional " or "casual sale" of surplus property outside the seller's regular business is not covered.

The rule stated in this section applies not only to sales transactions but also to other forms of product distribution that are the functional equivalent of product sales. Commercial lessors of products for consumer use are thus liable for injuries caused by defective products that they lease to consumers.

Interestingly, the drafters also state that the rule of this new section also applies to housing, although sales of real property historically have been within the ambit of product sales. But providers of services unaccompanied by products are not covered.

Another difference is that the new §402 has been phrased in terms of major categories of defects:

1) Manufacturing Defects

2) Design defects

3) Inadequate Instructions or Warnings

It is these major categories of defects that will have some different standards applied in later sections.

The first category of manufacturing defects has a long history and as drafters point out:

> By the early 1960s, American courts recognized that a seller of any product having a manufacturing defect should be liable in tort for harm caused by the defect regardless of the plaintiff's ability to maintain a traditional negligence or warranty action. Liability would attach even if the manufacturer's quality control in producing the defective product was reasonable.

The defenses of contractual privity or direct connection remain ineffective against strict liability.

In regard to the other two major categories or defect, the drafters state:

> Questions of design defect and defects based on inadequate instructions or warnings arise when the specific product unit conforms to the intended design but the intended design itself, or its sale without adequate instructions or warnings, renders the product not reasonably safe. If these forms of defect are found to exist, then every unit in the same product line is potentially defective.

Although the drafters still recognize these as defects in the product for which the purchaser can recover, they also see these defects as deserving slightly different treatment. The rule developed for manufacturing defects is inappropriate for these defects, they believe. Instead these cases require determinations that the product could have reasonably been made safer by a better design, instruction or warning. Sections 2(b) and (c) and 4(b) (2), (3), and (4) rely on a reasonableness test traditionally used in determining whether an actor (manufacturer or seller) has been negligent.

These standards for design of products and accompanying warnings would appear to be a negligence standard; however, the drafters point out that there are some differences dealing with design defects. If the product causes injury while being put to a reasonably foreseeable use, the seller is held to have known of the risks that attend such use. (See §2, Comment i).

Second, some courts have sought to limit the defense of comparative fault in certain products liability contexts. In furtherance of this objective, they have avoided characterizing the liability test as based in negligence, thereby affording freedom to fashion comparative or contributory fault doctrine in a more restrictive fashion. (See §7, Comment d). Third, some courts are concerned that a negligence standard might be too forgiving of a small manufacturer who might be excused for its ignorance of risk or for failing to take adequate precautions to avoid risk.

Some courts might focus negligence considerations on the conduct of the defendant and say it was not liable because its meager resources made it too burdensome to discover design risks or give warnings. But under the new 402A concept of strict liability reasonableness, a defendant is held to the standard of knowledge available to the relevant manufacturing community at the time the product was manufactured. Also, the liability of nonmanufacturing sellers in the distributive chain is strict in the sense that it is no defense that they acted reasonably and were not aware of a defect in the product, be it manufacturing, design, or failure to warn.

The drafters likewise acknowledge the overlap of legal theories of liability:

> As long as the functional criteria are met, courts may utilize the doc-

trines of negligence, strict liability, or the implied warranty of merchantability, or simply define liability in the functional terms set forth in the black letter.

The drafters continue that part of the law that limits this strict liability to personal injury or property damage. They exclude from this rule damage to the product itself, economic losses, or emotional upset.

Section 2 of the Restatement sets forth in more detail these three basic categories:

> For purposes of determining liability under §1:
>
> (a) A product contains a manufacturing defect when the product departs from its intended design even though all possible care was exercised in the preparation and marketing of the product;
>
> (b) A product is defective in design when the foreseeable risks of harm posed by the product could have been reduced by the adoption of a reasonable alternative design by the seller or a predecessor in the commercial chain of distribution and the omission of the alternative design renders the product not reasonably safe;
>
> (c) A product is defective because of inadequate instructions or warnings when the foreseeable risks of harm posed by the product could have been reduced by the provision of reasonable instructions or warnings by the seller or a predecessor in the commercial chain of distribution and the omission of the instructions or warnings renders the product not reasonably safe.

In regard to the last category (a), it is reemphasized that liability for the defective product exists regardless of the manufacturer's high standard of quality control and reasonableness.

It is also pointed out that the rationale for holding wholesalers and retailers strictly liable for harm caused by manufacturing defects is that, as between them and innocent victims who suffer harm because of defective products, the product sellers as business entities are in a better position than are individual users and consumers to insure against such losses. In most instances, wholesalers and retailers will be able to pass liability costs up the chain of product distribution to the manufacturer.

In regard to defect categories—defective design and defectiveness of warnings or instructions—the drafters set forth the different standards of reasonableness. They state that subsections (b) and (c), which impose liability for products that are defectively designed or sold without adequate warnings or instructions and are thus not reasonably safe, achieve the same general objectives as does liability predicted on negligence. Their goal can be seen in the following statement: The major emphasis is on creating incentives for manufacturers to achieve optimal levels of safety in designing and marketing products. Most would agree that society does not benefit from products that are excessively safe—automobiles designed with maximum speeds of 20 miles per hour—any more than it benefits from products that are too risky. Society benefits more when just the right, or optimal, amount of built-in product safety is achieved. They note that a reasonably designed product still carries with it some elements of risk that must be protected against by the user or consumer. If something risky cannot be designed out of the product at an acceptable cost then the user population bears the risk. However, what is an "acceptable" or an "unacceptable" cost is not indicated! But evidence of state of the art technology is relevant to show that a safer design for the product could have been used. Furthermore, even if the design is similar to others being used, it can still be shown by the purchaser that a safer design was feasible.

Where risks and benefits of less safe products are generally known, liability may be precluded. For example, John is seriously injured driving his small car, which is less crashworthy than some larger ones. The drafters note: product sellers must provide reasonable instructions and warnings about risks of injury associated with their products. If a design change is not a reasonable alternative for the particular style of a product that is being sold, such a change is not necessary. For example, sellers down the chain of distribution must warn when doing so is feasible and reasonably necessary. In any event, sellers down the chain are liable if the instructions and warnings provided by predecessors in the chain are inadequate.

Consumer expectations are a highly relevant factor in this reasonableness standard of risk-utility balancing in design issues. But consumer expectations alone are not the determinative factor in regard to design.

In terms of warnings, the drafters have made it clear that "product sellers must provide reasonable instructions and warnings about risks of injury associated with their products." Warnings of obvious risks or obvious risk avoidance are not required. But what is obvious? If the product is so misused, modified, or altered that this creates risks that are sufficiently unreasonable and unusual, liability for designs or warnings may be precluded.

Section 3 of the new §402 deals with inferences of manufacturing defectiveness without proof of specific defect. Section 4 deals specifically with drugs and medical devices. Section 5 deals with causation or causal connections problems. Did the defect cause the harm? Section 6 deals with defects that increase harm beyond what otherwise might have occurred. Was the careless driver more seriously injured because the car was defective? Because it is foreseeable that there will be some accidents, did the car manufacturer reasonably produce and design the car to give reasonable protection to those involved in accidents?

Section 7 deals with apportionment of liability where both parties have been at fault. This recognizes comparative fault where each must bear some of the responsibility and loss. This determination is up to the jury; or if there is no jury, it is up to the judge. It likewise will depend on the circumstances when the plaintiff's conduct is failure to discover a defect, or inattention to a danger that should have been eliminated by a safety feature. In such cases, a trier of fact may decide to allocate little or no responsibility to the plaintiff. Conversely, when the plaintiff voluntarily and unreasonably encounters a risk, the trier of fact may decide to attribute all or a substantial percentage of responsibility to the plaintiff.

Section 8 deals with disclaimers, waivers, and contractual defenses. It states disclaimers and limitations of remedies by product sellers, waivers by product purchasers, and other similar contractual exculpations, oral or written, do not bar or reduce otherwise valid products liability claims for harm to persons. This reaffirms the traditional §402A strict liability that overrides any contractual defenses, as the drafters point out. A commercial seller of a product is not permitted to escape liability for harm to persons through limiting terms in a contract governing the sale of a product. It is presumed that the plaintiff lacked sufficient information, bargaining power, or bargaining position necessary to execute a fair contractual limitation of rights to recover. There is an exception for used "as is" products. Also, the section may be inapplicable where the risk or waiver has been fully understood and negotiated by parties with equal bargaining power.

XX

Price and Credit Terms

PRICE

The legality of a contract for the purchase and sale of goods is not affected by the absence of a price term. The law has no problem declaring a contract enforceable when the price term is missing. The law has its own system of determining the price of the goods if none is stated.

Purchasing, on the other hand, has a keen interest in the price paid for a purchase. The object of the purchasing function is to satisfy the needs of the organization by obtaining the best value for each dollar expended. *Value*, as used in this context, is defined as being a function of quality, service, and price. After the proper quality and the essential service are determined, purchasing must acquire that item at the lowest possible price. The cost effectiveness of any purchasing department is measured by its ability to secure the best value for each purchase. Consequently, *price* is an important term to the purchasing officer.

Expressing the Price Term

Price, quantity, and the description of the goods are considered the "big-three" specifications in a contract for goods. When stated, price is also a "material" term in the contract. It gets into the contract as all terms and conditions do—through the offer and acceptance process. The offeree must accept the price as stated if there is to be a contract. Any price variation in the purported acceptance will constitute a rejection of the offer and become a counteroffer.

The price may be stated as a price per unit, as a total price only, or as a price per unit multiplied by the quantity and extended as a total price for the lot. Specific mention of the fact should be made if a special discounted price is offered as an inducement to purchase a group of items whose individual prices total more than the special price. This can be done by stating: "All for the total of $_____", "for a lump sum price of $_____," or "$_____ for the entire lot."

Applicable taxes must be considered when the price term is mentioned. Any applicable tax on a product must be paid by someone—either the buyer or the supplier. The only exception to this is if the party against whom the tax is levied happens to be a not-for-profit organization and is specifically exempted from the payment of that particular tax. Some taxes are levied against the buyer, others against the supplier; and then there are those that are levied solely on the transaction. The law requires that those taxes levied directly on one of the parties be paid for by the party, even though taxes are not mentioned in the stated price. But both parties must be careful of taxes that are levied solely on the transaction. There should be a statement to indicate if a stated price *includes* the applicable tax or if the taxes are to be *in addition* to that price. Failure to do so may result in one of the parties unknowingly being burdened with the tax. Take the case of a supplier to the Southern Railway Company who received a purchase order from them that showed a fixed price.[1] The railroad had this term printed on its purchase order:

> Prices: The prices indicated on this order are the maximum price at which the invoice will be paid unless an increase is specifically authorized by us prior to shipment

The supplier delivered the goods and sent the invoice for the fixed price shown. The railroad paid the invoice. Later the supplier was called upon to pay $6,709 in federal excise tax on the sale. The supplier billed the railroad for these taxes, but the railroad refused to pay the additional sum. The Georgia Supreme Court ruled that the Southern Railway Company did not have to pay the additional sum since the price term on the purchase order was quite clear. The court said the price term "resolves any ambiguity in separate billing of excise tax requirements."

The Georgia court reminds both purchasing officers and suppliers alike that a stated price term may mean more than the cost of the material involved in the transaction. Purchasing officers should qualify the price term with the statement "includes all applicable taxes," if that is the case. They should also insist that suppliers be equally clear on their statement of price as to whether or not the price includes the taxes. Clarity and understanding between the parties should be the goal. It is not a case of buyer or supplier attempting to make the other party pick up the tax bill.

---

[1]*Chatham v. Southern Ry. Co.*, Georgia, 278 S.E.2d 717 (1981).

A contract with a foreign supplier must specify whether the price stated is expressed in foreign currency or in U.S. dollars. It should also specify at what point in the life of the contract the exchange rate will be applied—if it is to be applied. Exchange rates fluctuate almost daily, and the price paid for the purchase by a U.S. buyer may vary considerably from the date the contract is signed until the date the goods are received. A purchasing officer needs to know the cost of a purchase. That cost, when dealing with an American supplier, is usually determined at the time the purchase order is issued. The same applies to a foreign supplier if the exchange rate is locked in at the time the order is issued or if the price is expressed in U.S. dollars. However, if the exchange rate is to be applied at the time the goods are shipped, then the cost will fluctuate. The purchasing officer and the company are at the mercy of the money markets. It is preferred that the cost be locked in at the time the purchase order is issued, but some foreign suppliers will not do business on that basis. If such is the case, the buyer must decide whether to seek an alternate supplier.

Price Escalation Clauses

Some U.S. suppliers also insist that the buyer pay for their products at the same prevailing price at the time of delivery. This attitude is understandable on the part of the supplier if there is a long lead time between the contract date and the actual delivery, or if a contract is to be performed over a long period of time. The buyer must price his product to his customers and even though he understands the supplier's plight, not knowing the final production cost of his product leaves him in a difficult, if not untenable, position. The buyer's customers must wait until delivery to find out the price they must pay, or the buyer must add a margin of safety to his selling price, or otherwise just take a gamble when setting his selling price. These are not palatable alternatives, but sometimes one must live with such uncertainties.

A *price escalation clause* in the contract is the avenue a supplier will utilize to avoid making a final commitment on his own selling price until the time of delivery. Price escalation clauses are not accepted very graciously by purchasing officers, but if such clauses are inevitable the purchasing officer should seek to negotiate the clause with the supplier under the most favorable circumstances. Four factors that should be in the contract pertaining to the escalation clause are as follows:

1. The "peg" according to which the price will be adjusted should be clearly established. It should be some well-known market quotation that is published regularly. If it is quoted with a high, low, and closing price, the one to be used should be specified. If it is to be pegged to some labor or material cost of the supplier that is not regularly published, the purchas-

ing officer must be satisfied as to its legitimacy and how it may be verified. By way of comment only, it should be noted that many purchasing officers find the consumers price index unsatisfactory because many of the items included in these indices are not directly related to industrial costs.

2. The "peg" reading at the time the contract is signed should be shown in the contract.

3. The effect a percentage change in the "peg" will create upon the contract price should be established. If, for example, the "peg" increases 10 percent between the contract and delivery dates, it does not follow that the total contract price will automatically be increased by the same amount. The supplier may be asking for the escalator clause because of a volatile market of a raw material. Raw materials may represent only 40 percent of the supplier's cost of production. If the price of that raw material increases 10 percent, the supplier should only be entitled to an increase of 4 percent in the contract price. He has no right to expect a 10 percent increase in labor costs, overhead, and profit as well. This point of view may not be received by the supplier with open arms, but it can be pursued with a strong sense of justice and fairness by both parties.

4. Provision should be included that the price is to be adjusted under the formula in both directions. Although the term "escalator clause" is a common term for such clauses, there is always the possibility that prices will decline. The buyer is entitled to consideration when this occurs and this fact should be included in the preamble to the escalator clause. A fair expression of such an eventuality would be: "The price shown herein is subject to upward or downward adjustment at the time of delivery. The following formula will be applied when determining the amount of any adjustment . . . "

One final comment. Subsection (1)(c) of Section 2-305, which is repeated in the following section of this text, provides the method for determining the price of a contract when the "peg" is unexpectedly unavailable.

Open-Price Orders

Purchase orders may be issued as offers to buy without any price shown. If such an offer to buy is accepted by the supplier, a firm contract is created. Even though no price is mentioned a valid contract is formed. The formation of a contract without a price term was not available under the common law since the contract would have failed by being considered indefinite. But Section 2-305(1) of the Uniform Commercial Code has changed this common law rule. It reads as follows:

> (1) The parties if they so intend can conclude a contract for sale even though the price is not settled. In such a case the price is a reasonable price at the time of delivery if
>
>> (a) nothing is said as to price; or
>>
>> (b) the price is left to be agreed by the parties and they fail to agree; or
>>
>> (c) the price is to be fixed in terms of some agreed market or other standard as set or recorded by a third person or agency and it is not so set or recorded.

This subsection allows the parties to create a valid contract with an open price term. All that is required is that the parties intend to create a contract. When a purchasing officer sends an unpriced purchase order, the intent is to make an offer to buy without specifying the price. The supplier's acceptance usually comes through the delivery of the goods since most of the time unpriced orders are used only for small purchases. The contract comes into existence and is performed without a price having been mentioned.

The charge is sometimes made that sending an unpriced purchase order is similar to sending a blank check to the supplier. Subsection (1) of 2-305 states that the price is to be "a reasonable price at the time of delivery." A *reasonable price* is not defined, but it has been interpreted to be the prevailing market price. Such a price is the prevailing price in the level of distribution when the buyer and the seller usually transact business, and giving due consideration to the quantity purchased. The supplier does not have the luxury of selecting a higher retail price for the item simply because there is no price stated on the purchase order. Thus subsection (1) provides protection to the purchaser.

Another restraint is placed on the amount to be charged on an unpriced purchase order in Subsection (2) of 2-305.

> (2) A price to be fixed by the seller or by the buyer means a price for him to fix in good faith.

This is a restatement of the obligation of good faith imposed many times by the Code upon all contracts. It is stated in Section 1-203:

> Every contract or duty with this Act imposes an obligation of good faith in its performance or enforcement.

Thus any supplier seeking to set an exorbitant price on an unpriced order must answer in court the questions: "Was this price set within the bounds of good faith?" and "Is it the prevailing market price in accordance with the standards of the industry?" A supplier challenged in this manner must be able to prove that his price is a good-faith price. Failure to do so will result in the establishing of a lower price by the court.

Nota Bene **to the Purchasing Officer.** Most purchasing officers find it prudent to issue unpriced purchase orders from time to time. Emergency purchases will arise where the time for negotiation of price is limited. There will also be small orders that may cost more to negotiate than the actual cost of the item being bought. The law, as has been seen, provides a safety net for such purchases. But there are also occasions when issuing an unpriced purchase order might be a hazardous procedure. The practice should be confined to established and continuing sources of supply. It should also be confined to the purchase of items that are regularly bought and sold, and thereby have established market prices. A new and unique product manufactured by only one source might have no other "prevailing price" than the one set by the manufacturer. Section 2-305 might be of little assistance in containing the unusually high price of a single source supplier. It is better first to negotiate the price for such an item. It is also prudent to fix prices when you are conducting business with that particular supplier for the first time.

No Price—No Contract. Subsection (4) of 2-305 emphasizes the importance of the *intent* of the parties when the unpriced contract is involved. You will recall that subsection (1) began with the statement: "The parties if they so intend can conclude a contract for sale even though the price is not settled." Subsection (4) follows up this necessity of intent by stating:

> (4) Where, however, the parties intend not to be bound unless the price be fixed or agreed and it is not fixed or agreed there is no contract.

CREDIT TERMS

Code Provisions for Credit Terms

The purchasing officer also needs to negotiate the credit terms with the supplier. Too often credit extension by a supplier is presumed by the buyer. Section 2-310(a) of the Uniform Commercial Code makes it clear that any extension of credit must be negotiated:

> Unless otherwise agreed
>
> > (a) payment is due at the time and place at which the buyer is to receive the goods even though the place of shipment is the place of delivery.

Under this Code section payment is presumed to be due when the buyer receives the goods. If there is to be a delay of payment after the goods have been received, it must come through the invitation stated in the preamble "Unless otherwise agreed."

You will note that payment for the purchase is due where and when the buyer is to receive the goods. Receipt of goods occurs when the buyer takes physical possession of them, as is defined in Section 2-103. Receipt does not refer to the time the buyer assumes responsibility for the goods as under an "F.O.B. Supplier's Plant" delivery contract. There the buyer becomes responsible for the goods when they are made available for shipment by the supplier, but under 2-310 payment is deferred until the buyer takes physical possession of them.

Some private organizations and most governmental agencies have a firm rule that no payment for purchases will be made until the goods have been received. Their purchasing officers must look carefully at the length of time the transportation of the goods will require when negotiating credit terms. It is possible that a longer period of time will be required to move the goods from the supplier to the buyer than the time provided in the credit terms. That would result in payment being due without the goods having been received. This often happens when shipments are made via barge on inland waterways, or when trucks or rail shipments get delayed en route. It can also occur when the credit period is extremely short.

All purchasing officers should keep this potential problem in mind, and also the fact that a credit period begins to run on the date the goods are shipped. (See 2-310(d) in the next section.) Credit terms should be negotiated that will allow payment to be made at some number of days *after the goods have been received*. This will allow a reasonable time to inspect the goods. It will also give the buyer the advantage of using the supplier's working capital rather than his own during the extension. One way to do this is to negotiate with the supplier for the credit period in the contract to begin to run after the goods have been received. One might consider having a term on the purchase order that reads

> *Terms:* Net 30 days unless otherwise stated. Credit period to run from date of receipt of goods and invoice in proper form.

There will be ample opportunity after the goods are received to inspect and process the invoice for payment, if this provision is included in every purchase. Such protection assumes greater importance if the supplier offers a cash discount for prompt payment of the invoice. Cash discounts are discussed in the following section.

A "reasonable time" for a credit period varies by industry. Thirty days is common for many, although 10 to 15 days is the rule for some.

There are situations where the credit period may be extended beyond 30 days, especially when the item is bought for resale. Every purchasing officer should consider including standard credit terms on the purchase order (similar to the one previously suggested for organizations requiring receipt of goods before payment). Credit must be negotiated for every purchase, and one way to bring the topic on the table is to show the terms stated on the purchase order. Those who are not interested in receipt of goods before payment may use a simple one-liner, such as "Terms net 30 days unless otherwise stated." This will get the credit period into the contract, unless the purchase order is used to accept the supplier's offer to sell, and the offer contains a different credit period of, say, net 10 days. Then the credit terms should be negotiated with the supplier before issuing the purchase order. Failure to do so may result in application of Section 2-207(1) whereby the contract is based on the supplier's credit terms, or of Section 2-207(3), which imposes the Code's credit terms that provide for immediate payment.

Counting the Days

Section 2-310(d) is quite explicit in designating the date a credit period begins to run:

> Unless otherwise agreed
>
> > (d) where the seller is required or authorized to ship the goods on credit the credit period runs from the time of shipment but post-dating the invoice or delaying its dispatch will correspondingly delay the starting of the credit period.

In other words—in a purchase agreement with 30-day credit terms—if the goods are shipped on July 10, and the invoice is dated the same date or earlier, payment is due on August 9. If the goods are shipped on July 10 but the invoice is dated July 12, payment is due on August 11. If the goods are shipped on July 10, and the invoice is dated July 12 but not mailed until July 14, the payment is due on August 13.

The Official Comment of the Code explains the reason for the delay in commencing the credit period if the invoice is dated after shipment has been made:

> Such conduct (delay in sending the invoice) results in depriving the buyer of his full notice and warning as to when he must be prepared to pay.

Cash Discounts

Some suppliers will offer a discount from the invoice price if payment is made promptly and in advance of the usual credit period. Such a discount is customarily expressed as "2/10,n/30." This means that the buyer is invited to pay the invoice within 10 days from its date (if that date coincides with the date of shipment of the goods), and to deduct 2 percent from the invoice price for such prompt advance payment. The full invoice price must be paid if the payment is sent from the eleventh to the thirtieth day after its date.

Cash discounts are a desirable reduction in the cost of the purchase. The invitation to take it should be accepted if your organization has adequate working capital. Getting a 2-percent discount for an advance payment of 20 days is the equivalent of a simple interest rate of 36 percent. Many suppliers willingly offer these discounts because such discounts reduce the amount of working capital invested in their accounts receivable. But a discount must be negotiated and included in the contract. Nowhere in the Code is a *cash discount* mentioned.

A cash discount term—usually 10 days—shortens a portion of the credit period. It also emphasizes the need to attempt to induce the supplier to have the entire credit period commence after the receipt of the goods and invoice in proper form. The insistence on the invoice being in proper form is included because most organizations find it difficult, if not impossible, to voucher for payment an amount due a supplier without having the invoice in hand.

Purchasing officers are encouraged to push hard for a cash discount allowance in every purchase. The following amended version of the purchase order term suggested in the preceding section is one way to begin this campaign.

> Terms: 2-percent discount if paid within 10 days, net 30 days. Credit period to run from receipt of goods and invoice in proper form.

***Nota Bene* to the Purchasing Officer**. It is important that the following suggestions be repeated one more time: You are urged to take advantage of the Code's many invitations to negotiate all purchases apart from the many provisions in the Code that are written in the *supplier's* favor. You are also urged to use caution when agreeing with a supplier to waive the protection the Code gives you as the *buyer.* One of the basic premises of the Code is that almost all provisions in a contract can be negotiated by the parties as long as the agreement is made in good faith and does not create an unconscionable contract. The Code assigns burdens and risks to one or the other party throughout its many sections. But this is done only to provide firm legal basis in the event the parties do not reach agreement on a particular topic or forget to include the topic in the contract. The Code is saying in effect that in the absence of agreement of the parties on a topic it assigns this burden (or risk) to the buyer or to the supplier, as the case may be. The presumptions in the Code are placed there so that the Code does not leave an essential provision of a contract "suspended in air," even though the parties did just that.

The importance of negotiating credit terms has been emphasized in this chapter. It is important for the buyer to get a credit period into the contract. Cash discount terms are also desirable. However, the protection of your rights of inspection given you by the Code is equally important. Do not lose the privilege of inspection before paying for the goods simply because too short a period of credit was negotiated. This will be discussed in Chapter XXI, "Delivery, Acceptance, and Payment." In any event—and inspection rights notwithstanding—the purchase order condition repeated above allows the credit and discount periods to begin after the goods have been received.

XXI

Delivery Terms
and Risk of Loss

Delivery terms are closely allied to price terms. The expense involved in getting the goods from the supplier to the buyer is a part of the price that the buyer must pay for the goods. The cost of delivery may be included in the supplier's selling price, it may be added onto the selling price, or it may be paid for separately by the buyer. The delivery term dictates which option is applied to a particular purchase.

The delivery term allocates expenses and duties of delivery between the buyer and the supplier. It also controls where and when the risk of loss to the goods is to be transferred from the supplier to the buyer when there is no special provision covering this phase of the transaction in the contract. The Uniform Commercial Code makes each term—the expense of delivery, the duties of the parties, and the location of the risk of loss to the goods—independently negotiable. The Code has provisions regarding the expense of the delivery if the parties have not included delivery terms in their agreement. The Code makes presumptions covering the location of the risk of loss based on the delivery expense terms, if there is no separate provision in the contract. The purchasing officer must take notice of the fact that these presumptive Code rules are written in favor of the *supplier*. The purchasing officer is therefore warned to negotiate delivery terms for every purchase so that the total purchase cost is determinable at the time the contract is made. This avoids *surprise* if the goods are lost, stolen, or damaged while in transit.

THE PROVISIONS OF THE UNIFORM COMMERCIAL CODE

The Code provides standard delivery terms for a variety of situations. These standard terms spell out the duties of the buyer and the seller, such as how the expenses will be met and where the risk of loss rests during the delivery process. The next sections of this chapter discuss these Code provisions and their legal impact on each party.

The Significance ot the Word "Delivery" in the Code

We begin the discussion of Code provisions for delivery by quoting Section 2-301:

> The obligation of the seller is to transfer and deliver and that of the
> buyer is to accept and pay in accordance with the contract.

Section 2-301 states that the delivery is the obligation of the supplier. But it does not tell us that the word *delivery* used here does not always involve the complete act of getting the goods from the supplier to the buyer's place of business. *Delivery* in the Code refers to when and where the seller voluntarily transfers effective ownership of the goods to the buyer. According to the Code, once delivery has taken place, the rights of ownership and the risk of loss of the goods rest with the buyer. The buyer then has the right to sell, to convert, to use, and to insure the goods. This effective transfer of control and ownership may occur at the seller's place of business, at the buyer's place of business, or somewhere in between these two locations. The physical transportation of the goods may commence either before or after the buyer receives control and ownership. Delivery, according to the Code then, is the intangible concept of the transfer of *ownership of goods*. It is to be distinguished from *receipt* of goods. The buyer is said to receive the goods when he obtains physical possession of them.

Rereading the above section with this definition of delivery in mind, we see that it refers only to the seller's obligation to transfer ownership of the goods to the buyer at some time and at some place. How the goods will get to the buyer's place of business may or may not be the supplier's obligation. That will depend upon the contract delivery terms or as presumed by the Code.

Tender of delivery is another Code expression that must be understood in our discussions of delivery terms. Section 2-503 states the following:

> (1) Tender of delivery requires that the seller put and hold conform-
> ing goods at the buyer's disposition and give the buyer any notifica-
> tion reasonably necessary to enable him to take delivery.

The Official Comment for this section takes an additional step by telling us that tender "contemplates an offer coupled with a present ability to fulfill all the conditions resting on the tendering party and must be followed by actual performance if the other party shows himself ready to proceed." The Official Comment adds that tender "connotes such performance by the tendering party as puts the other party in default if he fails to proceed in some manner."

Tender of delivery is the preliminary step to the actual transfer of control of the goods to the buyer. It is initiated by the supplier. To make a tender effective the supplier (1) must have "conforming goods" available for delivery and (2) must notify the buyer of their availability. Once the supplier tenders delivery, it is incumbent on the buyer to move forward in the transaction by receiving and accepting the goods. The buyer's failure to proceed will give the seller a claim for breach of contract. Section 2-507 points out the buyer's duties after tender is made by the supplier.

> (1) Tender of delivery is a condition to the buyer's duty to accept the goods and, unless otherwise agreed, to his duty to pay for them. Tender entitles the seller to acceptance of the goods and to payment according to the contract.

The purchasing officer should note, by the way, from this section how important it is to negotiate a credit term for the contract. This section states that "unless otherwise agreed" payment is due and can be demanded immediately upon tender of delivery.

Tender of delivery is a separate and distinct act only when the supplier is not required to ship the goods. Tender is then an announcement to the buyer that the goods ordered are ready for him to pick up. When it is the supplier's obligation to ship the goods, tender becomes more of a formality associated with the shipment process. After the goods have been shipped under a *shipment contract,* the supplier must send notification of their shipment to the buyer. This is regarded as the tender of delivery. When the goods are shipped under a *destination contract*, the supplier is said to tender the goods when the buyer is notified that they have reached that destination. Then tender amounts to a notice that the goods are ready for acceptance. But no matter how the buyer is to obtain possession of the goods, tender shifts the burden of proceeding with the transaction to the buyer.

The Place of Delivery as Presumed by the Code

The purchasing officer is alerted to the fact that the Code's presumptions regarding the *place of delivery* are written in favor of the *supplier.* Section 2-308, "Absence of Specified Place of Delivery," states:

> Unless otherwise agreed

(a) the place for delivery of goods is the seller's place of business or if he has none his residence; but

(b) in a contract for sale of identified goods which to the knowledge of the parties at the time of contracting are in some other place, that place is the place for their delivery.

Unless otherwise agreed, the supplier completes his contract obligation by tendering delivery and making the goods available at his place of business. If delivery terms have not been negotiated, the purchasing officer will have to make arrangements for the transportation of the goods and assume all of the related expenses. This conclusion reached by this section of the Code suggests that it might be prudent for the purchase order to contain the condition: "F.O.B. our receiving dock unless otherwise stated." This will give the purchasing officer some protection in the event the delivery term was accidentally not included in the negotiations with the supplier.

There is one protection the Code offers the buyer in such situations. This is provided by subsection (3) of Section 2-509, which states that in situations where the seller is not required to ship the goods and the goods are not held by a bailee "the risk of loss passes to the buyer on his receipt of the goods if the seller is a merchant." If the seller is not a merchant, then the risk of loss passes upon tender of delivery. Most purchasing officers do business with suppliers who qualify as merchants. Therefore, the goods will remain the responsibility of the supplier until they are picked up. The goods must be picked up from the supplier within a reasonable time after delivery has been tendered.

Standard Delivery Terms

The authors of the Uniform Commercial Code did not deliberately discriminate against the purchasing officer when they wrote the presumptive rule that "in the absence of a specified place of delivery the place for the delivery of goods is the seller's place of business." They believed that some rule had to be included because delivery terms are frequently left out of contracts. They therefore selected the law that prevailed prior to the adoption of the Code. The Code's authors provide statutory language for the delivery terms most frequently used in modern business. These delivery terms are spelled out in detail, and little inter-pretation is required. The duties of both parties are given—how expenses will be allocated and when the risk of loss to the goods is to be transferred to the buyer. The following delivery terms are recognized:

1. F.O.B. place of shipment (referred to as a *shipment contract*)

2. F.O.B. place of destination (referred to as a *destination contract*)

3. F.O.B. vessel, car, or other vehicle

4. F.A.S. vessel

5. C.I.F. destination

6. C&F destination

7. C.I.F. or C.A.F. net landed weights

8. Ex ship

9. "No arrival, no sale" (added to a destination contract).

An individual review of each of the above terms follows. (The reader should note that this is not an all-inclusive list of delivery terms, especially when overseas shipments are involved. Shipments from foreign vendors may be governed by a variety of terms, such as those promulgated by the International Chamber of Commerce entitled *Incoterms.*)

F.O.B. Place of Shipment. Section 2-319 of the Code entitled "F.O.B. and F.A.S. terms" contains the basic rules governing these familiar expressions. Subsection (1) begins with this general statement which the purchasing officer should keep in mind:

> (1) Unless otherwise agreed, the term F.O.B. (which means "free on board") at a named place, even though used only in connection with the stated price, is a delivery term.[1]

The preamble "unless otherwise agreed" is the oft-repeated invitation to the buyer and supplier to alter the general rules that follow in the section. It is suggested that any variation from the general rules should be expressed clearly in contract documents since the usual interpretation of F.O.B. and F.A.S. have wide general acceptance.

"At a named place" refers to any describable place. It does not have to be just mention of a city or a town. In fact, the statement: "Buyer's receiving dock at 111 Main Street, St. Louis, MO" is preferable to "St. Louis, MO." If only "St. Louis" was mentioned, the carrier would have completed the transportation contract when the goods arrived at their team tracks or their receiving terminal in St. Louis. Additional expense would be involved getting the goods from there to the buyer's receiving dock.

The phrase "even though used only in connection with the stated price" is included in the subsection because frequently price quotations by suppliers and listings of prices on purchase orders by buyers are given with the term "F.O.B. our plant" simply added at the end of the price. For example, there was a New York case[1] involving the destruction of some goods that were sent in response to a pur-

---

[1] *A M. Knitwear v. All America Export*, 390 N.Y.S. 2d 832 (New York 1976).

chase order that contained no delivery terms. However, the purchasing officer was able to show that the statement: "F.O.B. plant per lb. $1.35" appeared on the purchase order in a column headed "Price." The New York court ruled that the price term shown was a delivery term as well, and that the seller was obligated by the F.O.B. plant term to get the goods to the buyer before the risk of loss was transferred. Since the goods were destroyed en route to the buyer, it was the seller's goods that were destroyed. One may deduce from this case that there is a degree of magic to the use of the "F.O.B. our plant" designation. It may be shown anywhere on the purchase order and for any purpose—including determining the price—and it will be controlling as a delivery term as well. For the sake of clarity, it is suggested that the purchase order state "F.O.B. *our plant*" to distinguish it from the plant of the supplier.

Subsection (1) of Section 2-319 continues with the description of a shipment contract:

> (a) when the term is F.O.B. the place of shipment, the seller must at that place ship the goods in the manner provided in this Article (Section 2-504) and bear the expense and risk of putting them into the possession of the carrier.

Thus, under a shipment contract, the place of delivery is the supplier's place of business if the carrier picks up the goods there, or at the carrier's loading facilities if the seller uses his own truck to carry them there. The risk of loss passes to the buyer at the time the carrier gets the goods. Any expense the seller incurs in getting the goods to the carrier is his expense. The remainder of the expense involved in getting the goods from the carrier to the buyer is the buyer's responsibility.

Duties of the Seller Under a Shipment Contract. Section 2-504 is referred to in subsection (1)(a) of 2-319. Section 2-504 goes into greater detail on the seller's duties in a shipment contract. The section specifies that the seller must

> (a) put the goods in the possession of such a carrier and make such a contract for their transportation as may be reasonable having regard to the nature of the goods and other circumstances of the case; and

> (b) obtain and promptly deliver or tender in due form any document necessary to enable the buyer to obtain possession of the goods or otherwise required by the agreement or by usage of trade; and

> (c) promptly notify the buyer of the shipment.

Subsection (a) requires the supplier to exercise the above care in arranging for the carrier to ship the goods as may be necessary. Any special arrangements to care for the goods, such as refrigeration, must be arranged for by the supplier.

In addition, all other delivery terms of the agreement with the buyer must be followed as long as they are reasonable and realistic. The supplier is given a certain amount of latitude in assigning a literal and commercial meaning to such instructions. In the absence of any agreement to the contrary, the supplier has the liberty to select the carrier and designate the routing.

Subsection (b) expressly provides for the supplier to obtain all necessary shipping documents and forward them promptly to the buyer. This requirement is included so that the buyer is alerted to the fact that the shipment has been made and that he will be able to claim the goods shipped when they arrive.

The Official Comment in subsection (c) (which requires that the supplier notify the buyer when the shipment is made) states that in an open-credit shipment the mailing of the invoice is adequate notice to the buyer. The Official Comment also indicates that it is customary to forward a straight bill of lading, but that this is not required to meet the supplier's duty of prompt notification. The reader should note that if the supplier should fail to meet any of his duties relating to shipment and notification, the buyer must suffer material delay or loss to have grounds for rejection of the goods when they do arrive. A supplier who exercises all reasonable precautions in arranging the shipment is not held responsible for the minor mishaps that might occur during shipment. As long as his duties are performed in good faith and with due regard to the customs of the industry the shipper is regarded as having met the obligations imposed on him by this section. However, if a term requiring a special type of notification of shipment to be sent the buyer has been included in the original contract, such requirement must be followed by the supplier. The inclusion of such notification in the contract emphasizes the importance the buyer attaches to the notice. The supplier's omission of special notice could give the buyer grounds for rejection of the shipment.

F.O.B. Place of Destination. Subsection (b) of 2-319 details the Code's version of a destination contract:

> (b) when the term is F.O.B. the place of destination, the seller must at his own expense and risk transport the goods to that place and there tender delivery of them in the manner provided in this Article (Section 2-503).

A *destination contract* requires the seller to get the goods to the named destination before his obligations of delivery have been met. This must all be accomplished at his expense. Until the goods are at that destination, the supplier has the risk of loss of the goods. In fact, the risk of loss remains on the supplier's shoulders until the goods have been tendered and the buyer has had a reasonable opportunity to receive them.

Delivery terms that provide for a destination contract cause the buyer the least concern about delivery. The entire transportation burden is laid on the doorstep of the supplier. All the attendant costs must be assumed by the supplier, including cartage to the buyer's receiving dock if that is the named destination in the contract. The risk of loss also remains with the supplier until the goods are received by the buyer.

The above quoted subsection of 2-319 refers the reader to section 2-503 concerning the manner in which the seller should tender delivery. The first part of 2-503 and tender of delivery were reviewed earlier in this chapter. The seller must place conforming goods at the buyer's disposal and give the buyer reasonable notice of their availability. Section 2-503 also specifies that the seller's tender "must be at a reasonable hour," and the goods must be kept available "for the period reasonably necessary for the buyer to take possession." Subsection (1)(b) requires the buyer to "furnish facilities reasonably suited to the receipt of the goods." Usage of the trade and the circumstances of the particular transaction determine what is *reasonable* in both instances.

Nota Bene to the Purchasing Officer. The destination contract generally is to be preferred if it can be negotiated and if the supplier does not add more than a reasonable charge for the accommodation. A destination contract can be yours only if it is negotiated, since the shipment contract is presumed by the Code to be the normal arrangement between buyer and seller.

Whenever you give shipping instructions, designate the receiving point where you are best able to take possession of the goods. Most often this will be your receiving dock, and if so, it should be the named destination. Naming only the city where it is located may get the goods close to your dock, but not necessarily on it. Be precise in the statement of the location of that dock.

F.O.B. Vessel, Car or Other Vehicle. Subsection (c) of 2-319 states:

> (c) when under either (a) or (b) the term is also F.O.B. vessel, car or other vehicle, the seller must in addition at his own expense and risk load the goods on board. If the term is F.O.B. vessel the buyer must name the vessel and in an appropriate case the seller must comply with the provisions of this Article on the form of bill of lading (Section 2-323).

This section applies when the seller must load the goods on board before his obligations have been met either under a shipment contract or where the named destination is the point at which reshipment will occur. Thus, if the delivery terms are "F.O.B. vessel, San Francisco" with the probability of a reshipment to New York, the seller must get those goods on board the vessel at his expense and at his risk.

The seller also has certain duties regarding the bill of lading that must be obtained from the carrier. These duties are spelled out in Section 2-323, which requires the seller to obtain a negotiable bill of lading stating that the goods have been loaded on board. It also states that the buyer may demand the full set of the negotiable bill of lading unless the goods are to be shipped from abroad. (European shippers sometimes supply a bill of lading in what is known as a "set of parts." Such a bill usually has more than one (usually three) original parts. United States law frowns on this because of the possibility of fraud arising with three original bills having been issued. The Code insists on a full set for U.S. transactions, but it recognizes the "set of parts" custom that prevails in shipments from abroad. If only one of a "set of parts" is received by a U.S. buyer from a foreign supplier, Section 2-319 (2)(b) requires the buyer to pay on one of the set only if the supplier provides adequate indemnity to the buyer.) Section 2-323 is also applicable to C.I.F. and C.&F. shipments detailed in succeeding sections of this text.

Under an F.O.B. vessel delivery term the buyer is required to name the loading berth of the vessel, its name, and the shipping date. The buyer's failure to provide this information may subject him to certain penalties under Section 2-311. The buyer's failure might be regarded as a failure to cooperate, which could excuse the seller from delay on his own part. It would also give the seller the right to select his own shipping arrangements without penalty. The breach of contract is one more possible penalty against the buyer if the failure to cooperate makes the supplier's performance impossible.

The F.O.B. vessel delivery term with a bill of lading also brings forth and includes the procedure for "payment against documents" as a part of the delivery term. Subsection (4) of 2-319 states:

> Under the term F.O.B. Vessel or F.A.S. unless otherwise agreed the buyer must make payment against tender of the required documents and the seller may not tender nor the buyer demand delivery of the goods in substitution for the documents.

One of the conventional methods of making such shipments is to have a sight draft drawn on the buyer and sent along with the bill of lading to a bank in the buyer's city. The buyer must then pay the sight draft to the bank before obtaining the bill of lading. The bill of lading gives the buyer the right to claim the goods from the carrier on arrival. This results in the buyer's paying for the goods before having an opportunity to inspect them. His right of inspection is not lost, however. It is merely postponed until the goods can be claimed with the bill of lading. Payment against documents before delivery is customary in F.A.S. vessel, C.I.F. and C.&F. delivery terms, which are discussed in succeeding sections.

F.A.S. Vessel. The delivery term F.A.S. *vessel* relieves the seller of the duty of loading the goods as is required in the F.O.B. vessel term. Subsection (2) of 2-319 explains the term as follows:

> (2) Unless otherwise agreed, the term F.A.S. Vessel (which means "free alongside") at a named port, even though used in connection with the stated price, is a delivery term under which the seller must

(a) at his own expense and risk deliver the goods alongside the vessel in the manner usual in that port or on a dock designated and provided by the buyer; and

(b) obtain and tender a receipt for the goods in exchange for which the carrier is under a duty to issue a bill of lading.

Under the F.A.S. vessel term the buyer has the same duty to name the loading berth as he does in an F.O.B. vessel shipment. The buyer also has the same duty of payment against documents. The seller, however, is not required to secure an "on board" bill of lading. He must, however, "obtain and tender a receipt for the goods in exchange for which the carrier is under a duty to issue a bill of lading."

C.I.F. Destination. Section 2-320(1) provides for the commonly used C.I.F. term in overseas shipments.

(1) The term C.I.F. means that the price includes in a lump sum the cost of the goods and the insurance and freight to the named destination. The term C.&F. or C.F. means that the price so includes cost and freight to the named destination.

Subsection (2) of 2-320 details the duties of the seller in such a delivery term, "unless otherwise agreed." These duties include:

1. Putting the goods in possession of a carrier at the port for shipment.

2. Obtaining a negotiable bill of lading covering the entire transportation to the named destination. (This bill of lading must comply with all the requirements of Section 2-323 as detailed in the section above on the F.O.B. vessel delivery term.)

3. Loading the goods and obtain a receipt from the carrier showing that the freight has been paid or provided for.

4. Obtaining a policy of insurance in the amount of the currency of the contract. The insurance must provide for payment of any loss to the buyer.

5. Obtaining war risk insurance of a kind and on the terms then current at the port of shipment in the usual amount. The seller is permitted to add the amount of the premium for any such war risk insurance to the contract price.

6. Preparing an invoice for the goods and procuring any other documents required for shipment.

7. Forwarding and tendering with commercial promptness all the documents in due form and with any endorsement necessary to perfect the buyer's rights.

The C.I.F. delivery term, as pointed out in the Official Comment, is effectively a *shipment contract* as distinguished from a *destination contract.* The risk of loss is transferred to the buyer when the goods are delivered to the carrier. This is the reason why the insurance loss clause must state that the amount of any loss is payable to the buyer. Of course, this applies only if the seller meets all of his duties, as specified above.

The C.I.F. term relieves the buyer of the responsibility of arranging for the transportation of the goods, although the goods do become his risk once the carrier obtains possession. The buyer has the duty of payment against documents as specified in the F.O.B. vessel term stated above.

C.&F. Destination. The Code states: "The term C.&F. or C.F. means that the price so includes cost and freight to the named destination." It also repeats in subsection (3) of 2-320:

> (3) Unless otherwise agreed the term C.&F. or its equivalent has the same effect and imposes upon the seller the same obligations and risks as a C.I.F. term except the obligation as to insurance.

The same rules concerning the form of the bill of lading (2-323) as well as the rules for payment against documents, apply in the same way they do in C.I.F. and F.O.B. vessel terms (subsection (4) of 2-319).

C.I.F. or C.&F. Net Landed Weights. These are delivery terms that are based upon the quality or quantity of goods as they arrive at the place of destination. Section 2-321 clearly explains where they vary from the standard C.I.F. delivery terms.

> Under a contract containing a term C.I.F. or C.&F.
>
> (1) Where the price is based on or is to be adjusted according to "net landed weights," "delivered weights," "out turn" quantity or quality or the like, unless otherwise agreed the seller must reasonably estimate the price. The payment due on tender of the documents called for by the contract is the amount so estimated, but after final adjustment of the price a settlement must be made with commercial promptness.
>
> (2) An agreement described in subsection (1) or any warranty of quality or condition of the goods on arrival places upon the seller the risk of ordinary deterioration, shrinkage and the like in transportation but has no effect on the place or time of identification to the contract for sale or delivery or on the passing of the risk of loss.
>
> (3) Unless otherwise agreed where the contract provides for payment on or after arrival of the goods the seller must before payment allow such preliminary inspection as is feasible; but if the goods are lost delivery of the documents and payment are due when the goods should have arrived.

Ex-Ship. The delivery term *ex-ship* applies to the carrying of goods to the port of the named destination at the seller's expense and risk. Section 2-322 carries the statutory language that describes the term:

> (1) Unless otherwise agreed a term for delivery of goods "ex-ship" (which means from the carrying vessel) or in equivalent language is not restricted to a particular ship and requires delivery from a ship which has reached a place at the named port of destination where goods of the kind are usually discharged.
>
> (2) Under such a term unless otherwise agreed
>
> > (a) the seller must discharge all liens arising out of the carriage and furnish the buyer with a direction which puts the carrier under a duty to deliver the goods; and
> >
> > (b) the risk of loss does not pass to the buyer until the goods leave the ship's tackle or are otherwise properly unloaded.

There is little need to have a bill of lading with this delivery term since the seller is required to arrange for the carrier to deliver the goods to the buyer. Instructions to deliver issued to the carrier suffice for the buyer to obtain possession. Insurance to protect the buyer is also unnecessary. The risk of loss is to the seller during the transportation of the goods.

"No Arrival, No Sale." The last delivery term is "No arrival, no sale." It is offered in Section 2-324 as follows:

> Under a term "no arrival, no sale" or terms of like meaning, unless otherwise agreed
>
> > (a) the seller must properly ship conforming goods and if they arrive by any means he must tender them on arrival but he assumes no obligation that the goods will arrive unless he has caused the non-arrival; and
> >
> > (b) where without fault of the seller the goods are in part lost or have so deteriorated as no longer to conform to the contract or arrive after the contract time, the buyer may proceed as if there had been casualty to identified goods (Section 2-613).

The Official Comment on this section suggests that the "no arrival, no sale" term may be used when the seller is reselling goods that were bought by him as shipped by another, and the buyer is aware of this fact. This term confines the risk of loss to the seller. In this respect it could be a destination contract. The term does, however, keep the seller free of any breach of contract if the goods fail to arrive. For the seller to have this relief, it is essential to show that conforming goods were shipped, and that the failure of arrival is not the seller's fault. The latter proof is required to prevent the seller from selling the goods to another customer at a higher price and then claiming failure to arrive. The reference to Section 2-613 affirms the seller's exemption from breach if the loss is total; if the loss is partial, the buyer has the choice of accepting the remainder with a price allowance, or to reject all.

These then are the delivery terms recognized by the Code and placed in statutory language. Several other Code sections dealing with the particulars of delivery follow.

Delivery in Single Lot or Several Lots

Section 2-307 reads:

> Unless otherwise agreed all goods called for by a contract for sale must be tendered in a single delivery and payment is due only on such tender but where the circumstances give either party the right to make or demand delivery in lots the price if it can be apportioned may be demanded for each lot.

The Official Comment for this section begins by saying: This section applies where the parties have not specifically agreed whether delivery and payment are to be by lots." This places the obligation on the supplier to make a single delivery of the goods called for in the contract, "unless otherwise agreed." It assumes the parties intended delivery to be a single lot. The caveat in the section beginning with the words "But where the circumstances give either party" refers to the situations where it is not commercially feasible to deliver or receive the goods in a single lot. The Official Comment gives as examples of this exception: "Where ten carloads of coal are involved but only three cars are available at a given time," and, in a contract for bricks for a building, "The buyer's storage space may be limited so that it would be impossible to receive the entire amount of brick at once."

The Time for Shipment

Section 2-309 states:

> (1) The time for shipment or delivery or any other action under a contract if not provided in this Article or agreed upon shall be a reasonable time.

This Code section gives the purchasing officer some right to expect prompt delivery, but, once again it employs the vague phrase, "a reasonable time," when no specific time is agreed upon.

Obtaining prompt delivery from a supplier can pose a problem for the purchasing officer. Inexact terms, such as "Rush," "At once," or "As soon as possible" are often placed on a purchase order in an attempt to speed delivery. Such words often have little effect and do little to hasten the arrival of the goods. There are those suppliers who, especially during a sellers' market, respond silently to such terms with responses, such as "Your order will be handled in our customary expeditious manner," and "You will get your order when we deliver it." The law is of no assistance to the purchasing officer who uses such time-worn statements because it interprets them as requests for delivery within a reasonable time.

METHODS OF ENFORCING DELIVERY TERMS

Putting "Teeth" into Delivery Clauses

There are several approaches that you as a purchasing officer can take to assist in getting delivery more promptly. The first step is to establish a specific date when you want the.goods delivered. This should impress on the supplier the fact that you have carefully scheduled your need and want to enlist his cooperation. Be prepared to come up with a precise statement on the purchase order, such as "To be delivered at our receiving dock on or before June 10" or "To be delivered at our receiving dock during the week of June 10." Give the supplier some latitude in scheduling his production and deliveries, but be as precise as you can.

The next step is to place this delivery date on the table when negotiating the purchase with the supplier. Delivery terms can and should be negotiated as any other term of the purchase. Once the supplier has agreed to the date, make it a part of the purchase contract and place it on the purchase order. You have made it clear to the supplier that your scheduled June 10 date is a serious matter to you and to your company. Furthermore, you have made the delivery date a specific condition in the contract. Now you will get a bit of assistance from the law. If the term is expressed as "on or before June 10" and the goods have not arrived by then, your supplier is in technical default on the contract if the delivery is made on July 11.

The act of placing the supplier in technical default of his contract obligations does not get the goods delivered to your company, but it does serve as another reminder to him. The supplier does indeed become exposed to possible liability for damages in the event of default. However, this put the onus on you of proving the damages you have incurred because of nondelivery on the due date. Such damages are not easily provable, especially if you specified a delivery date in advance of the date your company would put the goods to use, which is standard operating procedure. There are also many purchases made where the failure to deliver on a specified date will not result in out-of-pocket expenses being incurred. Furthermore, in most instances the supplier will deliver in a reasonable time after the scheduled date, which further limits the amount of recoverable expenses incurred. This makes the threat of such a lawsuit nothing more than another persuasion to get the supplier to deliver on time. You will obtain broader legal rights for yourself and your company, and put pressure on the supplier to deliver an important order on time if you place the following statement on the purchase order.

> The goods ordered herein will be used in the purchaser's assembly line. As agreed, delivery is to be made at our receiving dock on or before June 10. Time is of the essence for delivery of these goods. This purchase order is subject to cancellation by the purchaser if the goods are not delivered by June 10. In the event the contract must be cancelled, the purchaser reserves the right to exercise all available remedies afforded by the Uniform Commercial Code including but not limited to the recovery of incidental and consequential damages.

The first sentence of the above stipulation can be altered to fit your particular need. The main thrust of the statement is that "time is of the essence" in the contract. This makes the agreed delivery date go to the very core and heart of the contract. It says to the supplier, "One of the major reasons I entered into this contract with you is to get the goods by June 10." The supplier's failure to perform as agreed now gives you the right to cancel the contract, and to

1. "Cover" by making a purchase of the goods from a competitor of the supplier in default; to recover as damages from the original supplier any excess costs to you between the new price paid and the original contract price plus any incidental or consequential damages; *or*

2. Recover damages for nondelivery plus any incidental or consequential damages incurred.

Use of this condition in the contract gives you a "bigger stick" to use on the supplier to obtain your delivery at the time promised. Obviously taking legal action of this nature is a major step and should be used only as a last resort. But you now have the power and right to do so if you believe it is essential.

The procedure to follow if the goods are not delivered by "June 10," is first to notify the supplier on June 11 that you are prepared to exercise your rights under the contract. You may have to threaten to cancel the contract. Then it is up to you as a reasonably prudent purchasing officer to "take it from there." If the supplier satisfies you with the explanation for the delay in delivery and offers you a satisfactory substitute delivery date, the clause has served its purpose. It is suggested that the promised new delivery date be reduced to writing and that you reserve all your rights under the original contract. Should there continue to be "foot dragging" on the part of the supplier, consult with your legal counsel. Work out with your legal counsel the procedure you should follow. It is to be hoped that the threat of canceling the contract is all that will be required to bring the supplier into a cooperative mood.

Liquidated Damages

Another effective tool a purchasing officer may utilize to protect his or her organization against loss due to delayed delivery is known as *liquidated damages*. The process involved is for the purchasing officer to establish the per-day loss the organization will suffer if the supplier does not deliver by the specified date. The loss figure must be a foreseeable and provable actual loss, and must not be based solely upon mere inconvenience or hardship. That figure is then placed into the contract with the supplier. Such a clause might read:

> The supplier and the purchaser agree that the purchaser will suffer irreparable damages in the amount of $1000 per day if delivery is not completed by June 10. The supplier thereby agrees to undertake to deliver all of the material covered by this contract by June 10. In the event delivery is not completed by that date, the supplier agrees to reimburse and pay to the purchaser the sum of $1000 per day for each workday beyond June 10 until delivery is completed as liquidated damages suffered by the purchaser because of the supplier's failure to meet this delivery date.

Liquidated damages is provided for in Section 2-718 of the Code and is discussed in Chapter XXII of this text. The purchasing officer is admonished that the amount of damages payable per day must be reasonable and provable. The procedure is not intended as a penalty against the supplier, but only as reimbursement to the buyer for the actual loss encountered because of the late delivery. The Code makes it quite clear that any unreasonably large amount that is set for liquidated damages could render the entire provision null and void, hence unenforceable.

SHIPMENT AND DELIVERY TERMS

Recently, a major development has taken place in regard to abbreviated shipment terms. The use of these terms has been discussed in Chapter XXI. With just a few letters, e.g. F.O.B, New York or C.I.F. St. Louis, major legal obligations and consequences ensue. Matters of price, delivery, risk of loss, insurance and other obligations are set forth in the law for these letters or abbreviated terms. The use of the definition in the Uniform Commercial Code remains the same and the discussion in the main text remains relevant as long as the purchasing manager makes sure it is specified in the contract that the UCC applies.

A new development is the issuance of new trade terms and definitions by the International Chamber of Commerce. These may be used in both domestic and foreign trade, and the purchasing manager will surely be encountering their proposed use by some suppliers. They are called "Incoterms 1990" and will undoubtedly be used during the last half of this century and into the next.

Nota Bene: The purchasing manager may prefer to use shipment terms which he or she is more familiar with and want to specify that the Uniform Commercial Code shipment terms apply as well as specifically contracting to precise duties and risks. Sometimes even the UCC shipment terms do not make it clear whose employees have the duty to load the goods into the truck or unload them, or who undertakes the risk while the goods are at the carrier's storage facility or dock. While custom or usage or past practice may be looked to under UCC §1-205, sometimes this is not clear and an express contract term on the matter is preferable.

However, the use of the shipment may be in the control of the other party and that party may insist on using a shipment term of the Incoterms. Or the purchasing manager who is engaged in numerous international purchases may find it to his or her advantage to use them.

Nota Bene: If the purchasing manager decides to use Incoterms, he or she should obtain a copy of them with the precise legal definitions contained therein. It is obtainable only from the International Chamber of Commerce, 38, Cours Albert ler, 75008 Paris, FRANCE (Phone (1) 49.53.28.28. or FAX (1) 42.25.86.63.) which controls its publication rights. The purchasing manager also should consult with the company lawyers to be sure of its understanding and consequences.

The type of terms which the purchasing manager may encounter are in four major groupings:

Group E Departure	EXW	Ex Works
Group F Main carriage unpaid	FCA	Free Carrier
	FAS	Free Alongside Ship
	FOB	Free On Board
Group C Main carriage paid	CFR	Cost and Freight
	CIF	Cost, Insurance and Freight
	CPT	Carriage Paid To
	CIP	Carriage and Insurance Paid To
Group D Arrival	DAF	Delivered At Frontier
	DES	Delivered EX Ship
	DEQ	Delivered EX Quay
	DDU	Delivered Duty Unpaid
	DDP	Delivered Duty Paid

Also, the ship with the port of destination named may be used or DEQ (Delivered Ex Quay) with the named port of destination.

There are some Incoterms which are applicable and may be used for any type of transportation or combinations thereof:

FCA   Free Carrier (. . . named place)
CPT   Carriage Paid To (. . . named place of destination)
CIP   Carriage and Insurance Paid To (. . . named place of destination)
DAF   Delivered At Frontier (. . . named place)
DDU   Delivered Duty Unpaid (. . . named place of destination)
DDP   Delivered Duty Paid (. . . named place of destination)

If the goods are to be picked up at the supplier's factory, warehouse, or place of business then the EXW or Ex Works term is appropriate with the place named immediately after those letters.

While the purchasing manager should consult the Incoterm publisher and the company attorney for precise meaning, a summary of the four major categories and their consequences is made here for general orientation. It is envisioned by the drafters of the Incoterms that these terms will be used most frequently with certain types of transportation. For example, if shipment is by air, then FCA (Free Carrier) may be used with the name of the city or place where shipment is made. If the shipment is by railroad, FCA likewise may be used. If the goods are shipped by sea or by inland waterway, there are some other specialized terms which may be used. There are the more common ones such as FAS (Free Alongside Ship) with the port of shipment named (e.g., St. Louis if goods are shipped from St. Louis to New Orleans), or FOB (Free on Board) with the port of shipment named. The CFR term is Cost and Freight with named city or port of destination following these letters. Or there is CIF (Cost, Insurance, and Freight) with the named port, the term DES (Delivered Ex Ship).

XXII

Letters of Credit

THE UTILITY OF THE LETTER OF CREDIT*

The letter of credit is a payment device often used in sales to facilitate the purchase of goods. While the use of letters of credit has been a standard practice in many international sales for decades, it now is found in some major domestic sales as well. Knowledge of their utility and the possibilities for preventing fraud is crucial for purchasers. Some general background on Article 5 and the Uniform Commercial Code (U.C.C.) is necessary so that purchasers clearly understand the unique character of the letter of credit. The importance of the letter of credit, as distinct from other payment devices, is that it is independent from the underlying transaction. As such, it serves as a mechanism for allocating risks among both the buyer and the seller. However, in absence of a clear definition of "fraud" in Article 5 of the U.C.C. such independence is undermined and, arguably, the utility of the letter of credit diminished.

One of the primary goals of the U.C.C. is to promote commerce by standardizing and streamlining the process by which commercial parties operate. The underlying presumption is that players in the commercial field can much more efficiently and appropriately address problems when they perform within the same conceptual framework as opposed to having fifty different commercial codes throughout the United States. Although the drafters of the U.C.C. pride

---

*Special Acknowledgment: Katherine Rader; Juris Doctor and Attorney-at-Law, St. Louis, Missouri.

themselves on achieving uniformity, they are faced with the competing interests of federalism. One of the basic precepts of federalism is the individual state's right to establish its own alternative solutions to problems commonly shared with other states. Thus, the success or failure of each article of the U.C.C. is often judged in terms of how well it achieves uniformity among the different states.

Accordingly, the great failure of the U.C.C. Article 5 has been the inability to attract the adherence of several states, including the world's banking center, New York. Some states have adopted nonconforming amendments to Article 5, while other states simply give preference to other law. The standard of compliance in this area has basically been left to case law and practice. Consequently, Article 5 is currently the subject of a comprehensive revision effort. The final revised draft has been placed before state legislatures for enactment.

Caveat Nota: For those entering into sales transactions requiring a letter of credit, it becomes important to specify what law is to govern.

Most pertinent to the revision effort is a proposal to define "fraud" under U.C.C. Section 5-114(2) (b), which permits injunctive relief against fraudulent draws on letters of credit. Buyers in particular are interested in this aspect since it is used to protect them against fraudulent actions of the seller, such as falsely presenting documents that conforming goods have been sent or sending virtually worthless goods. Courts throughout the country have struggled with the level, degree, and type of fraud necessary as a basis for an injunction of a letter of credit. As federalism has allowed individual states to experiment with different solutions, the California legislature has opted to deny injunctive relief altogether. California courts feared that unless injunctions were prohibited, courts would do "violence" to the most basic concept of the letter of credit, the independence principle: " . . . that the letter of credit agreement is independent of the underlying commercial transaction."

Therefore, any revision effort to create uniformity among the states in the application of Section 5-114 of the U.C.C. must contend with two competing objectives: preserving the independence principle that has forever been intrinsic to the letter of credit transaction versus protecting the letter of credit from being an instrument for fraud.

This chapter will discuss the different types of letters of credit, and will distinguish the letter of credit from other sureties, such as the performance bond. This chapter will further analyze the various court cases interpreting the language "fraud in the transaction" of Section 5-114(2) (b) of the U.C.C., and will address why the court has had such a difficult time defining fraud in this context. Finally, this chapter will examine the current revision efforts and proposed solutions for the proper definition of fraud in the letter of credit transaction in Article 5 of the U.C.C.

TYPES AND USE: WHAT IS A LETTER OF CREDIT?

There are basically two types of letters of credit: a commercial letter of credit and a standby letter of credit. Letters of credit are a type of commercial paper which merchants traditionally used to provide prompt payment for goods shipped long distances. Although the use of the letter of credit is by no means restricted, the device is most commonly used in international trade. The buyer and seller of goods and services may be located in different nations, and may not have previous business experience with one another. As a result, the seller may be uncertain about the buyer's ability to pay for the goods and may seek some sort of assurance of payment upon performance of a contract.

Caveat Nota: The buyer obtains a letter of credit for the benefit of the seller to assure payment. The letter of credit thus is for the advantage of the seller rather than for the purchaser. If the purchaser has the upper hand he may want to negotiate out of this term. However, in international sales the transaction is conditioned on the term and the buyer will have a difficult time negotiating an alternative means of payment.

A basic letter of credit transaction involves a customer (e.g., the purchaser), an issuer (e.g., the bank), and a beneficiary (e.g., the seller). The customer obtains credit from the bank. The issuer is the bank or other party to whom the customer has applied for credit. By issuing the letter of credit the bank basically guarantees payment to the beneficiary if the requirements in the letter are met, regardless of the customer's financial status. Since the bank or issuer and not the beneficiary bears the risk of the customer's potential insolvency, the beneficiary is protected by the guaranteed payment under the letter of credit.

In summary, there are three separate transactions. First, there is the underlying contract or transaction between the buyer and the seller. The second transaction is between the customer-buyer and the bank-issuer of a letter of credit. Finally, the letter of credit creates a relationship between the issuer and the beneficiary where the issuer is obligated to pay drafts when the beneficiary provides the required documents.

The letter of credit is a mandatory contract because the issuer's obligation to pay upon a conforming demand is not only unaffected by the insolvency of the customer, but also by any claims that the customer may have against the beneficiary on the underlying contract. Therefore, it is deemed to be completely "independent" of the sales contract. From the seller's perspective, the independence of the credit decreases the risk of nonpayment due to the buyer's asserting defenses to payment such as breach of warranty. This type of payment has been said to promote international trade because the bank rather than the customer is primarily liable for payment to the seller.

Caveat Nota: From the buyer's perspective, the independence of the letter of credit creates a risk that the issuer may honor a draft when the beneficiary has fraudulently failed to perform obligations.

A standby letter of credit operates under the same basic structure as the traditional letter of credit. Both are mechanisms for allocating risks among the parties. However, the standby letter of credit differs from the traditional letter of credit in the method by which it allocates those risks among the parties. The main difference is that the standby letter of credit is not used as an expected means of payment, rather it is used to secure payment or performance. The beneficiary may draw on the standby letter of credit only after the customer defaults on the underlying contract. The difference is particularly evident in the required documentation. In a documentary credit, the seller presents a bill of lading and invoice. In a standby letter of credit, the key document is a certificate of deposit indicating that the beneficiary is asserting a default and demands payment.

The difference between the documentary letter of credit and the standby letter of credit is crucial. In a documentary letter of credit, the customer-buyer relies on the protection of the required documents that must be presented by the beneficiary-seller. In a standby transaction, there are really no documents. Simple demand is virtually the only document required for payment. Thus, a standby customer does not look to the documents for protection. Consequently, the question discussed below as to whether the courts will enjoin payment only for documentary fraud or also for fraud in the "underlying" transaction becomes critical for the standby letter of credit customer.

In summary, the commercial utility of a letter of credit is two-fold: 1) the credit for the bank is substituted for the customer's credit; and 2) the letter of credit creates an obligation that is independent of any contractual defenses the customer may have in the primary or underlying contract. That is, the "independence principle" allows the seller to obtain payment even if he has breached his contractual obligation so seriously that no payment would be due under the primary contract.

WHAT IS FRAUD IN THE TRANSACTION?

In *Sztejn v. Henry Schroeder Banking Corporation,* the Court first established the exception to the independence principle. It held that the issuer-bank is permitted to dishonor the beneficiary's demand for payment if there has been "fraud in the transaction". In *Sztejn,* the customer-purchaser obtained an irrevocable letter of credit to buy bristles from an Indian corporation which required the issuing bank to pay the beneficiary-seller upon presentation of an invoice and a bill of lading. The beneficiary sent trash on a ship, procured the required documents and requested payment. The Court then enjoined payment of the letter of credit:

Transea filled the fifty crates with cow hair, other worthless material and rubbish with the intent to simulate genuine merchandise and defraud the plaintiff.

The Court concluded that the issuer is permitted to dishonor the beneficiary's demand for payment if there has been "fraud in the transaction."

The "fraud in the transaction" exception set forth in *Sztejn* was later codified in Section 5-114 of the Uniform Commercial Code. This section allows the issuer to dishonor in the situations of either demonstrated false or forged documents or where there has been "fraud in the transaction". Moreover, Section 5-114(2)(b) provides that an "issuer acting in good faith may honor the draft or payment" . . . "but a court of appropriate jurisdiction may enjoin such honor." However, neither the statute nor the official commentary on the U.C.C. section indicates the standard which the court should apply in determining whether to grant injunctive relief. Courts are faced with two competing principles: preserving the utility of the commercial letter of credit in the flow of commerce, and discouraging fraud by preventing a dishonest beneficiary from profiting at the expense of an innocent buyer. However, courts have given the "fraud in the transaction" exception a narrow reading, allowing its application to cases of "egregious fraud" on the part of the beneficiary.

It is not quite clear what exactly constitutes "egregious fraud" for the purposes of Section 5-114. The Court attempted to define more clearly this concept of fraud in *Intraworld Industries Inc. v. Girard Trust Bank*. In *Intraworld*, a standby letter of credit was issued to secure lease rental payments a year in advance. Intraworld, the lessee, claimed that there was fraud not apparent on the face of the documents, and sought to enjoin honor under U.C.C. 5-114(2) (b). The Court looked to the independence of the issuer's engagement and to the *Sztejn* case to determine whether an injunction should be issued. Thereby, the Court established a two-prong test to justify an injunction. First, the fraud must be that of the beneficiary of the credit; and second, the fraud must be of such a nature to have "vitiated" the entire transaction.

Courts have been in an agreement about the first prong of the *Intraworld* test—that the fraud must be that of the beneficiary. Courts, however, are still not in agreement about what type of fraud "vitiates" the entire transaction. Therefore, this is the issue that remains to be resolved: When determining whether there is fraud in the transaction, does the court look beyond the letter of credit to the underlying contract between the customer-buyer account party and the beneficiary.

Courts and commentators assert that the exception to the independence rule set out in *Sztejn* should be limited to cases where the beneficiary-seller committed active fraud rendering the document fraudulent. This theory limits the fraud that merits dishonor or injunction of the letter of credit to fraud in the documents themselves and not in the underlying transaction. The fraudulent document exception was first set forth in *Old Colony Trust Co. v. Lawyer's Title and Trust Co.*, which held that an issuer of credit cannot be called upon to recognize false documents or documents that are noncomplying as the result of fraud, as "falsified documents are the same as no documents at all."

By definition, "fraud in the documents" means that the documents which represent conforming merchandise that has been shipped are themselves fraudulent. In *O'Grady v. First Union National Bank*, the Court defined a fraudulent document for the purposes of U.C.C. 5-114: "such a document would be one that is completely forged or drawn up without any underlying basis in fact, one that is but partly spurious or a document which has been materially altered." In addition, the Court held that documents were fraudulent in *Voest-Alpine International Corp. v. Chase Manhattan Bank* stating " . . . deliberately backdated documents falsely indicating compliance with the terms of the credit" in order to have the documents accepted is outright fraud.

On the other hand, other experts in letter of credit law argue that "fraud in the transaction" is often mislabeled "fraud in the documents." Arguably, only documents that are initially genuine and later altered can be considered fraudulent. However, it is asserted that since this was not the case in *Sztejn*, and the Court still honored an injunction, the real source of fraud to justify enjoining a letter of credit must be in the underlying transaction. It is further argued that even if *Sztejn* stands only for the proposition that an injunction should be issued for fraudulent documents, a vast majority of cases have used it to support an injunction for fraud in the underlying transaction.

In *Dynamics Corp. v. Citizens & Southern Bank*, the account party sought to enjoin payment of a standby letter of credit arguing that the certificate which the foreign beneficiary had presented fraudulently stated the plaintiff had not performed, when performance had in fact occurred. The Court upheld the independence principle stating: "This Court has no business making an ultimate adjudication regarding compliance with the provisions of the underlying sale agreement." Thus, the Court pointed out that the decision of whether or not the applicant had breached the contract would not be the same decision as to the obligation to pay under the letter of credit. Yet, although the Court recognized the "independence rule," it granted the injunction arguing the beneficiary should not be allowed "to take unconscientious advantage of the situation and run off with the plaintiff's money". The case demonstrates a court's struggle to reach an outcome without adequate guidelines to specify what constitutes "fraud" in the context of a letter of credit transaction. Moreover, the Court in *Dynamics* made no attempt to set any guidelines.

In *United States v. Cambridge Sporting Goods* the New York Court held that a Pakistani company's shipment of "old unpadded and mildewed boxing gloves" rather than new boxing gloves constituted "fraud in the transaction" sufficient to satisfy the requirement of U.C.C. 5-114(2). The Court acknowledged that it was difficult to draw a bright line between cases involving "breach of warranty and outright fraudulent practices", and that a flexible standard was to be applied depending on the individual circumstances of each individual case.

The *Sztejn* and *Cambridge* cases are equally applicable to standby letters of credit. As discussed above, standby letters of credit are used to secure payment of goods. When standby letters of credit are used, the line between a genuine dispute and fraud that "vitiates" the transaction becomes even more difficult. It is important to identify the true source of fraud, especially in standby letter of credit cases because in a standby letter of credit there are few if any documents and thus documentary fraud is rare. It is argued that incorrectly reasoned documentary letter of credit cases fail to provide the precedent for enjoining payment in the underlying transaction in a standby letter of credit. This is so since injunctions have been honored in the standby letter of credit context merely to avoid unjust enrichment. Due to the unique character of the standby letter of credit, some authors have gone as far as to suggest a separate standard for standby letters of credit:

> The fraud exception should be applied whenever, given the conduct of the parties within the context of the underlying contract, there exists a high probability that payment to the beneficiary under the credit would result in unjust enrichment of the beneficiary at the expense of the customer.

The proposed standard for a standby letter of credit is the result of those cases in which the court honored an injunction as the result of the beneficiary demanding payment even when the customer-buyer had not at all breached the bargain in fact.

For example, cases involving the Islamic Government of Iran generated controversy over the proper application of the "fraud in the transaction" exception to the standby letter of credit. Early attempts to enjoin payment under the letter of credit were often met with strong judicial affirmation of the independence rule. However, courts and commentators pointed out the necessity of expanding the fraud in the transaction exception beyond the limit within which it was employed. Judicial criticism focused mainly on the fact that the independence rule would allow Iran to obtain payment even though the American companies were innocent of wrongdoing and, moreover, that there would be no meaningful remedy.

In *Harris v. National Iranian Radio and Television*, the Eleventh Circuit stated: " . . . unfortunately, one unsettled point in the law is what constitutes fraud in the transaction, in other words, what degree of objective performance justifies enjoining a letter of credit transaction in violation of the independence principle." The Court further held that granting an injunction was not contrary to the public interest of maintaining the market integrity and commercial utility of the letter of credit. However, the Court pointed out:

> That does not mean that the fraud exception should be restricted to allegations involving fraud in the underlying transaction, nor does it mean that the exception should be restricted to protecting the buyer in the framework of the traditional letter of credit.

The Court followed the *Cambridge* decision, asserting that the fraud exception is flexible and may be invoked on behalf of a customer seeking to prevent a beneficiary from fraudulently utilizing a standby letter of credit. In *Harris*, the corporation was unable to meet its fuel shipment dates to the Iranian purchaser. The Court found that the contract broke down, in this case, as a result of problems due to the Iranian Asset Control Regulation. Thus, the problem was attributed to the Iranian revolution rather than any fault of the Harris Corporation.

In *Itek Corp. v. First National Bank of Boston*, an injunction was granted against defendant First National Bank honoring the Iranian Bank Melli's demands under a letter of credit. The bank recognized that Itek's efforts to recover money legally owed by instituting a suit in the Iranian courts was futile, and thus no other remedy was available. *Itek* was also a unique case in that it fully summarized, as set forth below, the issues surrounding the letter of credit instruments. The *Itek* Court invoked these principles and determined that the account party had established that the beneficiary had no "plausible or colorable basis under the contract to call for payments of the letters."

In summary, *Intraworld* established the principle that letters of credit are independent of the underlying transaction. Consequently, *KMC International v. Chase Manhattan Bank* set forth that examining the rights and wrongs of a contract dispute to determine if a letter of credit should be paid "risks depriving its beneficiary of the very advantage for which he has bargained, namely that the dispute would be resolved while he is in the possession of the money." Nonetheless, *Harris* supported that the need for the fraud exception to the independence principle is apparent. Courts have not been hesitant to examine the documents that the credit calls for in order to ascertain fraud. *Sztejn* supports that courts have enjoined and will enjoin payment where there is fraud in the underlying transaction. The U.C.C. itself adopted the fraud exception and "recognizes the unfairness of allowing a beneficiary to call a letter of credit under circumstances where the underlying contract plainly shows that he is not to do so." Thus, courts have allowed "fraud in the transaction" exception when it so vitiates the entire transaction, or when "the legitimate purposes of the independence of the issuer's obligation would no longer be served."

THE LETTER OF CREDIT: WHY IS IT UNIQUE?

The adequacy of the U.C.C.'s fraud exceptions has created legitimate controversy. The above cases provide a compelling illustration of the need for further
clarification of the type of fraud which warrants injunctive relief. The courts face
this dilemma in response to the unique character that the letter of credit has over
other types of devices commonly used to allocate risks in commercial transactions.

The letter of credit can be compared to the performance bond. Both devices
protect and allocate risks in the case of nonperformance of another party's contractual obligations. However, unlike an issuer of a letter of credit, the surety of a
performance bond is not obligated to pay the buyer automatically upon the
buyer's claim that the seller has not performed. The surety may first explore the
validity of the allegation. If the surety finds that the seller has fulfilled the obligations under the contract, then the surety does not have to pay the buyer. All
defenses that are available to the principal against the buyer are also available to
be used by the surety against the buyer. Moreover, the surety has the right to
"actively intervene to ensure performance," for example, "by demanding that the
seller remedy the defect by completing the contract itself."

Comparatively, the standby letter of credit specifically allows the beneficiary to be paid on demand that the customer has defaulted except where the
fraud in the transaction exception applies. The issuer is not allowed to refuse payment based on the assertion that the request or demand is false or on the existence of any defenses the customer may have on the underlying contract.

Arguably, the difference between the standby letter of credit and the performance bond renders the standby letter of credit more attractive to the beneficiary for several reasons. First, under the standby letter of credit the beneficiary is
guaranteed prompt payment as the payment is not delayed by the inspection of
the underlying contract between the customer and the beneficiary. Moreover, a
standby letter of credit is often used in a wider and greater number of transactions. Finally, because the bank is merely responsible for evaluating the documents presented on demand and not for investigating the underlying contract, the
administrative expenses are lower as the bank avoids additional expenses of
monitoring the underlying contract. For these reasons the risk is much lower that
the issuer will be engaged in litigation with the beneficiary regarding the letter of
credit, as opposed to a performance bond where that risk is much greater. Finally,
a standby letter of credit is issued by a banking institution and thus is financially
insured. A performance bond cannot be issued by a bank; rather, it is issued by a
surety company.

The advantages of a letter of credit for the seller are numerous. When the
beneficiary-seller generates all the required documents, she can receive pay-

ment. Moreover, Section 5-114 requires no notice to the customer-buyer before payment, and thus the injunction remedy available in the fraud in the transaction exception is almost futile. This makes the letter of credit like having the cash in hand.

Caveat Nota: In summary, unlike a performance bond, a letter of credit gives the bank no control on the underlying contract and the bank has no right to refuse payment based on an opinion of the customer as to a false assertion. In this sense, the letter of credit has been viewed as similar to a cash deposit.

THE OPPOSING VIEWS

Some writers, therefore, contend that the letter of credit customer should be protected from fraud in the transaction despite the unique character of the independence rule that underpins the letter of credit. One commentator contends that a narrow exception to the independence rule has resulted in letters of credit being treated like "gold bullion." That is, the independence principle treats the letter of credit as something of intrinsic value, rather than a commercial instrument subject to statutory defenses. The commentator further argues that treating letters of credit as "gold bullion" undermines the policy decisions, as Section 5-114 was drafted specifically to provide protection to the customer.

It is further argued that there are competing interests of the commercial utility of the letter of credit, in light of an interest to preserve the commercial expectation of honesty and fair dealing. Thus, the U.C.C. supports that the independence principle must be subordinate to the strong policy against fraud both in the documents and in the underlying transaction. This is particularly so in a standby letter of credit, since a simple demand is the only document required for payment—the documents do not protect the customer as they do in a typical documentary letter of credit.

Therefore, a narrow protection of fraudulent documents does little for the standby customer who is not really looking to the documents for protection. Moreover, a narrow view requires the bank to pay when the customer may not even have destroyed the bargain in fact by breach or insolvency.

On the other hand, courts and commentators argue that a broad reliance on the fraud in the transaction exception impairs the independence of the issuers undertaking, "converts the standby letter of credit into a surety contract, and compromises the commercial utility of the credit device." Therefore, proponents of an absolute rule of independence seek a narrow definition of fraud in the transaction. Henry Harfield states:

> "an almost irresistible temptation is thus presented to rely on expansive interpretations of the word "fraud"; however relevant these inter-

> pretations are in a proceeding to surcharge a testamentary trustee, they are disastrously inappropriate in a letter of credit transaction."

Harfield has also pointed out the potential adverse affect on the ability of the United States to compete in foreign markets because " . . . there can be little doubt that an expansive reading and permissive application of Section 5-114(2)(b) could destroy the acceptability of credits established by United States issuers." Additionally, the issuer acts at its own peril when it opts to dishonor in reliance on the assertion of fraud by the customer account party.

It is further argued that a strict application of the "independence rule" is more in line with the parties' expectations because the parties who use letters of credit are well aware of the risks posed by the use. Moreover, commentators argue the beneficiary actually benefits from a strict application of the independence rule since the issuing bank charges a smaller fee due to less administration costs and no litigation threats. Furthermore, the beneficiary is assured the customer will not attempt to hold up payment; and finally, the beneficiary is protected from the bank mistakenly enjoining payment by finding its honest demand was made in bad faith.

The customer also benefits. First, the argument asserts that a customer does not agree to the use of the letter of credit in ignorance of the consequences or that the seller-beneficiary has superior bargaining power as a result of the transaction. Also, a customer-buyer is usually compensated for the risk inherent in the letter of credit which is posed by the "independence" of the instrument since it is a less expensive risk allocation device. In the case of a standby letter of credit, if the risk of an unjustified demand for payment by the beneficiary-seller is great, the customer could require some off-setting compensation for the risk. Of course, if the cost is too great to assure there would be no unjustified demand, this could make entering into the transaction undesirable for the beneficiary-seller.

Therefore, commentators contend that, logically, the letter of credit is used only when the customer has a high degree of confidence that the beneficiary would not make an unjustified demand for payment. Arguably, the reduced cost of the letter of credit, the certainty of operation, and the beneficiary's trustworthiness make the overall transaction much more beneficial and less costly than other risk allocation devices.

Finally, these commentators assert that if there is a broad definition of fraud, the risks inherent in the letter of credit will be more difficult to evaluate. Thus, the very risk shifting aspect that makes the letter of credit an assured predictable form of credit will be undermined by an uncertainty about how a court will decide in any one of the numerous situations in which demand for payment might be made. This destroys the very essence of the letter of credi—predictability. There is also a risk that payment will be frozen everytime a dispute arises, until the dispute between the parties is resolved. As a result, the cost of the letter of credit will increase because the bank is not insulated from the threats of litigation. Proponents of the narrow exception contend that although it may seem severe, customers may be better off dealing with the risks than using an alternative and more costly payment device.

As summarized by one Court:

> "One of the expected advantages and essential purposes of the letter of credit is that the beneficiary will be able to rely on assured prompt payment from a solvent party; necessarily, a part of this expectation of ready payment is that there will be a minimum of litigation and judicial interference, and this is one of the reasons for the value of the letter of credit device in financial transactions."

Finally, the commentator points out that it is important to note that the entities which use letter of credits are usually large corporations or governmental entities with access to resources that put them in a position to respond to the risks involved. Because of the sophistication involved, a strict rule of independence allows these players to reallocate risks according to the need of the particular transaction.

PROPOSED REVISIONS

The controversy regarding the "independence" principle of the letter of credit has caused courts throughout the country to struggle when it comes to determining the type of fraud necessary for the basis of injunction under Section 5-114 of the U.C.C. Many of these courts have broadly defined fraud. Other jurisdictions, in fear of complete erosion of the independence principle, have abolished the exception allowing injunctions for letters of credit in cases of fraud.

California is among those jurisdictions that deleted this exception to the independence principle stating:

> By giving courts the power to enjoin the honor of drafts drawn upon documents which appear to be regular on their face, the commissioners of Uniform State Laws do violence to one of the basic concepts of the letter of credit, to wit, that the letter of credit agreement is independent of the underlying contract.

In light of the strict adherence to the independence principle, it is noted that California would be willing to change its strict standard in lieu of a clarification of the proper standard in a revised Article 5 so as to assure courts of a proper understanding of the "fraud in the transaction" defense.

Therefore, any project to revise Article 5 or the official commentary must contain a definition of fraud. There is too much variance among the courts in this area resulting in uncertainty and confusion. The ABA Task Force on the study of the U.C.C. has deemed the Article 5 revision in this area to be one of the major issues in the current revision process. Alternative definitions of fraud have been proposed, with the goal to clarify and restrict the circumstances in which fraud can be raised as a defense to dishonor a letter of credit.

The Revision of Article 5 is a project of the American Law Institute and the National Conference of Commissioners on Uniform State Laws. Commentators agree that distinguishing a fraudulent transaction from a legitimate contract dispute is difficult. However, it is also agreed that an attempt must be made either in the statute or the official commentary to 5-114(2).

The proposed alternative definitions of fraud include:

"Fraud" means a presentment by one who has no colorable basis to be entitled to have the presentment honored.

or

"Fraud" means:

(i) the presentment of a document that is forged or materially altered.

or

(ii) presentment by one who has no colorable basis to be entitled to have the presentment honored.

or

"Fraud" means the presentment of a forged or materially fraudulent document by one who knows of the forgery or fraud.

or

"Fraud" means the presentment of a document that is forged or materially fraudulent.

or

Omit this subsection.

Despite attempts to achieve uniformity, it cannot be assured that stricter standards would promote the independence principle. The revisors of Article 5 would include language in the official comment to clarify that "fraud in the underlying transaction does not constitute fraud in the credit transaction." However, it has become apparent that such a distinction between the two transactions is not always possible. As discussed above, courts often confuse fraud in the transaction with fraud in the underlying documents. This is particularly evident in *Sztejn*, where the Court declared the documents were false because they did not properly define the fraudulently substituted goods. *Sztejn* suggests that fraud in the documentary transaction is the result of fraud in the underlying transaction. Commentators argue that there cannot be fraud in one place and not in the other: "once there is fraud in the underlying transaction, there is necessarily fraud in the credit documentation."

The need for uniformity in the development of the definition of fraud in a letter of credit transaction is clear. Consideration should be given to any policy regarding the formation of standards for traditional documentary and standby letters of credit. The Task Force contends that there may be different standards of documentary letters of credit as opposed to standby letters of credit. For example, in a documentary letter of credit, the question may be: Would the purpose of the underlying transaction be rendered virtually without value? In a standby letter of credit the question may be: Is there any colorable basis for the drawing?

Furthermore, proponents of reform contend that the real challenge the revisors face is to properly develop objective standards to determine whether the beneficiary has acted or performed adequately. The letter of credit is a unique instrument in the context of trade. The revisors recognize the challenging task of preserving the utility of the letter of credit, while at the same time encouraging the policy of the U.C.C. against fraud. If the Task Force fails to provide sufficient guidelines for courts to follow in cases of fraud, it could destroy the very element that distinguishes the letter of credit—the independence of the credit from the underlying contract.

CONCLUSION

In conclusion, although success of the U.C.C. is predicated on the ability to achieve uniformity among the different states, it is clear that lack of uniformity with regard to some aspects of the U.C.C. may not be so bad. This is evidenced by the nonuniformity that currently exists as to the application of Section 5-114 allowing injunctions against fraudulent draws on letters of credit.

It is apparent that allowing such variations among the different states in the application of Section 5-114 may be less problematic. Whether or not a state adopts the exception to the independence rule set out in Section 5-114(2) (b), allowing a customer in a letter of credit transaction to enjoin payment in the event of fraud, does not affect the letter's basic operation. Since the independence of the letter of credit governs its operation, a state's failure to adopt this exception to the independence rule in 5-114(2) (b) does not diminish the normal operation of the letter of credit, but rather assures the uniqueness and utility of the device.

As discussed above, the letter of credit is basically the buyer's bargain with the seller allowing the seller to maintain possession of funds in the period of time during which a legitimate dispute exists on the underlying contract. Maintaining this element of "independence" is essential to facilitate trade. Therefore, a clear and precise definition of fraud should be set forth in the statute for those states that do adopt the exception to the independence rule set forth in 5-114(2) (b). If courts do not have any guidance, they will continue to turn legitimate contract disputes into cases of "fraud." Ultimately, as the element of "independence" is diminished, the letter of credit will exist only in theory. In other words, unless courts recognize its "independence," the letter of credit will be no different from any other risk-allocation payment device.

For further information on this topic, reference may be made to the following sources:

James E. Byrne, U.C.C. *Article 5 Symposium: The Revision of U. C. C. Article 5: A Strategy for Success,* 56 BROOK L. REV. 13 (1990).

John F. Dolan, *THE LAW OF LETTERS OF CREDIT* sec. 7.04 (3) (b) (2d ed. 1991).

B. Kozolchyk, *Commercial Letters of Credit in the Americas* 394, 395, sec. 18.04 [1] (1966).

J. White and R. Summers, *UNIFORM COMMERCIAL CODE, PRACTITIONER TREATISE SERIES,* Vol. 3, (4th ed. 1995) ch. 26, p. 105.

Sztejn v. Henry Schroeder Banking Corporation, 177 Misc. 719, 31 N.Y.S. 2d 631 (Sup Ct. 1941).

Henry Harfield, *Enjoining Letter of Credit Transactions,* 95 BANKING L.J. 596, 599 (1978).

SECTION E

PERFORMANCE OF THE CONTRACT

XXIII

Delivery, Acceptance, and Payment

Previous chapters of this text have discussed the legal principles involved in the formation of a contract with the supplier and the terms of that contract. Our goal has been to demonstrate how to create a valid and enforceable contract, one that is sufficient to withstand the rigors of a courtroom battle, should such a battle arise. The major objective of the purchasing function is not to win a lawsuit in a courtroom but to fulfill the purchasing requirements of one's company by getting delivery of the goods we have ordered. *Performance* by the supplier is our real goal, and this chapter devotes attention to that objective.

PERFORMANCE DEFINED

Performance of a contract is the satisfaction of the duties each party assumed when the contract was formed. Performance of a contract to purchase goods is described succinctly by Section 2-301 of the Code.

> The obligation of the seller is to transfer and deliver and that of the buyer is to accept and pay in accordance with the contract.

> These duties are made interdependent by Section 2-507.

> (1) Tender of delivery is a condition to the buyer's duty to accept the goods and, unless otherwise agreed, to his duty to pay for them. Tender entitles the seller to acceptance of the goods by the buyer and to payment according to the contract.

Thus, the required performance of the buyer to accept and pay for the goods, is in most instances, dependent upon the seller tendering delivery of the goods. We say "in most instances" because the contract might call for partial or full payment by the buyer in advance of the seller's tender. Then the buyer must first perform the act of payment before the supplier must tender delivery. Note also that in situations where the goods are shipped C.I.F., C.&F., or C.O.D., the buyer has the duty to pay for the goods against the documents or upon demand before there is an opportunity to accept and inspect the goods. However, in these instances the supplier has already completed his performance by delivery of the goods to the carrier.

The seller's duty of tender of delivery is defined in Section 2-503:

> (1) Tender of delivery requires that the seller put and hold conforming goods at the buyer's disposition and give the buyer any notice reasonably necessary to enable him to take delivery.

The section goes on to state that such tender must be at a reasonable hour, and that the goods must be kept available for the buyer for a reasonable period of time. The important words are "conforming goods." The seller must tender goods that *conform* to the contract if the buyer is to be expected to perform the final act of payment. Payment more often follows acceptance of the goods by the buyer, but it could be after delivery and before acceptance.

The duties of the buyer in the performance of a contract are as follows:

1. The duty to take legal custody of the goods

2. The duty of physical receipt of the goods

3. The duty of acceptance of the goods

4. The duty of payment for the goods

These duties are not listed in any chronological order. Each duty will occur in every purchase. Payment may be required in advance of or simultaneously with the receipt of the goods. Acceptance of the goods may be made at the seller's premises before being delivered to the buyer. Taking legal custody could occur simultaneously with the receipt of the goods.

THE STEPS IN PERFORMANCE

Taking Legal Custody of the Goods

The buyer takes legal custody of the goods when the risk of loss is transferred from the seller. This might occur at the seller's place of business, at a warehouse, when delivered to a carrier, when unloaded from a vessel, or when received at the buyer's place of business. Taking legal custody, or title, to the goods is an intangible legal act. It is a transfer of the rights of ownership to the buyer, and is governed by the delivery terms.

Physical Receipt of the Goods

Physical receipt occurs when the goods arrive at the buyer's receiving dock. It may coincide with the act of taking legal custody of the goods, as in a destination shipment contract.

Acceptance of the Goods

The acceptance is another intangible legal act. It is said to occur in one of the following three circumstances:

1. The buyer notifies the seller that the goods are accepted.

2. The buyer treats the goods as his own, such as by using them or putting them into production.

3. A reasonable period of time has lapsed; the seller may therefore assume that the buyer has accepted the goods.

Payment for the goods after delivery may be evidence that the buyer has accepted the goods, but it is not conclusive evidence. Payment could be made even before the buyer has laid eyes on the goods. Payment as an act of acceptance is not absolute.

Payment for the Goods

The buyer must pay the supplier for the goods before his obligations under the contract are satisfied.

THE BUYER'S RESPONSIBILITIES IN PERFORMANCE

A purchasing officer is said not to be relieved of the responsibility for a purchase until the goods have been received, inspected, proven to be satisfactory, and the supplier has been paid the agreed-to amount. Most of these acts occur outside the purchasing office and are performed by personnel over whom the buyer may have little or no control. Nonetheless, because these activities directly affect the performance obligations of the contract that the purchasing officer executed on behalf of his or her organization, a continuing interest must be retained while these functions are being performed. The legal acts of performance are related to the legal relationships established when the contract was negotiated. The purchasing officer must be certain that both the supplier and his or her own organization perform properly. When a purchase goes awry, it is the purchasing officer who is called upon to correct the deficiency, wherever it occurs—in quantity, in quality, in service, or in price. The law relating to each of these performance activities must be followed.

Receipt of the Goods from the Carrier

The first step in accepting delivery of the goods from a carrier is to observe the general condition of the boxes or crates in which they were shipped, or the goods themselves, if not packaged. This preliminary inspection should be made before giving a receipt to the delivering agent. A "clean receipt" (a receiving signature on the dray ticket or other receiving form without any comment on the condition of the package) tells one and all that the package was received in apparent good condition. The delivery person is entitled to a clean receipt only if that is true.

On the other hand, if a part of the package is torn or dented, or if the package shows signs of having been exposed to water, that fact should be shown on the delivery receipt form. It is helpful if the driver of the delivery vehicle signs such damage notation to attest to your receiving person's observation of condition. It adds to your protection, if there is a damaged package, to unpack while the driver is present. Both your staff member and the driver can then verify if there is damage or not. Sometimes it is difficult to convince the driver to wait until it is unpacked and inspected. The driver's duty to his employer is to get a clean receipt and get out as quickly as possible. Some drivers can be convinced to wait for unpacking because if there is no apparent damage the interests of the carrier will have been well served.

Goods received in a damaged condition become a claim against the carrier because generally the carrier is an insuror of the goods while in its possession, acts of God and a common enemy excepted. The carrier has the right to go back to the shipper for indemnity if damage during shipment occurred because the goods were poorly packed. Therefore it is mandatory that your receiving personnel retain all of the packaging until the carrier has had the opportunity to inspect it. Section 2-515 of the code requires the buyer to preserve evidence of goods involved in a quality dispute; so retention of the complete package is advisable.

The actual preparation and filing of the claim report is the responsibility of the party who had the risk of loss while the goods were in transit. Thus, if they were shipped under a destination contract, the supplier has the duty to file the claim. If the delivery term was a shipment contract, it is the buyer's duty.

Inspection of the Goods

Once the apparent good condition of the packages delivered is determined, the next step for the buyer is to inspect the goods received for quality characteristics.

This is one of the most important functions that must be performed in any purchase. The purchasing officer expects the inspection to answer such questions as: Did the supplier fulfill all of his commitments to us? Were my specifications met? Did we get what we ordered? Is the entire shipment of uniform quality? If it was an equipment purchase: Does the item perform as specified and warranted? Answers to these and similar questions will enable the purchasing officer to decide whether the goods will be accepted.

The right to inspect goods delivered from a supplier is the inalienable right of every buyer. It is almost impossible to imagine a situation where the buyer does not have inspection rights. The place of inspection may vary among transactions, so too may the time of inspection. But somewhere and sometime before the buyer is required to take the legal step of accepting the goods there must be the opportunity to inspect. Section 2-513(1) of the Code states:

> (1) Unless otherwise agreed and subject to subsection (3) where goods are tendered or delivered or identified to the contract for sale, the buyer has a right before payment or acceptance to inspect them at any reasonable place and time and in any reasonable manner. When the seller is required or authorized to send the goods to the buyer, the inspection may be after their arrival.

The caveat at the beginning of the section: "Unless otherwise agreed and subject to subsection (3)" refers primarily to the fact that the terms of the contract may require payment before inspection. In subsection (3) of 2-513, for example, C.I.F. and C.O.C. sales are mentioned. These are delivery terms that do not permit inspection of the goods before payment is made. In such instances inspection is postponed until after payment has been made to the delivery agent or against documents. The buyer agrees to this postponement when he agrees to the delivery terms. However, the buyer cannot be asked to agree to a term specifying that acceptance must occur before the opportunity is given to inspect the goods.

Section 2-512 makes it quite clear that when the buyer has agreed to a delivery term that requires payment before inspection, that duty is absolute:

> (1) Where the contract requires payment before inspection nonconformity of the goods does not excuse the buyer from so making payment unless (a) the nonconformity appears without inspection.

But subsection (2) of 2-512 strongly states the buyer's right of inspection after payment:

> (2) Payment pursuant to subsection (1) does not constitute an acceptance of the goods or impair the buyer's right to inspect or suggest any of his remedies.

This confirms the buyer's right to inspection before the election to accept the goods is made.

Section 2-513(1) recognizes the conventional place of inspection to be at the buyer's location after delivery has been made. Actually, the buyer's right to inspection accrues when the seller tenders delivery (as at the supplier's place of business, in certain transactions) or when the seller appropriates or identifies the goods from a larger lot to the contract. As a matter of fact, the Code has a provision (Section 2-501) that gives the buyer an insurable interest in the goods when they are identified (designated, selected or marked) to the contract.

The time for inspection can range from when the goods are first identified to the contract to as late as a reasonable time after delivery. Even when the buyer has the right under the contract to inspect before payment but pays first, there still remains the right to inspect. As 2-513(1) states "The buyer has a right . . . to inspect . . . at any reasonable place and time and in any reasonable manner." But the buyer should be cautioned to make inspection and acceptance more promptly if payment is made voluntarily before the due date. Costs of inspection must be borne by the buyer. These costs may be recovered from the supplier if the goods do not conform and are rejected.

***Nota Bene* to the Purchasing Officer.** Inspection of the goods is the best opportunity you have to establish the fact that your supplier performed properly by delivering the proper quantity of the product in the right quality. Care must be taken in your inspection to discover any possible defects in the goods. Your rights vis-a-vis the supplier's are never as strong as they are prior to acceptance of goods. Based upon the results of inspection, you make the decision to accept or to reject the goods. Once you accept them you take one giant legal step forward in releasing the seller of his obligations to you. All is not lost if subsequent defects in the goods are discovered. But you have a more difficult task in establishing such failure, and your available remedies are somewhat limited. The opportune time to flag a defect in the goods is before acceptance. Proper and thorough inspection is rewarding to the purchasing officer and to his or her company.

The Acceptance Decision

The inspection results tell the buyer whether to accept or reject the goods. We will take the positive approach and assume that the goods received have been determined to be *conforming* to the contract. We will first review acceptance procedures and then follow with the procedure to follow to reject goods, if such is necessary.

The Official Comment to Section 2-606 defines acceptance by saying it "means that the buyer, pursuant to the contract, takes particular goods which have been appropriated to the contract as his own." Acceptance is the act the seller is entitled to if he has delivered conforming goods.

Acceptance may be made by the buyer in words, by action, or in silence when it is time to speak. Payment after receipt of the goods is one evidence of the possibility of acceptance, but as indicated previously it is never conclusive evidence. Section 2-606(1) states the following as to what constitutes acceptance of goods:

> (1) Acceptance of goods occurs when the buyer
>
>> (a) after a reasonable opportunity to inspect the goods signifies to the seller that the goods are conforming or that he will take or retain them in spite of their nonconformity; or
>>
>> (b) fails to make an effective rejection (subsection (1) of Section 2-602), but such acceptance does not occur until the buyer has had a reasonable opportunity to inspect them; or
>>
>> (c) does any act inconsistent with the seller's ownership.

In day-to-day purchasing operations items (b) and (c) are the commonly practiced methods of acceptance, along with payment. Once a supplier delivers what he considers to be conforming goods, he sits back and waits to hear if any complaints are forthcoming from his customer. When a check for payment arrives, he can take heart that things are moving along. Each day that passes without a complaint is one less day that the customer has to complain within a reasonable time. It would be nice if that supplier had something more definite to go on to be assured that the important act of acceptance had occurred, than the passage of a "reasonable time" but such is not the case. The supplier's only solace is that the continued silence of the buyer works in his favor.

The buyer, however, has strong pressure to notify the supplier promptly if the goods are nonconforming. Section 2-607 applies this pressure to the buyer under the title "Effect of Acceptance."

> (1) The buyer must pay at the contract rate for any goods accepted.
>
> (2) Acceptance of goods by the buyer precludes rejection of the goods accepted and if made with knowledge of a nonconformity cannot be revoked because of it unless the acceptance was on the reasonable assumption that the nonconformity would be seasonably cured but acceptance does not of itself impair any other remedy provided by this Article for nonconformity.
>
> (3) Where a tender has been accepted
>
>> (a) The buyer must within a reasonable time after he discovers or should have discovered any breach notify the seller of breach or be barred from any remedy;
>
> (4) The burden is on the buyer to establish any breach with respect to the goods accepted.

Subsection (1) applies only if payment has not already been made. Subsection (2) is the pressure applied to the buyer by Section 2-607. Once the goods are accepted by the buyer, subsection (2) prevents rejection of the goods at a later time. The buyer wanting to reject the goods subsequently must turn to "revocation of acceptance" which will be discussed shortly. Suffice it to say here that for the buyer to gain the right to *revoke* acceptance the nature of the breach must be more damaging than it would have to be to *reject* the goods originally. The Code has adopted what has been known through the years as the *perfect tender* rule. This rule requires the seller's tender of goods to meet the contract requirements exactly. Any variation, however slight, gives the buyer the right to reject the goods offered. This is to be distinguished from another rule, which had some credence prior to the code, known as *substantial performance*. Under the substantial-performance approach, the goods tendered or delivered did not have to be perfect to qualify as conforming goods. Minor defects were acceptable and would not give the right to reject.

The code takes a tougher stand once the buyer has accepted the goods. To be able to revoke acceptance, the defect in the goods must substantially impair their value to the buyer. Minor defects would not give the buyer the right to revoke acceptance, whereas the same minor defects would have supported a rejection before acceptance.

Nota Bene to the Purchasing Officer. The message here should be loud and clear: If inspection reveals any defect that could be interpreted to mean the goods do not measure up to your contract terms or standards rejection should be considered. Do not temporize. If you and your peers are uncomfortable or unhappy with what has been delivered, you should speak out before acceptance becomes a fact. Reject the goods.

REJECTION OF THE GOODS

Section 2-601 offers the buyer three options when nonconforming goods are tendered for delivery:

> if the goods or the tender of delivery fail in any respect to conform to the contract, the buyer may

(a) reject the whole; or

(b) accept the whole; or

(c) accept any commercial unit or units and reject the rest.

This section embraces the perfect tender rule. The goods may be rejected by the buyer if they *"fail in any respect to conform* to the contract." (Emphasis is the author's.) The variance of the delivered goods from the contract description does not have to be a major one to justify rejection by the buyer. All that is required is that there be a difference.

Section 2-601 allows the buyer to reject, accept, or partially reject and accept nonconforming goods. Acceptance of nonconforming goods may occur because the buyer believes the goods are usable in their condition. Therefore the buyer accepts them with the thought that a negotiation with the supplier will get a monetary allowance for the defect. The buyer has the authority granted by the Code to back up his claim for an allowance. Section 2-714 states that the buyer, when accepting nonconforming goods, may recover as damages the loss resulting from the seller's breach. The buyer does not lose a claim against the seller by accepting nonconforming goods. It is prudent, however, to notify the seller at the time of acceptance that an allowance is expected. Remedies will be discussed in the next chapter.

Reasonable Time

Code Section 2-602 details the manner in which the buyer should reject the goods:

> (1) Rejection of goods must be within a reasonable time after their delivery or tender. It is ineffective unless the buyer seasonably notifies the seller.

The fact that the rejection must be within a reasonable time is obvious. The longer the buyer remains mute, the more hopeful the supplier becomes that the goods have been accepted. Therefore the buyer should move as quickly as possible if he intends to reject the goods—not only for the supplier's benefit, but primarily to avoid having a rejection ruled *untimely* because of the passage of a reasonable period of time after delivery. At some point the seller is entitled to believe acceptance took place.

We remind you once more that the Code is not at all precise in defining *reasonable time*. Section 1-204 states: "What is a reasonable time for taking any action depends on the nature, purpose and circumstance of such action." Thus the reasonable time a purchasing officer has to reject goods may vary widely. The only sound advice that can be given is to make the rejection as expeditiously as possible.

Notice of Rejection

The second sentence in subsection (1) above should be memorized. Notice of rejection to the supplier is mandatory if the rejection is to be effective. Although the form of the notice is not specified here, it is always prudent to dispatch a written notice to the other party. This written notice should also confirm any verbal discussions. The content of the required notice is not specified in this Code section, but Section 2-605(1) imposes a severe penalty on the buyer if the notice does not state the reasons why the goods were rejected:

> (1) The buyer's failure to state in connection with rejection a particular defect which is ascertainable by reasonable inspection precludes him from relying on the unstated defect to justify rejection or to establish breach
>
> > (a) where the seller could have cured it if stated seasonably; or
> >
> > (b) between merchants when the seller has after rejection made a request in writing for a full and final statement of all defects on which the buyer proposes to rely.

The penalty herein imposed against the buyer is severe. He loses the legal justification for his action of rejection. Without this justification, the buyer could be forced to complete the contract with the goods "as is," or face an action by the seller for breach of contract. The rule is imposed because the buyer is expected to act in good faith. Concealing the reason for rejection may be construed as acting in bad faith.

We shall see shortly in the section of this chapter titled "Cure by the Seller of Defects" that the seller has a limited opportunity to cure (correct) any defect in the goods that are rejected. Obviously the seller is entitled to know why the buyer rejected them in order to be able to take corrective action. Therefore the mandatory notice of rejection should include not only a statement that the goods are being rejected but also the reason or reasons for the rejection. This statement should be written in the broadest possible language to allow subsequently discovered defects to be proven. Defects not covered by the statement cannot be used to prove rightful rejection unless such defects are concealed.

Rejected Goods That Remain in the Buyer's Possession

Subsection (2) of 2-602 continues with instructions to the buyer after rejection:

> (2) Subject to the provisions of the two following sections on rejected goods (Sections 2-603 and 2-604):
>
> > (a) after rejection any exercise of ownership by the buyer with respect to any commercial unit is wrongful against the seller; and
> >
> > (b) if the buyer has before rejection taken physical possession of goods . . . he is under a duty after rejection to hold them with reasonable care at the seller's disposition for a time sufficient to permit the seller to remove them; but
> >
> > (c) the buyer has no further obligations with regard to goods rightfully rejected.

Subsection (c) immediately above could be misleading to the merchant buyer whose rejected goods are on the receiving dock. Such a buyer, under certain circumstances, may have "further obligations with regard to goods rightfully rejected." These obligations are explained in Section 2-603. Subsection (1) of the section states:" . . . when the seller has no agent or place of business at the market of rejection a merchant buyer is under a duty after rejection of goods in his possession or control to follow any reasonable instructions received from the seller with respect to the goods and in the absence of such instructions to make reasonable efforts to sell them for the seller's account if they are perishable or threaten to decline in value speedily. Instructions are not reasonable if on demand indemnity for expenses is not forthcoming."

Any merchant buyer acting in good faith must give reasonable care to the seller's goods. Under the above subsection the merchant buyer must also follow an out-of-town seller's instructions for reshipping or storing the goods. This is one of the duties the Code imposes upon merchants in the interests of good faith in dealings with each other. The merchant buyer also has the duty to sell perishables and goods speedily declining in value (such as seasonal high-fashion clothes) if there are no instructions forthcoming from the seller. You will note that the merchant buyer has the right to demand indemnity for any expenses incurred in following the seller's instructions.

Subsection (2) of 2-603 specifies allowable expenses as those required reasonably to care for the goods and as those incurred in selling them. The buyer conducting such a sale is also entitled to a sales commission for goods sold. The subsection directs that the amount of the commission be "as is usual in the trade." If the usual commission is not known, up to a 10 percent commission is specified. The buyer is also expressly given permission to reimburse himself from the proceeds of the sale for all expenses and the commission due.

There are occasions when a supplier will not move promptly in giving instructions for the disposition of nonperishable goods. Section 2-604 suggests three alternatives for the buyer:

> Subject to the provisions of the immediately preceding section on perishables if the seller gives no instructions within a reasonable time after notification of rejection the buyer may store the goods for the seller's account or reship them to him or resell them for the seller's account with reimbursement as provided in the preceding section (Section 2-603). Such action is not acceptance or conversion.

Each of the three options mentioned above—to store, to ship back to the buyer, or to conduct a salvage sale—might pose problems if the supplier is considering abandoning the goods because the goods may not be resaleable nor reworkable in their present condition. Storage space may be available in a public warehouse, but if the supplier does not provide adequate assurances of paying the rental cost the warehouse will probably not accept them. Shipping the goods back to the supplier on a "collect" basis may be possible, but if the supplier refuses to pay the shipping costs, the buyer will be called upon to reimburse the carrier. The salvage sale may be the only answer, but the goods must have some value to make this worthwhile. In most situations the goods will have value and can be sold. The purchasing officer is advised to establish a reasonable per-day rental value of the space occupied in his receiving department or warehouse. Advise the supplier that this per-day cost is accruing and is attaching as a lien to the goods. Then arrange for the salvage sale and attempt to sell the goods on a good-faith basis. Keep an accurate accounting record of all units sold and of all expenses. Be certain to include as expenses the commissions earned and the storage costs.

The buyer's right to use any of these options is found in Section 2-604 and further in Section 2-711(3), which reads:

> (3) On rightful rejection or justifiable revocation of acceptance a buyer has a security interest in goods in his possession or control for any payments made for their price and any expenses reasonably incurred in their inspection, receipt, transportation, care and custody and may hold such goods and resell them in like manner as an aggrieved seller (Section 2-706).

Section 2-706 referred to above provides the details as to how a seller may resell goods wrongfully rejected by a buyer. It permits the seller to recover from the buyer any loss encountered in the resale. This would be determined by the contract price less the amount received on resale. Should the seller receive a price on resale in excess of the contract price, he is entitled to retain the profit. But subsection 2-706(b) limits the buyer's recovery to the amount of his security interest in the goods. The buyer must account for all resale proceeds, deduct his allowance expenses and commission and pay over any remaining funds to the seller.

The buyer's security interest in the rightfully rejected goods may consist of the following provable items:

1. Any payments made to the supplier under the contract

2. Costs of inspection

3. Costs of receiving the goods

4. Transportation of the goods if sent on a shipment contract

5. Costs of storing the goods

6. Any costs involved in caring for the goods

And, if the goods are resold, these items will be added:

7. Expenses of the sale

8. Allowable commissions to the buyer from the resale

The total of these expenses and commissions are a lien against the rejected goods. Should the goods have value, which they will have in most instances, there is a real incentive for the supplier to give prompt instructions as to their disposition. Failing to give reasonable notice to the buyer entitles the buyer to proceed with a salvage sale, as outlined above.

Two words of caution to the buyer should be given. Remember that the seller has the opportunity to cure defects on goods rejected. (This is the topic of the next section.) This deters the buyers from moving to a salvage sale too quickly. The other word of caution is that the buyer must be careful to preserve the evidence as to why the goods were rejected. The seller could later claim that the goods were conforming and should not have been rejected.

CURE BY THE SELLER OF DEFECTS IN THE GOODS

The seller, before "all is lost" after a rejection of the goods by the buyer, is given one last chance to correct any deficiencies or to replace the original goods with substitutes. The last chance is provided for in Section 2-508 of the Code entitled "Cure by Seller of Improper Tender or Delivery; Replacement."

> (1) Where any tender or delivery by the seller is rejected because nonconforming and the time for performance has not yet expired, the seller may seasonably notify the buyer of his intention to cure and may then within the contract time make a conforming delivery.

> (2) Where the buyer rejects a nonconforming tender which the seller had reasonable grounds to believe would be acceptable with or without money allowance, the seller may if he seasonably notifies the buyer have a further reasonable time to substitute a conforming tender.

This section provides two time periods for a seller to correct or "cure" a nonconforming delivery—before the time of performance has passed and after the time has passed. The seller's right to cure before the time of performance has passed is unconditional and absolute. The buyer must allow the seller this opportunity. After the time of performance has passed, the seller's right is conditional—conditional because the seller believed the goods delivered would have been acceptable. As a practical matter, most suppliers believe the goods they deliver will be acceptable to the buyer; otherwise they would not go to the effort and the expense of the delivery. Consequently, it is prudent for the buyer to plan on allowing the supplier time to cure either before or after the time of performance has passed.

The provision for cure is included in the Code for several reasons. One may believe that because the Code embraces the strict perfect tender rule in the case of rejection by the buyer, this two-barrel provision for cure by the supplier is included to ameliorate the harshness of perfect tender: The Code gives the buyer perfect tender and counterbalances it with the right of the supplier to cure. Another justification of the right to cure is that it provides the opportunity for further discussion and negotiation between the buyer and the seller. The Code is interested in having a completed transaction and abhors unresolved problems that lead to lawsuits. The seller's right to cure forces the buyer to meet with the supplier and attempt to find a solution to the problem.

The condition attached to the right to cure in subsection (2) of 2-508 is that the seller had "reasonable grounds to believe" the goods would be acceptable. The seller, to establish reasonable grounds, may not only lean on his own belief but also look to prior dealings with the buyer and with the usage of trade.

It is also interesting to note that the section even suggests "money allowance" by the seller in the event the goods do not fully conform to the contract. There are some industries and markets that provide for money allowances when there are variations in product quality, such as size and content. Such recognized variations are implicit in these contracts, and a money allowance is permitted. The Code suggests this approach for contracts in any industry where a completed contract is at stake.

The seller's two rights to cure do not last indefinitely. The unconditional right to cure expires when the time for performance of the contract has passed. The conditional right to cure in subsection (2) enables the seller to "have further reasonable time" to effect the cure. Once more this "reasonable" time limit is subject to the circumstances involved, and its only limitation is that it must not be a "manifestly unreasonable" time period.

The lack of a definite limit on time for cure raises uncertainty and problems for the buyer. The procedures for rejection of goods are inoperative until the seller's right to cure has passed. The seller could prolong this procedure by demanding written details of the cause for rejection. Then he has reasonable time to cure. All of this carries on while the buyer is anxiously waiting to be able to use the goods. The purchasing officer must be persistent in placing demands on the seller to complete the cure. He or she also must see to it that, when the seller has completed the cure, a prompt response is given to the seller regarding the acceptability of the goods as cured. If the goods continue to be unacceptable another formal notice of rejection should be given. This notice should include a statement of intention to exercise the buyer's right of rejection, to cancel the contract, to "cover" by making a similar purchase from a competitor or recover damages for breach of contract. These possible remedies are discussed in Chapter XXII.

The most potent weapon the purchasing officer has to secure prompt cure is the possibility of consequential damages arising because of delay in cure. The failure of the supplier to make the conforming goods available might cause the buyer's firm to lose a sale or to be subjected to damages for delay of delivery of its product to its customer. Such damages can accrue in alarming proportions. They are recoverable against a dilatory supplier unless a contract term precludes such damages. The threat of such liability might assist the purchasing officer in moving along the cure process. In any event, the time limit for cure by a seller does not go on indefinitely. The purchasing officer must take a firm stand and exercise the buyer's rights after the time for cure has passed.

REVOCATION OF ACCEPTANCE

We have discussed the buyer's duty to accept conforming goods and his right to reject nonconforming goods. There is one more possible situation. If a defect appears in a delivered goods after the buyer has accepted them, his recourse is to *revoke the acceptance.* This action is provided for in Section 2-608 entitled "Revocation of Acceptance in Whole or in Part."

> (1) The buyer may revoke his acceptance of a lot or commercial unit whose nonconformity substantially impairs its value to him if he has accepted it
>
>> (a) on the reasonable assumption that its nonconformity would be cured and it has not been seasonably cured;
>>
>> or
>>
>> (b) without discovery of such non-conformity if his acceptance was reasonably induced either by the difficulty of discovering before acceptance or by the seller's assurances.
>
> (2) Revocation of acceptance must occur within a reasonable time after the buyer discovers or should have discovered the ground for it and before any substantial change in condition of the goods which is not caused by their own defects. It is not effective until the buyer notifies the seller of it.
>
> (3) A buyer who so revokes has the same rights and duties with regard to the goods involved as if he has rejected them.

A revocation of acceptance gives the buyer a rougher road to travel than if the goods had been rejected when first delivered and inspected. The buyer now has a double burden: (1) He must prove the breach, and (2) he must prove that the breach substantially impairs the value of the goods to him. Minor defects or variances from the contract terms are now of no assistance. A *substantial impairment* of value is all that will prevail for the purchasing officer.

This section of the Code also places time limits and notice responsibilities on the buyer. Revocation must occur within a reasonable time after the buyer discovers the defect. It must also occur before there is any substantial change in the general condition of the goods. This rule, however, is subject to adaptation of the circumstances in any given situation. For example, if a buyer does not discover a defect in a raw material until it is processed, this change in condition of the goods sold should not affect the ability to revoke acceptance. The notice that must be given the supplier must be done as promptly as possible. The Official Comment to this Code section strongly emphasizes the need for quick notification to the supplier; so much so that the Comment suggests a relaxation of the rule requiring specific notice of the defects claimed. In other words, the strict requirement for specificity in a buyer's notice of rejection is relaxed in the case of revocation. The basic notice of revocation, though, is required before the revocation is effective.

Nothing is said about the seller's right to cure before revocation becomes effective. The Official Comment indicates that the assumption is made that in such situations revocation is the final act by the buyer after all attempts to cure by the seller have failed. This is true in most actual situations. When the problem with the goods is first discovered by the buyer, the seller will be called in to assist in solving it. The seller may make repeated attempts to cure and to assure the buyer that everything will be worked out to the buyer's satisfaction. The notice of revocation will come as the final move of surrender. The notice could come while the seller is in a repeated act of attempted cure.

Nota Bene **to the Purchasing Officer.** Do not depend upon revocation if your inspection reveals a defect. Reject and make the seller take the affirmative position of cure. Revocation is used only as a "last-ditch" measure, unless of course, the defect was only discovered at the time of revocation.

Risk of Loss to Rejected Goods

Section 2-510(1) provides that the risk of loss for goods rightfully rejected by the buyer remains on the supplier until the defect is cured or until the buyer accepts them. This applies to goods left in the buyer's possession after rejection. Of course, if the supplier repossesses the goods to correct the deficiency he has the risk of loss during that period of time.

Section 2-510(2) allocates the risk of loss for goods when the buyer rightfully revokes an acceptance. It provides that any loss not covered by the buyer's insurance falls on the supplier. This allocation of risk dates back to the time the buyer originally accepted the goods.

Wrongful Rejection or Revocation of Acceptance

The situation may arise where a buyer rejects delivered goods, or revokes an acceptance, without having the right to do so. If the seller can establish that the rejection or revocation was wrongful and not justified, the seller has a wide range of remedies available to him. These include damages, perhaps recovery of the price, and any lost profits. These and the buyer's remedies for rightful rejection or revocation are discussed in the next chapter.

RIGHT TO ADEQUATE ASSURANCE OF PERFORMANCE

Section 2-609, "Right to Adequate Assurance of Protection," covers situations such as those occurring when the credit standing of a buyer or a seller is in doubt, or when there are other circumstances present that give one party a doubt as to the other party's ability to perform his or her obligations under the contract. Section 2-609 gives the party learning of such eventuality the right to demand, in writing, adequate assurance of ability to perform from the other party. That other party must respond within 30 days giving such assurance of his ability to perform. Failure on the part of the seller to so respond gives the buyer the privilege to repudiate the contract.

Anticipatory Repudiation

Section 2-610 provides for the situation in which one party to a contract repudiates with respect to a performance not yet due. The other party to the contract is given the right to resort to any remedy for breach of contract and at the same time suspend his own performance.

Damage or Destruction to Contract Goods

Goods that are identified to a contract and are damaged or destroyed before the risk of loss passes to the buyer without the fault of either party are subject of Section 2-613. The section provides that if the loss is complete the contract is avoided. The seller is not responsible for a breach of contract nor does the buyer have any contract responsibilities. If only a portion of the goods are destroyed or damaged the buyer is given the right to inspect what remains and elect to accept or reject them.

FAILURE OF PRESUPPOSED CONDITIONS

Section 2-615 provides an exception to the seller's duty to perform his obligations under a contract. Subsection (a) reads;

(a) Delay in delivery or nondelivery in whole or in part by a seller who complies with paragraphs (b) and (c) is not a breach of his duty under a contract for sale if performance as agreed has been made impracticable by the occurrence of a contingency the nonoccurrence of which was a basic assumption on which the contract was made or by compliance in good faith with any applicable foreign or domestic governmental regulation or order whether or not it later proves to be invalid.

Should the contingency only partially impair the supplier's ability to perform, the section requires that the supplier allocate, in a fair and reasonable manner, the available supply among his contract and regular customers. It also requires the supplier to notify his customers of a delay or nondelivery. If allocation is necessary, the customers must be advised of their quotas. The law of this section is subject to the customary principles of good faith and commercial practicability. The buyer is given legal protection against the seller who overcommits his available supply to his customers and who uses this as an excuse for nonperformance. The cause for the excuse from performance must be one that was not within the contemplation of the parties at the time the contract was created. The fact of an increase in the costs of the supplier is generally not an excuse since the very purpose for which a buyer enters into a contract is to protect against a rise in the purchase price. Courts are given wide latitude in the enforcement of the provisions of this section.

PAYMENT

Payment and acceptance of the goods are the two performance obligations of the buyer. The time for payment should be and most often is negotiated at the time the contract is performed. If it is not negotiated, the Code presumes that delivery of and payment for the goods are concurrent conditions. Negotiated terms might call for advance payment, for payment on delivery under a C.O.D. sale, payment against documents, or payment at some date subsequent to delivery. Payment subsequent to delivery is made possible when credit terms are negotiated at the time of contracting. This was discussed in Chapter XIX.

Any creditor of the buyer has the right to demand payment in legal tender. *Legal tender* is that form of tender prescribed by law which the debtor can use and which the creditor must accept to satisfy a debt. Currency is the common form of legal tender. The Uniform Commercial Code continues to recognize the principle of legal tender, but it also recognizes that having large sums of currency available at all times is an aggravation and an unnecessary risk for the buyer. The Code observes that in modern business the practice is to pay invoices by check. Accordingly, subsection (2) of 2-511 provides that:

(2) Tender of payment is sufficient when made by any means or in any manner current in the ordinary course of business unless the seller demands payment in legal tender and gives any extension of time reasonably necessary to procure it.

The supplier insisting on payment in currency must wait until the buyer's representative can get to the bank during the bank's hours of doing business. "Up-front" negotiation for a credit period will save considerable aggravation.

There are many references and cross-references to various sections of the Code in this chapter. A reference guide to the Topics covered in these Code sections follows:

1. Acceptance of Goods: Section 2-606; 2-607.

2. Anticipatory Repudiation: Section 2-610.

3. Assurance of Performance: Section 2-609.

4. Buyer's Revocation of Acceptance: Section 2-608.

5. Casualty to the Goods: Section 2-613.

6. Failure of Presupposed Conditions: Section 2-615.

7. Payment: Sections 2-310; 2-511.

8. Rejection of the Goods: Sections 2-601; 2-714; 2-602; 2-605; 2-603; 2-604; 2-711; 2-706.

9. Right to Inspection: Sections 2-513(1); 2-512(1) (2).

10. Risk of Loss to Rejected Goods: Section 2-510.

11. Seller's Right to Cure Defects: Section 2-508.

SPECIAL TERMS AND CONDITIONS SUGGESTED PHRASEOLOGY

The author has a dislike for loading a purchase order with "boilerplate"—terms and conditions applicable to all purchases. In this chapter we have seen many of the performance problems that arise and that could be overcome if special terms addressed to the particular problems were included. Below are a few of the topics for which the purchasing officer might consider writing special terms. (Most are designed to counteract a specific term on the supplier's form addressed to the same problem but written in favor of the supplier. In the event of a dispute, both your term and the supplier's term would be stricken and the Code term substituted under operation of 2-207 (see Chapter XV). In these instances the substitution of the Code term would stand the purchasing officer in good stead.) The performance topic is followed by a suggested phraseology of the term.

1. A term reserving the right to recover for incidental and consequential damages in the event of a breach by the supplier: Many suppliers try to escape payment of any damages with a limitation clause. The code allows provable damages unless limited by the supplier. A purchasing officer's contra clause will clash with the supplier's term. Both would be eliminated under 2-207(3) in favor of the code presumption.

   Suggested term: Should the supplier breach any part of this purchase contract, including but not limited to the breach of any express or implied warranties, the buyer shall be entitled to recover all actual, incidental, and consequential damages arising from such breach.

2. A clause providing for a reasonable time for inspection and acceptance: Terms on many suppliers' forms attempt to reduce the number of days in which claims may be filed.

   Suggested term: The supplier agrees to give the buyer 30 days after receipt of the goods to inspect and accept goods delivered under this purchase order. The supplier further agrees that this does not preclude the buyer from revoking the acceptance after the expiration of this 30-day period for defects arising subsequent to that time.

3. A clause limiting the supplier's time for cure of a defect: It might also include a prohibition of a replacement for a defective item beyond a few number of days.

   Suggested term: Supplier's right to cure any defects or replace defective goods delivered is limited to 10 days after the supplier is notified of such defects. Any extension of that time must be agreed to in writing by the buyer.

4. A clause suggesting that you reserve the right to revoke any acceptances of delivered goods in the event they prove unsatisfactory after production or field testing: This applies only to goods that might be so tested. This is to counter the supplier's term "all sales final" and similar expressions of no continuing responsibility for their product.

   Suggested term: Same terms as item 2 above, adding to the end of the term, including those defects that may arise during production and/or field testing.

5. A clause affirmatively stating the risk of loss to rejected goods rests with

the supplier: A supplier clause may state the risk of loss remains with the buyer during attempts to cure or replace a part.

Suggested term: It is agreed the risk of loss will remain with the supplier for any properly rejected goods until accepted by the buyer after cure or replacement.

Each of these clauses should be written to fit your situation. The only limitation to the manner in which your terms are phrased is that they must be *reasonable*. An unconscionable restriction of the right of a supplier would be unenforceable. You are not permitted to eliminate a Code-given right, such as the supplier's right to cure. You may limit the time allowed, but you may not completely eliminate this right.

XXIV

Buyer's Remedies and Limitations on Remedies

It is appropriate that one of the chapters toward the end of this text discusses the last action the purchasing officer may take if all else fails to bring results in making a supplier perform his obligations in a contract. The purchasing officer works hard to make each contract result in a successful purchase—one that will satisfy the needs of the organization. Once the purchasing officer has made the decision to enter into a contract with a supplier, all efforts will be directed to making that contract successful for both the supplier and his or her company. Considerable time and effort are expended in preparing specifications, selecting potential sources of supply, securing price quotations, evaluating these quotations, and selecting the supplier to whom the award will be made. This investment of time makes it prudent to make certain that everything is done to make that investment have a productive conclusion. The purchasing officer will do all within his power to make the contract a successful one. Cooperation with the supplier will be given to help solve the problems that arise during production and to help correct the problems that remain in the delivered product. There may come the time that even after all of this effort the handwriting on the wall is clear that the contract has failed to achieve its purpose. It is then that the purchasing officer must turn to the law. Efforts must be made to legally disentangle the organization from the contract and to recover from the defaulting supplier any losses incurred because of his failure to complete the obligations of performance.

It is prudent for the purchasing officer contemplating cancellation of a contract to consult with his legal counsel for advice on how to proceed. Legal counsel will be required to "carry the ball" should legal action against the supplier be employed. This chapter is dedicated to reviewing the possible actions counsel will consider. The chapter is not intended as a substitute for counsel's opinion and judgment. It is offered only to make the purchasing officer aware that he has alternate solutions and that he does not need to continue working with a defaulting supplier beyond the point of sound business judgment. The chapter will also give the purchasing officer a few negotiating arguments while he continues to bargain with the supplier in the attempt to reach a satisfactory agreement. It will also advise what might be done if resort to legal action is essential.

BUYER'S REMEDIES

Counsel will tell a purchasing officer that legal action is more successful when there is a documented trail of the events that lead up to the rupture of negotiations with the supplier. The purchasing officer will find that important legal details occurred in a transaction long before there was any indication that legal action might be required against a supplier. These details will possibly have an important influence on the final outcome of a legal battle in the courtroom. Events that occurred prior to the formation of the contract could be significant. Therefore, it is prudent to keep a well-documented file of preliminary negotiations, selection of suppliers, requests for quotations and proposals for every major purchase. A copy of the purchase order and its signed acceptance copy, if any, or the supplier's acceptance form generally constitute the contract. These contract documents, plus any other integrated documents, are essential to have. From that point on in the transaction, any contacts or conversations with supplier's representatives should be noted. Any subsequent writings between the parties should be kept on file; these writings become increasingly important as the transaction moves toward an impasse or stalemate. Of course, copies of any formal notices of rejection of the goods or revocation of acceptance as detailed in the previous chapter are critical. A chronological reporting of the supplier's visits to your plant in his attempts to cure the defects should also be made and retained.

Section 2-711 of the Code details "Buyer's Remedies in General." This section gives the buyer the possible legal actions that may be considered when all hope of settlement with the supplier has vanished:

> (1) Where the seller fails to make delivery or repudiates or the buyer rightfully rejects or justifiably revokes acceptance then with respect to any goods involved, and with respect to the whole if the breach goes to the whole contract (Section 2-612), the buyer may cancel and whether or not he has done so may in addition to recovering so much of the price as has been paid
>
> > (a) "cover" and have damages under the next section as to all

the goods affected whether or not they have been identified to the contract; or

(b) recover damages for nondelivery as provided in this Article (Section 2-713).

(2) Where the seller fails to deliver or repudiates the buyer may also

(a) if the goods have been identified recover them as provided in this Article (Section 2-502); or

(b) in a proper case obtain specific performance or replevy the goods as provided in this Article (Section 2-716).

Subsection (1) gives the buyer the right to receive money damages for the supplier's breach of contract, and subsection (2) gives the buyer the right to go after the goods themselves. Subsection (2) applies only when the supplier has made no delivery, since the buyer would have had possession of the goods if he rejected or revoked acceptance.

The Official Comment points out a proper retender by the supplier "can effectively preclude the buyer's remedies under this section, except for any delay involved." This tells us that if the supplier submits conforming goods while we are contemplating legal action, our recoverable damages could be limited to those incurred because of the late delivery. Such damages may be minimal in the case of a prompt cure by the supplier.

Substitute Goods

One of the remedies suggested in Section 2-711 is "cover." Cover involves obtaining the same goods from a competitor of the defaulting supplier. Section 2-712 explains the cover remedy:

(1) After a breach within the preceding section the buyer may "cover" by making in good faith and without unreasonable delay any reasonable purchase of or contract to purchase goods in substitution for those due from the seller.

(2) The buyer may recover from the seller as damages the difference between the cost of cover and the contract price together with any incidental or consequential damages as hereinafter defined (Section 2-715).

(3) Failure of the buyer to effect cover within this section does not bar him from any other remedy.

Cover is the logical answer to the buyer's problem with a defaulting supplier. The item contracted for is required by the company. The supplier's failure to deliver conforming goods allows that need to go unfilled. It is only sensible to go elsewhere to make the purchase to "cover" the need. However, subsection (3) reminds us that cover is not mandatory. If the buyer no longer has a need for the goods, there is no requirement to cover. In such circumstances, though, the buyer continues to have a damages claim (provable damages) against the supplier for breach of contract.

The Official Comment reminds us, though, that there is a possible change in the buyer's position if the option of cover is not elected. It will give the seller the opportunity to claim that the failure of cover increased the buyer's consequential damages—or the reverse, that cover could have reduced the buyer's damages. This is a consideration the purchasing officer must contemplate when deciding whether or not to cover.

Section 2-715 makes several suggestions about the cover procedure. The purchase from a competitor of the defaulting supplier must be made in good faith. The buyer must follow the usual procedures in making the purchase so as to obtain the best value among the competition. Action to make the replacement purchase must be made without "unreasonable delay." This does not force the buyer to sacrifice the usual procedures in finding sources and evaluating alternatives. But it should be accomplished as expeditiously as possible, particularly when prices are on the rise. Finally, note the words "in substitution for those due from the seller." This tells us that the cover purchase need not be an identical replacement. The Official Comment states that products "commercially usable as reasonable substitutes under the circumstances of the particular case" are acceptable.

Damages for Nondelivery

Damages for the seller's breach by way of failure to deliver conforming goods is the alternate remedy suggested in Section 2-711. This remedy is explained in Section 2-713.

> (1) Subject to the provisions of this Article with respect to proof of market price (Section 2-723), the measure of damages for nondelivery or repudiation by the seller is the difference between the market price at the time when the buyer learned of the breach and the contract price together with incidental and consequential damages provided in this Article (Section 2-715), but less expenses saved in consequence of the seller's breach.
>
> (2) Market price is to be determined as of the place for tender or, in cases of rejection after arrival or revocation of acceptance, as of the place of arrival.

The important concepts in this section are:

1. The market price used to determine damages is that price at the time the

buyer learned of the breach. This might relate to the seller's communication of intent to repudiate the contract, or to the time the buyer rejected or
revoked acceptance.

2. The market price would be the San Francisco prices for example, if the
   supplier is located there and if the contract is a shipment contract that was
   breached through nondelivery. If the buyer is located in New York where
   the delivered goods were rejected or acceptance revoked, the New York
   market price would be applicable. (This price information should be
   noted by the buyer promptly.)

3. The Official Comment reminds us that here the market price is for goods
   of the same kind and in the same branch of trade.

The Official Comment makes another excellent suggestion for the purchasing officer to consider. If a market price is difficult to obtain because of the
scarcity of that type of product, a good case is normally made for specific performance. Legal counsel must be consulted on this alternative.

Damages for Breach in Accepted Goods

We have been considering up to this point the buyer's options for damages when
the goods have not been delivered or, if delivered, not accepted. Section 2-714
gives us the buyer's remedies in the event the goods were accepted, but a breach
was discovered after the time for revocation of acceptance has passed. The buyer
must have provided the seller with a proper notification of the breach as provided
in Section 2-607(3). Section 2-714 then allows the buyer to recover as damages
"the loss resulting in the ordinary course of events from the seller's breach in any
manner which is reasonable."

Subsection (2) of 2-714 defines the measure of damages as being "the difference at the time and place of acceptance between the value of the goods as
accepted and the value they would have had if they had been as warranted, unless
special circumstances show proximate damage of a different amount." Provision
is also made for the recovery of any incidental and consequential damages.

Incidental and Consequential Damages

The Code sections just reviewed allow damages to the buyer in cases of cover,
nondelivery of conforming goods, and for accepted nonconforming goods. Each
of these three sections also includes provision for the recovery of incidental and
consequential damages.

Section 2-715(1) details the types of incidental expenses that may be recovered. This list includes expenses incurred in (1) inspection, (2) receipt, (3) transportation, and (4) care and custody of goods rightfully rejected. It also includes
"any commercially reasonable charges, expenses or commissions in connection

with effecting cover." And finally, it provides for "other expense incident to the delay or other breach."

Subsection (2) of 2-715 spells out consequential damages:

> (2) Consequential damages resulting from the seller's breach include:
>
> (a) any loss resulting from general or particular requirements and needs of which the seller at the time of contracting had reason to know and which could not reasonably be prevented by cover or otherwise; and
>
> (b) injury to person or property proximately resulting from any breach of warranty.

It is essential that the seller be informed of the "particular requirements" of the buyer at the time of contracting for consequential damages to be allowed. The Official Comment suggests that "general needs must rarely be made known" to charge the seller with knowledge. Nonetheless it is the interests of protection of the purchasing officer's organization to make certain the use of the supplier's product is made known at the time the contract is negotiated.

***Nota Bene* to the Purchasing Officer.** Purchasing officers should also take note of this paragraph in the Official Comment to this section:

> Any seller who does not wish to take the risk of consequential damages has available the section on contractual limitation of remedy.

This suggests that the buyer's company be made to take the risk of consequential damages arising from a breach of warranty or poor condition of the seller's product. This does not seem to be an equitable conclusion.

The buyer's company should not be forced to assume the risk and liability arising from a defect in the supplier's product. But many suppliers take advantage of the above suggestion by insisting that no liability for consequential damages will be assumed by them. A term such as the following often appears in suppliers' proposals to sell or sales acceptances:

> Our liability in the event of defects in our product is limited to repair or replacement of the defective part. We assume no liability for incidental and consequential damages that might arise from such defect.

Such a limitation on damages is permitted by Section 2-719 of the Code, which will be discussed shortly.

It is suggested the purchasing officer take affirmative action and do what is possible to keep this liability in the supplier's hands. Perhaps the most sensible approach is to avoid doing business with a supplier who lacks confidence in the quality of his product by refusing to accept liability for such damages. Another approach is to negotiate with the supplier and attempt to convince him that the limitation should be removed. Finally, it is suggested the purchasing officer consider including a clause on the purchase order similar to the following:

> The seller guarantees that the goods supplied under this purchase order will meet all the express warranties and the implied warranties of merchantability and fitness for the intended purpose. The seller assumes responsibility for damages caused by any defective units supplied and/or for breach of these warranties, including incidental and consequential damages, that might arise.

Right to Specific Performance

There are circumstances involved in the nondelivery of an item where pure monetary damages are inadequate as a remedy for the buyer. This is especially true when the buyer is unable to effect a "cover" for the nondelivered goods. In such cases, a court of law is authorized by Section 2-716 to direct specific performance of the contract:

> (1) Specific performance may be decreed where the goods are unique or in other proper circumstances.

The term "or in other proper circumstances" broadens the scope of the types of goods that can be included in an action for specific performance. The action is not confined to "unique" or one-of-a-kind items. Modern commercial practice will include goods that are difficult to obtain which are covered in the contract with the supplier.

Liquidated Damages

Liquidated damages was discussed in Chapter XX. Section 2-718(1) provides for such damages:

> (1) Damages for breach by either party may be liquidated in the agreement but only at an amount which is reasonable in the light of the anticipated or actual harm caused by the breach, the difficulties of proof of loss, and the inconvenience or nonfeasibility of otherwise obtaining an adequate remedy. A term fixing unreasonably large damages is void as a penalty.

The law on liquidated damages is quite rigid in maintaining they not be used as a penalty against the defaulting party. The remedy is designed to reimburse the aggrieved party for the approximate actual loss suffered. As stated in Chapter XX, the buyer employing this remedy must stand ready to defend the reasonableness of the amount.

Either the buyer or the supplier may request that liquidated damages be placed in the contract at the time of formation. Contrary to popular belief, mutuality or fairness does not require that both parties benefit from liquidated damages. Thus, if the supplier agrees to pay as liquidated damages $5000 per day for each work day beyond June 10 before delivery is made, it is not necessary for the buyer to agree to pay the supplier $5000 for each day before June 10 the delivery is made.

Liquidated damages in a contract is an excellent approach to avoiding difficult legal trial procedures in proving damages by other means. It is also an excellent method to keep the obligations of the contract consistently in mind from the time the contract is signed.

LIMITATIONS ON REMEDIES

Section 2-719 contains three subsections that deal with limitations on remedies and the effectiveness of such limitations. We have discussed the topic previously. It is important that the purchasing officer have these provisions of the Code in mind when entering into a contract. The suggested limitations could wipe out for a purchasing officer most of the remedies we have covered in this section and leave him with little or nothing to cover any costs involved. The subsection reads as follows:

> (a) The agreement may provide for remedies in addition to or in substitution for those provided in this Article and may limit or alter the measure of damages recoverable under this Article, as by limiting the buyer's remedies to return of the goods and repayment of the price or to repair and replacement of nonconforming goods or parts; and

> (b) resort to a remedy as provided is optional unless the remedy is expressly agreed to be exclusive, in which case it is the sole remedy.

How the Supplier Will Attempt to Limit the Buyer's Remedies

Suppliers have leaped aboard the bandwagon to take advantage of the limitation of remedy suggested by subsection (a). Such phrases as these are often seen:

> Our liability is limited to acceptance of your return of a defective unit and to refund your purchase price. We assume no responsibility for incidental or consequential damages that you may incur because of the defective unit.

> or

> Our liability is limited to the repair or replacement of any defective unit or part. This is the sole and exclusive remedy offered by us. We assume no responsibility for incidental or consequential damages that may result from any use of our product.

The word "limited" is always included to take advantage of the suggestion in subsection (b) that the remedy offered is the sole remedy that will be made available to the buyer. It is seldom, if ever, offered as a remedy in addition to those provided in the Code.

It is difficult to find fault with the supplier who seeks to operate in this fashion. No matter how good a supplier's quality control program may be, mistakes can happen. When a defective unit is placed in use, it can cause all types of damage. Then the question becomes one of who should assume the risk of liability for the damage caused. The buyer will assert that the defective unit was the proximate cause of the damage. The supplier will say that the buyer's use of the product caused the damage because of the circumstances under which it was used, to which the buyer will respond that but for the defective unit no damage would have been done. Perhaps a case could be made for assessing responsibility against both parties. The Code takes the position that both parties should negotiate this liability problem at the time the contract is created. The buyer is offered the protection of Section 2-715, which gives the right to collect consequential damages. Now here Section 2-719 gives the seller the opportunity to avoid consequential damages. The Code tells both parties that the problem will only be solved through their negotiations.

Should the supplier be successful in avoiding liability through the use of 2-719, we are almost back to the days of *caveat emptor*. This must serve as a warning to all purchasing officers to read carefully the terms and conditions of sale proposed by the supplier. At the least, the buyer should not enter into a contract without the full realization that the remedies available may be severely limited in the event a defective product is received from the supplier.

How to Overcome the Supplier's Limitations

The only bright spot in this picture is that Section 2-719(2) of the Code may give relief from the restrictive provisions on remedies in the supplier's document. The section reads:

> (2) Where the circumstances cause an exclusive or limited remedy to fail of its essential purpose, remedy may be had as provided by this Act.

This subsection will give the purchasing officer an opportunity to "get out from under" a seller's provision that provides for an exclusive and limited remedy. A case heard before a federal court in 1978[1] contained this limitation of a warranted product in the supplier's terms:

> The seller's liability under valid warranty claims is limited to repair or replacement at seller's plant or buyer's location, all at the option of

---

[1]*A.E.S. Technology Systems v. Coherent Radiation,* 583 F.2d 933 (1978).

the seller. The foregoing warranty is exclusive in lieu of all other warranties and shall be buyer's sole remedy and seller's sole liability
under the contract.

The seller in this case shipped goods that did not meet the required performance standards. After many attempts to repair, a replacement was ordered that
took more than a year to arrive. (The repair attempts had already consumed four
or five months.) The buyer covered by purchase from another supplier, and the
original seller sued for the contract price. The buyer counterclaimed with damages for cover and also for incidental and consequential damages. The federal
court cited Section 2-719(2) and awarded the buyer the damages claimed. The
court pointed out that in this case the limited warranty had failed "of its essential
purpose," and the buyer was entitled to relief under any other section of the Code.
Therefore this subsection (2) has some value to the purchasing officer trapped in
a seller's limited warranty. The only question for the purchasing officer is how
bad the damages must be to have the court apply Section 2-719(2).

Subsection (3) of 2-719 is a section that specifically gives the supplier the
opportunity to limit incidental and consequential damages. It also contains an
exception for damages arising from personal injuries in consumer cases:

> (3) Consequential damages may be limited or excluded unless the
> limitation or exclusion is unconscionable. Limitation of consequential
> damages for injury to the person in the case of consumer goods is
> prima facie unconscionable, but limitation of damages where the loss
> is commercial is not.

This section is almost a restatement of subsection (2). One must assume
that any limitation to make subsection (2) effective would almost have to be
unconscionable.

Time Limitations on Remedies

The Uniform Commercial Code has a statute of limitations expressed in Section
2-725. It requires that an action for breach of contract in a sale must be commenced within four years after the cause of action has accrued. The cause of
action accrues at the time the breach occurs. A breach of warranty of quality is
said to occur when tender of delivery is made by the seller. Thus, under a shipment contract, the breach occurs when the goods are delivered to the carrier and
it is then that the four-year period begins. No action may be brought after the
four-year period has elapsed. In a destination contract, the statutory four-year
period begins when the goods are delivered to the buyer. Should the warranty be
to the future performance of the product, then the statute begins to run when performance begins and the defect is noted or should have been noted. The buyer
need not have knowledge of the defect when the quality warranty is breached.

The statute begins to toll when the risk of loss passes to the buyer.

You are reminded that non-Code contract claims may have a different statute of limitations in your state. In New York, for example, non-Code contract claims have a six-year limitation. Also note that most states have a different statute of limitations for tort claims, as well as a different time delay as to when the statute begins to toll. For example, as stated above, the Code limitation for breach of warranty begins to toll when the risk of loss passes to the buyer. However, if an injury results from the defect in the goods that was the breach of warranty, the statute of limitations for the tort claim for negligence begins to toll in most states from the date of the injury. The accident could occur long after the contract claim limitation began to run.

The supplier, if the purchasing officer agrees, may include in the contract a clause shortening the four-year period. However, the shorter period may not be less than one year. (The parties cannot agree to extend it longer than four years.)

Other Possible Remedies

The Code recognizes actionable fraud in Section 2-721. This includes material misrepresentation of facts, the falsity of which is known by the supplier at the time it is made, and the misrepresentation induces the buyer to enter into the contract to his disadvantage and damage. Section 2-721 of the Code provides remedies to the buyer in addition to any other remedies the buyer's legal counsel might elect.

Product liability is another source of remedy available to a buyer under certain circumstances. Discussion of this remedy is beyond the scope of this text and is mentioned here only as a suggestion for consideration by the buyer's legal counsel.

SELLER'S REMEDIES

This text is for purchasing officers and this chapter has devoted all attention to the buyer's remedies. However, the author wishes to remind the purchasing officer that the Code also includes an adequate list of remedies for the supplier. The supplier obtains a cause of action against the buyer if the buyer wrongfully rejects a conforming delivery, if the buyer wrongfully revokes acceptance, if the buyer fails to make a payment when due, and if the buyer refuses in any manner to perform his obligations under the contract. The seller's options for remedies against the buyer include the following:

1. Withhold delivery of the goods.

2. Stop delivery of any bailee (warehouse).

3. Sell partially manufactured goods for scrap.

4. Resell the goods and recover damages, including incidental damages.

5. Recover the price for nonacceptance.

6. Cancel the contract.

7. Stop and intercept any goods in transit, if the buyer is discovered to be insolvent.

At all times the supplier is entitled to the profit he would have made had the sale been completed. This is usually accomplished by the ability to recover the contract price for the goods.

Once more we remind the purchasing officer to consult legal counsel when considering breaching a contract with a supplier.

XXV

Buyer's Special Remedies

It is advantageous for a purchaser of goods to have a broad picture of the damages which he or his company may obtain if a seller breaches the sales contract. This is an examination and summary of the recent developments and trends in special or additional damage remedies. In particular, case law which interprets and supplements the Uniform Commercial Code will be considered with respect to incidental, consequential, liquidated and punitive damages.

Caveat Bene: This case law may not only give the purchaser a greater recovery, but also may serve to give the purchaser more leverage in insisting that the contract be carried out or an adequate settlement reached.

Under the Uniform Commercial Code, both buyer and seller have remedies that can be sought in the event that one party breaches the sales contract. There are both traditional and additional damage remedies. The standard damage remedies include:

1) Cover which allows the buyer to obtain substitute goods from a competitor of the seller, so long as the purchase is made in good faith and without unreasonable delay; the cover remedy is not mandatory (U.C.C. 2-712);

2) Cure which allows a breaching seller to correct a defective delivery (U.C.C. 2-608);

3) Damages for non-delivery equaling the difference between the market price (for a replacement) and the contract price, when the buyer has to purchase from another seller (U.C.C. 2-713);

Special Acknowledgment: Gloria J. McCollum, Juris Doctor

4) Specific performance where the goods are of a unique nature (U.C.C. 2-716) and

5) Deduction from the price (U.C.C. 2-717).

The non-traditional remedies include incidental, consequential, liquidated and punitive damages. Many Code sections provide that incidental and consequential damages can be sought by a non-breaching party. In order to better understand the purpose behind allowing an injured party to recover non-traditional damages we must look at the history of these remedies.

BACKGROUND

First, there is a distinction between general and special damages. Failure to properly draw the line could result in double recoveries. General damages must be distinguished from special damages especially in cases where the parties have agreed not to permit recovery for special damages.

There is often confusion when attempts are made to distinguish incidental from consequential damages. According to Roy Ryden Anderson, "the Code [itself] provides for a distinction . . . " While it is hard to draw a line that separates the differences between the two it should be noted that they are alike in the sense that they are both special damages, meaning, they "arise naturally but not necessarily as a result of the breach." In other words, it is the "special circumstances" of the injured party that cause these damages to arise.

In making further reference to the Code Anderson says that "incidental damages are normally incurred when a buyer (or seller) repudiates the contract or wrongfully rejects the goods, causing the other to incur such expenses as transporting, storing, or reselling the goods." A more detailed list is set out below in the reference to Code section 2-715(1-3). Incidental damages usually arise when there has been a revocation or rejection of acceptance. Consequential damages are generally sustained when the breach affects a party's dealing with third parties.

Caveat Nota: A claim by the purchaser for consequential damages presents a frightening threat to a breaching seller because such damages are more open-ended and can greatly exceed the value of the goods or the normal contract damages. Because there is money on the line courts imposed stricter standards of proof that must be met before recovery is permitted. As the information presented supra will show many courts require a claimant to prove that the "[(1)] . . . [I]njury was foreseeable; [(2)] that the loss was reasonably certain in amount; [(3)] that the loss could not have been reasonably avoided by the aggrieved party." Buyers are fortunate in the sense that they are likely the beneficiaries of the consequential damages provision under the Code. Contrarily, sellers have been permitted to only recover incidental damages.

Arguments have been made in support of allowing sellers to recover consequential damages. One such argument was also raised by Roy Anderson in an article entitled, "In Support of Consequential Damages for Sellers." More specifically, Anderson called for revision of Article 2 of the Code. He states that the courts' modern approach to interpreting section 1-106 of the Code is erroneous and unsupported by " . . . logic or fairness" because the provision states that the courts are to liberally administer remedies so that the aggrieved party is compensated. Therefore, when a buyer breaches and the seller is the aggrieved party he should be permitted to recover under various remedies including the consequential damages. Anderson says that the reason for the inconsistent treatment is based on the language in 1-106, which says that no recovery can be had for "consequential . . . damages . . . except as specifically provided in this Act or by other rule of law." Thus, there is no provision granting recovery in favor of sellers; therefore, they are excluded.

The article suggests, and rightly so, that Article 2 should be revised and the new version should be enacted that includes an expressed provision that will place " . . . sellers on equal footing with buyers with respect to consequential damages." The American Law Institute also has considered changing the Code so as to make it fair to sellers. In March 1988, the Institute summoned a study group to review and consider redrafting Article 2. In conclusion, Anderson urges that recovery be permitted for sellers because they occasionally suffer losses as a consequence of the breach. Moreover, the language in the Code does not deny recovery.

In the *Incidental and Consequential Damages* article, Roy Anderson states that it is the current trend for sellers to use "standardized form contract[s]" in an attempt to protect themselves by providing that buyers can only recover incidental damages in the event that there is a breach.

Courts have held that a disclaimer clause in a contract can bar recovery of incidental damages and only what is excluded will not be recoverable. Therefore, if the contract excludes incidental damages there still can be recovery of consequential damages.

It seems plausible that buyers would argue that an agreement limiting the recovery of consequential damages is fair but contracts limiting the recovery of incidental damages are unfair because the buyer ends up with less than he started with. In fact this dilemma was raised in *Durfee v. Rod Baxter Imports, Inc.*, 262 N.W.2d 349 (Minn. 1977). The *Durfee* court held that " . . . a clause limiting the recovery of incidental damages will not be effective against a buyer rightfully rejecting or revoking acceptance of non-conforming goods because denying this buyer incidental damages would leave him with less than an adequate remedy."

The modern trend among the courts is to recognize these types of agreements and deny recovery if damages were "properly disclaimed" in the contract. Anderson predicts that sellers will eventually begin to use standardized contract forms that contain disclaimer clauses for not only consequential but incidental damages as well. The article suggests that these total disclaimer types of contracts are being considered because buyers are having very little difficulty proving incidental damages because the standards imposed by the court are not as strict regarding such claims. As this paper will point out, consequential damages are more difficult to prove and many states require proof of reasonable certainty, foreseeability, and attempts by the buyer to mitigate his damages. Therefore, it is more difficult for a buyer to prove that he is entitled to consequential damages.

INCIDENTAL AND CONSEQUENTIAL DAMAGES

A closer look at the specific provisions that address these additional damages should be taken. First, let us consider the language of section 2-715(1) which states:

> (1) Incidental damages resulting from the seller's breach include expenses reasonably incurred in inspection, receipt, transportation and care and custody of goods rightfully rejected, and commercially reasonable charges, expenses or commissions in connection with effecting cover and any other reasonable expense incident to the delay or other breach. (2) Consequential damages resulting from the seller's breach include (a) a loss resulting from general or particular requirements and needs of which the seller at the time of contracting had reason to know and which could not reasonably be prevented by cover or otherwise; and (b) injury to person or property proximately resulting from any breach of warranty. U.C.C. sec. 2-715.

The official comments following this section state that subsection (1) was included to reimburse buyers that incur "reasonable expense" relating to goods where acceptance has been revoked, rejected, or cover has been sought.

Subsection (2) was modified in the sense that a buyer could no longer recover for consequential damages of which the seller had "reason to know" could be incurred; but a more restrictive approach was taken which only allows buyer to recover if he /she "could not reasonably have prevented the loss by cover or otherwise." In other words, this section imposes upon the buyer a duty to minimize damages in good faith.

If the seller had reason to know, at the time of contracting, that the buyer had "general or particular requirements" and damages are sustained that could not have been minimized by buyer, the seller is liable for such damages. In other words, knowledge need not be established regarding general needs. The Code imposes upon the buyer the burden of proving just how much was lost although such proof need not be calculated to a mathematical certainty.

Recent case law in both state and federal jurisdictions have taken varying approaches in interpreting section 2-715 of the U.C.C. An outline of the trends will now be examined. Specific sections of Article 2 of the U.C.C. relating to Buyer's remedies will be examined in this paper. In particular sections 2-715, 2-718 and 1-106 will be analyzed. If state is listed after various points, this means only that there are cases from those states that have a similar rule or have considered adopting a similar standard in relation to a particular issue.

THE CASE STUDIES

General

In considering section 2-715, there are numerous categories to be considered in search of trends. The first category contains cases that give a general overview of the incidental and consequential damage remedy. Some cases define the remedy under the Uniform Commercial Code. For example, Louisiana courts hold that the expenses incurred by buyer must be the "probable result" of the seller's breach or "arise from" the breach in order for the expense to be deemed incidental or consequential. Therefore, a buyer cannot recover these damages if the expense would have been incurred even in the absence of a breach. Missouri also has a similar standard that allows buyer to collect incidental and consequential damages only when such are proximately caused by the breach. The requirement is obviously for the purpose of providing consistency in decisions as well as cutting down on the number of incidents that can be claimed to result from the breach.

Many states allow special damages only when the damages can be calculated with "reasonable certainty"; however, they need not be calculated to a "mathematical" certainty. This requirement is in line with section 1-106 of the Code because it serves the purpose of providing expectancy to the nonbreaching party and nothing more.

Nota Bene: Section 1-106 is aimed at providing remedies to the aggrieved party such that will put him in the position he would have been in had the contract been performed. It is to be liberally administered to provide damages and mathematical certainty is not required to obtain relief.

Many states support the awarding of incidental and consequential damages to a buyer when the seller has delivered "nonconforming tender." States engaging in this trend are Maryland, California, Illinois, and Arkansas.

When a buyer "justifiably" revokes acceptance of nonconforming goods, both incidental and consequential damages can be sought for expenses incurred relating to the transaction (as in Ind., Minn., Ariz., N.C., Mo., and Tenn.). Furthermore, a buyer can recover the portion of the purchase price paid.

Foreseeability is another element considered by courts when determining whether or not to award incidental and consequential damages. Delaware and West Virginia have interpreted the U.C.C. as requiring that the parties reasonably foresee that such expenses will be incurred at the time of contracting. With regard to cases in which breach of warranty is alleged, courts generally hold that incidental and consequential damages can be recovered when such damages were proximately caused by the breach.

Typically, most of these cases allege breach of an implied warranty of fitness for a good bought from seller. Both incidental and consequential damages can be recovered under section 2-715 for such a claim. Currently there are 35 states which have adopted this rule.

Measure of Damages

The measure of damages generally is the "difference between the value of the goods accepted and the value of the goods as warranted." The common law "tacit agreement" for consequential damages test only held seller liable when he expressly or impliedly agreed to be liable.

Section 2-714 of the Code sets out the "usual though not exclusive" method of ascertaining damages for warranty breach. Several states recognize that circumstances may call for use of a different measure of damages and permits use of such so long as it is reasonable.

With regard to measure of damages there are no patterns of decisions. The case law suggests that different courts tend to look at the facts and circumstances of the case before them to calculate the damages.

Types of Expenses

There are reasonable popular expenses as well as some that are less popular. More specifically, courts hold that expenses incurred in inspecting, shipping, handling, storing, receipt, transportation, care and custody are all commercially reasonable and can be recovered as incidental damages.

Buyers are often reimbursed for the expense of purchasing insurance in instances where there has been a breach of warranty. Recovery has been allowed through both incidental and consequential damages.

Cost of Inspection

Cost of inspections (tests), as previously mentioned, are recoverable as an incidental damage where the inspection was "reasonable and necessary." The state of

Georgia has also allowed for such damages when the seller should have made the inspection anyway.

Storage

Storage charges are a form of incidental damages. Several states agree that such can be recovered so long as they are reasonable and provable.

Cost of Transportation

Regarding transportation expenses as an incidental damage, costs can be recovered for returning defective goods. Included in this amount would be the cost of shipping, handling and trucking. In other words, this rule says that a restriction on recovery would be imposed here against the buyer if he recovered the additional costs from a third party; therefore the seller would not be liable. New York courts impose this limitation.

Recovery of Sales Tax

Moreover, a buyer can recover amounts paid as sales tax in the event that there is a breach of warranty with respect to the delivered goods. Regarding resale commissions and measure of damages, there is very little case law and this suggests that there is no current trend in these areas.

Cost of Repair

However, where costs of repair are sought a buyer is allowed to recover as consequential damage for reasonable repairs made in good faith. This rule applies in cases brought based on both breach of warranty claims as well as breach of contract. The cost of the repair is the proper measure of damages under Texas law. Illinois courts hold that "damages based on [the] cost of repair are recoverable regardless of whether the repairs are actually undertaken . . . "

Lost Profits

A party to a contract that is effected by breach or delay can seek consequential damages for lost profits that are naturally caused by the breach when there is sufficient evidence to establish the loss with a reasonable amount of certainty.

In some isolated jurisdictions, like Minnesota, a buyer can only recover lost profits if the seller could foresee the same. However, foreseeability has not been a requisite imposed in all other jurisdictions in order to recover lost profits. Regarding lost profits, the question often comes up as to whether or not they are a past or future loss. The state of Delaware appears to have adopted the rule of Illinois and Florida which does not allow a buyer to recover lost profits if the business upon which he is basing his claim is not established. But an unestablished business is to be distinguished from a new business in the states of California and Ohio because with an established new business, loss of prospective profits can be recovered. Utah courts hold that "the absence of a record of past earnings should not preclude a new business from recovering lost profits, and the amount of lost profits shown does not have to be precise once the fact of loss and the cause of loss have been established."

Cover

Furthermore, limitations are imposed, in jurisdictions like Idaho, upon recovery when cover is possible. The buyer has to acquire substitute goods and can only acquire lost profits if no substitutes are available. But some hold that failure of buyer to effectuate cover is not a bar to recovery of consequential damages. The latter rule seems to be the fairer rule because even if substitutes can be obtained the goods may not comport to the purpose for which the buyer needs them. Substitutes, unlike replacements, are not the same product and therefore the features of the good may prove less useful.

In addition, a buyer can recover consequential damages for lost profits even if the seller did not agree contractually to be liable for such damages. However, a court can enforce a clause in a contract that limits consequential damages for lost profits in accordance with Code section 2-719(3).

In determining whether or not to award lost profits to a buyer, many courts require that the purchaser prove that the seller had "reason to know" of buyers' particular requirements/purposes (i.e. resale) at the time of contracting. Moreover, to recover lost profits a purchaser must come forward with evidence to support the claim that is not of a speculative nature. In other words, the amount of damages must be established with some degree of certainty. If losses are too speculative, recovery will be denied. This substantial certainty can be established through evidence such as history of profits which provides some reasonable method for ascertaining the loss.

Financing Costs

Often when a seller causes a delay or breach a buyer is forced to borrow money to complete a purchase or has already sought financing for the undelivered goods. The cost of financing as well as interest charges paid on the borrowed amount is recoverable as consequential damages if there is sufficient tying of the payment to the breach. The state of Kansas, in *Schatz* went further to say that the seller must have "reason to know" that additional financing will be needed to complete the purchase. The same knowledge requirement is required in the state of Florida. Case law from several states allows recovery for loss due to the payment of finance and interest charges.

Loss of Good Will

When a breach affects business, purchasers often seek damages from sellers for loss of good will. This type of damage would be sought under section 2-715 of the U.C.C. as a consequential damage. Some courts allow plaintiff to recover for losses to good will as well as expenses incurred in trying to restore it. A claim for loss based on good will is tough for a plaintiff to prove because such claims cannot easily be established. Courts often attempt to define good will to provide some guidance in determining the nature and extent of a loss. For example, in the state of Pennsylvania, good will "refers to profits lost on future sales rather than on sales of defective goods themselves; generally, "good will" refers to reputation that business has built over the course of time. That is reflected by return of customers to purchase goods and attendant profits that accompany such sales. The phrase good will is coextensive with prospective profits and loss of business reputation." The recovery of good will damages is a fairly recent development under Pennsylvania law.

In 1981, Pennsylvania "categorically denied recovery for loss of good will . . . " but in 1991 the state permitted such recovery. One New Jersey Court adopted Pennsylvania's old policy of completely denying recovery for loss of good will. Currently, no new case law from New Jersey suggests that it changed its policy when Pennsylvania changed its policy in 1991. Therefore, the no recovery for damages to good will rule appears to still stand in that state. It seems only fair that a breaching party be made to pay damages where the reputation or worth of a business is effected by breach. Good will can sustain harm just as property or goods can; just because it is intangible there is no reason for excluding these types of damages from recovery.

Florida, Illinois, and Delaware are states that do not currently permit recovery for damage to reputation and good will in connection with a breach.

In an attempt to streamline the vague definition of good will, courts take into account various factors. The Sixth Circuit, in *Poundhouse v. Owens-Illinois, Inc.,* 604 F.2d 990 (6th Cir.1979), held that relevant factors include lost profits and expert testimony as to the value of the good will. Washington courts hold that expert testimony is usually required to prove loss of good will. The state of Iowa denies recovery for loss of good will to "non-privity buyers who rely on express warranties" and limits their recovery to direct economic loss damage. . . . "

In some states where recovery is allowed, the plaintiff has the additional burden of proving that seller has "reason to know" that the breach would have an adverse effect on the reputation and good will of the establishment. Again we see courts imposing a knowledge standard that typically arises when a claim for consequential damages is made. Other cases do not specifically say that recovery is allowed for damages to good will/reputation but the same can be inferred because the cases considered plaintiff's claim and only rejected it because plaintiff did not come forward with evidence to establish the amount of damage. However, some cases from Michigan, New York, Oregon, Wyoming, and Washington hold that breaching party can be made to pay for loss of good will.

Interest

Another type of expense commonly sought under the incidental and consequential damages section of the U.C.C. is for the interest that accrues before a judgment on the claim is entered. No trend appears to exist. At best, the most that can be said about prejudgment interest is that it is allowed in some cases and denied in others.

Legal Expenses

When a purchaser brings a cause of action against a seller for breach, he or she will likely incur costly legal expenses consisting of attorney's fees, and court costs. In many cases, the purchaser requests that the cost of such fees be reimbursed by the seller as a consequential damage. The outcomes of these cases do not clearly define a trend among courts. Case law shows an award in some cases and a denial in others. It does not seem that courts in general are opposed to this type of recovery, but it is apparent that such a claim will undoubtedly be denied when the evidence is scant and does not clearly establish the amount spent. Before bringing such a claim for legal expenses a party should be aware that the traditional rule enforced by most courts requires each party to bear its own legal expenses.

Usually when a state denies a claim for attorney's fees it is because such were not provided for in either the contract, statute or case law. Sometimes these damages are rejected for other reasons at the reviewing court's discretion.

Although the Uniform Commercial Code in section 2-715 does not expressly mention litigation expenses as a recoverable consequential damage, some courts have awarded such expenses at their discretion. There are some states that deny plaintiffs right to seek incidental and consequential damages for legal fees based on the theory that this was not intended to be covered under section 2-715 of the U.C.C.

Loss of Use

Another expense claimed under consequential damages is for loss of use of a product, as a result of a seller's breach, where a defective condition exists. Several support loss of use damage award and do not deny the claim if the buyer provides sufficient information to prove his loss (i.e., giving seller notice). The state of Arizona takes a more restrictive approach requiring that the seller have "knowledge of buyer's intended use of goods at [the] time of contracting . . . "

Cost of Replacements

Another area worth mentioning deals with claims by buyers for damages for the cost of replacements. This type of expense can be recovered in some states as a consequential damage.

Delay in Delivery

When there is a delay in delivery, buyers can suffer substantial losses to their business and/or profits. In such instances, recovery is permitted for consequential damages caused by the delay. In *Halstead Hospital v. Northern Bank,* 680 F.2d 1307 (10th Cir. 1982), the court stated that because the U.C.C. is broadly drafted it provides for recovery of incidental and consequential damages for expense caused by delay.

In Colorado, plaintiff will be denied recovery for damages caused by delay if the delivery date was not established in advance and where the evidence fails to show that seller knew that the delivery was necessary on a certain date.

Foreseeability and Reason to Know Requirements

To be awarded incidental and consequential damages, a buyer often has to prove that such damages were within the contemplation of the parties at the time of contracting. The rule was best summarized by the Court in *Halstead,* 680 F.2d at 1307, which stated that even though the U.C.C could be construed broadly the court will also consider what the parties reasonably contemplated.

Along the same lines many courts require a plaintiff to prove that the damages sustained were foreseeable at the time of contracting. This section of the U.L.A. contains cases that impose a requisite of knowledge (either actual or constructive). An Ohio Bankruptcy court held in *Matter of Lifeguard Industries, Inc.,* 42 B.R 734 (1983), that under the U.C.C. consequential damages can be recovered for a breach and seller is liable for damages resulting therefrom where the seller had "reason to know." A number of states implemented a similar rule.

Some cases require the buyer to prove that the seller had knowledge before consequential damages can be recovered. A Delaware case best states the rule as it is applied in various jurisdictions. In *Beal v. General Motors Corp.,* 354 F. Supp. 423 (D.C.Del 1973), the court held " . . . that consequential damage resulting from requirements and needs which seller at time of contract had reason to know, if loss for which recovery is sought is one that results from general or particular requirements or needs of which seller at time of contract has reason to know, award of consequential damages is proper, provided that such damage could not have been reasonably prevented by action of buyer."

Contributory Negligence and Comparative Fault

In some states, when a claim for consequential damages is asserted, a buyer is scrutinized under a theory of contributory negligence or comparative fault. In other words, a buyer has to prove that damages were proximately caused by seller's breach of implied or expressed warranty and that such damages were not due to fault of buyer himself.

Minimization of Damages

A buyer can be barred from recovering consequential damages if he has not taken certain actions to prevent his loss. Under the Code, a buyer has a duty to attempt to prevent loss by attempting to cover. In other words, a buyer has to seek to find goods to use in the place of the goods for which he/she originally contracted. The purpose of the cover requirement is directly linked to causation. To summarize the connection between causation and cover: Damages the plaintiff could have avoided with reasonable effort are not caused by the breach, and therefore defendant cannot be liable for them.

The common law rule denies recovery to a buyer who does not reasonably attempt to minimize his consequential damages. Avoidance of consequential damages is expected of buyers in many states. The North Carolina Appellate Court in the case of *Stimpson Hosiery Mills, Inc. v. Pam Trading Corp.,* 392 S.E.2d 128 (N.C.App.1990), made a distinction between mitigation of damages and contributory negligence. With regard to the former, a buyer's remedies for recovery are lessened, whereas under the latter they are barred altogether.

Under the Code, a party can recover consequential damages if the same could not have been avoided through cover. However, a majority of courts hold that failure to cover is not a bar to an award of damages under certain circumstances. In other words, the duty to mitigate damages is limited and not extensive. For example, limits are imposed when circumstances suggest that there was no other reasonable replacement or cover that could be obtained by the buyer. So it is apparent that some courts will grant a buyer leeway especially when he has made a reasonable attempt to cover but to no avail.

On the other hand, if cover is not effectuated and the buyer's conduct was unreasonable or done in bad faith his/her remedies will be reduced. A buyer's duty to mitigate damages does not always mean that she/he must replace the defective goods so long as a reasonable effort is made to repair or replace in an attempt to minimize the loss.

Proximate Cause

Even though proximate cause is frequently mentioned in cases cited in the U.L.A. there is a specific section that outlines cases dealing with this issue. The prevailing rule holds that (under the Uniform Commercial Code) a buyer can only recover for incidental and consequential damages proximately caused by. the breach. Mere proof of breach alone is not enough.

Exclusionary Clauses

Sellers often place exclusionary clauses in their contracts, in an effort to limit their liability for consequential damages when there is a breach. Some states permit such clauses; however, a seller usually is required to assure that the buyer has notice of the provision. A court may hold the clause ineffective when notice of it was not received by the buyer at time seller's offer was accepted. Another court held that disclaimer on back of seller's acknowledgment form was not part of the contract because buyer was not a dealer in the business and therefore was unfamiliar with the terms.

Knowledge of Defect

In many cases where breach is alleged a buyer will use or continue to use the defective product. In such instances, the question often arises as to whether or not the buyer is entitled to consequential damages resulting from the breach. Several jurisdictions do not permit recovery of damages for loss when there is knowledge of defect prior to use. However, the contrary is true in the state of Illinois because a "Buyer's continued use of [a] machine did not require denying consequential damages for breach of warranty." The latter rule seems to be the most fair because the buyer could be attempting to mitigate his damages by using the product. If this is the case buyer should be allowed to recover.

Personal Injuries

A plaintiff that sustains personal injuries from a defective product due to a seller's breach of the implied warranty of merchantability is allowed to recover for such injuries in many jurisdictions. However, the cases listed in the U.L.A. do not set forth a trend of decisions in the states. The decisions cited tend to be very fact specific and show that the courts allow for such but only when the facts sufficiently prove the claim .

The U.C.C.D's section on breach of warranty resulting in personal injury or death cites several cases that permit recovery for consequential damages under the Code. Alabama adopted this approach, and went so far as to eliminate the requirement of privity altogether, thereby allowing third parties effected to recover damages. Contrarily, other states allow causes of action to be brought only by parties in privity of contract at the time of injury provided that the injury arose from the breach. Idaho requires that the claimant be in privity or a qualified beneficiary under the sales contract.

Although many states permit recovery when certain conditions are met, Massachusetts denies recovery for personal injuries (resulting in death) holding that such rights to recover for death are " . . . purely statutory" and no such damages are permitted for " . . . contractual breach of warranty alone."

Defective Title

Finally, under the breach of warranty category, come claims where the titles to goods are defective. Most of the cases cited deal with complaints about car titles. In these cases, state courts permit recovery of damages where the title turns out to be something other than what was represented to the buyer. In one case the seller claims to have title to a car that is stolen and buyer incurs attorney's fees defending a criminal charge of "possession of stolen property." Consequential damages are sought for different things such as in these cases although the claims are based on the breach of warranty of title.

Mental Suffering

Depending on the jurisdiction where a claim is filed, a plaintiff may be permitted to collect damages for mental suffering. U.C.C. section 2-715 permits recovery for personal injury although it does not specifically state that personal injuries include emotional disturbance. Under the common law of contracts, damages for mental suffering are not recoverable. This approach has roots in the Second Restatement of Contracts which holds that there can be no recovery for emotional disturbance unless " . . . the breach also caused bodily harm or the contract or the breach is of such a kind that serious emotional disturbance was a particularly likely result." This restriction is partially based on the causation requirement. In particular, some courts required that the claimant prove that there was some form of willful conduct on the part of the breaching party (held that there could be no recovery for mental distress absent willful conduct in a transaction involving a breach of contract in the sale of an automobile).

Compensation for mental anguish and suffering is sometimes sought as a consequential damage. Texas courts require a plaintiff to show that mental anguish was "more than ordinary regret or annoyance but is of a type commonly denominated as mental anguish, provided, the mental anguish was such a necessary and natural result of the breach of warranty as to have been within the contemplation of the defendant at the time the contract was made." Contrarily, the state of Missouri requires that the plaintiff suffer a physical injury before recovery is allowed.

Injury to Property

This type of consequential damage is specifically provided for in section 2-715(2) of the Code. Many of the cases in this area arise in cases where there has been fire damage to a buyer's home. The types of losses often result from defective products or goods. Examples of this include cases involving defective products like home appliances, or farming products/ equipment, which resulted in a loss.

Buyers often seek consequential damages for injury to property resulting from a seller's breach of implied/expressed warranty under section 2-715(2) (b) of the Code. At best, the rule with regard to such claims can be summarized as allowing recovery for damage to property that can be traced to the breach. The method of calculating damages to property most likely will depend on the state where the case is being heard. However, one example of a measure used is the costs of repairing or replacing the portion of the property damaged.

Injury to Animals

Purchasers often bring suit in instances where goods are supposed to be warranted but are not and such results in an injury to an animal. In most of the cases cattle or livestock were injured. Courts allow recovery for consequential damages for expenses like the cost of nursing the animal back to health (veterinarian), the diminution of the value of the animal, and the market cost of the animal (where the animal dies). Some other jurisdictions have addressed similar issues and have come to similar conclusions.

Sufficiency of Evidence

It is important that a purchaser alleging consequential damages for breach provide the reviewing court with sufficient evidence to support the claim. Even though this area was previously mentioned, it may be reiterated. In South Dakota, a "buyer need not prove consequential damages with mathematical certainty but must establish [a] basis for [a] reasonably certain computation."

The Ohio rule is similar in that it permits recovery of incidental damages when there is evidence to prove how damages were calculated "including [a] breakdown of the cost components of such damages." The rules are basically the same in many other states.

Burden of Proof

Generally, the buyer has the burden of proving seller's breach of warranty and proximate causation. In Arizona, a buyer can meet his or her burden of proof through his or her own testimony provided that the seller does not object or rebut. Case law in general suggests that the degree of proof is determined by the court, although many states start with the notion that at the very minimum the plaintiff must meet the Code's requirement of "reasonably certain" proof.

Pleading Consequential Damages

When consequential damages are sought under section 2-715 of the U.C.C., they must be specifically plead or they are waived. Arkansas, Colorado, Florida also have this type of rule. However, in other cases the court's position was not clear.

The plaintiff is commonly expected to carry the heaviest burden of proof in his case. Under the U.C.C., a buyer has the burden of proving consequential damages. In other words, the buyer must prove "the extent of loss from breach of contract . . . " Even though this is likely the rule in all states, only cases from a few states were cited in the U.L.A.

Admissibility of Evidence

With regard to the type of evidence that is admissible to support a claim for incidental and consequential damages under section 2-715, the cases listed in the U.L.A. under the section "Admissibility of Evidence" do not set forth a trend. There is a section on "Weight and Sufficiency of Evidence" that lists cases that spell out the requirements plaintiff needs to meet. However, the evidence issues are very fact specific and from the information provided, no trend is established with regard to what is or is not sufficient. Nevertheless, the prevailing rule seems to be that damages for breach still need to be proved with "reasonable certainty."

Waiver of Rights

Two cases cited under the U.L.A. section entitled "Waiver" hold that there can be a waiver of the right to sue for incidental and consequential damages when seller has breached his agreement to perform. Waivers that are bargained for at the time of contract are considered part of the arms length negotiation and therefore permitted.

Judge or Jury Issues

In cases alleging incidental and consequential damages several issues have to be decided. As a general rule questions of fact are to be determined by the trier of fact. The cases listed under this section point out specific questions that have been determined, and all were questions of fact. The following are examples of such questions: 1) Whether the buyer can be compensated for damages caused by the delay; 2) whether the buyer's consequential damages were foreseeable; 3) whether the damages were proximately caused by the breach; 4) whether the buyer was contributorily negligent; 5) whether plaintiff could have mitigated his or her damages resulting from an alleged breach: the mitigation of damages has been deemed a question of fact in many jurisdictions including Kansas, Arkansas, Michigan, Oregon; and 6) the amount of damages to Buyer as result of the breach.

PUNITIVE DAMAGES

In some cases in which there is a breach of warranty or contract, the breaching party's conduct amounts to some type of willful or intentional conduct. If the conduct is deemed to be of a tortious nature it is possible that the injured party will recover punitive damages. Clearly, this rule is based on common law principles grounded in tort. However, there are more restrictive provisions regarding recovery that may be codified in state statutes.

Many states have enacted prohibitions against "deceptive trade practices" that contain an exhausting list of the Do's and Don't's regarding the sale of goods to consumers. Moreover, many of these state statutes provide that punitive damages may be recovered if the specific provisions of the Act are violated. *Note:* The Anderson article suggests that Texas' Deceptive Trade Practices and Consumer Protection Act is probably the most liberal statute in the country. Under its provisions, a mere breach of warranty is actionable as a deceptive trade practice in the sale of goods, services, or real estate. The Texas statute provides that the first $1,000 of actual damages be trebled automatically, whether or not the seller had knowledge.

Regardless of how it may seem, punitive damages do not serve the purpose of compensating the plaintiff, but are in place to punish or deter the wrongdoer. Punitive damages are not authorized in section 2-715 of the Code because they are not consequential damages. Section 1-103 says that consequential damages cannot be penal in nature. Plaintiffs have tried, however, to claim punitives under 2-715 but courts have consistently " . . . section 2-715 creates no new right to punitive damages . . . "

Although no provision for punitive damages is specifically stated in the Code, such damages can be sought under section 1-106 which reads:

> (1) the remedies provided by this Act shall be liberally administered to the end that the aggrieved party may be put in as good a position as if the other party had fully performed but neither consequential or special nor penal damages may be had except as specifically provided in this Act or by other rule of law.

> (2) Any right or obligation declared by this Act is enforceable by action unless the provision declaring it specifies a different and limited effect.

To better understand how courts make awards for punitive damages, it is necessary that we consider the cases cited in the U.L.A. and the U.C.C.D. Looking first to the U.L.A. the applicable section can be found on page 475. The prevailing rule in the majority of jurisdictions (same as stated earlier) is that "Punitive damages may be recovered in exceptional cases involving a breach of contract when breach amounts to independent willful tort."

Under the U.C.C.D., the prevailing rule in the cases cited holds that punitive damages cannot be recovered for breach of warranty alone, but there must be evidence of tortious conduct. The limit on recovery that requires tortious conduct seems to be fair because it provides some predictability. This allows a party to know the types of conduct that will make him liable when there is a breach.

Furthermore, states following section 1-106 of the Code use it to allow a non-breaching party to gain his expectancy under the contract. This section attempts to place a party in the position it would have been in had the performance occurred. The U.C.C.D. also has a specific section that cites cases involving claims for punitive damages under 1-106. Many states adopted the rule from the Code as stated above.

The facts of the above cases are not included; however, it is helpful to note that the most common tort alleged with a breach of warranty action is the tort of "fraud or deceit." The "other types of torts dealt with in warranty cases under the Code are cases involving extortion or duress." Breach of good faith also has been used as a basis for punitive damages in some cases.

A major United States Supreme Court decision recently supported the principle of punitive damages, but held in a 5-4 decision an excessively high award of two million dollars was violative of due process. In that case the car manufacturer repainted new cars that were damaged in shipment and allowed them to be sold as brand new cars without any mention of the previous damage. A customer who found this out had expert testimony indicating such a car was worth $4,000 less. He recovered this amount and four million in punitive damages, which was later reduced to two million, to punish the major car manufacturer for such deceit. The Supreme Court recognized a state's interest in punishing and deterring unlawful conduct through the allowance of punitive damages. However, the amount should be based on several guideposts:

1) the degree of reprehensibility of defendant's conduct

2) the ratio of the punitive damage award to the amount of compensatory damages (in this case 500 to 1 is too high)

3) a comparison of the punitive damage award with other civil or criminal penalties

Still purchasers of goods using these criteria for the amount may find punitive damages still to be a powerful weapon.

LIQUIDATED DAMAGES

Liquidated damages are a category of special damages. Under U.C.C. section 2-718, parties to an agreement can provide therein that a set amount of money will be paid if the contract is breached. The statute specifically states that:

> (1) Damages for breach by either party may be liquidated in the agreement but only at an amount which is reasonable in the light of the anticipated or actual harm caused by the breach, the difficulties of proof of loss, and the inconvenience or nonfeasibility of otherwise obtaining an adequate remedy. A term fixing unreasonably large liquidated damages is void as a penalty.

The Official Comments to this section further states that clauses providing for liquidated damages are permitted if they are reasonable. If the term fixes the amount at a price that is too high or too low that term is void. The purpose behind the law on liquidated damages is not to penalize the breaching party but to "reimburse the aggrieved party for the approximate actual loss suffered. " With regard to subsection (2), the official comment explains its purpose being applicable to situations where there is a partial payment or deposit.

Many state courts have used section 2-718 to permit a party suffering damages to recover liquidated damages. In the U.L.A., there is a general category of cases that summarize the position of different states on the issue of liquidated damages and those states are listed above. There are two cases cited; one in Illinois and the other in New York. These cases suggest that even if the parties include a provision for liquidated damages, the same is not enforceable in the absence of a material breach. While these are the only two cases cited holding this way, it is important to note that this could be a trend that other states may follow.

In the U.C.C.D., several states permit reasonable liquidated damages agreements. Several states follow the rule that a provision made in advance for liquidated damages is only enforceable where "(a) damages caused by breach are very difficult to estimate accurately and (b) [The] amount so fixed is a reasonable forecast of the amount necessary to justly compensate one party for loss occasioned by breach of the other party."

Many courts generally agree that if a clause allowing liquidated damages is included in the contract for the purpose of imposing a penalty on a breaching party it is invalid.

New York courts established a test for determining if a clause providing for liquidated damages is a penalty. First if parties intended by their agreement to have the clause operate ("in lieu of performance"), it will be deemed a liquidated damages clause and therefore enforceable. However, if the clause is intended to penalize it will not be enforced.

CONCLUSION

It appears that almost every state has adopted some portion of Uniform Commercial Code. For the most part, the majority of states follow the same rules for awarding special damages. However, there are others that do not give the relevant sections of the Code liberal construction as suggested by section 1-106.

The trends adopted by each state are obviously based on the legislature's choice of law. Nevertheless, the Code sections really are useless in the absence of case law to interpret them. It would be very difficult to say that one trend in buyer's remedies is more popular than another because the courts' rulings are based on the particular facts of a case. However, the general approaches provide an essential framework to aid a buyer in understanding how and when he or she can collect special damages in the event of breach.

At best, one should be aware that there are rules that provide not only guidance for the buyers transacting business but for sellers as well. For the most part, the majority of states tend to huddle around the decisions of sister states, and by doing this, the trends stay fairly consistent.

SECTION F

LEASES

XXVI

Article 2A of the Uniform Commercial Code—Leases

GENERAL PROVISIONS

One of the fastest growing branches of business today is leasing. Over the past few years both businesses and consumers have discovered many advantages of leasing pieces of equipment rather than purchasing such items outright. For consumers, one of the most popular items to lease has been the automobile. Rather than using available cash or savings for the purchase of the auto, or for the required down payment, the buyer leases the automobile and pays a monthly rental fee. If the automobile is used partially for business purposes, that percentage of business use is applied to the total of the lease payments for the year. This figure then becomes a tax-deductible item. There is no need to calculate depreciation under the tax formulas provided, since the lease payments include both interest and depreciation. Amendments to our tax laws have eliminated 100 percent of the interest paid on a car loan as a tax deductible expense. Therefore the lease transaction should become even more popular, particularly for those who use their automobile for business purposes. The major disadvantage of the lease of an automobile is the fact that at the end of the lease period one has no equity in the car. But even that could be turned into an advantage, since the lessee can walk away from the car at the end of the lease. It is also possible to rent a new car at that time so that the lessee always has a bright and shiny car to drive about.

Businesses, too, find the lease arrangement to have advantages. For major plant assets there is no need to invest capital in the piece of equipment. The lease payments are fully deductible as an operating expense. There is no need to clutter one's financial statements with one of several types of depreciation methods that are allowed by tax regulations. Of course, here too, the disadvantage of the leasing process is that at the end of the lease term the lessee has no equity in the equipment. However many organizations do follow the lease program and find that because of the fact that they have no equity in the leased piece of equipment, their plants are equipped with more modern pieces of equipment.

Another disadvantage of the leasing procedure is that it has been difficult for some lessors and lessees to know what are their legal rights under a lease. There has been no body of law that addresses itself specifically to the rights and obligations of the parties to a lease. Under present conditions, leases are handled in one of four areas of the law:

1. Under common law principles

2. Under the law of bailments

3. Under Article 2 (Sales) of the Uniform Commercial Code

4. Under Article 9 (Secured Transactions) of the Uniform Commercial Code.

Having four alternatives as sources of available applicable law has left all parties, including the courts, scrambling for desperately needed assistance. Some courts have applied Article 2 to lease contracts since Article 2 applies to "transactions in goods" and they then follow with the reasoning that a lease of a piece of equipment is such a "transaction." But this approach has not been followed universally because there are too many inherent problems of applying Article 2 to every type of lease.

It is believed that assistance to the beleaguered lease participants is now at hand. The Commissioners who wrote the Uniform Commercial Code have written a new article—Article 2A—Leases—for adoption by the various states. If this article is adopted by all of the states, we will then have a uniform law pertaining exclusively to leases. Thus far, the following have adopted this article and made it the law in their jurisdiction:

Alabama	Nebraska
Alaska	Nevada
Arizona	New Hampshire
Arkansas	New Jersey
California	New Mexico
Colorado	New York
Connecticut	North Carolina

Delaware	Montana
District of Columbia	North Dakota
Florida (original 1987 Act)	Ohio
Georgia	Oklahoma
Hawaii	Oregon
Idaho	Pennsylvania
Illinois	Rhode Island
Indiana	South Carolina
Iowa	Tennessee
Kansas	Texas
Kentucky	Utah
Maine	Vermont
Maryland	Virginia
Michigan	Washington
Minnesota	West Virginia
Mississippi	Wisconsin
Missouri	Wyoming

Readers may want to check with the Commissioner's office, (312) 915-0195, as to any state not listed for an update on its status. This may be just the beginning of the parade for the adoption of the article. Thus far, the rate of adoption by the states has not proceeded as smoothly and as quickly as had been hoped for. It should also be pointed out that the adoptions by states have not been on a completely uniform basis. The State of California found it necessary to amend a few sections of the article, particularly sections dealing with remedies upon default, to have the law conform to the needs of the state. Oregon used the California version when they adopted Article 2A. However, the Commissioners have stuck tenaciously to their original version of the law, even after considering the California amendments.

Article 2A has six major parts to it, five of which are within the Article itself:

1. general provisions

2. formation and construction of the lease contract

3. effect of the lease contract

4. performance of the lease contract

5. default by either lessor or lessee

The sixth section of the lease provisions presented by Article 2A really appears in Article 1 of the Code. It is an amendment of Section 1-201(37) which is dedicated to the definition of "Security Interest." This definition is of importance not only to Article 2A, which deals with "true" leases, but also to Article 9 of the Code which is captioned "Secured Transactions." Leases covered by Article 9 are referred to as "security" leases—they are created by basically a sale of the piece of equipment, but it is designed as a lease for financing purposes. In other words, the seller is in a position if the goods were leased so that possession can be quickly reacquired if the buyer fails to make payments as promised. At one time such security protection was given by a "chattel" mortgage but now Article 9 considers all such devices as a secured transaction. Article 2A deals with true. leases and it is for such types of leases that the Article was written.

The amendment to Article 1-201(37) is lengthy but hopefully it will do much to clear the air as to what is a true lease and what is a security lease. Many lawsuits have been tried to determine whether a given lease is one type or the other type. The law has leaned rather heavily on "what was the intent of the parties" when the leasing agreement was entered into. Obviously this can be difficult to determine at times. Then the law was forced to go to other tests. One test, often resorted to, was to go to a whole battery of possible factual situations to determine whether the transaction was a true lease or a security lease. Here is a partial list of some of the factors considered in one case.[1] An affirmative answer to a question implies the transaction was intended to be a security lease.

1. Does the lessee have the option to purchase the item at the end of the lease for a nominal value?

2. Does the lessee have an equity or property interest in the item?

3. Is lessor's business primarily financing?

4. Did the lessee pay a sales tax?

5. Is lessee responsible for insurance?

6. Is entire risk of loss on lessee?

7. Could lessor accelerate payments if lessee is in default?

8. Did lessee select the equipment?

9. Did lessee pay a substantial security deposit?

10. Was the default provision very favorable to the lessor?

11. Was there provision for liquidated damages?

12. Were aggregate rentals equal to purchase price?

13. Did lessor disclaim warranties of merchantability and/or fitness?

---

[13]Bank 120 (1980), *In re Brookside Drug.*

14. Did lessee have to join lessor in executing the UCC financing statement?

15. Did lessee have to pay license fees and maintain the equipment?

Obviously one could give affirmative answers to some of these questions even if the transaction was not a security lease. Thus the use of such a list still left the law in a confusing state.

The revised section 1-201(37) should assist in making more clear what is a secured lease and what is not a secured lease. The definition leans heavily on the common law's requirement that there must be a residual interest in the goods that reverts to the lessor when the term expires in a true lease. There are many other distinguishing features between the two as you will note when reading Section 1-201(37)

The purchasing officer should study this section carefully and understand the difference between the two types of leases. When purchasing a piece of equipment where a security interest is created, you will note the differences and the lack of protection given the lessee. Actually such a transaction is really a sale by the lessor to the purchasing officer's company with stringent penalties provided for default by the lessee. Most of the transaction, because it is a sale should be covered by Article 2. However there are provisions in Article 9 that will be applicable too, such as the registration of the lien (security interest) by the seller or the financing agency. Corporate counsel should be able to guide the purchasing officer through these details. However it is up to the purchasing officer to negotiate the best possible deal for the purchase—including all of the terms and conditions of the purchase—except for payment. Counsel should handle the arrangements concerning this portion of the transaction. The purchasing officer should pay particular attention to warranties for the equipment. Many security leases try hard to do away with such assurances. Do not allow it to happen!

DEFINITION OF A LEASE

Article 2A applies to true leases. Section 2A-102, "Scope" reads this way:

> This Article applies to any transaction regardless of form, that creates a lease.

Then Article 2A-103(1)(j) defines a lease in this fashion:

> (j) "Lease" means a transfer of the right of possession and use of goods for a term in return for consideration, but a sale, including a sale on approval or a sale or return, or retention of creation of a security interest is not a lease. Unless the context clearly indicates otherwise, the term includes a sublease.

This definition makes it quite clear that only true leases are covered by Article 2A.

Article 2A closely resembles Article 2 with appropriate revisions to accommodate a lease transaction rather than a sale. Also because 2A was patterned after Article 2, we continue to have the same problems we had with Article 2, such as how to deal with lease contracts that cover partly goods and partly services.

SCOPE OF ARTICLE 2A

The scope of Article 2A was limited to leases. There was no need to include leases intended as security since they are adequately treated in Article 9, "Secured Transactions." The scope of Article 2A is limited to "any transaction, regardless of form, that creates a lease" of goods (U.C.C. Section 2A-102). It is important to determine whether a transaction is characterized as a "true lease" or a "secured sale." For example a lease [in the 2A sense] may be exempt from state usury laws. Moreover, the distinction may be necessary to determine if a U.C.C. filing is required (assuming it is a secured interest). Leases are treated differently in Section 365 of the Bankruptcy Code if the lessee goes into bankruptcy. When considering the scope of Article 2A, a purchaser or lessor should determine whether he has a meaningful economic interest in the residual or revisionary interest. A *lease* [covered by Article 2A] involves a certain use of goods, compounded with an expectation that the goods [still having some value] will be returned to the owner. A *sale* [covered by Article 2] on the other hand, constitutes an unconditional transfer of absolute title to goods, with the exception that the goods will remain with the buyer or new owner. Here a secured interest [covered by Article 9] may come into play if there is an inchoate interest contingent on default.

TYPES OF LEASES

Article 2A covers two distinct types of leases: (1) traditional contractual finance leases and (2) statutory finance leases. The traditional contractual lease is subject to all of the old-fashioned lease provisions under the Code. Traditional contract leases are covered by implied warranties and the standard rules expressed in the Code.

FINANCE LEASE

A *finance lease* is not subject to the same provisions as a traditional contractual lease. Certain leasing transactions substitute a financing organization for the supplier of the goods as the lessor. Normally the lessor would be the party responsible to the lessee with respect to warranties and the title. But in this situation, while the seller or manufacturer is so responsible, the finance lessor is not. The reason for this is that often under a finance lease arrangement a bank or finance company is technically the lessor. It was felt that it should be liable only for financing aspects and not for the quality of the goods. The definition of a finance lease [Section 2A-103(1)(g)] was developed to describe these transactions. The provisions generally immunize a qualifying finance lessor from implied warranties of fitness and merchantability other than warranty of title (U.C.C. Section 2A-212). A finance lessor may, however, still be liable for express warranties or negligent repairs. In a statutory finance lease, risk of loss passes to the lessee (Section 2A-219). "Hell or highwater" obligations to pay rent are imposed only in nonconsumer leases and only upon the lessee's acceptance of the goods. Under Section 2A-209(2)(a), the statutory finance lessor retains rights against the supplier under the supply contract. Three criteria must be met to qualify a transaction as a statutory finance lease:

1. The lessor must not select, manufacture or supply the goods.

2. The lessor must acquire the goods in conviction with the lease (not "out of inventory").

3. And the lessee must be given information at the outset about warranties covering the leased goods and whom to look to for warranties.

SALE AND LEASEBACK TRANSACTIONS

Sale and leaseback transactions are becoming increasingly common. A number of state statutes treat transactions in which possession is retained by the seller as fraudulent per se or *prima facie* fraudulent. That position is not in accord with modern practice and thus is changed by the article "if the buyer bought for value and in good faith."

STATUTE OF FRAUDS

Article 2A-201 provides that a lease contract is not enforceable by way of action or defense unless:

The total payments to be made under the lease contract, excluding payments for options to renew or try, are less than $1000.

Or there is a writing, signed either by the party against whom enforcement is sought or by that party's authorized agent, sufficient to indicate that a lease contract has been made between the parties and to describe the goods and the loan term.

Just as in the case for the sale of goods (Article Section 2-201), there are many exceptions to the statute of frauds [see Section 2A-201(4)]. For example, some specifically manufactured goods are not covered by the statute. Moreover, if the party against whom enforcement is sought admits in his pleadings, testimony or otherwise in court that a lease contract was made, then the statute is not enforceable to the extent (or quantity) that he admitted. Once goods have been accepted and received by the lessee, the statute is no longer applicable. It is worth noting that the statute's minimum requirement is $1000 for a lease, but only $500 for a sale. Further, unlike a buyer in a sales transaction, the lessee does not tender payment in full for goods delivered, but only payments of rent for one or more months.

Article 2A also contains a Parol Evidence Rule similar to Section 2-202 for sale of goods, which provides that the terms of a writing (intended to be a final expression by the parties) may not be contradicted by evidence of any prior agreement (see Section 2A-202).

REMEDIES

True lease remedies are different in form, and often more favorable to the lessor, than the remedies applicable to sales. The nature of the lease (that is, the future interest of the lessor) is what constitutes this differentiation. In sales the measure of damages is based on the buyer's equity in the goods. In a lease, the lessor's damages for the lessee's breach are equal to lost rentals plus any damage to the residual, while a lessee's damages for the lessor's breach are equal to the extra rental expense of renting substitute goods. The Article provides for the lessor's remedies upon default by the lessee (Sections 2A-523-2A 531). Further, it provides for the lessee's remedies upon default by the lessor (Sections 2A-508-2A-522). This is a significant departure from Article 9, "Secured Transactions," which provides remedies only for the secured part upon default by the debtor. This difference is compelled by the bilateral nature of the obligations between the parties to a lease.

DAMAGES

Two types of provisions on damages appear in Article 2A: (1) those that apply to contractually specified damages (see Section 2A-504), and (2) the statutory remedies provisions that apply when the lease contract is silent on damages. Article 2A will control the measure of damages only when the lease requirement is silent on damages. This is based on the fact that many leasing transactions are predicated in the parties' ability to stipulate an appropriate measure of damages in the event of default. This is consistent with the common law rule allowing greater flexibility for parties to anticipate damages in leases than for transactions for the sale of goods.

XXVII

Special Problems

UNCONSCIONABILITY IN LEASES

Article 2A on leases contains an unconscionability provision of its own in Section 2A-108. It is similar to the Article 2 definition on the sale of goods and gives the court the power to strike or modify the lease clause or the entire lease itself. However, this unconscionability section contains subsection 3, which is novel from an American point of view: If a lessee successfully asserts unconscionability, the court shall award reasonable attorney fees to him. Generally in U.S. law, each side must pay their own attorney fees—regardless of whether they win or lose.

The inclusion of attorney fees for those successfully asserting unconscionability should encourage attorneys to assert it more often and to use its added leverage in obtaining a fair settlement. If the lessor is made to realize that he may not only find the lease unenforceable because of unconscionability, but also may be liable for the lessee's attorney fees, more reasonableness may be the result.

Interestingly, this new subsection will apply under the U.C.C. only to leases under Article 2A. The basic U.C.C. section paragraph 2-302 in Article 2 on sales does not contain any term for attorney fees. Thus the lessee who successfully asserts unconscionability is markedly better off than the buyer who does likewise in regard to the sale of goods. There is, however, a new type of restriction that could seriously curtail its assertion. This restriction is found in another subsection 4 of Section 2A-108. It provides that, if the court does not find unconscionability and thinks the lessee knew the claim to be groundless, it shall award attorney fees to the lessor. While on the surface this restriction seems fair and of no great adverse consequence, a further analysis indicates that it could virtually "kill" unconscionability claims or defenses in lease situations. Some businesses may be deterred from raising legitimate unconscionability claims because of the uncertainty as to whether a conservative-minded judge may decide the claim is groundless and assesses this liability. Legal fees for opposing attorneys could run very high. Even if the claim is made in good faith, does the lessee dare to take such a risk? For the small business, the very possibility of this risk must be considered as a deterrent to raising the issue.

This type of clause also could hinder or even prevent the development of new legal theory. The term *groundless* should not include the advocacy of new legal theory. Would Brandeis or Warren when first proposing the unheard of theory of right of privacy (which has now developed into a legal right) be bringing a groundless action? Would the first strict liability case (the seeds of the famous 402A) be held to be groundless? Who will dare risk a new legal theory of unconscionability if their client may be subject to having opponent's legal fees assessed against him or her? It may well be, however, that one can ask for judicial recognition of penalties or damages if counsel frivolously asserts a groundless unconscionability claim made in good faith with supporting evidence and arguments.

FILING A LEASE

Article 2A does not require the filing of a lease so as to advise later creditors of the buyer of the lessor's interest in the goods. This means that creditors may be misled by an unfired or secret lease. It is true that a "lease" under the Uniform Commercial Code must be filed if it is determined that it is in fact a security interest, rather than a true lease as previously mentioned. This has led to considerable litigation in the past.

The drafters of Article 2A did not think a filing of leases was necessary. One reason appears to be that the leasing industry opposed it. But this is not a sufficient reason where there are other parties that may be hurt by the lack of filing. Another is that the Reporter viewed the current state filing systems as "very heavily overloaded." In this regard, the answer could have been simply to make those systems more efficient. Indeed, with the use of computers, this should have been no problem. Further, there has been no such assertion or any evidence of such overloading in most states.

OTHER RECENT LEASING PROBLEMS

More recently several other problems have developed in regard to the leasing of goods. The purchasing manager should be aware of these and guard against such problems.

One of the problems deals with the advertising which is done by some leasing companies. The advertising is not only over optimistic, but often does not reflect the nature of the agreement which a party is later asked to sign. It is, therefore, important to double check the contents and terms of the advertisement carefully against the more final written agreement.

A second problem has arisen in regard to "reasonable wear and tear provisions." Generally, a lessor should expect a lessee to put reasonable wear and tear on the equipment or vehicle involved. Indeed, in many leases there is a reasonable wear and tear clause which permits the lessee to return the goods at the end of the lease period with some deterioration that would normally be expected for such goods over that period of time. However, it appears that some lessors are charging the lessees for items which most people would consider to be reasonable wear and tear. For example in terms of a vehicle or a car, lessors or the financing company they are working with sometimes attempt to charge for small scratches, dings, dents, or scrapes. Indeed, this may even include a scrape on the bumper which is expected to be bumped at times to protect the vehicle generally. It may be wise for the Purchasing Manager and his counsel to expand on any such clause so as to make it clear that as a lessee there is no liability for this type of reasonable wear and tear.

If a Purchasing Manager is confronted with such a problem he should ask the company counsel to handle the matter. Counsel may insist on a more reasonable interpretation of the clause. In addition, counsel may attack its validity since it is often in boilerplate standard form print which has never been noticed by the lessee or actually agreed upon by him or her. Further, application of such a clause may well make it unconscionable and hence invalid.

In addition, the purchasing manager should check the clauses and agreements in the lease dealing with excess mileage charges. Often the allowable mileage is unrealistically low, so that excess mileage inevitably occurs. The charges for the excess mileage may be astronomical and in the thousands of dollars. This also is a type of clause which the purchasing manager may negotiate on or have handled by corporate counsel.

SECTION **G**

COMPUTERS AND ELECTRONIC DATA

XXVIII

Computer Purchases and Controversies

Purchasing computers for a business is a difficult and tedious task. This is especially true when you are buying a system to be used for a large company with many different departments whose needs and priorities vary. But even for smaller businesses, there are pitfalls to be avoided.

PURCHASE STRATEGY

Experts in the field of computer law recommend that when purchasing a computer one should map out a strategy and consider many factors.[1] Among other things, the purchaser is recommended to take the following steps and considerations:

1. *Create a study group:* Form a group within the company to bring the needs and priorities of the entire company into one setting. Discuss the need of each department. For example, the accounting department will have needs far different from the art department, and while colored screens mean nothing to the former, they are essential to the latter.

2. *Formulate a request for bids:* This should be put in a form that allows for uniformity. It should list various factors that are ranked in importance to

---

[1]David C. Tuniuk, *Computers and the Law, Cases and Materials,* John Marshall Publishing Company, 1991, pp. 1-7.

the study group. It might include price, delivery, maintenance, installation, updating, specialization, warranties and insurance.

3. *Figure in the cost of training:* Company employees will inevitably need training. Can the seller provide this? What is the cost? Will they retrain when the system is updated?

4. *Count on late delivery:* Often the delivery of software is not on time. This traditionally occurs when changes must be made in the programming. One should not expect delivery on time, but rather expect it to take as much as four times as long as predicted.

5. *Estimate the time to convert data:* Putting a company's prior records into the new system can be a tedious task. This is especially true when the previous system was not computerized.

6. *Include testing time:* Purchasers should contract for a period of time to test the new system. The system should be operated for a while not only to make sure it serves its intended purpose, but also to learn how to deal with user mistakes.

7. *Run the old system simultaneously:* Users should continue to run the old system simultaneously. This ensures against any "kinks" in the new system. Thus if mistakes are made during the learning process, the old system will ensure against problems.

8. *Provide for maintenance:* Malfunctions in the system often create problems between the seller and the purchaser. The contract can provide for maintenance time and cost. Parties can also take out insurance against system breakdowns.[2]

Applicability of the U.C.C.

The key article of the Code relating to computers is Article 2, "Sales." For a sale to fall within Article 2, it must be a "transactions in goods." *Goods* are defined in Article 2 as "all things (including specially manufactured goods) which are movable . . . " Computers, however, create many interesting problems to these relatively simple definitions.

The starting place for computers and the U.C.C. is the sale of computer hardware (screens, keyboards, printers and hard drives). The sale of these goods generally falls within the U.C.C.[3] However, when the sale also includes software,

---

[2]Ibid., pp. 1-7. This list is derived from the cited text; for a more in-depth discussion, see the relevant pages.
[3]Amelia H. Boss and Jeffrey B. Ritter, *Commercial Law Journal*, "A Legislative Response to the Issues of Software Contracting," p. 35.

the issue becomes difficult.

When attempting to meet the UCC's "goods" requirement, software can be broken down into three classes:[4] (1) off-the-shelf software, (2) bundled software, and (3) custom-designed software.[5]

Off-the-shelf software is often considered a good[6] for many reasons. This is the type of software the consumer buys when he walks into a store and pulls the preprogrammed software off the shelf. This software has been programmed for the use of anyone who walks in the store. There is no updating, maintenance or specific design plan. The item purchased is moveable and capable of identification at the time of the sale.[7]

The second type, *bundled software,* is a sale of both hardware and software that has been packaged together.[8] Under a variety of tests this sale has also been generally found to be a sale of goods.[9] Under such a ruling, courts have employed a "predominant" purpose of the contract test.[10] Such tests are used in many aspects in determining whether a particular sale constitutes the sale of goods versus services.

The issue of what test to use is exemplified in *Triangle Underwriters v. Honeywell, Inc.* [604 F.2d 737 (1979)]. In *Triangle* the plaintiff was induced to buy a computer package from the defendant consisting of hardware and software to be used along with it.[11] The representatives of the plaintiff were very excited for the new equipment and had high expectations for its use.[12] Much to plaintiff's regret, the system did not work as anticipated.[13] For example, the system was to process billings and productions.[14] After its initial use there were complaints and an immediate "panic" that the numbers were not accurate.[15] The defendant worked on the system but never did fix it.[16] Eventually litigation resulted.[17] In an attempt to avoid its suit from being barred by the Code's statute of limitation, the plaintiff argued the sale was one of services.[18]

In analyzing this issue the court stated, "A contract is for 'service' rather

---

[4]Ibid., pp. 39-43.
[5]Ibid., pp. 39-43.
[6]Ibid., p. 39.
[7]See *supra,* note 3, p. 39.
[8]Ibid. p. 39.
[9]See *Chatlos Systems Inc. v. Nat'l Cash Register Co.*, 479 F.Supp 738 (D.N.J. 1979).
[10]See *supra,* note 3, p. 40.
[11]*Triangle Underwriters, Inc. v. Honeywell, Inc.*, 604 F.2d 737, 740 (1979).
[12]Ibid., 740.
[13]Ibid.
[14]Ibid.
[15]Ibid.
[16]Ibid.
[17]Ibid.
[18]Ibid.

than 'sale' when 'service predominates'; and the sale of items is 'incidental.' " [19] The court, looking to the purpose for contracting, found that the plaintiff bought the new system because it would work better than the one it had. [20] Based on this fact, the court held it was a sale of goods. [21]

The court did acknowledge that, as part of the contract, the defendant was to perform certain services. [22] The court found and held that these services were merely incidental to the sale of the goods, and did not convert the sale of goods into one of services. [23] The court pointed out as a key factor that the contract price was for the purchase of the hardware and that no separate bill or pricing was indicated for services to be provided or so done. [24]

A few basic principles should be restated from the *Triangle* case because the tests employed can be very important. The initial step is the reason for entering into the contract and the expectations of the parties. In doing so, one must ask certain questions: What is the essence of the sale? What predominates? If the essence of the sale is determined to be goods, any services that go along with the sale can be deemed incidental, not determinative. If this is kept in mind, one can negotiate and contract in a way that keeps the sale under the U.C.C. and entails its protections.

Thus the purchaser should make it clear that the purpose and expectations are for the hardware and its production capabilities. A lump sum payment should be made for this and no additional amounts paid or contemplated for future maintenance or adjustments. The contract should also make clear that the services to be provided are incidental to the sale of the hardware.

The next area, *custom-designed software,* is the trickiest area for the courts. When the software is purchased from the shelf and then modified for a particular consumer, the transaction is still considered to be one in goods. [25] However, courts are split when the software is entirely customed-designed. [26] This can be seen by analyzing the cases of *Advent Systems, Ltd. v. Unisys Corp.* and *Data Processing v. L. H. Smith Oil Corp.* [27]

In *Advent*, Advent and Unisys agreed to certain documents outlining a sale by which the former provided the latter with computer software, marketing and

---

[19]Ibid.
[20]Ibid., pp. 742-743.
[21]Ibid., p. 743.
[22]Ibid.
[23]Ibid.
[24]Ibid.
[25]See *supra*, note 3, p. 43.
[26]Ibid.
[27]Ibid., pp. 45-46; *Advent Systems, Ltd v. Unisys Corp.,* 925 F.2d 670 (CA 3 1991), *Data Processing v. L. H. Smith Oil Corp.,* 492 N.E.2d 314 (Ind. App. rehearing denied 493 N.E. 2d 1272 (Ind. 1986)).

manpower,[28] and the latter was to build and install the programs.[29] Subsequently, Unisys terminated the relationship with Advent and Advent raised various claims.[30] To rule on the claims, the court was presented with the question of whether custom-designed software fell within the U.C.C.[31]

The court first pointed out that many problems are raised by the issue of software and goods.[32] The court stated that the Code is intended to clarify, not cause, confusion and that its provisions are to be read flexibly.[33] The court presented an interesting analogy between software, compact discs and textbooks.[34] The court stated that the music played by a musician and a lecture given by a professor are not goods, but when put into the form of a compact disc or a textbook, they become goods.[35] The court analogized this to the software, finding the same theory applicable. The court further found that mere customization did not change the good to something else, because the Code definition of goods includes the phrase "specially manufactured goods."[36] Thus, the court ultimately held that software is, per se, goods under the U.C.C.

However, the court in *Data Processing* reached a different conclusion.[37] In that case the plaintiff and defendant entered into a contract whereby the former was to develop software for the latter.[38] Subsequently, the defendant stopped making payments and plaintiff brought suit for breach of contract.[39] In reviewing the case, the court found the contract was not one for goods.[40]

The court first pointed out that no hardware was presented in the sale; rather it was for a data processing system designed specifically for the defendant.[41] The court made an important distinction that the *Advent* court glossed over. The *Data Processing* court, in determining what was bargained for, found that the defendant had contracted for the plaintiff's skill and expertise.[42] The court stated that the mere fact that this skill is eventually put onto disks was not important because, it was the actual expertise that was sought.[43] In a finding

---

[28]Ibid., p. 672.
[29]Ibid.
[30]Ibid.
[31]Ibid. p. 673.
[32]Ibid., p. 675.
[33]Ibid.
[34]Ibid.
[35]Ibid.
[36]Ibid.
[37]*Data Processing*, 492 N.E.2d 314.
[38]Ibid., p. 316.
[39]Ibid.
[40]Ibid.
[41]Ibid.
[42]Ibid., pp. 318-319.
[43]Ibid.

inapposite to that of other cases discussed, the court held that the means by which the knowledge and skill were given to the defendant (disks) was incidental to the sale of the skill.[44]

While the *Advent* court analogized to entertainers and professors, the *Data Processing* court analogized to doctors and lawyers.[45] The court stated that much as a lawyer and doctor are sought for advice, so is the computer programmer.[46] Thus, focusing on the object of the bargaining, not on the means for its transmission, the court found the sale of customized software to be the sale of services. Therefore, absent a revision to the U.C.C. or a Supreme Court decision, there is uncertainty on the applicable law for customized computer software.

EXPRESS WARRANTIES

Purchasers may attempt to invoke Code principles to hold sellers liable.[47] Purchasers can invoke three U.C.C. protections to serve three purposes:[48] (1) express warranties[49] (2) the implied warranty of merchantability,[50] and (3) the implied warranty of fitness for purpose.[51] These principles are invoked in order to:

1. Hold the vendor to an obligation to supply merchantable goods rather than the sample common law obligation to act reasonably.

2. Invoke the four-year limitations in Article 2.

3. Or avail themselves of the available U.C.C. remedies, which may be more extensive than those provided under the contract or common law.[52]

The first protection a purchaser may seek to invoke under the Code is an express warranty. Express warranties arise in two main respects. The first arises from an "affirmation of fact" made by the seller. This is the most frequently found basis arising as a result of statements concerning the product or its performance.[53] These statements may come prior to or concurrent with the sale.[54]

The statement need not be a guarantee but must be the "basis of the bargain."[55] When the statement is the basis of the bargain, reliance on the part of the

---

[44]Ibid., p. 319.
[45]Ibid.
[46]Ibid.
[47]Ibid. at 319.
[48]See *supra*, note 3, p. 53.
[49]Ibid., p. 53.
[50]Ibid., p. 53, U.C.C. Section 2-312.
[51]Ibid., p. U.C.C. 2-314.
[52]Ibid., p. U.C.C. 2-315.
[53]Ibid. p. 53.
[54]Scott and King, *Casenote Law Outlines, Sales*, Casenotes Publishing Co., 1992, 6-5, 6-7.
[55]Ibid., p. 6-5.

purchaser is not required.[56] For example, a statement made by the seller to the extent that a used computer is "very capable of performance" would constitute an express warranty and provide the purchaser protection in the event the computer does not work. Additionally, warranties may arise after the sale is completed.[57] These statements may be made by the seller or those acting for him.[58] The U.C.C. does not require consideration for the subsequent warranty because it is treated as a modification to the sales contract under Section 2-209.[59]

The second warranty that frequently arises is from the description of the goods and from a sample of the product that is the subject of the transaction.[60] One must be careful of a common problem that arises in proving that a particular description or name used is the actual one in the sale.[61] However, if it is proved to be the same, the purchaser is afforded a presumption that the sample, similar to an affirmation of fact, is intended by the parties to be a "basis of the bargain."[62] One must be aware that the seller may raise a question of fact whether the sample displayed was the general nature of the product versus a more precise representation that the character displayed is the actual product.[63] Thus, while an express warranty is possible as a result of description of the goods or the samples, various issues must be faced.

While the express warranty seems very "clean," the purchaser must be aware of the seller's defense that his statements were mere "sales talk."[64] Statements made by sellers regarding the product that cannot reasonably be taken literally are recognized as "sales talk" or "puffery" and do not amount to an express warranty.[65] The U.C.C. recognizes the distinction between affirmations of fact and sales talk or opinions.[66] This difference is often slight and often results in litigation.[67] A puzzling comparison is found in the area of valuation. In the case of *Hall v. T.L. Kemp Jewelry, Inc.* [322 S.E.2d 7 (1984)], the seller of a bracelet valued it at $2000. Subsequently it was appraised at $900.[68] The court held that the seller's valuation was an expression of an opinion and did not amount to a warranty.[69] However, in *Lawner v. Engelbach*, [433 Pa. 311, 249 A.2d 295 (1969)], a

---

[56]Ibid., p. 6-6.
[57]Ibid., p. 6-6.
[58]Ibid., p. 6-6.
[59]Ibid., p. 6-5.
[60]Ibid.
[61]Ibid.; see also *Keith v. Buchanan,* 220 Cal. Rptr. 392 (1985) where seller's statement that boat is "very seaworthy" amounted to an express warranty.
[62]Ibid. p. 6-7.
[63]Ibid.
[64]Ibid.
[65]Ibid.
[66]Ibid., p. 6-6.
[67]Ibid.
[68]Ibid.
[69]Ibid.

seller valued a ring at $30,000 and stated it would be so appraised by others.[70] After a later appraisal did not value the bracelet at such a high price, the court held that the seller's statements amounted to a warranty.[71] Thus, it is evident that the line between sales talk and affirmations of fact can be blurry. In terms of computers, statements as to value may raise the same types of issues.

IMPLIED WARRANTIES

The second protection the Code provides purchasers is the "implied warranty of merchantability."[72] Section 2-314 of the Uniform Commercial Code creates an implied warranty by a "merchant" that the goods sold will be "merchantable."[73] A *merchant* is defined by the Code as a "person who deals in goods of the kind or otherwise by his occupation hold himself out as having knowledge or skill peculiar to the practices or goods involved in the transaction . . . "[74] Merchant status can also be achieved through the use of an agent.[75] The key requirement for "merchantability" is that the goods be "fit for their ordinary purposes," as well as quality requirements.[76] If the purchaser can establish that the seller is a merchant, the implied warranty shifts the risk to the seller.

The implied warranty of merchantability to merchants presents the risk that, regardless of their efforts, the goods sold will not conform to the standard or customary uses of the purchaser. The policy behind this rationale is clear. The merchant is an expert as well as being in the best position to take cost-effective steps to reduce risks.

The third protection the purchaser seeks under the U.C.C. is the *implied warranty of fitness for particular purpose*.[77] Section 2-315 provides that, if a seller has reason to know of a particular or special purpose that the buyer has in mind for the goods, and that the buyer is relying on the seller's skill or judgment in selecting the appropriate goods, then the seller is liable if the goods are not suitable for the buyer's needs. This usually arises when the buyer makes known his needs and thereafter relies on the seller's judgment. Indeed, the seller may prevent the formation of a warranty by indicating that the buyer should not rely on the goods to meet his needs.

----

[70]Ibid.
[71]Ibid,
[72]Ibid.
[73]Ibid., p. 6-7.
[74]Ibid.
[75]U.C.C., Section 2-105.
[76]U.C.C., Section 2-105.
[77]U.C.C., Section 2-314(2).

The second way this warranty arises is for the protection of special services. This warranty protects against problems that occur when the goods are merchantable, yet not compatible with the particular needs of the buyer. For example, if the buyer informs the seller that he needs new computers to be used to perform tasks common to architectural design, a warranty will be formed. Thus, the buyer is protected if the computer's graphic design capabilities do not allow him to fully perform his specific needs.

The final way this warranty arises is when it coexists with an express warranty. A simple example would occur when the buyer informs the seller that he needs computers capable of being connected to other computers internationally, and the seller assures him that the particular goods will conform. As a result of the seller's knowledge and expression of assurance, both an express and implied warranty arise.

One of the key elements of the implied warranty of fitness for a particular purpose is whether the seller had reason to know of the particular use. As stated, the seller is not required to have actual knowledge of the particular purpose, rather "reason to know." This may arise from the relationship of the parties or perhaps on past dealings with the buyer.

Another key issue is whether the buyer actually relied on the expertise and judgment of the seller. If the buyer relies on some source apart from the seller, then the warranty does not exist. Problems arise when the buyer relies on multiple sources. When this occurs, the issue becomes one of degree. This problem is easily illustrated. Buyer needs a computer capable of highly technical images for designing aeronautic equipment. Buyer reads in a magazine that product X is capable of performing such tasks. Buyer further asks his neighbor, who is knowledgeable in computers, for advice. Neighbor says that X is perfect for the task. Buyer goes to seller and asks to see X. While negotiating the price, buyer informs seller of his needs and seller remains silent. Who did buyer rely on? Or even if the seller in this situation says X will do the task, did the buyer rely on his own reading and his neighbor, or on the seller? It is evident that, even if more facts are given, the question is not easily answered.

DISCLAIMERS

However, a purchaser must be careful not to contract away the liability. The Uniform Commercial Code has provisions allowing the parties to "otherwise agree." For example, if A is to buy computer hardware from B, and B is a merchant, the initial risk is that the computer will not conform to the ordinary uses for which people in B's industry need computers. However, if A and B agree that "any nonconformance of the computers with the business of B is to the detriment of B" or "that B is to insure against certain damages," then the U.C.C. will assign the risk as agreed. Note that the ability of merchant to disclaim the implied warranty of merchantability is limited by unconscionability and strict liability in tort.

LEGISLATIVE REFORM OF COMPUTER LAW

The current Article 2 of the Uniform Commercial Code (UCC) is not sufficient to handle transactions involving the sale and licensing of computer software. Under current law, several courts have even held that such transactions involving computer software do not fall within Article 2 of the UCC. These courts hold that such sales are not transactions in goods, but rather are transactions for services. This holding is common when the software contract entails substantial services (i.e., when the contract is for custom designed software).

Software contracts differ from contracts involving ordinary goods in two important features: 1) software contracts transfer intangible goods; and 2) software contracts often entail a license of rights to use rather than a sale. There needs to be a shift from case law to the legislative front to tackle these differences and resolve the problem of the scope of Article 2.

The Article 2 Drafting Committee had been given just this task. In November 1992, the Article 2 Drafting Committee decided to complete a section-by-section review of Article 2. The Drafting Committee asked the ABA Business Law Section Task Force on Software Contracting to prepare this analysis of Article 2 and make proposals regarding necessary changes and accommodations. These proposals will be summarized shortly.

The Drafting Committee has three alternatives which it could use to structure the additions and adjustments to Article 2 to handle computer software transactions.[78] The alternatives are:

(1) Defining Article 2 to include software licensing contracts; adjusting Article 2 sections to deal with the intangible character of the transactions; and adopting new sections to deal with licensing issues.

(2) Adopting a "hub and spoke" structure for Article 2, in which Article 2 would contain the fundamental principles applicable to all commercial contracts; and creating sub-articles which would deal with specific types of transactions, such as Article 2A (leases), Article 2B (sales), and Article 2C (licenses).

(3) Removing software contracts from Article 2 entirely and developing a

---

[78]These three possible approaches are set forth in: Raymond T. Nimmer, Donald A. Cohn, & Ellen Kirsch, *License Contracts Under Article 2 of the Uniform Commercial Code: A Proposal,* 19 Rutgers Comp. & Tech. L. J. 281, 283 (1993).

new article specifically for licensing of intangibles, including software contracts (Article 2B Licensing of Intangibles).

Because the Drafting Committee has proposed fewer changes in the area of contract formation and other basic issues, the "hub and spoke" approach seems feasible.

CATEGORIZING OF PROPOSED LEGISLATION

The Report of the ABA Task Force on Software Contracts is an important one. Instead of reviewing the proposal for changes, additions, and adjustments to Article 2 in a sequential fashion up the code section numbers, the proposal can best be understood by summarizing it in the following categories:

(1) General principles are different.

(2) General principles are same, but major changes are necessary.

(3) General principles are same, but minor technical changes are necessary.

(4) General principles of Article 2 are applicable without any changes.

(5) New sections need to be added.

This summary will not reflect every change, adjustment or difference. It is intended only to highlight important proposed changes in Article 2.[79]

General Principles Are Different

§2-201—In proposed revisions to Article 2 this section concerning the Statute of Frauds requirement is eliminated. However, this would be in conflict with the federal patent and copyright laws which require a writing to transfer ownership in intellectual property. Therefore, the ABA Task Force suggests that while the writing requirement be eliminated for other contracts, a writing could be mandated for some contracts to the extent mandated by federal patent and copyright laws.

§2-307—This "gap-filler" concerning delivery in lots is in direct contrast with the presumption of the custom developed software industry practice. Even with mass-marketed software, the industry practice is generally to contract, as part of the initial transaction, for upgrades, corrections, and enhancements. Therefore, this "gap-filler" is inappropriate for software transactions.

---

[79]To see the complete sectional analysis, see ABA Business Law Section Task Force on Software Contracting, UCC Article 2 Sectional Analysis, *Issues Relating to the Inclusion of Software Contracting*, Feb. 10,1993.

§2-309—Since licensing generally involves long-term or perpetual ongoing relationships as opposed to short-term purchases of goods, this gap-filler, providing for termination at any time by either party, will require significant redrafting to handle termination and cancellation of licensing relationships.

§2-401—This section concerns issues of transfer of title. Because title transfer is not applicable to many software transactions, as access to or use of the software is important, rather than physical transfer, the ABA Task Force suggests that rather than dealing with title transfer, the revisions should contain provisions determining when a license becomes binding, and determining when a licensee has access to an intangible would be necessary.

§2-403—Again, concepts of title transfer are not applicable to licensing. Also, there can be no good faith purchaser with regard to software licenses. The ABA Task Force suggests that mass-marketed software which resembles a good, may warrant separate treatment here than the custom software developed for a licensee.

General Principles Are Same, but Major Changes Necessary

§2-101 & §2-102—The short title and the scope of Article 2 shall have to be broadened to reach software contracts, including software licensing, and software assignments of intangible intellectual property, and the sections should be broadened to cover contracts, including licensing and assignments, of other types of intellectual property.

§2-103—The definition section for Article 2 will have to provide definitions for the new terms involving software contracts and licensing, such as licensor, licensee, license, intangible, intellectual property, etc. Terms already defined in this section may have to be modified. For example, "receipt" will have to be redefined to deal with different ways that intangible property is delivered (i.e., electronic transmission or "downloading").

§2-105—This section defining merchant will need to be broadened to cover software and other intangible property in light of the enlarged scope of Article 2. The drafters will need to decide which persons will be included in the merchant definition—the inventor, the designer or the author—and will need to decide whether a dealer who may have no specialized knowledge of the software and its application shall be considered a merchant.

§2-207—This section dealing with additional terms in acceptance should be revised to deal with the enforceability of "shrink wrap" licenses. A "shrink wrap" license is a preprinted set of vendor-oriented terms and conditions printed on the exterior of the mass-marketed software package or on the envelope containing the mass-marketed software. The license contains a warning which states that if the consumer breaks the package or envelope, she has agreed to the terms of the license.

§2-312—In this section on warranty of title, changes will be needed to address the right to use and access software and other intangible intellectual property without reference to "title." Changes will be needed to make clear that licensing of software does not involve any transfer of title. The section also has a provision providing a warranty against infringement and obliging buyer to hold a merchant seller harmless against claims arising out of compliance with buyer's specifications. This will need substantial revision, as it is in contrast with the actual practice of the software industry. The buyer's or licensee's specifications are only functional specifications as to what the program should do; it is the programmer who puts together the technical lines of computer code which can infringe upon the patent or copyright of other third parties. The drafters could consider adding a provision that would require licensor to warrant that licensee's use of the software will not infringe upon any patent or ownership rights of third parties.

§2-313, §2-314, §2-315, & §2-316—In these sections dealing with warranties, the ABA Task Force recommends that a "substantial conformity tender rule" be adopted for Article 2 as it relates to software contracting instead of the "perfect tender rule," with modifications to protect licensee, in event of less than perfect tender of intangibles. Because software generally does not operate without deficiencies or "bugs," the "perfect tender rule" is inappropriate to software transactions. This problem is particularly expected in the context of custom-developed software contracts in which there is an expected lengthy period of adjustment and refinement on a developed software program after the first operational testing. The drafters may wish to consider a substantial performance or a material impairment standard in light of the assumption that software is inherently "imperfect."

In the area of express warranties, there are questions as to whether the vendor should be held to the promises of a demonstration "shell" program (a non-working program which shows layout and proposed features of future software) of the non-working demonstration product. In the section on implied warranties, the drafters may provide protection for the consumer and licensee from the hidden presence of computer viruses and the resulting injury to the user's computer system. Because latent defects in software will be virtually impossible to discover by examination, drafters may wish to provide additional safeguards in the section on exclusion and modification of warranties to protect licensees and consumers.

§2-508—This section provides seller to cure improper delivery or tender. Again, the concept of delivery is not appropriate to contracts involving software licensing, and needs to be adjusted to reflect methods of transfer applicable to software transactions. Also, perfect tender should not be required by seller (see §2-313 supra), and a modified provision allowing for "substantial tender" should be drafted for software contracting.

§2-510—Because this section deals with the effect of breach, it will need to be modified to allow for use of a "substantial tender" rule for determining breach in software contracting. See §2-313 supra.

§2-512—Where buyer is to pay before inspection of software, the drafters will again wish to modify the perfect tender rule to a substantial conformity tender rule, to provide protection to the software seller. See §2-313 supra.

§2-513—The provision regarding buyer's inspection rights will have to be modified to adjust concept of delivery to include methods of transfer used in software transactions and to provide for a substantial tender rule (see 2-313 supra). Also, drafters will want to consider what inspection rights buyers and licensees should have considering that most defects in software and other intangible technology are latent defects and are not generally discoverable from a simple inspection.

§2-601-§2-617—These provisions which address breach, repudiation and excuse will all need to be adjusted to reflect the use of a "substantial performance" or "substantial conformity" test instead of the use of a perfect tender rule. See §2-313 supra. Also, in several of the sections, the concept of delivery needs to be adjusted to include transfers in software contracts. In §2-602 buyer's rightful rejection, the section needs revision to reflect the fact that in many software transactions there is no transfer of ownership. Section 2-603, dealing with the merchant buyer's obligations to rightfully rejected goods, will need substantial revisions for application to licensing contracts. Licensees have no rights to sell the software as they do not have title to goods, nor do licensees generally have greater rights than right of licensee alone to use or access the software. The section providing buyer's salvage rights in rightfully rejected goods (§2-604) will need much additional revision, in great part because the physical media of the software license is not the truest measure of the software's value. The drafters may wish to consider granting the licensee a right to continued use of the rightfully rejected software absent instructions from licensor; continued use of an intangible will likely not deteriorate the intangible property to the licensor's disadvantage. For the section defining acceptance (§2-606), the ABA Task Force suggests that different rules should apply to mass-marketed software, as there is no practical opportunity to inspect it before purchase without substantial opportunity to operate software. The Task Force suggests consideration of a partial acceptance notion. The ABA Task Force also questions the appropriateness of §2-607 in creating the obligations of buyer or licensee of mass-marketed software after acceptance where the buyer's inspection of the physical media and packaging will not discover latent defects or where transfer is done without opportunity to inspect.

§2-703—This section providing seller's remedies needs revision to adjust the definition of delivery to address the granting of use and access in software transactions. The concept of resale by the seller of wrongfully rejected goods, while it may apply to mass-marketed software, does not apply to the custom-developed software context. The drafters also need to consider what remedies they wish to provide for licensors. Licensors may generally be able to cancel licensee's access or use of software by means other than retaking physical possession. Also, with software and other intangible intellectual property licenses, a licensee's breach may involve more than just the user fee or royalty. For example, licensee could have wrongfully disclosed trade secrets of licensor. The drafters may wish to provide remedies for licensors in these and similar situations.

§2-711—Substantial revision will be necessary on this section which provides buyer's remedies when seller fails to deliver or buyer rightfully rejects goods. As is, this section provides the buyer with the right to hold goods after rightful rejection and to resell them. A licensee may not have the right to transfer his rights to a third party (see §2-603 supra). Besides, the transfer of the right to access the software may be valueless without the licensor's obligation to provide support and maintenance. The drafters need to provide the licensee with remedies when licensor defaults or when licensee rightfully rejects software. The drafters have many options for remedies, including granting the licensee: the right to refund payments; the right to continued use of software after licensor's default; or the right to contract with a third party to maintain the software program.

General Principles Are the Same, but Technical Changes Are Necessary

§2-204, §2-205, §2-206 & §2-208—These sections dealing with formation of contract, offer, acceptance, and course of performance need to be redefined so that the scope of the sections includes the transfer of, or granting rights to, software and other intangible intellectual property.

§2-301-This Section needs to be adjusted to include forms of transfer which are not done by physical delivery. For instance, the licensee of a software licensing contract expects only the right to access the intangible property, and the licensor's obligation is only to provide that access; there is no physical delivery.

§2-305—"Delivery" is an inappropriate measure to determine time of payment. Rather, transfer of right to use or access software or other intangibles should be the measure. Also, "price" should be redefined to reflect the software industry practice of making a continuing stream of payments, as royalties or user fees.

§2-308—This "gap-filler" provides for place of delivery in the absence of specification in the contract. Since the concept of physical delivery is not applicable to software transactions, drafters will need to take into account the means of tender of software and other intangibles, keeping in mind that right to access and right to use are generally the rights to be transferred.

§2-310—Again, this section will need to redefine delivery and receipt to include methods of transfer involved in software contracts and licensing. This section will also have to provide for relationships where the transfer is ongoing.

§2-503 & §2-504—These sections, which deal with the manner of seller's tender of delivery and shipment by seller, require adjustment so that the delivery concept will include transfers of rights to use or to access intangible intellectual property. The drafters may want to consider providing for the method of transfer for electronic or remote access contracts.

§2-511—No revisions are necessary to this section concerning tender of buyer's payment, other than adjusting the definition of delivery to include methods of software and other intellectual intangible property transfers.

General Principles Applicable Without Significant Changes

§2-202—The parol evidence section will not require revision to accommodate software contracts.

§2-302—The unconscionability section will not require revision to accommodate software contracts.

§2-303—The section allocating risk will not require revision to accommodate software contracts.

§2-304—The section providing how the purchase price may be payable will not require revision to accommodate software contracts.

§2-319-§2-323—These sections deal with shipment and delivery issues and are therefore either not relevant to most software contracts (e.g., licensing contracts where remote access rights are used), or are not unique in their impact upon software transfers where software is treated like any other commodity (e.g., mass-marketed software).

§2-326—Note that when dealing with intangibles, such as software, creditors may not have the right to a security interest.

§2-328—Provisions for sale by auction require no revision to accommodate software contracts.

§2-402—In this provision dealing with the rights of seller's creditors, there is some question as to whether a security interest can be created in intellectual property.

§2-509—Risk of loss during shipment is not important to many software transfers. Risk of loss might be important in the mass-marketed software transactions, and could probably be governed by the section's provisions as is.

New Sections Need to Be Added

Presumption of Confidentiality—The ABA Task Force proposes that the drafters may wish to consider a gap-filler which will provide a presumption of confidentiality in software or other intangible intellectual property contracts.

Default in Licensing of Intangibles—The default concept in the context of licensing intangibles is not currently defined in Article 2. The Task Force suggests looking to Article 2A for guidance with respect to rights to notice and cure and other similar provisions. Should the test of default be material breach or impairment of a license?

Mass-Marketed Software—Mass-marketed software could be treated separately from the licensing of intangibles. Sales of mass-marketed software could be treated as sales of goods.

Gap-Fillers—The revisions of Article 2 could provide provisions to fill in when the parties' contract is silent as to: location restrictions; revocability of license; term of license; number of users and copies; rights to future maintenance, support and enhancements; and licensee transfer rights.

Caveat Bene: It must be remembered that most license and computer contracts are printed ones. As such they are subject to the infirmities of standard form contracts, e.g., reality of consent; unconscionability; matters discussed in Chapters IX and XXVII of this book.

New Article 2B

The American Law Institute and the Commissioners on Uniform State Laws have recently decided to add a separate article called Article 2B, Licenses. These transactions involving the licensing of digital information differ significantly from transactions involving the sale of goods. Because of these differences, a body of law tailored to transactions whose primary goal is to pass title in tangible property from one party to another could not simply be adopted and applied to transactions whose primary purpose is to convey rights and privileges involving the use of intangible property and information assets. Seeing the need for a separate treatment of this commercially important class of transactions, the above parties decided to act.

There is now a working draft in place; however, the draft has not been reviewed by the Article 2B committee and may yet be modified.

PRAGMATIC AND LEGAL EFFECTS OF THE INFORMATION SUPERHIGHWAY*

The Information Age

A remarkable aspect of the information age is the speed at which it is impacting our lives. Less than five years ago the average American would have ventured to

---

*Special Acknowledgment A. James Wang, Juris Doctor, MBA, MS.

guess that the Internet was a network marketing scheme somehow connected to Amway Products. Now E-mail, World Wide Web, Gopher, and Mosaic are a regular part of the lives of millions. It is a means of communicating that has taken the world by storm.

It is estimated that by the year 2000, computers of various forms will outnumber people in the U.S. An estimated 35 million people in the world are already connected by the infobahn. Another estimate gives the median income of the Internet user as $55,000. The business world has been quick to take advantage of the superhighway or infobahn for efficiency and operational reasons. But now the prospect of reaching millions of well-to-do potential customers is another reason businesses are taking the infobahn seriously.

Internet dilettantes Speaker of the House Newt Gingrich and Vice President A1 Gore are but two of a growing number of politicians getting online. Now it is possible to send E-mail to President Clinton, read the latest legislation, or discuss deficit fighting with former Senators Rudman and Tsongas.

Electronic commerce is no longer just a catchy phrase. In the modern business world of international competition, satellite links, and laptop computers, high technology gives the business player the competitive edge and wider markets. And as expected, Commercial Sales law is being tested in ways that were not imagined when current laws were written.

Legal Role

Traditionally, law has usually played a more or less reactive catch-up role to technology. For instance, the invention of the telegraph in the 19th century had an enormous impact on business practices. Yet no clarification on the rules of business law were forthcoming for almost 30 years. In their 1868 treatise on the law of telegraphs, Scott and Jarnagen wrote, "It is becoming more and more important that the rules governing negotiations made by telegraph would be clearly defined and settled, as contracts thus made are constantly increasing in number and magnitude." History is repeating itself again as we watch legal rules struggle to maintain pace with advances in technology.

It is understandable why cyber-commerce has blossomed and grown. Modern businesses are adopting new technologies much faster than in the past. The old adage of "time is money" is ringing truer than ever. Just as the telegraph and telephone bridged buyer and seller located hundreds of miles apart, new communications technologies are making the world a much smaller place. Businesses are using the Internet to search throughout the globe for better bargains, employees, consultants, and to conduct market surveys. Most of all, businesses are looking to the Internet as a window to a broader market.

Purchasing managers may require their suppliers to meet the requirements of their computerization and electronics systems. For example, one of the requirements suppliers must meet to be qualified as potential vendors to General Motors is that they must be "electronically connected." Information must be up-to-date and instantly available for management schemes like just-in-time manufacturing to work properly. Information technology has become the competitive edge.

Going electronic is also more economical in many instances. The Internet is the giant computer network created by the Defense Department during the 1960s and 1970s. With proper access to the Internet, it is possible to send messages to every corner of the world at zero incremental cost. Although access to the Internet may cost the user a monthly fee, there are generally no further costs. The savings really add up for firms doing business globally. In some parts of the world (e.g., Eastern Europe), the Internet is often more reliable than the phone systems. Current estimates have the number of Internet users as over 25 million in the U.S. alone and growing. Practically every Fortune 500 company uses E-mail. A one-page E-mail sent from California to New York costs about 16 cents, compared with $1.86 by fax, $4.56 by Telex, and $13.00 by overnight express in 1992. The cost of access to the Internet has steadily been slashed as the three major providers—Prodigy, CompuServe, and American Online—compete aggressively. Computer software giant Microsoft is poised to enter the field in a few months and further depress access fees.

Even in the home, electronic commercial transactions will soon become as common as cable TV. Indeed, some of the home shopping channels have linked up with the cable companies to allow home viewers to purchase items being advertised on TV by entering codes into a controller box. Businesses are seeing green at the prospects of millions of consumers on the information superhighway. The astute consumer can search far and wide for the desired product as well as the best price. Shopping on the electronic malls is already existent. Electronic transactions will be the high-speed vehicle a considerable portion of commerce will ride in.

The boom in business done electronically means that an equivalently growing number of transactions are taking place without the traditional meeting of parties or even phone conversations. Electronic contracting becomes important as more people than ever before are making purchases over international boundaries. There is a broadening of horizons in search of the best products at the best prices.

What could possibly go wrong with commercial transactions done electronically? A guide to Internet purchasing appearing every five days on the "biz marketplace" news groups gives some advice on how to buy via the net. Of paramount importance in any Internet transaction is to save all E-mail and written correspondence relating to the transaction. The guide suggests the use of COD (Cash On Delivery), credit cards, or third-party escrow services. It also reports an average of one complaint per month concerning transaction fraud, a very low number considering the thousands of buy-sell matches negotiated through the net.

The legal difficulty with an electronic commercial transaction is that it is neither written nor signed as would be required by a strict reading of the Statute of Frauds. In addition, the Best Evidence Rule would require production of the original document. The question then is which document is the original document when it exists only in cyberspace and not in any file drawer? The authentication requirement places the burden on the proponent to prove that the document is what he or she claims it is.

U.C.C. 2-201(26) provides that a notice is deemed received when it is delivered at the place of business where the contract was made or at any other place held out by the recipient as the place for receipt of such communications, and U.C.C. 2-201(25) provides that the recipient has knowledge of a fact when the recipient has received notice of it. Considered together, this could prejudice the computer illiterate who fails to or is unable to read the electronic mail he or she has already received on his or her computer.

Statute of Frauds

The Statute of Frauds has its roots in 17th century England. Its purpose was to protect the unwary and unwitting from contractual obligations. The prevailing law of commercial transactions still upholds the statute: the Uniform Sales Act demands a memorandum in writing and the Uniform Commercial Code requires only a "writing."

The terms "memorandum in writing" and "writing," when applied to media other than ink and paper, raise some uncertainty. Telegraphs were eventually accepted as a valid means of memorializing a contract. The reasoning was that the mechanics of ink flowing through a pen was analogous to electricity flowing through a wire. When teletype came about, the courts readily held that the teletyped message satisfied the writing requirement. In addition, courts have shown a willingness to accept a bewildering variety of substitutes including scratchings on furniture and tractor fenders and writings on eggshells in rulings related to wills.

Telegraphs, facsimiles, and contracts on paper napkins all have a common denominator in that there is a physical object that is visually legible. The writing requirement reflected the central importance paper represented in commercial transactions. This was primarily so because it was easier to detect alterations made to the actual paper document. Electronic transactions are steadily becoming difficult to alter as the use of electronic safeguards has increased. Various computer security measures can be taken to keep tab of the primary document and to signal whether changes to the document have been made or whether the document has been displayed on a computer screen or printed on a printer.

The signature requirement of the Statute of Frauds requires the defendant party's signature on the contract. Ordinarily this implies a handwritten signature on paper in ink. Courts have accepted as substitutes letterheads, typewritten or printed names, stamp marks, and embossed marks. The basis is the parties' intent to use them as endorsements of the contract and therefore satisfies the signature requirement.

As a practical matter, signatures cannot be telegraphed but the courts are quick to accept typed signatures as signatures within the context of the Statute of Frauds. A natural progression in this line of thinking would place equal acceptance to the typed signature on an electronic document.

Because the U.C.C. defines "signed" to include any symbol executed or adopted by a party with present intention to authenticate a writing, a party may use an electronic identification code to signal that the transaction pertains to a particular party.

Best Evidence Rule

Modern commentators give a more narrow reading to the Best Evidence Rule, restricting it to a requirement that parties produce available original documents rather than copies. Electronic mail consists of electronic pulses instead of writings on paper. The determination of which—if any—of the transmissions should be considered an original document is difficult.

Federal evidence rules 1001 advisory committee's note reads:

> Present day techniques have expanded methods of storing data, yet the essential form which the information ultimately assumes for useable purposes is words and figures. Hence the considerations underlying the rule dictate its expansion to include computers, photographic systems, and other modern developments.

This advisory note, which would be looked to by courts utilizing the federal rules, recognizes that words and figures can be stored in media other than ink on paper. The federal rules also provide that if data is stored on a computer or similar device, any printout or output otherwise readable by sight, shown to reflect the data accurately, is an original. Therefore, E-mail and other forms of electronic communications should satisfy the Best Evidence requirements readily. The fact that electronic documents can be faithfully copied electronically without any degradation in quality should make the Best Evidence Rule an insignificant requirement.

Technology has a penchant of filling voids, especially where some financial reward exists. It seems only a matter of time before a more or less foolproof system of authenticating an electronic transaction will be developed. Recognition by the laws of Commerce will make electronic commerce safe and dependable.

Requirements that documents or communications be "written" or "in writing" are out of place in the context of modern commercial practices. The American Bar Association is currently working to revise the Uniform Commercial Code—especially Section 2-201—to accommodate electronic transactions. The working group on Electronic Writings and Notices of the subcommittee on Electronic Commercial Practices recently proposed an Article 2 redraft for comments by members. A revised definition of the term "record" was proposed. Many of the panel members felt that a "blanket" allowance of electronic transmission of notices may be inappropriate at the present time. A definition of "record," a new term, has been proposed:

> Record means a durable representation of information which is in, or
> is capable of being retrieved or reproduced in perceivable form. A
> record may be in writing or in any electronic or other media.

All references to "writing," "writings," and "confirmatory memoranda" are to be replaced by "record" or "records" from Section 2-201 through Section 2-207.

Likewise, the National Conference of Commissioners on Uniform State Laws (NCCUSL) in its draft for Revised Article 2 of the Uniform Commercial Code has offered the following new definition for "record":

> Record means information that is inscribed on a tangible medium or
> that is stored in an electronic or other medium and is retrievable in
> perceivable form.

These new definitions are designed to embrace all means of communicating or storing information including but not limited to E-mail, tapes, and disks.

The term "record" encompasses "writings"; that is, any writing is a record. The corollary is not true; that is, any record is not necessarily a writing. A record need not be permanent or indestructible, but does not include any oral or other communication that is not stored or preserved by any means. The information must be stored on paper or some other medium. Information that has not been retained other than through human memory does not qualify as a record.

The proposed revisions are a palpable improvement over the current definition and pave the way for electronic commerce to reach new levels in scope and effectiveness.

Authentication Requirement

The laws of evidence require the proponent of an article to provide proof that the submitted article is what the offering party claims it is and, therefore, authentic. Proof of the parties' signature using expert testimony is one way of authentication. Witnesses to the signing may testify as another means of authentication.

The authentication requirement raises the issues of fraud and deceit and reliability of transmission. The wide use of telegraph has resulted in ample contracts disputes involving fraudulent use of telegraphs and operator mistakes by the telegraph company. An alternate means of authentication are the telegraph forms that are filled out by the telegram senders. Faxes are still susceptible to transmission errors and the quality of the faxed document is still of inadequate quality to detect fraud.

The authentication requirement as applied to Internet transmissions is potentially tricky. There is almost no way to stop a determined criminal talented enough to commit fraud via the Internet. From a disgruntled coworker using the computer of someone who has just stepped away from their workstation to high-tech electronic eavesdropping to gain account passwords, the possibilities are too many to enumerate. Technological advances in preventing and fighting online fraud is indirectly providing means to meet the authentication requirement.

Notice

U.C.C. 1-201 (25) and U.C.C. 1-201 (26) taken together deem that a notice is received when delivered at the place of business where the contract was made or at any other place held out by the recipient as the place for the receipt of communications and that such receipt is knowledge of a fact. If the contract was transacted online, this presumes that the Internet address is a place held out as the place for the receipt of communications. This means that one is assumed to have read his or her E-mail. This substantially prejudices the computer illiterate who fails to or is unable to read the mail he or she has already received on his or her computer.

Conceivably, a person could enter into a commercial transaction over the Internet to buy a thousand widgets, and then fail to check his or her electronic mail thinking that all was well. Unbeknownst to the buyer; there is an E-mail message in his or her computer from the supplier informing the buyer that the price on the widgets has doubled. U.C.C. 1-201 (25) and U.C.C. 1-201 (26) applied here would imply that he or she had knowledge of the price increase.

U.C.C. 1-201 (25) and U.C.C. 1-201 (26) were designed to require that a person should read the mail he or she receives. It loses its practicality if it requires that just because a person uses an Internet address, he or she is required to use it faithfully. A feature that signals that a sent document was opened by the recipient would solve this dilemma. Or perhaps a return receipt note akin to certified mail.

Technology Aspects: Authentication and Security

Addressing the authentication requirement as one of the paramount problems with electronic commerce crosses several lines. The battle against crime may bring some benefits to safeguarding commercial transactions by meeting the authentication requirement. Computer security is a relatively new field that is growing rapidly. Fueled largely by industry and market demands, hundreds of hardware and software have been marketed and sold in the name of computer security. If judicial notice is granted to reliable forms of computer security, it would serve the dual purpose of satisfying the authentication requirements.

The federal government in its battle against computer crimes, economic crimes, and pornography has provided considerable funding to a variety of research efforts, sometimes even resorting to hiring hackers themselves. It has funded the creation of the Computer Emergency Response Team (CERT), a group formed to safeguard the Internet.

The boom in demand for the services of computer security experts is an indication of how seriously industry is taking the problems of computer security with regard to ex-employees, hackers and viruses. Concerns about unauthorized access—by hackers, competitors, and disgruntled employees—has been the main stumbling block for conducting business on the Internet.

The 1986 Electronic Communications Privacy Act (ECPA) makes it illegal for anyone other than the sender and the receiver of the message to read messages exchanged over public electronic mail systems. There is, however, the practical difficulty in its enforcement. Instead, the push has been to protect the information itself by various means.

Every innovation seems to have inspired the diabolical minds. For example, faxes have been used by forgers to defraud banks. Spurious individuals can easily cut and paste executives' signatures from company mailings onto payment orders and fax the orders to a bank. The quality of faxed documents is generally not good enough to discern whether the document and signature are authentic or not. For this reason, banks are unwilling to accept payments orders by fax.

Technical advances likewise have made it more efficient for criminals to ply their trade. Police in New York recently reeled in the head of one of the biggest illegal gambling operations known as "Spanish Raymond." His operation made good use of the indispensable fax machine, but police were able to bug his fax lines to gather the incriminating evidence against him.

In the battle against various types of crime, government and industry— often together—have persevered to come up with interesting solutions. For instance, not long after the first telephone system was in place, Bell's invention was probably used in some sort of crime. It invariably became desirable to ascertain whether a defendant placed a phone call from a particular place to another at a particular time. Today it is possible to obtain the Caller-ID service from the telephone company. All phone signals carry an electronic coded signal containing the phone number, listing name and time of call. By subscribing to the Caller-ID service, this data is displayed on an electronic device. E-mail users are assigned unique Internet addresses. The sender's address is electronically linked to whatever message is sent. Although this would probably meet the evidentiary requirement, there is always the possibility that a fraudulent user has obtained someone else's account and password. In addition, there are methods to disguise an Internet address to prevent traceability. This has created the need for cybersleuths like Tsutomu Shimomura who ensnared Kevin Mitnick, the wanted superhacker on the run since 1992.

Retinal scanners, voiceprint recorders, and cryptographic authentication are presently available. One ongoing study funded by the federal government looks into the feasibility of a grant plan requiring every computer, telephone, fax machine, and so on to incorporate an electronic chip that would provide a unique identification key. Two keys would be required to decrypt the coded information that will be appended to every transmission or record from the device. One of the keys is resident with the device and the other is a common key held by federal authorities. This plan would give every device a unique signature that only law enforcement authorities could decipher. This is comparable to a Caller-ID function usable only by law enforcement, a valuable crime-fighting tool against money laundering and computer crimes.

Another computer security measure under development is what is widely referred to as Public Key. This system was developed by the National Security Agency and licensed to a consortium called Public Key Partners consisting of companies such as the Silicon Valley firm Cylink. This is a signature system designed to ensure that transactions are made in good faith. The Department of Defense hopes to use this technique for its contracting and the Internal Revenue Service wants to incorporate this signature system to its electronically filed tax returns.

The electronic signature is created when the document is encrypted using a secret code. The difference is that, unlike conventional encryption/de-encryption routines, a different, public key is used to read the document. If the document has been altered in any way by someone without the secret code it will no longer produce exactly the same signature sequence when combined with the public key.

Signature authentication as a desired part of sealing a contract has spawned a multitude of hardware and software devices. United Parcel Service delivery persons carry specially designed hand-held computers that can digitally store the customer's signature. On receipt of the parcel, the customer signs on the special electronic writing pad and the signature is digitally transmitted back to the central office. Although this again is not altogether foolproof, the risk of fraud is slight and exists whether or not the customer signs on an electronic signature pad or a sheet of paper. The benefits of this technology far outweigh the drawbacks of fraud.

A race is on to develop the standard for Internet transaction security protocols. Two different security standards are emerging—the Secure HTTP (Hypertext Transfer Protocol) and SSL (Secure Sockets Layer).

SSL basically encrypts the customer's order and credit card number at the beginning of the transaction. Secure HTTP is a more sophisticated system. It includes authentication of the customer's identity by the server through digital signature verification and other features. A battle is brewing over which standard will emerge as the de facto standard for commercial net transactions. Although these security standards are primarily meant for retailing on the Internet, their applicability to other facets of commercial transactions in terms of the authentication and signature requirements is evident.

The growth of other computer technologies opens up more challenges to the Commercial Law. Artificial intelligence and neural networks could have far-reaching effects into commerce. A neural network can be made to learn the job functions of a purchasing agent by monitoring his or her activities over a period of time, and in due course, even perform them. This is a further test to existing commerce law because now the computer is not just the means of communicating a transaction but also involved in the direct formulation of contract.

PURCHASING DECISIONS BY COMPUTER

Computers making buying decisions? Hardly absurd considering the fateful Black Monday in October 1987 when computer programs of such pedigree caused the biggest one-day drop in the Dow Jones Industrial Average. Computers running artificial intelligent software make thousands of transactions on the stock market all around the world everyday without any human input. So much so that computer trading is suspended if a stock market crash is in progress. But the simple irony is that even the decision to suspend computer trading is computer triggered.

In the slim-profit grocery industry, managers monitor sales from data gleaned directly from the check-out registers and warehouses. More sophisticated systems have the added ability to automatically raise a flag if a particular item is selling very briskly or is sold out. It is not inconceivable that the computer can search the cybermall for the best prices, determine when and what quantity needs to be ordered, and send an electronic purchase order to the appropriate supplier.

Farfetched or not, it is possible for a personal computer to make purchasing decisions for man. Although the Statute of Frauds and the Best Evidence Rule requirements can be stretched to cover even these types of electronic transactions, it is evident that such technology advances can leave commercial law struggling to keep pace.

GENERAL CONCLUSION

Commercial transactions will experience more changes as technology continues to leapfrog itself. Perhaps a cue can be taken from copyright law, itself a victim of innumerable technological surprises. Surprises in the form of T.V., radio, compact discs, and video recorders when considered in the light of the original 1909 Copyright Act. The 1976 Copyright Act as well as the 1988 Berne Convention makes ample room for advances in technology. Flexible language such as " . . . ,now known or later developed, . . . " is found in multiple parts of the 1976 Copyright Act. Copyright law as it now stands is seemingly ready for the next barrage of gadgets and electronic toys Sony, Nintendo, and Disney come up with in the 21st century.

The Statute of Frauds requirement seems particularly out of place in the context of cyber-commerce. There is some talk about abolishing the requirement altogether. Even England, the birthplace of the Statute of Frauds, has dropped the requirement completely.

The Best Evidence Rule is at its maximum utility when applied to force a party to produce the murder weapon and not some replica of it. As applied to computer documents, the rule seems inappropriate. Of more value would be rules to require stating the original disposition of the electronic document; type of file whether test, graphic, etc., and location of document, where stored on a hard drive, removable disk, or the full Internet address if stored in cyberspace.

The scope of U.C.C. 2-201 (25) and U.C.C. 2-201 (26) should be limited to account for the fact that no one should be expected to religiously read his or her computer mail on a daily basis. A proper remedy instead would be to consider that computer mail sent to a person is considered unread unless the person acknowledges receipt by means of some response.

The spread at which electronic messages are transmitted and the possibility that all E-mail may not be read by the recipient also means that other rules (e.g., the Mailbox rule and the rules pertaining to revocation or withdrawal of offer) need to be reexamined.

Existing commercial law must be reexamined in the light of the growing numbers jumping on the information bandwagon. Otherwise,commercial law as it now stands will be a speedbump in the information superhighway.

PURCHASING VIA THE INTERNET

As previously pointed out by Dr. Wang, the speed with which the information age is affecting our lives is remarkable. Just in the past several months, numerous credit card companies have offered new methods to make purchases via the Internet.

MCI is one company that made an early effort to attempt to capitalize on this new market. The nation's second-largest long-distance carrier announced late in 1994 the offering of a new data network designed to carry its Internet traffic. The purpose of this particular network is to allow corporate users high-speed Internet connections. Other new companies have sprouted up, offering systems to enable customers to shop at home with a credit card.

However, the enthusiasm for this latest technology has been tempered as a result of consumer fears about using their credit cards to make purchases on the Internet. Many people have trouble allowing new technology to handle their money. In a USA Today/Intelliquest survey of technology users taken late in 1995, only five percent of those surveyed said they trust sending their credit card information over the Internet. Of course, as the authors of the article pointed out, consumers were also fearful of using Automated Teller Machines in the early days of electronic banking.

However, consumer confidence in this newest arena was so shaky it was enough to draw even the most competitive card associations together. Last June, Visa and Mastercard announced they were teaming up to develop a safe method for consumers to pay for products on the Internet by using their credit cards. The software the companies are developing scrambles payment messages, which the companies feel will discourage attempts by hackers to gather the information. Both companies have a guarded interest in seeing the project through: the two companies who together have nearly 700 million cards worldwide have made extremely large investments in developing global networks capable of handling electronic payments.

The efforts of Visa and Mastercard were dealt a blow last fall when the software company Netscape admitted that the transaction security built into its popular Internet software had been broken into by a couple of graduate students, once again raising questions about the safety of using credit-card numbers in Cyberspace. Netscape's problem was viewed as minor and easily correctable, and most experts insist that technology is now in place to make transactions secure. They say the main problem for companies hoping to increase sales using the new technology is perception. However, that appears to be a large problem. Immediately after Netscape announced its problems the impact was felt by some companies. NECX Direct, a company that sells computer products over the Internet, saw its sales fall and was put in the unenviable position of having to win back consumer trust.

More recently, Visa and Mastercard made another effort to attempt to remove impediments to credit card transactions. The companies announced in

February a new industry-standard technology designed to protect consumers making electronic payment. This standard brought together two previously feuding camps—Microsoft and Netscape—and is intended to give merchants of goods on the Internet the convenience of a single, universally employed method of protecting the privacy of on-line transactions. For customers, the new technology hopes to offer a much higher level of security for electronic purchases than has previously been offered.

Known as Secured Electronic Transactions, or S.E.T., this standard permits a user to send his or her credit card account numbers to a merchant in scrambled form. The idea is that this number will be unintelligible to hackers and electronic thieves. It will also be unreadable for the merchant—however, a special code will enable the merchant to automatically check with the bank that issued the card to ensure that it is a valid card number and the customer is authorized to make the transaction.

Although this new technology may put hackers at bay, it should not be a signal for Internet users to let their guard down. Electronic thievery comes in many forms. One should be particularly wary of offers of investment on the Internet. Many con artists have taken advantage of the Internet's low cost and broad reach to offer investment schemes. Although the Securities and Exchange Commission is aware of the problem, it is handicapped by several problems, primarily small staffs and a lack of technological expertise. Perhaps the biggest problem of all is attempting to prevent companies or individuals from another country from engaging Americans in business deals. That's one question among many that remains to be answered in the future.

The day may not be too far off—if it's not already here—where purchasing managers will make purchases using the Internet. If one is taking advantage of this new technology, the prudent course is to take whatever precautionary measures are necessary to ensure your purchase is secure from electronic spies.

The following sources were used in writing this section, and may be referenced for additional information:

1. Daniel King, "How to Conduct Transactions on the Usenet Marketplace," *biz.marketplace*, April 7, 1995.

2. "I Was a Hacker for the FBI," *Information Week*, March 13, 1995.

3. Edmund L. Andrews, *MCI to Offer One-Stop Shopping on the Internet;* N.Y. TIMES, November 21, 1994, D2.

4. John Markoff, *A Credit Card for On-Line Sprees:* N.Y. TIMES, October 15, 1994, A3.

5. Kevin Maney and Robyn Meredith, *Risky business on the Internet, Few feel safe making on-line transactions;* USA TODAY, September 20, 1995, B1.

6. *Credit card firms work to secure Internet;* USA TODAY, June 26, 1995, B4.

7. John Markoff, *Plan to Guard Credit Safety on Internet, Visa and Master-card Announcing a Standard;* N.Y. TIMES, February 1, 1996, C1.

8. Patrick McGeehan, *Cyber-swindles taking root, Business deals on the Internet hard to regulate;* USA TODAY, January 31, 1996, A1.

XXIX

Electronic Data Interchange

The electronic transmission and receipt of essential purchasing data is beginning to replace the long-standing practice of using paper-based documents to accomplish the same communication between purchaser and supplier. The use of computers by both buyer and seller to communicate with each other is leading the parade to establish a "paperless purchasing" operation and a sales office bereft of paper too.

COMMUNICATING THROUGH ELECTRONIC DATA

The process of talking to each other with a computer is known as *electronic data interchange (EDI)*. It is remarkably successful in accelerating the speed by which a purchase may be accomplished. The rapidity of communication makes the procurement process more efficient and enables it to meet the needs of the organization promptly. Because of the speed of the procurement process under EDI companies do not require inventories as large as previously. The process also eliminates much paper preparation and handling which enables the purchasing organization to take on an added volume of work or to handle the same volume with less personnel. It is a modern age answer to the search for efficiency and economy in today's business world.

There are some legal considerations that must be reckoned with before all of these accolades can be comfortably laid on the EDI process. Since almost all purchasing officers live in a paper-oriented society and under a body of business laws that place heavy emphasis on a "paper trail," it should come as no surprise that there are legal problems that are occasioned by our quest for the "paperless" purchasing operation. However, it is believed that most of the legal concerns can be satisfactorily dealt with under the existing bodies of contract and sales law that are now with us. It must be admitted that amending the Uniform Commercial Code would be a more feasible manner to achieve complete legal compliance for EDI processes. That will probably come in time but our need is now and we must use the law we have available on the subject.

The Electronic Messaging Services Task Force

The Electronic Messaging Task Force of the American Bar Association's Business Law Section has prepared and published a careful and extensive analysis of the legal considerations involved in the use of electronic data interchange for procurement and other related business activities. Their report is printed in *The Business Lawyer,* June 1990, Vol. 45 No. S, pp. 1645-1749. In these pages the Committee gives us a careful analysis of the potential legal involvement arising from the use of EDI in purchasing, and their opinion of how these problems can be overcome. At the conclusion of this article, the Committee presents a Model Agreement that is suggested as a pattern for trading partners (buyer and supplier) to execute. This agreement is suggested by the Committee as a model for attorneys to follow when writing a contract for their clients who are engaging in EDI procurement and sales. The purpose is to give their clients the fullest opportunity to have their transactions hold to the fullest legal effect possible. This Model Agreement, together with the Comments of the Committee and their suggestions of how the agreement should be used as a draft model, is something that your company's legal counsel should be able to adapt to your particular need without much difficulty.[1]

The Major Legal Hurdle

When one contemplates what legal problems could arise if a purchasing officer allows a computer to do the talking, the most obvious question would be whether the transaction would be enforceable in a court of law. That question arises because Section 2-201(1) of the Code requires that every contract for the sale of goods amounting to $500 or more be evidenced by a signed writing if the contract is to be enforceable in litigation. Both a "writing" and a "signature" are required by this Code section. This leads us to the question of whether a computer printout of a purchase order or a supplier's computer acceptance of an offer to buy meets the needs of Section 2-201(1).

---

[1]*45 Business Lawyer*, June 1990, No. S, p. 1690.

APPLICABLE PROVISIONS OF THE UNIFORM COMMERCIAL CODE

Case law generally does not answer the question of the need of a signed writing when a computer printout is used. There are some indications that this computer set-up is "almost the same" or "seems similar" to other situations, but no reliance should be placed on case law. When we turn to the Uniform Commercial Code itself we can again find many sections that indicate transactions accomplished by EDI should be legally proper and legally sound, but the exact words are not there to give such transactions proper credence. As a result of this absence of specificity the Electronic Messaging Services Task Force of the American Bar Association recommends that trading partners—buyers and suppliers—enter into an agreement similar to the one they have proposed and which is included at the end of this chapter. Their proposed Model Agreement takes advantage of all of the positive expressions of "probable" legality contained in various Code sections as well as providing for waivers to prevent either party from taking advantage of possible lapses of "all out" Code approval of EDI transactions. You will have a better understanding of these comments if you read some of the relevant sections of the Code that we quote here, with the thought in your mind that the Commissioners who wrote the Code were making room in the law to accommodate electronic data interchange. Your author believes such thoughts were there!

We can begin at the beginning of the Code to get the Commissioners' first instructions that are in the direction of our inquiry. Section 1-102(1) tells us "this Act shall be liberally construed and applied to promote its underlying purposes and policies." With these words the Commissioners tell us not to interpret the Code with the idea that EDI does not fall within it. Rather, we should think positively and find how to bring it within its folds. The next subsection, 1-102(2), when it states "the underlying purposes and policies of this Act are (b) to permit the continued expansion of commercial practices through custom, usage and agreement of the parties," plays right into our hands. EDI is an expansion of commercial practices of vast importance to modern business methods. It will become more and more widely used and we should make every effort to make this expansion possible under the protective fields of the Uniform Commercial Code.

You will also note that 1-102(2)(b) suggests "agreement of the parties" as one avenue for expanding the role of the Uniform Commercial Code in commercial practices. The next subsection (3) invites us to vary the effect of provisions of the Uniform Commercial Code by agreement. Subsection (3) reads as follows:

> (3) The effect of provisions of this Act may be varied by agreement, except as otherwise provided in this Act and except that the obligations of good faith, diligence, reasonableness and care prescribed by this Act may not be disclaimed by agreement but the parties may by

agreement determine the standards by which the performance of such obligations is to be measured if such standards are not manifestly unreasonable.

This subsection invites the buyer and the supplier to enter into a type of agreement such as the trading partner agreement we are showing at the end of this chapter. If that agreement perchance affects some of the provisions of the Code, subsection (3) says "so be it." As long as the fundamentals of good faith, diligence, reasonableness and care are not disturbed, subsection (3) gives us carte blanche to change any other nonrestricted provisions. (A restricted provision that is not changeable by agreement of the parties is one such as is in Section 2-725 the Statute of Limitations provisions, which establishes a four-year period to bring actions for breach. That section concludes with this " . . . the parties may reduce the period of limitation to not less than one year but may not extend it." The four-year period cannot be extended by agreement of the parties, no matter how desirable such a change might be to the both of them.) The Official Comment to Section 1-102 begins with this statement:[2]

> This Act is drawn to provide flexibility so that, since it is intended to be a semipermanent piece of legislation, it will provide its own machinery for expansion of commercial practices. It is intended to make it possible for the law embodied in this Act to be developed by the courts in the light of unforeseen and new circumstances and practices.

This Comment seems to suggest the writers of the Code had the uncanny feeling and belief that something akin to EDI was on the horizon. So much so that they made provision for it at the time the Code was being written in the 1950s.

The Electronic Messaging Task Force of the American Bar Association received encouragement for many of the provisions in their Model Agreement for Trading Partners from Subsection (3) of Section 1-102 (repeated above) and from Official Comment 2 which refers to that subsection. The Comment to Section 1-102 states in part:

> (2) Subsection 3 states affirmatively at the outset that freedom of contract is a principle of the Code: "the effect" of its provisions may be varied by "agreement" . . .
>   This principle of freedom of contract is subject to specific exceptions found elsewhere in the Act and to the general exception stated here. The specific exceptions vary in explicitness: the statute of frauds found in Section 2-201, for example, does not explicitly preclude oral

---

[2]Copyright 1989 by The American Law Institute and the National Conference of Commissioners on Uniform State Laws. Reprinted with the permission of the Permanent Editorial Board for the Uniform Commercial Code.

waiver of the requirement of a writing, but a fair reading denies enforcement to such a waiver as part of the "contract" made unenforceable, . . .

The above quote could be interpreted to mean that a written agreement to waive the Statute of Frauds probably would be enforceable. You will note later that this approach is made part of the Model Agreement.

The Official Comment continues by calling attention to Section 1-205 which defines a "course of dealing" between parties. Section 1-205(1) reads:

> (1) A course of dealing is a sequence of previous conduct between the parties to a particular transaction which is fairly to be regarded as establishing a common basis of understanding for interpreting their expressions and other conduct.

You will note Section 3.3.3 of the Model Agreement takes advantage of this suggestion contained in the Code.

Another section of the Code—2-208(1)—is also taken advantage of in the Model Agreement in the same Section 3.3.3. This Code section reads:

> (1) Where the contract for sale involves repeated occasions for performance by either party with knowledge of the nature of the performance and opportunity for objection to it by the other, any course of performance accepted or acquiesced in without objection shall be relevant to determine the meaning of the agreement.

Since EDI transactions normally occur between the same parties with some degree of regularity, the buyer and the supplier can readily establish a course of performance for doing business. When this course of performance is established there should be no concern about the validity and enforceability of each purchase and sale. You will see shortly how the Model Agreement takes advantage of these provisions.

We should also take note of the definitions of the two troublesome words—"signed" and "writing"—that appear in the Code. Section 1-201(46) defines a writing in this manner:

> (46) "Written" or "writing" includes printing, typewriting or any other intentional reduction to tangible form.

One must ask if this definition is broad enough to include a computer printout of a purchase order sent via the buyer's computer and received by either the "mailbox" or the seller's computer. We believe it is. Furthermore could the same print-out be signed according to the Uniform Commercial Code's definition of the word "signed"? Here is 1-201(9) which defines the word:

> (39) "Signed" includes any symbol executed or adopted by a party with present intention to authenticate a writing.

You will note Section 1.5 of the Model Agreement which is captioned "Signatures," requires each party to adopt an electronic identification as its official signature. Such official signature is to be affixed to any document that is transmitted by either party so that the other party will know that it is an authorized transmittal. This requirement conforms to the requirement of Section 1-201(9) that any official symbol be "adopted" by the party using it. When it is adopted by that party, it expresses the intention of that party that it be his or her official signature.

FEDERAL RULES OF EVIDENCE

Further evidence that the law is ready to receive advanced methods of modern communication such as EDI can be found in the Federal Rules of Evidence (FRE). FRE 1002 specifies that the original of a record of a transaction be used as evidence in a federal trial. In defining an original, Section 1001(1) of the FRE includes this among other sources:

> ...letters, words, or numbers or their equivalents set down
> by ... magnetic impulse, mechanical or electronic recording or other
> forms of data compilation.

Computer storage of data seems to satisfy this definition of an original. Section 1001(3) confirms this by including " . . . any print-out or other output readable by sight . . . "[3]

There is an additional suggestion in the Federal Rules of Evidence that computer data is acceptable for establishing document authenticity. In what is known as the "Business Records Exception" to the hearsay rule, certain types of business records qualify as acceptable evidence. FRE 803(6) states, *inter alia*, "A data compilation...made...from information transmitted by a person with knowledge, if kept in the course of regularly conducted business activity...is regular." Thus it would seem the person who programs the computer would be the reliable witness to testify to the validity of business records transmitted and maintained in a computer. There is much more involved in this legal documentation which your author is certain should be left to the legal counsel representing the purchasing officer's organization.

In summation the purchasing officer should recognize that although the computer and its output is probably within the folds of present legal boundaries, there always will remain some lingering doubts as to its full enforceability until there are some amendments made to existing laws. Therefore, the Model Agreement prepared by the American Bar Association's Task Force Committee appears

[3]Federal Rules of Evidence 1001(3).

to be just what we need to make certain our transaction accomplished by EDI complies with the existing law and will be enforceable in a court of law, if need be. It is suggested that you consult with your legal counsel with the Model Agreement in hand to plan what your operations will require to enable you to conduct your business transactions when feasible, via EDI and continue to remain legally proper. Remember that EDI is not for all seasons! Only certain repetitive transactions can be handled in this manner.

THE STRATEGY EMPLOYED BY THE TASK FORCE COMMITTEE

When you consult with your legal counsel, he or she will readily recognize that the Task Force Committee of the American Bar Association employed manifold legal strategies in making its Model Agreement responsive to the legal involvements of EDI transactions. This is particularly true where it concerns meeting the needs of the Statute of Frauds Section 2-201.[4] The first strategy employed is what the Task Force refers to as the "definition strategy."[5] You will note that Section 3.3.2 of the Model Agreement specifies that any document properly transmitted shall be considered to be a "writing" and if there is a signature attached, it shall be considered a "signed writing." Thus, if both parties agree via the Model Agreement that such documents are "signed writings," the Uniform Commercial Code will probably say "So be it!" Further, Section 3.3.2 of the Model Agreement also states the agreement of the parties is that such signed documents will constitute an "original" when printed from computer files.

The second strategy employed by the Task Force has the Model Agreement providing that the conduct of the parties shall evidence a course of dealing and a course of performance as provided in Section 3.3.3.[6] In this manner there will be a prior history of a contract performance that can be referred to if some problem arises in a current transaction.

The third strategy adopted by the Task Force is found in Section 3.3.4.[7] In this section the parties agree not to contest the enforceability of the signed documents used by the other party under provisions of Section 2-201 of the Uniform Commercial Code. By agreeing to this provision of the Model Agreement, a party is estopped (see pp. 208-10 in the original for an understanding of the doctrine of estoppel) or prevented from bringing up the question of the adequacy of the

---

[4]*45Business Lawyer,* June 1990, No. S. Section of Business Law, American Bar Association, p. 1690.
[5]Ibid, p. 1690.
[6]*45 Business Lawyer*, op. cit., p. 1693.
[7]Ibid., p. 1194

print-out as a signed writing. Each party has made this promise to the other party and the other party has acted in reliance of that promise. You will also note that the same section in the Model Agreement goes on to have each party not contest the admissibility of the signed documents under either the business records exception to the hearsay rule or to the best evidence rule. You can see from this strategy that the Task Force is implying that if strategies 1 or 2 do not work, there is always number 3 to fall back on. This model agreement is carefully drawn! But hold on! The Task Force has one more ace in the hole. They have provided for one last "fall back" provision. It is Section 4.2 of the Model Agreement.[8] That section is captioned "Severability" and provides that if any section of the entire agreement is found to be invalid or unenforceable, all of the remaining sections are to continue in full force and effect. Thus, the odds are all in favor of the agreement holding the parties to its terms. There remains little doubt after the parties sign the agreement and begin to perform under it, it should hold firm for a good period of time. It should cover all transactions between the parties.

Nota Bene **to the Purchasing Officer.** There are some provisions of the Model Agreement your author wishes to emphasize. First on this list is Section 3 captioned "Transaction Terms." The Task Force has given three options to handle the difficult topic of terms and conditions of a contract for the purchase and sale of goods. Your author encourages each purchasing officer entering into a trading partner agreement to opt for "Option A." When a purchasing officer and a supplier sit down together to work out their Trading Partner Agreement, they should "go all the way" in reaching agreement. Any differences between their respective terms and conditions should be resolved and agreed to as is every other provision of the agreement. They should reach agreement on all of the terms and conditions as they will apply to each and every transaction between them. This is an ideal opportunity to avoid the ugly consequences of Section 2-207! The parties are encouraged to take advantage of this feature.

Rule of "Acceptance" Under the Model Agreement

You will note that Sections 2.2 and 2.3 deal with "verification and acceptance." It should be pointed out that the Model Agreement is written to have two messages go from the supplier-receiver to the purchasing officer. First the original purchase (offer to buy) should be verified by the supplier-receiver. Then a second message need be sent accepting that offer to buy. You will note that the Task Force's comment for this section suggests the supplier may either send an acceptance of the purchase order or a shipping notice. Either form of acceptance is permitted under the Code and the Task Force makes the suggestion the trading partners agree on

---

[8]*Business Lawyer*, op. cit., p. 1194.

the use of one or the other.

You will also note that the acceptance rules under the agreement dictate that an acceptance is not effective until received by the offeror. This is the same rule that is followed under the Convention for the International Sale of Goods. Under the common law rule, which is followed in the United States, acceptance is effective when the acceptance document is "dispatched" from the offeree. (See Chapter XIV for an explanation of the "Dispatch" rule of acceptance of an offer.)

Applicability of the Model Agreement

The reader should note that the Model Agreement is prepared to make EDI transactions conform to the Uniform Commercial Code. You will recall in the original text on page 187 we remind you that the Uniform Commercial Code deals only with transactions in goods. Therefore you must realize that the Model Agreement is to be used only for transactions in goods with your supplier. You will also note the Task Force suggests the agreement not be used for sourcing with foreign suppliers.

Service Contracts

It is certain that the question "How about service contracts?" will arise. You are reminded that service contracts that are to be performed within one year from the date of the agreement do not have to be in writing to be enforceable in a court of law. Therefore all of the first part of Sections 3.3.2. and 3.3.4. of the Model Agreement would be unnecessary in a contract for services that may be performed within one year. The balance of the proposed agreement should be acceptable but your author counsels you to check this suggestion with your own legal counsel.

Foreign Sourcing

The Convention for the International Sale of Goods does not require contracts for the sale of goods to be in writing. (See Article 11.) Therefore, if you are trading with a supplier and using the C.I.S.G., the same exceptions to the Model Agreement as spelled out above will apply. However, the purchasing officer is advised to read the last page of this supplement that applies to the C.I.S.G. and note that there it is suggested the purchasing officer attempt to have the foreign supplier do business under the Uniform Commercial Code of your own state in some situations. Then the Model Agreement as presented would be applicable, but your legal counsel should review the Agreement for other necessary alterations made essential by dealing with a foreign supplier.

THE MODEL AGREEMENT

The Task Force, in their report, suggested the Model Trading Agreement could be used either for withdrawals under a requirements contract previously negotiated or as a repetitive transaction type of purchase and sale.[9] It is written carefully enough to "cover" both types of transactions. In either instance, the trading partners can be assured they are operating under a legal arrangement that should prove to be enforceable in a court of law, if it proves essential.

USE OF THE MODEL AGREEMENT AND COMMENTARY

The purchasing manager should ask corporate counsel to prepare the Model Agreement tailored to the particular needs of the company.

The following should be considered by counsel in reviewing and implementing the Model Agreement and Commentary:

1. Provisions of the Model Agreement contained in brackets ([ ]) identify options for counsel to consider; in several cases, the bracketed language represents alternatives presented within the Model Agreement, while in other instances the provisions are themselves presented as optional.

2. The Commentary has the following purposes: To explain how the Model Agreement works, the purposes of each section and the intended effect of certain provisions in the content of existing commercial law.

   To provide background technical information relating to certain aspects of EDI and prevailing general industry practices.

   To provide specific drafting considerations on the manner in which provisions of the Model Agreement may be utilized or modified in preparing a definitive agreement.

3. The Appendix is an essential component of the Model Agreement. The parties should use the Appendix to set forth information essential to the proposed trading relationship as well as additional terms and conditions. Counsel should not consider the Appendix merely a "technical" item; rather, it is the field upon which mutual business decisions which affect the substance of the relationship of the parties, as well as the validity and enforceability of the underlying transactions, are to be specified. For that reason, the format of the Appendix is a suggested format, but does not represent a required structure. Counsel is encouraged to adapt the form

---

[9]*Business Lawyer*, op. cit., p. 1657.

and content of the Appendix to meet the requirements of any particular business relationship.

Purchasing managers or corporate counsel can obtain a copy of the Model Agreement, Commentary and Report by phoning, faxing, and writing to:

American Bar Association
750 North Lake Shore Drive
Chicago, IL 60611
Tel. 312-988-5638 or 1-800-285-2221
Fax 312-988-6281 or 312-988-5528

ABSENCE OF AN EDI AGREEMENT

While having a trade agreement on electronic data interchange is the ideal situation, there still may be an enforceable agreement in many situations in which no such agreement exists.

The electronic exchange represents an agreement between the parties. Even though they have only a simple electronic exchange reflecting general agreement, this may be enough to form a contract. Under the Uniform Commercial Code, a contract may be formed in any manner. The Code section on the formation of contract allows for a number of terms often found in a contract to be missing— still there is a contract. Such terms as those relating to price, quality, time of payment and place of delivery may all be missing. Nevertheless, the courts may find a contract and "fill in" the missing terms by looking to trade usage, the course of dealing and the course of performance. Also, the court may look to standards of reasonableness. The electronic data exchange often easily satisfies the criteria of contract formation.

In regard to the Statute of Frauds, it should be noted that electronic data could satisfy the writing requirement when the liberal code definition is taken into account. It includes not only traditional writings, but any other intentional reduction to tangible form. The very transmission and its receipt constitute reduction to a tangible form. Already the courts have found tape recordings to satisfy the intentional reduction to tangible form. Tangible form can be in the form of recorded sound or recorded electronic messages. This is so even though the tangibleness is found in a tape, disk, or computer chip.

In regard to the signature, the Code definition is, again, a broad one. It includes any symbol of a party used to authenticate a writing. The parties sending the message are known through use of their names, symbols, codes, or numbers. They intend this to authenticate the message conveyed. It is adopted with the intention that the message conveyed is authenticated. Both parties intend to contract, and the use of the electronic symbol is intended to make the contract effective. It is intended as an electronic signature. As the comments state, the signature can be found in symbols such as those on letterheads or company logos. Electronically conveyed identifications are just as symbolic as these and qualify just as much as signatures.

SECTION H

CHANGING THEORIES OF AGREEMENT

Past, Present, and Future Contract Law

Although the basic contract principles have been set forth earlier, it should be kept in mind that they change gradually over the years as new theories are developed. Some judges may be influenced by earlier theories, while others by later ones. Therefore it is of importance to have some understanding of general theories as well as of the general principles.

A new model of contract law theory is currently developing, and it will continue to develop over the decades to come, having a profound effect on lawyers, judges, and professors. To see the progression in contract theory that is taking place, it is important to review some of the past theories of contract and sales law. This will also help in better understanding where contract theory stands at this point in time and where it may be going in the last few years of this decade and the first half of the twenty-first century.

THE CLASSICAL MODEL

The early development of contract law represents a type of Classical model.[1] Some of the leading commentators of contract law have recognized this. Perhaps one of the best discussions of the Classical model of contracts was by Professor Gilmore in his *Death of Contract*. In pointing out the Classical model, he noted its early development in the law and the establishment of rules and theory. The

---

[1]Gilmore, *Death of Contract* (Ohio State University Press, 1979).

framework of this model was set forth by Professor Langdell at Harvard in the 1870s. The Classical model is one that recognizes the enforcement of the promise, but in a very mechanical way and with firm enforcement of certain rules. The promises were enforced literally and no exceptions were made. An example of this is found in one of the very early cases where the court enforced the promise to pay in a lease contract, even though the land had been invaded by a foreign prince and could no longer be enjoyed by the leasing party. The law recognized the sanctity of the promise and its enforcement without any mitigating rules. The doctrines of frustration of contract or excuse did not exist at that time. In addition to the very literal enforcement of promises, the Classical model requires a definiteness to the contractual relationship; thus a number of terms are necessary for there to be an enforceable contract under this more traditional law. The concept of definiteness is also a very rigid and mechanical element of classical contracts law.

Furthermore, the Classical model narrowly restricts contractual liability. Such restrictions are partially achieved through the use of the doctrine of "consideration," which limits one's contractual liability unless legal consideration exists. "Bargained for consideration" further limits contractual liability. In addition, the Classical model severely limits damages and places stringent constraints on such things as consequential damages. This may be seen when a party is denied consequential damages because the party failed to expressly state its needs. As Gilmore has clearly pointed out, it is a model that is developed not only for enforcing promises, but for limiting liability as well.[2]

THE NEOCLASSICAL MODEL

A later development was the Neoclassical theory of contracts. While it may be called the New Classical model, it is generally referred to as *Neoclassical.* In this model, which began to develop even before the Classical model was fully formed and established, there is a modification of the rigidity and mechanical nature of the Classical model. For example, in regard to some of the rigid contractual rules, more flexible types of contract rules were founded by Corbin.[3] One of the examples of the Neoclassical model is found with the treatment of consideration. The Classical model requires consideration in order for there to be a contract. This also is true in the Neoclassical model, although the Neoclassical model recognizes other bases which may "substitute" for consideration. Section 90 allows one

---

[2]Ibid.

[3]Corbin, *Corbin on Contracts; a Comprehensive Treatise on the Rules of Contract Law* (West Publishing Co., 1992).

to satisfy consideration either through the traditional means, or through the less traditional means of promissory estoppel. Another modification of the Classical model may be found in Justice Cardozo's opinions.[4] In his opinions, there are serious inroads into the more traditional doctrine of consideration. Cardozo stretches the concept to find consideration in almost any case; allowing this may also be viewed as a modification that makes up part of the Neoclassical model.

The development of frustration of contract or the excuse doctrine is present in the Neoclassical model. It is recognized that, even with the sanctity of promises, they need not always be enforced; some situations will excuse performance. Thus, the Neoclassical theory clings to the framework of the Classical, giving only some slack in its rigid, taut hold in contract law.

THE U.C.C. OR FUNCTIONAL MODEL

The "Uniform Commercial Code" model evolved next. Some commentators would say this is an extension of the Neoclassical model or one facet of it; others would say it is based more on functionalism and reaching a desirable commercial result. Indeed, both of these models have many facets in common. The Uniform Commercial Code was born in part out of the old Neoclassical model, but also in part out of a realism or functionalism emphasized by Karl Llewellyn. Llewellyn emphasized "realist" jurisprudence and noted the artificiality of some of the commercial law concepts. The Uniform Commercial Code, for which Karl Llewellyn was Chief Reporter, deemphasizes the concept of title or property in the goods. The concept of title is modified and instead issues are dealt with in a functional step-by-step performance. The philosophy of the Uniform Commercial Code is different from that found in the earlier models, with their emphasis on mechanical sets of rules and logic. In addition, the Uniform Commercial Code emphasizes permitting surrounding circumstances to come into the contract and be viewed in its interpretation. The doctrine of consideration includes several major inroads. The fact that some firm offers need no consideration illustrates this,[5] just as a modification of contract requires no consideration.[6] These are all situations where exceptions have been made to the more traditional doctrine. In terms of the Statute of Frauds, while one may find a number of exceptions under case law, these have been extended by the Uniform Commercial Code.[7] Included are writings in confirmation of the contract by the party who is trying to enforce it, but who does not have any paper or contract signed by the other party. Addi-

---

[4]See discussion in Gilmore, The Death of Contract (Ohio State University Press, 1979).
[5]See Chap. XIII.
[6]See UCC Section 2-209.
[7]See Chap. XVI.

tional exceptions exist relating to admissions of the contractual relationship in court, special manufacture of goods and part performance through delivery of goods or payment.

The Uniform Commercial Code modifies other areas of contract formation as well. The Code no longer places emphasis on having all or nearly all of the terms of the contract present for the formation of the contract. Instead, formation can result from a more generalized agreement. Indeed, as emphasized by the comments, a number of terms such as price, time, place of delivery, and quality of goods can be left open while a contract is still formed.[8] The lack of terms with the possibility of the contract is recognized in the Statute of Frauds, which permits the writing to establish the contract, even though many of these terms are not present. The Uniform Commercial Code permits formation of a contract even though one party may not show the precise time an offer occurred or the precise time of acceptance.[9] Rather, it emphasizes formation occurring in any context and through any means including conduct, thereby not requiring the more formal meeting of an offer with an acceptance. In some instances an offer and acceptance may prove that a contract exists but the Code does not require this.

Thus, the Uniform Commercial Code created a new model of contracts that is more liberal than those of the past. Indeed, to the extent that it emphasizes looking to the functional aspects of the transaction, it frees one from the mechanical and logical basis of the Neoclassical model. On the other hand, the contract drafters did not abolish the legal requirement of consideration. It is still a recognized concept, and the inroads made in it may be viewed as slight, since the basic concept remains a part of contract law under the restatement and commercial law section (1-103) incorporating supplemental principles. Along with this, the Uniform Commercial Code retains the Statute of Frauds in Section 2-201, even though there are exceptions to it. Thus, the Code retains much of the past framework of contract law. On the other hand, many of its provisions recognize that the relationship of the parties is a crucial matter, are supportive of it and require some fairness and ethical behavior in the relationship. So the movement of the law to relational theory is not so difficult.

THE RELATIONAL MODEL

Now, having viewed the Classical theory, the Neoclassical theory, and the Extended Neoclassical or Uniform Commercial Code theory, one may turn to

---

[8]See UCC Section 2-204 Comments
[9]UCC Section 2-204

what some of the legal theorists have been looking to more recently. These theories might be viewed as new, but "relational" models will also serve as a transition for the theory models which may evolve in several decades. The term *relational* is used in a very broad sense; it includes not only the theories centering around the parties relations, but the economic and societal relations as well. Their recognition is that contracts involve something that the Classical, Neoclassical, and the Uniform Commercial Code models do not reflect.

One relational model is characterized by its emphasis on the fact that individuals who contract with one another having continuing contacts or relationships.[10] These are of a personal or businesslike nature. For instance, Professor Macaulay in Wisconsin noted that contracts are often a series of ongoing relationships.[11] Some of the different types of contracts in this category include the dealership or franchise, employment contracts, contracts of agency, to use best efforts contracts and certain output and requirement contracts.

Indeed, the long-term contracts often found in contemporary society require an occasional adjusting of the relationships. Professor Ian MacNeil appears to be one of the first to use and establish the term *relational contracts* with his landmark articles.[12] He noted that contracts often existed in the context of ongoing relationships and that the current models of contract law were not sufficient for some of the more modern needs. Other relationalists, such as Professor Robert Scott of Virginia, also pointed to the relational nature of contracts law.[13] However, he emphasized the economic nature of the relationships between parties. In this sense, it is a cross between relationship theory and economic relation theory (mentioned shortly). He pointed out that there were times when cooperative action took place, and other times when more antagonistic interests were reflected in contracts law, and regarded those relationships in those terms. He also defined the relational contract perhaps more narrowly in the sense that he looked at these as being generally ongoing contracts and not as the singular sale contract.

Professor Donald King of Saint Louis University noted the relationship

---

[10]For some articles on relational theory, see e.g., Macaulay, "Non-Contractual Relations in Business," 28 *Am. Soc. Rev.* 55 (1963); Macaulay, "Contracts in the Manufacturing Industry," 9 *Pract. Lawyer,* November, p. 14, 15; King, "The New Conceptualism of the Uniform Commercial Code,"10 *Saint Louis* L.J. 30(1965); 11 *Saint Louis* L.J. 15 (1966); MacNeil, "The Many Futures of Contracts," 47 *S. Cal. L. Rev.* 691,695 (1975); MacNeil Contracts: "Adjustment of Long-Term Economic Relations Under Classical Neo-classical, and Relational Contract Law," 72 *N.W.L. Rev.* 854; MacNeil, "A Brief Comment on Farnsworth's Suggestion for the Future," 38 *J. Legal Educ.* 301 (1988); Scott, "Conflict and Cooperation in Long-Term Contracts," 75 *Calif. L. Rev.* 2005 (1987); Scott, "A Relational Theory of Default Rules for Commercial Contracts," 19 *J. Leg. Studies,* 597 (1990).

[11]Macaulay, *supra,* note 22.

[12]MacNeil, *supra,* note 10.

[13]Scott, *supra,* note 10.

aspect of a single contract in his articles and book dealing with the new conceptualism of U.C.C.[14] In this regard, he pointed out that one should look in any contractual situation to the relationship of the parties in that particular setting. Further, that relationship should be viewed not only in light of its setting, but also in light of the overall setting of the trade or the community, and finally in light of the overall societal setting.

The relational model is not an established one, but it consists of fragments of various theories centering around the theories of understanding transactions in terms of the relationships involved.

It is important to realize that still some other relational models exist. This same period has also emphasized that in some relations, there is an overlap between contract and tort. Indeed some writers even phrased the term *contort* to describe these settings and the law to be applied.[15] The overlap can be seen in various areas of the law. For example, an overlap exists in the area of products liability between contract theory and tort theory.[16] Most view the warranty theory as being primarily contractual though entailing threads of tort. On the other hand, many view strict liability in tort for defective products as a tortious type of theory. Yet both may be applied to the single fact setting where one party sells defective goods to another. Often the relationships of manufacturer, seller and buyer are involved. Thus the theories overlap in regard to the specific facts. Indeed, even though different rationales are used and different defenses apply, the results reached are sometimes the same by either of these theories.

In some situations there have been debates as to whether the particular relationship is best handled by recognizing the "reliance interest," which is more tortious in nature or the "expectation interest," which is more contractual in nature.[17] It is a recognition that the solution shall be based on the relationship and on the solutions that are possible in these particular contract settings. In a sense these theorists who see contract and tort merging have also contributed to the breaking of more rigid categories of contracts or sales law theory, and toward an ultimate obligation theory.

The law and economics movement has also contributed to a relational the-

---

[14]*Supra*, note 10.

[15]E.g., "Contort: Tortious Breach of Simplified Covenant of Good Faith and Fair Dealing in Non-insurance, Commercial Contracts," 60 *Notre Dame L. Rev.* 510 (1985). Gilmore, *Death of Contracts*, p. 87; see also, O'Connell, "The Interlocking Death and Rebirth of Contract and Tort," 75 *Mich. L. Rev.* 659 (1977); Considine, "Some Implications from Recent Cases on the Differences Between Contract and Tort," 12 *U. Br. Col. L. Rev.* 85 (1978); Note, "Contractual Recovery for Negligent Injury," 29 *Ala. L. Rev.* 519 (1978).

[16]In many cases lawyers assert both breach of implied warranty (U.C.C. Sections 2-314 and 402A, "Restatement of Torts Second") For discussion of strategy, see King, *Missouri Products Liability*, Sections 1-5, "Major Theories," 7 (1983) and Supplements.

[17]*Supra*, note 15.

ory of its own. Indeed, it has become such a major force in discussions of theory that it might be termed either *Economic* or *Economic Relational theory* in the historic line of contract theory development. It views the relationship of the parties primarily in economic terms and efficient resource allocation.[18] It finds the self-interest of each party as the factor propelling him into an exchange, which each views as beneficial.[19] To some extent it supports the use of standard written form contracts since these may reduce transactional costs. But at the same time, its recognition of economic factors goes beyond the more mechanistic rules of Classical and Neoclassical or the functionalism of the U.C.C. It permits one to see that the nature of a contract can be based more on the question of what law should be imposed to achieve desired results.

The Critical Legal Studies movement also contributes to the relationist theory development.[20] It points to some of the relationships between various groups and interests in society; the unjustified influence of vested interests upon the law at the expense of weaker groups is brought to attention. The effect on the law of contracts by powerful economic forces can be seen in regard to the development of fictions to uphold the standard form contracts favoring manufacturers and businesses at the expense of the consumer.[21] The focus on the relationship of groups within society aids previously explored relational facets.

If you go beyond the expanded Neoclassical model, the Uniform Commercial Code model, and the Relational models just discussed, which exist to some extent at this time, you may ask what are the possible contractual models of the future? To the extent that old and new theories overlap, we may already see some of the beginnings of the new model in the law.

THE LAW MADE MODEL

It may well be that the next theoretical emphasis may be upon the *Law Made contract*. The basic structure of this new theory of contracts may be explained in the following manner.

Contracts are now viewed as being primarily consensual in nature. This view is not only in regard to their initial formation, but also to their content as well. Generally a contract is thought of as an entity, with the parties having agreed upon a number of terms.

---

[18]E.g., R. Posner, *The Economics of Justice* (Harvard University Press, 1981).

[19]E.g., *supra*, note 30; also see Goetz and Scott, "Liquidated Damages, Penalties and Just Compensation Principle. Some Notes on an Enforcement Model and a Theory of Efficient Breach," 77 *Col. L. Rev.* 554 (1977); Goetz and Scott, "Measuring Sellers Damages: The Lost Profits Puzzle," 31 *Stan. L. Rev.* 323 (1979).

[20]E.g., Dalton, "Deconstruction of Contracts," 94 *Yale L. Rev.* 997 (1979).

[21]King, "Standard Form Contracts: A New Perspective," 1 *Comm. L. Annual*, p. 137 (1991).

Instead, under the new theory, contract is thought of as primarily a relationship of parties recognized by law. While consent may be one part of the relationship, it is only one part. This requires analysis of the setting and the particular relationship in the transaction. Some parts of the relationship often are not agreed upon but this does not prevent a contractual relationship from being formed. Instead those are imposed by law and constitute the "law made" part of the contractual relationship. Consent or agreement is often very generalized in regard to the transaction. Rather than specific agreement or dove-tailing of consensual points, there is only this generalized consent. Once this general consent is present, the law then not only recognizes that a contract exists, but goes ahead and finds and is ready to enforce a much more thorough and detailed law made relationship. Thus the law at this initial point of time is recognizing a contract with a legal framework of reasonableness and fairness imposed by the law to create the major part of the contract. At this point, the contract consists of the general consent and terms formed from principles of trade usage,[22] course of dealing[23] and course of performance.[24] To the extent that these do not suffice to fill out the relationship, the Code gap-filling provisions[25] constitute the terms. This major part drawn from these various sources may be termed *law made,* as contrasted to consensual.

Thus at a very early point in most contracts, with only a generalized consent or "spark of consent," the contract is enforceable. Furthermore, at this very time a whole contractual relationship may be imposed as a type of law made contract.[26] But the matter does not end at this first stage, but rather proceeds to a second stage in the relationship.

It is important not to think of a contract as a single stage; instead, after the two parties have passed this first stage there is a second. This is the manner in which all contracts should be analyzed, rather than that of the contract once formed being thought of as complete. Even simple contracts "evolve" within themselves. Either of several basic directions may take place, with variations of degree between them.

First, the parties may simply go ahead and perform the contract without any further discussion of the more detailed aspects of it. The seller may go ahead

---

[22]U.C.C. Section 1-205.
[23]U.C.C. Section 1-205.
[24]U.C.C. Section 2-208.
[25]E.g., U.C.C. Sections 2-305, 2-307, 2-308, 2-309. See also, Hawkland, "Sale Contract Terms Under the Uniform Commercial Code," Chap. 4 in King, Commercial and Consumer Law from an International Perspective (1986), Farnsworth, "Omission in Contracts," 68 *Col. L. Rev.* 860 (1968 and Speidel, "Restatement Second: Omitted Terms and Contract Method," 67 *Cornell L R.* 785 (1982).
[26]King, "Standard Form Contracts Revisited," 2 *Comm. Law Annual* 87 (1992); King, "Standard Form Contracts: A New Perspective," 1 *Comm. Law Annual* 137 (1991).

and deliver his goods in the usual manner, and the buyer may simply pay for them in the usual manner. Assuming the buyer is satisfied with the quality of the goods and no problems develop in this regard or in respect to the seller's performance, the conduct of the parties is recognized by law as satisfying the contractual relationship.[27] This is the second stage that follows the first stage of general consent. In a sense, this legal recognition of ensuing conduct makes this a law made aspect of the contract. Since the parties' conduct or actions are creating this part of the contract, some might prefer to call it "recognized by law." But both in contrasting it with the "consensual" contract, as well as considering that the law is making such conduct a part of the enforceable contract, the general term *law made* still seems appropriate. Others might argue that the conduct of the parties is consensual in nature, but this is outside what is normally considered as consensual. Indeed one party's conduct often takes place without first consulting the other on particular points and there is no consent to it although there is an acquiescence and satisfaction at the end.

Another possible direction in this second stage is that the parties will talk later about various aspects of the transaction and reduce these to written terms. But it should be remembered that this is being done in a second stage, after the first stage in which an enforceable contract exists with only general consent and with the law ready to impose law made terms to fill in the terms. In essence, where the parties take this direction in the second stage, they are substituting their agreed terms for the law made ones that were present and available if necessary. These contracts have indeed become more consensual. Still the law made contract of the first stage plays an important role, even though the final result is a more consensual contract.

A third possible direction is that in the first stage there will be the generalized consent, but in the second stage the parties will not reach further agreement on many or all of these terms. In that situation, the law will still enforce the contract and will supply the law made terms.[28]

This third direction may occur in more settings than one might imagine. First, in a number of instances, the parties will agree to a sale and purchase mentioning the goods generally, but leaving out some details. In some instances even price may not be mentioned, with parties not even worried about it since they believe it will simply be the market price or the selling company's list price. Certainly in many contracts one or more terms related to matters of price, quality of goods, time of delivery, place of delivery, time of payment or credit adjustments, or remedies are not even discussed.

The group of contracts involved in this third direction becomes even larger

---

[27]U.C.C. Sections 2-204(1), 2-207(3).
[28]See supra, note 25.

when one considers the Battle of the Forms that occurs with a buyer's order form and a seller's acknowledgment form agreeing to the general transaction, but each containing their own terms with a general objection or negation of the others. When this happens, there still may be a contract under U.C.C. Section 2-207, but the various conflicting terms cancel each other out.[29] This leaves many gaps in the contract that must be filled by the Code provisions.[30] This means that a large portion of this agreement is "law made." Thus, in the "Battle of the Forms," the "law made" contract predominates.

In regard to standard form contracts, which are used both in business and consumer transactions and number in the millions, there is growing recognition that they are often one-sided and imposed unfairly on the other party who never really consents to those terms.[31] While there have been some legal fictions[32] used to make form contracts enforceable, it is imperative to recognize that in reality there is not agreement on most terms and that the law should not impose these one-sided standard forms on the other party. When the reality approach proposed by this writer[33] becomes more recognized and applied, then the generalized agreement will be enforced and the rest of the contract will be law made. And the law made portion will be through the Code gap-filling measures.[34]

In situations where contract clauses are declared unconscionable,[35] they may be replaced by other Code-mandated standards and terms. These become a law made part of the contract.

THE OBLIGATION MODEL

Eventually, contracts may move into a new Obligation theory. The law would no longer look to a consensual model of a contract, even in the more liberal sense of the Uniform Commercial Code. It would go far beyond the current thinking of contracts as being primarily consensual. While it would recognize the importance of relational theories in seeking solutions, it would go beyond them by emphasizing that law can create certain obligations. These obligations may support a generalized agreement, but go even beyond it. Obligations may arise before, during and after the currently recognized contractual relationship. The obligations created by law may supersede what are often thought of in today's legal world as being consensual. The law also may provide the machinery for

---

[29]Comment 6 to U.C.C. Section 2-207.
[30]See *supra*, note 25.
[31]See *supra*, note 26.
[32]See *supra*, note 26.
[33]Ibid.
[34]See King, *supra*, note 25.
[35]U.C.C. Section 3-302.

obligations to be determined, approved or negotiated by government representatives. In a sense, obligations theory is supported by law made contracts theory and utilizes much of it. It goes beyond that part of law made contracts that relies on the U.C.C. emphasis of looking to trade usage or U.C.C. gap-filling provisions, and initiates a reevaluation of what obligations should be.

It would impose by law an obligation on the basis that a general relationship has been created and place an emphasis on sustaining and enforcing that relationship. With the relationship at a certain point, there exists a duty towards each other as a matter of business ethics and a social desirability of upholding such transaction. In this sense, one can find a legally recognized and enforceable "obligation." The obligation exists not because of contract theory or tort theory but because law imposes it on the parties.

Within this "imposed-by-law" duty of dealing with each other, certain facets of obligation are currently reflected or developing in tort and contract law. Again, the imposed-by-law obligation is directed toward achieving a good relationship between parties. Parties must neither misrepresent nor act fraudulently within their dealing. Parties must disclose some of the facts surrounding the transaction. Indeed there must be a type of good faith between the parties in that precontractual stage.[36] Currently, the Uniform Commercial Code limits good faith to performance and enforcement[37]; it does not require good faith in the initial phase of the relationship. However, there is every reason to extend some facets of good faith into this earlier stage, and some of the civil law systems in Europe are now extending good faith to the precontract type of point of time.[38] Within the relational context, it is easy under an Obligation theory to establish the requirement of good faith at this point in time although certainly difficulty exists in determining what good faith means in regard to particular things at this point of time. Another facet is that what one considers the formation of the contract becomes instead the formulation of the relationship with imposed-by-law duties to carry out certain things. In this relationship setting the legal obligation to perform is imposed by law.

The general relationship is not based primarily on consent, as the contract has formerly been envisioned. Rather there is only the "spark of consent" to a generalized relationship. At this point in time a contract "imposed by law exists."[39]. It is the first, and sometimes final, stage of contract formation. Trade usage, course of dealing, course of performance or conduct fill in the details of that contract as it develops. Of course, once there is the generalized agreement imposed by law, the parties may enter a second stage by discussing some of the

---

[36]Hondius, *Precontractual Liability.* Devanter; Kluwer (Publishers) (1990).
[37]U.C.C. Section 1-203.
[38]*Supra*, note 36.
[39]My adopted terminology. See also U.C.C. Sections 2-204, 1-201(3) defining Agreement.

details and working out terms, which they put to writing. While this is often the case, it is still done under the umbrella of the imposed-by-law contract—a contract that is already in existence in the sense of an enforceable obligation.

The performance of that relationship continues to place an emphasis upon good faith.[40] However, the imposed-by-law "contract," or obligation, also requires an adjustment of that relationship and a flexibility where certain circumstances indicated that this is necessary. To a large extent this may draw from the excuse doctrine of the existing Uniform Commercial Code model.[41] But it is not recognized so much as an "excuse" of contract because of matters not considered when contracting, but rather as an imposed-by-law adjustment of the relationship. In that sense, certain circumstances may require more flexibility than the current section of the Code. Indeed, too, it would recognize the rights not just of the seller to excuse performance or adjustment, but also the rights of the buyer.[42] The obligation created is an adjustable one for both parties.

Finally, one other thing should be noted about the new model. In the area of remedies, there has been a debate between the expectation remedy of contract and the reliance remedies of tort.[43] Under the new model, we would not think of this in terms in either being a part of contract or tort, but rather of the new obligations theory. Therefore, the remedies could be fashioned to whatever would seem to be the best for those relationships and for society. One could readily draw in some situations from the expectations remedies and draw in others from the reliance remedies. The new theory would permit this greater flexibility and would not cause one theory, such as contracts, or another, such as torts, to dictate the most satisfactory solution.

In addition, whole new systems of remedies could develop. Some of the alternative dispute resolution mechanisms could be brought into the remedies area as a matter of the legally defined remedies system where it would seem advantageous. Currently, Article 2 remedies for sellers and buyers do not include alternative dispute resolution, nor does the restatement of contracts. Yet an Obligations theory permits a break from relying on more standard remedies or even on more traditional thinking as the courts decide on such problems. New systems can be built into the Code or statutory scheme of remedies. New specialized tribunals can be created to determine the obligations and remedies.

---

[40]U.C.C. Section 1-203.
[41]U.C.C. Section 2-615.
[42]U.C.C. Section 2-615 only mentions the seller's right to excuse, but does not mention buyer's rights in this regard.
[43]See Gilmore, *supra*, note 1, pp. 55-64 and 87-94.

SECTION I

SPECIAL PURCHASING SITUATIONS

XXXI

Purchasing from Foreign Vendors

The purchasing officer's first obligation is to his or her company or organization. The needs of the employer must be met properly and promptly, and at an economical price. Often American suppliers can be used. But on occasion the purchasing officer will find that these needs clearly can best be met by a foreign supplier. The required product may be manufactured abroad and marketed directly by the manufacturer. Better quality and better availability may sometimes be assured if a foreign supplier is used. And, of course, the purchasing officer may find that the total cost of acquisition may be considerably lower if bought in the foreign marketplace. Whatever the reason, and despite the fact that some groups may believe it is unpatriotic to ever buy abroad, the purchasing officer must be prepared to use foreign sources of supply in some settings.

This book has dealt exclusively with American law. This body of law will continue to be applicable to all foreign purchases, with one proviso. The caveat is that the purchasing officer must see to it that there is agreement with the foreign supplier that American law in the form of the laws of his state (including the Uniform Commercial Code) will govern the entire contract if it is determined that this is the most desirable law. Sometimes foreign or international law will be more advantageous and the purchasing manager should consult with corporate counsel on this matter. An appropriate clause to include in the contract is suggested in a succeeding section. If a foreign supplier insists that the law of his country be used, the purchasing officer must consider the consequences; if these are too adverse he may decide to avoid doing business with that supplier. The law in some foreign countries can be markedly different from American law. In addition, the requirement that the courts of that country would have jurisdiction in the event of a lawsuit makes the cost of such a trial increase exponentially. An attorney specializing in International Trade Law or Comparative Law should be consulted if doing business on that basis with such a foreign supplier is inevitable.

One other possibility is to agree to let the Convention in International Sale of Goods apply. This may be agreeable to both parties in many situations. This is discussed in more detail shortly. Indeed, if nothing is said as to what law applies, and both countries have adopted it, it will be applied.

Many unique facets are involved in doing business abroad, notwithstanding the fact that we can provide the contract that American law will be applicable. Some of the unusual situations and problems that arise are discussed in the following sections. Suggestions for coping with these problems are given. Throughout all of the following material, the basic assumption is that American law governs the agreement.

INHERENT PROBLEMS

Dealing with the representative of a foreign supplier might present some language problems, particularly if the representative is from the "home" office. Most foreign representatives have a good working knowledge of the English language. However, there may be an occasional word used that is misunderstood. The purchasing officer is advised to place all of the negotiated representations of the product and the performance in writing on the purchase order or in the contract. Cultural-legal difference are discussed in Chapter XXXIII.

Business practices and customs in a foreign country may differ from those of the United States. This is particularly true of commercial customs and usage of the trade. The Uniform Commercial Code places emphasis on these two traditions. Many foreign countries do the same. The difficulty arises because the purchasing officer may not be aware of what topics are covered by the foreign country and vice versa. The translation may be different than that in the United States. Conservative advice to the purchasing officer is not to assume that the commercial custom of the United States will be applicable in the purchases. It is to be preferred that any specific customs or trade practices that are relied on be spelled out in detail on the purchase order.

One typical example of variance between American law and that of foreign countries has to do with product liability. The product liability scene, as we know it here in America, is unique in the world. Consequently, foreign manufacturers may have little or no product liability insurance to cover potential liabilities. If the product being purchased is one that might create such exposure, precautions should be taken before making the purchase. Some protective measures will be discussed later.

DELIVERY CONSIDERATIONS

Adequate lead time must be provided for foreign purchases, particularly when shipment is to be made on water. Keep in mind that the goods must be shipped from the foreign supplier's plant to the seaport. If the supplier is located in a land-locked country, there is a problem of customs clearance at the intervening country's border. Then the goods must be loaded alongside the vessel, where they might remain for some period of time before being loaded. After loading, the shipment must be given port clearance. Time for the vessel to reach the port of delivery must be allowed. Then more time for unloading and customs clearance. Finally there is a transshipment to the buyer's plant. Considerable time will have elapsed between completion of manufacture of the goods and their eventual arrival at the receiving department in the United States.

The responsibility for delivery is determined by the negotiated contract with the supplier. In Chapter XX we discussed various delivery terms that might be employed for foreign shipments. In addition to those terms included in the Uniform Commercial Code, there are the variations contained in Incoterms. The purchasing officer should use the company's foreign traffic department, if one exists, to select the best possible terms for shipment. Consideration should be given to the following items in this selection of terms:

1. Where will the risk of loss be located at all times during the delivery process? Remember in an overseas shipment there could be as many as ten areas where the goods will be handled: (1) at the supplier's plant once the goods are identified for the buyer's use, (2) shipment from the supplier's plant to the seaport, (3) while the goods are transferred alongside the vessel, (4) while the goods are loaded, (5) while the goods are at sea, (6) while being unloaded at the port of entry, (7) while alongside ship awaiting transshipment, (8) while being loaded for transshipment to the buyer's plant, (9) during transshipment, and (10) while being transferred to the buyer's receiving dock.

   Proper selection of the desirable delivery terms will designate where the risk of loss should fall if there is damage at any of these possible sites. Once the delivery term is decided, proper precautions should be taken to cover the risk during the entire duration of transportation.

2. Which party will have the responsibility to obtain the necessary government clearances for the goods? Here the exposure is twofold—at the

exporting country and at the United States port of entry. Export licenses must be obtained and duties paid. Similar clearances must be made here. The purchasing officer is advised that there are import agents who will handle the problems if the responsibility is placed on the buyer.

3. Insurance of the goods must be provided either by the supplier or the buyer. Negotiations as to who obtains the insurance and at whose expense that insurance will be must be accomplished. In addition, the extent of the coverage must be settled. War risk insurance might be necessary as one example of the extent of the coverage.

4. Another responsibility of one of the parties is the selection and engagement of a vessel to carry the goods. It is not a simple matter to find a vessel suitable for carrying the goods that will be available at the time needed at the port of embarkation to go to the United States. There are agents, again, who can handle this if the duty is placed on the purchasing officer.

5. Allocation of the costs of the entire delivery process must be negotiated. If the price is a delivered price, obviously it would be the supplier's expense. But it could be a shipment contract when the entire cost rests with the buyer. These costs might also be divided between the buyer and the seller.

   Not only are these costs to be allocated but there may be considerable expenditures for export and import licenses and duties as well. Each cost must be carefully spelled out and an understanding reached between the parties. Some suppliers will prepay such costs for the benefit of the buyer if the obligation falls on the buyer.

Transit Financing

The possible lengthy period of transportation of the goods gives rise to the problem of financing while in transit. Will it be the supplier's or the buyer's working capital that is tied up in the value of the goods during this period of time? This must be looked at before the purchase is made. If the financing becomes the buyer's obligation, the cost of such investment must be added to the purchase cost.

DETERMINATION OF FINAL COST

Determining the total cost of a product purchased from a foreign source requires some mathematical skill. The many facets of the transaction must be considered before one arrives at the full cost. Of course, if the ,purchasing officer negotiates a firm price on a destination term, there is no doubt what the total cost will be. However, this type of an arrangement is not always possible to obtain, and some buyers believe that if you do get such terms, you may be paying more for the product than you should pay. Let us look at a few of the price problems that one might encounter.

The foreign supplier looks at his own costs in setting his sale price. That sales price first will be determined by the currency of the supplier's country. It will then be converted to American dollars by the rate of exchange prevailing at the time of conversion. Those who follow currency transactions know that exchange rates vary daily. While the conversion is a simple mathematical process, the purchased cost of the goods will vary depending on the day the conversion is made. That date could be the date the foreign supplier submits a firm price quotation and offer to sell, it could be the date the goods are ready for shipment, or it could be the date the goods arrive at the buyer's facility (or even after arrival). Given the lead time required for manufacturing and the time consumed by transportation, one or several months might elapse between the placing of the order and the arrival of the goods. During that time interval there could be major shifts in the exchange rate. Therefore, the first thing the purchasing officer should do is to determine when payment will be made. It also is prudent to specify the exact data source that will be used for the rate of exchange.

Next, it is important to determine which party is to assume the cost for the various licenses, duties, taxes, and fees associated with the purchase. This should all be part of the purchase contract. The purchasing officer should enumerate all of the various costs, even if the supplier has agreed to assume them. It is suggested a "catch-all" phrase be included, such as " . . . and any other licenses, fees, duties, and taxes that might be levied by any government, port authority customs, or other agency having authority over the goods involved herein."

Remember to include in the cost price the expense of transportation and insurance associated with the transaction.

PAYMENT OPTIONS

The next question to be determined, once the price and total costs are known, is the mechanics of how payment of the amount due is to be made and when it is to occur. We have discussed the conversion process so that the amount to be paid in American dollars is known. We have referred to the question of when payment is to be expected—in advance at the time the order is placed, when the goods are to be shipped, when they are received, or some time after their receipt.

Before determining the solutions to these questions, let us reflect on the credit scene when both the buyer and the supplier operate in the United States.

There are purchasing officers here who assume credit will be granted on every purchase they make. They do not even bother to negotiate the terms. This happens despite the fact that Section 2-310 of the Code assumes the buyer will pay the supplier at the time conforming goods are delivered, "unless otherwise agreed." Many purchasing officers will have printed on their purchase order the clause "Terms, net 30 days after goods are received unless otherwise stated," to cover this situation. The buyer who wants credit usually has little or no trouble obtaining it, if the buyer's credit rating is good.

Most American suppliers expect to and are usually willing to extend credit to their American customers. The credit rating of a buyer can easily be obtained through normal credit rating agencies. The bank accounts and assets of the buyer are easily accessible if that becomes necessary. If court action is required to do this, jurisdiction of the court can be obtained readily by simple process service at the company's home office. Yes, the average buyer can obtain credit terms to run for a period of time after delivery of the goods by the supplier.

Foreign suppliers, on the other hand, are not as willing to extend credit to an American buyer. They know that the credit process is expensive. Some are undercapitalized and simply do not have the working capital to finance the buyer for a reasonable time after the goods have been delivered. Lengthy periods of delivery compound the problem for them. The supplier could have multiple shipments at sea at the same time, and not have sufficient working capital to carry all of the related accounts receivable. There are some suppliers, too, who do not take the time to check a buyer's credit rating, and some do not know how to do it. Dealing with a new customer makes them cautious and consequently reluctant to assume a credit risk.

Despite all this, an American purchasing officer should make every effort to secure credit from a foreign supplier. Credit is as negotiable as price, quality, or delivery. It is another item to work out as part of the deal. In addition to the obvious monetary advantage of credit from a foreign supplier, it also has a strategic benefit. In a subsequent section, security devices for the buyer are discussed. These security measures are designed as protections for the buyer against possible breaches of contract that a foreign supplier might commit. A credit period that begins to run after the goods have been delivered, inspected, and accepted is one of the better security measures available to the buyer. Many or most defects in the foreign product can be ascertained by the time the credit period has run its course. Paying for the goods before they have been received loses this benefit. This credit period gives the buyer a safe and certain method to protect the company, particularly when dealing with a supplier for the first time. It is recommended that the purchasing officer always attempt to negotiate a credit period. It is also recommended that the buyer determines what the price would be if payment were made before the receipt of the goods. A foreign supplier may charge a high fee for credit.

In the event the foreign supplier will not do business on a credit basis, and it is necessary to do business with that supplier, then other payment arrangements must be made. There are a number of alternatives to be considered. First, the supplier might insist on an "up-front" deposit on the purchase, or cash for the full amount of the invoice price at the time the order is given. The purchasing officer will recognize this to be the least desirable of all possible payment arrangements and should be acceded to only as the last resort. When it is essential to do this, the purchasing officer should make every effort to learn everything about the supplier unless his company has done business with that supplier previously in that fashion. What assets does the supplier have in the United States? Does the supplier have an American bank account? What financial references can the supplier give? The balance sheet should be reviewed. Has it been audited by a recognized public accounting firm? The normal verifications with other American customers should be made, but care must be exercised when doing so.

One alternative to putting up cash in advance is to establish an escrow account. This escrow account could be set up at the buyer's bank, at the foreign supplier's bank, or at an international bank of recognized quality. The buyer's cash is transferred to that escrow account, subject to the call of the supplier under certain prearranged conditions. The most desirable call condition would be upon presentation of a bill of lading that shows conforming goods have been shipped to the buyer. The escrow amount could also be subject to the call of the supplier if the buyer cancels the order, or by any other manner attempts to repudiate the purchase contract. Partial calls might also be provided for in the event that the supplier's financial condition is poor.

A *letter of credit* is another device that may be used to give the supplier payment credit. It is less expensive to use than depositing funds in an escrow account. Here the buyer makes arrangements with his or her bank to issue a letter of credit subject to the call of the supplier under prearranged conditions. If the buyer's bank does an international business, this letter of credit will be transferred to the supplier's bank in the foreign country. Instructions are given with the letter of credit regarding when the funds may be accessed by the supplier. The most common, and best, payment trigger is the presentation of a bill of lading showing the goods have been loaded aboard a vessel for shipment to the buyer. The supplier's bank holding the letter of credit for the benefit of the supplier is also an agent for the buyer. It has the duty of ascertaining the validity of the bill of lading and that the material shipped is what the buyer ordered. However, the buyer cannot depend on the foreign bank to inspect the goods that are shipped. Only the "face" of the documents can be verified. The foreign bank will honor the payment request if there is some evidence on the bill of lading (and on the invoice that is usually attached) that the proper goods have been shipped. It should be noted that if the buyer's bank does not do an international business, it will have correspondent banks in New York City where the same accommodations can be made. Letters of Credit are further discussed in Chapter XXII.

The most common form of payment before the goods are received by the buyer is payment against "documents." This is a process that is recognized by the Uniform Commercial Code. The procedure to be followed is somewhat similar to that mentioned in the previous section, except that there is no need of an advance arrangement for credit. The foreign supplier must wait a few days longer for payment of the invoice, but not until the goods have been received by the buyer. The buyer must pay the amount due when the documents are presented by the bank. These documents come to the home bank via air mail and are received and presented long before the goods arrive, therefore the buyer must pay before the goods have been received.

There are three major documents involved: (1) an order bill of lading, (2) a sight draft, and (3) an invoice from the supplier. An order (or negotiable) bill of lading is a receipt from the carrier that the goods are in the carrier's possession. An *order bill* is one that must be presented to the carrier when claiming the goods. "Legal title" to the goods rests in the order bill of lading. The carrier or his representative will not surrender possession of the goods until the order bill is presented. The holder of an order bill of lading might sell the goods while they are still at sea, for example, by simply handing over the bill to the party buying the goods. The order bill is to be distinguished from a *straight bill* which authorizes the carrier to deliver the goods directly to the consignee without presentation of the bill.

The *sight draft* is a negotiable instrument involving three parties: (1) the drawer, (2) the drawee, and (3) the payee. The drawer is the one who draws the draft which directs the drawee, on whom the draft is drawn, to pay a sum of money to the payee. (The drawer, who is the supplier, and the payee may be the same party.) The draft is written in this form: "At sight pay to the order of Foreign Supplier the sum of $40,000." The draft can then be endorsed by the supplier "Pay to the order of my Bank" and then turned over for collection along with the order bill of lading and the invoice. The foreign bank will forward the documents to its correspondent bank in the buyer's home town. The home town bank will then notify the buyer to "Come take up the draft" by paying the amount due. When the invoice is paid, the home town bank hands over the bill of lading to the buyer. The bill of lading can then be given to the carrier to enable the buyer to claim the goods.

The foreign supplier, whose need for capital may be urgent, usually can arrange with the bank to borrow the money involved (less a bank charge) using the documents as security. A variation of the sight draft is written "Thirty days after sight pay to the order of Foreign Supplier the sum of $40,000." This is commonly known as a trade acceptance. It postpones the time the buyer must hand over the invoice price to the bank. The trade acceptance would be sent to the American bank in the buyer's home town with the documents attached. There the buyer must "accept" the draft before the bank will release the order bill of lading. Once accepted, the trade acceptance is a fully negotiable instrument and can be discounted by the foreign supplier to receive the funds before the trade acceptance must be paid by the buyer.

You will note that the ability of the foreign supplier to collect the funds from the sale is postponed when sold with the understanding that payment will be against documents. But the buyer must pay for the goods before they are received. Therefore, this system of payment may be termed a compromise between cash at the time of order and payment 30 days after the receipt of the goods. The foreign supplier takes some risks under this arrangement. The buyer could refuse to accept the draft—either refusing to pay the sight draft or refusing to accept the trade acceptance. The foreign supplier will then have an action for breach of contract against the buyer. And the buyer takes the risk of paying for the goods before ever laying eyes on them. If the goods turn out to be not in compliance with the purchase order, the buyer has a breach of warranty action against the foreign supplier. Both parties have some risk.

Payment terms should be negotiated at the same time the entire contract is negotiated and the entire agreement on payment should be included in the final contract between the parties.

BUYER'S PROTECTIVE DEVICES

There are risks the purchasing officer assumes in every purchase no matter where the supplier is located. That the supplier may not or will not deliver is one such risk. Another risk taken is that the supplier will be late with delivery. Finally, there is the risk that the goods delivered will not conform to the contract. These possibilities have been discussed in previous chapters and the buyer's remedies enumerated. These same problems can arise when a foreign supplier is used. There is the added complication with a foreign supplier in that there might be difficulty in enforcing the available remedies because of location in a foreign country. Obtaining jurisdiction over the supplier is one problem. Another is finding someone on whom legal papers may be served. Then there is the ever present worry that there may not be assets of the foreign supplier available for levying on a judgment once it's obtained. There are, however, protections against contingencies that are available to the purchasing officer if they are anticipated at the time of negotiation.

SUPPLIER SELECTION

The purchasing officer must not abandon all regular supplier qualification tests simply because the supplier is located in a foreign country. On the contrary, these investigations should be intensified. Financial statements must be obtained and evaluated. Bank references must be checked and verified. Lists of other customers of the supplier should be obtained and these reference sources should be checked. And, of course, the foreign supplier's product should be thoroughly tested. Samples, if possible, should be obtained, guarantees and warranties studied closely. In short, every test applied to a prospective American supplier should be followed with a prospective foreign supplier.

APPLICABLE LAW AND JURISDICTION

The contract with the foreign supplier should have a clause in it that makes the law of the purchasing officer's state applicable to the contract. Such a clause might read as follows, if the buyer is located in New York:

> The parties to this purchase contract agree that it is a New York contract and that the formation, interpretation, performance, and available remedies that might arise shall be governed by the laws of the State of New York.

There is no reason for the American buyer to look to the law of a foreign country when seeking to enforcing rights under a purchase. Establish your company's home state as the home grounds for the ball game.

An American buyer forced to go to court to enforce a contract with a foreign supplier may find that it is difficult to convince the court that it has jurisdiction over the supplier. Your legal counsel must advise you about this problem. However, one thing you can do to make counsel's job a bit easier is to determine if the supplier has an agent or representative within your state. If so, include a clause similar to the following in the contract:

> The seller represents to the buyer that it regularly does business within the State of New York, and that John Doe, located at 1234 Blank Street is its duly authorized agent empowered to accept process service for it.

Many states have what are known as "long arm" statutes. Such statutes allow the courts of the state to take jurisdiction over a foreign supplier and render judgment against it under certain circumstances. One of the tests these statutes apply is whether the foreign supplier "regularly does business" within the state. Finding an affirmative answer to this test will assist legal counsel in convincing a court that it does have jurisdiction.

Another possible method by which jurisdiction can be obtained in some states is to include a clause of mandatory arbitration in the contract. Some, but not all, states recognize an arbitration decision as being enforceable in a court of law. New York is such a state. Any dispute must first go to arbitration if the contract has a mandatory arbitration clause in it. If the buyer wins an award, he or she can then go into court to enforce that award. Then the court can take jurisdiction because of the arbitration. Should your state not so recognize an arbitration award, and if the foreign supplier does not have an agent within the boundaries of your state, consult your legal counsel about the wisdom of making the contract subject to the laws of the State of New York and include the arbitration clause.

The purchasing officer must realize that all of this effort may be for naught if the supplier does not have assets in the United States. Levying on a United States judgment in a foreign country where the supplier does have assets is time-consuming and expensive. Better ways to protect your company are suggested in the next four sections.

BONDS AND ESCROWS

One method of protecting your company is to obtain a performance bond from the foreign supplier. The purchasing officer, as a condition of doing business, can require the supplier to post a performance bond guaranteeing prompt delivery of goods that meet the specifications. Require the bond to be written with an American bonding company. The performance bond should guarantee delivery as agreed upon as well as assuring that the quality of the goods will be proper. Consider including liquidated damages as part of the delivery guarantee. (See Chapters XX and XXII for a discussion of liquidated damages.)

An alternative to the performance bond is an escrow account established by the foreign supplier. The supplier will deposit funds in an American bank as a guarantee of proper performance. Default conditions and appropriate penalties for nonconforming goods need to be spelled out in the contract and with the bank holding the escrow. It may be necessary for the buyer to agree to some type of arbitration or to the appointment of an independent arbiter to determine the amount of applicable penalties for various possible defaults. It is suggested again that liquidated damages be provided for delivery delays.

This is not a palatable alternative for the supplier because it requires tying up working capital to establish the escrow account. The next suggested security device usually finds more favor with foreign suppliers.

LETTER OF CREDIT

The purchasing officer could ask the foreign supplier to post a letter of credit with the buyer's bank in lieu of a performance bond or an escrow account. This probably will be the least expensive of the four alternatives for the foreign supplier. Although a bank does charge a fee for issuing a letter of credit, the supplier will find it may be less than a premium for a performance bond or the cost of the loss of the use of working capital tied up in an escrow account. As in the other alternatives, the letter of credit should spell out the conditions and penalties for the various possible defaults.

RETAINAGE

The final security device offered the buyer (there may be others that are not enumerated) is to retain part of the purchase price until the buyer is satisfied that all conditions agreed to by the foreign supplier have been met. It could be agreed between the parties that the buyer would not pay the final 10, 15, or 25 percent of the purchase price until he or she is satisfied that the proper goods have been received. The time limit on deferral of the final percentage withheld must be kept within reasonable bounds. This time limit should only be sufficiently long to give the buyer a reasonable opportunity to inspect and test the goods delivered.

The purchasing officer should note that retainage does not afford any protection against the foreign supplier not delivering the goods or refusing to deliver the goods. That protection is afforded only by the other three alternatives—a performance bond, an escrow account, or a letter of credit—and then only if failure to deliver is made a penalty under the agreement with the foreign supplier.

POSSIBLE SUPPLIER EXCUSES

The purchasing officer must recognize that even a foreign supplier may have valid excuses for nondelivery or late delivery. Once American law is made applicable to the contract, all of the excuses for failure of or late delivery become available to the foreign supplier. These include—but are not necessarily limited to—Acts of God, labor disputes, and acts of a common enemy. Failure of presupposed conditions (see Chapter XXI) is also available to the foreign supplier under the Uniform Commercial Code. Perhaps the only additional excuse for a foreign supplier would be government fiat—a decree of the foreign government that would prohibit him from delivering the goods to an American customer.

OTHER AMERICAN REGULATIONS

The purchasing officer is reminded that there are laws in the United States that may affect procurement from a foreign supplier. Without going into the details of each law, there are in effect the Buy American Act, the antibribery provisions, the trading with the enemy regulations, and certain prohibited imports. These may or may not affect the particular foreign procurement the purchasing officer is conducting.

XXXII

The Convention on the International Sale of Goods

A few years ago there were usually the two choices of applicable law available to the foreign supplier and the American purchasing officer when they were contracting with each other. "Your law or my law" remained one of the negotiable items in a foreign contract. Most of the time the final answer was determined by the party with the stronger negotiating power. Of course, the parties could agree to use a neutral third country's laws too. And then again—perhaps the two parties simply did not think of choosing an applicable law for their contract. If a legal question arose in the formation or performance of the contract, the law where the question arose would be applied by the courts.

Since January 1, 1988, there is a third alternative body of law that has become available for the American purchasing officers and some foreign suppliers. It is known as the "United Nations Convention for the International Sale of Goods." "The Convention" or "C.I.S.G." are shorter titles for this new body of law. No matter what it is called, it has become a third alternative; perhaps, a compromise of independent stature between American law and the law of the land of the foreign supplier.

GENESIS OF THE CONVENTION

Member states of the United Nations made strenuous efforts for more than 50 years to develop a uniform law governing the formation and performance of contracts for the international sale (and purchase) of goods.[1] Success of the project was finally realized in Vienna on April 11, 1980 when 42 states unanimously approved what is now known as the Convention for the International Sale of Goods. There were no dissenting votes but several states abstained from voting. It is suggested that perhaps many of the abstainers were in favor of the Convention but had not received formal approval from the "home government" to vote for it when the roll was called.

President Reagan submitted the Convention to the United States Senate for ratification in 1983. The Senate finally approved it in October 1986 and the United Nations Treaty Section recorded our formal ratification on December 11, 1986. This was the same day that the ratifications by China and Italy were also recorded. December 11, 1986 thus became the "trigger" date for the Convention to become effective. Article 99(1) of the Convention provides "This Convention enters into force . . . on the first day of the month following expiration of 12 months after the date of the deposit of the tenth instrument of ratification . . . "

The countries that have ratified thus far are:

Argentina	Italy
Australia	Lesotho
Austria	Mexico
Belorus	Netherlands
Bulgaria	Norway
Canada	Poland
Chile	Romania
China	Russian Federation
Czechoslovakia	Singapore
Denmark	Spain
Ecuador	Sweden
Egypt	Switzerland
Finland	Syrian Arab Republic
France	Uganda
Germany	Ukraine
Ghana	United States of America
Guinea	Venezuela
Hungary	Yugoslavia
Iraq	Zambia

Thus a total of 38 countries, including the United States of America, have

---

[1]For an excellent discussion of the history of the various attempts to get consensus on a body of international law, see John Honnold *Uniform Law for International Sales,* Kluwer Law and Taxation Publishers, 101 Philip Drive, Norwell, Mass 02061. The same text provides an excellent discussion of the various articles of the present Convention.

the Convention for the International Sale of Goods as part of the law of their land. Readers may want to check with the United Nations Treaty Section as to whether there are any new additions since the publication of this edition.

AN UNUSUAL SOURCE OF LAW

This law came on the books of the United States in an unusual manner. It was submitted to the Senate of the United States for approval as a treaty and was ratified as such! Thus, in one fell swoop, the Senate by exercising its Constitutionally granted prerogative of approving treaties, approved this treaty and applied this Convention for the International Sale of Goods to all of our 50 states, including the State of Louisiana which has not even adopted the Uniform Commercial Code. Purchasing officers and legal counsel must recognize that the Convention is a body of law we must live with when we are dealing with vendors from other ratifying countries. Suppose an American purchasing officer concludes a contract with a supplier whose place of business is located in one of the other 37 countries who have adopted the Convention. The C.I.S.G. is immediately applicable to that contract! The two parties might agree to apply the law of the state where the buyer is located. But this is ambiguous. It could be argued that would be the C.I.S.G.! Or the parties might agree to apply the law of the country where the supplier's business is located. Again, there is the ambiguity and chance that it will be held to be the C.I.S.G.

Should the parties want to eliminate the C.I.S.G. from their contract, they must be very specific about it. They must state positively that "the C.I.S.G. does not apply to this contract." Then they can specify which law they wish to apply. If no choice of law is selected for the contract by the parties, the contract in our example above automatically will have the C.I.S.G. applied by the American court if it has jurisdiction, or the court of the foreign country will apply it when it has jurisdiction.

***Nota Bene* to the Purchasing Officer Doing Foreign Sourcing**. The C.I.S.G. is with us and we need to learn its details. The succeeding sections in this chapter will discuss this law and compare some of its provisions with the Uniform Commercial Code. When you are doing business with a supplier from one of the countries that has adopted the C.I.S.G. you will be called upon to decide whether you and your company will be better off with the C.I.S.G. applying to your contracts. The alternatives for applicable law to a foreign contract are now these three:

1. The Convention (C.I.S.G.)

2. The law of your home state—the U.C.C. as enacted there or the sales law if your home state is Louisiana

3. The law of the land where the foreign supplier is located

(You and your supplier would also have the opportunity of selecting the law of some other foreign country that has not adopted the C.I.S.G. if the two of you are really searching for an independent law to apply.) As you read through these sections discussing the C.I.S.G., keep asking yourself the question "Am I better off with the U.C.C.?" There is a section at the end of this chapter that summarizes the areas in which the C.I.S.G. differs from the U.C.C. and where C.I.S.G. seems to favor the supplier. Review this section before making your final decision.

One more point to keep in mind. At the time of this writing, 38 countries have embraced the C.I.S.G. There is the possibility more countries will also get on the band wagon. For those who desire an up-to-date summary of the countries who have ratified this Convention, the place to write is Treaty Section, United Nations New York, NY 10017. Or one may phone (212) 963-7958.

WHAT IS THE C.I.S.G.?

The C.I.S.G. (the Convention) is a body of law dealing with contracts involving the international sale of goods. It was written by a representative group of members of the United Nations. In many respects it is a composite body of law that includes the civil law of Continental Europe, the common law of the United States and England, and the law of Third World countries. The C.I.S.G. covers much of the same subject matter as Article II (Sales) of the Uniform Commercial Code. There are some major differences, however, between the Code and the Convention. We will point out many of these variances as we proceed in the discussion of the C.I.S.G.

The C.I.S.G. has been written in six languages so that presumably everyone subject to the law will find it written in a language they can read. It is hoped the various judges who will be called upon to interpret and apply the law will interpret each part of it in the same manner. But it may take years to know whether that uniformity will come to pass.

SPHERE OF APPLICATION

The sphere of the Convention specifies the scope of application, the specific legal issues in and outside the Convention, and other agreements between the parties. This is covered in Articles 1 through 13 of the C.I.S.G.

Applicability of the Convention and Where Inapplicable. Article 1(1)(a) specifies that the Convention applies to contracts for the sale of goods between parties whose places of business are in different contracting states. (A contracting state would be one who has adopted the Convention.) Article 1(1)(b) expands the coverage of the Convention by providing it is applicable if only one of the contracting parties has its place of business in a contracting state. (Article 10 specifies that if a party does not have a place of business, reference is made to that party's habitual residence.) However, the United States rejected Article 1(1)(b) when it ratified the balance of the Convention. The ability of a contracting state to make this rejection is found in Article 95.

Article 2 lists six categories of sales of goods that are not covered by the Convention. Chief among these exceptions are sales to consumers. Also exempted are auction sales, sales of ships and vessels, electricity, investment securities, and forced sales by Court order.

The Convention makes it quite clear in Article 3(2) that sales of services also are not covered by the Convention. Where there is a mixture of goods and services in the contract, Article 3(2) specifies that the preponderant part of the contract governs the applicability or inapplicability of the Convention. If the preponderant part of the sale is goods, the Convention is applicable; if the preponderant part of the contract is the furnishing of services, the Convention is not applicable and local law will be utilized. Most courts in the United States follow the rule in Article 3(2) although the Uniform Commercial Code is not specific on that point. Section 2-102 of the Code states affirmatively that the Code applies to "transactions in goods," but no mention is made of mixed contracts for goods and services. It is the interpretations of the courts that make the U.C.C. applicable to mixed contracts where the supplying of services is not the major portion of the contract.

Specific Legal issues in and Outside the Convention. Article 4 asserts positively that the issues governed by the Convention include "the formation of the contract of sale and the rights and obligations of the seller and the buyer arising from such a contract." The Article goes on to specify that the Convention is not concerned with the validity of the contract (Article 4(a)) and the effect of the property in the goods sold (Article 4 (b)).

Thus Article 4(a) of the Convention tells us it is not concerned with the legality of the subject matter of the contract nor whether the parties possess the necessary authority to obligate their respective corporate organizations. This means that two of the generally accepted essentials of a valid contract—a legal subject matter and capable parties—are not covered by the Convention. (The other two essentials of a valid contract are mutual consideration and agreement of the parties.) The Convention allows these topics to be controlled by the law of the forum where the case is being tried. That means the controlling law could vary from one country to another.

Strange as it may seem, subject matter and capacity of the parties is not covered by the Uniform Commercial Code either, except by an indirect reference to them in Section 1-103. That section reminds the reader that unless replaced by provisions of the U.C.C., the "principles of law and equity, capacity to contract . . . " etc. shall supplement its provisions. That again means that the law of the forum in a contract between citizens of the United States will be governed by the laws of the state which is holding the trial.

In the United States local law would also control any products liability cases. That is because we basically bring products liability cases as actions in tort and avoid using the breach of contract or warranty approach. This is done for many reasons including a longer period of time in which to file suit, better legal theorems for the plaintiffs, and many other similar justifications. The Convention also follows this same lead. Article 5 states "This Convention does not apply to the liability of the seller for death or personal injury caused by the goods to any person."

"Unless Otherwise Agreed." These words are used in many sections of the Uniform Commercial Code to invite the contracting parties to write the contract in any manner they see fit. There is no need to make the contract conform to the general rules of the Uniform Commercial Code. Most of these rules can be changed by agreement of the parties. A few U.C.C. rules cannot be changed such as the manner in which a supplier may disclaim an implied warranty or the three months limit on firm offers in Section 2-205 or extending the Code's Statute of Limitations in Section 2-725 beyond the prescribed four years.

Article 6 of the Convention extends a similar invitation to the contracting parties to "make their own law." First off, the Article suggests the entire Convention may be excluded if the parties so desire. Then there is the provision that the parties may "derogate from or vary the effect of any of its provisions." (The Convention brought to your author's attention a new use of the word "derogate." *Webster's New Collegiate Dictionary* and *The Random House Dictionary of the English Language* gave us these definitions: "To lessen; to detract from; to take away a part.") Therefore, subject to one exception, the parties to a contract have a range of agreeing to the exclusion of from O to 100 percent of the text of the Convention, and, subject to the same exception, they are free to amend the effect of any part of it.

The one exception of this freedom to derogate or vary involves Articles 11 and 12. Article 11 does away with the Statute of Frauds, making a contract of sale enforceable without a writing. Article 12, however, permits any country who requires contracts of sale to be concluded in writing to make a declaration that Article 11 does not apply to contracts written by persons having their business within that state. Article 12 states "parties may not derogate from or vary the effect of this Article." (This explains our exception in the previous paragraph.) At this writing Argentina, Belorus, Chile, China, Hungary, and the Ukraine have taken advantage of Article 12. Therefore, if you are contracting with a person whose place of business is in one of these countries, and the two of you have agreed to apply the Convention, the contract must be in writing to be enforceable.

American purchasing officers should note that if you are contracting with someone whose place of business is in a country that has adopted the Convention, including Article 11, and the two of you have agreed to apply the Convention, the contract need not be in writing to be enforceable. This outcome results despite the fact that the U.C.C. requires the contract to be in writing. The Convention would override the U.C.C. provision. One further note on this assumption. When the two of you are contracting the Convention is applicable to the two of you, unless you have *both agreed to avoid the Convention.*

Excluding the Convention. We reminded you previously that one must be very specific in excluding the Convention from an international sales contract since the Convention is now American law. A clause similar to the following should be adequate to substitute Missouri law, for example, in an international contract:

> The parties to this contract agree specifically that the laws of the State of Missouri, except for the Convention for the International Sale of Goods which shall not be applicable, shall be applicable to the formation and the interpretation and application of this contract.

This phraseology clearly shows that the parties want to exclude the Convention and apply the regular Missouri law which is based on the UCC to the contract.

GENERAL PROVISIONS

The general provisions of the Convention relating to: interpretation and items not covered by the Convention, interpreting statements or conduct of a party, *Nota Bene to the Purchasing officer*: usages and course of dealing, and the Statute of Frauds are found in Articles 7 through 13.

Interpretation of the Convention. The Convention provides its own rules for its interpretation in Article 7(1). The suggestion is made in the Article to keep in mind regard for three general principles: (1) the Convention's international character, (2) the need for uniformity in application and (3) the observance of good faith.

Pertaining to the international character of the Convention, one must never forget, including the judiciary hearing cases under the C.I.S.G., that the convention was written by a diverse group of legal professionals—scholars and practicing attorneys—from many countries. Each coauthor no doubt has his or her own pet legal theories and approaches that they would like to have seen legislated into the law. Compound that fact with the different principles and concepts prevailing in common law, civil law, and Third World countries, and one can readily understand that much of the Convention represents compromises and adjustments from prevailing legal principles in any of the authors' contracting countries. Therefore, the Convention itself attempts to give courts some idea of how it should be interpreted, at least in broad-brushed terms. First, it reminds the courts of the "international character" of the Convention. Article 7(1) is telling the courts of all nations to interpret the Convention as it is written and not to attempt to bring into such interpretations the prevailing law of the country in which the court is located. Furthermore, the fact that it is international in character should emphasize the uniqueness of the law and that its terms are to be applied as written.

The article also reminds the courts that the Convention must be uniformly applied if it is to serve as a body of international law. In the translation from one of the six languages in which it is written, discrepancies could arise. Hopefully, these discrepancies and other types of possible variances will be discovered and corrected. This will happen only when there is some reporting service developed to uniformly report all cases decided under the law. Thus far there has been no public notice of such a service being developed.

Article 7(1) also reminds us of the need to observe good faith in the interpretation of the articles of the Convention. One wonders, though, why good faith in the Convention is limited only to the interpretation process? The Uniform Commercial Code, on the other hand, states in Section 1-203, "Every contract or duty within this Act imposes an obligation of good faith in its performance or enforcement." This is a broader expression of the need and the demand for good faith. It is hoped that the courts, in their interpretation of the Convention, will expand their conception of good faith much farther. In some of the articles of the Convention that follow there are bits of evidence of its concern for good faith, such as in communication by the buyer of defects in delivered goods and in the requirement of a party to mitigate damages whenever possible. Would that there was a much more positive expression that good faith was essential to the performance and enforcement of any international contract!

Items Not Covered by the Convention. Article 7(2) gives direction to find answers for legal questions not answered in the Convention itself. The Article reads:

> (2) Questions concerning matters governed by this Convention which are not expressly settled in it are to be settled in conformity with the general principles on which it is based, or, in the absence of such principles, in conformity with the law applicable by virtue of the rules of private international law.

Thus the law tells us in 7(2) to settle unanswered questions "in conformity with the general principles on which it is based . . . " ("It" refers to the Convention, one assumes.) Jurists from tribunals in different countries can search for "general principles" of term in the Sales Convention. There is a growing body of general principles internationally. A number of these have been stated by UNIDROIT in its new "International Restatement" of principles of contract law.

The second source that Article 7(2) suggests to find an answer to an unanswered question is in the domestic law of the jurisdiction where the case is being tried. This suggestion is consistent with the directions given in Article 4 to use domestic law when a question is not covered by the Convention. Again, though, this obviously raises problems of uniformity in the application of the Convention. "Plugging the hole" under French law, for example, could give a different result than if U.S. law were used to fill the same gap. Where there is a possible wide variety of jurisdictions that might hear a case to be decided under the C.I.S.G., using domestic law can only create manifold interpretations of the same question. The Convention fails in Article 7 to be consistent and to provide properly for uniformity in the law.

Interpreting Statements or Conduct of a Party. One of the essentials of a valid contract is that there must be a "meeting of the minds." The parties must first agree to form a contract and then they must agree on the various aspects of that contract, including the terms and conditions. However, even after this is done, there will be occasions when there will be doubts that the parties did agree to agree because one party will not be in full accord with the other party's interpretation of the words or the conduct. This is not unusual because people do react differently to the same words or to the same phrases. Misunderstandings can and do arise.

In the event a courtroom trial results from failures of the parties to agree, and the problem stems from the interpretation of the contract or conduct of the party, Article 8 of the Convention provides some ground rules for the tribunal to follow in settling the dispute. Article 8(1) reads:

> (1) For the purposes of this Convention statements made by and other conduct of a party are to be interpreted according to his intent where the other party knew or could not have been unaware what that intent was.

Since questions of interpretation usually arise because the other party was not in agreement with the thinking of the first party, your author believes this article will be of little value in settling such disputes. The other party is contesting the interpretation because he or she had not followed the intent of the party making such statements.

Article 8(2) adds what could be termed the "prudent person" ground rule in divining what is a party's intent. It reads:

(2) If the preceding paragraph is not applicable, statements made by and other conduct of a party are to be interpreted according to the understanding that a reasonable person of the same kind as the other party would have had in the same circumstances.

Thus we have here the instruction to determine what should have been the intent if he or she were a reasonable person of the same kind. It appears this is getting closer to determining the intent in an objective fashion.

Article 8(3) gives us the rules of what may be used and considered in determining a party's intent under 8(1) and 8(2):

(3) In determining the intent of a party or the understanding a reasonable person would have had, due consideration is to be given to all relevant circumstances of the case including the negotiations, any practices which the parties have established between themselves, usage, and any subsequent conduct of the parties.

This is a broad shopping list of sources to be used in interpreting a contract or portions of it, and is something every American purchasing officer should note. Before explaining the implications of the depth of the list of sources, let us first look at the similar provisions in U. S. law. United States contract law has long held to what is known as the "Parol Evidence Rule." Although this rule was not discussed in the original text we should become familiar with it now as well as with Article 8 of the Convention. *Parol evidence* is the term the legal community applies to verbal, word-of-mouth evidence. The Parol Evidence Rule, loosely stated, is that written contracts cannot be amended or altered by verbal testimony. The contract must be written and complete for this rule to apply. However, if a mistake occurred in the preparation of the written contract, or if fraud were involved in the construction of the contract, for example, verbal testimony can be offered to prove the extent of the original contract. This and other exceptions make the application of the rule somewhat discretionary by the courts.

Section 2-202 of the Uniform Commercial Code is now the governing statute in America on the parol evidence rule. The section is captioned "Final Written Expression: Parol or Extrinsic Evidence." It reads:

Terms . . . which are otherwise set forth in a writing intended by the parties as a final expression of their agreement with respect to such terms as are included therein may not be contradicted by evidence of any prior agreement or of a contemporaneous oral agreement but may be explained or supplemented

(a) by course of dealing or usage of trade or by course of performance and

(b) by evidence of consistent additional terms unless the court finds the writing to have been intended also as complete and exclusive statement of the terms of the agreement.

A comparison of Article 8 of the Convention with Section 2-202 shows clearly that Article 8 is much more permissive of what may be used to interpret the communications and conduct of a party. Both the Article and the U.C.C. section allow evidence of course of dealing, usage, and course of performance to be used. And it is certain both would allow evidence of mistake or fraud although it is not explicitly stated. But there the similarity ends. The Convention permits evidence of the "negotiations" while the U.C.C. specifically prohibits the use of "any prior agreement or contemporaneous oral agreement." The Convention's Article 8 also allows evidence of "subsequent conduct of the parties" while the Code is silent on the topic, which makes subsequent conduct inadmissible as evidence.

It is apparent the Convention through its Article 8 clearly intends to allow the parties to make known their interpretation or understanding of the written contract. The Code, on the other hand, attempts to emphasize the written word and carefully limits any attempt to bypass the writing with verbal testimony. Keep in mind though that the court, under the Code, always maintains the discretion to declare the writing "incomplete" and thereby avoid the Parol Evidence Rule.

***Nota Bene* to the Purchasing Officer.** We have devoted space in this supplement to explain the Parol Evidence Rule even though the purchasing officer is not particularly involved in its application in the court room. That is legal counsel's problem. Nonetheless the purchasing officer should discuss this topic with his or her counsel if any foreign sourcing is being done because Article 8 brings us some major changes in law. The legal rules you followed under the Uniform Commercial Code are changed drastically if you bring a purchase contract under the Convention. Article 8 really does away with all the customary limitations on evidence that are imposed by Section 2-202. Now that will not be all "bad" to some American counsel who dislike the limitations imposed by 2-202. On the other hand, many legal counselors not only applaud the limitations of Section 2-202 but insist purchasing officers include a merger clause in their contracts. A *merger clause* is a clause in the contract that brings all prior and contemporaneous agreements into the final written agreement. Such a merger clause should now include a reference to Article 8 if the contract is to be governed by the Convention. Here are suggested procedures for the purchasing officer to follow, depending upon whether you and your legal counsel are "in favor of" or "against" the Parol Evidence Rule:

> (1) *You wish to maintain the Parol Evidence Rule even in international transactions.* A clause similar in content to the following should be included in all of your *international* contracts:

>> The parties agree that this is the final and complete agreement between them; that it incorporates and replaces all of their prior and current formation statements and communications; and

that they further agree that Articles 8(1), 8(2), and 8(3) of the
C.I.S.G. are not applicable to this transaction.

The same clause, minus the reference to the Convention articles,
should be included in all of your domestic contracts. (Despite the use
of the merger clause, the purchasing officer is reminded that the court
will continue to have discretionary power to declare whether a contract is complete, or whether mistake and/or fraud entered into its formation. Therefore, use of the merger clause is not absolutely foolproof.)

(2) *You welcome the freedom of evidenciary procedures in the
Convention.* You will not require any merger clause in your purchase
orders because the full freedom of use of prior, current, and future
negotiations will be available to you in international contracts. This is
what you have bargained for. Your only concern will be to record and
to retain all communications and negotiations with your supplier. Your
legal counsel will find them invaluable in the event of a court trial and
you need to interpret an item in a contract by Article 8 law.
Remember, however, this is only applicable to international contracts
under the Convention. Section 2-202 of the Uniform Commercial
Code will continue to control your domestic contracts.

Usages and Course of Dealing. Article 8(3) previously discussed, and now
Article 9(1), bind the parties to any usages they have agreed to and also by any
practices which they have established between themselves. The Uniform Commercial Code also recognizes usage of trade and course of dealing. In Section 1-
205(3) both items are said to "supplement or qualify the terms of an agreement."
An American purchasing officer should note particularly that Article 9(2) of the
Convention makes applicable to any contract a usage widely known in international trade and regularly observed by parties in that type of industry. If the purchasing officer is not adept at international trade usages, it might be prudent to
add the following clause to the suggested merger clause above:

The parties further agree they will not be bound by an international
trade usage not repeated specifically in this contract despite the provisions of Articles 8 and 9 of the C.I.S.G.

The Need for a Writing: The Statute of Frauds. You are well aware of the
fact that Section 2-201 of the Uniform Commercial Code requires that a contract
for the sale of goods with a value of $500 or more must be in writing to be
enforceable in a court of law. The Convention has taken the opposite approach in
its Article 11. There it is stated that "a contract of sale need not be concluded in
writing . . . It may be proved by any means, including witnesses."

American purchasing officers must be alert to this change. An acceptance
of an offer need not be in writing. This could result in a contract being formed at
the moment the offeree states "I accept your offer" during the negotiations. Mod-

ification and termination of contracts by mutual consent also can be accomplished and proven by the verbal route as well as by the more tangible evidence of a writing.

One troublesome exception in the Convention's approach to the enforceability of an oral contract lies in Article 12. Article 12 permits a "Contracting Country" whose domestic law requires a written contract for the sale of goods, to declare "Article 11 inoperative in our country." As an example of this, the United States could have declared Article 11 inoperative in the United States when it adopted the C.I.S.G. The United States had the right to do this under the Convention because of Section 2-201 of the Uniform Commercial Code which requires the written contract. Then any foreign supplier dealing with an American purchasing officer would have to be certain that any resulting contract was in writing to be enforceable. For the sake of consistency, we can be thankful of the fact that the United States *did not* avail itself of the opportunity to make this reservation when it ratified the Convention. But already other countries have made this reservation. If we are dealing with a supplier from any one of these countries, we must remember their verbal commitments are unenforceable. But if we are dealing with the other adoptees of the Convention, then verbal commitments are enforceable. What confusion!

Nota Bene **to the Purchasing Officer.** Purchasing officers should consider whether eliminating the requirement of a writing is "good" or "bad." There has been considerable discussion of the pros and cons of the Statute of Frauds in the United States. Legal commentaries have long taken stands against the Statute, claiming it is archaic in nature and slows down the pace of business. England, where our Statute of Frauds originated, abandoned it in 1954. Louisiana, the holdout state on the Uniform Commercial Code, has long permitted oral contracts to be enforced in their courts. However, there are advantages to a writing that particularly serve the purchasing function well. You know what you are entitled to receive from your supplier when it is written. You avoid the age-old argument that begins with one party saying "But you said . . . " Yes, there are advantages of doing business in writing and we think it deeply applies in international trade. Still there may be some facets of the agreement that are not in writing and the Statute of Frauds may be a disadvantage.

FORMATION OF THE CONTRACT

Articles 14 through 17 cover "formation of the contract" which includes: the offer, revocable offers, firm offers, rejection of an offer, and acceptance.

The Convention's Definition of an Offer. Article 14(1) gives us this definition of an offer:

A proposal for concluding a contract addressed to one or more specific persons constitutes an offer if it is sufficiently definite and indicates the intention of the offeror to be bound in case of acceptance. A
proposal is sufficiently definite if it indicates the goods and expressly
or implicitly fixes or makes provision for determining the quantity
and the price.

This definition coincides with the one we have been accustomed to using in
America except for one major item—price. Under the Convention, price is an
essential term of any valid offer. Contract law in the United States, however, has
never been particularly concerned about price and many contracts have been
completed without it being mentioned. The prevailing market price at the time of
delivery is used in such cases. Section 2-305 of the Uniform Commercial Code
has codified this approach. It provides that the parties can conclude a contract
even though the price is not settled. Subsection (a) of this section further provides
that the price will be presumed to be a reasonable price at the time of delivery. We
therefore have a major difference here between the Convention and the Code.

It should be pointed out that Article 55 of the Convention provides for a
method of determining price where "a contract has been validly concluded."
Some authorities believe Article 55 overrides Article 14 and would thereby make
an offer without a price a valid offer, because it makes provision for determining
the price. It is difficult for your author to understand how a contract could be
"validly concluded" through the offer and acceptance routine, when the offer by
definition is invalid because of the lack of price. This will be explored further
when we discuss Article 55 in numerical order. Now, though, the American purchasing officer is advised to make certain any offer being made includes a price.
Also it is good advice to make any supplier's offer to you include the price. Without the mention of the price that offer may be only an invitation to do business,
and your supplier could withdraw from entering into a contract upon your acceptance.

Other than on the subject of price, the Convention and American contract
law are in remarkable agreement as to what constitutes a valid offer. Both emphasize the need for "intent" to make the offer and for the fact that communication of
the offer is required before it is valid. Article 14(2) of the Convention continues
this agreement with American contract law when it indicates that an advertisement or a catalog is only an invitation to do business.

Article 15(1) of the Convention also follows the American rule that an offer
is effective when it reaches the offeree.

Revocable Offers. Article 15(2) leads off our discussion of revocable and
nonrevocable offers by providing that an irrevocable offer can be withdrawn by
the offeror if the withdrawal reaches the offeree before the offer. This has never
been codified, to the author's knowledge, in American law. However the result
that the offer can be withdrawn seems equitable and provable because the intent

to make the offer has disappeared before the time the offer first reaches the offeree.

The Convention codifies a point of law in Article 16(1) that is part of the common law and followed in the United States:

> 16(1) Until a contract is concluded an offer may be revoked if the revocation reaches the offeree before he has dispatched an acceptance.

(To avoid confusion, the reader should take special note of the fact that 16(1) deals with revocation *after* the offer has been received by the offeree. Article 15(2) deals with the situation where the offer is revoked *before* the offeree receives the offer.) That Article 16(1) agrees with the common law in its initial thrust is a well-known fact. The common law permitted an offeror to withdraw an offer at will because no consideration passed from the offeree to the offeror to support keeping the offer open.

The latter portion of Article 16(1) that reads " . . . before he (the offeree) has dispatched an acceptance" also "appears" to support the common law rule that an acceptance becomes effective when it is dispatched. In Chapter I we presented the source of this common law rule in the case of *Adams v. Lindsell* decided in the English courts in 1818. Since that time most American jurisdictions have held fast to the notion that an acceptance is effective the moment it is mailed. (The only exceptions to this rule have been where the offeror has demanded acceptance to be made by telegram, telephone, or facsimile reproduction.)

Article 16(1) tricks its readers however. You will note that *it does not* state that an acceptance effectively creates a contract at the time it is dispatched. It merely states that an offer may be revoked before an acceptance is dispatched. A less than careful reader *will then assume* from this that a dispatched acceptance creates a contract. But alas! The Convention does not follow this assumption. It simply says that a dispatched acceptance only prevents a revocation from becoming effective. How do we know the Convention intends this? Because reading forward in the Convention we stumble upon Article 18(2) which tells us an acceptance " . . . becomes effective the moment the indication of asset reaches the offeror." Thus, under the Convention, receipt and not dispatch controls when an acceptance becomes effective.

If one follows Article 16(1) of the Convention to a logical conclusion, there is a period of time between the dispatch of an acceptance by the offeree and its receipt by the offeror when there is no contract. However during this time the offeror is bound to his offer because 16(1) will not allow its revocation. But during the same period of time the offeree remains free to change his mind about the contract. Article 22 permits an offeree to withdraw an acceptance any time before it becomes effective. In international trade it is not unusual for mail to take a week or more to be delivered. Thus an offeree under the Convention structure has an additional week to speculate on whether prices will increase or decrease. The offeree is free to act in his own best interest during that time. But the offeror is frozen to his offer.

***Nota Bene* to the Purchasing Officer.** If you are the offeror make certain your offer contains a time limit to which you will be held. Then you will not be taken advantage of by an unscrupulous offeree as detailed above. Or if you want even more control over your offer you might consider spelling out "this offer is subject to revocation by the offeror any time before a bona fide acceptance is received."

Firm Offers. Firm offers under the Convention are presented in Article 16(2). The reader will find that the Convention's version of a firm offer differs somewhat from Section 2-205 of the Uniform Commercial Code, where firm offers are defined. One cannot compare Article 16(2) with the common law or general contract law prior to the Code because firm offers were not available to offerees at that time because of the lack of consideration. Here is the way 16(2) reads:

> (2) However, an offer cannot be revoked:
>
>> (a) if it indicates, whether by stating a fixed time for acceptance or otherwise, that it is irrevocable; or
>>
>> (b) if it was reasonable for the offeree to rely on the offer being irrevocable and the offeree has acted in reliance on the offer.

Article 16(2)(a) makes any offer a firm offer simply "if it indicates . . . it is irrevocable." The article suggests the offeror might make such an indication of irrevocability "by stating a fixed time for acceptance or otherwise." This simplified approach to the creation of a firm offer is enticing but at the same time dangerous. The use of certain verbiage may create a firm offer as long as it qualifies as "or otherwise," and, then again, the same words may not rise to be a firm offer. One assumes the authors of the Convention are looking more to the intention of the offeror, past practices, usages of the trade, etc., to make an independent judgment in each instance whether the offer is firm. That approach can be faulted only because it leaves the offeror and offeree "up in the air." Was there a firm offer made or not?

The answer to that question in the Convention comes after it is too late—the parties may have acted in the belief that the intention was read properly only to later discover they were incorrect. The law should be more precise so that the parties may read their position without having to resort to the courtroom to determine what was the intent of one or both of the parties. Such an approach does not aid in developing uniformity either, Article 7(1) notwithstanding.

Parties operating under the Uniform Commercial Code, on the other hand, will find a list of requirements they must meet to create a firm offer. Section 2-205 enumerates these conditions that must be met:

1. The offer must be made by a merchant.

2. The offer must be in writing.

3. The offer must be signed.

4. The offer must have a reasonable time limitation not over three months.

5. The offer must give assurance it will be held open.

6. If made on the offeree's form, the assurance must be separately signed by the offeror.

You will note on this list of Code requirements only #5 is matched by Article 16(2)(a) of the Convention. The balance of the list is conspicuous by its absence in the article. There is no need for the offer to be in writing (or signed) to be valid under the Convention and no time limits are imposed. No mention is made in the Convention of offers that are submitted on the offeree's Request for Quotation form. Therefore we must assume there is no need for a second signature by the offeror if the "R.F.Q." specifies that the bidder is submitting a firm quotation. The purchasing officer's only restraint here is his or her own good conscience. Even "good faith" is not mandated—though probably assumed by the Convention.

***Nota Bene* to the Purchasing Officer.** The firm offer provision of the Convention, though loose and free, leaves much to be desired. Evidently it is another example of the many compromises that were made to get the Convention acceptable to all types and groups of countries. Your author suggests that the purchasing officer include in every request for quotation a statement similar to this:

> The supplier is required to submit this proposal to the buyer as a firm offer to sell. Supplier will complete the following statement:
>
>> Supplier agrees that this is a firm offer to sell and that it will be held firm and not be revocable until _____ (date) _____ .
>>
>> Buyer has until and including that date to notify supplier of acceptance
>> _____
>>   (signed)

The purchasing officer is also advised that if the supplier insists on using his own form or letterhead to submit the proposal, and includes a clause making it a firm offer, be certain the firm offer is written in a straight-forward manner. Do not accept statements that may seem to only "imply" the offer is firm. Make the supplier "stand up and be counted" as submitting a clear-cut, firm offer.

Firm Offers and the Doctrine of Promissory Estoppel. Article 16(2)(b) apparently codifies for international trade the doctrine of promissory estoppel (sometimes termed "detrimental reliance") in the United States. This topic is discussed in Chapter XIII. It is pointed out there that an offeror who knew his offer was being relied upon by the offeree could not revoke the offer because he was estopped from doing so since the offeror knew the offeree was depending on that offer. The doctrine of promissory estoppel is not recognized in all of the 50 states. Therefore, if an offeree is doing business in an industry where such protection of an offer is essential, use of the Convention is one way to be certain of the uniformity of application of this doctrine. The Convention would automatically be applied if the transaction occurred in international trade. The Convention, however, cannot be applied to domestic trade unless both parties expressly agree to be bound by it. The purchasing officer is advised to check with legal counsel to determine whether promissory estoppel is recognized under your state's laws.

Rejection of a Firm Offer. The Convention clarifies one issue about firm offers on which the Uniform Commercial Code is silent. Article 17 provides that an irrevocable offer is terminated when a rejection by the offeree reaches the offeror. Therefore, under the Convention, if a firm offer that is guaranteed firm until December 10 is rejected by the offeree on November 20, the offer is dead on November 20. The offeree cannot send an acceptance on December 1 and claim to have formed a contract. There was no offer alive on December 1 for the offeree to accept. By virtue of Article 17 the rejection killed the offer on November 20.

The same question is not covered by the Uniform Commercial Code and one would be required to apply general contract law to get the answer. Of course, under the common law there was no such thing as a "firm offer," unless consideration passed from the offeree to the offeror. If consideration did pass, then it was an option contract. Your author's opinion is that if this were an option contract then the offer would have had to be held open until December 10 unless the offeree signed some type of release, or the offeror returned the consideration and the offeree accepted its return. However, if the offer was a Section 2-205 firm offer where no consideration passed, then the answer would be the same as under the Convention. The offeror would not be bound to the offer after November 20. The rejection would kill the offer when it was communicated to the offeror.

Acceptance Under the Convention. Article 18 gives us the Convention's definition of acceptance and the several methods by which acceptance may be accomplished. In several of these areas the Convention differs from our understanding of acceptance in contract law and under the Uniform Commercial Code. Article 18(1) reads:

> A statement made by or other conduct of the offeree indicating assent to an offer is an acceptance. Silence or inactivity does not in itself amount to acceptance.

It is clear the Convention expects that there will be some positive expression of acceptance coming from the offeree to the offeror. One assumes that means "notice"—notice that the offeree has accepted the offer.

Article 18(2) begins by affirming this need of "notice." It reads "An acceptance of an offer becomes effective at the moment the indication of assent reaches the offeror." Therefore an acceptance is not effective until some notice "indicating assent" reaches the offeror. This changes the rule of the common law as we know and practice it in the United States. Our rule which comes from *Adams v. Lindsell* in 1818 makes the acceptance effective the moment it is dispatched. The one exception to this occurs if the offeror specified in the offer that the acceptance must be in his or her hands before it becomes effective. Requiring a specific mode of acceptance is the offeror's prerogative as "master of the offer."

The requirement in the Convention of the receipt of the acceptance by the offeror is apparently part of the compromise procedures used in obtaining its adoption. We have already seen in our discussion of Article 16(1) that an offer cannot be revoked after an offeree has dispatched an acceptance. This dispatch of the offer has some legal significance in the Convention when we are involved in the revocation of offers but absolutely no legal power to effect an acceptance. The Convention has embraced some of the dispatch theory of acceptance and some of the receipt theory.

Does this inconsistency of the Convention make any difference? The offeree, be it the buyer or the supplier, assumes the responsibility of seeing to the safe delivery of the acceptance under the Convention. The offer might lapse before the acceptance arrives if the mail fails to deliver the acceptance in a timely fashion. (This favors the offeror.) However the offer cannot be revoked once the acceptance is dispatched. (This favors the offeree.) Since buyers and suppliers both act as offerees some of the time and act as offerors the other times, the scales of justice hang evenly here. But the inconsistency of the Convention on this point is another annoyance for those who use the Convention.

Article 18(3) is another part of the Convention that is not entirely crisp and clear. Eliminating some of its many words, the Article in effect states that "by virtue of the offer, or as a result of past practices, the offeree may indicate assent by performing an act." The Article provides that the act of the offeree can be accomplished without notice to the offeror and still be effective. The Article provides that the acceptance is effective the moment the act is performed provided it is performed within the time limit of the offer or within a reasonable time after the offer has been received, if it does not contain a time for acceptance. The two acts referred to specifically in the Article are (1) delivery of the goods if the offeree is the supplier, and (2) payment of the price if the offeree is the buyer.

These two avenues of acceptance are commonplace to the American buyer (see Chapter XIV), so we are not dealing with a new approach to acceptance. But the wording of Article 18(3) imposes a limitation on the use of these two acts of acceptance. For example, the supplier may use the delivery of the goods as acceptance only if:

1. The offer specifically invites delivery; or

2. The parties have established a practice of accepting in this manner; or

3. By usage between the parties or usage as well-known in the trade.

Thus, if there has been no usage or past practice established between the parties on delivery of the goods as a means of acceptance of an offer to buy, the only way it can be used is if the purchasing officer states on the offer to buy "You may accept this offer to buy by delivering the goods." Must we be that specific? The answer is "yes" if one reads the article carefully. Acceptance without notice to the buyer can only be accomplished by delivery of the goods if that action is authorized. The buyer cannot be surprised. When acceptance is accomplished in this manner, it is effective immediately. Without the prior authorization, though, delivery is not an acceptable means of acceptance and the buyer may return the goods.

This vagueness as to what the offeree is to do to accept is not present under the Uniform Commercial Code. Section 2-206 clearly states:

> (a) an offer to make a contract shall be construed as inviting acceptance in any manner and by any medium reasonable . . .

> (b) an order or other offer to buy goods for prompt or current shipment shall be construed as inviting acceptance either by a prompt promise to ship or by the prompt or current shipment of conforming . . . goods.

Under the Uniform Commercial Code there is no doubt. The purchase order can be accepted by delivery of the goods or a written notice. Would that the Convention would take a stand instead of using "fiddle faddle" wording!

***Nota Bene* to the Purchasing Officer.** To avoid any problem with the mischievous wording of Article 18, it is suggested a prompt written notice of acceptance be sent for every offer to sell that you accept. For those offers you have held a close to a "reasonable" length of time before you accept, you might consider accepting them with a telegram or facsimile and then confirm with your purchase order. Remember when you are operating under the Convention, acceptance *does not* occur when you dispatch your purchase order. The acceptance must be received by the supplier to be effective. International mail may take a good deal of time to deliver considering how long it takes the U.S. mail to deliver a domestic letter. In any event, the monkey is on your back to get that acceptance to the supplier on time!

When you use your purchase order as an offer to buy in the international scene insist that the offeree put a written acceptance in your hands by a given date. Further, the term on your order should specify "This offer remains revocable until your acceptance is in our hands, Article 16(1) of the C.I.S.G. notwithstanding." By using the latter, you avoid being locked in a firm offer after an acceptance has been dispatched.

Finally, remember that if your purchase order is an offer to buy, you may want delivery to occur as soon as possible. Then give your supplier the word: "This order may be accepted by delivery of the goods. No notice is required."

The "Battle of the Forms." The Convention's Article 19, in three parts, covers the "nonconforming acceptance" as does Section 2-207 of the Uniform Commercial Code. Both cover the same topic and both have three subsections. There the similarity ends.

Article 19(1) codifies the "mirror-image" rule of the common law:

> (1) A reply to an offer which purports to be an acceptance but contains additions, limitations, or other modifications is a rejection of the offer and constitutes a counter-offer.

This is a recitation of the common law rule that requires an acceptance to be a mirror image of the offer to be effective. [See Chapter XIV for a decision of the Minnesota court in 1951 which restated the rule in almost the identical terms of Article 19(1)]. Subsection (1) of Section 2-207 of the Code was written in a deliberate attempt to end the legal problems created by application of the mirror image rule in a commercial world of buyers and sellers. The fact that these buyers and sellers have their own preprinted forms that they use in the attempt to satisfy the mirror image rule creates what is termed the "Battle of the Forms." Article 19(1) does nothing to bring peace to the situation—in fact the article tends to exacerbate the battle.

Article 19(2) does attempt to "wring out" part of the mess created by nonconforming acceptances:

> (2) However, a reply to an offer which purports to be an acceptance but contains additional or different terms which do not materially alter the terms of the offer constitutes an acceptance, unless the offeror, without undue delay, objects orally to the discrepancy or dispatches a notice to that effect. If he does not so object, the terms of the contract are the terms of the offer with the modifications contained in the acceptance.

"But for a few words" this portion of the article seems to reach the same result as subsections (1) and (2) of Code Section 2-207. It makes an acceptance out of a nonconforming acceptance that contains additional or different terms. For it to be able to make the nonconforming acceptance effective, the changes from the offer must not be material—that is, they should not materially alter the offer. The other requirement for it to be operative is that the offeror must consent to the adoption of the inconsistencies contained in the nonconforming acceptance. Without offeror approval, Article 19(2) does not create a contract.

The prerequisites for Article 19(2) to be operative and make a nonconforming acceptance effective are also found in Code Section 2-207(1) and (2). Nonmaterial additional terms become part of the final contract if both parties are merchants under 2-207(2)(b), and under Section 2-207(2)(c) the offeror is given the opportunity to object to any additional terms proposed by the offeror in the nonconforming acceptance. Thus the Convention and the Code, on the topic of nonconforming acceptances are closely aligned in procedure and result on this point, with one difference. "Different" terms in the nonconforming acceptance are treated differently under the two bodies of law. Under the Convention, "additional and different" terms are subject to approval of the offeror, and, if nonmaterial, become part of the final contract. Under the Code" only additional" terms are considered and "different" terms are discarded. Nonmaterial "additional" terms become part of the final contract if the parties are merchants.

The Convention goes the Code one step farther in its consideration of nonconforming acceptances. The Convention provides an official list of items "among other things" that are considered "material" in its Article 19(3):

> (3) Additional or different terms relating, among other things, to the price, payment, quality, and quantity of the goods, place and time of delivery, extent of one party's liability to the other, or the settlement of disputes are considered to alter the terms of the offer materially.

This is an extensive list of terms that are considered "material." It appears that the list covers most of the customary terms and conditions found in the contract for the purchase of goods. And when one considers the possibility of other nonlisted terms being included under the phrase used in this article "among other things," we come to the conclusion most terms in a sales contract could be "material" under the Article 19(3) definition. The net result of this is that many nonconforming acceptances with different or additional terms will fall into the category of counteroffers under article 19(1) because they are not "mirror-images" of the original offers.

This result is not all bad if it will make the supplier and the buyer resume negotiations until all differences between the two conflicting contract forms are resolved. This is the true meaning of "agreement" in a contract—both parties understanding and agreeing to their respective duties, commitments, and rights without any qualification or reservation. "We are in total agreement and bound in contract."

Alas and alack! We fear that getting on with the negotiations as outlined above will not always occur to iron out the wrinkles between the purported acceptance and the offer. More than likely the parties will move forward to perform the contract they believe their forms created. The seller will deliver the goods and the buyer will accept and pay the agreed price. If no problems arise after delivery, both parties will close their files on the transaction. The seller made a successful sale and the buyer satisfied a need. So be it.

However, if something goes wrong with the transaction, the parties will get out their files and for the first time, read the form the other party sent. That is when they first realize the papers they interchanged do not form a contract! They did not agree on the term that their dispute involves. And to compound the problem, they also discover that the Convention, unlike the Uniform Commercial Code, has no provision to settle such a dispute. The parties are left to their own devices and the domestic law to find the answer. If the problem arose under the Uniform Commercial Code, the dispute would be settled by subsection (3) of 2-207. Subsection (3) would say that the conduct of the parties created a contract and the final terms of this contract would be the terms on which the writings of the parties agree, plus any nonmaterial additional terms in the acceptance and then plus any needed supplementary terms from the Code. Those terms on which the parties had differed would be stricken.

Under the Convention and Article 19, the nonconforming acceptance (because of different or additional material terms) becomes a counteroffer. If the supplier is the offeree and delivers the goods after sending the nonconforming acceptance, it is the replay of the old "last shot" principle. The goods are delivered under the supplier's counteroffer, and therefore the supplier's terms will be applied to the contract. The supplier fired the last shot with the counteroffer.

On the other hand, if the buyer is the offeree and after sending a nonconforming acceptance, receives the goods, it could be said that the supplier has accepted the buyer's counteroffer. This conduct puts us right back to the common law problems associated with the mirror-image rule.

Such confusion has no place in modern business. The Convention is sadly deficient in not providing a solution to the problems created by the battle of the forms. One deduces that those who wrote the Convention are hoping purchasing officers and suppliers will thoroughly negotiate every term and condition when a purchase is made. Then there can be no nonconforming acceptances. But today— that is wishful thinking!

***Nota Bene* to the American Purchasing Officer.** When operating under the Convention, do not allow yourself to get trapped in a Battle of the Forms situation with a foreign supplier. A possible outcome of such an involvement could conclude by having the terms of your purchase contract determined by a foreign court applying foreign law. There follows here a few suggestions to assist you in avoiding such a trap.

1. Your first line of attack should be to send your foreign supplier two copies of your purchase order. One of these copies is an "Acceptance Copy" which the supplier is to accept by signing it and returning it to you. Your purchase order was an offer to buy when you sent it to the supplier. When

it is signed by the supplier, your offer—and your terms and conditions—are accepted by him. (See Chapter XIV.)

2a. If your foreign supplier will not agree to doing business with you in the manner suggested in #1 above, then include the following clauses on your purchase order if it is an offer to buy:

> The supplier may only accept this offer to buy in writing or by delivering the goods ordered. By doing so the supplier accepts all of the terms and conditions set forth on the face and reverse side of this purchase order. Any additional or different terms you may propose are rejected, unless they are accepted by the buyer in a separate writing.

2b. You can convert a supplier's offer to sell into an offer to buy from yourself by prefacing the above clause in this manner:

> Notwithstanding any prior negotiations, this is an offer to buy which you may accept only in writing or by delivering the goods ordered. By doing so the supplier accepts all of the terms and conditions set forth on the face and reverse side of this purchase order. Any additional or different terms you may propose are rejected, unless they are accepted by the buyer in a separate writing

Please remember that in converting a supplier's offer to sell to your own offer to buy you run the risk of losing that supplier's proposition. You have rejected his offer to sell and that extinguishes that offer. The supplier does not have to accept your new offer to buy even though it is identical to his proposal which you just rejected with your purchase order. At this point it is in the supplier's discretion whether to move forward with the transaction or abandon it.

3. A purchasing officer has a better opportunity to control the direction of the negotiations under the Convention from the offeror's position. Article 19(2) for example gives the offeror the opportunity to approve or reject additional or different terms that appear in the acceptance. In addition the common law maxim, "The offeror is master of the offer," is generally recognized and does give the party in that position some opportunity to control the procedures. Should the purchasing officer be forced to be the offeree in the transaction, however, there is less that can be done to control your destiny. You are generally at the mercy of the offeror-supplier under the Article 19(2) approval procedure plus the fact that as the supplier in the transaction, the offeror can set into motion the "conduct" procedures by delivering the goods. That is always the first step in firing the

"last shot." The buyer-offeree can utilize a conditional acceptance clause to keep some semblance of control over the situation. Following is a typical conditional acceptance clause:

> This acceptance of your offer to sell is subject to your acceptance of the additional and different conditions shown on the face and reverse side of this purchase order. By delivering the goods ordered, you accept these different and additional terms from those shown on your offer to sell.

If your supplier delivers the goods to you after receiving this conditional acceptance, you have gotten your terms and conditions included in the contract.

However, once more you are risking loss of a favorable offer to sell. Your supplier has every right to throw your conditional acceptance in the waste basket and sell the goods to another customer. That is the chance you take when you use a conditional acceptance.

4. If the purchasing officer does not want to risk this possible "walk away from it" by the supplier, you are at the bottom of the list of your alternatives to getting the goods on your terms and conditions. Now it is incumbent for you to decide how bad it would be for your organization to make the purchase under the supplier's terms and conditions. Attempt to negotiate any troublesome differences with the supplier. (As a matter of practicality, 90 percent of all terms and conditions are for the convenience and general good humor of the proposer and his or her counsel. Their use will cost the buyer nothing.)

Failing to "negotiate out" any unwelcome terms, your final option is to find another supplier. Alternate sourcing is always your last, but not insignificant, opportunity.

Some Acceptance "Housekeeping" Items. Articles 20 through 24 give us some of the rules of the Convention concerning acceptance. Article 20(1) states that a period of time fixed by the offeror for acceptance begins to run from the time (a) a telegram is handed in for dispatch, (b) the date is shown on a letter, or if none, (c) the date that is shown on an envelope. Article 20(2) states that holidays and nonbusiness days during an acceptance period are counted. Only if a notice of acceptance cannot be delivered on the last day it is due because that is a holiday or a nonbusiness day, does the period get extended to the first business day that follows.

Articles 21(1) and 21(2) deal with acceptances that are late. Both sections give options for consideration of the late acceptance to the offeror. Article 21(1) gives the offeror the option to regard a late acceptance as effective if he promptly notifies the offeree orally or in writing. Article 21(2) provides that if a late acceptance shows that if its transmission had been normal it would have reached the offeror in due time, it is effective *unless* the offeror, without delay, informs the offeree orally or by writing, that he considers the offer to have lapsed. This is in line with the Convention's approach to placing on the shoulders of the offeree the responsibility for the successful delivery of an acceptance.

Article 22 gives the offeree the right to withdraw an acceptance if it reaches the offeror before or at the same time as the acceptance would have been effective. Article 23 officially confirms that a contract is concluded when the acceptance becomes effective. The same pronouncement is contained in Article 18(2).

Article 24 defines when an offer or an acceptance officially "reaches" the addressee. The Article says this occurs when it is delivered to the addressee personally, to his mailing address, or to his place of habitual residence if he has no place of business. Any one of these three alternates constitute adequate delivery. This is similar to the definition of "receives" in Code Section 1-201 (26)(a) and (b). Article 24 concludes Part II of the Convention entitled "Formation of the Contract."

SALE OF GOODS

Articles 25 through 88 on "Sale of Goods," govern the rights and duties of the buyer and the supplier. Sections on breach, avoidance, specific performance, and modification are found here.

Fundamental Breach. This is a new term for American purchasing officers. The term is an important concept in Convention law. It is part of the system of remedies in the Convention.

"Fundamental breach" is a serious breach of contract in the Convention. The Convention recognizes more than one type of breach of contract because Article 25 defines a fundamental breach in this manner:

> A breach of contract committed by one of the parties is fundamental
> if it results in such detriment to the other party as substantially to
> deprive him of what he is entitled to expect under the contract, . . .

The only clue given in this definition on how to differentiate between a fundamental breach and other types of breach is that a fundamental breach "substantially deprives him of what he is entitled to expect." No definition is given of the word "substantially"—in fact, there are no word definitions given anywhere in the Convention. One can only assume that the phrase implies that the detriment to the other party must be really severe to merit the classification of a fundamental breach.

The degree of severity of breach necessary to be classified as fundamental under the Convention probably is comparable to the meaning of the same word "substantially" as used in Section 2-608(1) of the Uniform Commercial Code. The topic in the Code section is "revocation of acceptance" (see Chapter XIV). Section 2-608(1) allows the buyer to revoke his acceptance of the goods under certain circumstances. The section reads as follows:

> (1) The Buyer may revoke his acceptance of a lot or commercial unit whose nonconformity substantially impairs its value to him if he has accepted it . . .

You will recall that in the Code the buyer operates under the "perfect tender" rule when first receiving the goods. The buyer may reject the goods "if they fail in any respect to conform to the contract" when they are first delivered. But after the goods are once accepted by the buyer they can be returned to the seller under the Code only if the defects discovered after the original acceptance "substantially impairs their value to him."

Both the Convention and the Code use the word *substantially* to indicate a degree of severity. The Code uses it as a gradation of nonconformity of goods delivered by the supplier. The use of the word in Article 25 applies to deficient actions by either the buyer or the seller. However, nowhere is the word defined in either body of law and the decision would be made only in a lawsuit by the trier of fact. This makes it difficult for one who needs to know the precise meaning before taking action. One would like to determine it without the benefit of a lawsuit. All that can be said is for each purchasing officer confronted with the problem to be realistic in his or her appraisal of the severity of the breach.

"Foreseeability" is also included in Article 25 as one of the conditions for the breach to be fundamental. Article 25 concludes from that shown above with this:

> . . . unless the party in breach did not foresee and a reasonable person of the same kind in the same circumstance would not have foreseen such a result.

Thus a court, when determining whether a breach of contract is fundamental, must first ascertain "How bad was the breach?" If the court concludes it was "pretty bad" and deprived the aggrieved party of what he was entitled to expect under the contract, then it must go to the second question "Could the party who breached have foreseen what happened?" If the party who breached did not foresee what happened, and if the reasonably prudent person also could not have foreseen the event occurring, then one assumes there would be no fundamental breach. Then one must assume the injured party must be content with a smaller amount of damages or some other consolation because of the happening. This does not appear to bring a fair result to the party who is injured by the other party substantially breaching his or her obligations under the contract.

As a matter of interest there is no such requirement in the Code Section 2-608 for the supplier to have foreseen the substantial impairment of value. If the impairment occurs, the supplier is responsible and answerable for damages or must accept the return of the goods. It is the author's opinion that this portion of the Convention is written "pro" supplier.

Avoidance of the Contract. We mentioned at the beginning of this discussion on the Convention that we would discuss its provisions in the numerical order they are presented. Article 25, defining fundamental breach, is shown as one of the general provisions that is applicable to several sections in Part III which covers the rights and duties of both buyers and sellers. It is possible for a buyer as well as a supplier to commit a fundamental breach under the Convention. We will discuss this later as the numerical progression gets to those articles.

And along this line of numerical progression, we now come to Article 26, again in the general provisions chapter. It surprises the reader by stating:

> A declaration of avoidance of the contract is effective only if made by
> notice to the other party.

The authors of the Convention assume we all know what is "avoidance of a contract." Using our command of the English language, we would assume avoidance implies "side-stepping" the contract or "getting out of our obligations of the contract." If we look forward in the Convention to Article 8l, we get a better understanding of the term:

> (1) Avoidance of the contract releases both parties from their obliga-
> tions under it, subject to any damages which may be due. Avoidance
> does not affect any provision of the contract for the settlement of dis-
> putes or any other provision of the contract governing the rights and
> obligations of the parties consequent upon the avoidance of the con-
> tract.

Thus the parties are released from any further duties under the contract if the contract is avoided. Perhaps we should add, however, that the parties are still obligated to pay damages that are due, and, if the contract has been partially or wholly performed, the other party is required to make restitution. Restitution is provided for in Article 81(2).

Back to our sequential study of the Convention, we note that Article 26 makes it quite clear that notice is essential to make an effective declaration of avoidance. "We can live with this requirement of notice" because a purchasing officer is accustomed to several sections in the Uniform Commercial Code where notice is essential and, sometimes, penalties for failure to notify are particularly severe. Take for example Section 2-602(1) which states:

> (1) Rejection of goods must be within a reasonable time after their

delivery or tender. It is ineffective unless the buyer seasonably notifies the seller.

Section 2-605(1) spells out the penalty for failure of the notice to the seller stating the defects that occasioned the rejection of the goods:

> (1) The buyer's failure to state in connection with rejection a particular defect which is ascertainable by reasonable inspection precludes him from relying on the unstated defect to justify rejection or to establish breach.

We gather from this that the notice given by the buyer to the supplier upon rejection must detail the defect that caused the buyer to reject. One assumes this is to give the supplier the opportunity to cure. Section 2-608(2) is the section that requires notice to the supplier if the buyer revokes acceptance of the goods. Thus the Uniform Commercial Code parallels the Convention in requiring the buyer to notify the supplier promptly when something is wrong with the delivered goods. Probably the principal reason a buyer would seek avoidance of the contract is because of the failure of the goods to meet the contract description although the buyer could be concerned about the failure of the goods to be delivered seasonably. Keep in mind that under the Convention, avoidance of the contract may be an act of the supplier as well as the buyer. Avoidance of the contract will be discussed in more detail in succeeding sections.

When a Notice Is Effective. We must be careful to note that we are now discussing Part III of the Convention. Some of Part III's housekeeping rules are different from those in Part II. You will recall that in Article 18(2) of Part II the "receipt rule" is applied to acceptances. The offeror must be in receipt of an acceptance before it is effective. Now comes Article 27 in Part III where the "dispatch rule" is applied to notices we have been discussing as well as to other notices and communications required in most of Part III. The Article says that a delay in transmission of a notice or its failure to arrive does not deprive the party sending it of the right to rely upon it. Clearly Part III is embracing the "dispatch rule"—once mailed, it is effective. However, be on the alert because not all notices are treated in that manner. Article 27 has a preamble that reads "unless otherwise expressly provided in this Part of the Convention . . . " We will call your attention to variations in the "dispatch rule" in Part III.

Applicability of the Remedy of Specific Performance. These first few articles that comprise Chapter I of Part III cover topics on a random basis and are in no apparent order. You are reminded these are General Provisions that relate to subsequent articles of the succeeding chapters of Part III.

One of the major remedies offered by the Convention is that of specific performance. We will discover later that the remedy is available to both parties under the Convention—in Article 46 for the buyer and in Article 62 for the supplier.

One suspects that specific performance is a favorite remedy in some civil law and Third World countries. Common law countries recognize the remedy but limit its use. In the United States we much prefer to have monetary damages as a remedy. It is quicker and more direct. However, many countries opposed the inclusion of specific performance when the Convention was written, but its proponents won the battle.

A typical "olive branch" is offered to dissident countries who are not fond of the specific performance remedy. The olive branch is in the form of an article—Article 28—and is included here in the General Provisions of Chapter I. Article 28 provides that "a court is not bound to enter a judgment for specific performance unless the court would do so under its own law in respect of similar contracts of sale not governed by this Convention." You will note that the article does not direct the court to apply its own domestic law as it pertains to specific performance, but it simply states the court is "not bound" to order specific performance if its domestic law is different than the Convention.

Application of Article 28 will leave the parties in a quandary in many instances. One cannot be certain what a particular court will do when it finds itself "not bound" to follow the Convention. It seems a court would have four options: (1) apply the law of the Convention; (2) apply the law of the buyer's country; (3) apply the law of the supplier's country; and (4) apply the court's own domestic law if different from the first three alternatives. Which route the court will choose may seriously affect one or both parties' rights.

If one feels threatened by this, finding protection is no easy matter. A purchasing officer could see to it that a forum clause is included in the contract and the named forum would be the state court where his or her company is located. But there is no guarantee your own state court might not be inclined to apply the law of France where your supplier's office and manufacturing plant are located. Perhaps a clause whereby both parties agree not to seek the remedy of specific performance should a disagreement occur might be more effective. When all the cards are down, not very many parties want the remedy of specific performance anyhow. While the civil law writers may be inclined to push for the remedy, it remains to be seen whether their constituents in the business world feel the same way. Finally, there is always the option of writing your contract outside of the Convention. That leaves you to the devices of the Uniform Commercial Code and its provisions for specific performance by the buyer or by the supplier!

Modification of the Contract. This is one topic that both the Convention and the Uniform Commercial Code agree upon. Article 29(1) of the Convention provides that a contract may be modified or terminated by the mere agreement of the parties. One assumes "mere agreement" means without having consideration passing. Section 2-209(1) of the Code does the same and asserts positively that no consideration is necessary to modify a contract.

The second subsections of Article 29 and Section 2-209 provide that parties who agree in their original contract that all modifications must be in writing cannot otherwise modify such a contract. Any modification must then be in writing and signed by both parties.

***Note Bene* to the Purchasing Officer.** One should consider having a clause to this effect in every international contract where the Convention is to be applied. Remember there is no need to have a writing for a contract to be enforceable under the Convention. An oral agreement is valid and enforceable. To make certain there is no opportunity for "misunderstood oral discussions" with foreign vendors, we believe it is prudent to include a clause such as "All modifications or any termination of this contract must be in writing and signed by both parties signing this original contract."

OBLIGATIONS OF THE SELLER

This chapter spells out the specific obligations of the supplier in contracts for the sale of goods. It begins with Article 30 which repeats the customary obligations of the seller to (1) deliver the goods, (2) hand over any documents relating to them, and (3) transfer the property (title) in the goods to the buyer. Section I of Chapter II following, discusses the first two of these obligations.

Delivery of the Goods and Handing Over of Documents

Delivery Terms. The Convention does not offer the variety of delivery terms as does the Uniform Commercial Code in Sections 2-319 to 2-324. It is apparent the Convention depends first on the parties to make the necessary provisions for delivery in their contract. And although not mentioned in the text of the Convention, one may safely assume that the predominant guide for acceptable delivery terms is the group known as *Incoterms*. Incoterms has just been revised. The revised group of terms became effective June 1, 1990. Incoterms is a set of 13 different delivery terms that have a standard meaning in international trade. These terms were developed, standardized, and promulgated by the International Chamber of Commerce. The 13 terms have a wide range from "Ex-Works" which means the seller makes the goods available at his factory or warehouse to "Delivered Duty Paid, Buyer's Receiving Dock, U.S.A.," which requires the supplier to put the goods at the designated destination. "Ex-Works" represents the supplier's minimum obligation and risk under delivery, and of course "Delivered Duty Paid" imposes the most obligations and expenses, and the most risk on the supplier. The other terms listed have intermediate duties and obligations assigned to the parties. Purchasing officers involved in foreign sourcing should have a copy of *Incoterms*. It can be obtained from:

The ICC Publishing Company
156 5th Avenue
New York, N.Y. 10010

The Convention relies heavily on the contract between the buyer and the supplier to spell out the details of the delivery arrangements, or to select an Incoterm. In a purchase from a foreign supplier there are many details to be agreed upon that are not customarily found in a domestic purchase. The necessary licenses, duties, and taxes must be paid at the exporting country's boundary; if passage is required through a third country at both that country's entry and exit border, the same routine must be followed; and, finally, this routine is again necessary at the importing country's border. It is a tedious process that must be attended to by one or both of the parties to the contract, and by their import and/or export agents.

Absent clear-cut terms in the agreement, or if there are vagaries requiring interpretation in the agreement, the Convention has drawn a few rules that can be applied. Article 31(a) covers the supplier's duty if a shipment contract is involved requiring the supplier to send the goods on their way:

> If the seller is not bound to deliver the goods at any other particular place, his obligation to deliver consists:
>
> > (a) if the contract of sale involves carriage of the goods—in handing the goods over to the first carrier for transmission to the buyer.

One assumes the "carrier" mentioned in this article is the equivalent of a common carrier; that is, one capable of issuing a straight or order bill of lading at the time it accepts the goods from the supplier. Left "hanging" by this article is the question whether export licenses and fees must be satisfied by the buyer or the supplier. One would hope the two parties to the contract would be sufficiently cognizant of the need to make these arrangements and provide for the satisfaction of them in the original contract of sale. There will probably be times when such arrangements will not be made, and we then are left with the need to assign that responsibility. The Convention gives us no help. One can only suppose that the answer would be to lay such responsibility in the lap of the supplier. Since the supplier is the one who must hand over the goods to the carrier, it is doubtful the carrier would accept such goods for delivery to a foreign destination and issue a bill of lading unless all licenses, duties, and fees have been provided for by the shipper. Since the supplier is the shipper, we must assume he is left with this duty.

Article 32 requires the supplier to make certain shipping arrangements. 32(1) requires the supplier to clearly identify the goods shipped either by marking the goods, or identifying them in the shipping documents, or by giving the buyer notice of the consignment, specifying the goods. Article 32(2) places responsibility on the supplier for making proper contracts for the transportation of the goods, and to make any necessary special provisions for their transportation. This would include proper refrigeration if needed or protection against freezing and similar special provisions. This is similar to Section 2-504(a) and (b) of the Uniform Commercial Code. Article 32(3) calls for the cooperation of the seller if the buyer requests information and assistance in providing for insurance while the goods will be in transit. This would not be necessary if the original contract required the supplier to provide carriage insurance.

Time of Delivery of Goods. Article 33 (a) and (b) tells the supplier to deliver the goods on the date or within the period of time provided in the contract. If the contract does not specify the time for delivery, Article 33(c) says the goods must be delivered within a reasonable time after the contract is concluded. It is suggested that all contracts, whether international or domestic, contain some instructions for delivery and for the time of delivery. It is also suggested that phrases such as "deliver as soon as possible" or "please rush" are useless. Make a point to establish a specific date for delivery of the goods and add the phrase that "time is of the essence."

Documents Required by the Contract. Article 34 provides that the supplier must hand over any required documents relating to the goods at the time and the place stated in the contract. If the documents are delivered ahead of schedule and there are defects in them, the seller may cure any such lack of conformity. However, in such cases, the article provides that the buyer retains his rights to any damages for which he might be entitled.

Conformity of the Goods and Third-Party Claims

Warranties in the Convention. The word *warranty* does not appear in the Convention. Nonetheless there are a full set of what we know as warranties contained in Article 35. The writers of the Convention elected to avoid the use of the term but provided the buyer with the same group of quality assurances under the caption of "Obligations of the Seller." Article 35(1) begins the grand pronouncement by reminding the supplier to live up to his contract:

> (1) The seller must deliver goods which are of the quantity, quality, and description required by the contract and which are contained or packaged in the manner required by the contract.

The "quality and description required by the contract" is what the Uniform Commercial Code elects to term "express warranties." Section 2-313(1)(b) states that an express warranty by the seller is "Any description of the goods made part of the basis of the bargain."

However in 2-313(1)(a) the Code also states that "Any affirmation of fact or promise by the seller . . . " is also an express warranty. This type of express warranty is not specifically mentioned in the Convention. One assumes that such affirmations of fact and promises made by the supplier would be construed as part of the obligation of the seller under the Convention but we cannot allow ourselves to be lulled into believing this when we have the opportunity to make it a certainty. The purchasing officer must make certain such affirmations and promises that have been relied on become part of the written contract. This will leave no doubt but that they will then be enforced as an obligation of the supplier under Article 35(1).

Article 35(2) gets on with what might be termed the implied obligations of quality placed on the supplier. This subarticle begins with the preamble "Except where the parties have agreed otherwise." This should remind the purchasing officer to beware of disclaimers by the supplier from responsibility for quality. Disclaimers of warranties (or of supplier's obligations under the Convention) are discussed below. However, you will note this preamble to Article 35(2) is the closest mention of a disclaimer in the Convention. There are no rules given on how to do it or instructions to make it "conspicuous" as in the Code. Full reliance for disclaimers is placed on the wording of the contract.

Each of the four subarticles under Article 35(2) listed below begins with this full preamble:

> Except where the parties have agreed otherwise, the goods do not conform with the contract unless they:

It is interesting to note that this preamble ties each of the following four subarticles to the contract itself. A breach of any of the four conditions will constitute a breach of contract.

> Article 35(2)(a): Are fit for the purposes for which goods of the same description would ordinarily be used;

This implied obligation attached to the seller's goods closely resembles the implied warranty of merchantability under the Code [Section 2-314(2)(c)].

> Article 35(2)(b): Are fit for any particular purpose expressly or impliedly made known to the seller at the time of the conclusion of the contract, except where the circumstances show that the buyer did not rely, or that it was unreasonable for him to rely, on the seller's skill and judgment;

This article is almost identical to the Uniform Commercial Code Section 2-315. The Convention seems to be less restrictive in applying this obligation than the Code because it states the particular purpose need be expressly or impliedly made known to the supplier. The Code phraseology is "Where the seller at the time of contracting has reason to know any particular purpose for which the goods are required . . . " Other than that slight difference which would make it easier for the buyer to establish a breach, the two sections are identical.

> Article 35(2)(c): Possess the qualities of goods which the seller has held out to the buyer as a sample or model;

This subarticle reverts back to what we know as express warranties under the Code and suggests the goods supplied must possess the qualities of any sample or model submitted. This is Section 2-313(c) of the Code, with the one difference that the Code refers to "any sample or model which is made part of the basis of the bargain." You will note Article 35(2)(c) refers to " . . . qualities of goods which the seller has held out to the buyer as a sample or model." Quite often it is the buyer who has the sample and submits it to the supplier to be matched. Will the fact that it is the buyer's sample make any difference in the supplier's obligation to match its qualities? The Uniform Commercial Code accepts any sample—the buyer's or the seller's. And it makes an express warranty that the sample's quality aspects will be matched by what the seller delivers. The same result should be reached under the Convention. It is the seller's obligation to match the qualities of the buyer's sample if he contracts to do so. This makes it a seller's obligation under Article 35(1)—a part of the contract requirements. The seller has taken the buyer's sample and contracted to supply copies of that sample. Matching the qualities of the buyer's sample then is the seller's obligation under the Convention. It is not an implied obligation under 35(2)(c) but a contract obligation under 35(1).

> Article 35(2)(d): Are contained or packaged in the manner usual for such goods, or, where there is no such manner, in a manner adequate to preserve and protect the goods.

This implied obligation of the seller to properly package the goods is unique—and welcome. Section 2-314(2)(e) of the Code requires the seller to adequately package and label the goods "as the agreement may require." This is part of the section describing the attributes of merchantable goods. Absent any provision in the contract, the seller has no obligation under the Code to adequately package. All the seller needs to do is contain the goods in some manner to be able to deliver them. The Convention, under Article 35(2)(d) makes proper packaging an implied duty of the supplier in every instance there is a sale. This is a "plus" for the Convention insofar as the buyer is concerned.

The question might be asked about quality statements that appear on labels or on containers when one is working under the rules of the Convention. Under the Uniform Commercial Code, the implied warranty of merchantability makes the promises and affirmations of fact made on the container or label implied warranties. The goods contained in such packages must conform to these representations. This is Section 2-314(2)(f). The Convention, on the other hand, is silent on the subject of promises on labels or containers. Would such affirmations have any value to a buyer seeking to hold his or her supplier to the quality assurances printed thereon?

We think that it does if one uses the Convention's rules of evidence. When we were discussing Article 8(3), we called your attention to the fact that "any subsequent conduct of the parties" was allowable evidence under the Convention to prove the intent of the parties. It appears to your author that affirmations of fact or promises on the containers or the labels are admissible evidence to determine the extent of the supplier's quality responsibilities. However, to make use of this evidence possible, there cannot be a merger clause confining the court to use of the final written contract only.

One final reminder for purchasing officers seeking to establish the equivalent of warranties under the Convention. All the details of a contract do not have to be in writing under the Convention to be enforceable in a court of law. This is true of warranties as well as other details. They may be proven by verbal testimony. Oral statements made by the representatives of the supplier can become the equivalent of warranties by being made part of the contract.

Disclaimer of Warranties Under the Convention. As mentioned previously, nowhere in the Convention is there any mention of how a supplier is to disclaim any particular obligations (warranties) imposed by Article 35(2). (A supplier cannot disclaim any obligations to deliver goods as described in the contract. These are the equivalents of express warranties.) Of course, Article 35(3) does give the seller an excuse from any of the implied obligations in Article 35(2)(a to d):

> . . . if at the time of the conclusion of the contract the buyer knew or could not have been unaware of such lack of conformity.

With characteristic lack of clarity and explanation, the Convention "drops this one on us" and goes no farther. There is no indication from the Convention of what situations the writers had in mind with this pronouncement. Probably this is intended to cover the situation where a buyer has had an opportunity to inspect, noted the item's defects, and, notwithstanding, elected to complete the purchase. It could also cover the situation where the product is being offered for sale on an "as is" basis, or under other circumstances that are spelled out in Code Section 2-316(3). In any event it is apparent that Article 35(3) is designed to relieve the supplier of his obligations under Article 35(2) when there is an indication the buyer has assumed part of these obligations. In short, the buyer is taking a calculated risk by completing the purchase. Please note that Article 35(3) applies only to the implied obligations of the supplier stated in Article 35(22). It does not touch the express type of warranty by description in the contract under Article 35(1).

There is only one other section in the Convention that tells how a supplier may transfer such quality obligations and risk to the buyer, and that is the preamble phrase in Article 35(2)—"Except where the parties have agreed otherwise . . . " This is the invitation to the supplier to attempt to contract away the usual risks of the Convention associated with warranting the product he is selling. It is the invitation to get the buyer to assume the risks associated with not warranting the product by the implied obligations imposed by Article 35(2).

***Nota Bene* to the Purchasing Officer.** It makes no difference whether it is the Uniform Commercial Code's Section 2-316(2) telling the supplier the proper method of disclaiming implied warranties, or if the supplier must simply say in the contract with the buyer "I disclaim all of my implied obligations stated in Article 35(2) of the Convention." The result is the same—the risks are transferred to the buyer.

We have seen that there is a full set of the equivalent of express and implied warranties in the Convention. Recovery of all types of damages is also provided, including consequential damages that could be reasonably foreseen. Therefore, the purchasing officer is advised that any proposed disclaimers of warranties and/or limitations on damages are designed to take away from you and your organization benefits the Convention offers. It is to your advantage to strongly resist accepting any of such restrictions of your rights that might be proposed for inclusion in the contract with your supplier. Read carefully! Think carefully before you agree to such limitations and disclaimers!

Extent of Supplier's Quality Obligations. Article 36 contains two general rules concerning the period of time the seller is responsible for the quality of the goods.

Article 36(1) contains the well-known rule that the seller is responsible for any lack of conformity that exists in the goods at the time the risk passes to the buyer. The article reminds one that this responsibility continues even though the nonconformity is not discovered until after the risk has passed to the buyer. This obligation of the supplier extends not only to the nonconformity of the goods from the contract description that existed when the goods were appropriated to the contract, but also to any damage incurred in transportation of the goods to the point where the risk passes to the buyer. This is similar to the Code rules.

Article 36(2) simply reminds the supplier that the obligation for such nonconformity continues as long as the guarantee in the contract continues.

Supplier's Right to Cure. Article 37 is the first of two articles giving the supplier the right to cure defects in delivered goods. This article deals with the right to cure goods that were delivered before the required delivery date. (Article 48, to be discussed later in numerical order, covers cure after the delivery date.) This article suggests four methods by which the supplier may attempt to cure a nonconforming delivery:

1. Deliver any missing part.

2. Make up any deficiency in the quantity of goods supplied.

3. Deliver replacement goods for those deficient.

4. Remedy any lack of conformity in the goods delivered by repair.

Article 37 has one proviso in it that keeps the supplier's right to cure before delivery from being absolute. The proviso reads " . . . provided that the exercise of this right does not cause the buyer unreasonable inconvenience or unreasonable expense." Thus the purchasing officer can stop the supplier's attempts to cure even before delivery was due if he finds the "cure process" unreasonably interferes with his operations. In this respect the Convention rule is more restrictive on the supplier than is the Uniform Commercial Code. Under the Code, the supplier's right to cure before delivery is due is a "right" and cannot be interfered with by the buyer. See Section 2-508(1) of the Uniform Commercial Code.

Article 37 concludes with a general statement that the buyer retains the right to claim damages, notwithstanding the supplier's attempts to cure. We shall see later that the attempt to cure, if successful, denies the buyer the right to avoid the contract. All it states here is that it will not deny the buyer the right to claim damages.

Nota Bene **to the Purchasing Officer.** One of the obstacles purchasing officers face in the Convention is that there is a strong effort to make a delivery "hold" regardless of the nonconforming condition of the goods. The authors of the Convention recognize that much time, effort, and cost is involved in transportation of the goods from the supplier to the buyer in the international contract. Return of the goods, in most cases, would be sheer economic waste. It is much more practical to have the buyer "make do" with what was delivered—perhaps with some money allowance. This may be the reason why the right to damages clause is included in this article. Even though an attempt to cure might not be entirely successful to bring the goods to the condition demanded by the contract, it could make them usable enough to force the buyer to keep them and be satisfied by accepting some money damages.

Should a purchasing officer not be willing to accept goods under such conditions as above, it is suggested that the contract be taken out of the Convention and the Uniform Commercial Code be substituted as the applicable law. Remember, under the Uniform Commercial Code the buyer has the perfect tender rule going for him and can insist upon the delivery of goods that fully comply with the contract.

Time for Inspection of the Goods. The buyer is required to inspect the goods "within as short a period as practicable under the circumstances." This is Article 38(1). The second section in this article permits inspection to be accomplished after the goods have been delivered. The third section allows inspection to occur after the goods have arrived at their final destination, following redirection or redispatch by the buyer. This latter right applies only if the seller knew of the possibility the buyer might transship at the time of the conclusion of the original contract.

Notice of Nonconformity of the Goods. Article 39(1) of the Convention should be placed before every purchasing officer:

> (1) The buyer loses the right to rely on a lack of conformity of the goods if he does not give notice to the seller specifying the nature of the lack of conformity within a reasonable time after he has discovered it or ought to have discovered it.

A supplier is entitled to assume that a sale is completed within a reasonable time after he has accomplished delivery. Further, the supplier is entitled to a prompt notice of any defects in the goods so he has a reasonable opportunity to "cure" the defects. It is with these thoughts in mind that Article 39(1) is included in the Convention.

You will note that the notice (1) must specify the lack of conformity the goods suffer, and (2) must be sent within a reasonable time after being discovered. The penalty the buyer suffers for failure to report the defect is that he or she is not entitled to rely on the defect by way of affirmative action against the supplier, or in defense of a supplier action against the buyer. It forces the buyer to act as if the goods were conforming from the beginning if no notice is given to the supplier. The consequences for failure to notify are severe.

However, the article is no more harsh on the buyer than the provisions in the three sections of the Uniform Commercial Code on the same topic. In the event of a rejection of goods, Section 2-602(1) requires that the rejection must be made within a reasonable time after the goods have been delivered. The rejection is ineffective unless the buyer seasonably notifies the seller. Section 2-605 requires the buyer to list all the defects ascertainable in the nonconforming goods that are rejected. Failure to list a defect precludes the buyer from relying on it to justify rejection. Section 2-607 applies after the buyer has accepted the goods and then discovers a defect. The buyer must then notify the seller within a reasonable time after discovering the breach. If the buyer fails to notify the seller the buyer is barred from any remedy. Thus the Code as well as the Convention requires strict adherence to the need of notice to the supplier by the purchaser. And in both bodies of law, the penalty to the buyer is severe if he or she fails to notify promptly—that is, within a reasonable time.

Article 39(2) places an overall limitation of two years on the buyer to give notice, if that can be considered a reasonable time. That limit could be extended too, if the supplier has given the buyer a warranty that runs longer than two years.

Article 40 relaxes the rules against the buyer's failure to inspect promptly under Article 38 and to give notice of defects under Article 39. The relaxation occurs if the supplier knew of the defect or defects in the goods or "could not have been unaware" of such defects. Article 40 prohibits the seller from relying on Article 39's penalty against the buyer for failure to report defects of which the seller was cognizant.

The Warranty of Title—Third Party Claims. Another one of the supplier's obligations under the Convention is to deliver goods free from any right or claim of a third party, including rights or claims from patents or copyrights. The Convention distinguishes rights and claims arising from liens and encumbrances from those arising from patents and copyrights. Article 41 treats third-party claims arising from liens and encumbrances, and then specifically states that Article 42 governs claims from industrial property or other intellectual property.

The obligation of the supplier to deliver goods free of any right or claims of third parties seems to be absolute under Article 41. The only caveat to this is if the buyer "agreed to take the goods subject to that right or claim." One assumes a buyer might take goods subject to a lien only if the supplier gave the buyer a money allowance to be deducted from the cost of the goods to cover the lien.

The Uniform Commercial Code goes a bit farther in giving these types of assurances to the buyer than does the convention. First, Section 2-312(1)(a) gives the buyer an express warranty that the title conveyed to the buyer shall be good. Then Section 2-312(1)(b) gives another express warranty that the goods shall be delivered "free from any security interest or other lien or encumbrance of which the buyer at the time of contracting has no knowledge." These are express warranties and not implied. Such warranties are not reached by the usual broad disclaimers of implied warranties that are so fluently given by some suppliers. The supplier here must disclaim this warranty by specific language.

Patent and Copyright Infringement. Finally, Section 2-312(3) of the Code makes the seller, if a merchant, warrant "that the goods shall be delivered free of the rightful claim of any third person by way of infringement or the like." As stated above, Convention Article 41 "hands over" claims of patent and trademark infringement to Article 42. Article 42 deals with the same subject matter as Code Section 2-312(2) but does not impose the obligations on the seller without giving the seller three rather significant exceptions. Because of the complexity of patent law generally, and of international patent law specifically, one can understand the desire to lighten this obligation from infringement claims on the international supplier. But that in itself does not justify transferring these risks to the innocent buyer. This is what Article 42 will do in many instances.

We will not repeat the entire Article 42 verbatim here, but will only synopsize the pertinent provisions for our discussion:

1. The article begins with the pronouncement that the seller must deliver goods free of any right or claim of a third party based on industrial property.

2. Then comes the first major caveat for the supplier: he must deliver goods free from any right or claim of a third party "of which at the time of the conclusion of the contract *the seller knew or could not have been unaware.*" The seller has no obligation if a patent infringement claim surprised him.

3. The second caveat is that the obligation of the supplier must be based upon the law of the State where the parties contemplated the goods would be resold or used, or, in any other case, under the law of the State where the buyer has his residence.

4. And finally of course, this obligation of the seller does not extend to cases where the buyer knew or could not have been unaware of the right or claim of the third party.

You will note in point #2 above that for the seller to have the obligation for the penalties of a patent infringement, the seller must have known at the time of sale that the product he was selling did indeed infringe a patent. Article 42 states he has no obligation to the buyer if he did not know he was selling an infringement lawsuit to the buyer. One will challenge a supplier's good faith when he deliberately sells his customer a product that the supplier knows represents an infringement of a patent. But of course the Convention is not at all concerned about parties exercising good faith in their transactions; only in the interpretation process does the Convention suggest good faith. [See the discussion of Article 7(1).]

Article 42 is a supplier's dream world come true. The supplier makes a sale of a product and has no responsibility to the buyer for the consequences if the product is proven to be one that infringes on a third party's patent, unless the supplier knew from the beginning that it represents an infringement. A second caveat in this article limits the supplier's liability to the buyer for deliberate infringement only if it is an infringement under the country's laws where the product is to be used *and* if the supplier knew it was to be used in that country. If the supplier did not know in what country the product was to be used, then he is responsible to the buyer only if the product is an infringement in the country where the buyer has his place of business. Finally, Article 42(2)(a) presents a third caveat to allow a supplier to escape liability to the buyer for an infringement. That occurs when the buyer knew the product was an infringement. In such instances the supplier has no liability to the buyer but, of course, each of them individually and jointly have liability to the holder of the patent. This is when we like to observe that "it could not happen to a nicer pair of dishonest people" since both of them knowingly were involved in the infringement of a patent.

Article 42(2)(b) presents another instance where the supplier is relieved of infringement obligations. This is the situation where the buyer furnishes drawings or specifications which lead the supplier to infringement by compliance with such drawings or specifications. The article simply states the "obligation of the seller" does not extend to such a case. The buyer apparently incurs no liability for having given such specifications to his supplier even though they led the supplier down the primrose path to infringement.

Contrast this with the Uniform Commercial Code Sections 2-312(3) and 2-607(3), (4), (5), and (6). Here the merchant seller must warrant that the goods will be delivered free of the rightful claim of any third person by way of infringement. (Although the Uniform Commercial Code requires the seller to be a merchant to be responsible for infringement, remember that sales to consumers are not covered by the Convention. Therefore all suppliers under the Convention are the equivalent of merchants.) This subsection also says that a buyer who furnishes specifications to the seller must hold the seller harmless against any claim for infringement. Then Section 2-607(3 to 6) provides for notice to the other party when such a claim appears. It also provides that the infringing party (supplier or the buyer as the case may be) must defend the action, pay all expenses, and satisfy any judgment against the innocent party. This is good law and reaches an equitable result because it places the onus of the infringement upon the one who is in the best position to know most about the product.

Article 43(1) states the buyer loses the right to rely on the provisions of Article 41 (liens and encumbrances) or Article 42 (patent infringement) if he does not give notice to the seller specifying the nature of the right or claim of the third party within a reasonable time after he (the buyer) has became aware of it. Article 43(2) demonstrates that the authors of this portion of the Convention were "not with it" when writing it. 43(2) states the seller cannot rely on the provisions of 43(1) if he (the seller) knew of the right or claim of the third party. And yet, under Article 42(1) the seller has to know of the infringement claim at the time the contract is concluded if the buyer is to have a claim against the seller. It appears the writers of the Convention wasted the time of day by writing Article 43.

And now comes Article 44 which completes this discussion of notification of defects and liens and encumbrances. This article recognizes "reasonable excuses" which the buyer might claim prevented him from giving notice in a timely fashion. The article does not define what might be a reasonable excuse for failure to give the required notice. If the buyer can provide such a reason he is entitled to certain—but not all of—his remedies. Article 44 says "the buyer may reduce the price . . . or claim damages, except for loss of profit if he has a reasonable excuse . . . " Since we have not yet discussed damages, we must assume that some substantial types of damages are withheld from a buyer who has a reasonable excuse, chief among which is the right to avoid the contract.

Nota Bene **to the Purchasing Officer.** Article 42 does not represent the Convention's finest hour insofar as purchasing officers are concerned. But the same article certainly can endear the Convention to suppliers.

The possibilities of patent or copyright infringement claims in international trade are substantial. When one is purchasing a foreign-made product, the supplier and/or the manufacturer should know the most about the product, its derivation, and other related products in the industry classification. It would seem to be a logical *sequitur* that the buyer must depend upon the supplier for any patent knowledge pertaining to products in that field, because the supplier is the one who lives with the product and with the activities of competitors in the field. Yet the purchasing officer should not be required to depend solely upon the supplier's knowledge and good faith, whatever that might be under the Convention. Nor should the purchasing officer be required to live with the minimal protection against patent infringement given by the Convention. There are two suggestions we can give to add to the buyer's protection.

The first suggestion is to insert the following clause, or something similar, in every contract for goods that is covered by the Convention:

> The seller hereby agrees to defend and hold harmless the buyer should any claim of patent or copyright infringement be brought against the buyer because of the purchase, use, or resale of the goods or machinery purchased herein.

In all fairness, the buyer should give his or her foreign supplier the courtesy of the same protection if the supplier is furnished specifications developed by the buyer in the United States.

Of course, the second option available is to derogate 100 percent from the Convention and have the Uniform Commercial Code of your state become the applicable law for your international contracts.

REMEDIES FOR BREACH OF CONTRACT
BY THE SELLER

Articles 45 through 52 cover the remedies that the seller may elect subsequent to a breach by the buyer.

Index to Buyer's Remedies. Article 45 has three subsections. The first subsection reads this way:

> (1) If the seller fails to perform any of his obligations under the contract or this Convention, the buyer may:
>
> (a) exercise the rights provided in articles 46-52;
>
> (b) claim damages as provided in articles 74-77.

The "rights" mentioned in (1)(a) include the following:

1. To seek specific performance, require delivery of substitute goods, or to require the seller to repair the nonconforming goods. Article 46.

2. To fix an additional period of time for performance by the seller. Should the seller not perform within the additional period of time, the buyer may avoid the contract. Article 47.

3. To declare the contract "avoided." Article 49.

4. To reduce the price in the same proportion as the value of the goods had at the time of delivery to the value conforming goods would have had at that time. Article 50.

5. In the event of a partial delivery, to apply any of these rights to the quantity that has not been delivered. Article 51.

6. If the seller delivers before the due date, to refuse to take delivery. If the seller delivers more than the contract total, the buyer may refuse to take more. Article 52.

Here are the list of damages provided in the Convention as mentioned in (1)(b):

1. For the loss suffered, including lost profits. Article 74.

2. For any costs arising from cover, including the difference between the contract price and the cover price. Article 75.

3. In the case of avoidance, the difference between market price at the time of avoidance and contract price if the party has not taken over goods; otherwise, at time of taking over goods. Article 76.

You will note the articles pertaining to damages are carried much later in the Convention. This is because the various types of damages are available to both the seller and the buyer. Part III of the Convention lists obligations of the seller first (this is what we are presently involved in), then the obligations of the buyer and finally provisions common to both the seller and the buyer. We shall continue our discussion in the numerical sequence of the articles as they appear in the Convention.

Specific Performance. The buyer's right to demand specific performance of the seller is one of the remedies the common law recognized. But it is not favored nor encouraged by the Uniform Commercial Code. Section 2-716(1) reads:

> (1) Specific performance may be decreed where the goods are unique or in other proper circumstances.

The fact that the remedy is confined mainly to those cases where "the goods are unique" limits its applicability. Apparently the Commissioners who wrote the Code believed the right to damages and the right to cover was all a buyer needed to be "made whole" by a defaulting supplier. And there never has been much complaint heard that the remedy has been that limited in scope.

The Convention, on the other hand, takes a more favorable approach to a specific performance. Article 46(1) states that the buyer may require the supplier to perform his obligations "unless the buyer has resorted to a remedy which is inconsistent with this requirement." Nothing is said about the uniqueness of the goods—apparently it is a buyer's right to ask for specific performance. Later on we shall see in Article 62 that the seller has a similar right of specific performance against the buyer—that is, to make the buyer take the goods and pay the contract price for them. The Uniform Commercial Code does not give the supplier the same right in such precise terms.

One can only surmise that the right to specific performance is included in the Convention in such an unfettered state as a "sop" to civil law countries. Many civil law countries permit application of the remedy, although it is understood that not many buyers or suppliers avail themselves of this remedy. And, of course, Article 46(1) limits the application of the remedy if the buyer has resorted to an inconsistent remedy such as cover.

The reader is also reminded of our previous discussion of Article 28 at the beginning of Part III. Article 28 gives the court the opportunity of not following Article 46 and its specific performance remedy, if the court's own domestic law would not allow it to do so. While this is not a mandate to the court, it is an option some courts will have because of their own law. It places some vestige of ambiguity into the final disposition of such a case.

Two other possible remedies are given the buyer in Article 46. Subsection (2) gives the buyer the right to demand substitute goods from the supplier if the delivered goods' failure to conform to the contract is such as to constitute a fundamental breach of contract. (See the discussion of "fundamental breach" at the beginning of Chapter I, Article 25.) If the purchasing officer is convinced the defects in the goods are severe enough, this is a possible remedy.

Subsection (3) of Article 46 gives the buyer the right to require the supplier to remedy the lack of conformity of the delivered goods "by repair unless this would be an unreasonable request." One surmises the authors of the Convention believed this was a much more favored remedy because the section does not require the buyer to treat the defect as a fundamental breach to request it. However the Convention does protect the supplier by stating that this is a right of the buyer "unless this is unreasonable having regard to all the circumstances." In an international sale buyer and supplier could be thousands of miles apart. If repairs to an item require the attention of an individual located in the supplier's plant, travel expenses for that individual would be heavy. Perhaps it is suggesting to both buyer and supplier to look around the buyer's locale for a suitable repair person to do the proper repair job on the supplier's goods. Of course, such a repair would be at the supplier's expense. Furthermore, the supplier would have to assume full responsibility for the repair, since the repair person would be the supplier's agent or an independent contractor performing the repair for the supplier. The situation might occur where the buyer is asked by the supplier to recommend a "good" repair person to do the job. The buyer should be very careful in how this is done. Do not allow the supplier to make the repair person and the quality of the work the responsibility of the buyer.

An Additional Period of Time for Performance. The second "right" of a buyer listed in Article 45(1)(a) provides for a procedure that will be new to American purchasing officers. The Article reads this way:

> (1) The buyer may fix an additional period of time of reasonable length for performance by the seller of his obligations.

At first blush one may wonder how this action of fixing an additional period of time for the supplier to perform could possibly be related to a buyer's remedy against a breaching supplier. The truth of the matter is that this procedure is a preliminary step to securing one of the Convention's major remedies without taking some risk of falsely accusing a supplier of being in breach.

A bit later we shall discuss Article 49 which you will note from the list of remedies at the beginning of this section is "avoidance of the contract." Under Article 49 the buyer may declare the contract "avoided" if one of two possible events occurs. The first of these is that the seller may commit a "fundamental breach" that will allow the buyer to avoid the contract. (Fundamental breach was defined previously in Article 25 above.) The other happening to trigger "fundamental breach action" occurs when the seller does not perform his obligations within an "additional time period" fixed by the buyer under Article 47(1). Therefore, if the buyer wants to avoid the contract without having to speculate on whether the supplier's delay in delivery is sufficiently gross enough to meet the undefined test of "substantially . . . depriving him of what he is entitled to expect," the buyer has the "additional period notice" route as an alternative.

You will note that the buyer must fix the additional period of time at a "reasonable length." The "reasonableness" of the length of extension is one that is not spelled out in the Convention. One could refer to Article 7(1), which calls for good faith in international trading, as a guide. There are a myriad of different conditions that would need to be considered in each case before deciding whether any one extension is of reasonable length. For example, if the buyer is seeking the delivery of goods under an international contract, setting an additional period of three days beyond the contract date would not be reasonable unless the goods had already been shipped, or could be sent via air. Above all, when setting the additional period of time, the buyer should be specific on the closing date when delivery would be acceptable. "To be delivered no later than the close of business on June 10" is being specific.

Perhaps the purchasing officer should also be reminded that a precise delivery date for delivery of all of the goods should be on the original purchase order, as well as the precise place where the goods are to be delivered. (This is good purchasing practice for every purchase, domestic or international.) This places the responsibility of getting the goods there on that date on the supplier's shoulders. Article 33(1), you will recall, mandates this obligation. If no date is mentioned, then Article 33(3) allows the supplier "a reasonable time" to get the goods to that location. "A reasonable time" is always open to argument as to when it expires. A precise date is not arguable.

Giving an extension of additional performance time can also be helpful to the buyer if the supplier is lagging on the delivery of substitute goods under Article 46(2). A similar extension of time can be given for cure by repair by the supplier under Article 46(3). Using the time extension as a "cutoff" on a supplier who prolongs the cure process is also helpful. We have read cases in the United States where a supplier takes as long as six months in attempting a repair without success. Having a "turn-off" valve will stand the buyer in good stead.

The final section of Article 47(2) prohibits the buyer from resorting to any remedy for breach of contract while the additional period of time that was fixed is "running." The buyer, in effect, invites the supplier to perform when giving this additional time period. He should not be permitted to take a diverse action that is inconsistent with such an invitation to the supplier. Once the extension of time is given, the buyer must be patient until the extension has run its full course. Such patience on the part of the buyer, however, does not deny the buyer of the rights he may have to claim damages against the supplier for delays in performance.

Seller's Right to Cure After Delivery. We previously discussed Article 37 wherein the supplier is given the opportunity to cure any defect if the goods have been delivered before the date for delivery. His right to cure in any manner "up to" the delivery date is almost unlimited, subject only to unreasonable inconvenience or expense to the buyer. Now comes Article 48 which gives the supplier some opportunity to cure "after the delivery date has passed," subject to some caveats:

> (1) Subject to article 49, the seller may even after the date for delivery, remedy at his own expense any failure to perform his obligations, if he can do so without unreasonable delay and without causing the buyer unreasonable inconvenience or uncertainty of reimbursement by the seller of expenses advanced by the buyer. However, the buyer retains any right to claim damages as provided for in this Convention.

Article 49, referred to in Article 48, covers "avoidance of the contract by the buyer." Since avoidance is mentioned in an article dealing with cure, one wonders if and how the two are related. Does this article imply the seller's right to cure is based upon the buyer not having avoided the contract as yet, or does the seller's right to cure delay the ability of the buyer to avoid the contract? This is like the proverbial chicken and the egg problem.

There has to be a relationship between "cure" and a "fundamental breach." One would assume a proper cure of nonconforming goods would make them conforming. And, if the goods are conforming to the contract, the buyer would be unable to claim they "substantially deprive him of what he is entitled to expect." Realizing this fact, then perhaps the chicken and the egg problem is solved. The cure rightfully should come first, because if the cure is successful the buyer will not have the right to avoid the contract.

Completion of a contract is particularly encouraged in international trade. One way to have a completed contract is to permit the seller to correct any defects in his product so that the product will be acceptable to the buyer. Therefore it is reasonable to permit an attempted cure under Article 48(1) before a buyer is permitted to exercise his right to avoid the contract under Article 49(1). This interpretation is particularly true when one notices the last sentence in Article 48(1) which retains the right to claim damages by the buyer in the event the cure process takes too long.

During our discussion of Article 37, which gives the supplier the right to cure defects in goods delivered before the required delivery date, we mentioned Section 2-508(1) of the Uniform Commercial Code. That Code section gives the supplier the same right to cure prior to the delivery date. Section 2-508(2) also gives the supplier a limited right to cure after the time for delivery has passed. However, the Code section seems to be more strict on the supplier than does the Convention:

> (2) Where the buyer rejects a nonconforming tender which the seller had reasonable grounds to believe would be acceptable with or without money allowance, the seller may if he seasonably notifies the buyer have a further reasonable time to substitute conforming tender.

Subsection (2) must be read in light of subsection (1) which gives the supplier the right to cure within the contract time. Subsection (2) gives the supplier "a further reasonable time" to cure—which means after the contract time has passed. Presumably this right of the supplier to cure is more limited under the Code than in the Convention. First off the supplier is allowed to cure only if there was a surprise rejection of the goods by the buyer. Then and only then is the supplier allowed the opportunity to cure after the contract time for performance has passed.

As a matter of actual practice, no reasonable purchasing officer would deny a supplier the opportunity to cure if it can be done promptly and quickly. However, buyers are also aware that a supplier can "string out" cure for a long period of time. Persistent repairs of the same type often indicate a product is not capable of maintaining the required operating level. The buyer should have the ability to draw a "finish" line, declare the product nonconforming and of no value to him, whether it is purchased in the international market or a local market. Because of the propensity of some suppliers to take long periods of time for cure, some purchasing officers put a "no replacement" clause in a contract. This prevents the right of cure by the seller after the time for delivery has passed. One would assume a similar opportunity to use such a clause would be present under the Convention.

Seller's Notice of Intent to Cure. Articles 48(2 to 4) cover communication rules applicable to the seller's right to cure after the date of delivery. It is interesting to note that these rules are written so as to give the seller the right to cure in the event of no response by the buyer. Subarticle (2) states:

> (2) If the seller requests the buyer to make known whether he will accept performance and the buyer does not comply with the request within a reasonable time, the seller may perform within the time indicated in his request.

The article goes on to point out that if the buyer does not respond, the buyer cannot resort to any remedy inconsistent with the seller's attempts to cure. Subarticle (3) states:

> (3) A notice by the seller that he will perform within a specified period of time is assumed to include a request, under the preceding paragraph, that the buyer make known his decision.

These two subarticles tell every purchasing officer to immediately respond to any supplier's request to cure if cure is not desired. Else, the buyer will get cure whether he really wanted it or not. About the only solace to the buyer is that subarticle (4) requires that the onus is on the seller to make certain such communications about cure are *received* by the buyer. The Convention does not apply the dispatch rule to such notices of intent to cure—the notice must be received by the buyer.

The Convention's Rules on Avoidance of Contract. Article 49 of the Convention sets out the general rules for avoidance under the Convention. 49(1) tells *when* the buyer may declare the contract avoided:

> (a) if the failure by the seller to perform any of his obligations under the contract or this Convention amounts to a fundamental breach of contract; or

(b) in the case of nondelivery, if the seller does not deliver the goods within the additional period of time fixed by the buyer in accordance with paragraph (1) of Article 47 or declares that he will not deliver within the period so fixed.

The American purchasing officer should not be lulled into the belief that the right to avoid the contract under 49(a) is similar to the "perfect tender rule" of Code Section 2-601. In fact, there is no perfect tender rule for the buyer in the Convention. Under 49(1) (a) the buyer may avoid the contract only if the seller's breach is a fundamental breach. And a fundamental breach, you will recall, was defined in Article 25 of the Convention as one that "substantially deprives him of what he was entitled to expect under the contract." That wordage may be familiar to the American purchasing officer as coming from the Uniform Commercial Code. In fact, it is very similar to Section 2-608(1) of the Code which provides for revocation of acceptance by the buyer. Then the breach must be "substantial" to enable the buyer to revoke his acceptance of the goods. The buyer's right to avoidance under the Convention is based upon the same degree of substantial defect as is revocation of acceptance under the Code. That means there is no perfect tender rule in the Convention. The buyer must "make do" with less serious defects and does not have the option of rejecting such goods.

Article 49(1)(b) gives a buyer another opportunity to avoid a contract. This occurs only in cases of nondelivery of the goods. The occasion arises when the seller does not deliver the goods within an additional period of time for performance granted by the buyer under Article 47(1). Thus, even though failure to deliver promptly might not seriously injure the buyer, once the buyer gives the seller an additional period of time to perform under Article 47, the time of delivery becomes "of the essence" and goes to the core of the contract. After that warning, if the seller does not then perform in a timely manner, the buyer may avoid the contract. This procedure codifies the approach we follow under general contract law to make "time of the essence" in a contract. The procedure under the Convention is to be preferred because the result then becomes automatic.

When Buyer Must Declare Avoidance Where Seller Has Delivered Goods. Subsection 2 of Article 49 gives us some rules as to when the buyer must declare a contract avoided in those cases where the supplier has delivered the goods. These rules are:

1) when delivery is late, within a reasonable time after the buyer has become aware the delivery has been made.

2) in respect to any other breach than late delivery, within a reasonable time after the buyer knew or ought to have known about the breach, or

3) where an additional period of time for delivery was given under Article

47(1), within a reasonable period of time after that performance date has passed, or

4) where the seller has not performed the cure he promised under an Article 48(2) notice within the time he stated, the buyer within a reasonable time must declare the contract avoided.

Failure of the buyer to act within the "reasonable time" allowed results in the buyer's loss of the right to declare the contract avoided.

Nota *Bene* to the Purchasing Officer. Your author would be remiss if he did not remind you at this point that Article 26 which follows the article on fundamental breach is a "two liner" that states "A declaration . . . of avoidance is effective only if made by notice to the other party." The message to you is to send notice if you avoid a contract!

Reduction of Price. Article 50 presents another right of the aggrieved buyer, although it appears to be a right of very doubtful value. The article states:

> If the goods do not conform with the contract and whether or not the price has already been paid, the buyer may reduce the price in the same proportion as the value of the goods actually delivered had at the time of delivery bears to the value that conforming goods would have had at that time.

This section has very limited use under narrow circumstances. It may be of advantage to the buyer if his opportunity to recover damages under Article 74 (which we will be discussing in numerical order) is limited because the seller is not at fault for the breach. This would be similar to a situation that develops under the Uniform Commercial Code's Section 2-615, which refers to failure of presupposed conditions. In such cases the buyer has no breach of contract action against the seller.

Part of the Goods Are Not Delivered or Part Are Nonconforming. Article 51(1) covers the situation where the seller either does not deliver the complete contract quantity or a part of the delivered goods are nonconforming. The Article provides that the remedies offered in Articles 46 to 50 can be applied to the missing part or to the nonconforming portion. Thus the buyer can ask for delivery of substitute goods to replace the nonconforming goods or avoid the contract with respect to the missing or nonconforming goods. The buyer may also seek damages.

The buyer's right to avoid the contract with respect to the nonconforming or missing goods does not allow the right to avoid the complete contract. Article 51(2) states:

> The buyer may declare the contract avoided in its entirety only if the failure to make delivery completely or in conformity with the contract amounts to a fundamental breach of contract.

Thus, only if the missing part of the delivery or the conforming goods could make the delivered portion useless may the buyer have the right to avoid the entire contract. But avoidance because part of the goods were nonconforming gives the buyer the right to avoid only that portion of the contract.

What Article 51(2) does is to make it difficult for a buyer to return the portion of the goods that are conforming. This is in line with the thought that pervades throughout the Convention that it is costly to deliver goods in international trade, and once delivered, every attempt is made to make that delivery "hold." The Uniform Commercial Code, in comparison, does not attempt to force the buyer to retain any portion of goods if another portion of them is nonconforming. Section 2-601 states:

> . . . the buyer may:
>
> (a) reject the whole; or
>
> (b) accept the whole; or
>
> (c) accept any commercial unit and reject the rest
>
> if the goods or the tender of delivery fail in any respect to conform to the contract.

Thus the American buyer is able to dispose of any or all of the goods rather than being forced to accept "odd lots" as under the Convention or attempt to prove a partial nondelivery or a partial faulty delivery is a fundamental breach.

Nota Bene **to the Purchasing Officer.** Doing international business under the Convention may require you to accept something less than a complete delivery. A clause similar to the following could be inserted in your contract with the supplier to keep this from happening:

> Buyer insists on 100-percent delivery of conforming goods ordered under this purchase order, in one delivery. No over- or under-runs are acceptable. Buyer reserves the right to return the entire contract delivery if any portion of the goods are nonconforming.

Early Delivery and Overruns. Should a supplier deliver before the due date, the buyer has the right under article 52(1) to refuse to take delivery. It is suggested that unless the buyer has other requirements for the space where the goods are to be placed, delivery should be taken when tendered. Storage costs or demurrage could cause the seller to lose money on the contract.

Overruns are covered in Article 52(2). The buyer is not required to accept any overruns but may do so and pay the contract price for the excess quantity. No mention is made for exceptions to this rule where industry customs provide for over- or underruns, as in cases of the printing, cannery, and foundry industries.

OBLIGATIONS OF THE BUYER

The Convention presents the obligations of the seller in Chapter II. Now comes Chapter III which gives us the obligations of the buyer. We will not treat these in such detail unless the Convention makes unusual demands on the buyer.

Article 53 begins Chapter II by stating the fundamental obligations of the buyer:

> The buyer must pay the price for the goods and take delivery of them as required by the contract and this convention.

This comes as no surprise to purchasing officers. Section 2-301 of the Uniform Commercial Code places the same obligations on the buyer.

Payment of the Price

Buyer—Get Prepared to Pay! The section leads off with a single-sentence article that reminds the buyer to make all of the necessary arrangements for payment to the supplier:

> The buyer's obligation to pay the price includes taking such steps and complying with such formalities as may be required under the contract or any laws or regulations to enable payment to be made.

There are many details involved in arranging for credit and for payment when an international purchase is to be consummated. This can include clearance of government restrictions on money or goods going in and out of the parties' respective countries. Article 54 clearly reminds the buyer these are the buyer's obligations to handle. When the Convention does this it is also telling the supplier that any failure of the buyer to make these arrangements may be grounds for avoidance of the contract by the supplier.

***Nota Bene* to the Purchasing Officer.** Credit terms and details of how the supplier is to be paid should be negotiated at the time the purchase is made. This is especially true for international purchases unless you and your foreign supplier have an established routine of doing business with each other.

Open Price Contracts. Once again we come upon an Article dealing with open price contracts. This is Article 55 which is in the section dealing with the obligations of the buyer. You will remember that earlier in the Convention, in a section dealing with the Formation of a Contract, we found Article 14 which states that an offer "is sufficiently definite if it . . . expressly or impliedly fixes or makes provision for determining the quantity and the price." There we arrived at the conclusion that an offer under the Convention required a price in it to be valid.

Now comes Article 55 which states:

> Where a contract has been validly concluded but does not expressly
> or implicitly fix or make provision for determining the price, the par-
> ties are considered, in the absence of any indication to the contrary, to
> have impliedly made reference to the price generally charged at the
> time of the conclusion of the contract for such goods sold under com-
> parable circumstances in the trade concerned.

Authorities who have written law review articles on the Convention are mixed in their opinion of whether Article 55 is to be believed or that Article 14 controls. Is a price necessary to form a contract as in Article 14 or can the parties be assumed to have conjured in their minds that the price which is "generally charged" would be applied? The latter assumption is rather difficult to believe but in the interest of making the Convention a better document with one less loose end, let us grant that thesis.

As a matter of fact, your author can see some relationship between Articles 14 and 55 of the Convention on the one hand, and Section 2-207(3) of the Uniform Commercial Code on the other. Article 55 begins with "Where a contract has been validly concluded . . . " We compare this with Section 2-207(3) "Conduct by both parties which recognizes the existence of a contract is sufficient to establish a contract for sale . . . " and we come to the conclusion it is similar logic that is "stretched a bit." Somehow the parties conclude a contract by performance and conduct. The Convention says "here is the manner in which we will determine the price of that contract in this instance. "Article 55 assumes the parties meant to apply the price generally prevailing in the trade because they made the assumption they were in contract. While this may be placing words in the mouths of the writers of the Convention, it is one way to explain Article 55. We can certainly vouch that no self-respecting purchasing officer is going to purchase something and agree to pay a price that is considerably above the current market price. Likewise we know that no self-respecting supplier will be caught giving his product to the buyer.

You will note that Article 55 specifies the price to be applied is the one prevailing at the time "of the conclusion on the contract." Recall that the Uniform Commercial Code (Section 2-305) applies the price prevailing at the time of delivery.

Manner of Payment—Place. The settlement of the amount owing the seller is usually spelled out in a contract involving the international sale of goods. Both buyer and seller could face governmental obstacles in the settlement of their debt and usually will face up to the problem at the time they are contracting. Should there be no provision for the place where settlement is to be made, the following rules are set by Article 57:

(l)(a) if no place for payment is provided, the buyer must pay at the seller's place of business;

(l)(b) if payment is to be made against the handing over of the goods or documents, the buyer must pay where the handing over occurs.

Time for Payment and Inspection of Goods. Article 58 spells out the rules of the Convention about time of payment and the inspection of the goods when the contract is silent on these issues. Here again the parties are free to agree on such issues in their contract. The Uniform Commercial Code usually preambles a section with "Unless otherwise agreed, . . . " The Convention does much the same by stating "if the buyer is not bound to pay the price . . . ," so under either codified law, the parties are first given the opportunity to establish their own rules on time for payment and where inspection is to occur. If they do not take advantage of this invitation, then the Convention, in Article 58, provides these guides to time of payment and time of inspection:

(1) If the buyer is not bound to pay the price at any other specific time, he must pay it when the seller places either the goods or documents controlling their disposition at the buyer's disposal . . .

(2) If the contract involves carriage of the goods, the seller may dispatch the goods on terms whereby the goods, or documents controlling their disposition, will not be handed over to the buyer except against payment of the price.

(3) The buyer is not bound to pay the price until he has had an opportunity to examine the goods, unless the procedures for delivery or payment agreed upon by the parties are inconsistent with his having such an opportunity.

We can put 57(1)(a) together with 58(1) and assert with some authority that the Convention requires the buyer to pay for the goods at the seller's place of business when the seller makes the goods available to the buyer. We can also assert that where the goods are to be shipped by the seller, the seller can ship the goods against documents of title that require the buyer to pay for the goods in exchange for the title documents. Article 58(3) spells out the fact that the buyer is not bound to pay the price until he has had an opportunity to inspect the goods, unless the payment procedures agreed upon in the buyer-seller contract prevent this from happening. And this usually happens to the buyer—the buyer waives the right to inspect before paying for the goods when agreeing to allow the seller to ship against documents of title.

The provisions of Article 58 are similar to those in the Uniform Commercial Code—Sections 2-310(1) and (2). Subsection 2-310(2) repeats the buyer's right to inspect before payment, but Section 2-508(3) specifically states that:

> ...the buyer is not entitled to inspect the goods before payment of the price when the contract provides
>
> (b) for payment against documents of title...

Therefore under both the Convention and the Code the buyer waives the right of inspection before payment when the contract provides for shipment against documents of title.

The problems of payment and inspection in foreign purchases were discussed earlier. In every purchase, whether domestic or international, there is always the desire to protect oneself against the other party. The buyer does not want to pay for the goods until the goods have been inspected and are known to conform to the contract. On the other hand, the supplier is not willing to release the goods before the buyer has paid the price. The Convention and the Code, in general, provide for the *exchange* of the price and the goods. These acts are supposedly simultaneous so that neither the buyer nor the supplier have any advantage or take any unusual risk.

Variations from this "exchange" pattern are manifold. The seller will sell on credit and the buyer is thereby given time to inspect the goods before payment. On the other hand, arrangements could be made for the seller to "ship against documents" which results in the buyer having to pay for the goods long before ever laying eyes upon them. In domestic transactions, either of these assumptions is a relatively safe and conservative procedure for the parties; that is, if the buyer and the seller have both done their "homework" and verified each other's credit standing.

International trade presents more problems that are not as easily solved. Greater distances between buyer and seller mean that transportation costs are greater, cure costs of the supplier are greater, and the supplier's ability to dispose of unwanted goods is much more limited. In addition, there may be governmental restrictions on currency transactions. Determining the credit standings of the buyer and the seller are also more difficult. Therefore there is less willingness by either party to place as much trust in each other, and substitute procedures must be found.

We suggested one method for American buyers to follow in the original text. The funds are made available to the seller in the seller's country via a letter of credit or some similar financing device. This can be arranged for through the buyer's local bank and its correspondent banks that have a branch in the seller's country. When the seller ships the goods, the money can be obtained from the correspondent bank in the seller's country. When the seller ships the goods to the buyer, the seller can obtain his money from the bank in his country by presenting the order bill of lading the seller received from the transportation company. This bill of lading should show that conforming goods have been sent by the seller. Remember that the bank in the seller's country, who has the buyer's letter of credit, is a representative or agent of the buyer's bank. That bank is under the duty not to release the funds to the seller without receiving in return a proper bill of lading showing that conforming goods have been sent. This is some protection for the buyer, but it is not a real substitute for inspection. Of course, the buyer could go the full step and employ someone in the supplier's country to make the inspection for the buyer.

Nota Bene **to the Purchasing Officer.** You will find that the Convention tries very hard to protect both parties in an international sale, but when that is impossible to accomplish, the nod then seems to go to the supplier. Here in Article 58, the buyer's right of inspection first is lost so that the seller can be properly protected.

Section I of Chapter III of the Convention concludes with Article 59. This Article makes the simple observation and rule that the buyer must pay for the goods on the due date without any "demand for payment" being made by the supplier. Your author is unaware of any similar section in the Uniform Commercial Code except for Section 2-511(2) which permits the seller to demand payment in legal tender if sufficient time is given the buyer to obtain legal tender.

Taking Delivery

Section II consists of one article—60—which states that the buyer's obligation to take delivery consists of doing all the acts which could reasonably be expected of him in order for the seller to make delivery and for the buyer to take over the goods. There is no section of the Uniform Commercial Code exactly like this, although Section 2-319(3) requires the buyer to give the seller any needed instructions for making delivery. Failure of the buyer to do this could render the buyer in default under Section 2-311(3)(b), which gives the seller certain rights to complete or avoid the contract.

REMEDIES FOR BREACH OF CONTRACT BY THE BUYER

Articles 61 through 65 cover the remedies available to the seller for a breach of contract by the buyer.

Remedies Available to the Seller. Section III of this chapter (which is III) is almost a mirror image of Section III in Chapter II. The difference is that Chapter II covered the remedies available to the buyer, and Chapter III, Section III deals with the remedies of the seller. Article 61 indexes the remedies available to the seller. Its first subsection reads this way:

(1) If the buyer fails to perform any of his obligations under the contract or this Convention, the seller may

    (a) exercise the rights provided in Articles 62 to 65;

    (b) claim damages as provided in Articles 74 to 77.

The "rights" mentioned in 61(1)(a) include the following:

1. The right to require the buyer to pay the price, take delivery, or perform his other obligations. Article 62.

2. To fix an additional period of time of reasonable length for performance by the buyer of his obligations. Article 63.

3. To declare the contract avoided. Article 64.

4. To supply missing specifications that the buyer fails to supply. Article 65.

The list of damages provided for the seller in the Convention are the same as those provided the buyer in Article 45. This is one of the fine features of the Convention—damages are the same for the buyer and for the seller.

Seller's Right to the Equivalent of Specific Performance. Article 62 states:

> The seller may require the buyer to pay the price, take delivery, or perform his other obligations.

The seller will probably use this Article only to enforce payment by the buyer if the buyer has already received and accepted the goods. Although the Article is basically the seller's right to obtain and enforce specific performance (to parallel the buyer's right under Article 46), its use to enforce specific performance will seldom be used. Section 2-709(1) of the Uniform Commercial Code gives the seller the same opportunity to claim the price if the goods have been delivered and accepted by the buyer.

Additional Period of Time for Buyer to Perform. Article 63 gives the seller the right to grant buyer a reasonable amount of additional time to perform his or her obligations. If after the expiration of that additional time the buyer has not performed, the seller may declare the contract avoided. This is similar to the buyer's right to do this in Article 47. You will recall that we said that right was needed if the buyer wanted to declare the contract avoided and was not certain the seller's breach was deep enough to warrant an outright declaration of avoidance. By giving the additional period of time to perform, the party giving that time is assured of the right to declare the contract avoided if the other party does not perform within that time period.

Seller's Right to Avoid the Contract. Article 64 spells out the seller's right to avoid the contract if the failure of the buyer to perform his obligations under the contract amounts to a fundamental breach of contract. It also provides the seller with the opportunity to avoid as we pointed out in the previous paragraph. These provisions for the seller are the same as were given the buyer in Article 49.

Supplying Missing Specifications. Article 65 gives the seller the right to supply missing specifications for the goods if the buyer fails to do so. The seller is required to inform the buyer what he has done in this respect. The Uniform Commercial Code in Section 2-311 gives the party awaiting such instructions the right to supply the instructions or they have the right to declare the other party to be in breach.

PASSING OF RISK OF LOSS

The Articles pertaining to passing risk of loss are covered in Articles 66 to 70.

Damage After Risk Passed to Buyer. The first basic rule we encounter is in Article 66:

> Loss of or damage to the goods after the risk has passed to the buyer does not discharge him from his obligation to pay the price, unless the loss or damage is due to an act or omission of the seller.

This article is self-explanatory and within our understanding of the risk of loss as it is applied under the Uniform Commercial Code.

Risk of Loss When Goods Are in Transit. The general rule of the Convention concerning risk of loss while the goods are in transit is contained in Artcle 67:

> (1) If the contract of sale involves carriage of the goods and the seller is not bound to hand them over at a particular place, the risk passes to the buyer when the goods are handed over to the first carrier for transmission to the buyer in accordance with the contract of sale. If the seller is bound to hand the goods over to a carrier at a particular place, the risk does not pass to the buyer until the goods are handed over to the carrier at that place. The fact that the seller is authorized to retain documents controlling the disposition of the goods does not affect the passage of the risk.

You will note the risk of loss passes to the buyer "when the goods are handed over to the first carrier for transmission to the buyer." To your author this appears to be much more precise than the Uniform Commercial Code's expression in Section 2-509(1)(a) "when the goods are duly delivered to the carrier..." The Code's definition lacks the preciseness of exactly when in "delivery" does the risk pass to the buyer.

The reader will note that even though the seller makes the shipment under reservation, as with documents, the risk of loss still passes to the buyer at the time the goods are handed over to the first carrier. This is in line too with section 2-509(1)(a).

Miscellaneous Rules Regarding Breach. The final three articles in this chapter on the passage of the risk contain miscellaneous rules involved in the action. Article 68 presents a special rule where the goods are sold while in transit. Article 69(2) covers the case where the buyer is to take over the goods at a place other than the seller's place of business. This subarticle states that the risk passes to the buyer when delivery is due and the buyer has been made aware that his goods are available to him.

Article 69(2), by the process of elimination, also points out that Article 69(1) refers to the situation where the buyer is to take over the goods at the seller's place of business. The rule states the risk passes to the buyer when he takes the goods or when he breaches his contract by failing to take delivery. These rules are the same as in the Uniform Commercial Code.

Article 70 covers the situation when the seller hands over nonconforming goods to the carrier. If the nonconformity is such as to give the buyer the right to avoid the contract, that right continues despite the fact that the goods may be damaged in transit. Though technically the damaged goods were the buyer's goods, the fundamental breach of the seller causes the loss to fall back on him. Section 2-510(1) of the Uniform Commercial Code protects the buyer in the same fashion—except that the seller's default need not be such a serious breach to enable the buyer to reject or revoke his acceptance of the goods.

ANTICIPATORY BREACH AND INSTALLMENT CONTRACTS

Articles 71 through 88 cover anticipatory breaches and installment contracts. Article 71 provides some general rules regarding anticipatory breach. Subarticle (1) states that:

> (1) A party may suspend the performance of his obligations if, after the conclusion of the contract, it becomes apparent that the other party will not perform a substantial part of his obligations as a result of:
>
>> (a) a serious deficiency in his ability to perform, or in his credit worthiness; or
>> (b) his conduct in preparing to perform or in performing the contract.

Note the permissive words " . . . may suspend performance . . . ", which implies the party may only temporarily interrupt his or her performance because the other party, under subarticle (3), may provide adequate assurance of his ability to perform. 71(3) makes it mandatory that the party suspending performance must notify the other party of his action. The Uniform Commercial Code has a similar provision in Section 2-609(1).

Nowhere in these articles is there any definition of what is adequate notice of suspension, whether it has to be in writing, and who is responsible for its delivery. The suggestion to the American purchasing officer is (1) put in writing, (2) give all of the necessary facts of why you are questioning the possibility of performance, and (3) make certain that your message is delivered to your supplier by sending it via "return receipt requested" mail.

You will also note that subarticle (2) of Article 71 provides for stoppage of delivery when the goods are in transit and the buyer is proven to be insolvent. A similar section 2-705(1), is in the Uniform Commercial Code.

Avoidance of Contract Prior to Date of Performance. Article 72 goes one step farther than Article 71. It provides the aggrieved party may declare the contract avoided if it is clear the other party "will commit a fundamental breach of contract." The aggrieved party must give notice to the other party if time allows. No notice is required if the breaching party has declared he will not perform his obligations.

Avoidance in Installment Contracts. Article 73 of the Convention provides that the failure of one party to perform any of his obligations in respect to any installment constitutes a fundamental breach in respect to that installment. Subarticle (2) provides that if this gives the aggrieved party good grounds to conclude future installments will likewise be violated, the aggrieved party may declare all future installments avoided. Subarticle (3) provides for the aggrieved party to declare the entire contract avoided if each installment is interdependent of the other. This is all similar to Section 2-612 of the Uniform Commercial Code.

DAMAGES AND INTEREST

Articles 74 through 77 cover the damages available for a breach of contract under the Convention. Article 74 begins Section II on damages. This article states the general rule for damages under the Convention and, with one caveat, coincides with the Uniform Commercial Code:

> Damages for breach of contract by one party consist of a sum equal to the loss, including loss of profit, suffered by the other party as a consequence of the breach.

The caveat, if it may be called that, is found in the second sentence of Article 74:

> Such damages may not exceed the loss which the party in breach foresaw or ought to have foreseen at the time of the conclusion of the contract, in the light of the facts and matters of which he then knew or ought to have known, as possible consequence of the breach of contract.

The basic rule of damages included in the first sentence is incontrovertible. Note particularly that loss of profit is specifically mentioned as an element of damages for either party. Also note that the Uniform Commercial Code does not permit the buyer to receive damages for loss of profit. This is a plus for the Convention, although your author can see some difficulties of proof for a buyer seeking to collect loss of profit as damages. We have had cases in the United States under the Uniform Commercial Code where the courts have specifically denied recovery for the buyer's overhead or profits.

The second sentence of the Article places a strong limit on the amount of consequential damages that can be recovered by an aggrieved party. This Article required the breaching party to have some knowledge of the possibility of the occurrence before he can be held liable for the consequences. We believe this is a bit of hardship on the buyer particularly.

Those knowledgeable in matters of the Convention, with some manner of correctness, will say this necessary foreseeability of the consequence is written into Section 2-715 of the Code. This subsection reads:

> (2) Consequential damages resulting from the seller's breach include:
>
>> (a) any loss resulting from general or particular requirements and needs of which the seller at the time of contracting had reason to know and which could not reasonably be prevented by cover or otherwise; and
>>
>> (b) injury to person or property proximately resulting from any breach of warranty.

Section 2-715 makes only the seller liable for consequential damages. (2)(a) says the seller is liable only if he had reason to know the consequence and it could not be prevented by cover or otherwise. However (2)(b) says that where an injury to a person or property is involved because of a breach of warranty, no such knowledge requirement is imposed on the seller before being found liable for damage.

Damages Where Buyer Has Executed a Cover. Article 75 deals with the damages due where the seller has resold the goods or the buyer has executed a "cover" purchase. In such instances the damages are the difference between the contract price and the price in the substitute transaction as well as any further damages recoverable under Article 74. While the phrase "further damages under Article 74" is not explained, one assumes it has reference to regaining the full measure of profits lost. This would be of advantage to the supplier, although it may be possible for the buyer to prove lost profits too.

Damages Where Contract Is Avoided and There Is No Cover Transaction. Article 76 covers this topic. The measure of damages in such instances is the difference between the contract price and the current price at the time of avoidance, plus anything more that might be recoverable under Article 74. Again, that probably refers to lost profits. Although this article is written for both buyers and sellers, one would assume the seller will derive the most advantage from it.

The section concludes with Article 77, which imposes upon either party claiming under Articles 74 to 76, the duty to mitigate damages, including loss of profit, wherever possible. Failure of the aggrieved party to do so gives the other party the right to claim an equivalent reduction in damages recoverable.

Interest

Interest is provided as a penalty against any party who fails to pay the price or any other sum that is in arrears. This is Article 78. No rate of interest is specified. There is no similar provision in the Uniform Commercial Code although interest may be awarded by the Court in appropriate circumstances.

EXCUSE

The Convention, under the caption of "Exemptions," presents its version of the Uniform Commercial Code's Section 2-615 which the American purchasing officer knows as "Failure of Presupposed Conditions." There is some difference in the approaches the Convention follows versus the Code.

The Convention, in the first subarticle of Article 79, details the circumstances that must exist for either party to be given an exemption:

   a) The failure is due to an impediment beyond his control.

   b) He could not have been expected to take the impediment into account at the time of contracting.

   c) He could not have avoided its consequences.

Subarticle (2) gives the defaulting party another exemption. Here the rule is that if the party in default was depending on a third person's performance to complete his own performance, and if the third person could not perform because of an impediment described in subarticle (1), the defaulting party then has an exemption. In other words, the third party's exemption becomes the defaulting party's exemption too.

Subarticle (3) provides that the exemption lasts as long as the impediment lasts. One assumes the defaulting party must perform after the impediment is removed if the other party continues to demand performance. One also assumes the defaulting party would be given an extension of his or her performance date equal to the length the impediment continues.

The fourth subarticle requires the defaulting party to give notice to the injured party within a reasonable time after the impediment appears. Failure to give such notice or failure of the injured party to receive such notice, subjects the defaulting party to exposure for damages.

Finally, subarticle (5) makes it quite clear that the exemption exempts the defaulting party from payment of damages only. The injured party may pursue any other right available under the Convention. This might be the right to avoid the contract so that the injured party will not have to await removal of the impediment. Such party can go elsewhere, if desired, to fulfill the need, such as having the right to cover.

There are differences between Article 79 and the applicable Code sections. The basic Code section on this topic is 2-615 and it is written only as an exemption for the supplier. The buyer has none. We will not go into discussions of the differences between the Convention and the Code on this topic, since 2-615 is discussed in Chapter 15 under "Failure of Presupposed Conditions."

Article 80 simply prevents an injured party from relying on the failure of the other party to perform if such delay has been occasioned by the aggrieved party.

EFFECTS OF AVOIDANCE

Articles 81 through 84 cover the effects of avoidance of a contract. These four sections give miscellaneous rules concerning the effects of avoidance of a contract. We will simply enumerate such rules and show the appropriate article in parentheses.

1. Avoidance releases both parties from their obligations under the contract. Of course, this does not apply to any damages that may have accrued. (31)

2. Avoidance does not affect any other provision of the contract that governs the rights and obligations of the parties, or how disputes are to be settled. (81)

3. A party who has performed may claim restitution from the other party. (81)

4. The buyer loses the right to declare the contract avoided or to require the seller to deliver substitute goods if it is impossible for him to make restitution of the goods substantially in the condition in which he received them. This does not apply if the impossibility of making restitution is not due to the buyer's act, or if the goods have perished, or if the goods have been sold in the normal course of business. (82)

5. A buyer who has lost the right to declare the contract avoided or to require the seller to deliver substitute goods in accordance with Article 82, retains all other remedies under the convention. (83)

6. If the seller is bound to refund the price, he must also pay interest on it. (84)

Nota Bene **to the Purchasing Officer.** The manner in which this section is written poses some interesting questions about breaches of warranty that are discovered after the goods have gone into production. The American buyer should protect against the need to return goods after having worked them partially, by including a clause in the contract giving the buyer the opportunity to return any goods at any point in production when a breach from the contract description is discovered.

PRESERVATION OF THE GOODS

Articles 85 through 88 cover preservation of goods. These are four articles at the conclusion of the Convention that require the party in possession to take reasonable care of the goods even though the other party has defaulted in one manner or another. These rules are similar to those in the Uniform Commercial Code in Sections 2-603 and 2-515. (See Chapter XXI.)

SOME GENERAL OBSERVATIONS

The C.I.S.G. and the American Purchasing Officer. Now that we have dissected the Convention as well as compared its major provisions with the Uniform Commercial Code, the next questions to be faced are "Can we live with it?" and "Should we contract under its principles of law?" The answer to the first question would be affirmative. We can live with the Convention. Although it is not a perfect law by any measure of the imagination, it is not all "bad." It has some good features going for it that the purchasing officer will find advantageous. But there are also places in the Convention where its laws are written in favor of the supplier and against the buyer. Before making a final decision on "good or bad," let us enumerate the advantages and disadvantages in the use of the Convention, and then point out where the Convention can be said to be written against the best interests of the purchasing officer.

The Good Word About the Convention. Perhaps the finest thing that can be said about the Convention is that it is now a uniform law in 38 different countries of the world, including the United States. That is a sizeable portion of the world. There must be merit in the Convention because it enables us to sit in our offices located in any one of the 50 United States and contract under the same body of law with suppliers in any one of 37 foreign countries. The fact that there is "one law" that governs all of us in that circle helps us considerably. The possibility of either party acting in ignorance of the applicable law is minimized.

The Bad Piece of Business About the Convention. Perhaps the most worrisome feature about the Convention is the fact that it may not be uniformly interpreted and applied. The probability that the Courts of 38 different countries will interpret each section of the Convention in identically the same manner is remote. If it does happen, it will be a huge surprise. There are two major problems that militate against uniformity. The first is the fact that some articles in the Convention depend upon the application of domestic law to the problem in litigation. We all know that domestic law varies. We also know that the domestic law to be applied can be the law of the plaintiff's country or that of the defendant's. So there is a built-in possibility of diversity of application.

The other factor pointing to nonuniformity is that at the present time there are not yet enough decisions rendered under the Convention. It is essential that jurists, attorneys, and all parties involved in litigation have the opportunity to learn how other countries, as well as their own country, have applied specific articles of the Convention. Without such experiences, each party and their legal counsel begin a transaction in uncharted seas. Such a situation also limits the ability of legal counsel to give proper legal advice on how to proceed.

MAJOR DIFFERENCES BETWEEN THE CONVENTION AND THE UNIFORM COMMERCIAL CODE

Before itemizing these major differences between these two bodies of law, your author wishes to make one general observation. The American purchasing officer is advised to expect in the Convention a great desire to have the contract completed without too many, if any, adjustments being made. Some of the Articles are written with the deliberate intent to place responsibility for safe transportation of the goods on the shoulder of the buyer. Another Article wants to make certain the buyer accepts nonconforming goods if they are at all useable regardless of their deviation from the contract description.

The general thrust of the Convention is that it recognizes that there is considerable effort and expense expended by the supplier in preparing the goods for shipment and forwarding them. Because of that fact the Convention wants to exert every pressure possible on the buyer to accept and utilize the goods if at all possible, no matter whether the goods are conforming or nonconforming. Of course all buyers subscribe to the general approach that economic waste should be avoided whenever possible. Therefore it is good business to try to "make do" with what has been delivered by a supplier, but particularly by a foreign supplier. On the other hand, the American purchasing officer does not want to be forced into accepting goods that will result in his or her company's product not being up to acceptable standards. It is in this area that we should be concerned about the effect of the Convention on the quality of our products. In any event the American purchasing officer can protect against such eventualities by appropriate clauses in the purchase contract. But then, that is not living totally within the Convention.

There follows here a list of major differences in the Convention. We have listed them by their appropriate Article numerical sequence.

1. Article 2(a) states the Convention does not apply to consumer purchases and sales. This difference does not affect purchasing officers in their daily routine.

2. Article 3(2) codifies in the Convention that if the predominant part of a contract is for services, the Convention is not applicable. This is not so stated in the Code but is now generally applied by the courts. The clarification of this point in the Convention enures to the benefit of both buyer and supplier.

3. Article 8(3) overturns the parol evidence rule of the Code by providing, *inter alia*, that " . . . the negotiations, . . . usages, and any subsequent conduct of the parties" may be used in determining the intent of a contracting party. Both buyer and supplier are equally affected by this change.

4. Article 9(2) brings "international usages" into any contract unless excluded by agreement of the parties. This affects both parties.

5. Article 11 does away with the Statute of Frauds as we know it in the Code. An oral contract for the sale of goods is now possible.

6. Article 12 permits Article 11 from becoming effective in any country that requires a writing (such as in the United States) for an enforceable contract. The United States did not take advantage of this caveat but other countries did. This makes another nonuniform application of the Code.

7. Article 14(1) requires a price to be included in a valid offer. This may prolong negotiations between the buyer and the supplier.

8. Article 16(2)(a) apparently makes it more simple for a firm offer to be created than under the Code. This is a plus for the buyer.

9. Article 16(2)(b) codifies the doctrine of promissory estoppel in the topic on revocation of an offer. This is a plus for the buyer, since the Code is silent on the doctrine and some states recognize it while others do not.

10. Article 17 provides that a rejection terminates a firm offer. The Code is silent on this. Probably it is an assist to the supplier.

11. Article 18(2) changes the dispatch rule for acceptances. It demands the acceptance be received by the offeror before becoming effective. This change may work to the detriment of the buyer because more acceptances come from the buyer. Whoever accepts an offer is at the mercy of the postal service unless facsimiles are utilized.

12. Article 19(1) restates the mirror image rule for acceptance of an offer. The Code in Section 2-207 attempted to eliminate this. A backward step for both the buyer and the supplier.

13. Article 19(2) restates the Code's Section 2-207(1) but adds "subject to the offeror's approval." This is a detriment to the buyer who more often sends the acceptance. Should it be delayed, the buyer should not be required to depend upon the supplier to decide whether it will be accepted. This gives the supplier the opportunity to speculate on "up and down" prices.

14. Article 19(3) does the buyer and supplier a favor by spelling out what different or additional terms will be considered "material." This is an improvement over Section 2-207, which lets one guess. However, Article 19(3) lists so many items that it makes most additional or different terms "material," thereby losing the 19(2) rule of contract completion.

15. Article 25, defining a fundamental breach, requires the breach to "substantially deprive the other party..." This works against the buyer because it impliedly does away with the perfect tender rule and gives redress only when there is a substantial defect.

16. Article 25 also favors the supplier by giving him the right to a fundamental breach only if the results could have been "foreseen" by him. This works against the buyer in many instances.

17. Article 29 on modification of a contract follows the Code by not requiring consideration to pass for a contract modification. But because of Article 11 (abandoning the Statute of Frauds), the amended contract does not have to be in writing.

18. The Convention contains no delivery terms, depending entirely on Incoterms. This is not all bad except that Incoterms are amended from time to time with little or no notice.

19. Article 35 gives a full set of Code warranties to each contract and makes these warranties part of the contract. This is definitely a buyer's advantage. However, nowhere in the Convention is there any prescribed method of disclaiming warranties. The buyer must be alert to the wording the supplier gives concerning warranties.

20. Article 37 gives the supplier the opportunity to "cure" defects before the time for delivery has passed. Article 48 gives the seller the same opportunity to "cure" after the time for delivery has passed. The latter right generally prevents the buyer from declaring a fundamental breach until the rights of "cure" have been exhausted. All of this works against the buyer.

21. Article 42 gives the buyer protection against patent infringement but only if the supplier knew of the possible infringement suit. This is definitely against the buyer.

22. Article 47(1) allows the buyer to grant the supplier additional time for performance of his obligations under the contract. This is new to the American purchasing officer. It gives a precise time to declare a fundamental breach but it prolongs completion of the contract.

23. Article 52(2) prohibits the supplier from delivering and charging for "overruns." An advantage for buyers.

24. Article 54 emphasizes the buyer's payment problems of foreign sourcing by making the buyer alert to "being prepared to pay" and comply with all formalities of import and export.

25. Article 55 applies a price where the contract is silent. It applies the price prevailing at the time of contracting; not at the time of delivery as does the Code. It works for and against both parties.

26. Article 74 makes the supplier liable for consequential damages only if he could have foreseen them. This definitely works against the buyer.

Conclusion for the American Purchasing Officer. It is apparent that the price you pay for foreign sourcing is not overwhelming. If contracting and performing under the Convention is the only way your supplier will do business—and you want to do business with that supplier—then attempt to protect yourself as we have indicated in the body of this text.

Since most purchasing officers do more domestic than foreign sourcing, they live under the Uniform Commercial Code daily. One can only ask the question "Is it essential to also learn the confusing vagaries of the Convention?" to do business with some foreign suppliers. Some of your suppliers will agree to do business on your terms and under your state's version of the Uniform Commercial Code. But as foreign transactions increase, you will want to learn more about the Convention.

***Nota Bene* to the Purchasing Officer.** It is suggested that before the first negotiation with any supplier occurs which might be covered by the Convention, the two parties sign an agreement as to which law will be applicable. (Uniform

Commercial Code, the foreign law, or the Convention). An analysis of which law is most desirable for you in the particular transaction should be made. Perhaps you, the purchasing officer, should take the offensive on this and hand the supplier a paper making your own state law (the Uniform Commercial Code and not the Convention) applicable to any business you might do if that is the law you favor. Furthermore, if you do a continuing business with a supplier, why not execute one "Overriding Agreement for All Purchases" agreement with that supplier. Settle your problems once and for all time with such an overriding agreement.

XXXIII

Cultural-Legal Problems in Foreign Purchasing

The purchasing manager who purchases goods from abroad will readily discover that not only is it wise to understand the law of that country, but also some of its culture. These cultural aspects may affect the negotiation, forming, and carrying out of the contract. While this is true of many cultures throughout the world, a particularly good illustration is found in the Chinese laws and culture. It may be well to first consider some general matters, and then proceed to a consideration of some other pragmatic considerations.

NEGOTIATING AND CONTRACTING IN THE PEOPLE'S REPUBLIC OF CHINA*

Major reforms have been carried out to transform the Chinese economic and legal system to adapt to the international standards and practice. As a result of its "open door" policy, China has established trade relations with most Western trading nations and has become one of the key trading partners of the United States.

With its enormous population and low cost labor, China possesses the possibility of becoming America's major supplier of goods, and the supplier for many American companies. It thus becomes most important for purchasing managers. Yet the purchasing manager may be dealing with someone who sees business transactions and legal obligations very differently.

---

*Acknowledgment: Shukang Zou, Juris Doctor.

While the Chinese emphasize "friendship" as a precursor to a business relationship, Westerners use explicit forms such as the external procedures provided by laws and courts. Westerners approach everyone as a stranger, and, hence, use the short-term and fall-back reliance on the formalism of contract and law. Western businessmen build relationships on complementary interests. They begin with nothing personal, but, rather, an assumption of mutual interests: you have something I want or need and I have something you want or need. Interaction depends not on you or me as individuals, but on my ability to meet your needs. If there is to be a relationship, it will develop over our interaction meeting each other's needs.

Since implementing the open door policy, China has placed a high priority on the codification of its law. China enacted economic, trade, and investment legislation covering contracts, trademarks, patents, joint ventures, wholly owned foreign enterprises, taxation of foreign enterprises, and also promulgated miscellaneous related regulations. The Law of the People's Republic of China on Economic Contracts Involving Foreign Interest ("Foreign Economic Contract Law," hereinafter "FECL") is one of the most significant laws in this series.

Foreign Economic Contract Law

While Chinese domestic Economic Contract Law governs contracts concluded between domestic enterprises, individuals or enterprises, and other individuals, FECL only governs contracts concluded between Chinese corporations or enterprises and foreign companies or individuals, provided Chinese law applies to such contracts. (The FECL may also govern contracts concluded between foreign companies if the parties decided to apply the FECL or the law applies because of private international law rules.) Otherwise, it should be remembered that China also has adopted the Convention on the International Sale of Goods.

The Scope of the FECL

Except for international transportation contracts, all other international economic or commercial contracts will generally be governed by the FECL. Joint ventures (including the exploration and development of natural resources), the sale of goods, insurance, processing and assembling arrangements, and compensation trade are within the FECL's scope. It also extends to other contracts including leasing, co-production, technology transfer, licensing, engineering projects, provision of credits, consignment sales, agency cooperative research, and storage.

The FECL has seven chapters containing forty-three articles. The provisions are written in broad terms and are quite flexible, leaving the parties to their creative abilities to form or fashion contracts to fit the transactions. All the basic concepts and principles of contract normally used in the West are firmly embedded in the FECL, such as contract formation, performance and remedy consideration, contract assignment, contract modification, contract termination, dispute settlement and statute of limitations. While exposition of each of these concepts contained in the FECL would require a whole book, the major provisions regarding contract formation, performance and remedy consideration, contract assignment and contract modification and termination are briefly explained below.

Contract Formation Under the FECL

The first issue concerning contract formation is contract validity. The FECL provides that if the contract is entered into without the requisite authority, then the Chinese contract law would invalidate it. The FECL will also invalidate foreign economic contracts if they: violate Chinese law; are contrary to the public interest of Chinese society; or are concluded by means of fraud or duress.

Contract validity is inherently intertwined with choice of law problems. Although Article 5 of the FECL provides that the parties may select the law to be applied to the settlement of disputes arising from the contract, parties to the contract must also decide whether Chinese law and public policy will determine the contract validity. Nonetheless, contract validity under China's new economic laws and regulations is not yet clear, and the application of such rules and policies to foreign economic contracts is still in the early stages of development, and there is an insufficient body of legal precedent, case law, to fill the gap.

Performance, Breach and Remedies

Consistent with the American common law and the Uniform Commercial Code (UCC), the FECL provides for the suspension of performance in anticipation of another party's breach—the doctrine of anticipatory breach or repudiation. The party suspending performance without a proper basis must notify the other party and is liable for damages for breach of contract.

Like other legal systems all over the world, China's law recognizes the principle that parties impeded in their performance of contractual obligations by unpredictable and unpreventable events—force majeure—may be exonerated to an appropriate extent from liability for breach of contract.

> Article 24: When a party cannot perform all or part of its contractual obligations because of an event of force majeure, it shall be fully or partially relieved from liability.
>
> When a party cannot perform in accordance with the contractually agreed time periods because of an event of force majeure, it shall be relieved of liability for delayed performance during the period of continued influence of the effects of the event.
>
> An event of force majeure means an event that the parties could

not foresee at the time of conclusion of the contract and the occurrence and effects of which cannot be avoided and cannot be overcome.

The scope of events of force majeure may be agreed to in the contract.

Article 25: When one party cannot perform all or part of its contractual obligations because of an event of force majeure, it shall promptly inform the other party in order to diminish the losses that might be caused to the other party, and it must within a reasonable period provide evidence issued by the relevant agency . . .

Article 29: In any one of the following circumstances, a party shall have the right to inform the other party of the rescission of the contract:

> (1) The other party has breached the contract, to the extent that such breach has seriously affected the economic benefits expected when concluding the contract;
>
> (2) The other party has not performed the contract during the period agreed to in the contract, and has still not performed within a reasonable time period allowed for delayed performance;
>
> (3) An event of force majeure has occurred, with the result that none of the contractual obligations can be performed; or
>
> (4) The conditions agreed on in the contract for rescission of the contract have arisen.[1]

Thus, the FECL defines an event of force majeure in Article 24 as an event that is (1) unforeseeable as of the time when the contract was executed; and (2) the effects of which are (a) unavoidable and (b) insurmountable by the party or parties to the contract. Furthermore, the parties may stipulate the scope of force majeure events in the contract to suit their particular requirements.

However, neither the scope of events of force majeure nor the mechanism by which this principle may actually be implemented is explicitly set forth in the FECL, and neither Chinese arbitration tribunals nor Chinese courts of law have expanded on these issues in their published opinions. The FECL leaves to the contracting parties the task of spelling out detailed provisions on force majeure in their contracts.

With regard to damages, the FECL does not include a provision for specific performance as a remedy. But, reference to losses or damages in many situations is made in Chapter 3. Thus, the FECL basically intends to conform to Western common law and international practice.

Choice of Law Provisions and Dispute Settlement

Historically, China has shown reluctance to apply Western law to commercial

---

[1]FECL, *supra* note 95, arts. 24, 25, 29.

transactions. Given the past Chinese practices, the FECL has made a major concession for the foreign party in choice of law rules.

Article 5 provides for party autonomy in selecting the law to govern the contract. The same article applies the law of the country with the most significant contacts, a practice consistent with private international conflict of laws rules. However, the FECL prohibits the parties from selecting the governing law if the transaction is a joint venture contract, or a contract for Chinese-foreign cooperative exploration and development of natural resources.

It appears that Chinese law will apply to a substantial number of foreign trade transactions, but in the absence of a relevant provision of Chinese law governing a specific contractual dispute, the FECL provides that "international practice" shall apply.

Consistent with prior and current Chinese practices, the FECL encourages informal dispute settlements as opposed to arbitration or litigation.

While China has recently made significant progress in codifying economic laws, it is still in the initial stages of developing a uniform system to protect foreign creditors' rights. As China's FECL is still relatively new, its interpretation by domestic courts and domestic and foreign arbitration tribunals presents both uncertainties and opportunities for the international transactions practitioners.

Legal Dispute Resolution

The Chinese are generally loath to resort to legal proceedings. They feel the relationship between the parties involved should prevent any insoluble confrontations from arising. Although adjudication is becoming more acceptable to the Chinese, precipitous lawsuits involving Chinese defendants may result in a potential loss of friendship or advantageous business relationships.

China's foreign economic laws offer several alternative dispute resolution options in an effort to discourage courtroom litigation. First, if possible, the parties should attempt to settle differences through "friendly consultation or mediation." Only when this proves unachievable should the parties turn to arbitration or to the courts.

A Western investor may better understand Chinese dispute resolution by envisioning a system utilizing a continuum of methods of increasing formality and coercion: friendly consultation, then friendly consultation with outside help, non-binding conciliation, arbitration, and finally, litigation.

The Chinese abhor compulsion or coercion and do not rely upon it. Instead, Chinese culture orders society by standards called "li." Good people aspire to conform to Confucian "li"; no honest person behaves so badly that "fa," or law, limits action. In addition to "li," Buddhist-Taoist doctrine requires the Chinese to choose compromise over conflict. As a result, the Chinese ideally resolve all disputes by understanding the needs of the other party, taking their own needs into consideration, and agreeing on an equitable solution. Third party arbitration and litigation are anathema to orderly society, and signal hostility and rejection.

Accordingly, solving disputes by conciliation or arbitration in civil cases, as well as in commercial and maritime cases, has long been a tradition in China. The country's history of arbitration also makes it largely preferable to litigation because of the risks of facing court-appointed officials lacking experience in solving sophisticated economic disputes.

Arbitration is not the only, nor is it necessarily the best, method of resolving disputes with Chinese business partners. Conciliation provides a cheaper, quicker, more flexible, and more friendly means to settle problems than arbitration or litigation. Moreover, the Chinese see the settlement of a dispute either in the courts or through arbitration as a failure of the relationship which reflects badly on both sides.

Most commercial contracts with the Chinese do not mention conciliation directly; instead, it is usually considered an optional step between "friendly negotiations" and "arbitration"—both of which are usually mentioned explicitly in contracts. According to an investor in China, "[i]n arbitration you have to accept the tribunal's decision, which from a businessman's point of view, may not be the best solution, while in conciliation you are free to work out your own."

The process of conciliation or mediation, closely identified with traditional Chinese culture, is considered to be a particularly good method for resolving China-related disputes. When disputes arise, Chinese firms will normally be the first to initiate consultation with their foreign counterparts so as to solve them in a friendly manner. If consultation is unsuccessful, a third party is sometimes asked to mediate. However, in most cases in which consultations fail, a third party will not be invited to mediate and the concerned parties directly seek arbitration or bring the case before the court.

Arbitration is resorted to only when negotiation, consultation, conciliation, or mediation fails or when they are inappropriate to the settlement of a dispute. Infrequently, the parties may choose to resolve their dispute exclusively by arbitration.

Most contracts signed by the Chinese and their foreign counterparts contain arbitration clauses. This illustrates the Chinese preference for arbitration over litigation. Arbitration cases do not necessarily have to be conducted in China. Arbitration may be carried out either in China or in other countries, as decided by the contracting parties through consultation. This is clearly affirmed in the FECL. Cases conducted in China are handled by the Foreign Trade Arbitration Commission (FTAC) and the Maritime Arbitration Commission (MAC). The FTAC deals with disputes in Sino-foreign economic and trade cooperation. Most of the cases are in the area of business contracts, such as product quality, late delivery, and nonperformance. Disputes arising from joint venture contracts are fewer in number, and are mainly grounded on failure to discharge the obligation of making the pledged investment, shortage of circulation funds, poor quality of equipment contributed in lieu of cash, and procurement matters. The MAC deals with Sino-foreign marine disputes. Cases in marine transport are primarily disputes concerning ship leasing contracts and bills of lading, remuneration for salvage work, and collisions. There are also cases concerning freight losses from foreign ships in Chinese. harbors, debts, and other trading cases, sometimes in which both parties are foreign.

Over the 1980s, China's FTAC and MAC have made fair and equitable settlements of many cases, contributing to China's enjoyment of a good reputation in the world.

Contract Administration and Enforcement vs. Government Red Tape

While it is not too difficult to nail down detailed agreements on all aspects of a business transaction through persistent negotiation, such as shareholding structure, product, technology transfer, local content, whether products are to be exported, marketing, finance, tax, access to foreign currency, recruitment and training, the resulting contract does not have the weight that it would have in the West because China lacks the necessary body of law as well as an adequate judicial system. Virtually anything is negotiable. Topics which had been closed can be reopened, although there could be seeking of redress for breaches of contract through the courts.

Despite China's establishment of active judicial and arbitration systems and many laws regulating commercial contracts with foreigners, in practice contracts concluded with Chinese entities lack legal enforceability. China's inability to provide contract security to potential investors has hindered its efforts to attract the steady inflow of the much-needed hard currency. Foreign businessmen accustomed to Western standards of legal protection have found Beijing's inconsistent attitude toward contracts among the most frustrating aspects of investment.

Implementing contracts in China is not a simple process, either. In implementing the investment contracts, foreign investors that are not familiar with the importance of personal relationships in China especially encounter all sorts of bureaucratic hurdles after the conclusion of their contracts.

Sometimes, government agencies will directly interfere with the performance of the contract by imposing new rules, conditions or fees that affect the profitability of the venture. The sources of supply of raw materials or other Chinese inputs may be selected by the department-in-charge of the venture, preempting what should normally be a commercial decision by the venture itself. Or the costs of local inputs may be arbitrarily increased if the official hierarchy thinks that the venture is making too much profit.

Perhaps the most baffling and irritating aspect of the administration of contracts concluded with China is the frequency with which either the Chinese parties or Chinese officials insist that signed and approved contracts later be renegotiated. Because of this it is frequently said that contract negotiation never ends in China, and this unenviable reputation is a deterrent to prospective investors.

Caveat Bene: To the Chinese, a signed contract merely marks the end of the initial stage of negotiations, and will be followed by more discussions. More compromises and more concessions are to be expected, as nothing is ever set in stone. Westerners, in particular, are often caught unprepared for frequent Chinese requests to continue negotiations that have supposedly already concluded.

Obtaining a Binding Contract

Careful and studied consideration of legal issues should be prominent on the agenda of any companies interested in doing businesses in China. Within the context of the FECL, as well as other general considerations involved in doing business with China, the following recommendations must be considered for negotiation purposes.

Get a good contract including a reasonable amount of detail. Even though Chinese and Western views of a contract may differ, the Chinese are likely to treat it as a framework for discussion in the event of problems.

In an effort to insulate their contracts from any changes in the legal regime, many foreign companies have even attempted to negotiate clauses that "freeze" the law applicable to the contract as of the date of signature. Such a practice is guaranteed by the FECL which provides that where there is a conflict between the provisions of laws promulgated after an investment contract's approval and those of the contract, the contract "may" continue to be implemented according to its terms.

Resolve problems through negotiation. There is little point in pursuing a claim through courts in China, and few cases in which a judgment in a foreign court or arbitration tribunal have been enforced in China.

Use litigation only as a last resort. Unless the foreign party has no choice or no concern about ending the relationship, addressing problems through the courts should be last on the list of possible solutions.

Use experts and retain legal counsels. A growing number of foreign consultants, law and accountancy firms have established offices in China and can provide considerable expertise as well as access to Chinese contacts. When a contract with the Chinese parties is concluded, the foreign investor should consider consulting lawyers working for Chinese law offices to review for possible conflicts with Chinese rules or regulations. In negotiating a commercial transaction in China, an attorney should be prepared to assume a secondary role, allowing the business parties to negotiate face-to-face as is customary in Asian countries.

A DETAILED APPROACH TO ROLES AND CONTRACTING WITH THE CHINESE*

Although there is some writing on contracting generally with Chinese businessmen, negotiation skills and role playing in the contracting process have not received sufficient emphasis. An international business negotiation involves style, procedure, and substance. A good plan for style and procedure will be determinative.

International business negotiators should decide upon a plan for general negotiating style and procedure in advance and for different roles assigned to members of the negotiating team. The negotiators should also consider alternative plans to adjust to changing circumstances or needs during the negotiation process. There is, of course, no "one-size-fits-all" negotiation plan. Different cultures and contexts require different styles and plans.

In negotiating with the Chinese counterparts, Western business negotiators should keep in mind three facts: 1) the Chinese usually value a long relationship, either business or personal, with their business counterparts, rather than just a transient one; 2) the Chinese are proud of their culture and at the same time resentful of the past invasions of China by the Western "imperialists;" and 3) the Chinese are resilient negotiators and Western negotiators should have sufficient patience during the negotiation.

Place

The place of negotiation is usually determined by the following factors: 1) the subject matter of the negotiation; 2) the intended choice of law; and 3) other cultural considerations.

The Subject Matter of the Negotiation. This may involve prenegotiation inspection of the subject matter. In case of a sale of goods, the negotiating parties may want to investigate the quality and quantity of goods, the manufacturing facility and work force, and the access to ports and other means of transportation. In case of a joint venture project, the parties also need to carry out on-the-spot inspection of the proposed work site, availability of competent work force and management personnel, access to market and highways and railroads, and sufficient power supply. Because these are essential aspects of the negotiation, it is

*Acknowledgment: Xiaoxue Zhao, Juris Doctor, Attorney-at-Law, St. Louis, Missouri.

hard to imagine that the negotiation should be held in another country away from the subject matter.

The Intended Choice of Law. The Uniform Commercial Code (Sec. 1-105) permits the parties to choose the law governing the contract, as long as the transaction bears "a reasonable relation" to the jurisdiction providing the governing law. One factor usually considered in determining the reasonable relation to a jurisdiction is the place of negotiation.

The Convention on International Sale of Goods permits unlimited party autonomy. Both the U.S. and China are member states under the Convention. Therefore, the merchants in the U.S.-Chinese transaction can choose U.S. law, Chinese law, the law of a third country, or simply remain under the law of the Convention. The place of negotiation is always a factor to be considered in choice of law questions. Thus, to achieve more predictability and to avoid confusion on the choice of law issue, the negotiating parties' are well-advised to take it into account when choosing the place of negotiation.

Other Cultural Considerations. If the parties are negotiating a long-term project like a joint venture, the first negotiation is usually a good opportunity for the parties to better understand each other and each other's culture. The place of negotiation should depend on the respective parties' knowledge about the other's culture. It should appear to be necessary for the party who has less knowledge of the other country or culture to offer to go to that country to hold the negotiation there. This will be a good opportunity to personally investigate not only the conditions of the project site but also the cultural and political environment of that country.

Finally, an agreement between the parties is always needed on the place of negotiation because a consensus on this very first issue may set the general tone of the start of the negotiation.

Styles

Negotiating styles differ from culture to culture and person to person. The styles can be categorized into two: 1) the adversarial standoff style (or confrontational style); and 2) the consensus-building style. Each style is effective for its own purpose and in its own context.

Confrontational Style. This style is often counterproductive when negotiating an international business transaction with the Chinese. This style is extracting the most from the other party by using bluffs, threats, procedural manipulations, purposeful ambiguity, and repetitive demands, with little or no desire for interpersonal relations. All of this occurs in the broader context of attempts to extract as much information as can be gained while revealing no information before agreement is reached on any point.

This style's emphasis upon pressing maximum advantage to the point of conquest is often inappropriate when measured against other, more important factors. These factors include the efficient use of time, political and cultural differences, the volatility of international markets, currency exchange fluctuations, and expenses that must be paid by a client along the way to shaping a satisfactory international agreement.

In addition, the ill will engendered by this style may prejudicially color the opponent's judgment, in some cases "killing" the deal. Because the style places parties in unequal positions, it very often reminds the Chinese of their ancestors' humiliating experiences at negotiating tables where they had to pay for the costs of foreign invading armies. The negative connotations of confrontational style are counterproductive, particularly in countries of oriental cultures.

A Chinese attorney witnessed a negotiation where a Western negotiation team was negotiating a joint venture with a Chinese factory. The Western company would provide technology to the joint venture and the Chinese factory would provide facilities. The Western negotiators tried repeatedly to raise the estimated price of their technology and to keep down the valuation prices of Chinese equipment and facilities. They also threatened again and again to unilaterally end the negotiation if their demands were not satisfied.

The Chinese negotiators did not expressly object to the Westerners' demands. In the end, the parties agreed to discuss the details further through fax and the Western negotiators left thinking that a tentative agreement had been reached. However, the moment they left the negotiation room, their Chinese counterparts dumped all documents and memoranda of negotiation.

The Western company soon sent numerous follow-up fax messages requesting further discussion, but got no response at all from the Chinese factory.

The Chinese negotiators later recounted that during the negotiation they had come to regard their counterparts as insincere and difficult to get along with and that they did not raise any objections because they saw no point in continuing the negotiation, but did not want to say so expressly so that both sides could save face.

This is an example of adversarial negotiation style killing a business deal that would otherwise have been viable. The Western negotiators neglected a very crucial aspect of Oriental Culture in general and Chinese Culture in particular: the importance of saving one's face. To allow the other side "to save one's face" does not mean giving them whatever they want, but it does require some efforts and considerations to leave them enough space to make concessions or enough grounds upon which they can make such concessions. They should not hesitate to make their demands if they think they are justified, but they should use facts to support their demands, instead of threats to end the negotiation. With statistics to support their demands, it would make it easier for the Chinese negotiator to justify his concessions to his superiors.

There is also considerable cultural diversity about the meaning in international negotiations of silence and delay. The common law rule that, under appropriate circumstances, "silence is acceptance" is not shared in many countries, certainly not in China. In China, people are particularly reluctant to say "no" in front of the person making a request, while in other countries periods of silence are an acceptable and common occasion during which thoughts are arranged and rearranged. In the above example, the Chinese negotiators went as far as agreeing to negotiate in the future to avoid saying "no" during the negotiation while their silence after the negotiation was an unequivocal "no."

The Westerners mentioned above have made every mistake possible in the negotiation. Confrontational style is the best way to break, not to make, a deal.

Consensus-Building Style. The consensus-building style emphasizes finding some kernels of agreement and expanding upon those areas with a view to building a momentum toward complete agreement. For example, in the first phase of the negotiation, the parties should concentrate on such points of consensus as the mutual willingness to mutually seek opportunities, to develop a business relation and cooperation between each other. Such emphasis upon common ground helps to finesse such pitfalls as a "hidden dimension" in a negotiation.

Of course, one problem is that there may be no initial consensus about the reason for negotiating at all. In such a situation, the Western negotiators should prepare for the upcoming negotiation by making a plan for different stages of the negotiation.

Preparations for the Negotiation. Although in the West, the market is usually dictated by demand and supply, doing business with the Chinese is not so impersonal and has an added aspect of personal relation. The Chinese value continuing personal relation not only in social contexts but also in business contexts. There is a Chinese saying, "Strive for friendly relation even when business negotiation fails." A good personal relation will not only give you a friendly starting point but will also help the mutual understanding throughout the negotiation.

There are numerous ways to build a rapport but several are most effective. The first and most common is the exchange of gifts or souvenirs. The Chinese usually present gifts to the other party if they are serious in building a continuing relation with their counterparts. It is not just a ceremonial routine, but a meaningful message and should be reciprocated by the other side.

In China, the guest should always present his or her gift to the host first. Then the host presents his or her gift to the guest. The host should always be notified in advance of the presentation of the gift so as to avoid the possible embarrassment where the host is not prepared with a gift.

The second way to build a rapport, less common than the first but also very important, is to have dinners together so that both sides can know each other better. It is an unwritten rule that the host should give a welcome dinner to show respect to the guest and the guest should later give a thank-you dinner to show respect to the host and appreciation of the host's hospitality regardless of the outcome of the negotiation.

Even when there seems no possibility that the two sides will do business with each other in near future, the guest should reciprocate with a thank-you dinner. It is not necessary for the host to give the guest an advance notice of the welcome dinner because the two dinners do not take place on the same day.

The advantages of exchanging gifts and giving dinners are: 1) a more reliable relation has been established and the relation will bring benefits with it; 2) a good reputation has also been built among the host's trade or industry, which will bring more customers. The last point is especially true in China where everyone judges each other not only by their business ability but also by their social behavior.

It is important to note a cultural difference that in China, people do not share a meal and split the bill as is common in the U.S. Anyone who does so in China would appear too impersonal and unwilling to develop a continuing relationship. Therefore, it may be all right to have no meals together with the counterparts at all, but it will be absolutely destructive to "go Dutch" with them at a restaurant in China.

The Negotiation Stage. If, for any reason, Western negotiators fail to do the above preparations before the negotiation, they will have to build a rapport during the first 10 minutes of the negotiation. They should always remember it is courteous to tell people what they want to hear to start building consensus at the negotiation table. They can start with minor subjects like the most favorite Chinese relics or ancient buildings to show their knowledge and appreciation of Chinese culture so as to build up personal rapport, which can lead to more common ground to build more consensus.

Of course, having a pleasant personality and knowledge of Chinese culture alone will not accomplish everything you want. The personal and cultural aspects of negotiations are emphasized because they have not received sufficient attention. Sufficient knowledge of the management structure in China is also important.

The Chinese economy is still very much centralized. The government still has the last word on the finality of many contracts, especially in imports and joint ventures in basic industries.

Normally, a chief Chinese negotiator would be an upper-middle or middle management officer with a considerable amount of discretion, but who does not have unlimited power to finalize the deal. This will have three advantages for the Chinese: 1) they have someone well-informed and experienced leading the negotiation team; 2) there is sufficient guard against abuse because the chief negotiator does not have all the power to make the deal right on the spot; 3) a flip side of 2) is the chief negotiator can always be ambiguous or say "sorry" when he or she wants to, by saying he or she would have to "get the approval from bosses upstairs," so as to create more space and time for them to maneuver.

W. Averell Harriman pointed out from his negotiating experiences that "You have to put yourself in the other fellow's shoes . . . You also have to consider how to make it possible for him to make a concession . . . .But the idea that you can whip your negotiating opposite into agreeing with you is nonsense . . . . If you call a hand, you must recognize that you may lose it."

The same applies to negotiations with the Chinese. The consensus building style is most productive. The key to the consensus building style is an advance. determination of: 1) what your negotiating opposites really want; 2) what they really must have; 3) what they may offer in return; 4) what they really cannot offer either because they lack authority to do so or because it would be unacceptable for enterprise, national or international reasons.

Negotiating Teams and Role Playing

The Negotiation Team. Negotiation teams are most often used with direct foreign investments, joint ventures, and large licensing or sales transactions because these involve complex legal issues. Knowing in advance what minimum *quid pro quo* a negotiating opposite really must have to join in an international business agreement makes it easier to decide upon the necessary members of the negotiating team.

One should appreciate all of the personal, cultural, and linguistic meanings in any conversation, quite apart from the substance of whatever subject matter is under discussion. For example, a team too big may be intimidating and suggest "imperialist" overtones; a team too small can be insulting and also suggest "imperialist" overtones.

The best way to determine the size of a negotiation team is to measure these factors: 1) the complexity of issues involved in the negotiation; and 2) the status and importance of possible members on the opposite team.

This is in fact a balancing test between legal and cultural needs. If the negotiation involves complex issues in securities law, merger or licensing, legal need outweighs cultural need and any necessary number of legal, accounting, and engineering experts should be suitable. On the other hand, if the negotiation involves only a small sales transaction, a single negotiator should suffice. Generally, a negotiation team of three is the most appropriate size in most situations.

Of course, if the formation of the opposite negotiation team is known, it is important to staff your own team with members of equal status and importance so as to avoid offending the opposite side. The higher the status of the chief negotiator, the smaller the number of extra team members he or she may need because presumably he or she has enough power and knowledge to finalize the transaction. In any case, the team should have one member with enough status or importance to convey a sufficient impression of sincerity of purpose and of respect for the dignity of those who will be the negotiating opposites.

In China, lawyers are not welcome at the negotiation table because "transaction lawyers," as opposed to "litigation lawyers," are a new phenomenon in China. At the very mention of lawyers, the Chinese would have an image of the litigators ready to fight in a dispute. A lawyer's presence on a negotiation team, therefore, symbolizes a "hired gun" and may thus indicate a lack of sincerity and trust on the part of the negotiation team. So when a lawyer is absolutely necessary on the team, he or she can participate as "consultant" so as to avoid misunderstanding.

Role Playing. All team members must know about and agree upon the negotiating strategy. However, it is inevitable that at some point during the negotiation an unplanned decision will have to be taken extemporaneously. Therefore, it is essential that team members agree in advance upon the person who will be the team's "voice" to make that decision. If the situation fits one of the alternative plans pre-determined, the "voice" of the team will announce that decision. If the situation goes beyond the imagination of the negotiators, the "voice" of the team should also make a decision either to call a recess or adjourn the negotiation.

Other roles, such as the "compromiser" or the "diplomat," should also be preassigned so as to avoid confusion in the course of the negotiation. As mentioned above, the Chinese are resilient negotiators and are familiar with such role assigning. At a point where the negotiation seems to stall, a compromiser would try to reconcile by shifting the subject to more pleasant ones. In tough moments during a negotiation, courtesy alone may keep a consensus momentum going, especially in China. Enduring courtesy is the essential lubricant of international negotiations. Many negotiations have been saved by this old trick.

Such procedures that are flexible enough to allow time to work out such problems may cultivate ego, avoid loss of "face" and continue participation in the negotiations. On a negotiation team, a person playing the role of compromiser is a must.

Conclusion

The above thoughts should give some practical guidelines to follow and correct approaches to take while negotiating with the Chinese, Of course, as China opens more and more to the outside world, its culture and legal system are bound to change. But while Western influence is strong in China and is still growing, the Chinese culture and thinking is still present.

Caveat Bene: No matter how drastic the changes may be in China, some of the fundamental traditional philosophy will endure for a long time. Therefore the basic principles mentioned here will continue to be useful.

RECENT DEVELOPMENTS

Of course, negotiating with foreign investors can be an adventure even on American soil. A real-estate broker in New York found this out recently. The broker thought he was on the brink of closing a $14-million sale with a group of Taiwanese investors. He then found out that before the deal would be closed, a Chinese mystic had to be flown in to determine if the building's qi, or life force, would be acceptable. This ancient practice of feng shui is still practiced quite a bit in areas on the West Coast with large Chinese populations, and those negotiating with Chinese investors should be aware of it.

More and more companies are exploring China. Dozens of companies with headquarters in St. Louis—including Anheuser-Busch, Emerson Electronic, HOK, McDonnell Douglas, Ralston Purina and Monsanto—view China as a land of opportunity. The U.S. companies have used Chinese-Americans to represent them in making inroads into China. Already, China purchases more than $50 million worth of Missouri exports a year. Some estimate that one business trip to China generates at least $25 million and 100 new jobs in the community.

The following sources were used in writing this section, and may be referenced for additional information:

1. Ralph H. Folsom, Michael W. Gordon, and John A. Spanogle, *International Business Transactions,* (1992).

2. The Uniform Commercial Code.

3. Ashley Dunn, *Ancient Chinese Craft Reshaping Building Design and Sales in U.S.*; N.Y. TIMES, Sept. 22, 1994, A1.

4. Charlotte Grimes, *Gateway To The East, As China Embraces Western Style Markets,* Many St. Louis Businesses Are Setting Up Shop—And Hoping For Profits; ST. LOUIS POST-DISPATCH, January 21, 1996, C1

XXXIV

Purchasing for Government Agencies

Procurement for government agencies and government contractors must conform to the statutes, rules, and regulations established by the cognizant unit. The Federal government, for example, has the Federal Acquisitions Regulation System, which was passed by the Congress on April 1, 1984, as the controlling statute for procurement. Most states have procurement statutes, too, and these must be adhered to by the various state agencies in their purchase of materials, services, and equipment. Other governmental units will have similar controls and regulations.

The Law of Agency and general contract law, as well as the Uniform Commercial Code, continue to be applicable for government procurement. The general principles of law enunciated from the beginning of this book to this chapter are applicable for the government procurement officer. (Probably the only exception to this generalization would be the sections dealing with antitrust exposures.) Superimposed on the general body of law for all purchasing officers are these various statutes, rules, and regulations. The government simply takes advantage of the invitations within the law to establish the special conditions under which they will do business. Suppliers that want to sell to the government must agree to abide by such rules. They have no choice.

In addition there is a host of laws and statutes to which the government procurement officer must assure compliance by the supplier in any contract document. The supplier must agree to conform to these laws. The topics that these laws cover range far and wide, including but not limited to federal and state equal employment opportunity, anti-sex discrimination, small business, minority-owned business, labor standards, and the like. The specifics of each law must be adhered to by the supplier. It is the duty of the government procurement officer to see that each law is included in any contract documents.

The following sections will give some examples of how this is accomplished and what are some of the rules given. The government purchasing officer is reminded that the sections that follow are not an all inclusive discussion of the variations in the field. Each purchasing officer is advised to study and learn the applicable statutes, rules, and regulations. The limited space in this book does not permit an exhaustive recount of these practices.

THE PROCUREMENT AGENT

Appointment of the Procurement Agent

The statutes spell out how the procurement officials are to be appointed. Many times some type of civil service structure also will be involved. Some will require appointment and then confirmation by a legislative group for senior officials. It is important that whatever appointment procedures might be in place be followed to the letter of the law. An imperfect appointment could jeopardize an entire procurement function. Appointment of purchasing officers for private businesses who act as government contractors follow the customary route for all organizations as detailed in Chapter III.

Authority of the Procurement Officer

The general rule of agency law is that the principal has the right to select the agent and determine what authority that agent is to be given. This rule is applicable to governmental agencies. Most agencies, including the Federal government, are quite precise in designating where the final contract authority lies. Some agencies will differentiate contracting authority by the amount of the purchase or by the type of purchase being made. It is always within the province of the governmental unit, as the principal, to establish any variations in the authority of the agent as desired.

Suppliers to governmental agencies, particularly to federal contractors, are advised to determine the hierarchy in the agency to be able to know "when" a contract has been finalized. Statutory authority and funding capabilities may range far and wide, as will the office where the final approval is given. All of these possibilities should be determined by the supplier before money is spent for production of the product.

SELECTION

Competition in Government Procurement

The taxpayer assumes final responsibility for payment of a purchase. Government procurement statutes are geared to develop the greatest measure of competition possible to attain. Therefore, all of the various avenues of negotiation and notice to prospective suppliers are provided for in the purchasing procedures. "Get the most for the taxpayer's dollar" is the goal of every governmental procurement officer. They are given wide latitude in procedures for developing and encouraging the American concept of a competitive economy.

Supplier Selection

One of the cardinal principles in government procurement is that every supplier is entitled to the opportunity of doing business with the entity. As a taxpayer, each supplier should have this right and they are given it. Such an open door policy creates problems for the purchasing officer. The nongovernmental purchasing officer has wide latitude in the election of potential suppliers. There is no law that says a private business must consider any and every supplier that expresses an interest in selling his or her product. Therefore the purchasing officer is free to choose, discard, or ignore some suppliers and favor others. The private business purchasing officer can ignore a low bidder and place the contract with a higher bidder, restrained only by the ethical considerations of such action.

Not so with the governmental procurement officer. Everyone qualified is entitled to submit proposals to fill the agency's needs. Once the bids are opened, the government buyer is required to make the award to the "lowest responsible bidder." There is no discretion given in making the award. When required to allow anyone to quote, the low bidder may not be one with whom the purchasing officer would want to contract. But the law says the award must be made on that basis.

Some procurement statutes, particularly the federal act, provide for prequalification of suppliers. Detailed procedures and applicable test standards are provided. Prequalification gives the procurement officers some assurance that the suppliers who "measure up" have the potential to be satisfactory sources of supply.

There is little the purchasing officer can do about "weeding out" undesirable suppliers, absent any provisions for prequalification. It is difficult—and fraught with problems—to declare a supplier a "nonresponsible" seller. A poor performance record on a prior contract is usually insufficient to disqualify a supplier. It takes more than one failure to declare a supplier nonresponsible. The government procurement officer is advised to consult the Attorney General's office before making a decision on excluding any supplier. An unsustainable decision on a supplier can seriously damage the supplier's business reputation and cause a loss of profits for him. It might expose the purchasing officer to liability for such an unsustainable action. Therefore the suggestion of assistance from the Attorney General is good advice.

One possible justification for exclusion is a violation of a federal or state statute with which the supplier must comply. For example, if a supplier is proven to have made an attempt to bribe a procurement officer or to have violated Equal Employment Opportunity regulations, the government purchasing officer could disbar (as said in law when an attorney loses the license to practice law) that supplier from doing further business. But even if the supplier is caught with a clear violation of the law, he still has certain rights to protect his position as a supplier. These would include the right to appeal the disbarment. Your author repeats the suggestion to the purchasing officer that has been made several times—the advice and counsel of the Attorney General's office should be sought and followed.

FORMATION OF THE CONTRACT

The Offer. Government procurement officers must take positive action in the solicitation of offers to sell to their agency. The need to generate competition among suppliers, the need to get the best value for the government dollar, and the need to be certain all eligible suppliers have the opportunity to submit offers to sell dictate that all avenues of notice be made for every purchase. Fair and impartial competition must be assured.

QUALITY CONTROL

Warranties under the Uniform Commercial Code are available to government purchasing officers. These are discussed in Chapter XVIII. At one time federal procurement officials did not overly concern themselves with warranties because of the strict inspection programs in place for most major purchases. The more modern Code warranties are of such value that they are now considered to be worthwhile.

The prime quality control criteria should be conformance to the specifications. No relaxation of conformance to the specifications should be tolerated. The using department, the taxpayer, and the unsuccessful suppliers all have major stakes in the fact that the successful supplier conforms to the specifications.

MODIFICATION OF A CONTRACT

One of the conditions often imposed on suppliers is that the government must be able to modify a contract even though it has been signed, sealed, and delivered. We talk in law of the sanctity of a contract once it has been created. But there are circumstances in which it can be modified by one of the parties. The government simply makes this a condition within the contract and the supplier, if he wants to do business, must agree to such a clause. Provision is made to recompense the supplier for any costs incurred by the modification. The various provisions regarding how this will be determined are detailed in the contract with the supplier.

SUMMARY

Only some of the areas of government procurement have been discussed here, and then only in a superficial manner. The government purchasing officer must supplement general contract principles with the statutory requirements of the cognizant government entity, as well as with the rules and regulations that may be promulgated by administrative departments. Variations from legal principles that are followed by everyone are minimal. The government agency primarily establishes and publishes the ground rules under which it will do business. These terms and conditions are included in the contract "boilerplate" and then followed strictly.

Most statutes mandate how a purchase is to be accomplished, beginning with public advertising for offers to sell. Certain purchases require sealed bids be submitted; other may be accomplished with less formal written proposals. Only under most unusual conditions may a single source of supply be considered. A minimum of three proposals must be obtained.

Specifications must be prepared that clearly express what is to be purchased. At the same time, such specifications cannot be too restrictive as that will result in some suppliers not being able to compete. Yet tightly drawn specifications are the one protection the agency has at its command to get exactly what is required. The specifications must keep a "would-be wayfaring supplier" in bounds in order to give conforming suppliers a fair opportunity. Obviously some compromise must be found to make the specifications serve all purposes. The use of trade names is discouraged but the saving clause "or equal" often is sufficient. Sealed proposals are required on major purchases. The statute or regulations will dictate the conditions when sealed proposals must be used. A closing time for the receipt of bids must be established and enforced to the precise second. Prospective suppliers are allowed to withdraw or change their proposals at any time before the closing deadline. Bid bonds are a commonplace requirement.

Lesser dollar value purchases can be made on written bids. The agency can require such suppliers offering proposals to make their prices "firm" for a limited period of time. This is provided for in the Uniform Commercial Code (Section 2-205, see Chapter XIII). Under very restrictive conditions, small or emergency purchases can be made without negotiation.

Acceptance of Offers

The time for making the award and the procedure to be followed are customarily contained in the statute. It is not unusual for a series of reviews and approvals to be obtained before the final contract is official. Tie bids are decided by pro-scribed procedures.

One of the unusual features of evaluating quotations and making awards in most state agencies is the preference given to "in-state suppliers." Many states specify that an award be given to an in-state supplier even though an out-of-state supplier has submitted a somewhat lower price. Usually a variation of 2 to 4 percent in favor of the in-state supplier will be allowed. The definition of an in-state supplier must be closely followed.

Index